Instructor's Manual
Volume I, Chapters 1–11

to accompany

Understanding Business

Fifth Edition

William G. Nickels
University of Maryland

James M. McHugh
St. Louis Community College at Forest Park

Susan M. McHugh
Applied Learning Systems

Prepared by
Gayle M. Ross
Copiah-Lincoln Community College

Boston Burr Ridge, IL Dubuque, IA Madison, WI New York San Francisco St. Louis
Bangkok Bogotá Caracas Lisbon London Madrid
Mexico City Milan New Delhi Seoul Singapore Sydney Taipei Toronto

Irwin/McGraw-Hill

A Division of The McGraw-Hill Companies

Instructor's Manual, Volume I, Chapters 1–11 to accompany
UNDERSTANDING BUSINESS

5 6 7 8 9 BKM BKM 9 0 9 8 7 6 5 4 3 2 1 0

ISBN 0-07-289218-8

http://www.mhhe.com

Preface

Introduction to the Instructor's Manual

Teaching an introduction to business class can be satisfying and challenging because this is the first business course for many of your students. You have the important task of introducing them to a broad range of topics and helping them learn the business terms necessary to understand the business literature. Throughout the course, you will be helping them explore and prepare for their careers.

The volume and speed of changes in today's world requires that continuous education be an integral part of each of our lives. We cannot tell our students as we hand them their degrees, Here, now you know all you need to know. Even if we were successful in teaching them what we thought they needed to know, much of it will be obsolete before their diplomas are framed. The best way that we can make sure that our students develop the skills needed to succeed is to teach them how to learn, how to think, how to question.

Helping students learn how to think is what *Understanding Business,* 5th edition, strives to do. The design of the text and this instructor's manual is based on learning principles that put the responsibility for learning where it belongs on the students shoulders.

Secretary's Commission on Achieving Necessary Skills (SCANS)

The Secretary of Labor appointed a commission, the Secretary's Commission on Achieving Necessary Skills (SCANS), to identify the skills people need to succeed in the workplace. SCANS fundamental purpose is to encourage a high-performance economy characterized by high-skill, high-wage employment. The commission's message to educators is this: Help your students connect what they learn in class to the world outside.

To help educators prepare their students for the workplace, SCANS identified five workplace competencies that should be taught: (1) Resources ability to allocate time, money, materials, space, and staff; (2) Interpersonal skills ability to work on teams, teach others, serve customers, lead, negotiate, and work well with people from culturally diverse backgrounds; (3) Information ability to acquire and evaluate data, organize and maintain files, interpret and communicate, and use computers to process information; (4) Systems understanding of social, organizational, and technological systems; ability to monitor and correct performance and to design or improve systems; and (5) Technology ability to select equipment and tools, apply technology to specific tasks, and maintain and troubleshoot equipment. The pedagogical tools in the text and this instructor's manual are designed to facilitate these SCANS competencies.

Perhaps it is because we use these materials in our own classrooms that we were so meticulous with their preparation. Jim teaches traditional-size classes of 30-50 students in an urban community college and Bill teaches large classes of 250 in lecture halls in a four-year institution. As a result, everything in this instructor's manual is designed to help instructors be more effective and make this course more practical and interesting for students. To accomplish this integration, the authors designed and contributed to the instructor's manual by implementing suggestions from other users and focus group participants. We want to thank Gayle Ross for the stellar job she did in revising the lecture outlines, adding many fine lecture enhancers, and putting the numerous pieces of this complicated document together in such an attractive and functional format.

Components of the Instructor's Manual

The following is a brief overview of the components for each chapter:

FOLDER CONTENTS:

The first page of each chapter answers the question, What's in this thing anyway? The list of folder contents lists all of the materials contained in the folder. The second portion of this list includes all of the resources available for each chapter contained in the folder (videos, Student Assessment and Learning Guide, and technology elements). This list makes it easy to choose the resources you want to use. There is no need to flip through half a dozen sources to find what supplementary material is available for a particular chapter.

ASSOCIATED WEB SITES:

This list of Web sites is included for the purpose of analysis and critical thinking of issues related to the concepts presented in the chapter.

WHAT'S NEW IN THIS EDITION:

If you used the fourth edition of Nickels/McHugh/McHugh, this section will tell you exactly what changes were made in the transition to the fifth edition. In many cases, you may need to make only minor changes in your previous notes. In other cases, the text's discussion of evolving business concepts may require some restructuring of your notes. In either case, the What's New section will explain how the text is different.

BRIEF CHAPTER OUTLINE/LEARNING GOALS

- **BRIEF CHAPTER OUTLINE:**

This one-page outline provides a quick overview of the topics covered in the chapter.

- **LEARNING GOALS:**

The entire text and instructional package revolves around the learning goals. The learning goals outline what students are expected to be able to do after reading each chapter.

KEY TERMS:

This is a list of the key terms that are printed in bold in the body of the text, reproduced in the text margin, and listed at the end of each chapter of the book.

LECTURE OUTLINE/LECTURE NOTES:

To make the system easy to use, the detailed lecture outline contains marginal notes recommending where to use acetates, transparency masters, supplementary cases, lecture enhancers, and critical thinking exercises. When the instructor's manual is opened flat, the lecture outline is on the left-side page. If all you want is a thorough outline of the chapter, you can ignore the notations and material on the facing page. The lecture outline remains uninterrupted since all of the references to supplements and article summaries, etc are on the right-side Lecture Notes pages. (If you would like to use a word processor to reorganize the lecture outline, the outline is available on the Presentation CD-ROM.)

- **OVERHEAD TRANSPARENCY ACETATES:**

  There are more than 260 color acetates available to augment the concepts presented in the text. All of these visual aids were taken from sources outside of the text. Teaching suggestions for using this acetates are appropriately integrated throughout the chapter. The teaching suggestions are also supplied on the slip sheets that accompany the acetates in case you prefer to organize your lecture without the aid of this manual. Thumbnail sketches of the acetates appear near their suggested placement in the lecture notes to help you judge their relevance to your needs without having to rummage through the actual acetates.

- **TRANSPARENCY MASTERS:**

  In addition to the acetates, most of the charts and graphs in the text are reproduced as transparency masters for your use in the classroom.

- **LECTURE ENHANCERS:**

  The lecture enhancers are fresh examples or extended discussions of topics in the text that you can use to enhance your lectures. A brief description of each lecture enhancer is integrated in the lecture notes pages (of course, they include page references for where you can find the complete lecture enhancer in the folder).

ANSWERS TO PRACTICING MANAGEMENT DECISIONS:

This section provides the answers to the cases presented in the text. These are only possible answers. You and your students are likely to have a variety of answers to the case questions.

CRITICAL THINKING EXERCISES:

These exercises are designed to get the students actively involved in the learning process as recommended by SCANS. The exercises help students relate the concepts covered in the text to their own experiences in their own communities. The critical thinking exercises can be used as class activities or outside assignments for individual students or teams of students. Of course, possible answers are provided.

SUPPLEMENTAL CASES:

These cases provide opportunity for additional discussion. The cases can be reproduced for seminar-style classes or for outside assignments. Instructors who prefer to have students create their own case questions will find the supplemental cases easy to reproduce since our suggested questions appear on separate pages than the cases themselves.

You will find that there is much more material than you could possibly use in this manual. That gives you the flexibility to pick and choose what to cover and how to cover it.

Standford Erickson says in his book, *The Essence of Teaching*, that students learn what they care about and remember what they understand. Our job as teachers, therefore, is to show students why they should care about a subject and then help them understand it. We sincerely hope this instructor's manual and the entire integrated teaching and testing system provides you with the materials you need to make your job easier and your students the most caring you've had in your career!

Bill Nickels

Jim McHugh

Susan McHugh

Table of Contents

Table of Contents

Table of Contents

CHAPTER 5.
FORMS OF BUSINESS OWNERSHIP

Table of Contents

Table of Contents

Table of Contents

CHAPTER 10.

MOTIVATING EMPLOYEES AND BUILDING SELF-MANAGED TEAMS

Table of Contents

CHAPTER 11.

HUMAN RESOURCE MANAGEMENT: FINDING AND KEEPING THE BEST EMPLOYEES

What's New in This Edition

The transition from the fourth to the fifth edition is much more subtle than those of previous editions that saw major text reorganizations. Focus groups participants and reviewers sent us a clear message: "You've got the organization right! Enhance, update, and refine—but do not move a thing." In response to their recommendations, the following changes were made:

- The most unexpected request, and one that came from many schools, was to focus attention on the need for students to develop proper business etiquette and professional behavior. We address these important issues in the new "Secrets to Your Success" prologue. To highlight this important theme, which we carry throughout the text, a special video was created to show students proper professional behavior and etiquette.
- More coverage of technology was integrated throughout the text beginning with a new appendix, Driver's Ed for the Information Superhighway. This brief overview of how to use the Internet is organized in a question-and-answer format so that new as well as experienced net surfers can quickly access the information they need.
- Taking It to the Net exercises were added to the end of each chapter. These Internet exercises encourage students to surf the Web to find information and other tools that will enhance the concepts in the text.
- Internet addresses for companies featured as examples in the text are listed in an index at the end of the book. Web addresses for companies profiled in chapter boxes are included on the box title band.
- Business Week boxes featuring summaries of articles from this popular publication are included to provide more "real world" examples of companies that use the concepts presented in the text. (Instructors now have the option of offering their students discounted Business Week subscriptions as well.)
- A slang glossary was added to assist English-as-a-second-language students. In addition to this glossary, audiotapes of the text are available that will help these students learn the English language while learning about business.
- The latest business topics were integrated throughout the text. Examples of the new topics include:
- Economic problems in Asia
- ISO 14000
- Latest uses of the Internet, intranets and extranets
- Year 2000 problems (Y2K)
- Learning organizations
- Contingent workers
- Hoteling/hot desks
- Customer relationship management

- Micropreneurs and home-based businesses
- Most recent fiscal and monetary policies in the United States
- Internet 2
- Cookies
- Internet security issues
- Push technology
- Proposed merger of Nasdaq and Amex
- 1997 stock market downturn
- Diluted earnings per share
- Roth IRAs

These and other changes resulted in a more efficient text than the previous editions without losing the personal, interactive tone. Detailed explanations of chapter changes can be found in the What's New section for each chapter.

Suggested Class Schedule

16-WEEK TERM

WEEK	TOPICS	CHAPTER ASSIGNMENT
1	Introduction to Course & Text	Prologue
	Finding Opportunities in Today's Dynamic Business Environments	1
	Economics: The Creation and Distribution of Wealth	2
2	Economics: The Creation and Distribution of Wealth	(2 cont'd)
	Competing in Global Markets	3
	Overcoming Hurdles in Global Markets	(3 cont'd)
3	Demonstrating Ethical Behavior and Social Responsibility	4
	Section Review and Recap	
	Exam I	
4	Forms of Business Ownership	5
	Franchising	(5 cont'd)
	Entrepreneurship and Starting a Small Business	6
5	Starting a Small Business	(6 cont'd)
	Section Review and Recap	
	Exam II	
6	Management, Leadership, and Employee Empowerment	7
	Building Management Skills	(7 cont'd)
	Organizing a Customer-Driven Business	8
7	Organizational Models, Restructuring, and Quality	(8 cont'd)
	Using the Latest Technology to Produce World-Class Products and Services	9
	Section Review and Recap	
8	Exam III	
	Motivating Employees and Building Self-Managed Teams	10
	Applying Theories of Motivation	(10 cont'd)

WEEK	TOPICS	CHAPTER ASSIGNMENT
9	Human Resource Management: Finding and Keeping the Best Employees	11
	Dealing with Employment-Management Issues and Relationships	12
	Section Review and Recap	
10	Exam IV	
	Marketing: Building Customer Relationships	13
	Developing and Pricing Quality Products and Services	14
11	Product Life Cycles and Competitive Pricing	(14 cont'd)
	Distributing Products Efficiently and Competitively	15
	Understanding Functions of Middlemen	(15 cont'd)
12	Promoting Products Using Integrated Marketing Communication	16
	Section Review and Recap	
	Exam V	
13	Using Technology to Manage Information	17
	Understanding Financial Information and Accounting	18
	Using Ratio Analysis	(18 cont'd)
14	Section Review and Recap	
	Exam VI	
	Using Financial Resources	19
15	Financing and Investing Through Securities Market	20
	Choosing the Right Investments	(20 cont'd)
	Understanding Money and Financial Institutions	21
16	Developing and Managing Your Personal Finances	22
	Section Review and Recap	
	Exam VII or Final Exam	

14-WEEK TERM

WEEK	TOPICS	CHAPTER ASSIGNMENT
1	Introduction to Course & Text Prologue	
	Finding Opportunities in Today's Dynamic Business Environment	1
	Economics: The Creation and Distribution of Wealth	2
2	Economics: The Creation and Distribution of Wealth	(2 cont'd)
	Competing in Global Markets	3
	Overcoming Hurdles in Global Markets	(3 cont'd)
3	Demonstrating Ethical Behavior And Social Responsibility	4
	Forms of Business Ownership	5
	Franchising	(5 cont'd)
4	Entrepreneurship and Starting a Small Business	6
	Starting a Small Business	(6 cont'd)
	Section Review and Recap	
5	Exam I	
	Management, Leadership, and Employee Empowerment	7
	Building Management Skills	(7 cont'd)
6	Organizing a Customer-Driven Business	8
	Organizational Models, Restructuring, and Quality	(8 cont'd)
	Using the Latest Technology Produce World-Class Products and Services	9
7	Motivating Employees and Building Self-Managed Teams	10
	Applying Theories of Motivation	(10 cont'd)
	Human Resource Management: Finding and Keeping the Best Employees	11
8	Dealing with Employment-Management Issues and Relationships	12
	Section Review and Recap	
	Exam II	
9	Marketing: Building Customer Relationships	13
	Developing and Pricing Quality Products and Services	14
	Product Life Cycles and Competitive Pricing	(14 cont'd)

WEEK	TOPICS	CHAPTER ASSIGNMENT
10	Distributing Products Efficiently and Competitively	15
	Understanding Functions of Middlemen	(15 cont'd)
	Promoting Products Using Integrated Marketing Communication	16
11	Section Review and Recap	
	Exam III	
	Using Technology to Manage Information	17
12	Understanding Financial Information and Accounting	18
	Using Ratio Analysis	(18 cont'd)
	Using Financial Resources	19
13	Financing and Investing Through Securities Markets	20
	Choosing the Right Investments	(20 cont'd)
	Understanding Money and Financial Institutions	21
14	Developing and Managing Your Personal Finances	22
	Section Review and Recap	
	Exam IV or Final Exam	

10-WEEK TERM

WEEK	TOPICS	CHAPTER ASSIGNMENT
1	Introduction to Course & Text	Prologue
	Finding Opportunities in Today's Dynamic Business Environments	1
	Economics: The Creation and Distribution of Wealth	2
2	Economics: The Creation and Distribution of Wealth	(2 cont'd)
	Competing in Global Markets	3
	Overcoming Hurdles in Global Markets	(3 cont'd)
3	Demonstrating Ethical Behavior And Social Responsibility	4
	Forms of Business Ownership	5
	Entrepreneurship and Starting a Small Business	6
4	Starting a Small Business	(6 cont'd)
	Exam I	
	Management, Leadership, and Employee Empowerment	7
5	Organizing a Customer-Driven Business	8
	Using the Latest Technology to Produce World-Class Products and Services	9
	Motivating Employees and Building Self-Managed Teams	10
6	Human Resource Management: Finding and Keeping the Best Employees	11
	Dealing with Employment-Management Issues and Relationships	12
	Exam II	
7	Marketing: Building Customer Relationships	13
	Developing and Pricing Quality Products and Services	14
	Distributing Products Efficiently and Competitively	15
8	Promoting Products Using Integrated Marketing Communication	16
	Exam III	
	Using Technology to Manage Information	17
9	Understanding Financial Information and Accounting	18
	Using Financial Resources	19
	Financing and Investing Through Securities Markets	20

WEEK	TOPICS	CHAPTER ASSIGNMENT
10	Understanding Money and Financial Institutions	21
	Developing and Managing Your Personal Finances	22
	Exam IV or Final Exam	

8-WEEK TERM

WEEK	TOPICS	CHAPTER ASSIGNMENT
1	Introduction to Course & Text and Finding Opportunities in Today's Dynamic Business Environments	Prologue and 1
	Economics: The Creation and Distribution of Wealth	2
	Competing in Global Markets	3
2	Demonstrating Ethical Behavior and Social Responsibility	4
	Forms of Business Ownership	5
	Entrepreneurship and Starting a Small Business	6
3	Management, Leadership, and Employee Empowerment	7
	Organizing a Customer-Driven Business	8
	Using the Latest Technology to Produce World-Class Products and Services	9
4	Motivating Employees and Building Self-Managed Teams	10
	Human Resource Management: Finding and Keeping the Best Employees	11
	Dealing with Employment-Management Issues and Relationships	12
5	Mid-Term	
	Marketing: Building Customer Relationships	13
	Developing and Pricing Quality Products and Services	14
6	Distributing Products Efficiently and Competitively	15
	Promoting Products Using Integrated Marketing Communication	16
	Using Technology to Manage Information	17
7	Understanding Financial Information and Accounting	18
	Using Financial Resources	19
	Financing and Investing Through Securities Markets	20
8	Understanding Money and Financial Institutions	21
	Developing and Managing Your Personal Finances	22
	Final Exam	

6-WEEK TERM

WEEK	TOPICS	CHAPTER ASSIGNMENT
1	Introduction to Course & Text and Finding Opportunities in Today's Dynamic Business Environments	Prologue and 1
	Economics: The Creation and Distribution of Wealth	2
	Competing in Global Markets	3
	Demonstrating Ethical Behavior And Social Responsibility	4
2	Forms of Business Ownership	5
	Entrepreneurship and Starting a Small Business	6
	Management, Leadership, and Employee Empowerment	7
	Organizing a Customer-Driven Business	8
3	Using the Latest Technology to Produce World-Class Products and Services	9
	Motivating Employees and Building Self-Managed Teams	10
	Human Resource Management: Finding and Keeping the Best Employees	11
	Dealing with Employment-Management Issues and Relationships	12
4	Mid-Term	
	Marketing: Building Customer Relationships	13
	Developing and Pricing Quality Products and Services	14
	Distributing Products Efficiently and Competitively	15
	Promoting Products Using Integrated Marketing Communication	16
5	Using Technology to Manage Information	17
	Understanding Financial Information and Accounting	18
	Using Financial Resources	19
	Financing and Investing Through Securities Markets	20
6	Understanding Money and Financial Institutions	21
	Developing and Managing Your Personal Finances	22
	Final Exam	

(Confidential for Students Using This Text)

Prologue

Folder Contents

OT ACETATE P-4 Career Expectations and Opportunities Analysis

OT ACETATE P-5 Six Keys to Career Self Reliance

OT ACETATE P-6 Planning For a Return to the Workforce

OT ACETATE P-7 Where Are the Jobs of the Future

OT ACETATE P-8 Enrollments in Higher Education

OT ACETATE P-9 Number of Students Completing 4-Year Degrees

(Acetates and Transparency Masters are also available as PowerPoint slides on disk and on the Presentation CD-ROM.)

(Resources Available are also referenced in the expanded lecture outline later in this chapter.)

Other Resources Available

Video Case - "Business Etiquette." Start students off on the right foot with this video that portrays examples of effective and ineffective behaviors in the workplace. (The **Media Resource Guide** contains a summary of the Video and suggested discussion questions.)

Student Assessment and Learning Guide: Contains matching key term and definition questions, write-in retention questions, write-in critical thinking questions, and practice test of multiple choice and true/false questions.

Technology:

Zapitalism CD-ROM - Simulation program.

Concept Mastery Exam Preparation Disk - Practice test and tutorial.

Business Essentials Disk - Hyperlinks Understanding Business with seven other leading business texts.

Presentation CD-ROM - Contains PowerPoint slides of acetates and transparency masters, video clips, lecture materials. This tool allows you to customize your lecture presentations.

***Business Week* Web Site Access with the *Business Week* edition.**

***Understanding Business* Home Page - http:/www.mhhe.com/ub5e.**

Audiotape: Abridged chapter (Text minus profile, boxes, and end-of-chapter material.

What's New in This Edition

Additions:

- Section "Another Secret Weapon: Good Manners"
- Section "Learning to Act Like a Professional"

Revisions:

Statistical data and examples throughout the chapter were updated to reflect current information. In addition:

- The list of outside readings was revised and updated.
- The Section "Resources for the Course" was expanded to include discussions of working in teams and researching on the Internet.
- Section "The Secret To Getting The Most From This Text (And An A In The Course)" was revised to include a list of all the elements of the text and a description of how to use them.

Deletions:

- Profile
- Section "Which College is Best for Me?

Brief Chapter Outline/Learning Goals

PROLOGUE

SECRETS TO YOUR SUCCESS (CONFIDENTIAL FOR STUDENT USING THIS TEXT)

I. YOU ALREADY KNOW ONE SECRET: THE VALUE OF A COLLEGE EDUCATION.

II. THE SECRET TO STARTING A SUCCESSFUL CAREER.

A. Getting Started.

B. Assessing Your Skills and Personality.

C. Learning Professional Business Strategies.

III. ANOTHER SECRET WEAPON: GOOD MANNERS.

A. Good Manners Are Back.

B. Learning to Act Like a Professional.

IV. THE SECRET OF THE RESOURCES FOR THIS COURSE.

A. The Professor as a Resource.

B. The Text and the Study Guide as a Resource.

C. Outside Readings as a Resource.

D. Your Experience and That of Your Classmates as Resources.

E. Outside Contacts as a Resource.

F. The Internet as a Resource.

G. The Library or Learning Resource Center as a Resource.

V. THE SECRET TO GETTING THE MOST FROM THIS TEXT (AND IN THE COURSE).

A. List of Learning Goals.

B. Self-test Questions.

C. Key Terms.

D. Boxes.

E. End-of-Chapter Summaries.

F. Developing Workplace Skills Exercises.

G. Taking it to the Net Exercises.

H. Practicing Management Decisions.

Lecture Outline

I. YOU ALREADY KNOW ONE SECRET: THE VALUE OF A COLLEGE EDUCATION.

A. **BUSINESS OPPORTUNITIES HAVE NEVER BEEN GREATER**—and there have never been more challenges.

1. The purpose of this text is to help you learn some **SECRETS OF SUCCESS** that will help you in this course and in your career.
2. Because college graduates will hold seven or eight different jobs in their lifetimes, you will have to **BE FLEXIBLE** and **ADJUST YOUR TALENTS** to new opportunities.
3. You don't have to be in business to use business principles.
4. The skills learned in this course will help you not only in a business career, but in all areas of your life.

B. **THE VALUE OF A COLLEGE EDUCATION.**

1. The gap between the earnings of high school graduates and college graduates is now from 60% to 70%.
2. To get the most out of your college education, you must **BECOME FAMILIAR WITH COMPUTERS.**

Lecture Notes

TRANSPARENCY MASTER 1
Chapter Outline

Transparency Masters begin on page P.27.

OT ACETATE P-1
Business Training For the 21st Century

Business Training for the 21st Century

Changes in business education should include:

- A greater emphasis on people skills.
- More global perspectives.
- The fostering of creativity & innovation.
- Real-world problem solving.
- Examining business issues from the viewpoint of several disciplines.

Comments:

1. This acetate focuses on the ever-changing curriculum in business administration. The proposed changes in training were suggested by the University of Pennsylvania's Wharton School.
2. You can go over each of these principles one by one and solicit student comments. An interesting question students could be asked is, "which of these principles will be most appropriate in your own career and why?"
3. It's also helpful to point out at this stage that the textbook makes a concerted effort to cover each of these changes in the chapter-by-chapter analysis. Students could keep a running diary of how information they read in the text relates to one or more of the specific criteria cited by the Wharton school.
4. This is also a good time to remind students of the boxed inserts that appear in each chapter. The 5th edition of Understanding Business includes in each chapter a box on global business, small business, ethical decisions, and a new feature from the pages of Business Week Magazine, and a legal briefcase box where appropriate. Remind students to read these and note the application of the boxes to the material covered in the chapter. The 5th edition test bank will include questions from the boxed material. They read the boxed material more intensely if they feel test questions are forthcoming.

Lecture Outline

II. THE SECRET TO STARTING A SUCCESSFUL CAREER.

A. One purpose of this course is to help you become aware of **DIFFERENT CAREER OPTIONS**.

1. You will learn about production, marketing, finance, accounting, economics, personnel, management, and more.
2. You will also be prepared to use basic business terms and concepts that are necessary in any organization.
3. Your textbook is a **GUIDE TO UNDERSTANDING BUSINESS.**

B. **GETTING STARTED.**

1. Each chapter will begin with a profile of someone in the business world.
2. Each section of the book ends with a profile of a recent student who used the concepts of this course to begin their careers.
3. These stories are a good way to learn from the experiences of others.

C. **ASSESSING YOUR SKILLS AND PERSONALITY.**

1. There are a variety of **ASSESSMENT PROGRAMS** you can take to help you find out what careers might interest you (i.e. SIGI,

Lecture Notes

OT ACETATE P-2
Key Career Questions

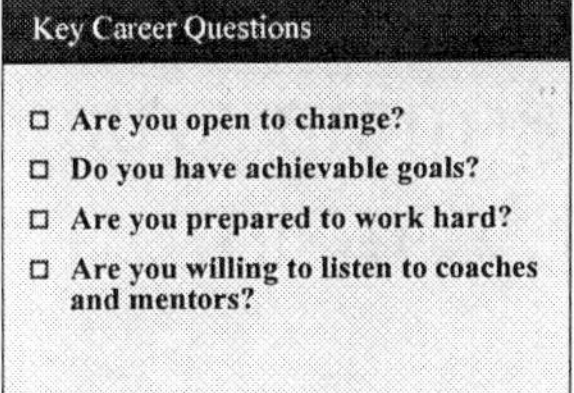

Comments:

1. The information here provides a good self-test for students. The four points can be discussed either during class or as an outside assignment.
2. It's important to remind students that honesty is the key to providing an accurate assessment of where they stand at this point in their careers. There will most likely be pointed differences between day and evening classes as they assess where they stand presently. Evening students tend to be much more focused in their answers and assessments.
3. A couple of questions you may consider implementing here include. What do you think "prepared to work hard" actually means? What must be considered in setting goals that are achievable? How hard should you push yourself to attain your goals and objectives? Lots of opportunities here.

LECTURE ENHANCER P-1
Success of Women Entrepreneurs

Three women entrepreneurs represent a growing trend today: people of all ages are discovering the rewards, and challenges, of owning and building their own businesses. (See complete lecture enhancer on page P.26).

DISCOVER, Strong-Campbell Interest Inventory.)

2. It would be helpful to take such assessment programs early so you can determine which business fields most closely fit your interests and skills.

3. These assessment tests can be accessed by most college placement centers, career labs, and libraries.

D. **LEARNING PROFESSIONAL BUSINESS STRATEGIES.**

1. **TWO SECRETS** to success that you should be practicing now are **NETWORKING** and **KEEPING FILES ON SUBJECTS THAT ARE IMPORTANT TO YOU.**

    a. Also important is keeping names of **CONTACT PEOPLE** at various organizations.

    b. You may want to **KEEP FACTS AND FIGURES** of all kinds of economy and business related subjects.

2. One good way to become an expert on almost any business subject is to **CREATE YOUR OWN INFORMATION SYSTEM.**

    a. Eventually you may want to store data on computer disks.

Lecture Notes

OT ACETATE P-3
How to Grow a Career

How to Grow in a Career

- Enjoy what you do.
- Never stop learning about technology and management skills.
- Try to get some international experience.
- Think about new business opportunities.
- Be willing to work in teams and help others grow on the job.

Comments:

1. Since career development is a key theme of the text, the focus on careers continues with this acetate.
2. The acetate provides a sort of how to get where you want to go format. Students often neglect to think of specifics such as doing something you like enhances the potential to do well. They instead tend to focus on factors such as money and prestige.
3. Points two and three highlight the importance of learning and education in relation to career growth and development. It's important at this point for students to realize that education and learning are life-long processes. As the workplace changes and job requirements expand, continuous growth and development is the key. Students can also hone from this acetate the necessity of learning about technology and the global market. Again, these two points are key themes of the text.
4. You may want to introduce just briefly the idea of critical or conceptual thinking through points four and five in the acetate. It may be useful to point out that throughout the text students will face critical thinking challenges that test their full understanding concerning a situation or important concept.

OT ACETATE P-4
Career Expectations and Opportunities Analysis

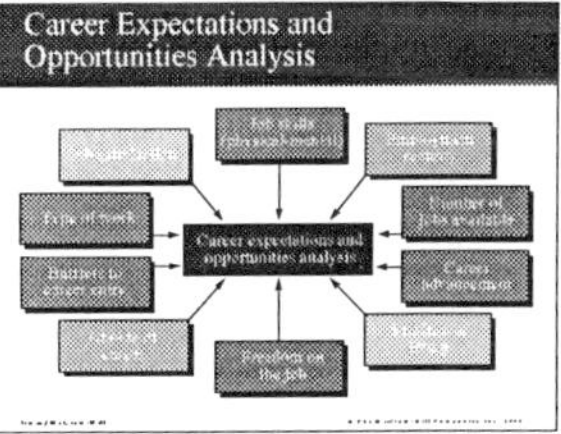

Comments:

1. This acetate outlines some of the questions that students must ask themselves concerning their career expectations.
2. It also serves as an effective checklist in evaluating opportunities associated with specific career decisions.
3. This is also a good starting point to direct students toward a "future perspective" in approaching career decisions. Questions such as number of jobs available, employment security, barriers to career entry, etc. in the future can be successfully approached from this acetate.
4. The economic problems of the early 1990s, the job shifts of the mid-1990s, and the employment boom of the late 1990s, should reinforce the information in the acetate. Students should be keenly aware of the challenge of selecting the proper career focus. It's possible many in the class will be already working on their second or third careers. An interesting exercise could be to have students relate to the class any career shifts that have occurred in their lives and why they occurred.

Lecture Outline

b. Cut out or copy stories that interest you put them in an appropriate file.

c. This will save a lot of research time when you need the information.

3. You should have a personal data file titled **"CREDENTIALS FOR MY RESUME"** containing reference letters and other job-related information.

4. Developing this habit is one of the most effective ways of educating yourself and having the information available when you need it.

5. Watching programs such as "Wall $treet Week" and Adam Smith's "Money World" is like getting a free graduate education in business.

III. ANOTHER SECRET WEAPON: GOOD MANNERS.

A. **GOOD MANNERS ARE BACK.**

1. The **PERSON WHO MAKES A GOOD IMPRESSION** will be the one who gets the job, wins the promotion, or clinches the deal.

2. It is important to **MAINTAIN YOUR COMPOSURE** at work and not lose your temper.

Lecture Notes

OT ACETATE P-5
Six Keys to Career Self Reliance

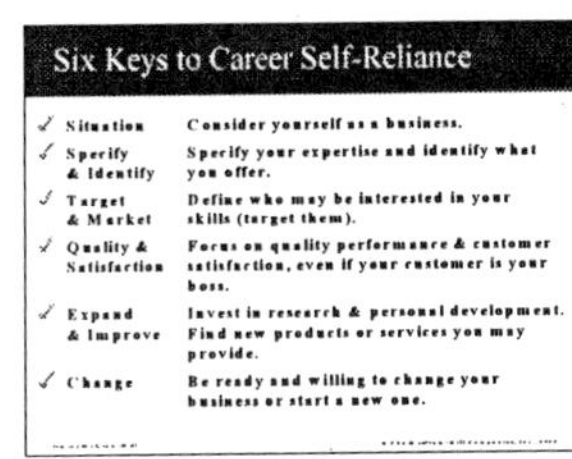

Comments:

1. Vicky Farrow, director of executive and work force development at Sun Microsystems, developed these keys for employees at Sun to follow. It was her intention that employees assume a sense of personal responsibility for their own careers.
2. You might want to work through each of these assumptions one-by-one and advise students how to apply each concept. Student comments and suggestions can also be generated. (It's often surprising what students will come up with.)
3. The premise of the worker as a full-functioning business, fits well with the discussion of empowerment that students will be exposed to in the text. You could give the students a class assignment to take these six points and develop a profile of themselves as businesses. It would be interesting to see what they note as their key strengths.

B. **LEARNING TO ACT LIKE A PROFESSIONAL.**

1. You can learn about good and bad manners from watching professional sports.

2. Business professionals also follow rules; many are not formally written, but every successful businessperson knows them.

3. **HABITS THAT WILL MAKE FOR SUCCESS IN YOUR CAREER INCLUDE:**

   a. Making a Good First Impression.

   b. Focus on Good Grooming.

   c. Being on Time.

   d. Practicing Considerate Behavior.

   e. Being Prepared.

4. Business etiquette has **DIFFERENT MEANINGS IN DIFFERENT COUNTRIES;** it is important to learn the proper etiquette for each.

5. Honesty, high ethical standards, and good character are important ingredients to success in any country.

IV. THE SECRET OF THE RESOURCES FOR THIS COURSE.

A. College courses such as this are best at teaching concepts and ways of thinking about business.

Lecture Notes

Lecture Outline

1. Textbooks are like **COMPREHENSIVE TOUR GUIDES**, but they can't replace experience.
2. There are **SEVEN BASIC RESOURCES** for the class in addition to the text.

B. **THE PROFESSOR AS A RESOURCE.**

1. While you are taking this course, your professor can help you find materials and answer questions.
2. After the course, professors often pass on job leads and write job references.
3. Your professor can help you find resource materials and answer questions.

C. **THE TEXT AND THE STUDY GUIDE AS A RESOURCE.**

1. The **STUDY GUIDE** will help you review and interpret key material and give you practice in answering test questions.

D. **OUTSIDE READINGS AS A RESOURCE.**

1. Reading outside journals and magazines will help you understand the relationship of the concepts in the text.
2. Such resources include: *The Wall Street Journal, Forbes, Inc., Business Week, Fortune, The Harvard Business Review,*

Lecture Notes

Lecture Outline

Nation's Business, Black Enterprise, and *Entrepreneur* as well as the business section of your local paper.

3. One secret to success in business is **STAYING CURRENT**, and these magazines will help.

E. **YOUR EXPERIENCE AND THAT OF YOUR CLASSMATES AS RESOURCES**.

1. **WORKING WITH OTHERS** is an important business skill.

   a. Some of your fellow students have experience that can be beneficial for you.

   b. **SHARE YOUR EXPERIENCES** with each other and you will all benefit.

2. By working with students from other countries, you can **LEARN ABOUT DIFFERENT CULTURES AND DIFFERENT APPROACHES** to handling business problems.

F. **OUTSIDE CONTACTS AS A RESOURCE**.

1. The best way to find out about specific careers is to **GO OUT AND TALK TO PEOPLE** in those jobs.

2. You will learn more about career opportunities later in the course.

OT ACETATE P-6
Planning a Return to the Workforce

Planning for a Return to the Workforce

- Volunteer or work freelance.
- Get involved in professional organizations and associations.
- Clearly define your specific skills.
- Research employers' most pressing needs and priorities.
- Plan on how to apply your past experience to the current workplace.
- Do some public speaking.

Comments:

1. This acetate is particularly important for returning students such as displaced or downsized workers, returning home-makers, or any others pursuing work via the traditional job search or through and entrepreneurial venture.
2. The things students should like about this acetate is that the majority of the information included is just straight common sense. Often returning students are so intimidated about their job quest that it's hard for them to remain focused.
3. This is an ideal time if you have a guest speaker (especially a former student) address the class about the challenges of returning to the workforce or for some breaking into the workplace. The speaker could use this acetate as the foundation for his/her discussion.
4. The acetate is particularly helpful in focusing on students researching their skills, needs of particular employers, and the demands of the current workplace. Often students have no idea where to start in beginning a job search.
5. The information also recommends active student involvement in terms of doing volunteer or free lance work, developing public speaking skills, and learning the benefits of professional associations and organizations.

OT ACETATE P-7
Where Are the Jobs of the Future?

Comments:

1. A question that virtually all students are interested in. This information is from an article in Business Week magazine. If you would like a copy of the article, please call or e-mail one of the authors and we will get you a copy as soon as possible.
2. Students may be a bit surprised at the growth of jobs in education. It might be helpful to point out that a new "boom" is expected at the elementary school level. However an additional growth in the population under age 17 will also create significant demand for teachers. Fastest growing areas math, science, business, and English as a second language.
3. They may also question the "growth" in jobs in manufacturing. It's important to remind them that specialty manufacturing is different from what they perceive of the old assembly lines. An assignment to find a specialty manufacturer and prepare a short report on what this manufacturer does could reinforce the growing opportunities in this area.
4. This could be an appropriate time to challenge students understanding of demographic trends in our economy. They should be able to identify that opportunities will grow in health care, social services, and financial consulting due to the aging of the U.S. population.

Lecture Outline

3. You will even be given a step-by-step procedure for getting a job.

G. **THE INTERNET AS A RESOURCE.**

1. Never have students had access to information as easily as today.
2. Once you've learned to surf the Internet, you can search through library catalogues, find articles in business journals, and more.
3. The information changes very rapidly, and **IT IS UP TO YOU TO STAY CURRENT.**

H. **THE LIBRARY OR LEARNING RESOURCE CENTER AS A RESOURCE.**

1. The library is a great complement to the Internet as a resource.
2. **WORKING AS AN INTERN** in a firm can give you a better feel for what people do.
3. The library has a wealth of resources to use in your career search.
   a. The text lists a number of them.
   b. There are many more you can add to the list yourself.

V. **THE SECRET TO GETTING THE MOST FROM THIS TEXT (AND IN THE COURSE).**

Lecture Notes

OT ACETATE P-8
Enrollments in Higher Education

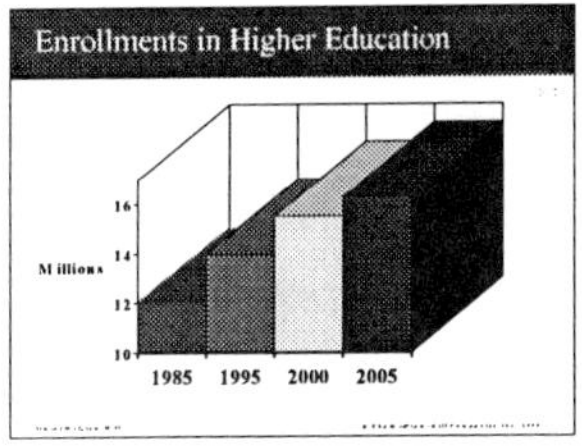

Comments:

1. Students can see from this acetate that higher education is no longer a luxury but instead is a necessity. As the numbers indicate, more and more Americans are seeking advanced education.
2. You may want to question students why the numbers in higher education continue to accelerate. They should be able to figure out from the previous acetate that the workplace is dictating that workers of the future be more skilled with higher levels of education.
3. This could be an opportune time to ask students how the delivery and presentation of higher education may change by the year 2005. Many will identify that the Internet will allow for different teaching methods and offer significant opportunities in distance learning. It's interesting to see if your students would prefer the traditional format of higher education versus the high-tech applications promised in the future.
4. Information is available from the U.S. Census Bureau concerning the lifetime earnings of workers with different levels of education. As you may expect, the spread is growing between college-educated workers and those that lack a college degree. E-mail the authors if you would like more specific information.

OT ACETATE P-9
Number of Students Completing 4-Year Degrees

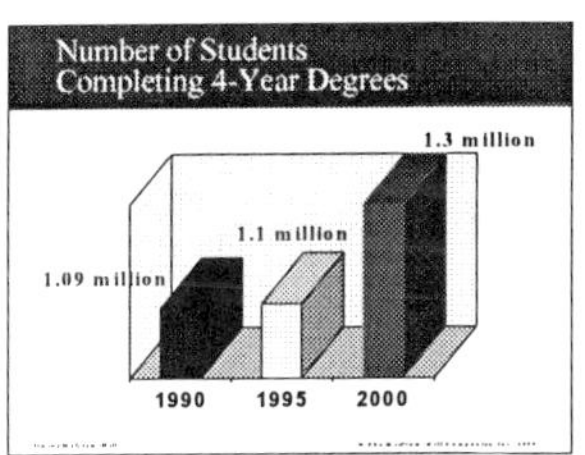

Comments:

1. As this acetate highlights, the number of Americans with degrees is accelerating. They may be interested in knowing that by 2000, it's expected the number of degreed persons in the U.S. could increase to more than 30 percent of the population.
2. It could be interesting to look around your class and observe the numbers of non-traditional students present in the course. Check and see how many students represent the following groups:
   a. Veterans upgrading job skills.
   b. Workers displaced from jobs.
   c. Workers looking to upgrade their skills.
   d. Displaced homemakers, single parents, etc.
3. An interesting discussion can be pursued pertaining to why the different groups of students are seeking degrees and how they can help each other in attaining a common goal of all groups to understand the course.
4. Other topics that can be addressed from the acetate include the importance of updating skills, the growth at many campuses of part-time students, the importance of education at any age, etc.

Lecture Outline

A. **LIST OF LEARNING GOALS**—These let you know what you are supposed to learn in each chapter.

B. **SELF-TEST QUESTIONS**—APPEARING periodically throughout each chapter, these sections give you a chance to stop and think about what you just read.

C. **KEY TERMS**—These vocabulary words are highlighted in boldface and defined in the margins the first time they appear in the text.

D. **BOXES**—Each chapter contains numerous boxes that contain extended examples of the concepts in the text.

1. **ETHICS** (Making Ethical Decisions)
2. **ENTREPRENEURSHIP** (From the Pages of *Business Week* Magazine)
3. **SMALL BUSINESS** (Spotlight on Small Business)
4. **LEGAL ENVIRONMENT OF BUSINESS** (Legal Briefcase)
5. **GLOBAL BUSINESS** (Reaching Beyond Our Borders)

E. **END-OF-CHAPTER SUMMARIES**—Written in a question and answer format, these summaries are keyed to the chapter's learning goals.

Lecture Notes

Lecture Outline

F. **DEVELOPING WORKPLACE SKILLS EXERCISES**—These exercises are designed to reinforce what you have learned by having you get involved by applying the concepts in outside activities.

G. **TAKING IT TO THE NET EXERCISES**—These exercises serve to enhance your understanding of the concepts presented in the chapter and build your Internet skills.

H. **PRACTICING MANAGEMENT DECISIONS**—These end-of-the-chapter cases apply the concepts to real-life situations.

Lecture Notes

Lecture Enhancers

LECTURE ENHANCER P-1

SUCCESS OF WOMEN ENTREPRENEURS

Kelly Stratico-Smith and Laura Biondi-Williams each has two children. Like many mothers today, they were both busy carting their children to school, music lessons, dentist appointments, and more. Unable to obtain help or relief from these transportation duties, Kelly and Laura decided to assist other mothers in the area with similar needs. They started a part-time service in Santa Cruz, California, that for a fee would pickup children at their homes and take them to various activities. They bought a couple of white vans and put signs on them saying, "KART! Kids Area Rapid Transit."

Smith and Williams didn't do any special marketing research before starting their business. They simply saw a need and filed it. It turned out that there was no competition in the area, and their service increased to 400 rides a week (at $6 a ride) and seven employees. Now these entrepreneurs are planning to expand into all of California's major cities. These two women represent a major trend in the country today. People of all ages are discovering the rewards, and the challenges, of owning and building their own businesses.

Linda Grabill is another entrepreneur who, as an 18-year-old student, decided to start her own summer lawn-care company. Her motivation to do so came from the realization that, if successful, she could make $30 an hour rather than the $6 she could earn as a store cashier. Linda's Lawn Care is a success, has two additional employees, and pays tor many of her college expenses.

For various reasons beyond their control, many students and young married people are finding it harder to find attractive jobs in local businesses. The result has been positive for many, however, because the scarcity of jobs has opened their eyes to the opportunities of owning their own businesses.

Colleges and universities throughout the country are responding to the desire for students to own their own businesses. Community demand led Montgomery College in Rockville, Maryland, to offer a summer course that teaches students how to develop business plans and to learn other business skills. Howard University in Washington, D.C. has a Small Business Development Center that teaches teenagers how to start and manage businesses. Students lineup early in the morning to register for the University of Southern California's Entrepreneurship Program.

A survey by the Higher Education Research Institute at the University of California at Los Angeles found that 42 percent of college freshmen said that eventually owning their own business was very important to them. Many of today's students are individualistic and idealistic. To them, starting a business is more than a way to make money. It is also a way to be on your own and to make a difference in the world.

There are many risks involved in starting your own business and much that you must earn. For those who don't want to assume that much risk, there are many excellent opportunities working for others in business firms, nonprofit organizations, and government.

Transparency Masters

TRANSPARENCY MASTER 1 Chapter Outline

Chapter Outline

PROLOGUE
SECRETS TO YOUR SUCCESS

I. YOU ALREADY KNOW ONE SECRET: THE VALUE OF A COLLEGE EDUCATION.

II. THE SECRET TO STARTING A SUCCESSFUL CAREER.

A. Getting Started.

B. Assessing Your Skills and Personality.

C. Learning Professional Business Strategies.

III. ANOTHER SECRET WEAPON: GOOD MANNERS.

A. Good Manners Are Back.

B. Learning to Act Like a Professional.

IV. THE SECRET OF THE RESOURCES FOR THIS COURSE.

A. The Professor as a Resource.

B. The Text and the Study Guide as a Resource.

C. Outside Readings as a Resource.

D. Your Experience and That of Your Classmates as Resources.

E. Outside Contacts as a Resource.

F. The Internet as a Resource.

G. The Library or Learning Resource Center as a Resource.

V. THE SECRET TO GETTING THE MOST FROM THIS TEXT (AND IN THE COURSE).

A. List of Learning Goals.

B. Self-test Questions.

C. Key Terms.

D. Boxes.

E. End-of-Chapter Summaries.

F. Developing Workplace Skills Exercises.

G. Taking it to the Net Exercises.

H. Practicing Management Decisions.

Appendix
Getting the Job You Want

Folder Contents

TM 4 Interview Rating Sheet *(Figure A.4 on text page P-17)*

TM 5 Sample Résumé *(Figure A.5 on text page P-19)*

TM 6 Sample Cover Letter *(Figure A.6 on text page P-20)*

TM 7 Be Prepared for These Frequently Asked Questions *(Figure A.7 on text page P-21)*

Overhead Transparency Acetates

OT ACETATE P-10 Fastest Growing Areas in Job Growth For the Next 15 Years

(Acetates and Transparency Masters are also available as PowerPoint slides on disk and on the Presentation CD-ROM.)

(Resources Available are also referenced in the expanded lecture outline later in this chapter.)

Other Resources Available

Student Assessment and Learning Guide: Contains matching key term and definition Questions, write-in retention Questions, write-in critical thinking Questions, and practice test of multiple choice and true/false Questions.

Technology:

Zapitalism CD-ROM – Simulation program.

Concept Mastery Exam Preparation Disk – Practice test and tutorial.

Business Essentials Disk – Hyperlinks Understanding Business with seven other leading business texts.

Presentation CD-ROM – Contains PowerPoint slides of acetates and transparency masters, video clips, lecture materials. This tool allows you to customize your lecture presentations.

Business Week **Web Site Access with the** ***Business Week*** **edition.**

Understanding Business **Home Page – http:/www.mhhe.com/ub5e.**

Audiotape: Abridged chapter (Text minus profile, boxes, and end-of-chapter material.

What's New in This Edition

Additions

- Instructions on how to access job search information on the Internet was added to the section "A Five-Step Job Search Strategy."

Revisions

- Statistical data and examples throughout the chapter were updated to reflect current information.

Brief Chapter Outline

APPENDIX A

GETTING THE JOB YOU WANT

I. GETTING THE JOB YOU WANT.

II. A JOB SEARCH STRATEGY.

A. The Job Search.

B. Writing a Résumé

C. Writing a Cover Letter.

III. PREPARING FOR JOB INTERVIEWS.

IV. BE PREPARED TO CHANGE JOBS.

(Learning Objectives are also referenced in the expanded lecture outline later in this chapter)

Lecture Outline

I. GETTING THE JOB YOU WANT.

A. One important objectives of this text is to **HELP YOU GET THE JOB THAT YOU WANT**.

1. First, **DECIDE WHAT JOB YOU WANT**.
2. Do a self-assessment to determine what kind of career would be best for you.

B. If you're older, your assessment probably will reveal that you have handicaps and blessings that younger students do not have.

C. Whatever your age, it is time to develop a **STRATEGY FOR FINDING AND OBTAINING A PERSONALLY SATISFYING JOB**.

II. A JOB SEARCH STRATEGY.

A. **IMPORTANT STEPS:**

1. Complete a self-analysis inventory.
2. Search for jobs you would enjoy.
3. Begin the networking process.
4. Begin investigating companies on the Internet.
5. Find companies looking for people on the Internet.
6. Prepare a good cover letter and résumé.
7. Develop interviewing skills.

Lecture Notes

TRANSPARENCY MASTER 2
Appendix Outline

Transparency Masters begin on page A.18.

OT ACETATE A-10
Fastest Growing Areas in Job Growth For the Next 15 Years

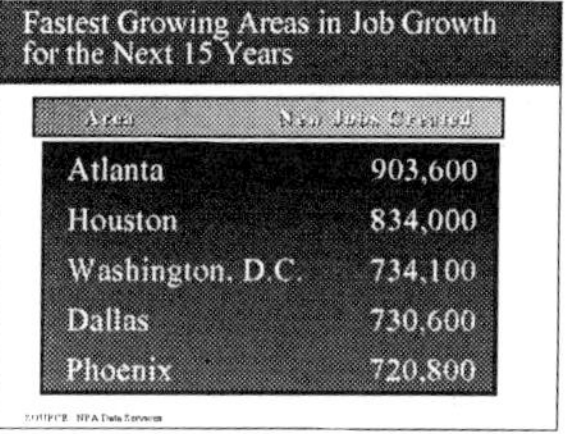

Fastest Growing Areas in Job Growth for the Next 15 Years

Area	New Jobs Created
Atlanta	903,600
Houston	834,000
Washington, D.C.	734,100
Dallas	730,600
Phoenix	720,800

Comments:

1. This acetate is perfect for a short, written or oral quiz in class. It's interesting to note the selections of students and their rationale for suggesting the cities they picked.
2. Students may not be too surprised that Atlanta is at the top the list. Consistent growth and economic strength are the key reasons it ranked first on the list. Since the beginning of the decade, Atlanta has added thousands of jobs to its economy. A good deal of the job shift has happened as many residents have left the mid west and northeast and moved to the emerging south.
3. Houston may cause some moderate surprise among students. Some may see Houston as a rather sleepy, non-dynamic town. However, the truth is the city has a strongly diversified economy that is growing at a fast pace.
4. It's interesting to note that three Southern cities round out the top five metro areas. All have very reasonable costs of living, good educational facilities, and expanding local economies. I suspect we have to violate Horace Greeley's command to go west, and advise students to go south and southwest.
5. The information for this acetate was provided by NPA Data Services, a Washington D.C. research firm. For a list of the top ten, contact the authors.

Lecture Outline

8. Keep after companies in which you have an interest.

B. **THE JOB SEARCH.**

1. The **PLACEMENT BUREAU** at your school is a good place to begin reading about potential employers.
2. **ON-CAMPUS INTERVIEWING** is by far the number one source of jobs.
3. An important source of jobs is **NETWORKING**; that is, finding someone in a firm to recommend you.
4. **OTHER GOOD SOURCES** include the want ads, job fairs, internship programs, placement bureaus, and visiting firms.
5. Check the **INTERVIEW RATING SHEET** in Figure A.4 to see what recruiters want.
6. It is never too early to begin designing a résumé and thinking of cover letters.

C. **WRITING A RÉSUMÉ.**

1. A **RÉSUMÉ** is a document that lists information an employer would need to evaluate you and your background.
2. You must be **COMPREHENSIVE AND CLEAR** if you are to communicate all your attributes.

Lecture Notes

TRANSPARENCY MASTER 3
Where College Students Find Jobs
(Figure A.3 on text page P-15)

TM 3

Transparency Masters begin on page A.18.

TRANSPARENCY MASTER 4
Interview Rating Sheet
(Figure A.4 on text page P-17)

Transparency Masters begin on page A.18.

TRANSPARENCY MASTER 5
Sample Résumé
(Figure A.5 on text page P-19)

Transparency Masters begin on page A.18.

Lecture Outline

3. Your résumé is an **ADVERTISEMENT FOR YOURSELF**—Make yourself look as good on paper as you are in reality.

D. **WRITING A COVER LETTER.**

1. A cover letter is used to **ANNOUNCE YOUR AVAILABILITY** and to introduce the résumé.
2. The cover letter should indicate that you've researched the organization and are interested in a job there.
3. In the description of yourself, be sure to say **HOW YOUR ATTRIBUTES WILL BENEFIT THE ORGANIZATION.**
4. Be sure to say that you are available for an interview.
5. **PRINCIPLES TO FOLLOW IN WRITING A COVER LETTER.**
   a. Be self-confident.
   b. Don't be apologetic or negative.
   c. Research every prospective employer thoroughly before writing anything.
   d. Have your materials prepared by an experienced keyboarder if you are not highly skilled yourself.
   e. Don't send the names of references until asked.

Lecture Notes

LECTURE ENHANCER A-1
More Résumé Guidelines

Résumés should be short, sweet, and to the point. Other do's and don'ts are discussed. (See complete lecture enhancer on page A.14.)

LECTURE ENHANCER A-2
Using the Internet for Résumés

Tens of thousands of college graduates have uploaded their résumés onto the World Wide Web in a high-tech move to attract potential employers. (See complete lecture enhancer on page A.16)

TRANSPARENCY MASTER 6
Sample Cover Letter *(Figure A.6 on text page P-20)*

Transparency Masters begin on page A.18.

Lecture Outline

III. PREPARING FOR JOB INTERVIEWS.

A. Companies usually don't conduct job interviews unless they are somewhat sure the candidate has the requirements for the job.

B. There are **FIVE STAGES OF INTERVIEW PREPARATION.**

1. Research the Prospective Employers.
2. Practice the Interview.
3. Be Professional During the Interview.
4. Follow Up on the Interview.
5. Be Prepared to Act.

IV. BE PREPARED TO CHANGE JOBS.

A. You will probably follow **SEVERAL DIFFERENT CAREER PATHS** over your lifetime.

B. The key to moving forward is a willingness to change jobs, searching for the career that will bring the most satisfaction.

LECTURE ENHANCER A-3
Grade Honesty Becoming More Important

The high school transcript—the document voted most likely to gather dust—is becoming required reading for many employers. (See complete lecture enhancer on page A.17.)

TRANSPARENCY MASTER 7
Be Prepared for These Frequently Asked Questions
(Figure A.7 on text page P-21)

Transparency Masters begin on page A.18.

Lecture Enhancers

LECTURE ENHANCER A-1

MORE RÉSUMÉ GUIDELINES

Having your résumé delivered by a President Clinton look-alike or tailoring it to resemble the Sunday comic strip may get you noticed, but it won't guarantee you an interview. In fact, it may ensure that you don't get one, according to Jerry Brockert, career counselor at Brevard Community College in Melbourne, Fla.

"If you're applying for a professional position, gimmicks like that are not very effective," Brockert said. "Employers don't really want anything cutesy-putesy. It may give them a good laugh, but more than likely your résumé will wind up in the trash."

What is most important, Brockert said, is what is on your résumé and how it is presented. "Résumés must be short, sweet, and to the point," Brockert explained. "In a way, it's a lot like buying a man's suit. We don't have much choice. It's usually blue, black, or gray."

According to Brockert, the average employer spends 30 seconds looking at a résumé. He offered the following advice on making your 30 seconds count:

- **Start with a strong objective.** Besides your name, this is the first thing a prospective employer reads, so make it catchy. Use action words, such as manage or command, to grab their attention. Avoid "seeking a position in . . ." It's also a good idea to list several positions in which you are interested.
- **Under education, list your degree and specialization.** Add your grade point average only if it is a 3.0 or higher. Be sure to mention any extra-curricular activities or club memberships. Also, list any academic achievements.
- **Include a separate section highlighting specific aspects of your qualifications**, including academic or other awards, special projects, independent study, work citations or extensive community service.
- **When listing your work experience, consider using a functional rather than a chronological format**. For example, list types of jobs, such as journalist, and then detail what you've done in that field.
- **Be as accurate as possible.** And definitely do not lie about work experience or academic qualifications. Companies spend an average of $100 to research the background of a new hire.
- **Use keywords or buzzwords,** such as types of software you've used, whether you're PC or Mac literate, speak a foreign language, even model numbers of equipment you're proficient at handling. Many companies now scan their résumés onto computers and catalog them according to keywords.
- **Limit your résumé to one page.** Use standard fonts and avoid printing on paper with designs, such as flowers or kittens. Proofread

your résumé carefully because a spelling mistake could end your chances.

- **Send your résumé to the right person.** Do some research and find out who is hiring for the position. Call and determine the exact requirements to fill the position, then draft a short cover letter showing how you meet those requirements.
- **Consider placing your résumé on-line.**

Brockert warns:

- Do not send employers pictures of yourself.
- Do not send your résumé via fax machine or e-mail unless told to do so.
- Do not list references.
- Do not include personal information, such as, height, weight, marital status, or political/religious ideology.

LECTURE ENHANCER 10-2

USING THE INTERNET FOR RÉSUMÉS

Tens of thousands of college graduates have uploaded their résumés onto the World Wide Web in a high-tech move to attract potential employers. "It's a cost-effective way to broadcast your résumé," said Yolanda Lewis, owner of Net-Connect Information Services Inc. in Maryland. Lewis estimates more than 2,000 companies cruise the Internet daily looking for job applicants.

She said this recent phenomenon has been an overwhelming success in helping to connect recent graduates with the people who count at large companies. "It's been very successful for people who use it not only for submitting résumés, but for networking," Lewis said. "Since you're communicating on line, you don't necessarily have all the barriers you would normally face getting to the decision-makers."

Most college career offices can help students place their résumés on the Internet. Those interested also can call the major Internet access providers for information on their bulletin boards and Web addresses. In addition, there are many private résumé writing services that do everything from writing your résumé to placing it directly into company Web sites, typically for $40 to $80.

But don't rely too heavily on the Internet. Use it as a supplement to traditional methods, she recommends.

LECTURE ENHANCER 10-3

GRADE HONESTY BECOMING MORE IMPORTANT

High-school students who plan to go to college have long worried about the grades they earn. But students who plan to hit the job market right out of high school have had little incentive to do more than the minimum to earn a diploma. That's about to change. The high school transcript—the document voted most likely to gather dust—is becoming required reading for many employers.

IBM has announced that it will begin checking transcripts of job applicants at plants in six states. Entergy, an electric utility with headquarters in New Orleans, said it will require transcripts and will pressure its contractors to do the same.

Studies show a strong correlation between high school grades, attendance, and job performance. By the time graduates with no college are in their 30s, those who got Bs in high school earn an average $6,000 more a year than those who got Ds, says John Bishop, chairman of human resources study at Cornell University. "Most kids don't perceive it to be the case, but in the long run, you'll lose out if you don't study," he said.

The economy has undergone dramatic changes, with the best jobs going to the best trained and educated workers. Companies have cut heavily from middle management, and workers at all levels are expected to be able to communicate effectively and understand technology. "Even ditch diggers need to know how to read a blueprint," said Billy Harper, CEO of Harper Industries in Paduesh, Kentucky, which requires transcripts for all job applicants.

In 1995, only 18 percent of 300 corporate executives surveyed by Cannon Consulting said they would hire a high school graduate for an entry-level job. But with unemployment at a 23-year low, companies cannot ignore recent high school grads in favor of experienced workers or graduates of technical schools and colleges.

Although educators and employers believe requiring transcripts will help motivate students, some question whether enough employers will embrace the practice to make it effective. Although the Green Bay Chamber of Commerce said more than 100 local businesses have pledged to ask to see grades, corporate commitment has been slow in coming.

Inertia can also be found among educators. In Colorado, a bill died in committee in 1997 that would have required that diplomas be printed with grade-point average, attendance, and non-academic achievements, such as an artistic awards.

Transparency Masters

TRANSPARENCY MASTER 2	Appendix Outline
TRANSPARENCY MASTER 3	Where College Students Find Jobs *(Figure A.3 on text page P-15)*
TRANSPARENCY MASTER 4	Interview Rating Sheet *(Figure A.4 on text page P-17)*
TRANSPARENCY MASTER 5	Sample Résumé *(Figure A.5 on text page P-19)*
TRANSPARENCY MASTER 6	Sample Cover Letter *(Figure A.6 on text page P-20)*
TRANSPARENCY MASTER 7	Be Prepared for These Frequently Asked Questions *(Figure A.7 on text page P-21)*

Appendix Outline

APPENDIX
GETTING THE JOB YOU WANT

I. GETTING THE JOB YOU WANT.

II. A JOB SEARCH STRATEGY.

A. The Job Search.

B. Writing a Résumé

C. Writing a Cover Letter.

III. PREPARING FOR JOB INTERVIEWS.

IV. BE PREPARED TO CHANGE JOBS.

Where College Students Find Jobs
(Figure A.3 on text page P-15)

WHERE COLLEGE STUDENTS FIND JOBS

When looking for a job, be sure to check the sources listed below.

SOURCE OF JOB	PERCENTAGE OF NEW EMPLOYEES
On-campus interviewing	49.3%
Write-ins	9.8
Current employee referrals	7.2
Job listings with placement office	6.5
Responses from want ads	5.6
Walk-ins	5.5
Cooperative education programs	4.8
Summer employment	4.7
College faculty/staff referrals	4.5
Internship programs	4.5
High-demand major programs	4.4
Minority career programs	2.9
Part-time employment	2.4
Unsolicited referrals from placement	2.1
Women's career programs	2.1
Job listings with employment agencies	1.9
Referrals from campus organizations	1.8

TM-4

Interview Rating Sheet

(Figure A.4 on text page P-17)

Candidate: "For each characteristic listed below there is a rating scale of 1 through 7, where '1' is generally the most unfavorable rating of the characteristic and '7' the most favorable. Rate each characteristic by *circling* just *one* number to represent the impression you gave in the interview that you have just completed."

Name of Candidate ____________________

1.	Appearance								
	Sloppy	1	2	3	4	5	6	7	Neat
2.	Attitude								
	Unfriendly	1	2	3	4	5	6	7	Friendly
3.	Assertiveness/Verbal Ability								
a.	Responded completely to questions asked								
	Poor	1	2	3	4	5	6	7	Excellent
b.	Clarified personal background and related to job opening and description								
	Poor	1	2	3	4	5	6	7	Excellent
c.	Able to explain and sell job abilities								
	Poor	1	2	3	4	5	6	7	Excellent
d.	Initiated questions regarding position and ?rm								
	Poor	1	2	3	4	5	6	7	Excellent
e.	Expressed thorough knowledge of personal goals and abilities								
	Poor	1	2	3	4	5	6	7	Excellent
4.	Motivation								
	Poor	1	2	3	4	5	6	7	High
5.	Subject/Academic Knowledge								
	Poor	1	2	3	4	5	6	7	Good
6.	Stability								
	Poor	1	2	3	4	5	6	7	Good
7.	Composure								
	Ill at ease	1	2	3	4	5	6	7	Relaxed
8.	Personal Involvement/Activities, Clubs, Etc.								
	Low	1	2	3	4	5	6	7	Very high
9.	Mental Impression								
	Dull	1	2	3	4	5	6	7	Alert
10.	Adaptability								
	Poor	1	2	3	4	5	6	7	Good
11.	Speech Pronunciation								
	Poor	1	2	3	4	5	6	7	Good
12.	Overall Impression								
	Unsatisfactory	1	2	3	4	5	6	7	Highly satisfactory

13. Would you hire this individual if you were permitted to make a decision right now?

Yes No

Sample Résumé
(Figure A.5 on text page P-19)

Yann Ng
345 Big Bend Boulevard
Kirkwood, Missouri, 63122
314-921-5385

Job objective: Sales representative in business to business marketing

Education:

St. Louis Community College at Meramec
A.A. in Business (3.6 grade point average)
Served on Student Representative Board

University of Missouri, St. Louis
B.S. in Business: Marketing major (3.2 grade point average, 3.5 in major)
Earned 100 percent of college expenses working 35 hours a week.
Member of Student American Marketing Association
Vice President of Student Government Association
Dean's List for two semesters

Work experience:

Schnuck's Supermarket: Worked checkout evenings and weekends for four years while in school. Learned to respond to customer requests quickly, and communicate with them in a friendly and helpful manner.

Mary Tuttle's Flowers: For two summers, I made flower arrangements, managed sales transactions, and acted as Assistant to the Manager. I trained and supervised three employees. Often handled customer inquiries and complaints.

Special skills:

I am fluent in Vietnamese, French, and English. I'm proficient at using WordPerfect and Word. I've developed my own Web site (www.yan@stilnet.com) and use the Internet often to do research for papers and for personal interests.

Other interests:

I'm an excellent cook and often prepare meals for my family and friends. I enjoy reading the classics. I play the piano and do aerobics. I've traveled extensively in Asia, Europe, and America. I also enjoy doing research on the Internet.

References furnished upon request

TM-6

Sample Cover Letter

(Figure A.6 on text page P-20)

Yann Ng
345 Big Bend Boulevard
Kirkwood, Missouri, 63122
314-921-5385

Dear Mr. Karlinski: [Note: it's best to know whom to write by name.]

Recent articles in Inc. and Success magazine have praised your company for its innovative products and strong customer orientation. I'm familiar with your creative display materials. In fact, we've used them at Mary Tuttle's Flower Shop, where I have worked for the last two summers. I talked to Christie Bouchard, your local sales representative, and she told me all about your products and your training program at Premier Designs.

Christie mentioned the kind of salespeople you are seeking. She said you want men and women with proven sales ability. I've had great success making and selling flower arrangements at Mary Tuttle's, and I've learned customer relations at Schnuck's. As you know, they have one of the best customer-oriented training programs in the industry. Christie also said that you wanted self-motivated people with leadership ability. I've paid my way through college working nights and summers. I was selected to be on the Student Representative Board at St. Louis Community College at Meramec and was active in student government at Missouri. I have also paid my own way to Asia, Europe, and the Americas. I am very independent and self-motivated.

I know that I could be a successful salesperson at Premier Designs. I'll be in the Chicago area the week of January 4–9. What time and date would be most convenient for you to discuss career opportunities at Premier? I'll phone your secretary to set up an appointment.

Sincerely,

Yann Ng

TM-7

Be Prepared for These Frequently Asked Questions
(Figure A.7 on text page P-21)

BE PREPARED FOR THESE FREQUENTLY ASKED QUESTIONS

- **How would you describe yourself?**
- **What are your greatest strengths and weaknesses?**
- **How did you choose this company?**
- **What do you know about the company?**
- **What are your long-range career goals?**
- **What courses did you like best? Least?**
- **What are your hobbies?**
- **Do you prefer a specifc geographic location?**
- **Are you willing to travel (or move)?**
- **Which accomplishments have given you the most satisfaction?**
- **What things are most important to you in a job?**
- **Why should I hire you?**
- **What experience have you had in this type of work?**
- **How much do you expect to earn?**

Finding Opportunities in Today's Dynamic Business Environment

Chapter 1

Folder Contents

OT ACETATE 1-3	How Government Affects Business
OT ACETATE 1-4	Government As An Overseer and Regulator
OT ACETATE 1-5	Did You Know?
OT ACETATE 1-6	Projected Required Average Skill Level by 2000
OT ACETATE 1-7	Current Skill Level of Workers
OT ACETATE 1-8	Growing Number of Telecommuters
OT ACETATE 1-9	Dealing With a Multi-Cultural Workforce
OT ACETATE 1-10	The Changing Workforce
OT ACETATE 1-11	U.S. Population by Generations
OT ACETATE 1-12	Ethical Questions to Ask

(Acetates and Transparency Masters are also available as PowerPoint slides on disk and on the Presentation CD-ROM.)

(Resources Available are also referenced in the expanded lecture outline later in this chapter.)

Other Resources Available

Video Cases

"Starbucks." Many of us dream of starting a business and watching it grow. This video shows how Howard Schultz, CEO of Starbucks, made his dreams come true.

"Getting the Job You Want Online." Shows how people are using the World Wide Web using an example which explores the ins and outs of online career resources, such as researching company web pages, posting a resume on the WWW, and networking online.

(The **Media Resource Guide** contains a summary of the Video and suggested discussion questions.)

Student Assessment and Learning Guide: Contains matching key term and definition questions, write-in retention questions, write-in critical thinking questions, and practice test of multiple choice and true/false questions.

Technology:

Zapitalism CD-ROM - Simulation program.

Concept Mastery Exam Preparation Disk - Practice test and tutorial.

Business Essentials Disk - Hyperlinks Understanding Business with seven other leading business texts.

Presentation CD-ROM – Contains PowerPoint slides of acetates and transparency masters, video clips, lecture materials. This tool allows you to customize your lecture presentations.

***Business Week* Web Site Access with the *Business Week* edition.**

Understanding Business **Home Page – http:/www.mhhe.com/ub5e.**

Audiotape: Abridged chapter (Text minus profile, boxes, and end-of-chapter material.

Associated Web Sites

These sites are provided to students for the purpose of analysis and critical thinking of the issues. Students are encouraged to explore other sites. As with any Web site, some may be inactive now.

Career Planning:

Five Steps in Good Career Planning:

http://www.cudenver.edu/public/career/5step.html

Best Businesses to Start:

10 best:

http://www.incomeops.com/online/contents9601/bestbiz/bestbiz.html

16 best:

http://www.oncomdis.on.ca/homentre/homent.htm

Make a Profit:

Can't miss propositions:

http://www.worldprofit.com/infomall/inbaily.htm

Business Plans:

Recommendations:

http://www.educ.utas.edu.au/~Bob.Boocock/Tech&SmallBus.html# The Business Plan

Risky Businesses:

5 riskiest:

http://www.realgame.com/hp-ra-ri.htm

Wealth:

Share the wealth - a social perspective:

http://www.stw.org/

Entrepreneurship:

Frequently Asked Questions about starting a business:

http://www.liraz.com/q&a.htm

Social changes affecting business:

Women in the workforce:

http://www.econ.ag.gov/epubs/htmlsum/aib732.htm

Violence in the workplace:

http://www.state.il.us/ISP/viowkplc/vwpp4.htm

Understanding Business Home Page:

http:/www.mhhe.com/ub5e.

What's New in This Edition

Additions:

- Profile of Herman Cain of Godfather's Pizza
- Discussion of ISO 14000 standards in the subsection "Quality, ISO 9000, and ISO 14000"
- Taking It to the Net exercises
- Video case: Starbucks
- Spotlight On Small Business: From Disability To Opportunity
- Legal Briefcase: Freedom Equals Prosperity
- Reaching Beyond Our Borders: Competing in Cyberspace, Keeping up with Technology
- From the Pages of *Business Week:* Marketing on the Internet

Revisions:

Statistical data and examples throughout the chapter were updated to reflect current information. In addition:

- The chapter was reorganized to begin with definition of business and build upon the concepts of risk, profit, and loss and how business affects a country's standard of living and quality of life.
- The label of the fifth factor of production was changed from information to knowledge to reflect the growing importance of knowledge in today's economy.
- The NAFTA discussion in the section "The Global Environment" was expanded to include what has happened since NAFTA was passed.

Deletions:

- Profile of LaVan Hawkins
- Video Case "Opportunity Unlimited"
- Most of the boxes were replaced
- Figures "Where Your Money Goes When You Buy a Coke," "Per Capita Income Adjusted for Purchasing Power," and "Numbers for the Nineties"

APPENDIX

- This appendix is completely new to this edition. The appendix is designed to direct novices toward the on-ramp to the information superhighway. The question and answer format makes it easy for students to access the information they need.
- Novices should read this appendix before attempting the new Taking It to the Net exercises at the end of each chapter. Experienced Internet users may want to just skim this material for some features they may not have used yet.

Brief Chapter Outline/Learning Goals

CHAPTER 1

FINDING OPPORTUNITIES IN TODAY'S DYNAMIC BUSINESS ENVIRONMENT

PROFILE: Herman Cain of Godfather's Pizza

I. WHAT IS A BUSINESS?

LEARNING GOAL 1. Describe how businesses and nonprofit organizations add to the standard of living and quality of life.

A. Businesses Can Provide Wealth and a High Quality of Life for Almost Everyone.

B. Nonprofit Organizations Use Business Principles.

II. THE IMPORTANCE OF ENTREPRENEURSHIP TO WEALTH.

LEARNING GOAL 2. Explain the importance of entrepreneurship to the wealth of an economy and show the relationship of profit to risk assumption.

A. Opportunities for Entrepreneurs.

B. Matching Risk with Profit.

C. The Role of the Factors of Production in Creating Wealth.

III. THE BUSINESS ENVIRONMENT.

LEARNING GOAL 3. Examine how the economic environment and taxes affect businesses.

A. The Economic Environment.

IV. THE TECHNOLOGICAL ENVIRONMENT.

LEARNING GOAL 4. Illustrate how the technological environment has affected businesses.

A. The Importance of Information Technology.

B. Responding to Customers.

V. THE COMPETITIVE ENVIRONMENT.

LEARNING GOAL 5. Identify various ways that businesses can meet and beat competition.

A. Competing by Delighting the Customer.

B. Competing by Meeting the Needs of the Community.

C. Competing by Restructuring and Meeting the Needs of Employees.

D. Competing by Concern for the Natural Environment.

VI. THE SOCIAL ENVIRONMENT.

LEARNING GOAL 6. Demonstrate how the social environment has changed and what the reaction of business has been.

A. Multiculturalism and Its Advantages for Business.

B. The Increase in the Number of Older Americans.

C. Two-Income Families.

VII. THE GLOBAL ENVIRONMENT.

LEARNING GOAL 7. Analyze what businesses must do to meet the global challenge.

A. Global Opportunities and Free Trade Agreements.

B. How Global Changes Affect You.

VIII. THE QUALITY IMPERATIVE.

LEARNING GOAL 8. Compare the new quality standards and identify what businesses are doing to meet those standards.

A. The Quality Standard: The Baldrige Award.

B. Quality, ISO 9000, and ISO 14000 Standards.

IX. THE EVOLUTION OF AMERICAN BUSINESS.

LEARNING GOAL 9. Review how trends from the past are being repeated in the present and what that will mean for the service sector.

A. Progress in the Agricultural and Manufacturing Industries.

B. Progress in Service Industries.

C. Your Future in the Global Economy.

X. SUMMARY AND REVIEW.

XI. APPENDIX: DRIVER'S ED FOR THE INFORMATION SUPERHIGHWAY.

(Learning Objectives are also referenced in the expanded lecture outline later in this chapter)

Key Terms

business *(text page 1)*
databank *(text page 10)*
demography *(text page 14)*
downsizing *(text page 4)*
entrepreneur *(text page 4)*
factors of production *(text page 6)*
goods *(text page 20)*
Internet *(text page 9)*
ISO 9000 *(text page 19)*
ISO 14000 *(text page 20)*
loss *(text page 5)*
multiculturalism *(text page 14)*
nonprofit organization *(text page 3)*
productivity *(text page 16)*
profit *(text page 4)*
quality *(text page 19)*
quality of life *(text page 2)*
revenue *(text page 5)*
risk *(text page 5)*
services *(text page 21)*
stakeholders *(text page 12)*
standard of living *(text page 2)*
telecommuting *(text page 15)*

Lecture Outline

The **PROFILE** at the beginning of this chapter focuses on **HERMAN CAIN OF GODFATHER'S PIZZA.** By rising through the ranks at Pillsbury's Burger King division, Cain became the president of Pillsbury's Godfather's Pizza. Cain and a partner eventually bought the franchise and have doubled the value of the company.

I. WHAT IS A BUSINESS?

▶ **LEARNING GOAL 1.** Describe how businesses and nonprofit organizations add to the standard of living and quality of life.

A. A **BUSINESS** is any activity that seeks profit by providing goods and services to others.

B. **BUSINESSES CAN PROVIDE WEALTH AND A HIGH QUALITY OF LIFE FOR ALMOST EVERYONE.**

1. Entrepreneurs may not only become wealthy themselves, but also provide employment for other people.
2. Businesses are a part of an economic system that helps to create a higher standard of living and quality of life for everyone.
3. The **STANDARD OF LIVING** of a country refers to the amount of goods and services people can buy with the money they have.
4. The **QUALITY OF LIFE** of a country refers to the general well-being of a society.

Lecture Notes

TRANSPARENCY MASTER 8
Chapter Outline

TM 8

Transparency Masters begin on page 1.72.

OT ACETATE 1-1
Herman Cain's Rules for Successful Leadership

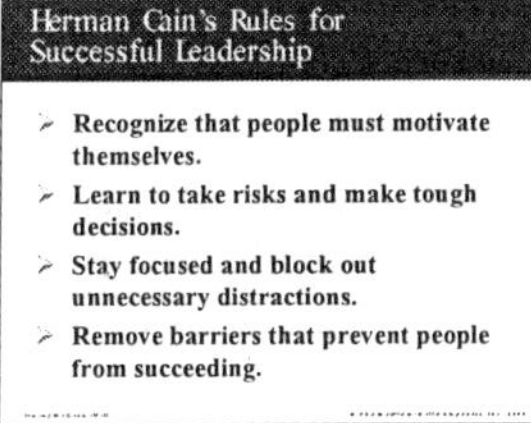

Comments:

1. You might want to remind students that Herman Cain is the profile that starts off chapter one. His story is attention grabbing and one that relates many of the career principles listed in the prologue.
2. Mr. Cain learned leadership principles the hard way—by trial and error and hard work--in businesses both large and small. Students can use this information as a basis for reinforcing the concept of career planning and continuous lifetime learning.
3. Herman Cain is also a great believer in communication. He encourages the value of the spoken word to inspire people and encourages students to become solid communicators fluent in both verbal and writing skills.

OT ACETATE 1-2
Objectives of Business

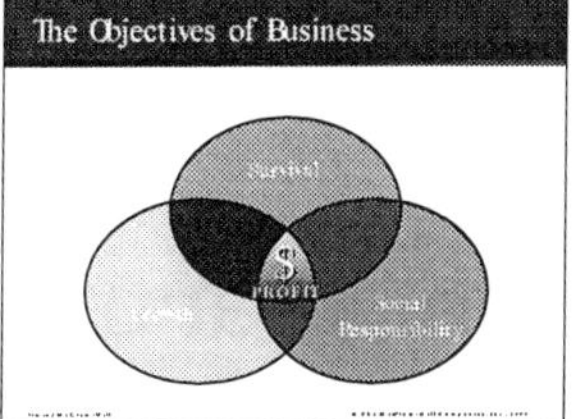

Comments:

1. This acetate highlights the four key objectives of business in our free enterprise economy.
2. It's important to point out to students that survival is the ultimate objective of any business large or small. As they progress in the text, it will become very apparent that survival is by no means guaranteed, and businesses must constantly adapt to changing environments and trends to avoid failure and dissolution.
3. Growth is an interesting word to pursue. Some students may question, "does a business have to grow? What if an owner has no incentive to expand?" It is important to note that growth does not always mean expansion or acceleration of the business. Surely, the businessperson must grow in skill and competency to compete in an ever-changing market. Also, growth can relate to needs of customers in the market. You may want to press students to explain how many businesses they can think of have grown to meet the challenges of their environment.
4. Profit is a critical part of a capitalist system. This is discussed fully in the next chapter. A good point of discussion here is "do non-profit businesses need to seek profits?" Many will answer no. Ask the students that respond yes to expand on their answers.
5. This is a good time to make students aware that chapter four in the text deals with ethics and social responsibility. You can take the time to deal with this issue now or perhaps hold it until the expanded analysis in chapter four.

Lecture Outline

C. **NONPROFIT ORGANIZATIONS USE BUSINESS PRINCIPLES.**

1. Nonprofit organizations such as government agencies, public schools, charities, and social causes help make a country more responsive to all the needs of citizens.
2. A **NONPROFIT ORGANIZATION** is an organization whose goals don't include making a profit for its owners.
3. You need the **SAME SKILLS** to work in nonprofit organizations that you need in business. Skills needed include information management, leadership, marketing, and financial management.
4. Businesses, nonprofit organizations, and volunteer groups often help to accomplish the same objectives.

II. THE IMPORTANCE OF ENTREPRENEURSHIP TO WEALTH.

▶ **LEARNING GOAL 2.** Explain the importance of entrepreneurship to the wealth of an economy and show the relationship of profit to risk assumption.

A. **OPPORTUNITIES FOR ENTREPRENEURS.**

1. An **ENTREPRENEUR** is a person who risks time and money to start and manage a business.

CRITICAL THINKING
(page 3 in text)

Presently, many people are sacrificing a higher standard of living (having more "things") for a higher quality of life (having more time). They are buying smaller homes and smaller cars, but are taking more vacations and spending more time with the family. As you approach your career, how can you balance having a high standard of living and still maintain a quality of life that makes life more worthwhile?

2. Entrepreneurs have come from all over the world to prosper in America.

   a. The number of Latino-owned businesses in the United States grew by 76% in the 1990s.

   b. Increases have also been made by Asians, Pacific Islanders, American Indians, and Alaskan Natives.

3. Corporate **DOWNSIZING**, eliminating some workers or managers to make a business more efficient, is a factor contributing to the increasing number of entrepreneurs.

4. Such reductions are creating new opportunities for entrepreneurs.

5. The 21st century will provide more opportunities, and challenges, for those who understand how the business system works.

B. **MATCHING RISK WITH PROFIT**.

1. **PROFIT** is money a business earns above and beyond what is spends for salaries, expenses, and other costs.

2. A **LOSS** occurs when a business's costs and expenses are more than its *revenue*, the money a business earns by selling its products.

SPOTLIGHT ON SMALL BUSINESS
(Box in text, page 5)
"Business: From Disability to Opportunity"

The needs of disabled Americans have created a huge market for specially designed or adapted products (there are some 48 million people with various disabilities). Evan Kemp, former head of the Equal Employment Opportunity Commission, understands this market because he has muscular dystrophy.

CRITICAL THINKING EXERCISE 1-1
How Much Profit?

See complete exercise on page 1.60.

Lecture Outline

3. **RISK** is the chance you take of losing time and money on a business that may not prove profitable.

4. Not all companies make the same profit.

   a. Those companies that take the most risk may make the most profit.

   b. As a potential business owner, you should do research to find the right balance between risk and profit.

C. **THE ROLE OF THE FACTORS OF PRODUCTION IN CREATING WEALTH.**

1. **THE FACTORS OF PRODUCTION** the resources businesses use to create wealth.

   a. **LAND** (and other natural resources)

   b. **LABOR** (workers)

   c. **CAPITAL** (e.g., money, machines, tools, and buildings)

   d. **ENTREPRENEURSHIP**.

   e. **KNOWLEDGE**.

2. Some experts believe that the most important factor of production is **KNOWLEDGE**.

3. Entrepreneurship and knowledge are key compoents in enriching today's countries.

Lecture Notes

PROGRESS CHECK
(page 5 in text)

- What at is profit and who gets the profits businesses make? What is the difference between revenue and profit?
- What is risk and how is it related to profit?
- What is the difference between standard of living and quality of life?

TRANSPARENCY MASTER 9
The Five Factors of Production
(Figure 1.1 on text page 6)

Transparency Masters begin on page 1.72.

A recent study found that the freer a country is, the wealthier its citizens are. One country that had great freedom, Hong Kong, also had the highest per capita income ($27,202). It will be interesting to see how much freedom Hong Kong is able to maintain now that it has become a part of the People's Republic of China.

4. Entrepreneurship also helps make some states and cities rich while others remain relatively poor.

III. THE BUSINESS ENVIRONMENT.

▶ **LEARNING GOAL 3.** Examine how the economic environment and taxes affect businesses.

A. The **FIVE KEY ENVIRONMENTAL FACTORS** critical to the success of business are:

1. Economic environment, including taxes and regulation.
2. Technological environment.
3. Competitive environment.
4. Social environment.
5. Global business environment.

B. Business prospers in a healthy environment.

C. **THE ECONOMIC ENVIRONMENT.**

1. People are willing to take the risk of starting businesses if they feel that the risk isn't too great.
2. **GOVERNMENTS CAN LESSEN THE RISK** of starting a businesses thereby increasing entrepreneurship and wealth by:

   a. **ALLOWING PRIVATE OWNERSHIP OF BUSINESS.**

TRANSPARENCY MASTER 10
The Business Environment
(Figure 1.2 on text page 8)

Transparency Masters begin on page 1.72.

OT ACETATE 1-3
How Government Affects Business

Comments:

1. It's important that students understand the influence government exerts on business. Chapter two will cover this topic in more depth.
2. Students may be interested to know that the federal government is the largest single buyer of goods and services in the world. State and local governments are also significant buyers (customers) that many businesses depend on.
3. Government also plays a significant role as regulator and overseer. It may be a good time to point out to students that throughout the text they will encounter boxed inserts referred to as legal briefcases that discuss many issues of law and regulation business must follow. **ACETATE 1-4** also gets into this topic with a bit more depth. Chapter-by-chapter the influence of government and law will become more obvious to students.
4. Government obtains its resources through taxation. Students may be interested to know that government in essence does not produce anything. It stays afloat through taxes imposed on businesses and individuals. More on this topic will be covered in chapter two.

OT ACETATE 1-4
Government As An Overseer and Regulator

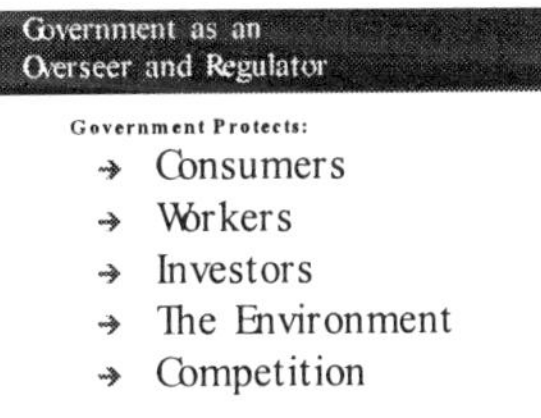

Comments:

1. Government's role in the economy has increased significantly over the years. Today regulations and laws protect all the stakeholders listed in the acetate.
2. Students may be interested to know that we will cover the extent of government protection and involvement of all five groups listed in the acetate throughout the text.
3. You might challenge students knowledge of government involvement as an overseer and protector by asking them if they can name laws or regulations that affect each of the five groups noted on the acetate. Some suggestions:
   - **Consumers** - consumer protection laws abound
   - **Workers** - workers are covered by minimum wage laws, worker's compensation laws, workplace safety rules, etc.
   - **Investors** - protected by federal deposit insurance, securities laws, etc.
   - **Environmental** laws cover air, water, pollution, and other issues.
   - **Competition** - is protected by antitrust laws, predatory pricing laws, etc.

b. **PASSING LAWS THAT ENABLE BUSINESSPEOPLE TO WRITE CONTRACTS THAT ARE ENFORCEABLE IN COURT.**

c. **ESTABLISH A TRADABLE CURRENCY.**

d. **ELIMINATE CORRUPTION IN BUSINESS AND GOVERNMENT.**

e. **KEEP TAXES AND REGULATIONS TO A MINIMUM.**

IV. THE TECHNOLOGICAL ENVIRONMENT.

▶ **LEARNING GOAL 4.** Illustrate how the technological environment has affected businesses.

A. The **INTERNET** is the network of computer and telecommunication equipment that links people throughout the world into one unified communications system.

B. **THE IMPORTANCE OF INFORMATION TECHNOLOGY.**

1. Many companies now have a chief information officer responsible for getting workers the information they need.

2. That information includes information about customers, competitors, and the changing business environment.

3. The problem today is that few businesses are managing information well.

Lecture Notes

OT ACETATE 1-5
Did You Know?

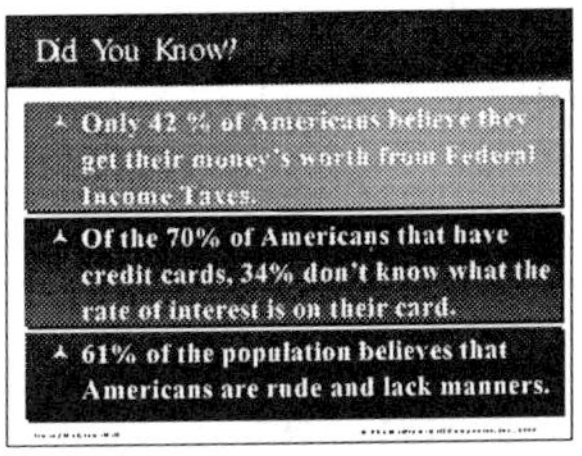

Comments:

1. Three points of interest are included here for student information and general interest. This acetate highlights that most Americans are similar in attitudes and often in what they do not know.
2. In relation to the third comment, a new objective of this edition is a focus on student etiquette. A new video will accompany the text and special sections of the text will deal with this issue. It's interesting that over 60 percent of Americans believe that manners and etiquette are lacking.
3. Statements one and two are good discussion topics. Why don't Americans feel they are getting their money's worth from taxes? See what students think and see if they think the tax code may be changed. You can also ask those with credit cards if they know the rate of interest they pay.

LECTURE ENHANCER 1-1
The Internet Is Here To Stay

The Net traffic jam is for real. In 1998 there are almost 37 million PCS regularly accessing the Internet, up 19 percent from 1996. (See complete lecture enhancer on page 1.46.)

LECTURE ENHANCER 1-2
The Job Skill Gap

As America changes from an industrial economy to a service economy, 25 million American workers will need to upgrade their job skills by the end of the century. (See complete lecture enhancer on page 1.47.)

OT ACETATE 1-6
Projected Required Average Skill Level by 2000 and **OT ACETATE 1-7**
Current Skill Level

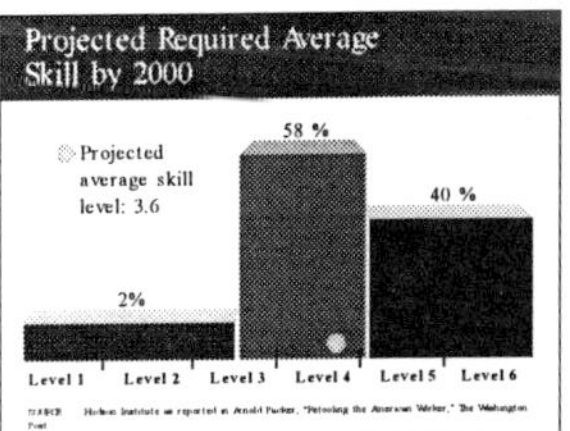

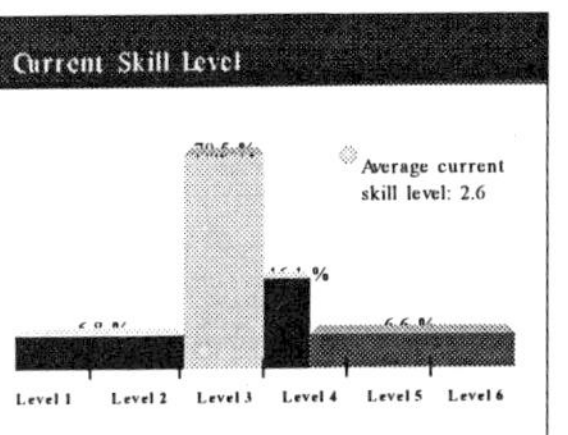

Comments:

OT ACETATES 1-6 and **1-7** are referenced in **LECTURE ENHANCER 1-2** on page 1.47.

Lecture Outline

4. Because information technology is so central to an organization's success, we will devote Chapter 17 to that issue.

C. **RESPONDING TO CUSTOMERS.**

1. Technology has also made it possible for businesses to become more responsive to customers.

2. A **DATABANK**, an electronic storage file where information is kept, can be used to store vast amounts of information about customers.

3. **ELECTRONIC DATA INTERCHANGE** involves data from bar codes being sent directly to manufacturers, which then replace the items quickly.

4. Growing use of this technology is making it possible for businesses to save time and money, resulting in less expensive products. (This is discussed in detail in Chapter 15.)

V. THE COMPETITIVE ENVIRONMENT.

▶ **LEARNING GOAL 5.** Identify various ways that businesses can meet and beat competition.

A. Making quality products is not enough to stay competitive in world markets. Now you have to offer quality products and outstanding service at competitive prices.

Lecture Notes

LECTURE ENHANCER 1-3
Keeping the Customer Happy

What should a company do for angry customers? According to experts: just about anything it can. (See complete lecture enhancer on page 1.49.)

TRANSPARENCY MASTER 10
The Business Environment
(Figure 1.2 on text page 8)

Transparency Masters begin on page 1.72.

MAKING ETHICAL DECISIONS
(Box in text, page 12)

"Ethics Begin with You"

Television, movies, and the print media all paint a dismal picture of ethics among businesspeople, government officials, and citizens in general. It is more difficult to see the moral and ethical misbehavior of your own social group. What are some of the behaviors of your friends that you find morally or ethically questionable?

TRANSPARENCY MASTER 11
A Business and Its Stakeholders
(Figure 1.4 on text page 13)

Transparency Masters begin on page 1.72.

Lecture Outline

B. **COMPETING BY DELIGHTING THE CUSTOMER.**

1. Successful companies must listen to customers to determine their wants and needs and then adjust their products, policies, and practices to meet these demands.
2. Business is becoming customer-driven—this means that customers' wants and needs come first.

C. **COMPETING BY MEETING THE NEEDS OF THE COMMUNITY.**

1. **STAKEHOLDERS** are all the people who are affected by the policies and activities of an organization.
2. Stakeholders include customers, employees, stockholders, suppliers, environmentalists, and elected officials.
3. The challenge for companies in the 21st century will be to ensure that all stakeholders' needs are considered and satisfied.

D. **COMPETING BY RESTRUCTURING AND MEETING THE NEEDS OF EMPLOYEES.**

1. To meet the needs of customers, firms must give their front-line workers more freedom to respond quickly to customer requests.

Lecture Notes

LECTURE ENHANCER 1-4
How to Build a Strong Ethical Base

The first step toward improving a negative social condition is to admit that it exists. The next step is to do something about it. (See complete lecture enhancer on page 1.50.)

CRITICAL THINKING EXERCISE 1-2
Making Ethical Decisions

See complete exercise on page 1.62.

From the Pages of BusinessWeek
(Box in text, page 11)
"Marketing on the Internet"

Business Week magazine did a survey in 1997 to determine what people were doing on the Internet.

CRITICAL THINKING
(page 13 in text)

The current business books talk about having teams of employees work together to satisfy the needs of all stakeholders, including the community. Some recommend having environmentalists and community leaders sit in on team discussions so that businesses can respond more quickly to community needs. What community needs aren't being met by businesses in your area? Can you see the benefit of having community leaders sit in on planning sessions to see that those needs are met? What, if any, drawbacks to such a policy can you see from the company's perspective?

OT ACETATE 1-8
Growing Number of Telecommuters

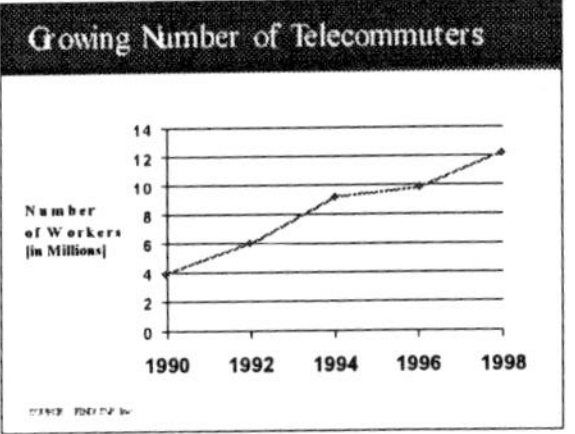

Comments:

1. The workplace is changing in many ways. This acetate highlights one of the key changes occurring in the workplace of the future. Telecommuting has more than quadrupled in the past eight years.
2. It's easy to quiz students regarding what jobs are most prone toward telecommuting. Also see which type of job they would prefer, a more traditional type job situation or one that involves telecommuting. It would be interesting to debate the pro's and con's of the issue.
3. This acetate also indirectly highlights the growth of empowerment in the workplace. As more workers balance time at the office with time at home, it requires a certain degree of independence and responsibility.

Lecture Outline

2. In many companies this has meant **EMPOWERING** employees and using **CROSS-FUNCTIONAL, SELF-MANAGED TEAMS.** (Discussions of these concepts are woven throughout the entire text.)

3. It sometimes takes years to restructure and organization so that managers are willing to give up some of their authority.

E. **COMPETING BY CONCERN FOR THE NATURAL ENVIRONMENT.**

1. Environmental issues include the potential benefits and hazards of nuclear power, recycling, management of forests, ethical treatment of animals, and protection of the air we breathe and the water we drink.

2. Environmentalism must be a major focus of everyone, and is becoming increasingly so.

VI. THE SOCIAL ENVIRONMENT.

▶ **LEARNING GOAL 6.** Demonstrate how the social environment has changed and what the reaction of business has been.

A. **DEMOGRAPHY** is the statistical study of the human population to learn its size, density, and characteristics.

B. **MULTICULTURALISM AND ITS ADVANTAGES FOR BUSINESS.**

Lecture Notes

LECTURE ENHANCER 1-5
Teams Lead to Responsiveness

Small teams of employees make it possible for large firms to get close to internal and external customers and respond to their needs quickly. (See complete lecture enhancer on page 1.51.)

OT ACETATE 1-9
Dealing With a Multi-Cultural Workforce

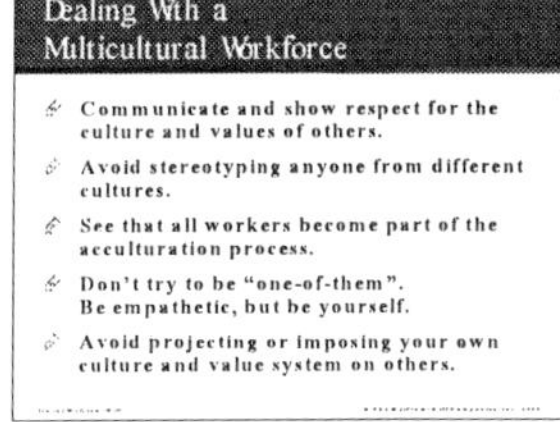

Comments:

1. The workforce in the future will be more multi-cultural than in the past. This acetate offers advice on how to deal with the challenges of multiple cultures in the workplace.
2. It's advisable to work through the acetate point-by-point with a bit of elaboration on each of the statements. Student input and comments should be encouraged.
3. Ask students if they have first-hand experience with other cultures. For example, students with military experience often spend time in foreign countries. See if any students presently work in multi-cultural environments and have experiences to share with the rest of the class.

Lecture Outline

1. The U.S. of the future will be very different from what it is today.
   a. Our population will increase by approximately 50%. As the population grows, there will be a greater need for goods and services, creating more jobs.
   b. The Hispanic, Latino, and Asian populations will increase.
2. **MULTICULTURALISM** is the process of optimizing the contributions of people from different cultures.
3. As American workers learn to work with people of all nations, they gain an **ADVANTAGE WHEN IT COMES TO NEGOTIATING AND WORKING WITH PEOPLE IN GLOBAL MARKETS.**
4. A diverse population is a strong population—there is strength in different views and perspectives.

C. **THE INCREASE IN THE NUMBER OF OLDER AMERICANS.**

1. By 2030, the 76 million baby boomers will be senior citizens.
2. Think of the career opportunities of providing goods and services for older adults.

Lecture Notes

LECTURE ENHANCER 1-6
The Aging of the Baby Boomers

The bumper crop of 64 million infants born between 1946 and 1961 is now 40 to 55 years old. They are by far the largest generation in American history—and the effects they have had are widespread. (See complete lecture enhancer on page 1.52.)

OT ACETATE 1-10
The Changing Workforce

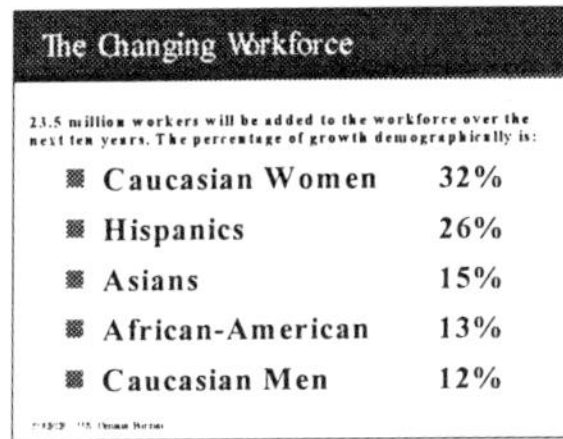

Comments:

1. This acetate previews for students the workplace of the future. As the numbers indicate, it will be much more diverse than previous generations. Dealing with growing diversity in the work force will be dealt with throughout the text. It will also be a key challenge of business in the next century.
2. This might be a good time to look around your classroom and observe the diversity that may exist. Students are often very willing to involve themselves in discussions about how businesses could do more to address the needs of its diverse populations. A cost/benefit analysis of the situation could be very appropriate here.
3. A question concerning training that managers need in dealing with work force diversity might be appropriate here. You may invite students to offer suggestions how business schools need adjustments to programs to meet the challenge.
4. The next acetate provides additional information about the changing U.S. population in the next century.

LECTURE ENHANCER 1-7
Older People Are Becoming More Influential

Older people are playing a more important role in the labor force. (See complete lecture enhancer on page 1.54.)

CRITICAL THINKING EXERCISE 1-3
The Effects of Trends

See complete exercise on page 1.64.

What opportunities do a wealthy, older market offer retailers, recreation specialist, etc.?

D. **TWO-INCOME FAMILIES**

1. The high costs of housing have made it difficult for many households to live on just one income.

2. Many companies are implementing programs to assist two-income families.

   a. Many employers provide child care benefits of some type, some through cafeteria benefits packages.

   b. Other companies provide parental leave, flexible work schedules, and elder care programs.

3. Some companies are increasing the number of part-time workers by allowing workers to stay home and send in their work by telecommunications, a practice known as **TELECOMMUTING**.

VII. THE GLOBAL ENVIRONMENT.

▶ **LEARNING GOAL 7.** Analyze what businesses must do to meet the global challenge.

A. The global environment of business affects all other environmental influences.

1. The number one global environmental change today is the growth of international

Lecture Notes

OT ACETATE 1-11
U.S. Population by Generations

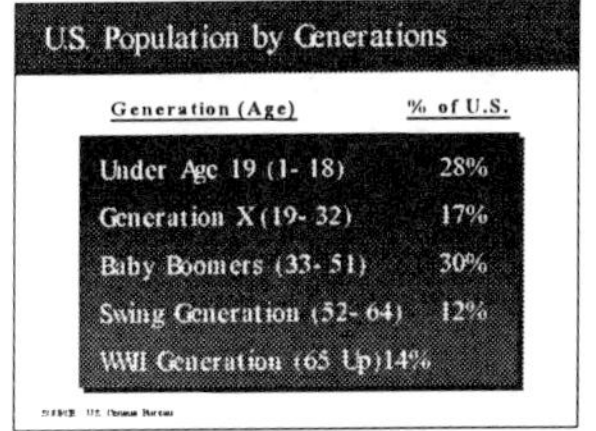

Comments:

1. By the year 2020 almost one third of the U.S. population is expected to be at least age 55. This acetate supports the previous illustration and can be used to generate further discussion concerning the diverse work force of the next century.
2. An obvious question that may bother younger workers is, "how will the aging work force affect opportunities for younger workers?" For example, "If more older workers are in the work force, won't younger workers find it harder to gain opportunity for employment and particularly advancement?"
3. Additional issues involve questions surrounding the need for elder care for older employees, parents and other relatives since this segment of the population is growing. Further insight could address the growing burdens on systems such as social security when this aging population reaches retirement age. These topics will be addressed and expanded in later chapters.

LECTURE ENHANCER 1-8
Men, Families, and "Women's Issues"

Men want improved benefits in the workplace to help with child and dependent care just as much as women do. What has been seen as a women's issue is now a family concern. (See complete lecture enhancer on page 1.55.)

SUPPLEMENTAL CASE 1-1
Dealing With Changing Family Structures

See complete case on page 1.66.

PROGRESS CHECK
(page 16 in text)

- What are the five factors of production?
- How can government encourage entrepreneurial growth?
- How does information technology help businesses to be more customer-oriented?
- What is the advantage of multiculturalism to today's businesses?

Lecture Outline

competition and the increase in free trade among nations.

2. U.S. manufacturers have implemented the most advanced quality methods, after analyzing the best practices throughout the world.
3. U.S. workers in many industries are more productive than workers in Japan and other countries.
4. **PRODUCTIVITY** is the volume of goods an services that one worker can produce.
5. Businesses have gone beyond simply **COMPETING** with organizations in other countries to learning to **COOPERATE** with international firms.

B. **GLOBAL OPPORTUNITIES AND FREE TRADE AGREEMENTS**.

1. **NAFTA,** signed in 1994, opened trade between the United States, Canada, and Mexico. (NAFTA is discussed in more detail in Chapter 3.)
2. The intended goal was for consumers and businesses in all three countries to benefit from unrestricted trade.
3. In general, NAFTA has not been the success imagined by some, nor the disaster proposed by others.

SUPPLEMENTAL CASE 1-2 The Travel and Tourism Industry	See complete case on page 1.69.
LECTURE ENHANCER 1-9 Global Opportunities for the Smaller Competitor	As national borders become increasingly invisible to businesses, a smaller company may succeed where larger companies have encountered problems. (See complete lecture enhancer on page 1.57.)

4. Trying to protect manufacturers from international competition often leads to stagnation and the inability to compete globally.

5. European leaders recognize the benefits of free trade and have negotiated free trade agreements creating the **EUROPEAN UNION (EU)**.

C. **HOW GLOBAL CHANGES AFFECT YOU**.

1. Many think that the fair trade agreements will lead to many **CAREER OPPORTUNITIES** for American college graduates.

2. Students must **PREPARE** themselves to compete in changing global environments.

VIII. THE QUALITY IMPERATIVE.

▶ **LEARNING GOAL 8.** Compare the new quality standards and identify what businesses are doing to meet those standards.

A. **QUALITY** in is defined as providing customers with high quality goods and services that go beyond the expected.

B. **THE QUALITY STANDARD: THE BALDRIGE AWARD**.

1. One standard for quality was set with the introduction in 1987 of the Malcolm Baldrige National Quality Awards.

2. The award measures quality in three ways:

Lecture Notes

REACHING BEYOND OUR BORDERS
(Box in text, page 18)
"Competing in Cyberspace—Keeping up with Technology"

Tropical Jim's Remake-Shop, a small business that designs Web sites for businesses, is located in Caracas, Venezuela. Jim MacIntyre, the owner, says that the firm wasn't profitable until it began to sell in the U.S. market.

TRANSPARENCY MASTER 12
Members of the European Union
(Figure 1.5 on text page 18)

Transparency Masters begin on page 1.72.

LECTURE ENHANCER 1-10
The Impact of the Baldrige Awards

Some experts question the wisdom of small companies pursuing the Baldrige award. (See complete lecture enhancer on page 1.58.)

a. By customer satisfaction

b. By product and service quality

c. By quality of internal operations.

C. **QUALITY, ISO 9000, AND ISO 14000 STANDARDS**.

1. The new global measures for quality are called ISO 9000 standards.

2. **ISO 9000** refers to quality management and assurance standards published by the International Organization for Standardization.

   a. ISO standards provide a "common denominator" of business quality accepted around the world.

   b. The European Union is demanding that companies doing business with the EU be certified by ISO standards.

3. **ISO 14000** is a collection of the best practices for managing and organization's environmental impacts.

IX. THE EVOLUTION OF AMERICAN BUSINESS.

▶ **LEARNING GOAL 9.** Review how trends from the past are being repeated in the present and what that will mean for the service sector.

OT ACETATE 1-12
Ethical Questions to Ask

Ethical Questions to Ask Yourself

- What are the alternatives?
- What are the effects of each alternative?
- Which alternatives do you choose?
- Is your decision ethical?

Comments:

1. This acetate suggests a method to help students reach their decisions concerning the situations in the "Making Ethical Decisions" box in each chapter. Students should keep these four questions in mind when making their decisions:
   - **WHAT ARE THE ALTERNATIVES?** What are your choices?
   - **WHAT ARE THE EFFECTS OF EACH ALTERNATIVE?** What will happen because of this action?
   - **WHICH ALTERNATIVE DO YOU CHOOSE?**
   - **IS YOUR DECISION ETHICAL?** Would you want your family to know of your decision? Would you want it printed in the newspaper? Is it fair to all parties involved?
2. You may consider referring students to the "ETHICS BOX" in chapter one and discuss some of their ideas according to the four questions listed in the text and on the acetate. It might help to remind them that an ethics box appears in each chapter of the text.

Lecture Outline

A. Businesses in the U.S. have become so productive that fewer workers are needed to product **GOODS**, or tangible products.

B. **PROGRESS IN THE AGRICULTURAL AND MANUFACTURING INDUSTRIES.**

1. The use of **TECHNOLOGY** allowed the agricultural industry to become so **PRODUCTIVE** that the number of farmers dropped for about a third of the population to less than 2 percent.
2. **AGRICULTURE** is still a major industry in the U.S., but **MILLIONS OF SMALL FARMS HAVE BEEN REPLACED BY FEWER AND LARGER FARMS.**
3. **FARMERS LOST THEIR JOBS** and went to work in factories.
4. **TECHNOLOGY** made manufacturing more productive and workers lost their jobs.

C. **PROGRESS IN SERVICE INDUSTRIES**

1. Many workers who lost their manufacturing jobs found jobs in service industries.
2. **SERVICES** are intangible products.
3. Since the mid-1980s, the **SERVICE SECTOR HAS GENERATED ALMOST ALL OF OUR ECONOMY'S INCREASES IN EMPLOYMENT.**

TRANSPARENCY MASTER 13
Future Employment Opportunities
(Figure 1.7 on text page 23)

TM 13

Transparency Masters begin on page 1.72.

Lecture Outline

4. Projections are that the service section **WILL GROW SLOWLY** in the coming decades.
5. The service era is quickly losing out to a new **GLOBAL INFORMATION REVOLUTION** that is breaking down barriers between nations.

D. **YOUR FUTURE IN THE GLOBAL ECONOMY.**

1. This information-based global revolution will alter the way business is done in the future.
2. Most of the **CONCEPTS AND PRINCIPLES** that make business more effective and efficient are applicable in government agencies and nonprofit organizations.

X. SUMMARY AND REVIEW.

XI. APPENDIX: DRIVER'S ED FOR THE INFORMATION SUPERHIGHWAY.

PROGRESS CHECK
(page 23 in text)

- How has NAFTA affected the U.S. and Mexican economies?
- What is the Baldrige Award?
- What is the difference between ISO 9000 and ISO 14000 standards?
- If the service sector is in decline, where will future job opportunities be?

SEE APPENDIX: DRIVER'S ED FOR THE INFORMATION SUPER-HIGHWAY
(text page 29)

Due to the nature of this appendix, no lecture notes have been provided.

TRANSPARENCY MASTER 14
Hypertext Links and a Uniform Resource Locator (URL)
(Figure A1.2 on text page 32)

(Transparency Masters begin on page 1.72.)

TRANSPARENCY MASTER 15
E-Mail Form
(Figure A1.3 on text page 37.)

(Transparency Masters begin on page 1.72.)

Answers to Practicing Management Decisions

CASE ONE

WOMEN ENTREPRENEURS IN SMALL BUSINESS

1. *The number of women in developing countries who are becoming entrepreneurs is increasing. What can the governments of these developing countries do to promote and encourage such risk taking among their entrepreneurs?*

It is important for all entrepreneurs to be able to own the land and buildings they use for business. Otherwise, they won't invest a lot of money in the business for fear of losing it to the government. That is why there are so many street vendors in third world countries. Secondly, the government should keep taxes low to encourage people to take the risk of starting a business. Taxes can get as high as 85 percent, discouraging anyone from trying to make a lot of money (and hiring others). Also, the government should get rid of the bureaucracy that makes starting a business so difficult. In some countries, the process of getting licenses, permits, and such takes years.

2. *What progress, if any, can you cite in breaking the glass ceiling for women in U.S. businesses, government agencies, and nonprofit organizations?*

First of all, there are more women in college today than men, so the future for women managers is great. This is a relatively new phenomenon, so women haven't reached the top ranks of business, government, and nonprofits yet. But they are making progress. While there are only a few women as CEO of top organizations, there are thousands of women who own and manage their own firms. Childless women 27-33 now make 98 percent of their male counterparts. In the past 10 years, the number of female executive vice-presidents has doubled and senior vice presidents by 75 percent. Women also take home 40 percent of the degrees in areas such as medicine and law and 35 percent in dentistry and medicine. See *The Wall Street Journal* of January 15, 1997, p. A16.

3. *What advantages and/or disadvantages do you see from women taking over top positions in business, nonprofit organizations, and government?*

The goal should be to have the best people in the job regardless of age, gender, or other characteristics. Students may enjoy talking about what they perceive as the advantages and disadvantages nonetheless.

4. *Minority women small business owners are one of the fastest-growing categories. What affect will such a trend have on the economy in general?*

Whether an entrepreneur is a woman or a minority has little bearing on the overall economy. But the fact that women, young people, and others are increasingly looking to entrepreneurship means more jobs, more competition, more wealth, and a surging economy—in the United States and throughout the world. Women often hire other women, creating more jobs and more wealth. Entrepreneurship should be encouraged among all people in all countries.

CASE TWO

VIDEO CASE: STARBUCKS

1. *How does Schultz attempt to meet the needs of his employees? How might his action affect Starbuck's employee performance?*

Schultz calls his workers "partners" and gives them all (even part-timers) stock options. They also receive health care. Employees recognize such outstanding benefits by being more loyal and working hard to make the stores work. The more money the stores make, the more the employees make through the stock options.

2. *How will the competitive environment affect the future performance of Starbucks?*

The competitive environment is getting quite stiff. Other coffee shops with similar products are being opened, often in the same block as Starbucks. Furthermore, companies are now selling comparable coffee for home brewing. Soon the high prices at Starbucks may make them less competitive

3. *How did Schultz balance risk and profit potential while pursuing his vision of Starbucks?*

It is not easy to keep a business going when you lose millions of dollars in the first few years. But that is not unusual for big-time entrepreneurs. Schultz saw the potential and forged on, and his later success shows his vision was correct. The way that business works is this: The more risk you take, the more profit potential you find--and the greater your chances for loss.

Lecture Enhancers

LECTURE ENHANCER 1-1

THE INTERNET IS HERE TO STAY

The Net traffic jam is for real. In 1998 there are almost 37 million PCs regularly accessing the Internet, up 19 percent from 1996. Figures compiled by the research firm Computer Intelligence (CI) show that Internet usage continues to grow, but at a more moderate pace than in past years.

"While the Internet remains the nexus of activity in the PC and telecommunications industries, the growth in the number of users of the Internet is clearly slowing," said CI Senior Industry Analyst Dave Tremblay.

CI's research showed that in January 1997, 31.1 million U.S. PCs regularly connected to the Internet, an increase of nearly 70 percent over January 1996. By August 1997, the number of personal computers linking to the Net had grown to 36.9 million—only a 19 percent jump from January.

LECTURE 1-2

THE JOB SKILL GAP

(**OT ACETATE 1-6** and **OT ACETATE 1-7** are used with this Lecture Enhancer.)

As America changes from an industrial economy to a service economy, 25 million American workers will need to upgrade their job skills by the end of the century. Service and high-tech jobs are replacing lower skilled manufacturing jobs. These new jobs require higher job skills.

The Labor Department identified six skill levels that the job market requires. Understanding what the skills are at each level is not as important as understanding that on a scale of one to six the average job requirement skill is 3.6. Unfortunately, the average skill level of American workers falls significantly below this point at 2.6. **OT ACETATE 1-6** and **OT ACETATE 1-7** illustrate this gap in job skill levels.

Looking at **OT ACETATE 1-6** you will note:

- 40 percent of the American jobs by the year 2000 will require high levels of skill (Levels 5 & 6).
- 58 percent of the jobs will require medium levels of skill (Levels 3 & 4).
- Only 2 percent of the jobs can be filled with workers with low levels of skill (Levels 1 & 2).
- This graph shows the needs of marketplace. These are the skills needed to do the jobs of the future. Will the workers have those skills? One way to get an idea if workers will have the necessary skills is to look at the skills of the current workforce.

If the current skills overlap with the skills needed, we are in business. If not, we have a problem. Lay **OT ACETATE 1-6** on top of **OT ACETATE 1-7. OT ACETATE 1-7** charts the skills of the current workforce. Oh, oh—when you lay the two graphs together this is what you see:

- Only 6.6 percent of the workers have high levels of skills while the market needs 40 percent of its workers having such skills. Unless the future workers receive higher levels of training, businesses will have a tough time filling these jobs.
- Over 76 percent of the workers have medium levels of skills while the market needs only 58 percent with such skills. That means 18 percent of the workers with this skill level will not have jobs waiting for them.
- Things will be even tougher for workers with low levels of skill. Almost 7 percent fall in this category, but they will only qualify for two percent of the jobs. That's more than three job applicants for every one low level job.
- Briefly, when these two transparencies are laid together, the area that remains yellow indicates the jobs that will not have workers with adequate skills to fill them. The area that remains blue indicates the workers with low skills that won't be able to find jobs. The overlapping areas (green) indicate a match of skills. The message: *The jobs of tomorrow require high levels of skill. Wise students will prepare themselves now.*

Secretary of Labor, Alexis Herman has identified this skill gap as one of the key deficiencies facing U.S. business as it moves into the next century.

We are including the following in case you are interested in the actual skills the Labor Department assigned each level:

Level 1: Vocabulary of 2500 words. Reading rate of 95-125 words per/min. Ability to write simple sentences.

Level 2: Vocabulary of 5,000-6,000 words. Reading rate of 190-215 words/per min. Ability to write compound sentences.

Level 3: Ability to read safety rules and equipment instructions. Able to write simple reports.

Level 4: Ability to read journals and manuals. Able to write business letters and reports.

Level 5: Ability to read scientific/technical journals and financial reports. Able to write journals and speeches.

Level 6: Same skills as number five, but more advanced.

LECTURE ENHANCER 1-3

KEEPING THE CUSTOMER HAPPY

What should a company do for angry customers? According to experts: just about anything it can. Studies show customers tell twice as many people about bad experiences as good ones, so complainers left unhappy can send a company's image crashing. Simply listening to complaints boosts brand loyalty and a customer's tendency to buy again.

One research firm calculated the return on company dollars invested in customer complaints and inquiries. The average return for makers of consumer durables like washing machines and refrigerators was 100 percent. In other words, if manufacturers spent $1 million handling consumer complaints, they reaped $2 million in benefits. For banks it was as high is 170 percent.

LECTURE ENHANCER 1-4

HOW TO BUILD A STRONG ETHICAL BASE

In recent years we have seen many instances of scandal and unethical behavior among business leaders throughout the world. Immoral and unethical behavior among government officials is also global in scope. One positive element in all this sordid behavior is that much of it is being reported, and the public seems genuinely upset at the findings. The first step toward improving a negative social condition is to admit that it exists. The next step is to do something about it. The second step is now being implemented. Business schools across the country have made ethics an integral part of the curriculum. Many businesses are working hard to alter their behavior in a positive way. There is a growing trend toward greater commitment to ethics policies—written codes that clearly communicate management expectations—programs to implement these guidelines, and surveys to monitor compliance.

Ethical business behavior is much more than not doing what society (customers) concludes is improper. It means getting involved in something to help improve conditions. A national poll by the Gallup organization found that half the people who were surveyed were involved in charitable or social service activities such as helping the poor, the sick, or the elderly. This healthy sign indicates that businesspeople aren't just talking about moral and ethical behavior; they're starting to do something about it.

LECTURE ENHANCER 1-5

TEAMS LEAD TO RESPONSIVENESS

When we read about Sam Walton and Wal-Mart and the thousands of jobs he created for employees, we tend to forget that Sam Walton started out as a small business owner. His entrepreneurial skills are what led his company to its extraordinary growth. But big companies like Wal-Mart aren't the major job creators in the United States. Small and medium-sized companies were responsible for generating 58 million new jobs from 1987 to 1992. Larger companies with more than 500 employees had a net loss of 2.3 million jobs in 1993, small companies added 17 million jobs while big companies were losing 300,000. In short, small companies represent the fastest-growing and major job-creating sector of the U. S. economy.

Small businesses are growing partly because they're faster at responding to customers' needs. A recent survey showed that small companies produce 2.4 times as many innovations as large companies. So small companies not only produce jobs, but they produce the technological change that keeps America strong.

Competition from small businesses is forcing larger businesses to become more responsive and entrepreneurial. That is, they're firing middle managers who historically have slowed the decision-making process. One trend in business is toward more intrapreneuring and intraprise. This means that firms are encouraging employees to take more risks inside larger firms. Management gives these innovators the resources and support they need to make large firms more creative, responsive, and competitive.

Intraprise is the creation of small businesses within larger firms to service other workers within the firms. For example, the accounting department may become an intraprise that competes with accounting firms from the outside. If the intraprise fails to please its customers (employees), the company will give the accounting function to an outside firm. Small teams of employees make it possible for large firms to get close to internal and external customers and respond to their needs quickly. Such teams, if successful, will make it possible for these larger businesses to be flexible and responsive, similar to small businesses, and to begin expanding and generating more jobs.

LECTURE ENHANCER 1-6

THE AGING OF THE BABY BOOMERS

The bumper crop of 64 million infants born between 1946 and 1961 is now 40 to 55 years old. They are by far the largest generation in American history—nearly one-third of the U.S. population today. In the 1950s they made the United States a child-oriented society of new schools and station wagons. Between 1950 and 1970, that generation caused a 70 percent jump in the number of elementary- and high-school-aged children. During the 1960s, their social consciousness and alternate lifestyles rocked American society.

The effects of the baby boom have been widespread. Some economists blame the armies of new adults, at least in part, for the inflation of the late-1970s. Young, inexperienced workers flooded the job market, depressing productivity rates just when they are stimulating demand for consumer goods. During the 1980s the boomers also tended to be hard-pressed for money, borrowing a lot and creating a staggering demand for consumer credit and home mortgages. Their low savings rates depressed the supply of capital for investment. Criminologists say that their vast numbers in the crime-prone ages of 15 to 24 contributed heavily to the record crime rates of the late 1970s.

As boomers reach their 30s and 40s, their productivity rates rise. This improves their wages, improves their savings rates, and provides the Federal Treasury with a boost as their taxable incomes increases. During the 1980s they flocked to buy houses, fueling a construction boom. Their passage through middle age has made retirement planning seem more urgent. They embraced the stock market with enthusiasm, helping fuel the long-running bull market of the 1980s and 1990s.

One thing is certain: the baby boomers are getting older. The first boomers turned 50 in 1996 and another four million will cross that threshold each year through 2004. Beyond that fact, there is little agreement about what the future will look like.

CONSUMER SPENDING:

Older workers generally earn more than young ones. Almost one in three Americans today is a baby boomer, and a little extra income for each means a lot more money in consumer spending for the economy as a whole. And baby boomers have notorious big-spending ways. Middle-aged families also register above average spending on food, clothing, and home furnishings.

Except that the real wages of aging baby boomers haven't climbed as rapidly as their parents' did. Wages for all workers have been stagnating in recent years. The consumer spending kick from this age group may be overrated.

SAVINGS AND INVESTMENT:

Boomers won't spend all they earn. Some analysts expect that the stock market will be flooded with more money in baby-boomer investments. Others feel that boomers will borrow less and save more when they have children. Wealthier boomers tend to borrow a lot to buy or expand houses when their children are young, but after that they save readily.

However, there isn't any evidence that older baby boomers are saving any more than they did when they were younger. Comparing the savings behavior of the past generation to the baby boom generation may not be valid. People in their sixties and seventies today were Depression babies. They formed their savings habits in a very different time.

HOUSING:

Most baby boomers have reached the age where they have already bought a home. Thus there has been reduced demand for houses built in the 1990s. There will be 14 percent fewer households headed by 25 to 34-year-olds in the year 2000 than in 1995. That age bracket spans the prime first-home buying years. Builders reason that the growth market of tomorrow will be fancier "trade-up" homes with bigger master bedrooms, higher ceilings, and bigger and snazzier kitchens.

But some economists and lenders say the scenario of baby-boom homeowners moving up to better homes isn't a sure thing. Many boomers may be unable to follow their parents' trade-up pattern because they won't be able to sell their first houses for enough money to buy a bigger one. And business realignment and downsizing could force many to remain in their first homes longer and longer.

Some experts are worried more about the baby bust of the past two decades. With a drop of 6.5 million in the school-aged population in the 1980s, elementary schools and colleges closed for lack of students. Businesses and industry were hit by a severe labor shortage in the late 1980s, forcing them to raise more money for investment in labor-saving devices. The labor shortages have driven up wages for the baby-bust generation.

LECTURE ENHANCER 1-7

OLDER PEOPLE ARE BECOMING MORE INFLUENTIAL

Older people are playing a more important role in the labor force. One of the traditional sources for new jobs was through the retirement of older persons. But because of various factors, older persons are returning and staying longer in the work force. Part of the reason for the return of the senior citizen to the work force is the lack of interest of younger persons in some of the more mundane jobs in the service sector, especially in the food service and retailing industries.

More important reasons, however, include: (1) employers offer fewer early retirement incentives than in previous years; (2) insecurity of their work lives frustrate workers ability to build up retirement resources; (3) later child bearing extends heaviest family and financial responsibilities to later years; (4) aging parents that are living longer than earlier generations require more care; and (5) the Social Security system is gradually increasing the retirement age to receive maximum benefits to age 67.

The return of senior citizens is putting more pressure on younger people and also those in the middle-aged groups. Older workers are also demonstrating two key virtues: experience and dependability.

LECTURE ENHANCER 1-8

MEN, FAMILIES, AND "WOMEN'S ISSUES"

Men want improved benefits in the workplace to help with child and dependent care just as much as women do. What has been seen as a women's issue is now a family concern, with benefits, such as flexible spending accounts for dependent care, as important to fathers as they are to mothers. They have become the kind of benefits that both men and women are willing to switch jobs to get.

These are just some of the conclusions drawn by the National Study of the Changing Workingforce, an examination of nearly 3,000 workers that was conducted by the New York-based Families and Work Institute. "The pattern here suggests that men will trade wages and salaries for equivalent benefits," said James T. Bond, senior researcher for the study. "If men are willing to make those kind of tradeoffs, that's new." While men and women with children younger than 13 seem to agree on the importance of child care benefits at work, the study found that women were "much more willing" than men to sacrifice earnings and advancement for flexible work arrangements.

Other findings of the study:

- Despite massive increases in women's work outside the home, women's responsibilities inside the home have not changed much. And the issue is not generational—young men do not cook or clean any than older men.
- Single working mothers and married working mothers exhibit "no significant difference" in the time they miss from work.
- Workers younger than 25 are more willing to make sacrifices in their education, jobs and career than in their personal and family lives.
- "Few employed men . . . take primary responsibility for the main household chores of cooking, cleaning and shopping," the study concludes. However, 43 percent of the men in families where both parents work said they share child-care responsibility with their spouses. Only 19 percent of those families agreed that their spouses shared that much.
- As for younger married men, the only thing they took responsibility for in greater number than their older counterparts was household repairs.
- The survey indicated that women did not miss much work because of their at home responsibilities. Working parents with children younger than 13 missed very little time because of child-care responsibilities. Single mothers and married mothers missed about the same amount of time a year because of their children: four days.
- Of the working mothers with children younger than six, 54 percent said they "needed" to work, that it would be "quite difficult or extremely difficult for their families" if they did not have a job.
- Working parents in the study exhibited higher levels of stress than workers without children and do not cope as well as other workers. In contrast, workers with children feel "somewhat more successful" in their personal and family lives than workers without children.

- Younger workers—those under 25—were found more willing to sacrifice for their personal and family lives (82 percent) than for their jobs and careers (76 percent).

LECTURE ENHANCER 1-9

GLOBAL OPPORTUNITIES FOR THE SMALLER COMPETITOR

As national borders become increasingly invisible to businesses, a smaller company may succeed where larger companies have encountered problems. WorldCom, the nation's fourth largest telecommunications company, outpaces Sprint, AT&T, and MCI in foreign markets. (Of course, if the proposed WorldCom-MCI merger goes through, these rankings will change.) The 15-year-old company operates in more than 50 countries and in 1996 derived about 12 percent of its $5.6 billion annual revenues from international markets.

While competition for overseas customers is heated, WorldCom has a distinct advantage over the major carriers, claims CEO Bernie Ebbers. "The advantage we have or the basis on which we are building our international business is as one company owning our own facilities. The others are doing it as consortiums, joining up with other foreign companies or existing telecommunication systems."

Because WorldCom is smaller and perceived as less of a threat that the big three, it has been allowed direct access to territories Sprint, MCI, and AT&T can only reach through alliances. For example, Sprint joined France Telecom and Deutsche Telekom to create Global One, and a partnership between MCI and British Telecom has produced Concert. Local companies have resisted letting the big telecommunication companies come in on a direct basis. Under pressure to let someone in, they chose the smaller WorldCom, which at that time only controlled five percent of the U.S. telecommunication market.

WorldCom was the first American telecommunications company to get cross-border licenses to build and own facilities in several key European markets—the United Kingdom, France, Sweden, Germany, and Netherlands. Two-thirds of the $60 billion European business is concentrated in France, Germany, Italy, and the United Kingdom.

Owning the network allows WorldCom to control costs and quality. WorldCom's local phone service subsidiary, MFS, has been active in opening up monopolized markets in the U.S. This experience gave them a leg up in international markets, where deregulation and privatization are opening up, just as it did in the U.S. ten years ago. According to one telecommunication industry analyst, MFS "knows how to get around the red herrings, stall tactics, and bureaucratic manipulations" that come with the process.

About 78 percent of the top 1,000 multinational companies are located in the U.S., Europe, and Japan, according to the U.S. Department of Commerce. Tapping into foreign markets is critical for growth-oriented companies, such as WorldCom.

LECTURE ENHANCER 1-10

THE IMPACT OF THE BALDRIGE AWARDS

The text discusses the trend toward quality. The Malcolm Baldrige National Quality Award is one of the highest honors a company can earn. The Wallace Co., a family-owned distributor of industrial pipes and valves in Houston, won a Baldrige award in 1990. By 1992, the company was in Chapter 11 bankruptcy. What happened? Some problems could be blamed on the hard times in the petrochemical industry. However, chairman John Wallace places most of the blame on himself and his other top managers. They were so busy traveling for speaking engagements about their success that no one was minding the store.

Some experts question the wisdom of small companies pursuing the Baldrige award. "Breaking the attention span at a company that doesn't have layers of management is a big-time cost. It can kill you," says consultant Gail Cooper. The Wallace Company is now out of business.

Listed below are the **Baldrige Award Winners for 1988 through 1997.**

ADAC Laboratories (1996)

Armstrong World Industries Building Products Operations (1995)

AT&T Consumer Communications Services (now part of the Consumer Markets Division of AT&T) (1994)

AT&T Network Systems Group - Transmission Systems Business Unit (now part of Lucent Technologies, Network Systems) (1992)

AT&T Universal Card Services (1992)

Cadillac Motor Car Company (1990)

Corning Telecommunications Products Division (1995)

Custom Research, Inc. (1996)

Dana Commercial Credit Corporation (1996)

Eastman Chemical Company (1993)

Federal Express Corporation (1990)

Globe Metallurgical Inc. (1988)

Granite Rock Company (1992)

GTE Directories Corporation (1994)

IBM Rochester - AS/400 Division (1990)

Marlow Industries, Inc. (1991)

Merrill Lynch Credit Corporation (1997)

Milliken & Company (1989)

Motorola Inc. (1988)

3M Dental Products Division (1997)

The Ritz-Carlton Hotel Company (1992)

Solectron Corporation (1991 and 1997)

Texas Instruments Incorporated - Defense Systems & Electronics Group (now Raytheon TI Systems) (1992)

Trident Precision Manufacturing, Inc. (1996)

Wainwright Industries, Inc. (1994)

Wallace Co., Inc. (1990)

Westinghouse Electric Corporation - Commercial Nuclear Fuel Division (1988)

Xerox Corporation - Business Products & Systems (1989 and 1997)

Zytec Corporation (1991)

Critical Thinking Exercises

Name: ____________________

Date: ____________________

CRITICAL THINKING EXERCISE 1-1

HOW MUCH PROFIT?

The text defines *profit* as "money a business earns above and beyond what it spends for salaries, expenses, and other costs. Choose a large corporation representing each of the following types of companies. Using the above profit definition, how much profit as a percentage of sales do you think each corporation earns? In other words, out of every dollar a company earns, how much does it keep?

1. **AUTOMOBILE MANUFACTURER**

   Corporation ____________________ Percent Estimated Profit ____________

2. **GROCERY CHAIN**

   Corporation ____________________ Percent Estimated Profit ____________

3. **AIRLINE**

   Corporation ____________________ Percent Estimated Profit ____________

4. **COMPUTER COMPANY**

   Corporation ____________________ Percent Estimated Profit ____________

ANSWERS TO CRITICAL THINKING EXERCISE 1-1

Students often have a very exaggerated idea of the amount of profit big corporations make. This exercise should help set the record straight.

Each spring, *Fortune* magazine publishes a comprehensive listing of the largest U.S. corporations along with annual income, profit, employees, etc. There are also numerous financial references on the Web. These resource can provide the most recent profit figures for comparison. Below are the published figures for 1997:

AUTOMOBILE MANUFACTURER: *Ford Motors Corp*, 4.1 percent annual profit.

GROCERY CHAIN: *Albertsons Inc.*, 3.4 percent annual profit.

AIRLINE: *Delta Airlines*, 6.3 percent annual profit.

COMPUTER COMPANY: *Compaq Computer* 7.2 percent annual profit. (However, *Apple Computer* suffered a *negative* 15 percent annual loss.)

Name: ____________________

Date: ____________________

CRITICAL THINKING EXERCISE 1-2

MAKING ETHICAL DECISIONS

Throughout the textbook, you will see a box in each chapter called "Making Ethical Decisions." You will be given a short description of a situation and then asked what you would do in that situation. These boxes may or may not be assigned by your professor, but you will benefit greatly by reading them and answering the questions. If they are assigned, you probably won't be required to hand in a written report. Your professor will probably have no real way of knowing if you read the boxes and answered the questions. You are likely to be "on your honor."

This is your first ethical situation in this course: You come to a "Making Ethical Decisions" box in your text. What do you decide to do? Read and answer the questions or skip it and go on?

Use the questions below to help you make your decision.

1. What is the problem?

2. What are your alternatives?

3. What are the effects of each alternative? (What will happen if you choose that alternative?)

4. Which alternative will you choose? Why?

5. Is your choice ethical? (Would you want your family and professor to know of your decision? Would you want it printed in the school paper? Is it fair to all parties involved?)

ANSWERS TO CRITICAL THINKING EXERCISE 1-2

It is easy to skip ethical boxes in a text because they don't seem to have any direct relationship to your main goal in this class—to learn about business so you can get a good job and make good money. The problem is that businesspeople tend to have the same attitude. They don't want to waste their time making ethical decisions—they want to make decisions that result in more profit for the firm. There comes a time, however, when society must recognize the need for making moral and ethical decisions and puts so much pressure on people that they conform. This can take the form of laws, but it is much easier to permit more freedom for people to choose to act morally and ethically on their own. You should encourage your students to choose what is right always and what is right in this case is to consider the moral and ethical ramifications of their business decisions so that it becomes automatic. "Is it right?" should be heard in corporate offices as often as "Is it profitable?"

Name: ______________________

Date: ______________________

CRITICAL THINKING EXERCISE 1.3

EFFECTS OF TRENDS

The text describes the trend toward increasing numbers of businesses in the service sector. Look through your local phone book and list five businesses that provide services in your town.

1. ______________________ 4. ______________________

2. ______________________ 5. ______________________

3. ______________________

The text also describes how certain demographic and social changes affect businesses. Look at your list of local service businesses and consider how the trends listed below affect them. Below each trend, write the name of the business(es) that are positively affected by the trend and then those that are negatively affected by it. Explain your answers.

A. **MULTICULTURALISM**

Positively affected: ______________________

Negatively affected: ______________________

B. **INCREASING NUMBER OF OLDER AMERICANS**

Positively affected: ______________________

Negatively affected: ______________________

C. **MORE TWO-INCOME FAMILIES.**

Positively affected: ______________________

Negatively affected: ______________________

ANSWERS TO CRITICAL THINKING EXERCISE 1-3

Answers will depend upon the specific businesses selected by the student.

Supplemental Cases

CASE 1-1

DEALING WITH CHANGING FAMILY STRUCTURES

Economic and social changes have had a dramatic impact on the nature of the family. It used to be that a "typical" family was one with a mother, father and two kids. Only 11 percent of all families now fit that description! In 1970, 40 percent of the families consisted of a husband, a wife, and children. Today, about 28 percent match that description. To show you how significant that change is, let's look at another figure. Since 1970, there has been an increase in "families" of 22 million, but a decrease of over 1 million in married-couple families with children. The number of single-person households has increased by about 9 million since 1970 and now accounts for 23 percent of all households.

Today, couples with no children are the largest group of American households (30 percent). These are mostly older couples (two or three are over 50). About 4 percent of American households consist of unmarried couples living together. If we were to add up all those people who live alone with those married couples without children (including those who live together without being married), we find that 57 percent of all households fall into a category that might be called new-style family.

Think what that means when communities are trying to get more money for schools. Some 57 percent of the voters have no children in school and could resist the increase. Think also of how many schools are closing because of declining enrollments. Family changes are affecting all kinds of institutions in society.

Think also of the economic potential of two-income families with no children. These people have been called "yuppies," or young urban professionals, and are stereotyped as driving fancy sports cars, living in elaborately decorated apartments, and enjoying the good life. There is some truth in that image. On the other hand, such couples tend to work long hours and seem to have no time for starting a family.

The tensions of having two-income families plus the social changes that have happened over the last 25 years or so have led to divorce and the phenomenon called the single-parent family. The number of households headed by a woman with one or more children has doubled since 1970. There are about 6 million such families, and most of them live in poverty. Another 800,000 single-parent households are headed by a man. These are the statistics. What do they mean for business?

DISCUSSION QUESTIONS FOR CASE 1-1:

1. What effects have the changes in family structure had on businesses thus far? Think of the products that have been designed for couples with no children and for individuals living alone. Think also of the working woman phenomenon. What does that mean in the long run for businesses?

2. Couples are having fewer and fewer children, and are beginning to have children later. What effect will these changes have on schools and businesses?

3. What is the significance of the fact that two of three of the married couples with no children at home are over 50? What market opportunities does that create?

4. What is the relationship between the breakup of the family and poverty in the United States?

ANSWERS TO DISCUSSION QUESTIONS FOR CASE 1-1:

1. *What effects have the changes in family structure had on businesses thus far?*

   Many new products such as meals for one have been designed for individuals and couples. Apartments are often smaller to accommodate smaller families, and many amenities such as weight rooms, swimming pools, and game rooms have been added. Businesses have added more flextime, part-time jobs, and day care centers.

2. *Couples are having fewer and fewer children, and are beginning to have children later. What effect will these changes have on schools and businesses?*

   Young couples often have much money when they are both working and spend it on cars, clothes, apartments, travel, and other such items. The name given such people in the 1980s was "Yuppies" for young urban professionals. These children of the "baby boom" era (after World War II) are now having their own children. They are likely to have fewer children than their parents and to spend more money on them. There are so many people in this category that this will be a boom for toy makers, children's clothing manufacturers, baby food producers, and so on. Schools are likely to go from underutilized to overcrowded as the yuppies have children.

3. *What is the significance of the fact that two of three of the married couples with no children at home are over 50? What market opportunities does that create?*

   It may be more difficult to get school tax referendums passed, but businesses may benefit because these couples tend to have much discretionary income. No children at home may also increase the desire for condominiums and smaller homes.

4. *What is the relationship between the breakup of the family and poverty in the United States?*

   The majority of those living in poverty are in single-parent families. Many are young women who have never married: others are divorced individuals with children who are not receiving support from the father. It is important to follow family trends because they will indicate much about the strength of the economy and the future of business. Strong family units are good for the economy and society.

CASE 1-2

THE TRAVEL AND TOURISM INDUSTRY

Tourism employees 204 million people worldwide, or one in nine workers. Tourism is the world's leading economic contributor, producing over 10 percent of global gross national product. It is the world's largest industry in terms of gross output—about $3.4 trillion. Tourism generates some $655 billion in tax revenues. Finally, travel and tourism will generate 144 million new jobs between now and 2005, 112 million in the regions of Asia and the Pacific alone.

If these statistics didn't surprise you, let's consider some more figures from the United States alone. Travel and tourism is America's leading exporter. It's the nation's number two employer and the third largest retail industry. Domestic and international travel and tourism generate $23.5 billion in federal taxes, $12.1 billion in state taxes, and $7.08 billion in local taxes. Travel and tourism is the largest employer in 11 states and is one of the top three employers in 34 states.

Travel and tourism, therefore, is a critical part of the world and U.S. economies. Not only does the industry create jobs, but it creates a significant percentage of the wealth that federal, state, and local governments can use to build roads, feed the hungry, and so forth. Therefore, you might think our governments would do all they could to help the travel and tourism industry prosper and grow, but that's not always the case. In 1994, some 1,500 members of the industry marched on Washington, D.C., to urge legislators to cut taxes on the industry and help them prevent fraud. The president of the American Society of Travel Agents (ASTA) encouraged Congress to cut taxes because high taxes kill jobs. Most of the 10 percent tax on all domestic airfares goes to an infrequently used Airport and Airway Trust Fund. Much of this tax is actually used to reduce the federal deficit.

Travel-related taxes have increased by 75 percent over the past five years. Airfare taxes alone increased by 25 percent. Many airlines are on the verge of bankruptcy, yet a fuel tax increase of 4.3 cents a gallon went into effect in 1995. Current air travel and shippers fees and taxes include a ten percent tax on domestic airline tickets, $3 passenger facility charge, $6 international departure tax, $6.50 customs fee for travelers entering the United States, $6 immigration fee, $61 aircraft fee, and a 6.25 percent air freight tax.

DISCUSSION QUESTIONS FOR CASE 1-2:

1. Given the importance of the travel and tourism industry, should the government encourage more growth and more jobs through less taxation or should it tax the industry more to pay for other social programs or reduction of our national debt?

2. If travel expenses remain high and the government doesn't allow more than the current 50 percent deduction for meals and entertainment, business travelers may turn to alternatives such as teleconferencing and E-mail conferences. Should the government lower travel taxes and increase deductions to encourage more business-related travel?

3. What careers in the travel and tourism industry are most appealing to you?

4. What could travel and tourism companies do to make your travel more enjoyable?

ANSWERS TO DISCUSSION QUESTIONS FOR CASE 1-2:

1. *Given the importance of the travel and tourism industry, should the government encourage more growth and more jobs through less taxation or should it tax the industry more to pay for other social programs or reduction of our national debt?*

   Student answers will be individual.

2. *If travel expenses remain high and the government doesn't allow more than the current 50 percent deduction for meals and entertainment, business travelers may turn to alternatives such as teleconferencing and E-mail conferences. Should the government lower travel taxes and increase deductions to encourage more business-related travel?*

Again, answers will be individual. Teleconferencing and E-mail are low-cost alternatives to physical travel. They do not, however, have the advantage of face-to-face communication with one's customers.

3. *What careers in the travel and tourism industry are most appealing to you?*

   Students answers will be individual.

4. *What could travel and tourism companies do to make your travel more enjoyable?*

The majority of those living in poverty are in single-parent families. Many are young women who have never married; others are divorced individuals with children who are not receiving support from the father. It is important to follow family trends because they will indicate much about the strength of the economy and the future of business. Strong family units are good for the economy and society.

Transparency Masters

Chapter Outline

CHAPTER 1
FINDING OPPORTUNITIES IN TODAY'S DYNAMIC BUSINESS ENVIRONMENT

PROFILE: Herman Cain of Godfather's Pizza

I. WHAT IS A BUSINESS?

A. Businesses Can Provide Wealth and a High Quality of Life for Almost Everyone.

B. Nonprofit Organizations Use Business Principles.

II. THE IMPORTANCE OF ENTREPRENEURSHIP TO WEALTH.

A. Opportunities for Entrepreneurs.

B. Matching Risk with Profit.

C. The Role of the Factors of Production in Creating Wealth.

III. THE BUSINESS ENVIRONMENT.

A. The Economic Environment.

IV. THE TECHNOLOGICAL ENVIRONMENT.

A. The Importance of Information Technology.

B. Responding to Customers.

V. THE COMPETITIVE ENVIRONMENT.

A. Competing by Delighting the Customer.

B. Competing by Meeting the Needs of the Community.

C. Competing by Restructuring and Meeting the Needs of Employees.

D. Competing by Concern for the Natural Environment.

VI. THE SOCIAL ENVIRONMENT.

A. Multiculturalism and Its Advantages for Business.

B. The Increase in the Number of Older Americans.

C. Two-Income Families.

VII. THE GLOBAL ENVIRONMENT.

A. Global Opportunities and Free Trade Agreements.

B. How Global Changes Affect You.

VIII. THE QUALITY IMPERATIVE.

A. The Quality Standard: The Baldrige Award.

B. Quality, ISO 9000, and ISO 14000 Standards.

IX. THE EVOLUTION OF AMERICAN BUSINESS.

A. Progress in the Agricultural and Manufacturing Industries.

B. Progress in Service Industries.

C. Your Future in the Global Economy.

X. SUMMARY AND REVIEW.

The Five Factors of Production
(Figure 1.1 on text page 6)

THE FIVE FACTORS OF PRODUCTION

Land:	Land and other natural resources are used to make homes, cars, and other products.
Labor:	People have always been an important resource in producing goods and services, but many people are now being replaced by technology.
Capital:	Capital includes machines, tools, buildings, and other means of manufacturing.
Entrepreneurship:	All the resources in the world have little value unless entrepreneurs are willing to take the risk of starting businesses to use those resources.
Knowledge:	Information technology has revolutionized business, making it possible to quickly determine wants and needs and to respond with desired goods and services.

TM-10

The Business Environment

(Figure 1.2 on text page 8)

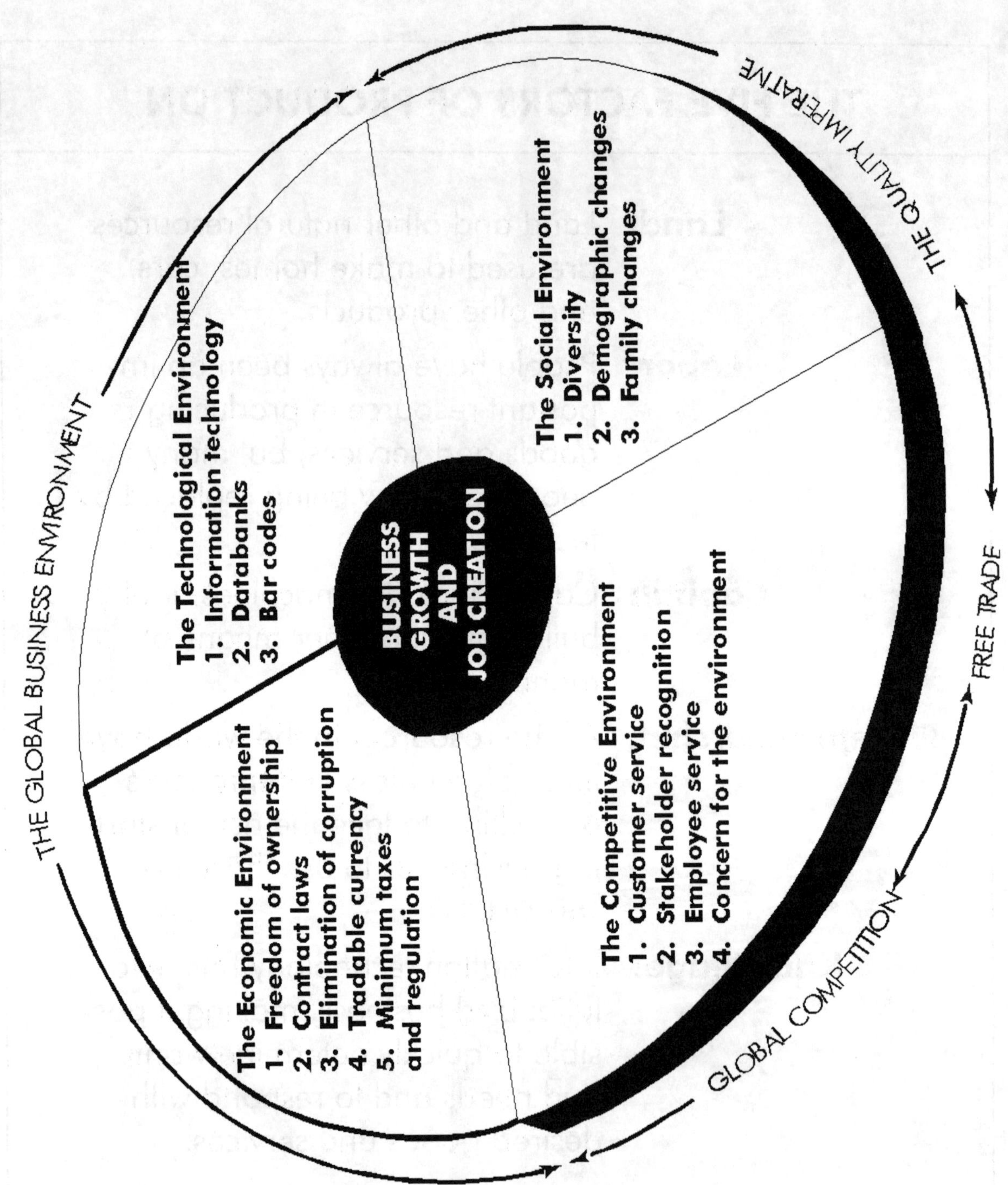

TM-11

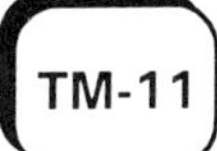

A Business and Its Stakeholders
(Figure 1.4 on text page 13)

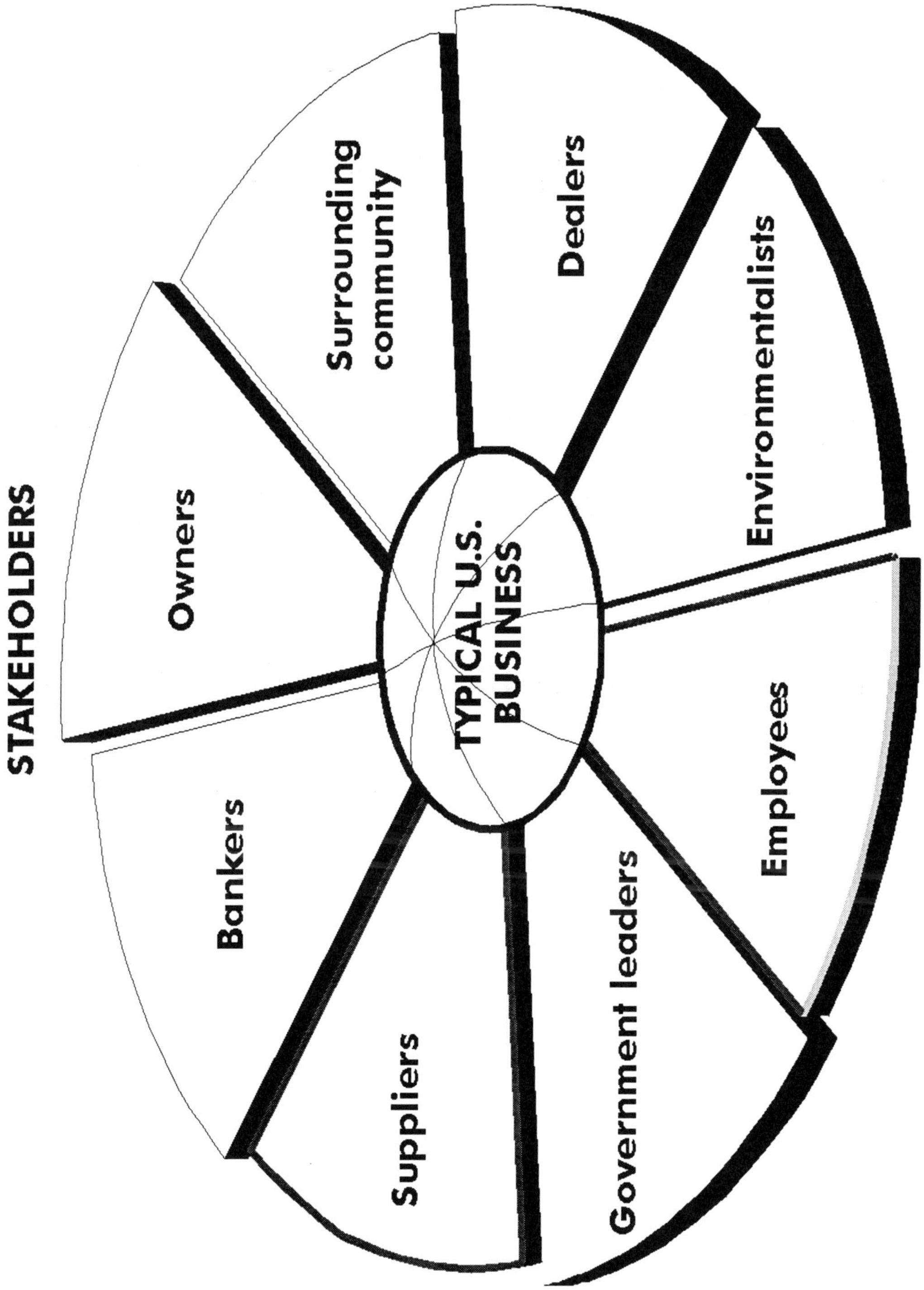
STAKEHOLDERS
TYPICAL U.S. BUSINESS
Owners
Surrounding community
Dealers
Environmentalists
Employees
Government leaders
Suppliers
Bankers

Members of the European Union
(Figure 1.5 on text page 18)

MEMBERS OF THE EUROPEAN UNION		
Austria	Germany	Luxembourg
Belgium	Great Britain	Netherlands
Denmark	Greece	Portugal
Finland	Ireland	Spain
France	Italy	Sweden

TM-13

Future Employment Opportunities
(Figure 1.7 on text page 23)

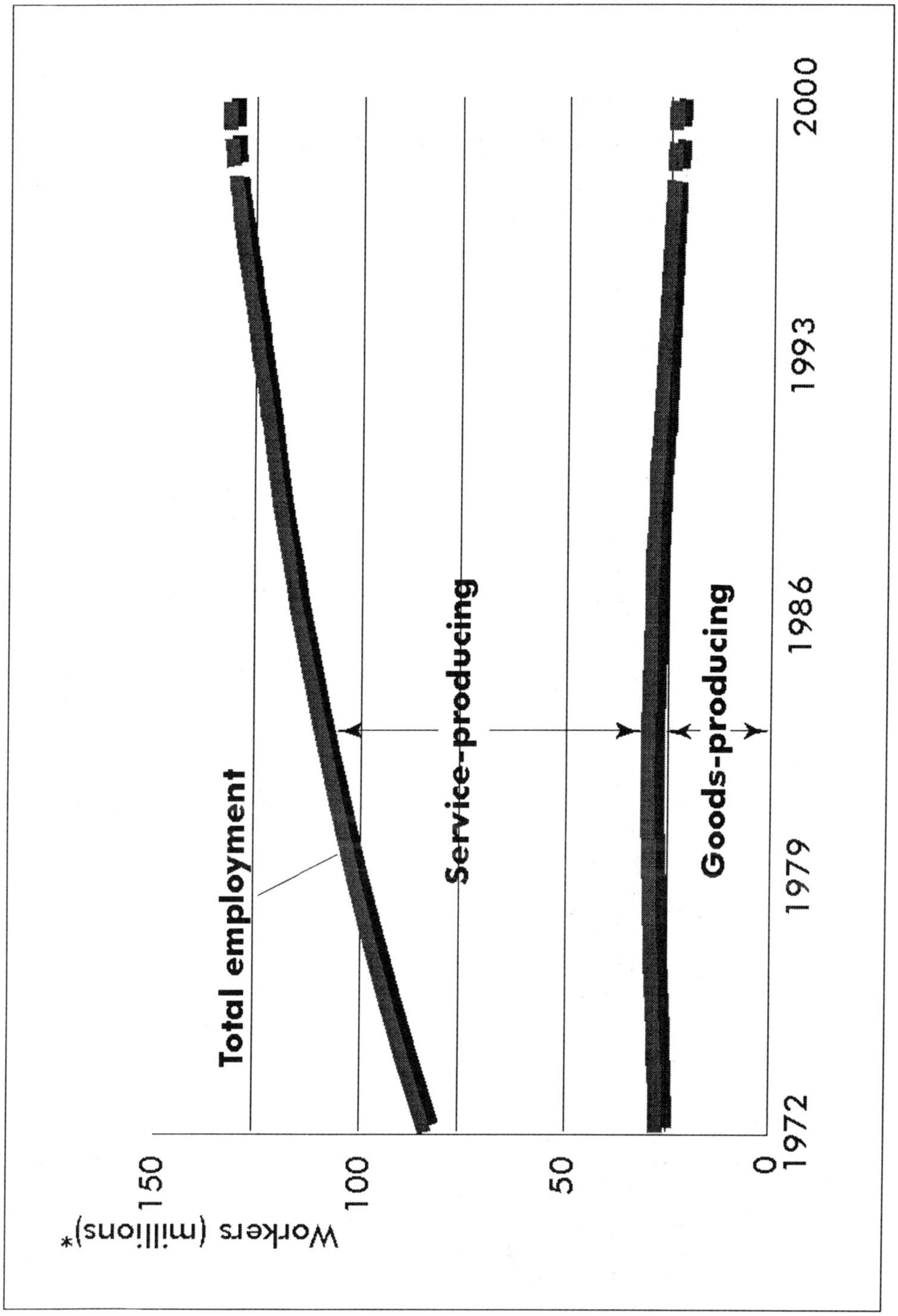
Total employment
Service-producing
Goods-producing
Workers (millions)*
150
100
50
0
1972
1979
1986
1993
2000

TM-14

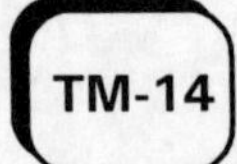

Hypertext Links and a Uniform Resource Locator (URL)

(Figure A.2 on text page 32)

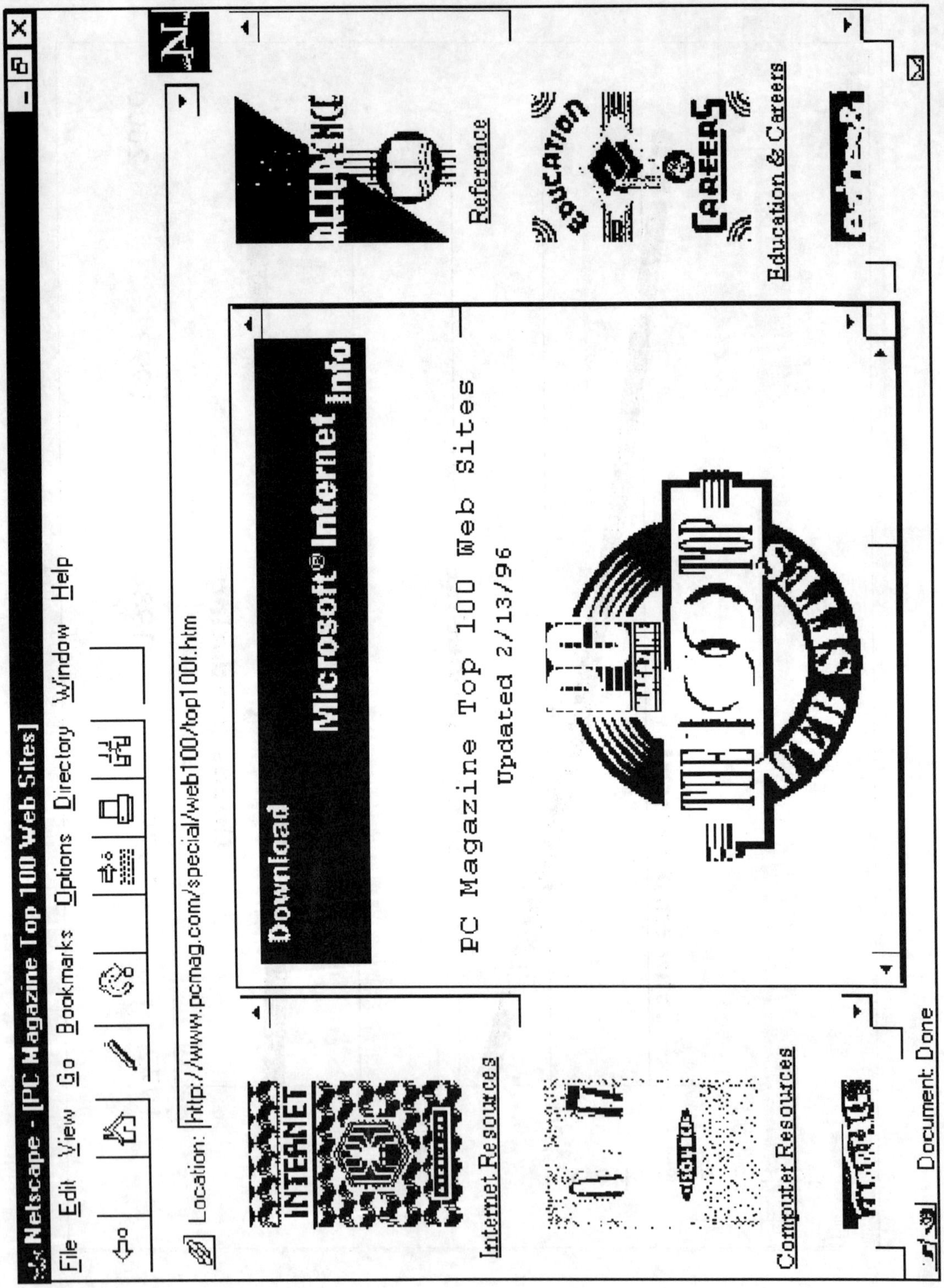
Netscape - [PC Magazine Top 100 Web Sites]
File Edit View Go Bookmarks Options Directory Window Help
Location: http://www.pcmag.com/special/web100/top100f.htm
Internet Resources
Download Microsoft® Internet Info
PC Magazine Top 100 Web Sites
Updated 2/13/96
Reference
Education & Careers
Computer Resources
Document: Done

TM-15

E-Mail Form

(Figure A.3 on text page 37)

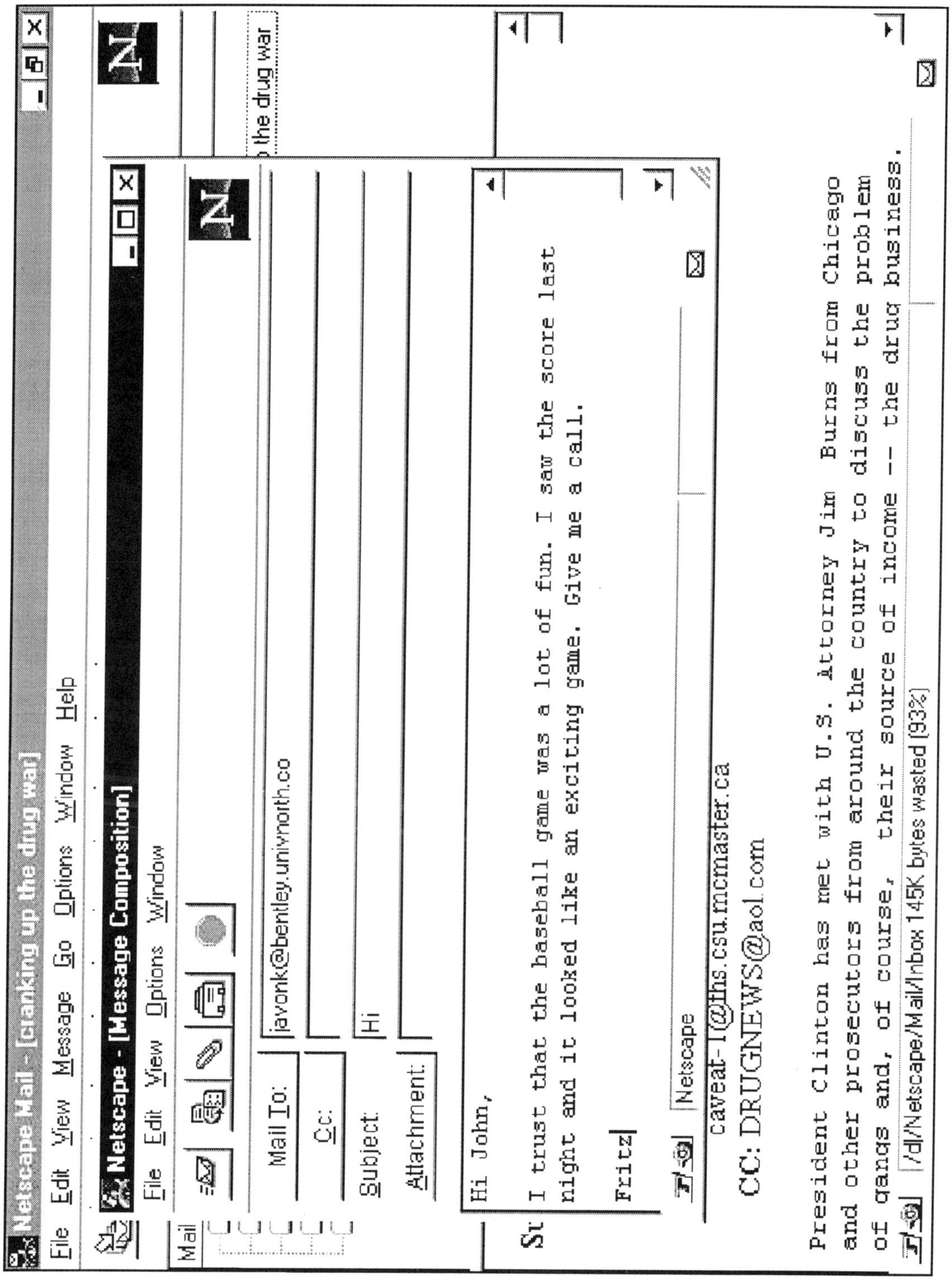

Netscape Mail - [cranking up the drug war]

File Edit View Message Go Options Window Help

Netscape - [Message Composition]

File Edit View Options Window

Mail To: javonk@bentley.univnorth.co

Cc:

Subject: Hi

Attachment:

Hi John,

I trust that the baseball game was a lot of fun. I saw the score last night and it looked like an exciting game. Give me a call.

Fritz

Netscape

caveat-l@lhs.csu.mcmaster.ca

CC: DRUGNEWS@aol.com

President Clinton has met with U.S. Attorney Jim Burns from Chicago and other prosecutors from around the country to discuss the problem of gangs and, of course, their source of income -- the drug business.

/dl/Netscape/Mail/Inbox 145K bytes wasted (93%)

Economics: The Creation and Distribution of Wealth

Chapter 2

Folder Contents

OT ACETATE 2-6 How Inflation Affects Buying Power

OT ACETATE 2-7 Where Does the Government Get Its Money?

OT ACETATE 2-8 What $1 Billion Can Buy

OT ACETATE 2-9 How Much Is the Federal Debt?

OT ACETATE 2-10 Top Expenditures of the Federal Government

OT ACETATE 2-11 The Changing Composition of the Federal Budget

(Acetates and Transparency Masters are also available as PowerPoint slides on disk and on the Presentation CD-ROM.)

(Resources Available are also referenced in the expanded lecture outline later in this chapter.)

Other Resources Available

Video Case - "Breaking Down the Great Wall." Dramatizes the situation in Hong Kong, where after 150 years of British control the capitalist Mecca of the far east returned to China's rule. This changeover may be a giant step in bridging gaps that have separated China from global markets in the past. (The **Media Resource Guide** contains a summary of the Video and suggested discussion questions.)

Student Assessment and Learning Guide: Contains matching key term and definition questions, write-in retention questions, write-in critical thinking questions, and practice test of multiple choice and true/false questions.

Technology:

Zapitalism CD-ROM - Simulation program.

Concept Mastery Exam Preparation Disk - Practice test and tutorial.

Business Essentials Disk - Hyperlinks Understanding Business with seven other leading business texts.

Presentation CD-ROM - Contains PowerPoint slides of acetates and transparency masters, video clips, lecture materials. This tool allows you to customize your lecture presentations.

***Business Week* Web Site Access with the *Business Week* edition.**

***Understanding Business* Home Page - http:/www.mhhe.com/ub5e.**

Audiotape: Abridged chapter (Text minus profile, boxes, and end-of-chapter material.

Associated Web Sites

These sites are provided to students for the purpose of analysis and critical thinking of the issues. Students are encouraged to explore other sites. As with any Web site, some may be inactive now.

Balance of Payment - Trends:

http://www.clev.frb.org/research/jul96et/curact.htm

The Distribution of Wealth

General Perspective:

http://pompano.pcola.gulfnet/~middlesware/economic.htm

The Distribution of Wealth: Increasing Inequality?:

http://www.aei.org/cs6808.htm

Capitalism:

Strategy (interesting perspective):

http://www.pcgamer.com/s_capita.html

Capitalism and the Alternatives:

http://www.mcspotlight.org/debate/capitalism/messages/15.html

ANOVA Group believes "Greed is good" look at their Scam of the month article:

http://www.anovagroup.com/

Socialism:

Comprehensive site for many topics on soclalirn:

http://www.stile.lut.ac.uk/~gyedb/STILE/t0000461.html

Free-Market Economy (Chinese perspective):

http.//www.forerunner.com/mandate/ X0030_Moving_to_a_Market_e.html

Social Economy:

http://www.cdu.de/englisch/gp/gp3-3.html

Gross Domestic Product and Gross National Product:

Frequently Askcd Qtnstions:

http://www.bus.ucf.edu/eco/ecofaqs/macro/20l3c6.htm

Consumer Price Indexes:

Government indexes and frequently asked questions:

http:/stats.bls.gov/cpihome.htm

Productivity - Labor:

U.S. Department Labor:

http://bubba.dol.gov/

Federal Reserve System:

Federal Reserve Board:

http://www.ncs.gov/~ncs/html/frb.html

Inflation:

Factors which influence inflation:

http://ns.hm-treasury.gov.uk/pub/html/top/top6/inf.html

Affects of inflation:

http://www.minnesotamutual.com/solindiv/retire/inflatn.html

Recession:

The Joys of Recession - review of economics:

http://epn.org/prospect/16/16gal2.html

Welfare Capitalism:

Poverty in America (newsletter):

http://www2.ari.net/home/poverty/news.html

***Understanding Business* Home Page**

http:/www.mhhe.com/ub5e

What's New in This Edition

Additions:

- Profile of Rosa Alvardo, Village Banker in Guatemala
- Section "The Birth of Communism"
- Section "The Attraction of Socialism" to introduce the section on the consequences of socialism
- Section "Just Tax the Rich and Pay Off the Debt?"
- Making Ethical Decisions box
- Spotlight on Small Business: The Internet Creates a One-World Market"
- Legal Briefcase: Exploring the Tax Laws
- Taking It to the Net exercises

Revisions:

Statistical data and examples throughout the chapter were updated to reflect current information. In addition:

- Profile of Pablo Tesak was transferred to the Reaching Beyond Our Borders box.
- Section "Inflation and the Rule of 72" was converted to an end-of-chapter case.
- Section on Competition (perfect competition, monopolistic competition, oligopoly, and monopoly) was moved from the Business Law appendix.
- Consumer price index (CPI) discussion was expanded.
- Figure 2.1 Comparison of key economic systems was revised to include communism.
- Video case about breaking down the Great Wall of China was revised and moved from Chapter 3.

Deletions:

- All boxes were replaced.
- Section "Emergence of Welfare Capitalism"
- Section "Regulation the Hidden Tax"

Brief Chapter Outline/Learning Goals

CHAPTER 2

ECONOMICS: THE CREATION AND DISTRIBUTION OF WEALTH

PROFILE: Rosa Alvardo—Village Banker

I. THE IMPORTANCE OF THE STUDY OF ECONOMICS.

LEARNING GOAL 1. Explain how wealth is created in an economy.

A. What Is Economics?

B. The Economic Theory of Wealth Creation: Adam Smith.

C. The "Invisible Hand."

II. THE HISTORY OF BUSINESS AND ECONOMICS.

LEARNING GOAL 2. Discuss the major differences between capitalism, socialism, communism, and a mixed economy.

A. The Search for Equality.

B. The Birth of Communism.

III. THE ATTRACTION OF SOCIALISM.

A. The Negative Consequences of Socialism.

B. The Trend Toward Mixed Economies.

IV. THE FOUNDATIONS OF CAPITALISM.

LEARNING GOAL 3. Describe how the free-market system works.

A. How Free Markets Work.

B. How Prices Are Determined.

1. Supply.
2. Demand.
3. Equilibrium Point.

C. Competition Within Free Markets.

V. WORLD MARKETS: SUPPLY AND DEMAND.

A. Limitations of the Free-Market System.

VI. UNDERSTANDING THE ECONOMIC SYSTEM OF THE UNITED STATES.

LEARNING GOAL 4. Use key terms (e.g., GDP and productivity) to explain the U.S. economic condition.

A. Key Economic Indicators.

   1. Gross Domestic Product (GDP).

   2. The Unemployment Rate.

B. The Price Indexes.

C. Distribution of GDP.

D. Productivity in the United States.

E. Productivity in the Service Sector.

VII. INFLATION AND THE CONSUMER PRICE INDEX.

A. The Issue of Recession Versus Inflation.

VIII. THE ISSUE OF MONETARY POLICY.

LEARNING GOAL 5. Describe monetary policy and its importance to the economy.

A. Tight Versus Loose Monetary Policy.

IX. THE ISSUE OF FISCAL POLICY.

LEARNING GOAL 6. Discuss fiscal policy and its importance to the economy.

A. How Taxes and Spending Affect Businesspeople.

B. The Federal Deficit.

C. The National Debt.

D. Just Tax the Rich and Pay Off the Debt?

X. SUMMARY AND REVIEW.

(Learning Objectives are also referenced in the expanded lecture outline later in this chapter)

Key Terms

capitalism *(text page 45)*
command economies *(text page 48)*
communism *(text page 47)*
consumer price index (CPI) *(text page 59)*
demand *(text page 53)*
deflation *(text page 61)*
depression *(text page 62)*
disinflation *(text page 61)*
economics *(text page 44)*
federal deficit *(text page 63)*
fiscal policy *(text page 62)*
free-market economies *(text page 48)*
gross domestic product (GDP) *(text page 58)*
inflation *(text page 61)*
invisible hand *(text page 45)*
mixed economies *(text page 49)*
monetary policy *(text page 62)*
monopolistic competition *(text page 55)*
monopoly *(text page 56)*
national debt *(text page 63)*
oligopoly *(text page 55)*
perfect competition *(text page 55)*
recession *(text page 62)*
socialism *(text page 47)*
supply *(text page 53)*
unemployment rate *(text page 58)*

Lecture Outline

The **PROFILE** at the beginning of this chapter focuses on **ROSA ALVARDO**, one of the founders of a Guatemala village bank. The purpose of this chapter is to understand how free markets work and how businesses and government can work together to encourage entrepreneurship and growth.

I. THE IMPORTANCE OF THE STUDY OF ECONOMICS.

▶ **LEARNING GOAL 1.** Explain how wealth is created in an economy.

A. Any change in the economic or political system has a major influence on the success of the business system.

   1. The world economic situation and world politics have a major influence on U.S. business.

   2. The three basic objectives of this chapter are to teach students:

      a. **HOW FREE MARKETS WORK.**

      b. **HOW FREE MARKETS DIFFER FROM GOVERNMENT-CONTROLLED MARKETS.**

      c. **SOME BASIC ECONOMIC TERMS AND CONCEPTS THAT STUDENTS WILL READ IN BUSINESS PERIODICALS.**

B. **WHAT IS ECONOMICS?**

   1. **ECONOMICS** is the study of how society chooses to employ resources to produce

Lecture Notes

TRANSPARENCY MASTER 16
Chapter Outline

Transparency Masters begin on page 2.81.

LECTURE ENHANCER 2-1
The Need for Economic Education

Sylvia Porter says, "Most people do not know what the gross national product is. Nor do they understand the causes of the current federal budget deficit." (See complete lecture enhancer on page 2.56.)

OT ACETATE 2-1
The Four *"Whats"* of an Economic System

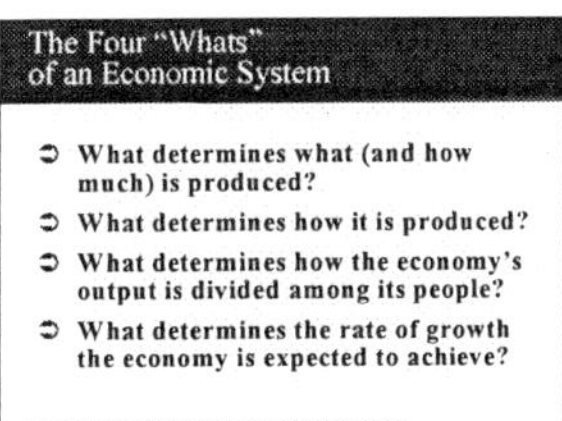

Comments:

1. Societies and economists are concerned with these four basic questions in evaluating an economic system. With globalization becoming a fact of business life evaluation of these principles is even more important.
2. These four questions form the basic core of economics because they address the primary characteristics of economic systems. Consider developing economies such as the Peoples' Republic of China. How might this nation address each of these questions?
3. See if students can relate the four "what's" to the U.S. system and evaluate why the U.S. economy operates as it does.

REACHING BEYOND OUR BORDERS
(Box in text, page 44)
"Pablo Tesak, Entrepreneur from El Salvador"

When Pablo Tesak came to El Salvador in 1951, the majority of consumer products were imported from the United States and Europe. Tesak decided to develop a line of snack products for the poor people of El Salvador. He knew these snacks would have to be simple and cheap. Tesak began making such snacks and prospered. Later, a civil war in the country caused dissent among his workers. In order to stabilize his work force Tesak raised salaries, but discovered that his employees needed more.

various goods and services and to distribute them for consumption among various competing groups and individuals.

2. There aren't enough known resources merely to divide resources among all nations.
3. **RESOURCE DEVELOPMENT** is the study of how to use technology to increase the known resources of the world and to create the conditions that will make better use of those resources.

C. **THE ECONOMIC THEORY OF WEALTH CREATION: ADAM SMITH.**

1. **ADAM SMITH** advocated creating wealth through entrepreneurship.
   a. Rather than divide fixed resources, Smith envisioned creating *more* resources so that everyone could be wealthier.
   b. In 1776, Smith wrote a book called ***THE WEALTH OF NATIONS*** in which he outlined steps for creating prosperity.
2. Smith is called the **FATHER OF CAPITALISM.**
3. **CAPITALISM** is an economic system in which all or most of the means of production and distribution are privately owned and operated for profit.

Lecture Notes

LECTURE ENHANCER 2-2
The Study of Economics

The relationship of macroeconomics and microeconomics are discussed. (See the complete lecture enhancer on page 2.57.)

OT ACETATE 2-2
Key Principles of Economics

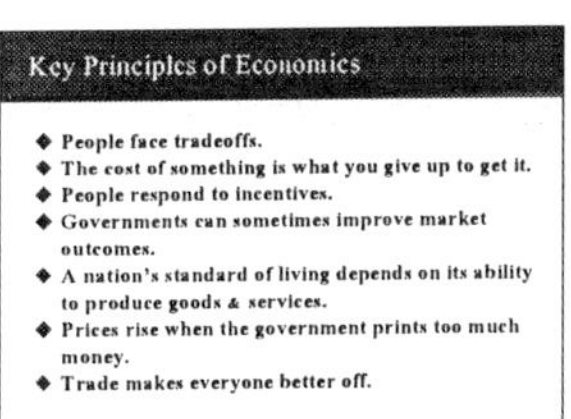

Comments:

1. This acetate lists several key principles of economics as proposed by N. Gregory Mankiw. Professor Mankiw teaches at Harvard University and has written a principles of economics textbook.
2. These concepts are easy for students to follow and generally make common sense to them. It's interesting to ask students if they disagree with any of the principles and why they disagree. Asking students for examples of the principles in action help clarify if students fully comprehend the material.
3. This is also an opportune time to explain the basic differences between business and economics. Students often assume both disciplines are the same. It's also a good idea to discuss why students need a clear understanding of economics before we tackle specific business topics. This is the reason economics is covered up front in chapter two.

OT ACETATE 2-3
Economics: Macro and Micro

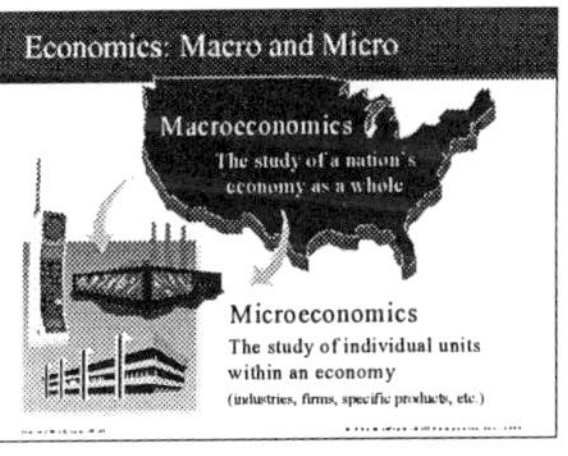

Comments:

1. The distinctions and relationship of macroeconomics and microeconomics are highlighted in this acetate.
2. Topics such as gross domestic product, consumer price indexes, profit maximization, pricing in competitive markets, etc., can be introduced as macro and micro topics important to the study of business.
3. Since this is not a course in economics, students may question why they must study economics first? You may want to relate to them the importance of understanding basic economic principles in applying business decisions. It might also be advisable to apprise them that they will have to take two courses in economics as part of most business programs: anyone awake should be able to figure out the two courses are Macro and Micro.

LECTURE ENHANCER 2-3
The Spirit of Adam Smith

Adam Smith is known as the Father of Capitalism, but he was far from being anti-government. (See complete lecture enhancer on page 2.58.)

Lecture Outline

a. In capitalist countries, businesspeople decide how to use their resources and how much to charge.

b. No country is purely capitalist, but the **FOUNDATION OF THE U.S. IS CAPITALISM.**

4. What are the driving forces behind wealth creation, according to Adam Smith?

   a. **FREEDOM** (to keep the profits from what you produce and sell and freedom to own land).

   b. **INCENTIVES**. One has much more incentive to work long hours and to work hard when one gets to keep the profit from one's labor. The more one works, or course, the more that gets produced for others (the invisible hand).

D. **THE "INVISIBLE HAND."**

1. Adam Smith called the mechanism for creating wealth and jobs an **INVISIBLE HAND**, which turns self-directed gain into social and economic benefits for all.

2. Basically, what this meant was that a person working hard to make money for his or her own personal interest would (like an invisible hand) also benefit others.

Lecture Notes

a. For example, a farmer trying to make money would grow as many crops as possible.

b. This provides needed food for others.

c. If everyone worked hard in his or her own self interest, Smith said, society as a whole would prosper.

3. Many U.S. businesspeople are becoming concerned about social issues and their obligation to return to society some of what they've earned.

II. THE HISTORY OF BUSINESS AND ECONOMICS.

▶ **LEARNING GOAL 2.** Discuss the major differences between capitalism, socialism, communism, and a mixed economy.

A. Following the ideas of Adam Smith, businesspeople created more wealth than every before.

1. Great disparities in wealth began to appear.

2. Although it is not easy, opportunities to start one's own business have always been there, especially in a free market.

B. THE SEARCH FOR EQUALITY.

1. **FREE-MARKET CAPITALISM** (capitalism without any government regulation) naturally leads to **INEQUALITY OF WEALTH**.

Lecture Notes

SUPPLEMENTAL CASE 2-1
Foundations of the Capitalist System

See complete case on page 2.73.

Lecture Outline

2. Free-market capitalism may also lead to environmental damage.

3. Some government rules and regulations are necessary to protect people and the environment.

C. THE BIRTH OF COMMUNISM.

1. **KARL MARX** decided that workers should take over ownership of businesses and share in the wealth.

   a. He wrote ***THE COMMUNIST MANIFESTO*** in 1848, becoming the **FATHER OF COMMUNISM.**

   b. **COMMUNISM** is a system where all economic decisions are made by the state and the state owns all the major forms of production.

2. Communist countries include China, North Korea, and Cuba.

3. Communism doesn't inspire businesspeople to work hard, and is slowly disappearing as an alternative economic form.

III. THE ATTRACTION OF SOCIALISM.

A. **SOCIALISM** is an economic system based on the premise that some businesses should be owned by the government.

Lecture Notes

LECTURE ENHANCER 2-4
Red Dawn for Hong Kong

American Craft Brewing International Ltd., based in Metairie, Louisiana, concocted a special beer to celebrate the 1997 takeover of Hong Kong by China. The red-colored lager was created as "the perfect toast to the beginning of a new chapter in Hong Kong's history," the company said. (See complete lecture enhancer on page 2.60.)

LECTURE ENHANCER 2-5
Post-Communist Russia: Some Statistics

The old Soviet Union has been broken up into 89 republics and regions, and parliamentary elections have replaced the iron control of the Kremlin. This enhancer gives several key statistics that illustrate some of the other changes that have taken place. (See complete lecture enhancer on page 2.61.)

Lecture Outline

1. Socialists believe that the **GOVERNMENT SHOULD DECIDE**:
   a. What gets produced.
   b. How much workers should be paid.
   c. How much trade should take place between and among nations.
2. Advocates of socialism acknowledge the major benefits of capitalism, but believe that wealth should be more evenly distributed.
3. Socialism became the economic platform from countries such as Holland, Sweden, and France.
4. Socialist nations rely heavily on government to provide education, health care, retirement, and care for those not able to work.

B. THE NEGATIVE CONSEQUENCES OF SOCIALISM.

1. Socialism creates more equality, but it takes away some work incentives.
2. The motto of socialism is, "From each according to his or her ability; to each according to his or her need."
3. Marginal tax rates (the rate you pay on the additional money earned after a certain income level) in Sweden once reached 85%.

CRITICAL THINKING EXERCISE 2-1
Standard of Living Comparison

See complete exercise on page 2.69.

SUPPLEMENTAL CASE 2-2
Economic Consequences of Communist Systems

See complete case on page 2.76.

Lecture Outline

4. Socialism did not create the jobs or the wealth that capitalism did.

C. **THE TREND TOWARD MIXED ECONOMIES.**

1. There are two economic systems vying for dominance in the world:

   a. **FREE MARKET ECONOMIES.**

      (i) The marketplace largely determines what goods and services get produced, who gets them, and how the economy grows.

      (ii) Commonly known as **CAPITALISM**, these economies are based on the principles of Adam Smith.

   b. **COMMAND ECONOMIES.**

      (i) The government largely decides what goods and services will be produced, who'll get them, and how the economy will grow.

      (ii) These economies, known as **SOCIALISM** and **COMMUNISM**, are based on the principles of Karl Marx.

2. **NO ONE ECONOMIC SYSTEM IS PERFECT BY ITSELF.**

LECTURE ENHANCER 2-6
Shenzhen: China Experiments With Economic Reform

Shenzhen province, directly adjacent to Hong Kong, is one of China's Special Economic Zones—a successful experiment in market economics. (See complete lecture enhancer on page 2.62.)

Lecture Outline

a. Free-market mechanisms weren't responsive enough to a nation's social and economic needs.

b. Socialism and communism didn't create enough jobs or wealth to keep economies growing fast enough.

c. No country is purely capitalist or purely capitalist, rather some mix of the two systems.

d. However, the long-term global trend is toward a **BLEND OF CAPITALISM AND SOCIALISM.**

3. **MIXED ECONOMIES** exist where some allocation of resources is made by the market and some by government.

4. **THE U.S. HAS A MIXED ECONOMY.**

   a. There is much debate about the role of government in many parts of the economy.

   b. The basic principles of freedom and opportunity remain so that economic growth is sustainable.

5. In the U.S., the government serves as a means to *supplement* the basic capitalist system.

Lecture Notes

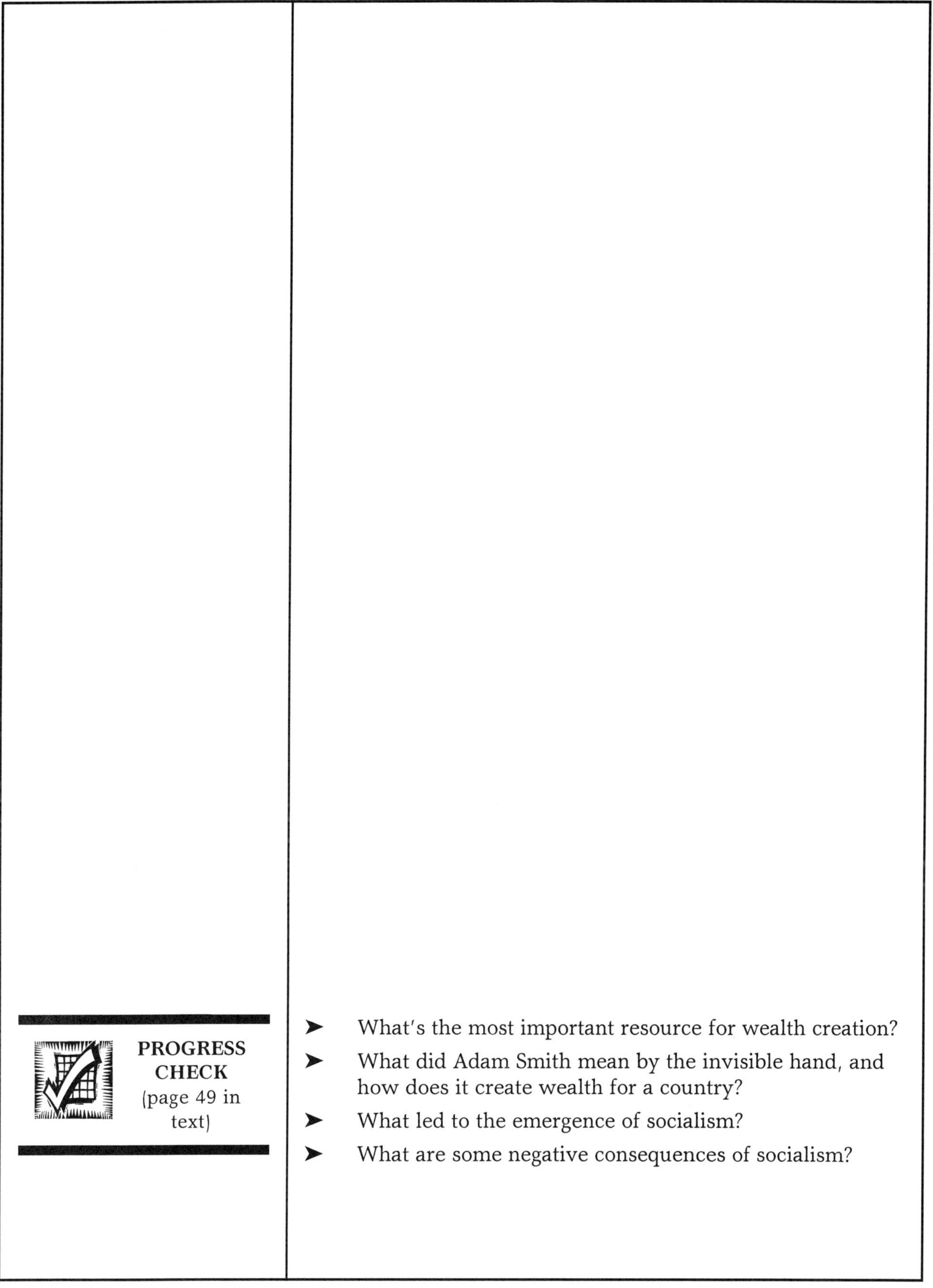

- What's the most important resource for wealth creation?
- What did Adam Smith mean by the invisible hand, and how does it create wealth for a country?
- What led to the emergence of socialism?
- What are some negative consequences of socialism?

Lecture Outline

IV. THE FOUNDATIONS OF CAPITALISM.

▶ **LEARNING GOAL 3.** Describe how the free-market system works.

A. Individuals living in a capitalist system have **FOUR BASIC RIGHTS:**

1. **THE RIGHT TO PRIVATE PROPERTY.**
2. **THE RIGHT TO KEEP ALL OF A BUSINESS'S PROFITS AFTER TAXES.**
3. **THE RIGHT TO FREEDOM OF COMPETITION.**
4. **THE RIGHT TO FREEDOM OF CHOICE.**

B. **HOW FREE MARKETS WORK.**

1. In a free-market system, decisions about what to produce and in what quantities are made by the market.
2. Consumers send signals to producers what to make, how many, and so on through the mechanism of **PRICE**.
3. In the U.S. the *price* tells producers how much to produce, reducing the changes of a long-term shortage of goods.

C. **HOW PRICES ARE DETERMINED.**

1. **SUPPLY** refers to the quantity of products that manufacturers or owners are willing to sell at different prices at a specific time.

COMPARISONS OF KEY ECONOMIC SYSTEMS
(Text figure 2.1, page 50)

This figure compares capitalism, mixed economies, socialism, and communism across five key dimensions.

SPOTLIGHT ON SMALL BUSINESS
(Box in text, page 51)

"The Internet Creates a One-World Market"

The World Wide Web (WWW) is a relatively new phenomenon, but one that will have a profound affect on the world's economies. In the past, a small business was fairly confined in its market reach. It couldn't afford to advertise nationally, much less globally. In such a setting, it was possible for a country to become rather isolated from other countries, and the government could regulate businesses closely. Today, however, even small businesses have established Web sites where they can reach global markets quickly and easily.

TRANSPARENCY MASTER 17
The Supply Curve at Various Prices
(Figure 2.2 on text page 53)

Transparency Masters begin on page 2.81.

Lecture Outline

a. The amount supplied will increase as the price increases.

b. The quantity producers are willing to supply a certain prices are illustrated on a **SUPPLY CURVE.**

2. **DEMAND** refers to the quantity of products that people are willing to buy at different prices at a specific time.

   a. The quantity demanded will decrease as the price increases.

   b. The quantity consumers are willing to buy at certain prices are illustrated on a **DEMAND CURVE.**

3. **THE EQUILIBRIUM PRICE** or **MARKET PRICE** is the price at which the quantity demanded and the quantity supplied are equal.

4. It is the interaction between supply and demand that determines the market price in the long-run.

   a. If surpluses develop, a signal is sent to sellers to lower the price.

   b. If shortages develop, a signal is sent to sellers to increase the price.

D. COMPETITION WITHIN FREE MARKETS.

Lecture Notes

TRANSPARENCY MASTER 18
The Demand Curve at Various Prices
(Figure 2.3 on text page 54)

Transparency Masters begin on page 2.81.

TRANSPARENCY MASTER 19
The Equilibrium Point
(Figure 2.4 on text page 55)

Transparency Masters begin on page 2.81.

LECTURE ENHANCER 2-7
Supply and Demand: Coffee

The concepts of supply, demand, shortages, surpluses, and equilibrium prices are often best illustrated in the agricultural commodities markets. (See complete lecture enhancer on page 2.63.)

Lecture Outline

1. Competition exists in different degrees, ranging from perfect to nonexistent.
2. **PERFECT COMPETITION** exists when there are many sellers in the market and no seller is large enough to dictate the price of a product.
   a. Sellers produce products that appear to be identical.
   b. There are no true examples of perfect competition, but agricultural products are often used as an example.
3. **MONOPOLISTIC COMPETITION** exists when a large number of sellers produce products that are very similar but are perceived by buyers as different.
   a. Product differentiation, making buyers think similar products are different, is a key to success.
   b. Under monopolistic competition, individual sellers set prices.
   c. The fast food industry is an example.
4. An **OLIGOPOLY** is a form of competition in which just a few sellers dominate a market.
   a. The initial investment is usually high.

Lecture Notes

OT ACETATE 2-4
Competitive Market Structures

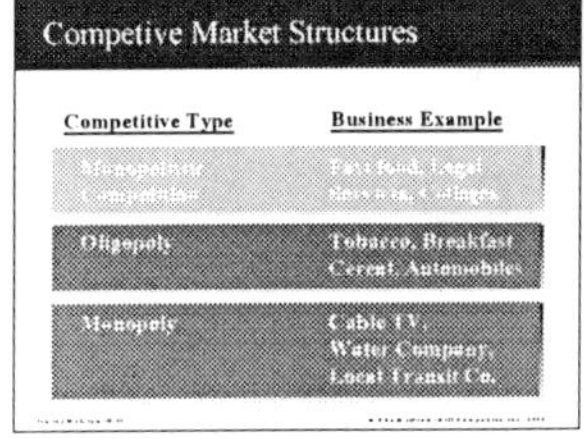

Comments:

1. Students often get confused in discussing competitive market structures. This acetate helps students see what types of firms compete in the different competitive structures.
2. It's helpful to clarify the difference between monopoly and monopolistic competition. With both terms containing the word monopoly, students often get very confused.
3. See if students can add more examples to the various categories on the acetate. Students will frequently ask about approved or regulated monopolies such as power companies or cable television companies that have monopoly power in a market. They want to know why under antitrust laws they have such power and would the market be better off if these services were deregulated.
4. It may be helpful to divide the class into groups and debate the economic and consumer benefits of competition. Ask what the market situation would be like if there were just one college in a city.

Lecture Outline

b. Prices tend to be close to the same.

c. Examples include breakfast cereal, beer, automobiles, and soft drinks.

5. A **MONOPOLY** occurs when there is only one seller for a product or service.

   a. In the U.S. laws prohibit the creation of monopolies, but do permit approved monopolies such as public utilities.

   b. New legislation is likely to result in fewer, larger utilities and lower prices.

6. Competition works best when **ORGANIZATIONS KNOW WHAT CONSUMERS WANT.**

V. WORLD MARKETS: SUPPLY AND DEMAND.

A. Consumers send signals to producers telling them what they (the consumers) want.

1. There are interferences to the free exchange of goods and services among countries.

2. This results in surpluses in some countries and shortages in others.

B. LIMITATIONS OF THE FREE-MARKET SYSTEM.

1. Capitalism brought prosperity to the U.S. and much of the world, but it brought inequality as well.

LECTURE ENHANCER 2-8
Handicaps of the U.S. Economy

In spite of the wonderful advances the U.S. has experienced in its economy, there are underlying problems that must be solved before the country can be a true beacon for others to follow. (See complete lecture enhancer on page 2.64.)

2. When countries introduced capitalist principles, inequality increased dramatically, causing national and world tension.

3. Government entities also take a large share of total national output and reallocate it to create more equality.

4. A major question is, **WHAT'S THE PROPER BLEND OF GOVERNMENT AND FREE MARKETS?**

VI. UNDERSTANDING THE ECONOMIC SYSTEM OF THE UNITED STATES.

A. While most of the world was moving toward freer markets, in recent years the U.S. was moving toward more social programs.

1. There was much conflict between business leaders and government leaders on issues such as taxes, regulations, and social programs.

2. Currently the U.S. economic system is in a state of flux.

B. KEY ECONOMIC INDICATORS.

▶ **LEARNING GOAL 4.** Use key terms (e.g., GDP and productivity) to explain the U.S. economic condition.

1. **GROSS DOMESTIC PRODUCT (GDP).**

PROGRESS CHECK
(page 57 in text)

- What are the four basic rights a person has under capitalism?
- What is the signal businesspeople use to know what to produce and in what quantity?
- How are prices determined?
- What are the limitations to a free-market system.

CRITICAL THINKING
(page 57 in text)

Adam Smith anticipated that businesspeople would be like Pablo Tesak and would voluntarily support those in need. In the past, churches, temples, and other nonprofit organizations took a leadership position in supporting those in need. If the government were to stop supporting the needy, would those organizations provide the extra needed support? What are the advantages and disadvantages of the government being the major source of welfare?

LECTURE ENHANCER 2-9
Economic Indicators

The business cycle moves from recession to recovery to peak to decline. Economists search long and hard for signs of a coming change in economic performance. (See complete lecture enhancer on page 2.65.)

Lecture Outline

a. **GDP** is the total value of a country's output of goods and services in a given year.

b. A major influence on the growth of GDP is how productive the work force is.

c. The major figure used until recently was the **GROSS NATIONAL PRODUCT (GNP)**—the U.S. adopted GDP to be compatible with the rest of the world.

2. **THE UNEMPLOYMENT RATE.**

a. The **UNEMPLOYMENT RATE** refers to the number of civilians, 16 years old or older, who are unemployed and tried to find a job within the prior four weeks.

b. **FOUR TYPES OF UNEMPLOYMENT**

(i) **FRICTIONAL UNEMPLOYMENT**—refers to those people who have quit work because they did not like the job, the boss, or working conditions.

(ii) **STRUCTURAL UNEMPLOYMENT**—refers to unemployment caused by restructuring of businesses or by a mismatch between the skills (or location) of job seekers and the requirements (or location) of available jobs

LECTURE ENHANCER 2-10
Creating Jobs

Small businesses have the potential to create the jobs needed to substantially reduce the U.S. unemployment rate. (See complete lecture enhancer on page 2.66.)

Lecture Outline

(i.e. coal miners in areas where mines have been closed.)

(iii) **CYCLICAL UNEMPLOYMENT**—unemployment caused by a recession or similar downturn in the business cycle.

(iv) **SEASONAL UNEMPLOYMENT**—unemployment which occurs when the demand for labor varies over the year (i.e. harvesting of crops.)

3. **THE PRICE INDEXES.**

   a. The **CONSUMER PRICE INDEX (CPI)** consists of monthly statistics that measure the pace of inflation or deflation.

      (i) Some government benefits, wages, and interest rates are based on the CPI.

      (ii) However, experts argue that CPI overstates inflation and there is a call for an adjustment of the figure.

   b. The **PRODUCER PRICE INDEX (PPI)** measures prices at the wholesale level.

C. **DISTRIBUTION OF GDP.**

   1. The percentage of GDP taken by all levels of government in the U.S. is around 33%.

Lecture Notes

CRITICAL THINKING
(page 59 in text)

Would the United States be better off today if we hadn't introduced modern farm machinery? There would be more people employed on the farm if we hadn't. Would the world be better off in the future if we didn't introduce new computers, robots, and machinery? They do take away jobs in the short run. What happened to the farmers who were displaced by machines? What will happen to today's workers who are being replaced by machines?

OT ACETATE 2-5
What Makes Up the Consumer Price Index?

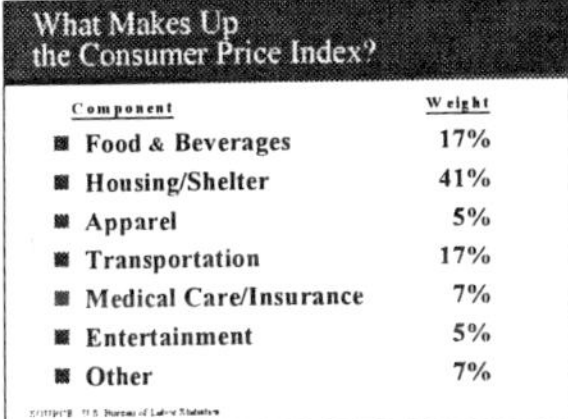

Comments:

1. The consumer price index is the government's key indicator to gauge the rate of inflation in the economy. Students should be familiar with the importance of inflation from the discussion in chapter two. If you wish to implement ideas such as cost-push and demand-pull inflation in your course, this is a good time to do it.
2. Students often question how the consumer price index is compiled. This acetate should help in discussing this question. It might help to briefly go over the purpose of the percentages attached to the various goods and services and how the final numbers are derived.
3. It's important to note that the components of the CPI are reconsidered every few years to reflect changes in such things as consumer lifestyles or increase in cost. Health Care is a component of the CPI that has experienced significant growth in terms of cost. The reorganization of the CPI may require a bit more explanation.

2. When you add in all the fees and sales taxes, the government's share can exceed 50%.

3. One of the sources of prosperity is increased productivity.

D. PRODUCTIVITY IN THE UNITED STATES.

1. **PRODUCTIVITY** is the total volume of goods and services one worker can produce in a given period of time.

2. The same amount of labor producing more goods and services is known as an **INCREASE IN PRODUCTIVITY.**

   a. An increase in farm productivity used to be the basis of American economic growth.

   b. The use of machines led to the increase in productivity in the manufacturing industry.

3. We are now focusing on ways to increase productivity in the service sector.

E. PRODUCTIVITY IN THE SERVICE SECTOR.

1. The service sector uses machines such as word processors and computers to increase productivity. Actually these machines may add to the quality of the services but not

Lecture Notes

to the output per worker which is the definition of productivity.

2. New measures of productivity for the service economy need to be developed that include quality as well as quantity of output.

VII. INFLATION AND THE CONSUMER PRICE INDEX.

A. **INFLATION** refers to a general rise in the price level of goods and services over time.

1. The CPI measures the price of an average market basket of goods for an average family over time.

2. **DISINFLATION** describes a condition where the increase in prices is slowing (the inflation rate is declining.)

3. **DEFLATION** means that prices are actually declining, occurring when countries produce so many goods that people cannot afford to buy them all.

B. **THE ISSUE OF RECESSION VERSUS INFLATION.**

1. A **RECESSION** is two consecutive quarters of decline in the GNP.

Lecture Notes

OT ACETATE 2-6
How Inflation Affects Buying Power

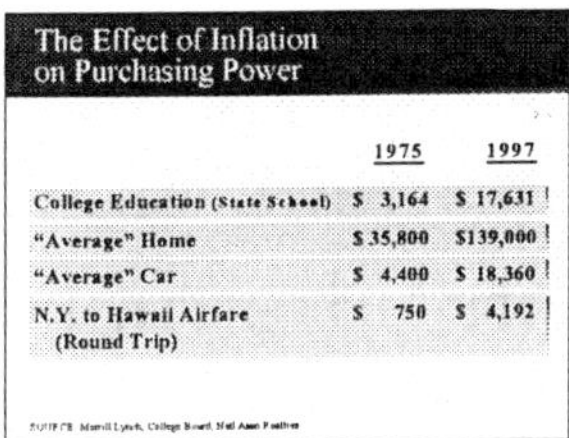

The Effect of Inflation on Purchasing Power

	1975	1997
College Education (State School)	$ 3,164	$ 17,631
"Average" Home	$ 35,800	$139,000
"Average" Car	$ 4,400	$ 18,360
N.Y. to Hawaii Airfare (Round Trip)	$ 750	$ 4,192

Comments:

1. This acetate helps students see the effect of inflation at a 5% annual rate for a ten year period. A discussion of the rule of 72 could easily assist here.
2. It is challenging to question students concerning what prices they would be paying for products such as rock concerts, Big Mac Hamburgers, running shoes, jeans and other items in 2008 if the rate of inflation continued at 5 percent for 10 years. They are very surprised how much that 5% changes prices.
3. The consumer price index is a topic that can easily be wedged back into the discussion at this point. A review of the previous acetate will also help with this discussion.

LECTURE 2-11
The Great Depression: Capitalism in Crisis

The worldwide business slump of the 1930s ranked as the worst and longest period of high unemployment and low business activity in modern times. The U.S. economic system seemed inadequate to deal with massive economic disruption. John Maynard Keynes suggested changing the role of central government to ease the crisis. (See complete lecture enhancer on page 2.67.)

2. For years the government has tried to prevent another recession or depression.

3. A **DEPRESSION** is a severe recession.

VIII. THE ISSUE OF MONETARY POLICY.

▶ **LEARNING GOAL 5.** Describe monetary policy and its importance to the economy.

A. **MONETARY POLICY** is the management of the money placed into the economy and the management of interest rates.

1. The Federal Reserve System is responsible for managing the money supply.

2. The Fed is one of the sources of money in the economy; it can add or subtract money from the economy as it sees fit.

3. The Federal Reserve System operates independently of the president and Congress and has the goal of keeping the economy growing without causing inflation.

B. **TIGHT VERSUS LOOSE MONETARY POLICY.**

1. The Fed can curb inflation by decreasing the money available and discouraging borrowing.

   a. It does this by cutting the money supply and raising interest rates.

OT ACETATE 2-7
How Does the Government Get Its Money?

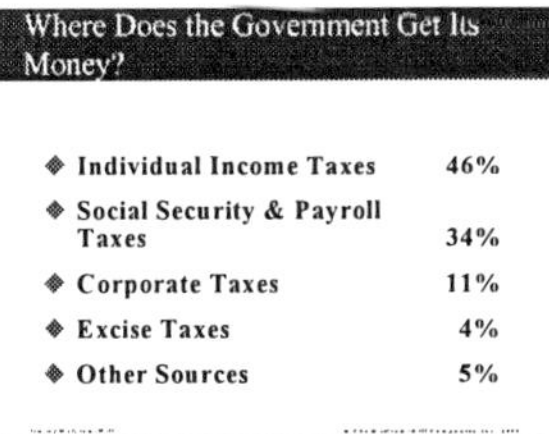

Comments:

1. Again the point of emphasis here is the government gets its money from taxes. Students should be able to appreciate the controversy that's generated when tax policy is discussed.
2. Students may be surprised that individual income taxes provide almost half the revenue that the federal government generates. They also may be a bit surprised to see that corporate taxes only provide approximately 13% of federal revenues.
3. You may need to explain what an excise tax is all about. Students can be advised that the excise taxes are covered in the Legal Environment of Business appendix following chapter four.
4. Another good opportunity to gets the student's opinions concerning taxes. We always find an interesting discrepancy between day and evening students. It might be interesting to have both groups discuss the subject and relate the conclusions to all the classes.

Lecture Outline

b. Production is cut back slowing the economy and lowering inflation.

2. When the Fed **"LOOSENS UP THE MONEY SUPPLY,"** it tries to stimulate the economy.

3. A **"TIGHT MONETARY POLICY"** is one in which the Fed is restricting the supply of money.

IX. THE ISSUE OF FISCAL POLICY.

▶ **LEARNING GOAL 6.** Discuss fiscal policy and its importance to the economy.

A. **FISCAL POLICY** refers to the Federal government's efforts to keep the economy stable by increasing or decreasing taxes and/or government spending.

1. For many years, federal expenses have been exceeding federal revenues—the result is an increasing federal debt.

2. The money paid for interest on the debt is so high that it drains money from the economy.

B. **HOW TAXES AND SPENDING AFFECT BUSINESSPEOPLE.**

1. Higher taxes lower the amount available for investment.

Imagine that you've been out of school for a while and you and your spouse are now earning $50,000 a year. To get to that point, you both paid your way through college. You look forward to buying a home, cars, and other goods and services that you've been postponing all these years to get your education. You decide to buy a nice home. The government allows you to deduct all the mortgage interest charges on that home and the property taxes from your taxable income. That makes the payments much easier at first. In fact, almost all the money you're paying into the home the first few years goes for taxes and mortgage interest, and all of that is tax deductible. That means that you won't have to give the government as much money in taxes.

MAKING ETHICAL DECISIONS
(Box in text, page 66)

"Exploring the Tax Laws"

TRANSPARENCY MASTER 20
1998 Government Revenue and Expenses
(Figure 2.5 on text page 64)

Transparency Masters begin on page 2.81.

CRITICAL THINKING EXERCISE 2-2
Balancing the Federal Budget

See complete exercise on page 2.71.

2. The government is spending more each year, even though the rate of growth in spending is slowing.

3. Fiscal policy has a major influence of businesses.

C. THE FEDERAL DEFICIT.

1. The **FEDERAL DEFICIT** is the difference between federal revenue and federal spending in any given year.

2. The **NATIONAL DEBT** is the sum of all the federal deficits over time.

D. THE NATIONAL DEBT.

1. The national debt is now about $6 trillion.

2. A stack of $1000 bills a mere 4 inches high would make you a millionaire, but the stack would have to be 67 miles high to make you a trillionaire!

3. The national debt is so high because the government grew faster than the economy's ability to pay for it.

4. The question is: "What are our national priorities?" We can't afford everything. Which programs to we keep and which must we cut?

Lecture Notes

OT ACETATE 2-8
What $1 Billion Can Buy

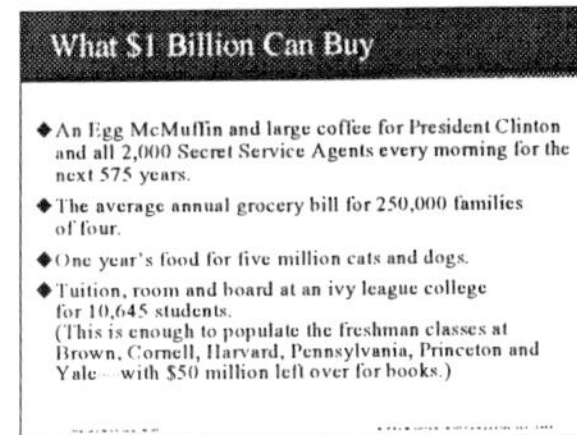

Comments:

1. This is a fun acetate students will enjoy. However, it's very useful that they absorb the extent of how much money one billion dollars is. Often hearing all the bantering about billions going here and there, Everett Dirksen's words (a billion here, a billion there, pretty soon you're talking some real money) makes students rather indifferent about the size and scope of a billion dollars. They have little, if any perception of what a billion dollars actually amounts to.
2. You could assign students a short project to go to the library and get a copy of *Fortune Magazine's* annual report on the world's richest people. After viewing the information in this acetate, they will be astounded at the wealth of many Americans and global leaders. The Sultan of Brunei is estimated to be worth approximately $40 billion. Sam Walton, before his death, was the wealthiest American with a net worth of approximately $24 Billion. Bill Gates of Microsoft is estimated to be worth approximately $36 Billion (give or take a few billion). Students can see why presidential candidate Ross Perot had little trouble financing both of his presidential campaigns from his personal war chest of over $3 Billion.
3. If you would like to stay abreast of such interesting class information, stay tuned to the UB5E web site that will keep you up with such information and class ideas.

OT ACETATE 2-9
How Much Is the Federal Debt

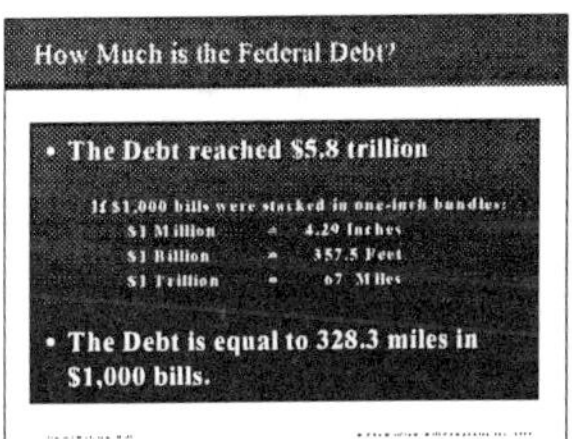

Comments:

1. Again, students should love the information in this acetate. They are fascinated when such examples are presented in class.
2. Quiz the class and see if they have any ideas how this massive debt can be reduced. Information from the previous acetate dealing with expenditures can be reintroduced here. Also **ACETATE 2-11** will give them a key perspective of the changing composition of the federal budget.

TRANSPARENCY MASTER 21
The National Debt
(Figure 2.6 on text page 65)

Transparency Masters begin on page 2.81.

Lecture Outline

E. **JUST TAX THE RICH.**

1. For years, economic was defined as the allocation of *scarce* resources among competing groups and individuals.
   a. Feeling among many people is that the rich got rich by exploiting the poor.
   b. Some people suggest increasing taxes on the rich and giving the additional money to the poor.
   c. Such was the thinking behind most socialist governments.
2. However, there aren't enough wealthy people making enough money to pay for all government programs.
3. Wealthy people make most of their money from investing in business.
   a. If taxes were increased, that investment money would no longer be there.
   b. Taxing the rich isn't a solution.
   c. The tax burden always falls on the middle class, who are already struggling.
   d. Recent tax bills have cut the taxes on the middle class or offered them more benefits.

Lecture Notes

OT ACETATE 2-10
Top Expenditures of the Federal Government

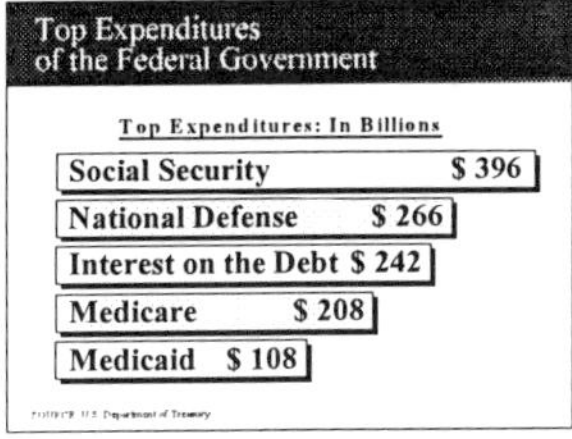

Comments:

1. This acetate helps support the information in the previous acetate. You can quiz students to see if they can identify the six largest entitlements. It will be interesting to note how many suspect foreign aid ranks high.
2. An interesting discussion could be initiated among the class concerning which entitlements they would choose to cut if given the option. Considerable disagreement will most likely ensue.
3. If you choose to expand a bit beyond the information on the acetate, ask students their opinion concerning National Health Insurance. With Medicare and Medicaid ranking two and three in entitlement disbursements, the issue could likely surface again. What do they note as the pro's and con's of government involvement in health care?

OT ACETATE 2-11
The Changing Composition of the Federal Budget

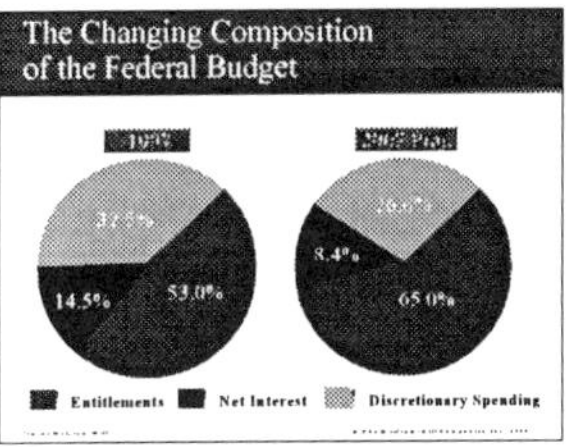

Comments:

1. You may want to get into the discussion of **Entitlement Programs** and their relationship to the federal budget. The first question students may ask related to this acetate is "what is an entitlement program?" **ACETATE 2-10** highlights three large entitlement programs. A good discussion question at this point is "why do entitlement programs continue to grow?" One answer is that people have become accustomed to these programs and expect their continued service no matter what the cost or availability of funds. You might also relate the political sensitivity of these programs to the electorate. Congress often cringes at the thought of suggesting cuts in Medicare, Social Security, Student loan programs etc. Will entitlements continue to grow? Best bet is probably so.
2. The information in this acetate reinforces the discussions going on in the U.S. Congress as this text goes to press. What can the government do about growing entitlement programs and the federal debt?
3. You might ask students what they would do about the accelerating cost of entitlements. The differences likely to be raised in class will easily illustrate to them the problems Congress has in addressing the same issue.
4. Another sore spot worthy of discussion, the percentage of the budget that goes for interest on the federal deficit. Approximately fourteen cents of every dollar is a formidable amount. If the economy can keep its momentum, this will be reduced in the future. The key to point out to students is the need for growth in the economy.

4. The only long-term solution is for the economy to grow.
   a. That increases the size of the economic pie and everyone benefits.
   b. Growth strategies, however, are in conflict with goals of more equality.
5. The economic goal in the future is to keep the economy growing so:
   a. More and more people can rise up the economic ladder.
   b. Pay their share of taxes.
   c. Cut the federal deficit and debt.

IX. SUMMARY AND REVIEW.

Lecture Notes

PROGRESS CHECK
(page 60 in text)

- ➤ What's the difference between a recession and a depression?
- ➤ How does the government manage the economy using monetary policy?
- ➤ How does the government manage the economy using fiscal policy?
- ➤ How big is the U.S. national debt? What's the difference between the federal deficit and the federal debt?

SUPPLEMENTAL CASE 2-3
Just Tax the Rich and Pay Off the Debt? (Revisited)

See complete case on page 2.79.

Answers to Practicing Management Decisions

CASE ONE

THE RULE OF 72

1. *If the cost of a college education is about $15,000 per year now, what will it cost your children per year if costs go up 9 percent a year and your children go to college 24 years from now?*

Using the rule of 72, costs would double in 8 years (72 divided by 9). There are three 8-year periods in 24 years, meaning that costs would double three times: $30,000, $60,000, $120,000 per year. So the cost would be $120,000 per year. Scary huh?

2. *If the value of a home doubles in 12 years, what is the annual rate of return?*

Using the rule of 72, you divide 12 into 72 and get the rate of return, which is 6 percent.

3. *If a bank is charging 7 percent to borrow money for your mortgage, how do you know whether or not you will make money on the home when you sell it?*

You determine how much the home increases each year (in percent) and divide that into 72 to see how many years it would take to double. Then you calculate how much it would be worth after 30 years when the mortgage is paid. Then you subtract the total cost of the mortgage to see if you gained or lost.

4. *If interest on the national debt is 7 percent a year, how long would it take for the debt to double? How long would it take if interest rates went up to 8 percent.*

Again, using the rule of 72, it would take about 10 years at 7 percent (72 divided by 7) and 9 years at 8 percent (72 divided by 8).

CASE TWO

VIDEO CASE: BREAKING DOWN THE GREAT WALL

1. *What elements of Communism prevent the spread of entrepreneurship? What adjustments will China need to make to conform to the cultural, economic, and social practices of free market countries?*

Communism prevents entrepreneurs from owning their own land or businesses. The incentive to get up early and work late is not there because everyone makes the same amount no matter how hard they work. And people are not free to change jobs or to invent new products and make them on their own. For China to become part of the economic and cultural norm of free-market countries, it would have to establish property rights, allow wages to seek their own level, create laws of contract, and free labor to go and do what is wants, where it wants.

2. *If the Chinese impose stiff trade policies what might be the reaction of its global trading partners?*

If the Chinese have strict trade policies, other countries are likely to do the same. Since China sells much more than it imports, it would lose much revenue and the country would suffer economic disaster. It is best for China and the world for trade to be fair, open, and free.

3. *Implementing capitalism in China would lead almost immediately to great disparities in wealth between the rich and the poor. Is this necessarily a negative outcome? What can be done to minimize the reaction to such disparities?*

Capitalism creates huge differences between rich and poor. But there are huge differences between the capabilities of the best athletes and the general population and the smartest people and the general population. Differences are not bad. They are good in that each person has the opportunity to do best what he or she does best—no limits. If the outcome is unequal, that's because the contributions are unequal. Entrepreneurs and entertainers contribute much more to society than they take out, even though they get quite rich doing so. Entrepreneurs create jobs and wealth far beyond what they personally get. Pointing out the benefits of allowing each person to optimize his or her opportunities would lead to more prosperity for all. Note the United States and Hong Kong, for examples.

Lecture Enhancers

LECTURE ENHANCER 2-1

THE NEED FOR ECONOMIC EDUCATION

Sylvia Porter gives expert opinion on how to invest your money on TV, in books, and in articles. In one article, she discussed the lack of knowledge of economics among the citizenry. She said, "Most people do not know what the gross national product is. Nor do they understand the causes of the current federal budget deficit." She praises the Academy for Economic Education in Richmond, Virginia as a good step in the right direction. Some of the basic principles the Academy teaches include:

- **The principle that "there is no such thing as a free lunch."** Every decision involves a choice between benefits received and benefits foregone (costs).
- **The behavioral principle.** People act in their own self-interest and choose the course that maximizes their own satisfaction.
- **The economic welfare principle.** Voluntary, non-fraudulent exchanges leave both parties better off. A maximum level of exchange in any market maximizes voluntary exchanges.
- **The market system and general economic welfare.** In a market economy goods and services make their way from low-value to high-value uses, via a series of voluntary exchanges.
- **Demand creates supply.** If people are willing to pay a price for any good or service that exceeds its cost of production, then the market will respond by supplying that good or service.
- **The law of demand or "the principle of substitution."** When the price of some good rises relative to the price of a similar good, both consumers and business firms will demand less of it by substituting other goods.
- **The principle of competition.** In the long run, risk-adjusted rates of return among industries will equalize at a "normal" level of price and profit by the entry and exit of productive capacity.

If you know these basics, you know much more than the average person about economics and how the economic system works. Can you give examples of each principle?

LECTURE ENHANCER 2-2

THE STUDY OF ECONOMICS

If you were to go through the course list in economics at most colleges, you would find courses in both macroeconomics and microeconomics. You would likely find other courses on the history of economic thought. The following sections define some basic terms in economics and give you some feel for what is covered in various economics courses.

MACROECONOMICS

What causes one country to prosper and grow while other countries, with similar resources, remain poor? What causes unemployment? How much of a country's wealth should be spent on government programs such as defense, welfare, and education? How can the newly formed Commonwealth of Independent States (the former Soviet Union) and the various Central European countries (i.e., the countries that were formerly called Eastern European, such as Poland and Czechoslovakia) manage the transition from communism to some form of free-market capitalism? These and similar questions are the subject of macroeconomics.

Macroeconomics is the study of a nation's economy as a whole. Macroeconomics can be a fascinating subject to study because it looks at such important issues as whether or not taxes should be raised, how to handle the problems of inflation and depression, and much more. Nearly every major social, political, or economic issue can be discussed more intelligently and objectively once one understands basic macroeconomics. We shall explore various macroeconomic systems in this chapter, including capitalism, socialism, and communism.

MICROECONOMICS

What happens to the price of corn when there is a drought in the Midwest? What happens to the supply of farm products when the government subsidizes farmers or keeps farm prices artificially low? What is the impact of income taxes versus sales taxes on consumers? How does one determine the value of leisure time? These and similar questions are the subject of microeconomics. Microeconomics is the study of the behavior of people and organizations in particular markets. It looks at how prices are determined and how people and businesses respond to changes in the market (for example, changes in the demand for and supply of products).

Microeconomics can also be challenging to study because it teaches principles that can be used in everyday buying and selling transactions with others. Microeconomics also explains how free markets work. Many countries in the world today are trying to introduce market economies. We explain such systems in this chapter so that you can follow the progress (or lack of same) in introducing such systems worldwide.

(**OT ACETATE 2-3** is used with this Learning Enhancer.)

LECTURE ENHANCER 2-3

THE SPIRIT OF ADAM SMITH

Adam Smith (1723-1790) is best know for championing free markets, but he also cared about much more. Smith was also concerned with constructing a decent society. Free markets were only one means to that end. Government was another, and Smith constantly probed the proper roles for government and the market.

Some liberal economists today are so protective of government that they cannot concede the great power of Smith's "invisible hand." Self-interest is not simply greed, selfishness, or narcissism. If properly constrained, it is an immense force for social good, and much human progress stems from the independent exertions and creative energies of individuals and enterprises.

Meanwhile, conservatives are so contemptuous of government that they cannot admit that it is often more than a necessary evil. It creates the legal and political framework without which tolerably free markets could not survive. It also supplies the collective services—from defense to roads—that the private market doesn't and deals with the market's unwanted "excesses." Smith realized that government produced these benefits, but many conservatives who cite him seem oblivious to their existence or importance.

In his work *Adam Smith in His Time and Ours*, Jerry Muller demolishes the stereotype of Smith as an anti-government zealot. That image founders on one fact: Smith served for years as a bureaucrat, Scotland's Commissioner of Customs. He collected import duties, then the government's largest source of revenue. The job was akin to the head of the IRS today.

Smith's theories explained changes that had already occurred. In 18th-century Britain, feudalism had collapsed. Farm production rose, as did living standards. In England, people felt ashamed to go without shoes; in France, being shoeless was still common. Blankets, linens, and ironware became common in England. Smith attributed the new wealth to the triumph of the market; buying and selling. Before, food was mostly consumed by those who produced it or their feudal lords. Manufacturing was also transformed. Goods once produced laboriously at home—clothes, beer, candles, furniture—could then be purchased.

The market multiplied wealth, Smith reasoned, because it led to economic specialization: the "division of labor" that—through more knowledge, experience, and customized machinery—raised production. None of this was planned. It flowed (as if by an invisible hand) from the striving of sellers to maximize their wealth. "It is not from the benevolence of the butcher, the brewer, or the baker, that we expect our dinner," Smith wrote, "but from their regard to their own interest." Smith grasped that incentives count: that is, how people are motivated and toward what ends.

Government's ability to cripple the market appalled Smith. *The Wealth of Nations* aimed to fortify legislators against "the pressures of economic groups" for special privileges, Muller says. But Smith's skepticism of government wasn't a revulsion for it. He "enjoyed the work" as customs commissioner, writes Muller. This was not hypocrisy, because Smith saw three vital roles for government: (1) providing defense, (2) ensuring justice and protecting property, and (3) building roads, canals, harbors—"infrastructure." Government had to be properly financed.

Nor did Smith believe that wealth was all that mattered. Quite the opposite. He wanted a society that would be less violent and more civil—one that tempered people's worst passions. Greater wealth, by relieving suffering, enabled people to be more "benevolent." And though the market could be cruel and crass, it also encouraged stable commercial relations. That was a civilizing influence, Smith argued. Finally, Smith believed in the primacy of the family as a moral force (the place where children learn self-control) and as a source of personal happiness.

Deciding what government should do is harder in our era than Smith's, precisely because its activities—ranging from the social safety net to environmental regulation—are so much greater. But Smith's pragmatic approach can still be applied. He assigned social tasks where he thought they could best be met, whether that be the market or government.

LECTURE ENHANCER 2-4

RED DAWN FOR HONG KONG

American Craft Brewing International Ltd., based in Metairie, Louisiana, concocted a special beer to celebrate the 1997 takeover of Hong Kong by China. Brewed at the company's Hong Kong microbrewery, the red-colored lager was created for consumption as the transition took place at the end of June 1997. It was "the perfect toast to the beginning of a new chapter in Hong Kong's history," the company said.

The beer was called Red Dawn, a name selected as a positive message about the new era. Red is associated with weddings and festivals in China, while dawn is a metaphor for change.

But for some, the name was all too appropriate. Within China, red is also associated with the Communist Party, which many in Hong Kong fear will come to dominate life on their small island. In fact, the name also evoked an anthem from the Cultural Revolution, says one expert. The song "Dong Fang Hong," which once played at the end of television broadcasts the way the "Star-Spangled Banner" once did in the U.S., includes the lyrics "The east is red, the sun is rising, China has produced Chairman Mao."

For its part, AmBrew took steps to reduce problems. It sent cases of Red Dawn to Chief Executive-designate Tung Chee Hwa and ex-governor Chris Patten to serve at transition events.

The last laugh may be AmBrew's. The company brewed 10,000 cases and sold them all.

LECTURE ENHANCER 2-5

POST-COMMUNIST RUSSIA: SOME STATISTICS

The old Soviet Union has been broken up into 89 republics and regions, and parliamentary elections have replaced the iron control of the Kremlin. Below are several key statistics that illustrate some of the other changes that have taken place.

- Military spending as a percentage of the GDP has decreased from 17 percent in 1985 to less than 10 percent in 1995.
- Oil production has declined from 10 million barrels per day in 1990 to less than 6 million in 1995.
- Exports in 1991 amounted to about $105 billion U.S. dollars; in 1995 exports were less than $80 billion.
- About 10 percent of Russian workers between 25 and 29 years old earn more than $200 per month; around 38 percent of Russian workers over 65 earn less than $20 monthly.
- Consumer goods are becoming more available: 37 percent of Russians have TVS, 34 percent have radios, 16 percent have telephones, and 9 percent have cars.

LECTURE ENHANCER 2-6

SHENZHEN: CHINA EXPERIMENTS WITH ECONOMIC REFORM

China remains one of the few remaining Communist economies. However, even in China, some experiments with free markets have been undertaken. On the southern China coast, Shenzhen province has been designated a "Special Economic Zone (SEZ)." This status, plus its close proximity to Hong Kong, have profoundly influenced the region's economy.

China's SEZs are modeled on the export-processing zones established, with varying degrees of success, in South Korea, Taiwan, the Philippines, Thailand, Malaysia, Singapore, Pakistan, India, and Sri Lanka. They also draw on a Leninist tradition of economic pragmatism, invoking memories of Lenin's New Economic Policy and Zhou Enlai's commitment to economic modernization in 1963.

Established in 1980 under China's Open Door policy, the Shenzhen SEZ is designed as a foreign-exchange earner—both as an export-processing zone and as a tourist destination for neighboring Hong Kong. The SEZ attracts foreign investment by granting special privileges involving land use, business registration, technology transfers, the regulation of immigration, and taxes. While profits are taxed at 30 percent on the mainland, they are taxed at only 15 percent in the SEZ.

The importance of the SEZ's success to the rest of China is seen in a number of ways. In 1993, Shenzhen replaced Shanghai as China's top exporter and as the region with the highest per-capita income. Deng Xiaoping's first public appearance after two years of seclusion was a highly publicized visit in early 1992 to Shenzhen, where he announced that economic reform and modernization continued to be China's top priorities. He also used the occasion to warn reform opponents that their obstructionism would lead to expulsion from public office.

China's first special laws for foreign economic contracts were drafted for the Shenzhen SEZ and then applied nationally. In 1986, Shenzhen became the first Chinese city to regularize the circulation of bills of exchange. The first officially approved private law firm was established in Shenzhen in May 1988. While the SEZ still adheres to the principles of the Chinese Communist Party (CCP), it has copied the legal system of its capitalist neighbor to remedy the lack of legal infrastructure in the newly formed SEZ.

LECTURE ENHANCER 2-7

SUPPLY AND DEMAND: COFFEE

The concepts of supply, demand, shortages, surpluses, and equilibrium prices are often best illustrated in the agricultural commodities markets.

In early 1997, global supply and demand for coffee beans sent commodity prices on a roller coaster ride. In January 1997 damaging rains in Central and South America were blamed by a spike in coffee prices. Supermarket coffee brands such as Folgers and Maxwell House soared by more than 20 percent. Starbucks Coffee Company upped the price of a cup of coffee by a nickel.

The supply squeeze that had begun in early winter boosted futures prices to record levels—on the perception that beans would not be available. Panicked roasters began buying, sending the price of green coffee beans to a 30-month high of $2.27 per pound, more than twice what it was three months earlier. Growers then unloaded their stockpiles to take advantage of the high prices.

Coffee investors and speculators were happier than coffee drinkers. Starbucks' stock rose in response to the price increase, in anticipation of higher revenues.

LECTURE ENHANCER 2-8

HANDICAPS OF THE U.S. ECONOMY

In spite of the wonderful advances the U.S. has experienced in its economy, there are underlying problems that must be solved before the country can be a true beacon for others to follow. Capitalism with all of its freedoms has led to the following situations:

1. No modern, industrialized society has the rate of drug addiction, teenage pregnancy and functional illiteracy we do.
2. We are the most violent, crime ridden society in the industrialized world.
3. The U.S. spends far more than any of our international competitors on health care.
4. No other society spends as much time in court or as much money defending and insuring itself against lawsuits. Two thirds of the lawyers in the world work in the U.S.

America is still a major competitor in world markets, but its competitive edge is slipping. Other nations are apprehensive about adopting capitalist principles for fear that the other problems—drugs, crime, etc.—will creep in as well. Can a society be free and prosperous and yet be tough on crime and drugs? What would it take for that to happen?

LECTURE ENHANCER 2-9

ECONOMIC INDICATORS

The business cycle moves from recession to recovery to peak to decline. Economists search long and hard for signs of a coming change in economic performance. Traditionally twelve "leading economic indicators" have been studied. These include:

- The average workweek of production workers
- Initial claims for unemployment insurance
- Change in prices of sensitive crude materials such as steel and iron scrap
- Stock prices
- Money supply
- Residential building permits for private housing.

Changes in these indicators tend to occur several months before the economy has a whole reacts. Thus an increase in stock prices may indicate that the economy will enter a recovery period six to twelve months in the future.

While these indicators provide the soundest objective evidence of coming changes, some economists track lesser known, even eccentric, indicators. One of these secondary indicators is cardboard box shipments. Because boxes are used to package other products, an increase in shipments seems to indicate that business people anticipate increased sales. Prices for old newspapers also point to economic changes. Recycled newspapers go into roofing, insulation, auto panels, and newsprint. Another indicator is the index of help-wanted advertising. Still other economists swear the best economic indicators is a speech by Arthur Greenspan, chairman of the Federal Reserve System Board of Governors.

LECTURE ENHANCER 2-10

CREATING JOBS

Small businesses have the potential to create the jobs needed to substantially reduce the U.S. unemployment rate. There are about 15 million small enterprises that don't have any workers other than the owner. If the country's economic, tax, and budget policies encouraged each of those businesses to hire just one employee, that would be 15 million new jobs.

There are 6.3 million businesses in the U.S. with under 100 employees. If each of those businesses added just one employee, there would be another 6 million workers. Add that number to the 15 million and you'd have about 21 million new jobs. That's more than the number of workers added throughout the 1980s, a period of rapid expansion in the U.S. Much of the growth in business employment will come from mid-size companies.

In other words, unemployment in the U.S. could be improved by giving small and mid-sized businesses some incentive to hire new worker. The problem in the past has been that some government programs did just the opposite. Businesses have frequently been faced with new taxes and regulations. Business leaders are now trying to work with government leaders to devise job growth legislation.

LECTURE ENHANCER 2-11

THE GREAT DEPRESSION: CAPITALISM IN CRISIS

The worldwide business slump of the 1930's ranked as the worst and longest period of high unemployment and low business activity in modern times. Many causes contributed to making the Great Depression as severe as it was. During the 1920s many bank failures, together with low incomes among farmers and factory workers, helped set the stage. Uneven distribution of income among workers also contributed.

The Great Depression differed in both length and harshness from previous depressions in the United States. In earlier depressions, business activity had started to pick up after one or two years. But from October 1929 until Franklin D. Roosevelt became president in March 1933, the economy slumped almost every month. From 1930 to 1933 prices of industrial stocks fell about 80 percent. Banks and individuals with investments in the stock market lost large sums. Banks had also loaned money to many people who could not repay it. The deepening depression forced large numbers of people to withdraw their savings. Banks had difficulty meeting the withdrawals, which came at a time when the banks were unable to collect on many loans. Between January 1930 and March 1933, about 9,000 banks failed. The bank failures wiped out the savings of millions of people.

Bank failures made less money available for loans to industry. The decline in available money caused a drop in production and a further rise in unemployment. From 1929 to 1933, the total value of goods and services produced annually in the United States fell from about $104 billion to about $56 billion. In 1932, the number of business closings was almost a third higher than the 1929 level.

In 1925, about three percent of the nation's workers were unemployed. The unemployment rate reached about nine percent in 1930 and about 25 percent—or about 13 million persons—in 1933. Many people who kept or found jobs had to take salary cuts. In 1932, wage cuts averaged about 18 percent. In 1932, the New York City Police Department estimated that 7,000 persons over the age of 17 shined shoes for a living.

Human suffering became a reality for millions of Americans as the depression continued. Many died of disease resulting from malnutrition. Thousands lost their homes because they could not pay the mortgage. Severe droughts and dust storms hit parts of the Midwest and Southwest during the 1930s. The afflicted region became known as the Dust Bowl, and thousands of farm families were wiped out.

President Herbert Hoover held office as the Depression began. America had operated for 150 years under Adam Smith's philosophy of laissez faire, or free competition. Hoover believed that business, if left alone to operate without government supervision, would correct the economic conditions. He vetoed several bills aimed at relieving the depression because he felt they gave the federal government too much power. Most Americans felt that Hoover did not do enough to fight the depression and elected Franklin D. Roosevelt president in 1932.

America was at a crossroads. The existing economic system had proved inadequate to deal with massive economic disruption. Capitalism seemed to be discredited as business failures and unemployment escalated. For many Americans without a job the teachings of Karl Marx and Frederick Engles held tremendous appeal—"from each according to his ability, to each according to his need." Many questioned whether capitalism would survive.

It is this environment that influenced the ideas of John Maynard Keynes, a British economist at Cambridge University. His General Theory of Employment, Interest, and Money (1936) ranks among the most important books on economics. The book changed economic theory and policy, and became the basis of economic policies of most nations today.

The basis of Keynesian economics is simple. The level of economic activity depends on the total spending of consumers, business, and government. If business expectations are poor, investment spending will be cut, causing a series of reductions in total spending. If this should happen, the economy can move into a depression and stay there. To avoid a depression, Keynes urged increased government spending and easy money. These actions, he argued, would encourage investment, increase employment, and enable consumers to spend more. Keynes sought not to destroy capitalism, but to save it.

President Roosevelt also believed the federal government had the chief responsibility of fighting the Great Depression. He called Congress into a special session to pass laws to relieve the suffering, which became known as the New Deal.

New Deal programs not only helped relieve the depression, but also renewed the confidence of Americans in the government. But about 15 percent of the nations working force still did not have a job in 1940. The Great Depression did not end in the United States until 1942, after the country had entered World War II.

New government policies increased federal control over banks and the stock market. Laws of the New Deal also gave the government more power to provide money for the needy. Since the depression, the powers of the federal government have been broadened. This shift can be dramatically seen in the pattern of government spending. In 1929, government spending made up less than five percent of the gross domestic product—by the early 1990s this percent had grown to over one-fourth.

The depression also changed the attitudes of many Americans toward business and the federal government. Before the depression, most people regarded bankers and business executives as the nation's leaders. After the stock market crashed and these leaders could not relieve the depression, Americans lost faith in them. The government finally succeeded in improving conditions. As a result many Americans decided that the government—not business—had the responsibility to maintain the national economy.

Critical Thinking Exercises

Name: ____________________

Date: ____________________

CRITICAL THINKING EXERCISE 2-1

STANDARD OF LIVING COMPARISON

Is the standard of living different in capitalist, socialist, and communist economies? Which economic system provides the highest standard of living? One way of answering these questions is by comparing economic data you might find in the library. Use the following chart to record your findings.

	CAPITALIST COUNTRIES	SOCIALIST COUNTRIES	COMMUNIST COUNTRIES
Gross National Product			
Consumer Prices			
Unemployment Rate			
Average Income			
Average Education			

ANSWERS TO CRITICAL THINKING EXERCISE 2-1

In searching for the answers to this exercise, students should go to the library and talk to the librarian about possible sources. As they go through those sources, they can record the latest information they can find. Even if they cannot find the answers, encourage them to note what information is available in those sources so they can refer to them again in the future. In fact, the official unemployment rate in the Soviet Union is zero because they claim everyone has a job. Consumer prices are meaningless in an economy with scarcities in most consumer goods. The official price and the price paid to unofficial sellers working underground are two radically different things. One lesson from a case like this is that information is often difficult to obtain from a controlled government and the information you do get may not be accurate.

Name: ______________________

Date: ______________________

CRITICAL THINKING EXERCISE 2-2

BALANCING THE FEDERAL BUDGET

There has been much discussion regarding the Federal government's historical budget deficit and possible future surpluses. Everyone has an opinion as to how to balance the budget. Below are actual figures for fiscal year 1997 expenditures and income. Rearrange the figures to eliminate the $140,000,000,000 deficit and balance the budget. You can either cut money going out or increase money coming in. (Note: Numbers may not add up to the totals due to rounding.)

MONEY COMING IN: (all figures in $ billions)

SOURCE	AMOUNT	PROPOSED VALUE
Individual Income Taxes	645	______
Corporate Income Taxes	185	______
Payroll Taxes	536	______
Excise Taxes	60	______
Estate and Gift Taxes	17	______
Customs Duties	20	______
Miscellaneous Taxes	32	______
TOTAL	1,495	______

MONEY GOING OUT: (all figures in $ billions)

PROGRAM	AMOUNT	PROPOSED VALUE
National Defense	259	______
International Affairs	15	______
General Science, Space, Technology	17	______
Energy	2	______
Natural Resources and Environment	22	______
Agriculture	8	______
Commerce and Housing	6	______
Transportation	39	______
Community and Regional Development	12	______
Education, Training, Social Services	54	______
Health	135	______
Medicare	190	______
Income Security	237	______
Social Security	368	______
Veterans Benefits	40	______
Administration of Justice	22	______
General Government	15	______
Net Interest	238	______
Credits and Miscellaneous	-41	______
TOTAL	1,635	______

DEFICIT:	-140	______

ANSWERS TO CRITICAL THINKING EXERCISE 2-2

There are no right or wrong answers to this exercise. Each student will have a different opinion as to how to reduce the deficit. It is an interesting exercise in setting priorities and the difficulty involved in solving a long-standing, complex problem.

Current figures for expenditures and income are published monthly in the *Federal Reserve Bulletin*. These figures are also available on the Federal Reserve System web site (**http://www.ncs.gov/~ncs/html/frb.html**.) Another good Web resource is "A Citizen's Guide to the Federal Budget" **(http://www.http://cher.eda.doc.gov/BudgetFY97/guidetoc.html.)** You might want to update the previous figures with current ones.

Supplemental Cases

CASE 2-1

FOUNDATIONS OF THE CAPITALIST SYSTEM

Throughout history of capitalism, there has been one persistent criticism. The whole system seems to be based on selfishness—the more one works, the more one prospers. If one is unable to work, the system seems to have no answer to his or her problems. Furthermore, there does not seem to be any moral or spiritual foundation to the system. Where do businesses get their values? What about concepts such as sharing, helping neighbors, and protecting the environment?

It is important to make a distinction between plain capitalism and democratic capitalism. Democratic capitalism is a system based on three components: (1) free enterprise; that is, freedom to own your own businesses and farms and freedom to keep the profits, (2) a freely elected government that has internal checks and balances, and (3) moral, ethical, and spiritual values that are part of the very fabric of the country and the business system. Plain capitalism is a system where there is free enterprise, but no freely elected government and no foundation of moral, ethical, and spiritual values. There are several "capitalist" countries headed by right-wing dictators that do not have democratic capitalism and do not have the relative prosperity and social justice that we have in the United States.

Let's explore democratic capitalism in more detail so that you can understand how the system works. One of the most important elements of democratic capitalism is its moral and spiritual base. When the U.S. was being settled, there was so much religious debate and rivalry among religions that people were tortured and killed for their beliefs. When it came time to establish a free and separate U. S., however, the founding fathers were adamant about freedom of religion. They were very religious people themselves.

Thomas Jefferson was proud of his religious heritage and his fight for religious freedom in the U.S. He asked that his epitaph should read: "Author of the Declaration of Independence, of the Statute of Virginia for Religious Freedom, and Father of the University of Virginia." Jefferson felt that freedom of religion was one of his most important contributions. He felt it was as important as being President of the United States.

Democratic capitalism cannot work effectively and fairly without all three components. With all three, the democratic capitalist system can become the most fair and equitable economic system in the world. Not everyone agrees on the role of government in the democratic system and on how much of the total gross national product the government should control. (Recent history indicates that somewhere between 20 percent and 25 percent of GNP gives the government the funds it needs to create more social justice and more equitable distribution of wealth.) A freely elected government is important to democratic capitalism because if the people feel that the system is not fair, they can elect new politicians to change the rules.

DISCUSSION QUESTIONS FOR CASE 2-1:

1. Do you see any evidence that the moral, ethical, and spiritual foundation of the American democratic capitalist system is eroding? How does that affect the ability of capitalist proponents to promote capitalism in other countries such as China and India?

2. Why is it so necessary to have a freely elected government for democratic capitalism to create a prosperous and fair economy?

3. Go through the three components of democratic capitalism and picture an economy without each one. What happens to freedom, fairness, and moral and ethical behavior? Which part of the system seems weakest today? What can be done about it?

ANSWERS TO DISCUSSION QUESTIONS FOR CASE 2-1:

1. *Do you see any evidence that the moral, ethical, and spiritual foundation of the American democratic capitalist system is eroding? How does that affect the ability of capitalist proponents to promote capitalism in other countries such as China and India?*

When one of the authors was in elementary school, the codes of what was moral forbid him to see "The Moon Is Blue" because the movie used the word "virgin" in it. Now movies for children have swear words and portray immoral conduct of all kinds. In fact, many such movies are now available in prime time on TV. There does seem to be an erosion of moral and ethical behavior in business. It could be a function of more media reporting of such behavior, but the impression is clear—moral decay is spreading.

When other countries see moral decay in capitalist countries, they are hesitant to adopt capitalism. They do not want the immorality, the pregnancies among teenagers, the crime, and the music that they see as corrupting of the spiritual values of their countries.

2. *Why is it so necessary to have a freely elected government for democratic capitalism to create a prosperous and fair economy?*

Because any kind of dictatorship hinders the operation of free markets, or at least tends to do so. Free choice in the market is based on a value system that includes free choice in it, including free choice of leaders.

3. *Go through the three components of democratic capitalism and picture an economy without each one. What happens to freedom, fairness, and moral and ethical behavior? Which part of the system seems weakest today? What can be done about it?*

Without free enterprise, shortages develop and the whole economy tends to slow. Poverty, hunger and starvation often result. Without a freely-elected government, the arbitrary allocation of resources can lead to the same problems as an absence of free markets. But what is needed in any economy is a moral and ethical base. Without that base, the market mechanism falters. People cheat, mislead, lie and engage in immoral and unethical behavior. The consequences are crime, drug-related incidents and a collapse of the very foundations of society. We see that happening in some cities today.

CASE 2-2

ECONOMIC CONSEQUENCES OF COMMUNIST SYSTEMS

Although the capitalism system led to prosperity in much of the world, there were some people, especially Karl Marx, who felt that capitalism would eventually be replaced by socialism. He felt that the wealth of capitalism should be distributed more evenly and that the people should own businesses and forms collectively. Socialism got a real boost in the 1930s when the United States went through the Great Depression. Government involvement in the economy increased greatly in the United States and even more so in socialist countries.

In the former Soviet Union, China, and a few other countries, socialism took the form of communism. That is, the government became the principal mechanism for allocating resources, and the government (not the people) owned businesses and farms.

To create a more equal distribution of wealth, communist governments felt they had to suppress many of the freedoms enjoyed in capitalist nations. That included freedom of religion, press, travel, expression, and business ownership. The government became very powerful. The problem is that government allocation of resources is not as fast, efficient, or effective as free market choices. As a consequence, shortages and surpluses occur in many goods and services.

A major problem of communism is that the suppression of freedom also takes away the incentive to produce quality goods and to maintain them. Therefore, many goods produced in communist countries are of inferior quality and suffer from lack of service. Government directives simply cannot motivate people to work as hard and as carefully as the profit motive.

DISCUSSION QUESTIONS FOR CASE 2-2:

1. Given the apparent economic success of capitalist countries and the relative economic failure of communist countries, why would a Third World nation adopt the communist system?

2. What happens as communist countries introduce capitalist concepts?

3. Could more open exchange of goods and services between the United States and the former Soviet Union improve international relationships? Are there two sides to this question?

ANSWERS TO DISCUSSION QUESTIONS FOR CASE 2-2:

1. *Given the apparent economic success of capitalist countries and the relative economic failure of communist countries, why would a Third World nation adopt the communist system?*

   Communist systems give almost total power to the government, so government officials who want power naturally turn to communism. Furthermore, the communist system has always had the promise of creating a utopia where everyone is equal and shares the product of his or her labor with everyone else. The problem is that the promise and the reality are far apart.

2. *What happens as communist countries introduced capitalist concepts?*

   In China, the result was a sudden surge in the economy, with food production increasing dramatically and thousands of new retail shops opening. The government loses some power and control, however, and inequality creeps in. In China, for example, there are several millionaires in the midst of poverty. Perhaps there will be less poverty with the freedom and incentives now being introduced.

3. *Could more open exchange of goods and services between the United States and the former Soviet Union improve international relationships? Are there two sides to this question?*

   The differences between the United States and the former Soviet Union are more than economic. The basic difference is in government philosophy. The U.S. believes in a freely elected government where politicians can lose their jobs if they don't please the people. The former Soviet government wanted total control to the extent that it allowed no freedom of the press, religion, travel, or dissent. No trade policy would change those differences. Now that the political system in the Soviet Union is changing, the economic system will also change. Free trade could help facilitate these changes while improving international relationships. Today there is heated debate concerning regarding the United States' role in help the former Soviet Union with its political and economic transitions. Some favor economic aid with humanitarian arguments and others oppose it with arguments based on distrust of a former enemy. Events are quickly changing the identity and role of the former Soviet Union leadership. It should be interesting for students to note the changes in the former Soviet Union and our evolving relationship with the region since this was published.

CASE 2-3

JUST TAX THE RICH AND PAY OFF THE DEBT? (Revisited)

Using the information from the final section of the text (pages 65 to 66), answer the following questions.

1. Recently Sweden joined many of the other nations in the world in cutting taxes. The Swedish people also voted against a socialist government. Taxing the rich is no longer the preferred way to balance government budgets. What are the alternatives?

2. There are thousands of millionaires and some billionaires in the United States. What are the advantages and disadvantages of taxing such people at much higher rates than now prevail?

3. There is a notion that "a rising tide lifts all ships." That is true in the United States for all but 3 percent of the population. What can be done to help raise those people as well?

4. Every year, there seems to be a call for a cut in "government waste and corruption." Years pass, and no such cuts appear to be made. What steps would you recommend for making local, state, and federal government agencies more efficient and effective?

ANSWERS TO DISCUSSION QUESTIONS FOR CASE 2-3:

1. *Recently Sweden joined many of the other nations in the world in cutting taxes. The Swedish people also voted against a socialist government. Taxing the rich is no longer the preferred way to balance government budgets. What are the alternatives?*

There are several other income sources. Excise taxes could be increased, but would provide only a small increase in revenue. Some suggest instituting a value added tax, in essence a national sales tax. This would generate huge amounts of income, but, as all sales taxes do, hit lower-income families the hardest. The best way to balance government budgets would probably be to increase the nation's productivity and maintain steady economic growth.

2. *There are thousands of millionaires and some billionaires in the United States. What are the advantages and disadvantages of taxing such people at much higher rates than now prevail?*

Our federal income tax system is designed to be progressive. In other words, as people earn more money, they pay an increasingly large portion as income tax. The theory proposes that those best able to pay shoulder the greatest burden. Whether or not this is fair or necessary can be debated. What has become clear is that as income tax rates increase, tax payers put more effort into avoiding tax and less productive effort into increasing wealth. Thus, in theory, more wealth would be created if tax rates were leveled.

3. *There is a notion that "a rising tide lifts all ships." That is true in the United States for all but 3 percent of the population. What can be done to help raise those people as well?*

Our national conscience has always provided a "safety net" for those who are who are temporarily unemployed or are truly unable to work. The debate now is how best to help these persons. Many argue that distributing money without training advances no ones' interests. Investment in education and vocational training would, in the long run, increase the work force's skill level and productivity.

4. *Every year, there seems to be a call for a cut in "government waste and corruption." Years pass, and no such cuts appear to be made. What steps would you recommend for making local, state, and federal government agencies more efficient and effective?*

Students will have differing opinions as to how make government more responsible and efficient. An interesting exercise is to allow students to "balance" the federal budget by setting priorities and rearrange income and outflow. **CRITICAL THINKING EXERCISE 2-2** in this manual can be used for this purpose. Most students find it extremely difficult to bring the figures in line and better understand the difficult choices the nation must make.

Transparency Masters

Chapter Outline

CHAPTER 2

ECONOMICS: THE CREATION AND DISTRIBUTION OF WEALTH

PROFILE: Rosa Alvardo—Village Banker

I. THE IMPORTANCE OF THE STUDY OF ECONOMICS.

A. What Is Economics?

B. The Economic Theory of Wealth Creation: Adam Smith.

C. The "Invisible Hand."

II. THE HISTORY OF BUSINESS AND ECONOMICS.

A. The Search for Equality.

B. The Birth of Communism.

III. THE ATTRACTION OF SOCIALISM.

A. The Negative Consequences of Socialism.

B. The Trend Toward Mixed Economies.

IV. THE FOUNDATIONS OF CAPITALISM.

A. How Free Markets Work.

B. How Prices Are Determined.

1. Supply.
2. Demand.
3. Equilibrium Point.

C. Competition Within Free Markets.

V. WORLD MARKETS: SUPPLY AND DEMAND.

A. Limitations of the Free-Market System.

TM-16B

Chapter Outline (continued)

VI. UNDERSTANDING THE ECONOMIC SYSTEM OF THE UNITED STATES.

A. Key Economic Indicators.
   1. Gross Domestic Product (GDP).
   2. The Unemployment Rate.

B. The Price Indexes.

C. Distribution of GDP.

D. Productivity in the United States.

E. Productivity in the Service Sector.

VII. INFLATION AND THE CONSUMER PRICE INDEX.

A. The Issue of Recession Versus Inflation.

VIII. THE ISSUE OF MONETARY POLICY.

A. Tight Versus Loose Monetary Policy.

IX. THE ISSUE OF FISCAL POLICY.

A. How Taxes and Spending Affect Businesspeople.

B. The Federal Deficit.

C. The National Debt.

D. Just Tax the Rich and Pay Off the Debt?

X. SUMMARY AND REVIEW.

TM-17

The Supply Curve At Various Prices

(Figure 2.2 on text page 53)

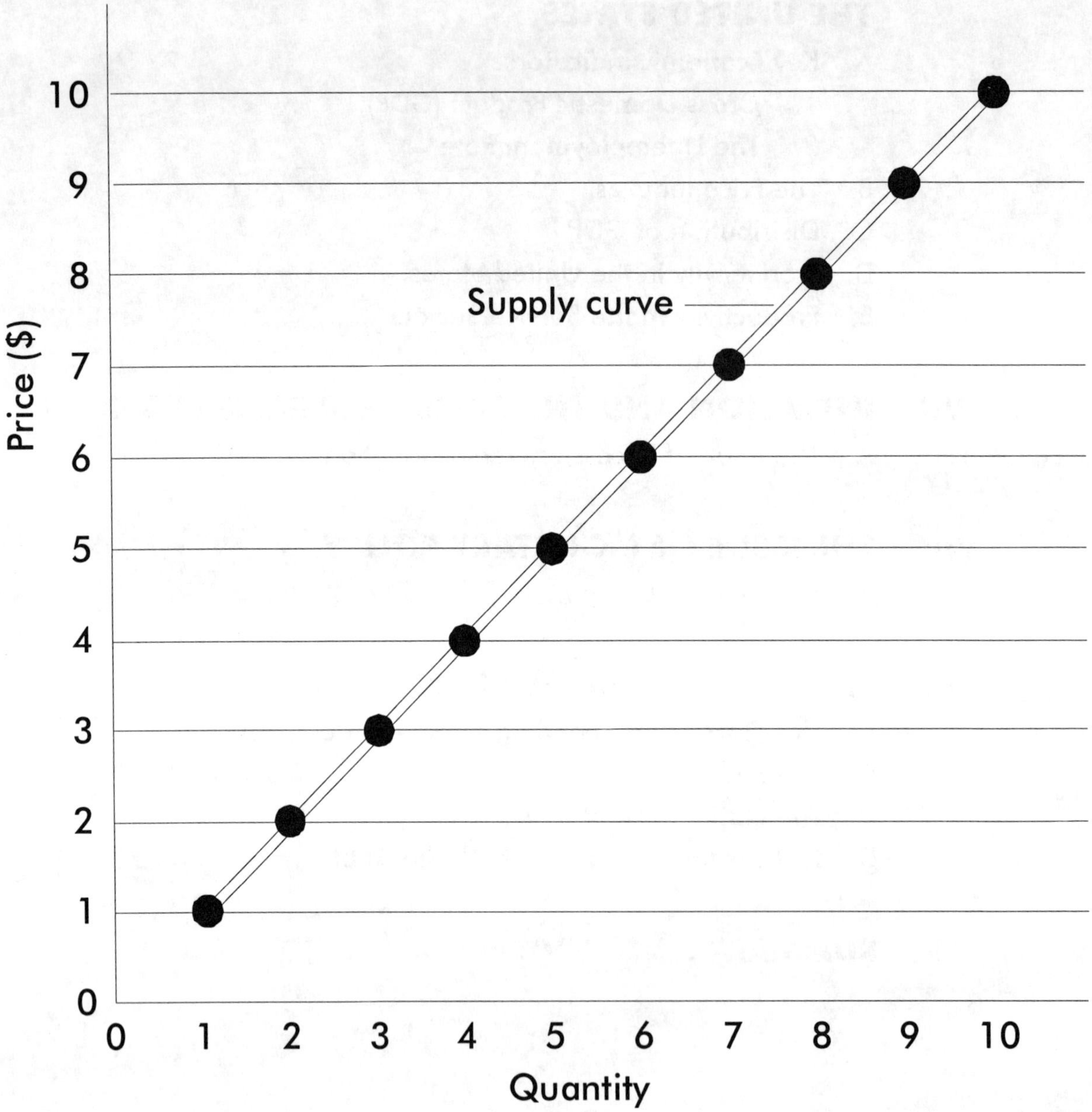

TM-18

The Demand Curve at Various Prices

(Figure 2.3 on text page 54)

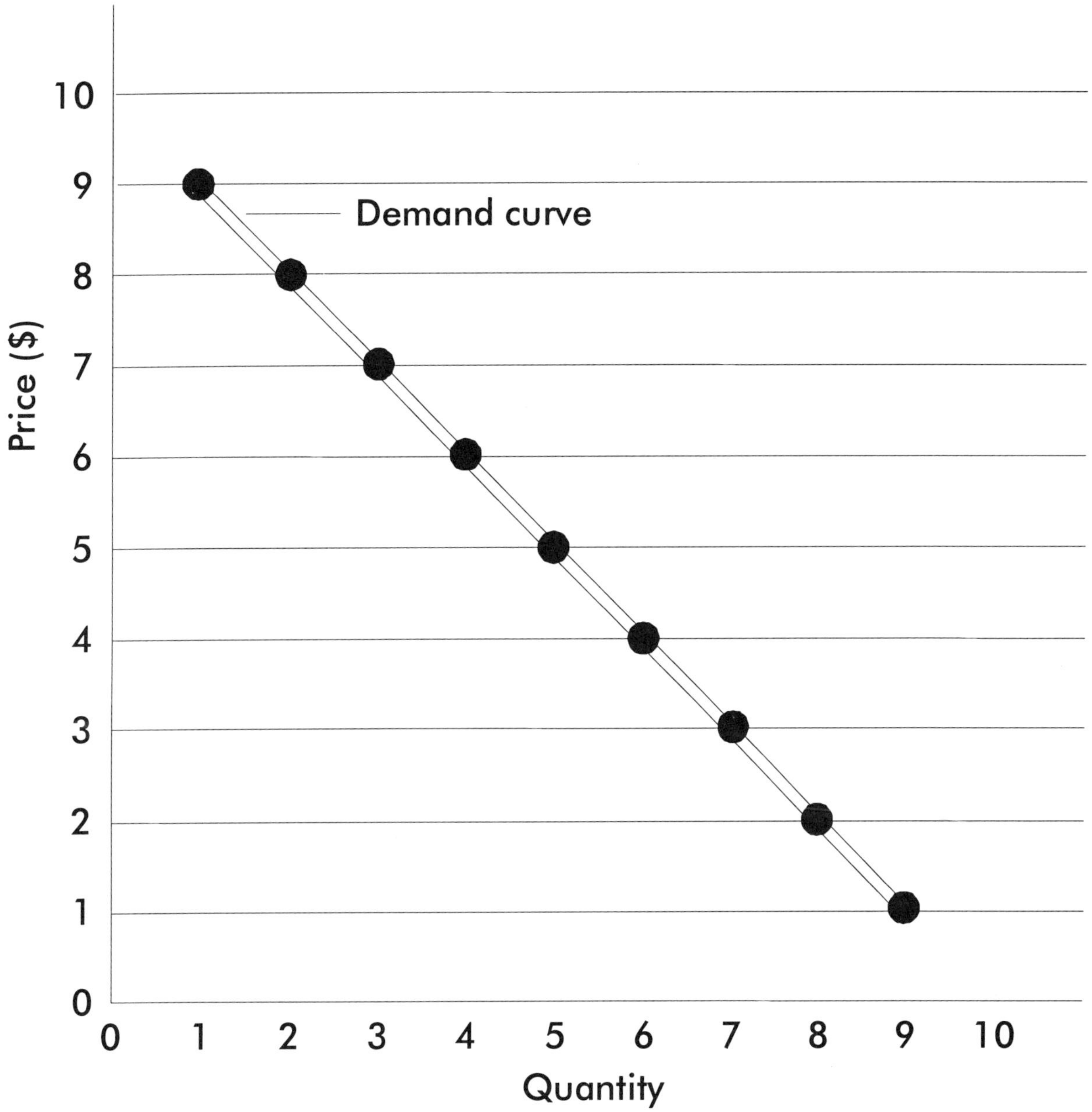

10
9
8
7
6
5
4
3
2
1
0
Price ($)
Demand curve
0 1 2 3 4 5 6 7 8 9 10
Quantity

The Equilibrium Point
(Figure 2.4 on text page 55)

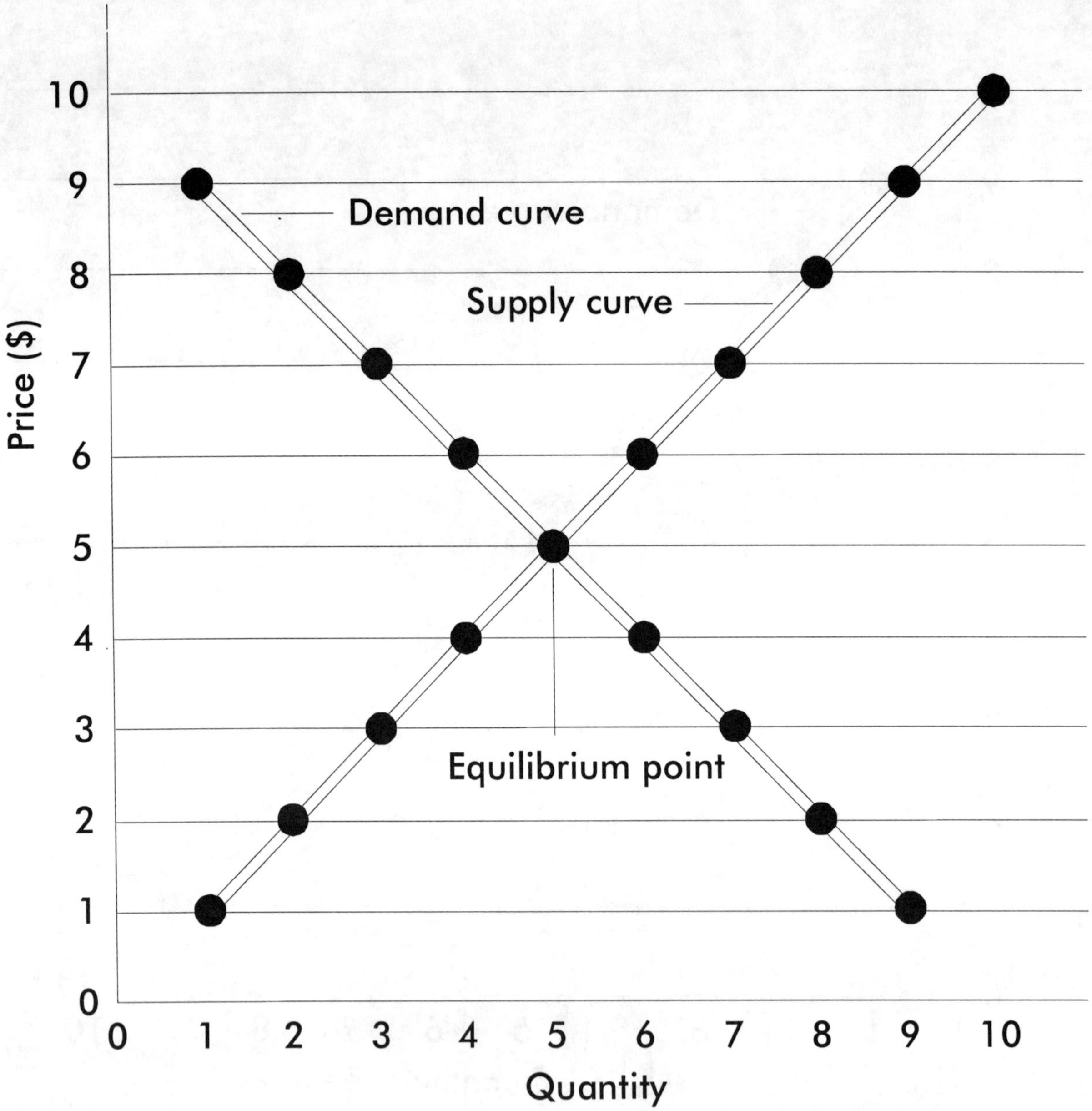

Demand curve

Supply curve

Equilibrium point

Price ($)

10 9 8 7 6 5 4 3 2 1 0

0 1 2 3 4 5 6 7 8 9 10

Quantity

TM-20

1998 Government Revenue and Expenses

(Figure 2.5 on text page 64)

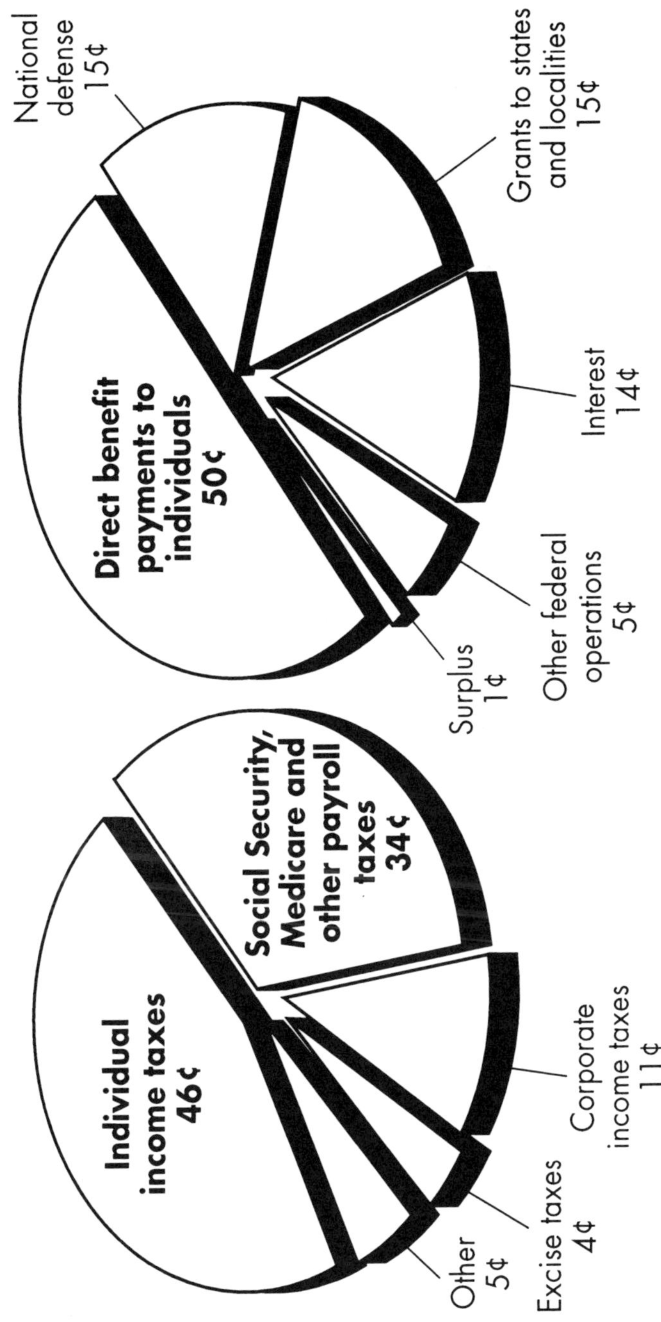

TM-21

The National Debt

(Figure 2.6 on text page 65)

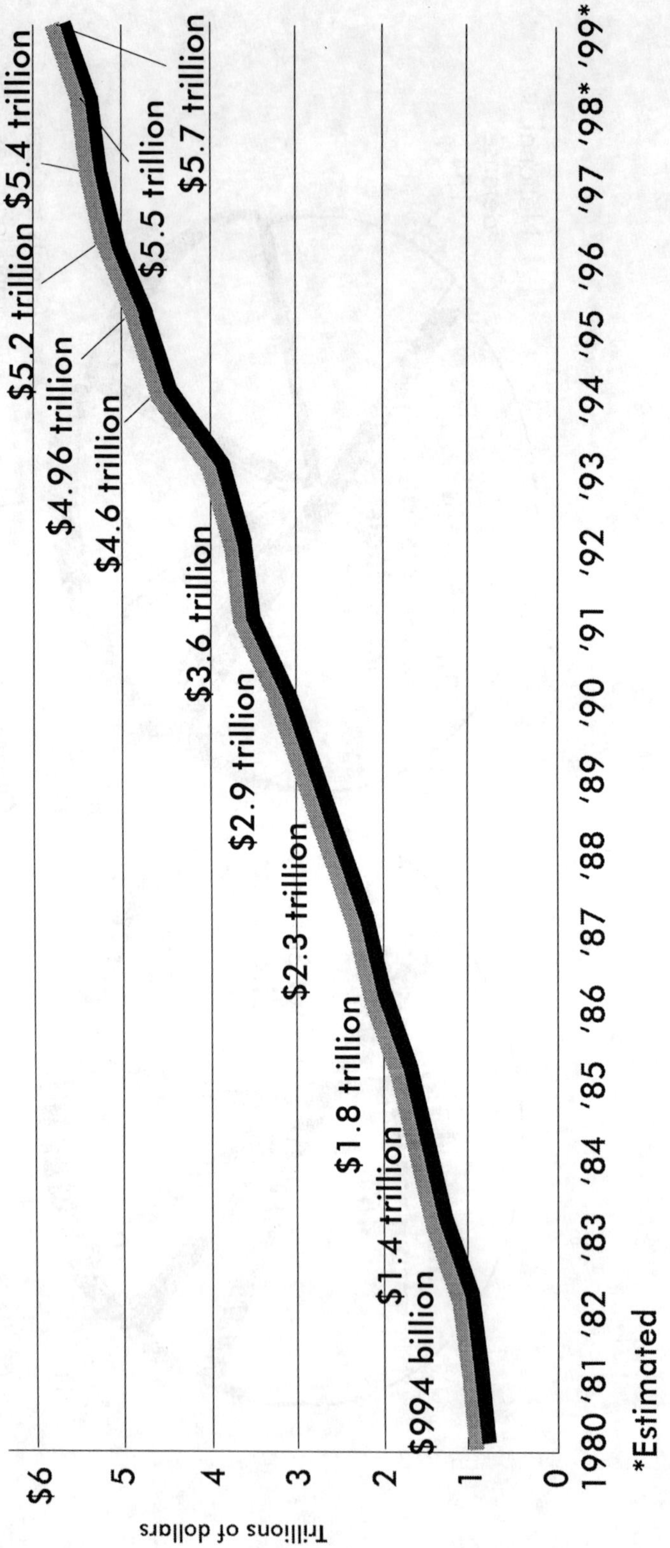
$6
5
4
3
2
1
0
Trillions of dollars
1980 '81 '82 '83 '84 '85 '86 '87 '88 '89 '90 '91 '92 '93 '94 '95 '96 '97 '98* '99*
$994 billion
$1.4 trillion
$1.8 trillion
$2.3 trillion
$2.9 trillion
$3.6 trillion
$4.6 trillion
$4.96 trillion
$5.2 trillion
$5.4 trillion
$5.5 trillion
$5.7 trillion
*Estimated

Competing in Global Markets

Chapter 3

Folder Contents

OT ACETATE 3-8 Cultural Differences in Global Markets

OT ACETATE 3-9 Did You Know?

OT ACETATE 3-10 Favorite Campbell Soups Around the World

OT ACETATE 3-11 Who's Got the Worst Reputation Globally?

OT ACETATE 3-12 Familiar Multinational Companies

OT ACETATE 3-13 What's the Second Most Valuable Language in Business Globally?

(Acetates and Transparency Masters are also available as PowerPoint slides on disk and on the Presentation CD-ROM.)

(Resources Available are also referenced in the expanded lecture outline later in this chapter.)

Other Resources Available

Video Case - "Coca-Cola in Japan." Coca-Cola and Pepsi are major competitors throughout the world as well as in the U.S. When it comes to Japan, however, Coke is the clear winner. This video demonstrates that what made Coke a success in Japan was its willingness to partner with local businesspeople. (The **Media Resource Guide** contains a summary of the Video and suggested discussion questions.)

Student Assessment and Learning Guide: Contains matching key term and definition questions, write-in retention questions, write-in critical thinking questions, and practice test of multiple choice and true/false questions.

Technology:

Zapitalism CD-ROM - Simulation program.

Concept Mastery Exam Preparation Disk - Practice test and tutorial.

Business Essentials Disk - Hyperlinks Understanding Business with seven other leading business texts.

Presentation CD-ROM - Contains PowerPoint slides of acetates and transparency masters, video clips, lecture materials. This tool allows you to customize your lecture presentations.

***Business Week* Web Site Access with the *Business Week* edition.**

***Understanding Business* Home Page - http:/www.mhhe.com/ub5e.**

Audiotape: Abridged chapter (Text minus profile, boxes, and end-of-chapter material.

Associated Web Sites

These sites are provided to students for the purpose of analysis and critical thinking of the issues. Students are encouraged to explore other sites. As with any Web site, some may be inactive now.

U.S. Department of Commerce - International Trade Administration

http://www.ita.doc.gov/

Balance of Payment - Trends:

http://www.clev.frb.org/research/jul96et/curact.htm

Balance of Trade:

http://206.31.84.75/drlinn/trade.htm

Common Markets:

Trade with the U.S.:

http://www.ita.doc.gov/media/emerge.htm

Embargos:

Keep the arms embargo on Cuba:

http://www.heritage.org/heritage/library/categories/forpol/cbrief14.html

Lifting embargo against Vietman:

http://www.serve.net/vietnam/pages/viet1205.htm

Import and Export:

Latin America (look for business and commerce for each country):

http://www.latin-america.com/

Connecting buyer and seller (International trading floor):

http//trading.wmw.com/

World Trade Organization:

http://www.ustr.gove/reports/tpa/1996/wto_8.html

GATT:

GATT and democracy:

http://tdg.uoguelph.ca/polstudies/readings/gattndemo.html

GATT's affect on the U.S. economy:

http://dc.smu.edu/Rhetoric/hzrubek.essay.html

NAFTA:

http://www.naftaconnect.com/

Tariffs:

Food tariffs:

http://www.spb.su/suppress/114/newtarif.html

Free Trade and Protectionism:

Heritage Foundation's perspective (liberal):

http://www.heritage.org/heritage/commentary/op-bj2.html

Phyllis Schlafly's perspective (conservative):

http://www.ups.edu/polgov/oneil/class/schlafly.htm

Understanding Business **Home Page**

http:/www.mhhe.com/ub5e.

What's New in This Edition

Additions

- A profile of Dary Rees, global entrepreneur
- Export Assistance Centers (EACs) to the subsection "Exporting."
- The new role of the World Trade Organization in mediating trade disputes in the subsection "General Agreement on Tariffs and Trade (GATT)."
- "Euro," the new European Monetary Union currency to the subsection "Common Markets"
- Taking It to the Net exercises.
- Video case to complement "Coca Cola in Russia."
- Reaching Beyond Our Borders: Looking for a Kick from the Global Market.
- From the Pages of Business Week Magazine: Merger Mania Rocks the Continent
- Spotlight on Small Business
- Figure 3-2 The Major Trading Economies of the World
- Figure 3-4 Oops, Did We Say That?

Revisions

- Statistical data and examples throughout the chapter were updated to reflect current information. In addition:
- The subsection "Countertrading" contains a more detailed discussion of the differences between bartering and countertrading.
- The subsection "North American Trade Agreement NAFTA" contains a revised discussion of the effects of NAFTA since 1994.
- The section "The Future of Global Trade" contains a new discussion of the future of trade with Asia particularly with the People's Republic of China.
- The Practicing Management Decisions case was revised and retitled "Protecting or Risking Your Future?"
- Legal Briefcase box was condensed.

Deletions

- Profile of Virginia Kamsky
- Video case "Learning to Do Business Globally"
- Reaching Beyond Our Borders: Where's the Beef? Not in India!
- Spotlight On Small Business: A Place to Call Home
- From the Pages of Entrepreneur Magazine: Funding Global Ventures
- Figure Market Share of Foreign Companies in Five Major Countries

Brief Chapter Outline/Learning Goals

CHAPTER 3

COMPETING IN GLOBAL MARKETS

PROFILE: Dary Rees, Global Entrepreneur

I. THE DYNAMIC GLOBAL MARKET.

LEARNING GOAL 1. Discuss the increasing importance of the global market and the roles of comparative advantage and absolute advantage in international trade.

II. WHY TRADE WITH OTHER NATIONS?

LEARNING GOAL 2. Explain how the marketing motto "Find a need and fill it" applies to global markets and understand key terms used in international business.

A. The Theories of Comparative and Absolute Advantage.

III. GETTING INVOLVED IN GLOBAL TRADE.

LEARNING GOAL 3. Describe the current status of the United States in global business.

A. Importing Goods and Services.

B. Exporting Goods and Services.

C. Measuring Global Trade.

IV. TRADING IN GLOBAL MARKETS: THE U.S. EXPERIENCE.

V. STRATEGIES FOR REACHING GLOBAL MARKETS.

LEARNING GOAL 4. Illustrate the strategies used in reaching global markets.

A. Exporting.

B. Licensing.

C. Creating Subsidiaries.

D. Contract Manufacturing.

E. Franchising.

F. International Joint Ventures.

G. Countertrading.

VI. HURDLES OF TRADING IN GLOBAL MARKETS.

LEARNING GOAL 5. Evaluate the hurdles of trading in world markets.

A. Cultural Differences.

B. Societal and Economic Differences.

C. Legal and Regulatory Differences.

D. Problems With Currency Shifts.

VII. TRADE PROTECTIONISM.

LEARNING GOAL 6. Debate the advantages and disadvantages of trade protectionism.

A. General Agreement on Tariffs and Trade (GATT).

B. Common Markets.

C. The North American Free Trade Agreement (NAFTA).

VIII. MULTINATIONAL CORPORATIONS.

LEARNING GOAL 7. Explain the role of multinational corporations in global markets.

IX. THE FUTURE OF GLOBAL TRADE.

A. Globalization and You.

X. SUMMARY AND REVIEW.

(Learning Objectives are also referenced in the expanded lecture outline later in this chapter)

Key Terms

absolute advantage *(text page 75)*
balance of payments *(text page 77)*
balance of trade *(text page 77)*
bartering *(text page 82)*
common market *(text page 90)*
comparative advantage theory *(text page 74)*
contract manufacturing *(text page 81)*
countertrading *(text page 82)*
debtor nation *(text page 79)*
devaluation *(text page 87)*
dumping *(text page 78)*
embargo *(text page 89)*
exchange rate *(text page 86)*
Export Assistance Centers (EACs) *(text page 80)*
export trading companies *(text page 80)*
exporting *(text page 74)*
floating exchange rate *(text page 87)*
Foreign Corrupt Practices Act of 1978 *(text page 85)*
foreign direct investment *(text page 79)*
foreign subsidiary *(text page 81)*
free trade *(text page 74)*
free-trade area *(text page 92)*
General Agreement on Tariffs and Trade (GATT) *(text page 90)*
global marketing *(text page 84)*
import quota *(text page 89)*
importing *(text page 74)*
International Organization for Standardization (ISO) *(text page 89)*
joint venture *(text page 82)*
licensing *(text page 80)*
mercantilism *(text page 89)*
multinational corporation (MNC) *(text page 92)*
protective tariff *(text page 89)*
revenue tariff *(text page 89)*
trade deficit *(text page 77)*
trade protectionism *(text page 88)*
World Trade Organization *(text page 90)*

Lecture Outline

The **PROFILE** at the beginning of this chapter focuses on **DARY REES, a GLOBAL ENTREPRENEUR.** Dary represents a growing number of successful U.S. businesspersons that have identified the opportunities that exist in global markets.

I. THE DYNAMIC GLOBAL MARKET.

▶ **LEARNING GOAL 1.** Discuss the increasing importance of the global market and the roles of comparative advantage and absolute advantage in international trade.

A. A few statistics can help illustrate the **IMPORTANCE OF INTERNATIONAL MARKETS:**

1. Whereas there are 260 million people in the U.S., **THERE ARE 6 BILLION POTENTIAL CUSTOMERS IN THE WORLD.**

2. Of these, approximately 75% live in developing areas.

3. The **U.S. IS THE LARGEST IMPORTER** in the world. It is often the world's largest exporter as well.

   a. **IMPORTING** is buying products from another country.

   b. **EXPORTING** is selling products to another country.

4. **COMPETITION IS INTENSE**—The U.S. must compete against aggressive exporters.

Lecture Notes

TRANSPARENCY MASTER 22
Chapter Outline

Transparency Masters begin on page 3.76.

OT ACETATE 3-1
Growing World Population

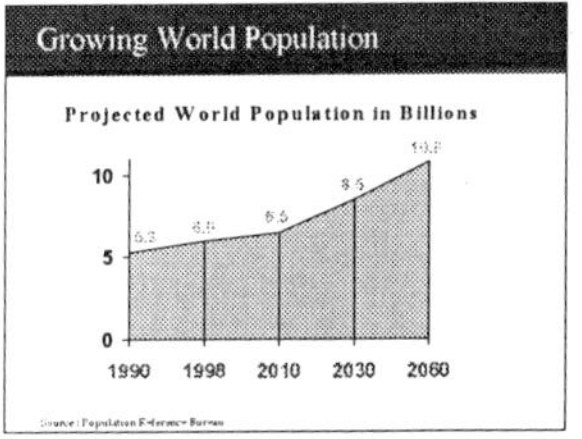

Comments:

1. World population reached 6 billion in 1998. In approximately 40 years another 3 billion people will be added to the total. An interesting point to note to students is that, when today's newborn children reach age 70, there will be almost 11 billion people in the world.
2. What makes this information more striking is the population of the U.S. is approximately 262 million. In other words, the U.S. is only 5 percent of the world population. Also, you may want to note that much of the growth in world population is occurring in less-developed countries. Another interesting piece of information students might enjoy, one out of every five persons in the world now lives in one country, China.
3. You might want to ask students what opportunities and problems will be created by this incredible growth.

B. The purpose of this chapter is to discuss the **POTENTIAL AND PROBLEMS OF INTERNATIONAL BUSINESS.**

II. WHY TRADE WITH OTHER NATIONS?

▶ **LEARNING GOAL 2.** Explain how the marketing motto "Find a need and fill it" applies to global markets and define the terms used in international business.

A. Reasons for trading with other nations include:

1. **NO NATION CAN PRODUCE ALL THE PRODUCTS IT NEEDS.**
2. **NATIONS DEMAND TRADE WITH COUNTRIES TO MEET THE NEEDS OF THEIR PEOPLE.**
3. **TRADE RELATIONS ENABLE COUNTRIES TO PRODUCE WHAT THEY CAN AND BUY THE REST IN A MUTUALLY BENEFICIAL EXCHANGE.**

B. **FREE TRADE** is the movement of goods and services among nations without political or economic obstruction.

C. **THE THEORIES OF COMPARATIVE AND ABSOLUTE ADVANTAGE.**

1. **COMPARATIVE ADVANTAGE THEORY** states that a country should produce and sell to other countries those products that it produces most efficiently and should buy

Lecture Notes

LECTURE ENHANCER 3-1
Is Free Trade Still the Answer?

For the past 50 years, the U.S. has been committed to free trade. Now, shifts in global commerce have eroded that commitment. (See complete lecture enhancer on page 3.51.)

LECTURE ENHANCER 3-2
Arguments for and Against Free Trade

There are many arguments that can be presented on behalf of free trade and on behalf of protectionism. Arguments on both sides are presented. (See complete lecture enhancer on page 3.52.)

OT ACETATE 3-2
Largest Global Companies in the World by Industry

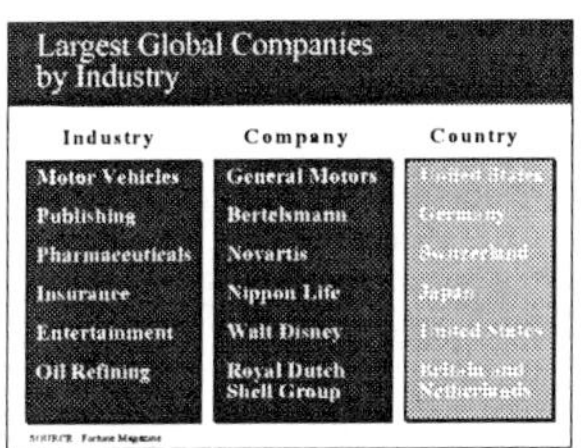

Comments:

1. This is a challenging acetate that tests students knowledge of global markets. It's probably best to uncover the industries identified in the acetate if you choose. See if the students are able to get any of the answers beyond perhaps the first one, General Motors.
2. For additional information concerning leading companies in other world industries, contact the U.S. Commerce Department, the World Bank, or call or e-mail one of the authors. We will get you the information as fast as we can.

TRANSPARENCY MASTER 23
Successful
U.S. Exporters
(Figure 3.1 on text page 75)

TM 23

Transparency Masters begin on page 3.76.

from other countries those products it cannot produce as effectively or efficiently.

2. **ABSOLUTE ADVANTAGE** exists when a country has a monopoly on producing a product or is able to produce it at a cost below that of all other countries.

III. GETTING INVOLVED IN GLOBAL TRADE.

▶ **LEARNING GOAL 3.** Describe the current status of the United States in global business.

A. The real potential in global markets may be with **SMALL BUSINESSES**, which generate about half of the private sector commerce, but account for only 20% of exports.

B. Getting started in global trade is often a matter of observation, determination, and risk.

C. **IMPORTING GOODS AND SERVICES.**

1. Foreign students attending U.S. schools often notice some products widely available in their countries are not available here.
2. Importing these goods into the U.S. can be quite profitable.

D. **EXPORTING GOODS AND SERVICES.**

1. **EXPORTING** is selling products to another country.

Lecture Notes

Lecture Outline

2. **WHAT CAN YOU SELL TO OTHER COUNTRIES?**
   a. Just about anything of quality you can sell in the United States.
   b. The text offers the example of sand sold to Saudi Arabia for swimming pool filters.
3. Selling in global markets involves many hurdles.
4. The text supplies several sources for information about exporting including a government pamphlet, a trade magazine, and the SBA.

E. **MEASURING GLOBAL TRADE.**

1. **BALANCE OF TRADE** is the relationship of exports to imports.
2. **TRADE DEFICIT** is buying more goods from other nations than are sold to them.
3. **BALANCE OF PAYMENTS** is the difference between money coming into a country (from exports) and money leaving the country (for imports plus money flows from other factors such as tourism, foreign aid, and military expenditures.)
   a. **A FAVORABLE BALANCE OF PAYMENTS** means more money is flowing into than flowing out of the country.

Lecture Notes

REACHING BEYOND OUR BORDERS
(Box in text, page 77)
"Looking for a Kick From the Global Market"

Nike is the number one athletic shoe seller in the U.S. Its products made by foreign contractors are sold in over 100 foreign countries. The objective of the company is to compete with Coca-Cola and McDonald's to become the best-known brand on the planet.

OT ACETATE 3-3
Comparing India, China, and the U.S.

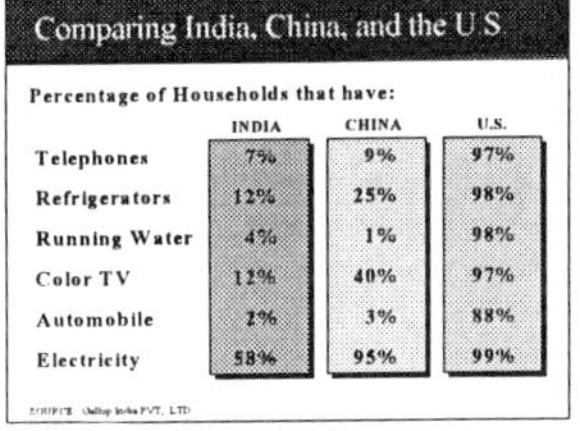

Comparing India, China, and the U.S

Percentage of Households that have:

	INDIA	CHINA	U.S.
Telephones	7%	9%	97%
Refrigerators	12%	25%	98%
Running Water	4%	1%	98%
Color TV	12%	40%	97%
Automobile	2%	3%	88%
Electricity	58%	95%	99%

Comments:

1. This acetate helps to point out the wide discrepancies that exist in the global market. Students will most likely be surprised to see that what we consider simple necessities of life are often luxuries in other countries.
2. Another interesting issue that can be raised from this acetate is the potential that global markets offer. China and India have almost one-third of the world's population in the world. With such opportunities, it's easy to see why so many American companies have flocked into China and have their sights set on India.
3. It might be fun to give the students a brief pretest before disclosing the information on the acetate. They may be surprised when you provide the actual data from the acetate.

b. Likewise, an **UNFAVORABLE BALANCE OF PAYMENTS** means more is leaving than coming into the country.

4. **DUMPING** is the practice of selling products for less in a foreign country than is charged in the producing country.

   a. The U.S. has laws against dumping by foreign firms.

   b. Dumping can take time to prove as some governments subsidize certain industries to sell goods in global markets for less.

IV. TRADING IN GLOBAL MARKETS: THE U.S. EXPERIENCE.

A. Even though 95% of the world's population lives outside of the U.S., **AMERICA HAS NEVER BEEN VERY GOOD AT EXPORTING**.

1. In the early 1980s, no more than 10% of American businesses exported products.

2. Now a majority of large businesses are involved in global trade and growing numbers of small businesses are going global.

B. Although the **UNITED STATES IS THE WORLD'S LARGEST EXPORTER**, it does not export a significant percentage of its gross domestic product (GDP).

Lecture Notes

OT ACETATE 3-4
Nations That Have Not Converted to the Metric System

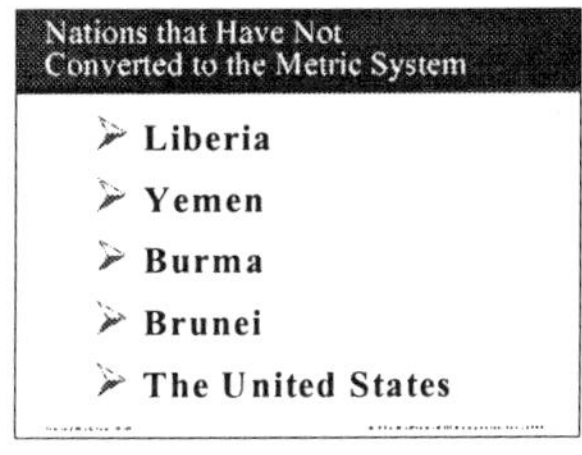

Comments:

1. Students most likely will be rightfully shocked by the information on this acetate. It's a bit of a national embarrassment that the U.S. is one of the few countries in the world that has not converted to the metric system.
2. A very logical, yet pointed, question for students is "why?" Many argue it's simple resistance to change that has kept the U.S. as a non-metric nation. With the size of the U.S. market, it's also easy to see why other nations have agreed to accommodate our resistance.
3. You can assign students the task of finding evidence of the metric system at work in the U.S. economy. If some students have foreign cars, they are probably aware of the differences in tools that must be used. Also, students are keenly aware of two liter bottles of their favorite soft drinks. See how far the list can go.

PROGRESS CHECK
(page 78 in text)

- ➤ Can you explain why statistics (world population, size of market, etc.) support the expansion of U.S. businesses into global markets?
- ➤ Evaluate the concept of comparative advantage and state some examples of this concept in actual global markets.
- ➤ How do you determine the difference between a nation's balance of trade and balance of payments?

TRANSPARENCY MASTER 24
The Major Trading Economies of the World
(Figure 3.2 on text page 79)

Transparency Masters begin on page 3.76.

LECTURE ENHANCER 3-3
International Relations Gunboat Style

International debt crises have lately been handled through a combination of diplomacy and negotiation, rather than by force. But such modern methods are in sharp contrast to the actions of bankers and presidents in the early part of this century. (See complete lecture enhancer on page 3.54.)

Lecture Outline

1. The U.S. buys more goods from other nations that it sells to other nations—called a **TRADE DEFICIT** or **UNFAVORABLE BALANCE OF TRADE.**

C. During the 1980s, it was widely reported that the United States had become a **DEBTOR NATION**, that is, a country that owes more money to other nations than they owe it.

1. This is not necessarily a bad sign when foreign businesses invest here.

2. There is a trend emerging toward more foreign direct investment in the U.S.

D. **FOREIGN DIRECT INVESTMENT** is the buying of permanent property and businesses in foreign nations. Some view foreign purchase of American assets as **"SELLING OF AMERICA."**

E. Others view foreign investment in the U.S. as a **SIGN OF STRENGTH.**

F. Is this confusing? You bet! That's why students interested in international business should take courses in international economics.

V. STRATEGIES FOR REACHING GLOBAL MARKETS.

▶ **LEARNING GOAL 4.** Illustrate the strategies used in reaching global markets.

Lecture Notes

TRANSPARENCY MASTER 25
Countries with the Highest Foreign Direct Investment in the United States
(Figure 3.3 on text page 79)

TM 25

Transparency Masters begin on page 3.76.

SUPPLEMENTAL CASE 3-1
Entering the Import/Export Business

See complete case on page 3.70.

CRITICAL THINKING
(page 80 in text)

You have read that some 95 percent of the world's population lives outside the United States, but still many U.S. companies do not engage in world trade. Why is that? What do such figures indicate about the future potential for increasing U.S. exports? What do they say about future careers international business?

OT ACETATE 3-5
Checklist for Exporters

A Checklist for Potential Exporters

- Analyze your companies' capabilities.
- Clearly define the export potential of your product.
- Identify foreign markets that would be best for your company.
- Use all available government assistance.
- Study entry strategies and export procedures.

Comments:

1. An effective checklist to use in building student awareness of what goes into an export venture.
2. Students interested in global business should be keenly interested in this information. Stay tuned to the UB5E web page for updates related to exporting and global trade. If you have information you believe we can use, we would love to hear from you.

Lecture Outline

A. **EXPORTING.**

1. **EXPORT ASSISTANCE CENTERS (EAC's)** were created to provide hands-on exporting assistance and trade-finance support for small and medium-sized businesses.

2. **EXPORT TRADING COMPANIES** serve the role of matching buyers and sellers from different countries.

3. An export trading company is a good place to get career training in international trade.

B. **LICENSING.**

1. **LICENSING** involves granting to a foreign company the right to manufacture its product or use its trademark on a fee basis.

2. The **ADVANTAGES** of licensing are:

   a. A company can gain **ADDITIONAL REVENUES** from a product it would not have normally produced domestically.

   b. A company can gain **ADDITIONAL REVENUES** from the Sale of startup supplies, component materials, and consulting services from the licensing firm.

   c. **LICENSOR SPENDS LITTLE OR NO MONEY** to produce and market the product.

LECTURE ENHANCER 3-4
Harley Davidson Cigarettes

Japan's motorcycle fans can now smoke what they ride: Harley-Davidson cigarettes. (See complete lecture enhancer on page 3.55.)

LECTURE ENHANCER 3-5
Drug Dealing, Swiss Style

Drug pioneer Elmer H. Bobst describes two run-ins with the Swiss managers of Hoffman-La Roche when he discovered the company's legitimate pharmaceuticals were ending up as illegal street drugs. (See complete lecture enhancer on page 3.56.)

Lecture Outline

3. The **DISADVANTAGES** of licensing are:
   a. Often a firm must **GRANT LICENSING RIGHTS** to its product for an extended period.
   b. If a product experiences remarkable growth in the foreign market, the **BULK OF THE REVENUES GO TO THE LICENSEE.**
   c. If the foreign licensor learns the technology, it may **BREAK THE AGREEMENT AND BEGIN TO PRODUCE A SIMILAR PRODUCT ON ITS OWN**. The licensing firm loses its trade secrets, plus the royalties.

C. **CREATING SUBSIDIARIES.**

1. A **FOREIGN SUBSIDIARY** is a company owned by another company (parent company) in a foreign country.
2. **THE LEGAL REQUIREMENTS OF BOTH THE HOME AND THE HOST COUNTRY MUST BE OBSERVED.**
3. The **ADVANTAGES** of foreign subsidiaries include that the **COMPANY MAINTAINS COMPLETE CONTROL** over any technology or expertise it may possess.

Lecture Notes

LECTURE ENHANCER 3-6
The Growth in Pet Food Exports

Pet owners around the world are buying more prepared pet food, and much of it comes from the United States. (See complete lecture enhancer on page 3.57.)

OT ACETATE 3-6
Proposed Global Labor Standards

Proposed Global Labor Standards

- Do not use child or forced labor.
- Provide a safe working environment.
- Respect workers' right to unionize.
- Do not regularly require more than 48-hour work weeks.
- Pay fair wages to meet workers' basic needs.

Comments:

1. The question of global labor standards should pique student's interest and attention. Many are aware of the problems companies such as Nike have faced. Kathy Lee Gifford's problems should also come to mind. The standards proposed in this acetate were devised by a group of companies and human rights organizations.
2. The issue that seems to generate the most intense response from developed nations is the use of child labor. It's perhaps useful to note that U.S. law strictly prohibits abuses in terms of child labor. A good question for students is did the U.S. always have such prohibition of child labor? Remind students of publications such as Upton Sinclair's novel, *The Jungle.*
3. Another interesting question that students might enjoy dealing with, is the question of paying wages sufficient to meet workers' basic needs. It will be interesting to see what they consider "fair" wages.

4. The major **DISADVANTAGE** is: The firm's **ASSETS COULD BE TAKEN OVER BY THE FOREIGN GOVERNMENT** if relations with the host country fail.

D. **CONTRACT MANUFACTURING.**

1. **CONTRACT MANUFACTURING**, also referred to as **OUTSOURCING**, involves the production of private-label goods by a foreign company to which a company then attaches its brand name or trademark.

2. Through contract manufacturing a company can often experiment in a new market without heavy start-up costs.

E. **FRANCHISING.**

1. Franchising is popular both domestically and in global markets.

2. **FRANCHISERS MUST ADAPT IN THE COUNTRIES THEY SERVE.**

3. Domino's Pizza found that Germans like small individual pies and Japanese enjoyed squid and sweet mayonaisse pizza.

F. **INTERNATIONAL JOINT VENTURES.**

1. A **JOINT VENTURE** is a partnership in which companies (often from different countries) join to undertake a major project.

LECTURE ENHANCER 3-7 Beijing Big Mac	Beijing is evicting McDonalds. (See complete lecture enhancer on page 3.58.)

Lecture Outline

2. The text offers the example of the 35-year joint venture between Xerox Corporation and Fuji Photo Film Co.

3. The **ADVANTAGES** of joint venture include:

   a. **SHARED TECHNOLOGY,**

   b. **SHARED MARKETING EXPERTISE,**

   c. **ENTRY INTO MARKETS WHERE FOREIGN GOODS ARE NOT ALLOWED UNLESS PRODUCED LOCALLY,** and

   d. **SHARED RISK.**

4. The **DISADVANTAGES** are:

   a. One partner can learn the technology and practices of the other and **LEAVE TO BECOME A COMPETITOR;**

   b. The **TECHNOLOGY** may become **OBSOLETE**; and

   c. the partnership may be **TOO LARGE TO BE AS FLEXIBLE** as needed.

G. **COUNTERTRADING.**

1. **BARTERING** is the exchange of merchandise for merchandise or service for service with no money involved.

2. **COUNTERTRADING** is more complex in that several countries may be involved.

LECTURE ENHANCER 3-8
Differences in Culture

One of the hottest topics in international business today is the effect of culture on business behavior. (See complete lecture enhancer on page 3.59.)

OT ACETATE 3-7
U.S. Foreign Direct Investments

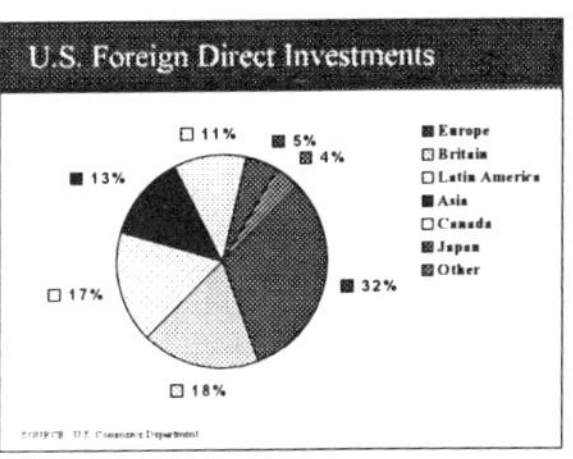

Comments:

1. The acetate will support material in the textbook dealing with foreign direct investment in the United States. Students often ask where the U.S. has the majority of its foreign investment after looking at the figure in the text.
2. Ask students if they feel the comment in the text regarding foreign direct investment is accurate. The text notes that the U.S. has attracted such large amounts of foreign direct investment because other nations see the U.S. as having great potential for growth.
3. Students may pick up on the fact that we have very limited amounts of foreign direct investment in developing or less-developed countries. You might quiz students why that is the case if such great global opportunities exist in these areas.

3. Approximately 25% of the international exchanges involve countertrading.
4. The text uses the example of Chrysler trading vehicles in Jamaica for bauxite.
5. Barter is especially important to **POOR COUNTRIES** that have little cash for trade.

VI. HURDLES OF TRADING IN GLOBAL MARKETS.

▶ **LEARNING GOAL 5.** Evaluate the hurdles of trading in world markets.

A. **CULTURAL DIFFERENCES.**

1. American businesspeople are notoriously bad at adapting to cultural differences among nations.
2. American businesspeople have been accused of **ETHNOCENTRICITY**, feeling that our culture is superior to all others and our job is to teach others the American way.
   a. **RELIGION** is an important part of any society's culture and can have a significant impact on business operations.
   b. **CULTURAL DIFFERENCES** can also have an impact on business functions such as human resource management.
   c. Learning about cultural perspectives about time, change, competition, natural

Lecture Notes

LECTURE ENHANCER 3-9
Ground Breaking and The Smiling Pig

In their search for global markets and low cost production sites, American companies have come face to face with some interesting local ground breaking customs. (See complete lecture enhancer on page 3.60.)

OT ACETATE 3-8
Cultural Differences in Global Markets

Cultural Differences in Global Markets

- Language
- Religion
- Values & Attitudes
- Aesthetics
- Materialism

Comments:

1. This acetate highlights information concerning one of the most important variables in international business.
2. It's helpful to go over each of the elements of culture one-by-one and offer insight into the important aspects of each factor:
   - **Language** can refer to specifics such as spoken language, written language, official languages, etc. Even unspoken language (body language) can have a significant effect on the success of foreign business operations. Often if two different languages are spoken in a country, two totally different cultures exist. Canada and Belgium are good examples of this. Switzerland actually has four different languages that perpetuate four different cultures.
   - **Religion** influences many of the attitudes and beliefs that affect human behavior in a culture. In the U.S., the Protestant Ethic has dominated economic development. Religions such as Islam have tremendous impact on policy making and attitudes in other cultures. For example, American businesspeople often have difficulty understanding Middle East businesspeople's attitudes toward such factors as time.
   - **Values and attitudes** of a society are reflected in its culture. Attitudes toward deadlines, achievement, work itself, and change are clearly the result of cultural values and attitudes.
   - **Aesthetics** relate to a culture's sense of beauty and refinement as reflected in a society's arts, drama, music, folklore, and dances. Attitudes toward natural resources and the treatment of national resources are closely related to aesthetic attitudes. For example, the Nile River in Egypt is looked upon not only as a natural resource, but a gift from the heavens. To throw a cigarette butt in the Nile would be considered a punishable offense.
   - **Materialism** is also an important factor to be evaluated. Islamic cultures prohibit usury (charging interest on borrowed money), and value spiritual success much more earnestly than material success or wealth. Material culture refers to who makes what and why. Cultures will vary in attitude and application.

Lecture Outline

resources, achievement, and even work itself can be of great assistance.

3. Cultural differences affect not only management behaviors but **INTERNATIONAL MARKETING STRATEGIES** as well.
   a. **GLOBAL MARKETING** is used to describe selling the same product in essentially the same way everywhere in the world.
   b. **BRAND NAMES** such as Coca-Cola, Disney, and IBM have widespread global appeal and recognition.
   c. However, translating a theme into a different language can be disastrous (the text gives the examples of "Body by Fisher" becoming "Corpse by Fisher" and "Nova" becoming "it doesn't go.")

B. **SOCIETAL AND ECONOMIC DIFFERENCES.**

1. A sound global philosophy is "never assume what works in one country will work in another."
2. Certain **TECHNOLOGICAL DIFFERENCES** affect the nature of exportable products (examples in the text include 110 volts versus 220 volts and use of the metric system.)

C. **LEGAL AND REGULATORY DIFFERENCES.**

OT ACETATE 3-9
Did You Know?

Did You Know?

- In Turkey it's rude to cross your arms while you are facing someone.
- In the Arab world, the left hand is considered unclean; don't eat with it.
- In Greece, "Yes" is indicated by tilting your head to either side.
- In India, never pat someone's head: It's the seat of the soul.
- The Chinese associate gifts such as straw sandals, clocks and handkerchiefs with funerals.

Comments:

1. Another straightforward acetate that offers students some simple facts about global markets and some of the cultural and social differences that exist in such areas.
2. It's useful to go over each specific point individually and ask students whether its important for U.S. business men and women to be aware of such cultural and social quid nuncs. A couple of other interesting points you may want to bring up include:
3. French-Canadian homes are divided into public and private rooms. The kitchen is often such a private room. Only enter if invited.
4. In Switzerland it's considered quite rude to ever talk with your hands in your pockets.
5. In Thailand never point your foot at someone; it's considered very rude.
6. It might be interesting to see if students in your class have other examples to add to the discussion. Other students are usually particularly interested in hearing from their classmates.

SUPPLEMENTAL CASE 3-2
Differences in Management Methods

See complete case on page 3.73.

From the Pages of BusinessWeek
(Box in Text, page 86)
"Merger Mania Rocks the Continent"

This time it's Europe where mergermania is just beginning.

OT ACETATE 3-10
Favorite Campbell Soups

Favorite Campbell Soups Around the World

- Britain — Tomato soup
- Japan — Corn soup
- South America — Cream of Asparagus soup
- Australia — Cream of Pumpkin soup
- Hong Kong — Watercress & Duck Gizzard
- United States — Chicken Noodle, Cream of Mushroom soups

Comments:

1. Students should enjoy and learn from this acetate as they explore soup preferences around the globe. Again, cultural differences form the primary focus of the acetate.
2. You might want to point out to students that Campbell also uses such diversification in the U.S. according to geographic or cultural tastes. For example, soups in the southwest are often spicier than similar brands of the same soup on the east coast.
3. Additional information you may want to add include KFC's problem in dealing with markets such as Singapore where eating with your fingers is considered unclean. As you can guess, "finger lickin' good," didn't work very well.

Lecture Outline

1. In global markets, several groups of laws and regulations may apply.
2. Businesspeople find global markets governed by a myriad of **LAWS AND REGULATIONS** that are often **INCONSISTENT**.
3. American businesspeople are bound to follow U.S. laws and regulations. The **FOREIGN CORRUPT PRACTICES ACT OF 1978** prohibits "questionable" or "dubious" payments to foreign officials to secure business contracts.

D. **PROBLEMS WITH CURRENCY SHIFTS.**

1. The global market does **NOT HAVE A UNIVERSAL CURRENCY**. Currencies **FLUCTUATE** in value daily.
2. Understanding currency fluctuations and financing opportunities is vital to success in the global market.
   a. The **EXCHANGE RATE** is the value of one currency relative to the currencies of other countries.
   b. Global markets operate under a system of **FLOATING EXCHANGE RATES** in which currencies "float" according to supply and demand in the currency market.

Lecture Notes

LECTURE ENHANCER 3-10
Japan and Music Copyrights

"All You Need Is Love" blasts out of the speakers at a tiny stall in a bustling Tokyo subway station. And all you need is 490 yen—$4.60—to buy a CD of that and other old Beatles tunes. (See complete lecture enhancer on page 3.61.)

MAKING ETHICAL DECISIONS
(Box in text, page 87)

"Deciding the Fate of Nightie Nite Nightgowns"

A manager of Nightie Nite, maker of children's sleepwear, must decide whether to export a questionable product.

CRITICAL THINKING EXERCISE 3-1
Currency Shifts

See complete exercise on page 3.64.

Lecture Outline

c. **DEVALUATION** is lowering the value of a nation's currency relative to other currencies.

3. Changes in currencies causes other problems—labor costs can vary considerably as currency values shift.

4. Understanding currency fluctuations and financing opportunities is vital to success in the global market.

VII. TRADE PROTECTIONISM.

▶ **LEARNING GOAL 6.** Debate the advantages and disadvantages of trade protectionism.

A. **TRADE PROTECTIONISM** is the use of government regulations to limit the import of goods and services.

1. Countries often use trade protectionism measures to protect their industries against dumping and foreign competition.

2. Another barrier to international trade is the overall political atmosphere between nations.

B. For centuries businesspeople advocated an economic principle called **MERCANTILISM.**

1. **MERCANTILISM** is selling more goods to other nations than you bought from them; that is, to have a favorable balance of trade.

Lecture Notes

TRANSPARENCY MASTER 26
U.S. Government, Multilateral, and Interregional Sources of Global Financing
(Figure 3.5 on text page 88)

Transparency Masters begin on page 3.76.

CRITICAL THINKING
(page 88 in text)

Many countries in the world are called less developed countries. Why are they less developed? Is it because they lack natural resources? Then how do you explain the success of Japan, which has few natural resources?

CRITICAL THINKING EXERCISE 3-2
Trade Protectionism

See complete exercise on page 3.67.

Lecture Outline

2. Governments charged a tariff on imports, making them more expensive.

C. There are two kinds of **TARIFFS**:

1. **PROTECTIVE TARIFFS** are import taxes designed to raise the price of imported products so that domestic products are more competitive.

2. **REVENUE TARIFFS** are import taxes designed to raise money for the government.

D. There is much debate about the degree of protectionism a government should practice.

1. One form, the **IMPORT QUOTA**, describes limiting the number of products in certain categories that can be imported.

2. **EMBARGO** is a complete ban on the import or export of certain products.

3. Some say that as much as half of all trade is limited by **NONTARIFF BARRIERS** (including requiring imports to go through undermanned, out-of-the-way customs posts and unusual packaging regulations.)

E. **GENERAL AGREEMENT ON TARIFFS AND TRADE (GATT) AND WTO.**

1. In 1948, the **GENERAL AGREEMENT ON TARIFFS AND TRADE (GATT)** was established.

Lecture Notes

OT ACETATE 3-11
Who's Got the Worst Reputation Globally

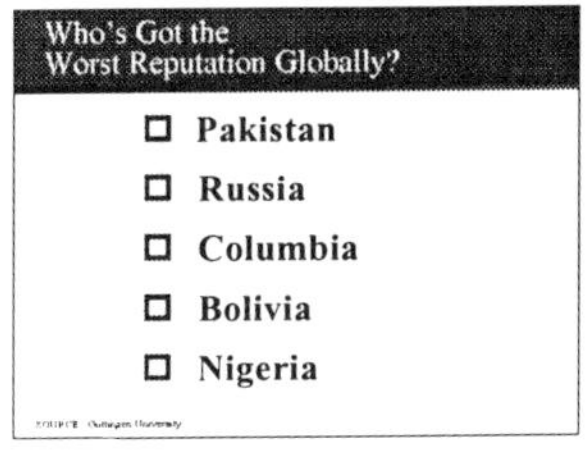

Comments:

1. This acetate looks at the other side of global business. Many countries have unfavorable reputations that deter other nations from trading with them. The top of the unfavorable list is noted here.
2. It's important that students know that such reputations for corruption is what stops economic development in such countries.
3. In case you want to point out to the class, the remaining 5 countries in the top ten in order are:

   Cameroon

   Venezuela

   Russia

   India

   Indonesia
4. The U. S. ranked number 40. New Zealand was considered the least corrupt.

Lecture Outline

2. This agreement among 23 countries provided a forum for negotiating mutual reductions in trade restrictions.
3. The 1986 Uruguay Round of GATT talks were convened to renegotiate trade agreements.
   a. After eight years, 124 nations agreed to a new GATT agreement.
   b. The U.S. House of Representatives and Senate approved the pact in 1994.
4. **THE NEW GATT AGREEMENT:**
   a. **LOWERS TARIFFS** on average by 38% worldwide.
   b. **EXTENDS GATT RULES** to new areas such as agriculture, services and the protection of copyrights and patents.
5. On January 1, 1995 the **WORLD TRADE ORGANIZATION (WTO)** replaced GATT and was assigned the primary task of mediating trade disputes.
6. The GATT agreement did not resolve many of the internal national laws that impede trade expansion.

F. **COMMON MARKETS.**

1. **A COMMON MARKET** is a regional group of countries that have no internal tariffs, a

LEGAL BRIEFCASE
(Box in Text, page 29)
"To Tariff or Not to Tariff. That Is the Question"

Some people feel that tariffs are necessary to protect national markets from foreign competition. Others point to the negative effects such as trade reduction and foreign retaliation. Arguments for both sides are highlighted.

common external tariff, and the coordination of laws to facilitate exchange among countries.

2. The **EUROPEAN UNION (EU)** is a group of nations in Western Europe that dissolved their economic borders in the early 1990s.

3. The path to unification has been slow and difficult, yet significant progress has been made.

4. One advantage for Americans is that English has become Europe's common business language.

5. Some fear that a European protectionist superstate may emerge.

G. The **NORTH AMERICAN FREE TRADE AGREEMENT (NAFTA)**.

1. The **PRIMARY CONCERNS OF NAFTA OPPONENTS REVOLVE AROUND THE ISSUES OF U.S. EMPLOYMENT, EXPORTS, AND THE ENVIRONMENT.**

2. **PROPONENTS PREDICT A VAST NEW MARKET FOR EXPORTS THAT WOULD CREATE JOBS AND OPPORTUNITIES** in the long term.

3. The combination of the United States, Canada, and Mexico created a market of over 370 million people with a gross domestic product of $7.2 trillion.

LECTURE ENHANCER 3-11
Vintage NAFTA

For one venture group, the North American Free Trade Agreement is bearing fruit—fermented fruit. Raise a glass to NAFTA brand wines made from California grapes, carrying a Mexican-made label, and topped with caps and corks processed in Canada. (See complete lecture enhancer on page 3.62.)

Lecture Outline

4. **NAFTA** creates a **FREE TRADE AREA** where nations can trade freely with each other without tariffs or other trade barriers.

5. The emergence of economic blocs like NAFTA has changed the landscape of global trade.

VIII. MULTINATIONAL CORPORATIONS.

▶ **LEARNING GOAL 7.** Discuss the role of multinational corporations in global markets.

A. **A MULTINATIONAL CORPORATION (MNC)** is an organization that does **MANUFACTURING AND MARKETING** in many different countries; it has multinational stock ownership and multinational management.

B. The more multinational a company is, the more it attempts to operate without being influenced by restrictions from various governments.

IX. THE FUTURE OF GLOBAL TRADE.

A. New markets present new opportunities for trade and development, particularly in the emerging nations in Asia.

B. The **FALL OF COMMUNISM** created enormous possibilities for opening new markets.

C. **GLOBALIZATION AND YOU.**

Lecture Notes

PROGRESS CHECK
(page 92 in text)

- ➤ What are the major hurdles to successful global trade?
- ➤ What exactly is meant by ethnocentricity?
- ➤ Identify at least two cultural and societal differences that can affect global trade efforts.
- ➤ What are the advantages and disadvantages of trade protectionism?

OT ACETATE 3-12
Familiar Multinational Companies

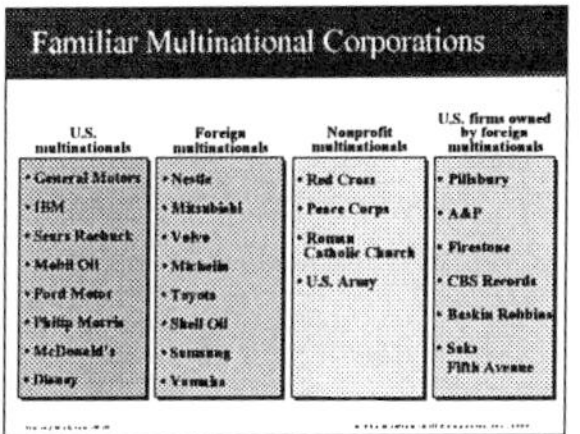

Comments:

1. This acetate identifies multinational corporations students should be able to identify.
2. It might surprise some students to find out that Nestle', Michelin, and Shell are foreign multinationals. The country of origin for the foreign multinationals is:

   Nestle' .... Switzerland
   Mitsubishi .... Japan
   Volvo .... Sweden
   Michelin .... France
   Royal Dutch Shell .. Great Britain/Netherlands
   Toyota .... Japan
   Samsun .... South Korea
   Yamaha .... Japan

3. Students will probably not think of non-profit firms as being multinationals. Nonetheless, the Red Cross is Swiss, the Roman Catholic Church (Italian), and the Peace Corps (USA), in terms of origin. The U.S. Army's classification as a nonprofit multinational will undoubtedly surprise many students.
4. Probably the category that will most intrigue students is the number of American firms that are now owned by foreign multinationals. The Pillsbury Doughboy is now British since the takeover of the Pillsbury Company. Michael Jackson sings for a Japanese company since Sony purchased CBS Records from the Columbia Broadcasting System.

1. Those students who are prepared to manage global operations will have an advantage over other graduates.

2. Students are encouraged to study foreign languages, foreign cultures, and international business.

X. SUMMARY AND REVIEW.

SPOTLIGHT ON SMALL BUSINESS
(Box in Text, page 94)

"Utah: Global Trade Player"

Can you name a state with explosive growth in global trade, lots of foreign-language speaking citizens, and an emerging breed of global entrepreneurs? Would you believe Utah?

OT ACETATE 3-13
What's the Second Most Valuable Language of Business Globally?

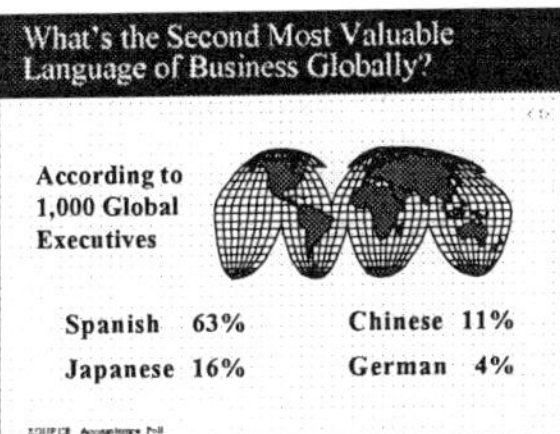

Comments:

1. We expect students will be able to identify English as the dominant language used in business globally. In fact the EU has mandated that English will be the language of the EU much to the chagrin of such members as the French.
2. See if students can name in order the next important languages as identified on the acetate. They are doing better than we were if they are able to do so.
3. This is also a good time, if you choose, to pitch to students the importance of learning a foreign language if they would like to work in global business. There's a tremendous advantage to the businessperson that knows the language of a Japanese or Chinese businessperson. Remember that language is a very important cultural factor.

PROGRESS CHECK
Page 94 in text

- ➤ What is a multinational corporation (MNC)? Can you name at least three multinational corporations?
- ➤ What are the major risks doing business in countries like the People's Republic of China or Russia?
- ➤ What might be some important factors that will have an impact on global trading?

LECTURE ENHANCER 3-12
Web Watch: Big Emerging Markets

There are numerous Web sites for tracking emerging global markets. (See complete lecture enhancer on page 3.63.)

Answers to Practicing Management Decisions

CASE ONE

PROTECTING OR RISKING YOUR FUTURE

1. *Why do you suppose some politicians are pushing for trade protection? What are the economic conditions that would call for protectionism?*

There are political agendas among politicians in Washington. Pat Buchanan and Congressman Gephardt are just two politicians that have pushed trade issues. Congressmen must be re-elected every two years; Senators every six. So no matter what the effect of trade protectionism on America's economy as a whole, politicians are responsible to their constituencies back home. If Oregon's lumber industry or Michigan's automobile industry(and their jobs) are threatened by foreign imports, the congressmen from Oregon and Michigan are going to have a difficult time voting against protection for American jobs.

2. *Is there a lesson to be learned from the early 1930s concerning restrictive legislation on world trade? What forces could cause Congress to reverse itself on this issue?*

The Great Depression is a constant memory in the history of U.S. economics. It is doubtful that any Congress would vote to reinstate a sixty percent import tariff such as was passed under Smoot-Hawley in 1930. That's not to say that trade protectionism could not become popular if the U.S. trade deficit begins to bloat further and the U.S. economy experiences such problems as a severe recession. Economic crises seem to invite radical responses from the government for solution. Another fear of a depression could also trigger renewed calls for trade protectionism.

3. *What should the role of the U.S. government be with regard to world trade? How much effort should be made to protect American workers from foreign competition? When should such efforts take effect?*

Americans can no longer look at itself as a country isolated from global influences. The Asian economic crisis of late 1997 proved that. Global currencies are interrelated, and government actions in other countries inevitably affect the U.S. economy. The U.S. government's role should be one of facilitating world trade and minimizing trade restrictions among America's trading partners. The temptation to protect American jobs is intense, however. The theory of comparative advantage should provide one answer. The U.S. worker is educated, skilled, and imaginative. Jobs that rely on those characteristics will never move to a lower wage economy.

CASE TWO

VIDEO CASE: BREAKING DOWN THE GREAT WALL

1. *Hong Kong's reentry into China should help the Chinese economy make use of the economic theory of comparative advantage. How might China make use of this important global economic theory? Cite some examples.*

Comparative advantage theory states that countries should produce and sell to other countries products that it produces most efficiently and buy from other countries those products it cannot produce as efficiently. China, with its population of 1.2 billion people can certainly make use of comparative advantage theory. On obvious advantage China possesses is labor. Many of you probably note how many textile, toy, and other manufactured goods are now produced in China. It also has many undeveloped natural resources that can be openly traded on the global market once they are extracted and developed.

Unfortunately, China lacks technology and other specialized skills to expand its economy and improve its quality of life. This is where using its comparative advantages (labor, natural resources, market size) should help the Chinese economy grow and prosper. It's also where the inclusion of Hong Kong, long an established trader in global markets, should help in easing China's transition into an emerging economy. Hong Kong's experience in distribution, financing, and trade can move China's development along at a faster than normal pace.

2. *What adjustments will China need to make to conform to the cultural, economic, and social practices of other countries?*

China chose to isolate itself from the outside world for approximately 50 years. This self-imposed isolation is certain to make the transition into the global economy difficult.

Adjusting to cultural, economic, and social practices in other countries will be a formidable challenge. The U.S. as an example has questioned China's policies concerning human-rights violations (child labor, prison labor, etc.) and has even threatened trade sanctions against them. Its also difficult for businesses that have lived under strict central planning and economic controls for many years to ease into free trade policies. Holder of patents and copyrights demand that China live with decisions negotiated under the GATT agreement and now governed by the World Trade Organization (WTO) that protect such intellectual property.

These and other cultural, economic, and social practices are bound to cause some consternation in China as it adjusts to world markets. Again, the assistance of Hong Kong could be invaluable here.

3. *If the Chinese impose stiff trade policies, what might be the reaction of their global trading partners?*

If China imposes strict trade policies such as tariffs, subsidies, import quotas, etc., against other countries, it can probably expect its trade partners to do the same. The principle of free trade is to enhance the quality of life and standard of living of all economies in the global market by using economic applications such as comparative advantage theory. It will be important for China to develop trade policies that help it adapt to practices established by its prospective trade partners.

CASE THREE

VIDEO CASE: SELLING COCA-COLA IN JAPAN

1. *What evidence can you cite showing that foreign firms have been very careful to adapt to U.S. culture when marketing their products here?*

Names like Sony, Mitsubishi, and Volvo are very familiar in the United States. Volvo cars, for example, advertise their safety features to those in the U.S. who desire such things. Every effort if made to adapt the cars to U.S. tastes, including, for example, having the steering wheel on the left, the speed in miles per hour vs. kilometers, and so on. Students should be able to think of their own examples that would be more fun to discuss since they thought of them.

2. *Many U.S. firms have had difficulty establishing relationships in Japan. Do you think that they could learn from Coke's experience and try again? Would a similar approach work for U.S. automakers?*

It is always a good idea to copy those who are successful in any venture and learn from them. Coke took its time to establish relationships in Japan. Every firm could learn from that. Automakers may have a more difficult time because Japanese automakers resist the competition. Nonetheless, patience pays, as does establishing relationships with suppliers and adapting to the culture.

3. *Talk with a local storeowner or manager who sells products from various parts of the world. Ask him or her what foreign manufacturers do to establish and maintain good relationships with that store and its suppliers.*

This is a great exercise for students to learn more about foreign goods and how they are sold in the United States.

Lecture Enhancers

LECTURE ENHANCER 3-1

FREE TRADE STILL THE ANSWER?

For the past 50 years, the U.S. has been the most steadfast preacher of Adam Smith's gospel in global markets. The commitment to free trade has been a cornerstone of the administrations of both Ronald Reagan and George Bush. The fact is though, shifts in global commerce have caused changes in trade policies that involve considerable amounts of governmental meddling. American government is no exception.

According to American University economist Stephen Cohen, if there is enough political pressure on the government, it diverts from its policy of follow the marketplace, to let's cut a deal. A good example of this involves the U.S. automobile industry. Recently the Big 3 U.S. automakers met privately in Chicago with Japan's Big 5 automakers. Officially the purpose of the meeting was to discuss the sale of more U.S. cars in Japan and increased purchase of U.S.-made parts by Japanese producers in the U.S. Most informed analysts would find it hard to believe that the issue of what an appropriate Japanese share of the U.S. auto market would be did not work its way into the discussions. It seems apparent the U.S. and other nations are realizing that free trade in its pure economic state is the path to higher global economic development. However, sometimes free trade principles are too hard to impose on nations due to internal obstacles. That's one reason why the term managed trade seems to be working its way into many nation's global trade policies.

Many argue that managed trade makes common sense and is the only way to address a rapidly changing global environment. Policies such as landing rights at international airports have long been examples of managed trade. For example, if the U.S. had not forced reciprocal rights with competing nations, many government-controlled airlines could have flooded the U.S. market with cut-rate fares and denied access rights to major U.S. carriers. Nonetheless, many trade purists want the U.S. to be the bastion of free trade and raise their voice against what they see as the mounting pressure for more managed trade. The reality may be the U.S. has no choice.

If the U.S. still dominated global commerce, free trade would seem more logical. However, today with governments targeting industries and offering subsides, a flexible, yet managed trade policy may be the only path to compete. After all, the U.S. position on free trade didn't influence European nations to limit their subsides to aircraft manufacturer Airbus Industrie. By the way, Airbus recently overtook McDonnell-Douglas Corp. and became the No. 2 aircraft maker in the world.

LECTURE ENHANCER 3-2

ARGUMENTS FOR AND AGAINST FREE TRADE

There are many arguments that can be presented on behalf of free trade and on behalf of protectionism. Some arguments for free trade have more merit than others. Some arguments for protectionist measures also have merit. The text discussed several of these arguments in the Legal Briefcase "To Tariff or Not to Tariff; That is the Question." Additional arguments include:

FOR FREE TRADE:

1. **The trade, specialization, and efficiency argument.** Free trade permits the markets in which goods and services are bought and sold to operate effectively and efficiently. Free trade permits the full use of comparative advantage and specialization. Free trade enables more goods and services to be produced and distributed, reducing the problem of scarcity.

2. **The economies of scale argument.** Free trade allows more goods to be produced; thus permitting economies of scale. When there are limited or restricted markets, less goods are demanded and the economies of scale are not as great as when free markets exists.

3. **The new products argument.** Competition leads to suppliers and manufacturers seeking to gain a competitive edge. One way to do so is by coming up with new products and services or new distribution methods. Free trade not only promotes more goods at lower prices, but it also encourages more innovation in order to keep up with competitive forces.

4. **The comparative advantage argument.** Absolute advantage is an abstract concept that is hardly ever found to exist in world markets. Most trade occurs because of the comparative advantage theory. When there are restrictions to trade, there are also interferences with the practice of comparative advantage. The heart of comparative advantage is free trade.

FOR PROTECTIONISM:

1. **Diversification argument.** This argument is a variation of "not putting all your eggs in one basket". Most stock market portfolio managers recommend that a person have a variety of issues to prevent against the stock of sudden losses to one of the firms. The same argument can be applied to protectionism. According to this argument, there are risks associated with developing a dependency on foreign countries for goods and services, as we have seen with petroleum, because changes in price and supply can greatly interfere with domestic markets. Protectionists argue that while some specialization is desirable, a nation should keep a well rounded industrial and service base and special steps should be taken to ensure a diversity continues, even in the fact of foreign competition, by special help, as given through protectionist measures.

2. **The equalization of costs and prices argument**. This argument states that protectionist measures, such as tariffs, tend to equalize costs of goods at home and abroad. This argument is the very counter of the comparative advantage theory. Tariffs transfer cost burdens but do not equalize costs. Consumers in the

nation that uses tariffs will pay more for the goods. The costs do not get any lower.

3. **Countering subsidies from foreign countries and dumping practices.** Protectionist measures to counter subsidies of foreign products and dumping can increase the costs of the products to consumers or reduce the price of goods sent abroad. In either case the subsidies must be borne by the consumers and taxpayers.

4. **The "deliver a message" doctrine.** This argument is that by applying restrictions we are notifying foreign countries that we will not buy their goods as long as they use subsidies to support them or place restrictions on our goods. The only message that is really delivered seems to be higher prices for all. Sometimes this argument works, but then the countries practicing the subsidies just send in higher priced items that are still in great demand, such as firms like Honda and Toyota have done with cars. The message is send over the more expensive models and maximize profits on the units sold. The producers gain and the consumers lose.

5. **Restricting imports may lead to lower prices.** While the U.S. got the prices of petroleum and relative products to come down as a result of conservation measures by consumers, there were few direct trade restrictions placed on oil imports. Recommendations by some economists to use revenue tariffs on oil to protect the domestic petroleum industry and build up funds to help displace workers due to trade, have been rejected by the administration. While some large countries like the U.S. may be successful in driving prices down by restricting the demand for goods, what happens when the price falls? Will the tariffs or other restrictions be eliminated? Not very likely. Furthermore, there are liable to be retaliatory efforts.

LECTURE ENHANCER 3-3

INTERNATIONAL RELATIONS GUNBOAT STYLE

International debt crises have lately been handled through a combination of diplomacy and negotiation, rather than by force. In 1995 Mexico's currency crisis sent international financial markets into a frenzy, eased only when President Clinton arranged $20 billion in U.S. support to stabilize the Mexican peso. But such modern methods are in sharp contrast to the actions of bankers and presidents in the early part of this century.

In 1904, when the Dominican Republic threatened to renege on $32 million in loans, President Theodore Roosevelt didn't waste time talking. He dispatched troops, took over the Caribbean nation's customs services, and diverted 55 percent of duties collected to the repayment of debts. "The mere fact that the collectors of customs are Americans gives a certain moral power to the government of Santo Domingo which it hasn't had before," President Roosevelt said. He claimed that the Dominican government "is actually getting more from the 45 percent that the American collectors turn over to it than it got formerly when it took the entire revenue."

And consider what happened to Ismail, the pasha of Egypt. A century ago, he flooded Europe with bonds to finance border skirmishes with Sudan and to remake Cairo as a sort of Paris on the Nile. He also bought a great deal of cotton-growing land. Things went well for a while. But then the price of cotton crashed, and the pasha couldn't make the interest payments on his bonds. The pasha's default provoked a rapid response in European capitals. Britain and France sent a commission to oversee Egypt's economy. But the pasha resisted, so Britain and France took the next logical step—they dispatched troops to storm the pasha's palace. And for the next 30 years, Britain and France diverted a large part of Egypt's tax revenues to the repayment of his bonds.

Elsewhere in the world, European powers were quick to use the prospect of default as an excuse for taking over debtor nations. In 1881, a group of European countries forced Turkey to put its revenues into receivership. They took income from the government's salt and tobacco monopolies, taxes on spirits and fishing, and levies on raw-silk production. They even confiscated an annual tribute due Turkey from Bulgaria. Through their debt commission, the Europeans, in effect, ran Turkey for the next 25 years.

LECTURE ENHANCER 3-4

HARLEY DAVIDSON CIGARETTES

Japan's motorcycle fans can now smoke what they ride: Harley-Davidson cigarettes. Japanese consumers are avid fans of the American motorcycle, paying premium prices along with import tariffs to purchase a Harley. Now Carolina Cigarette is exporting its Harley-Davidson cigarettes to satisfy the Harley urge through PBI International.

The biker cigarettes come in white packages emblazoned with the Harley motif and are licensed by the motorcycle maker. They are popular in Japan, considered an American authentic, with American taste and American spirit. Americans may be somewhat perplexed by the slogan "Have you, Harley." Grammar wasn't a priority PBI International chose the slogan because it used the name, which is very famous in Japan, to its best advantage.

Japan's smokers are sucking up the brand: PBI sells about 10 million cigarettes monthly, and foresees tripling that figure to grab 2 percent of the imported cigarette market.

LECTURE ENHANCER 3-5

DRUG DEALING, SWISS STYLE

Do the drugs made by legitimate pharmaceutical companies—narcotics, for example—sometimes end up in illegal street traffic? In his autobiography Bobst, published by David McKay & Co. in 1973, drug industry pioneer Elmer H. Bobst described two run-ins he had on this question with the Swiss managers of Hoffman-La Roche.

The first came in 1923 when Bobst, then head of U.S. operations for Roche, made his first trip to the company headquarters in Basle. Prior to going he had been informed by the U.S. commissioner of narcotics that Roche had been shipping illegal opiates to Mexico, Canada, and the United States. Bobst, the son of a Lutheran minister, told the Swiss that they must stop these shipments or else the U.S. government would stop all imports from Roche. According to Bobst, Dr. Emil Barell of Roche replied: "Mr. Bobst, you did not know this, but we make $200,000 or more a year on those sales. We get a dollar, sometimes two dollars, more per ounce from those purchasers than through normal channels. Why must it stop? It's perfectly legal for us in Switzerland to fill any orders we receive."

Roche finally agreed to sign a statement saying they would not ship narcotics to illegal purchasers in Mexico, Canada, or the United States after Bobst told them: "If you attempt to carry on this trade that is degrading this company, there will be no Roche in America."

Twenty years later, when Dr. Barell had come to Nutley, New Jersey, to sit out World War II, Bobst was tipped off by Harry Anslinger, the U.S. narcotics commissioner, that Roche had planted acres of poppy plants in Argentina from which they were planning to harvest the straw to produce morphine—all of which was contrary to the rules of the Geneva Convention on narcotics. Upon returning from Washington to Nutley, Bobst said he gave a dressing down to Dr. Barell and his brother-in-law, who also worked for the company, by declaring: "We have a fence around this plant and a guard at the gate. If either of you engage in any action of this sort again, I will instruct the guards to lock you out for good."

Barell, according to Bobst's account, was later hauled before the Alien Property Commission and told that if he didn't stop fooling around with narcotics he would either be thrown out of the country or interned. Barell was head of Hoffmann-La Roche from 1920 to 1953.

LECTURE ENHANCER 3-6

THE GROWTH IN PET FOOD EXPORTS

Pet owners around the world are buying more prepared pet food, and much of it comes from the United States. Statistics from the U.S. Agriculture Department show that pet food is one of the fastest-growing American farm exports, multiplying more than eightfold in the last decade.

The obstacles to growth include new restrictions on making products from animal wastes in Europe, tariffs and other trade restrictions, exports by other countries, and taste preferences of pets and their owners.

Prepared pet food is replacing table scraps in many international markets. The trend reflects growing affluence in Asia and a trend toward pampering pets more in Europe and Canada. Canada, Japan, and the European Union are the largest markets for U.S.-made pet food. About half of all Canadian, Japanese, and British households have pets.

Much of the future growth in pet-food exports could come in markets like Mexico, Taiwan, Hong Kong, and Korea. Imports account for half of the Mexican market, and Koreans are beginning to see dogs as attractive pets rather than tasty ingredients for human dishes.

LECTURE ENHANCER 3-7

BEIJING BIG MAC

Beijing is evicting McDonalds. In 1994, two years into a 20-year lease, the municipal government handed the fast food franchise an eviction notice from its prime location near Tiananmen Square. One of the few Western companies willing to do business with China after the 1989 crackdown on the democracy movement, McDonalds opened its largest restaurant in the world at the corner of Wangfunjing Street and the Avenue of Eternal Peace. Now the city has turned over the real estate to Hong Kong developer Li Ka-shing, who plans a huge office and commercial complex called Oriental Plaza.

The eviction shows how difficult it can be to do business in Beijing. Other U.S. companies are feeling a bit vulnerable of late, thanks to the way Chinese authorities have set up the rules of commerce. "If you want complete legal protection, you shouldn't be investing in China,"says one businessman in Beijing.

McDonalds doesn't have much of a legal case for appealing the eviction. China only passed a law on land-use rights in 1992—after the company negotiated its deal. Under those circumstances, "approval for 20 years is not a contract" and can be revoked at any time. McDonald's probably won't sue. It doesn't want to wreck its plan to add ten Beijing restaurants to the seven it already operates.

LECTURE ENHANCER 3-8

DIFFERENCES IN CULTURE

One of the hottest topics in international business today is the effect of culture on business behavior. Dr. Edward T. Hall, anthropology professor emeritus at Northwestern University, has made a lifelong study of the cultural biases and behavior patterns of other cultures.

Dr. Hall draws a distinction between what he calls monochronic cultures and polychronic cultures. Schedules, punctuality, a sense that time forms a purposeful straight line are all characteristics of monochronic cultures. Americans, Germans, Swiss, and certain other Europeans are among the more monochronic people. In polychronic cultures business and government people are more likely to nurture human relations and to do work simultaneously on several fronts rather than doggedly pursuing a single task.

When an American is kept waiting 45 minutes for a business appointment while his Latin-American host remains with another visitor, the American's perception likely will be that he is being ignored. But, Hall says, the Latin American host most likely is simply operating from his own cultural assumption that it would be unnatural, and perhaps insulting to someone else, if he cut off the conversation he already was having just because the schedule said it was time to talk to someone else. Seasoned American businesspersons in Latin America know they're not being insulted and are willing to wait.

A central distinction among cultures, he believes, is whether or not a culture handles information in a direct, linear fashion. A German seeking detailed information from a Japanese counterpart might feel that the Japanese is refusing to cooperate. In fact, the Japanese might feel that being too direct is offensive and getting down to substantive business might be premature if no personal relationship has yet been established.

LECTURE ENHANCER 3-9

GROUND BREAKING AND THE SMILING PIG

In their search for global markets and low cost production sites, American companies have come face to face with some interesting local ground breaking customs. In Taiwan, at a ground breaking ceremony of a building site, monks and priests chant and perform rituals to appease the earth god and encourage good fortune. Even good old American McDonalds followed this practice when it opened its branches in Taiwan.

In 1991 a kosa ceremony was performed in front of a modern stadium built for the 1988 Olympics. This ceremony is performed in Korea for everything from industrial plant dedications to ground breaking at building sites. In this case a baseball team was inaugurating two large buses to bring good fortune. In front of the buses a makeshift altar held a large smiling pig's head. It must be smiling, everyone agreed. There was also a large drinking vessel and a jug of wine. The owners, shareholders, captains, and other players were all there. One by one they all knelt down, bowed to the pig, drank a little wine, and then poured the rest of it on to the wheels and the front of the buses. It was a very happy occasion.

These rituals may seem like small things, but it is important to respect them and participate as the locals do if your business is to be successful in other countries.

LECTURE ENHANCER 3-10

JAPAN AND MUSIC COPYRIGHTS

"All You Need Is Love" blasts out of the speakers at a tiny stall in a bustling Tokyo subway station. And all you need is 490 yen—$4.60—to buy a CD of that and other old Beatles tunes. Officially licensed Beatles records sell for 3,000 yen—$28—but the ones sold in the subway aren't pirated. They're perfectly legal in Japan, where copyright protection lasts only 25 years. That means anything from before 1971 is fair game.

The Japanese law has come under fire from the United States, which says it is depriving American recording companies of hundreds of millions of dollars in fees. The cheap CDS are made by copying original recordings, bypassing recording companies and artists alike.

In February 1996, the U.S. filed a complaint with the World Trade Organization, demanding that Japan honor copyrights for 50 years. Under a World Trade Organization agreement effective January 1, 1996, developed countries must protect the rights of recording artists for that period.

The U.S. says Japan is bound by that agreement. Tokyo maintains it interpreted new global trade rules to mean Japan wouldn't have to abide by the 50-year protection policy. Former U.S. Trade Representative Mickey Kantor says the lack of protection allows "piracy" of "one of the most vibrant—and popular—periods in the history of American music."

LECTURE ENHANCER 3-11

VINTAGE NAFTA

For one venture group, the North American Free Trade Agreement is bearing fruit—fermented fruit. Raise a glass to NAFTA brand wines made from California grapes, carrying a Mexican-made label, and topped with caps and corks processed in Canada.

The 1993 NAFTA chardonnay and 1993 NAFTA Cabernet Sauvignon are the "first true North American wines" say its producers, The NAFTA Venture Group of Sonoita, Arizona. Wines are sold in 20 states; negotiations are under way to sell them in Canada and Mexico.

"We didn't set out to make a political or sociological statement," says Tom Brady, one of three partners, representing American, Mexican, and Canadian heritages. "It started out a little bit as a gimmick, but it's turned serious."

Kautz Vineyards in the Sierra foothills supplied the grapes, which were fermented at Ironstone Winery in Murphys, California. Labels were designed and printed in Nogales, Mexico, and closures come from British Columbia.

LECTURE ENHANCER 3-12

WEB WATCH: BIG EMERGING MARKETS

If you are interested in searching the Web for info on emerging global markets, start with the Big Emerging Markets home page at **http://www.stat-usa.gov/itabems.html.** Aside from a broad overview, the BEM home page also offers sector- and country-specific information.

If you haven't yet bookmarked it, STAT-USA is a government organization that provides free access to the National Trade Databank (NTDB). The NTDB contains over 100,000 trade-related documents including detailed market research by country and product, comprehensive U.S. export and import statistics broken down by country and product, a complete list of Harmonized System Tariff Numbers and other resources valuable to exporters.

You'll find additional emerging market information in the Trade Compass library at **http://www.tradecompass.com/library/doc/ltbam**. Try also the Emerging Markets Companion available at **http://ps.ucdavis.edu/classes/poll29/SWE/SWE-bems .htm.**

While online, you can also order what has quickly become the Big Emerging Market bible: "The Big Emerging Markets Outlook and Sourcebook," available for $45 at **http:/www.fedworld.gov/ntis/bemsntis.html.**

For high-tech-specific international marketing info and advice, stop by the site of the information Technology Team, a division of the Commerce Department's International Trade Administration at **http://www.ita.doc.gov/infotech.** The site offers trade leads, trade statistics, and country-by-country updates, as well as phone numbers of regionally-located ITA consultants.

Critical Thinking Exercises

Name: ______________________

Date: ______________________

CRITICAL THINKING EXERCISE 3.1

CURRENCY SHIFTS

As the text discusses, one of the hurdles of international trade is the constant shift in exchange rates. Just how much do exchange rates change over a 30-day period? Let's find out by choosing five countries of interest to you and recording the exchange rate for their currency (Austria's schilling, Italy's lira, Japan's yen, Mexico's peso, etc.) for 30 days. The rates are available daily in *The Wall Street Journal* (in the "Currency Markets" chart in the "Money and Investing" section.) The chart shows the amount of foreign currency per dollar. What effect would such currency shifts have on your business trade with each of these countries?

	Country (Currency)	Country (Currency)	Country (Currency)	Country (Currency)	Country (Currency)
	________	________	________	________	________
	________	________	________	________	________
1.	________	________	________	________	________
2.	________	________	________	________	________
3.	________	________	________	________	________
4.	________	________	________	________	________
5.	________	________	________	________	________
6.	________	________	________	________	________
7.	________	________	________	________	________
8.	________	________	________	________	________
9.	________	________	________	________	________
10.	________	________	________	________	________
11.	________	________	________	________	________
12.	________	________	________	________	________

CRITICAL THINKING EXERCISE 3.1 (continued)

	Country (Currency)	Country (Currency)	Country (Currency)	Country (Currency)	Country (Currency)
	__________	__________	__________	__________	__________
	__________	__________	__________	__________	__________
13.	__________	__________	__________	__________	__________
14.	__________	__________	__________	__________	__________
15.	__________	__________	__________	__________	__________
16.	__________	__________	__________	__________	__________
17.	__________	__________	__________	__________	__________
18.	__________	__________	__________	__________	__________
19.	__________	__________	__________	__________	__________
20.	__________	__________	__________	__________	__________
21.	__________	__________	__________	__________	__________
22.	__________	__________	__________	__________	__________
23.	__________	__________	__________	__________	__________
24.	__________	__________	__________	__________	__________
25.	__________	__________	__________	__________	__________
26.	__________	__________	__________	__________	__________
27.	__________	__________	__________	__________	__________
29.	__________	__________	__________	__________	__________
30.	__________	__________	__________	__________	__________

ANSWERS TO CRITICAL THINKING EXERCISE 3-1

What effect would such currency shifts have on your business trade with each of these countries?

The principle is this: If the currency of another country goes up, that means they can buy more U.S. goods more cheaply and that is good for exporters. If the value of their currency goes down, that means that goods and services from the United States are more expensive, and that would hurt your business.

Name: ______________________

Date: ______________________

CRITICAL THINKING EXERCISE 3-2

TRADE PROTECTIONISM

I.M. Windy is a candidate for the U.S. House of Representatives from your district. He just delivered an excellent speech at your college. He spoke at great length on the topic of international trade. His major points were:

1. We need tariffs to:
   a. provide revenues
   b. protect our young industries
   c. make people buy at home because it is patriotic
   d. keep us militarily strong
   e. protect American workers and wages
   f. help us maintain a favorable balance of trade
   g. create a favorable balance of payments
2. We should eliminate embargoes (like the one against selling wheat to the U.S.S.R. in 1979-80) because they accomplish little, but we should keep quotas and tariffs.
3. The American standard of living would be greatly increased if we eliminated foreign competition.
4. The tide of foreign goods washing across our nation should be stopped at once. We are a self-sufficient nation that can stand alone without trading with foreigners.

Do you agree or disagree with Mr. Windy? Evaluate each of the candidate's major points by indicating whether you consider it valid or invalid. Justify your position.

CRITICAL THINKING EXERCISE 3.2 (continued)

Do you agree or disagree with Mr. Windy? Evaluate each of the candidate's major points by indicating whether you consider it valid or invalid. Justify your position.

		VALID	INVALID	JUSTIFICATION
1.	a.	________	________	________________________
	b.	________	________	________________________
	c.	________	________	________________________
	d.	________	________	________________________
	e.	________	________	________________________
	f.	________	________	________________________
	g.	________	________	________________________
2.		________	________	________________________
3.		________	________	________________________
4.		________	________	________________________

ANSWERS TO CRITICAL THINKING EXERCISE 3-1

1. a. ***Invalid.*** In the long run a tariff will decrease a country's revenues as other nations enact their own trade restrictions.

   b. ***Valid.*** Tariffs are ways to protect or give support to a nation's infant industries. Quite often this support is needed until the domestic industry can compete effectively with global competitors.

   c. ***Invalid.*** This argument might sound good to workers in specific industries who may have lost their jobs due to foreign imports, but the simple reality is you cannot force people to buy goods they may not want or perceive to be as good as competing foreign products.

   d. ***Valid.*** In some industries it is important to have tariffs that protect domestic operations. This is particularly true in sensitive industries such as defense where secrecy is vital. Also, if military hardware is shifted overseas, in a national emergency it may be difficult to obtain important equipment or materials.

   e. ***Invalid.*** True, workers in some industries will suffer due to cheaper foreign labor causing a shift in consumer demand. However, as workers progress to jobs that require more involvement and training their standard of living may actually increase. The theory of comparative advantage is quite appropriate here.

   f. ***Invalid.*** This argument might sound good, but in reality it could cause retribution on the part of our trading partners. This could cause our balance of trade to fall even further. Additionally, Americans have become more dependent on foreign products for use in everyday life. Loss of many products due to excessive tariffs would severely dent our standard of living and quality of life.

   g. ***Invalid.*** This is invalid for many of the reasons mentioned in the previous answer. Strong trading policy spurred on by a free market increases such industries as tourism that help the balance of payments.

2. ***Invalid.*** Embargoes, tariffs, and quotas all tend to hinder international trade. They also tend to lead to retribution on the part of competing nations. Quota and tariff policies should only be used sparingly, if at all.

3. ***Invalid.*** The American standard of living would severely deteriorate if we eliminated foreign competition. We would become very dependent on foreign products such as petroleum. The oil embargo of the 1970s illustrated this clearly. It also showed that we are not a totally self-sufficient nation even though we produce many goods and have vast natural resources.

4. ***Invalid.*** It would be virtually impossible to stop all foreign trade. Consumers are big buyers of foreign-made products and rely on the constant flow of new products and replacement part products. We are also seeing growth in foreign producers located in the U.S. market. Toyota and Nissan are just a few that come to mind. The U.S. will most likely fall further from self-sufficiency in the future than it has in many years past.

Supplemental Cases

CASE 3-1

ENTERING THE IMPORT/EXPORT BUSINESS

Gordon and Carole Segal went to the Caribbean on their honeymoon. While there, they were fascinated by the variety of elegant, functional housewares they saw: French copper, German cutlery, and so on. A few months later, Gordon was doing the dishes (Arzberg dinnerware) when he got the inspiration to start an importing firm. He had experience in restaurants and real estate. Carole was a teacher. Neither had any experience in retailing.

With $17,000 in capital and one employee, the couple opened the first Crate & Barrel store in an old elevator factory in Chicago's Old Town district. It took a while to learn the business. In fact, the couple forgot to buy a cash register and went several days without one. This was in 1962.

At first, the Segals and their company, Euromarket Designs, Inc., imported only quality items they had seen and used themselves. Eventually, they toured the continent searching for more items. They learned that European tradespeople were often reluctant to sell to Americans because of past bad experiences with department store buyers. For example, these buyers would place large orders; the manufacturers would expand to fill the orders; and then, when there were no reorders, the manufacturers were stuck. Often, the Segals had to spend days negotiating to buy goods.

When the store opened, sales were $8,000 the first month. The second month they fell to $4,000, the third month to $2,000. About half the initial inventory was sold at cost due to ignorance, not charity. Eventually things got straightened out, and the Segals opened a second store in 1968 in suburban Wilmette, Illinois (outside Chicago). A third store opened in 1971.

The Segals now have 32 stores. They were the ones who set the image for new housewares stores. Glassware, dinnerware, flatware, and cookware are piled floor to ceiling on open shelves. Emphasis is on the product, not the display case.

The Segals' honeymoon shopping trip in the Caribbean led to a major retail chain in the United States. By 1990, Crate & Barrel reported sales of $150 million. The Segals are considering taking the company public by 1994. Maybe you can buy in when the Segals cash out.

DISCUSSION QUESTIONS FOR CASE 3-1:

1. How much thought have you given to the import/export business as a career? The Segals imported European goods to America. Would you enjoy selling American goods in Europe?

2. What are some of the successful stores you have seen that sell imported goods? Have you ever talked to the owners about their experiences? Do so and report back to the class.

3. Why is the global market an attractive career possibility for tomorrow's college graduates relative to the U.S. market?

ANSWERS TO DISCUSSION QUESTIONS FOR CASE 3-1:

1. *How much thought have you given to the import/export business as a career? The Segals imported European goods to America. Would you enjoy selling American goods in Europe?*

This is a good opportunity to discuss living conditions in other countries and the kinds of products available in America not often found in other countries, including air conditioning, large refrigerators and freezers, certain franchises such as taco places and copy services, and so on.

2. *What are some of the successful stores you have seen that sell imported goods? Have you ever talked to the owners about their experiences? Do so and report back to the class.*

This is a good project for the class. Because you are dealing with local businesses, class interest should be high.

3. *Why is the global market an attractive career possibility for tomorrow's college graduates relative to the U.S. market?*

The world market is much larger (5 billion versus 240 million people), growing much faster, less competitive, more in need of available goods and services, and potentially more interesting and challenging. At least, it is a subject worth talking about and investigating.

CASE 3-2

DIFFERENCES IN MANAGEMENT METHODS

International business can create conflicts simply in describing what is a "good" manager. Americans are accustomed to stressing achievement, results, experience, and professional traits. Europeans, on the other hand, emphasize stature, schools, degrees, being known in the community, a high level of intelligence, and style.

One of the biggest potential problems is the difference in U.S. and foreign management methods—such things as how executives deal with one another, how they make decisions, how they use an organization to get things done. These differences can be seen as well in foreign countries operating in the United States.

Bernard Mitchell, who is vice-chairman and president of Advent Corporation of Cambridge, Massachusetts, is one who knows; he used to run the U.S. unit of Pioneer Electronic Corporation, a Japanese company. "It's really like becoming an astronaut," Mr. Mitchell says. "You get to visit the other side of the moon." He explains that Japanese managers are accustomed to a slow and deliberate kind of consensual decision making that can be frustrating to an American executive.

The day he was named president of U.S. Pioneer Electronics, Mr. Mitchell recalls, there was a meeting of the subsidiary's board of directors—all Japanese except him. As any assertive American manager might, he took the opportunity to lay out just what he wanted to do with the company as its new president. The Japanese, used to more discreet assertions of authority, were "incensed and outraged," he remembers. "At the time, I thought my chances of surviving another four hours were less than 2 percent," he says.

DISCUSSION QUESTIONS FOR CASE 3-2:

1. What could Mitchell have done to ensure support for his plans?

2. Would stock options be a positive way to motivate Japanese workers?

3. If your company offered you the opportunity to move to Tokyo, would you take it? What factors would you need to consider?

ANSWERS TO DISCUSSION QUESTIONS FOR CASE 3-2:

1. *What could Mitchell have done to ensure support for his plans?*

   The Japanese management style is based on consensus building. If Mitchell had spent some time discussing his plans with the directors, building support, and anticipating objections, his chances of success would have been greatly increased. Many companies routinely prepare international managers for such cultural conflicts by attending pre-transfer cultural sensitivity programs.

2. *Would stock options be a positive way to motivate Japanese workers?*

   Mr. Mitchell spent four years trying to introduce stock options as compensation, finally giving up after deciding the idea was "so strange and alien to them that I don't think it was ever mastered."

3. *If your company offered you the opportunity to move to Tokyo, would you take it? What factors would you need to consider?*

   This will be answered individually by each student. Factors to consider include cultural differences and Japan's high cost of living. Women used to America's climate of acceptance would find the Japanese male-dominated business world stifling. Our business schools train executives to make bold decisions, not build consensus; skills carefully learned and practiced may prove ineffective in Japanese business.

   Other considerations could include family priorities and spouse's careers. The manager who spends several years overseas may also find that his or her career progress within the company has slowed.

   On the positive side are the many benefits gained by exposure to another culture. The manager who has worked in another economic system will be a prime candidate for advancement in today's multinational corporations.

Transparency Masters

TRANSPARENCY MASTER 22	Chapter Outline
TRANSPARENCY MASTER 23	Successful U.S. Exporters *(Figure 3.1 on text page 75)*
TRANSPARENCY MASTER 24	The Major Trading Economies of the World *(Figure 3.2 on text page 79)*
TRANSPARENCY MASTER 25	Countries With the Highest Foreign Direct Investment in the United States *(Figure 3.3 on text page 79)*
TRANSPARENCY MASTER 26	U.S. Government, Multilateral, and Interregional Sources of Global Financing *(Figure 3.5 on text page 88)*

Chapter Outline

CHAPTER 3
COMPETING IN GLOBAL MARKETS

PROFILE: Dary Rees, Global Entrepreneur

I. THE DYNAMIC GLOBAL MARKET.

II. WHY TRADE WITH OTHER NATIONS?

A. The Theories of Comparative and Absolute Advantage.

III. GETTING INVOLVED IN GLOBAL TRADE.

A. Importing Goods and Services.

B. Exporting Goods and Services.

C. Measuring Global Trade.

IV. TRADING IN GLOBAL MARKETS: THE U.S. EXPERIENCE.

V. STRATEGIES FOR REACHING GLOBAL MARKETS.

A. Exporting.

B. Licensing.

C. Creating Subsidiaries.

D. Contract Manufacturing.

E. Franchising.

F. International Joint Ventures.

G. Countertrading.

VI. HURDLES OF TRADING IN GLOBAL MARKETS.

A. Cultural Differences.

B. Societal and Economic Differences.

C. Legal and Regulatory Differences.

D. Problems With Currency Shifts.

Chapter Outline (continued)

VII. TRADE PROTECTIONISM.

A. General Agreement on Tariffs and Trade (GATT).

B. Common Markets.

C. The North American Free Trade Agreement (NAFTA).

VIII. MULTINATIONAL CORPORATIONS.

IX. THE FUTURE OF GLOBAL TRADE.

A. Globalization and You.

X. SUMMARY AND REVIEW.

TM-23

Successful U.S. Exporters

(Figure 3.1 on text page 75)

COMPANY	EXPORTS AS A PERCENTAGE OF TOTAL SALES
Boeing	57.5%
Sun Microsystems	49.2
Intel	39.1
Caterpillar	32.8
Hewlett-Packard	22.6
Chrysler	19.1
General Electric	13.2

TM-24

The Major Trading Economies of the World
(Figure 3.2 on text page 79)

THE MAJOR TRADING ECONOMIES OF THE WORLD	
European Union	Republic of Korea
United States	Singapore
Japan	Taiwan
Hong Kong and China	Switzerland
Canada	

Countries With the Highest Foreign Direct Investment in the United States

(Figure 3.3 on text page 79)

United Kingdom	$110 billion
Japan	$80 billion
Netherlands	$68 billion
Canada	$38 billion

U.S. Government, Multilateral, and Interregional Sources of Global Financing

(Figure 3.5 on text page 88)

U.S. GOVERNMENT, MULTILATERAL, AND INTERREGIONAL SOURCES OF GLOBAL FINANCING

EXPORT-IMPORT BANK This bank makes loans to exporters that can't secure financing through private sources and to foreign countries that use the funds to buy American goods.

INTERNATIONAL FINANCE CORPORATION (IFC) This organization makes loans to private businesses when they can't obtain loans from more conventional sources. It's affiliated with the World Bank.

INTERNATIONAL DEVELOPMENT ASSOCIATION (IDA) This organization makes loans to private businesses and to member countries of the World Bank.

INTER-AMERICAN INVESTMENT CORPORATION (IIC) This organization operates as an autonomous merchant banking corporation that will give preference to small and midsized companies that wish to expand.

EUROPEAN BANK FOR RECONSTRUCTION AND DEVELOPMENT Based in London, this bank has a mandate to devote 60 percent of its investment activity to private-sector loans.

OVERSEAS PRIVATE INVESTMENT CORPORATION This organization sells insurance to U.S. firms that operate overseas. It covers damages caused by war, revolution, or insurrection; inability to convert local currencies to U.S. dollars; and expropriation (takeover by foreign governments).

Demonstrating Ethical Behavior and Social Responsibility

Chapter 4

Folder Contents

TM 29 Strategies for Ethics Management *(Figure 4.2 on text page 106)*

TM 30 Socially Responsible Business Activities *(Figure 4.3 on text page 111)*

Overhead Transparency Acetates

ACETATE 4-1 Classifying Business Decisions by Ethical and Legal Relationships

ACETATE 4-2 Factors Influences Managerial Ethics

ACETATE 4-3 Who Are the Most Generous Business Tycoons?

ACETATE 4-4 Why People Volunteer

ACETATE 4-5 Factors that Cause Workers to Behave Unethically

ACETATE 4-6 Top Five Unethical/Illegal Behaviors of Workers

ACETATE 4-7 Where Employers Lose the Most

ACETATE 4-8 What Concerns Workers Most on the Job?

ACETATE 4-9 Three Concepts of Social Responsibility

ACETATE 4-10 Most Admired Companies by Industry

(Acetates and Transparency Masters are also available as PowerPoint slides on disk and on the Presentation CD-ROM.)

(Resources Available are also referenced in the expanded lecture outline later in this chapter.)

Other Resources Available

Video Case - "Ethics in the Workplace." Three interactive video vignettes—"Electo Plus," "The Pension Fund," and "The Sexist Campaign"—explore ethical dilemmas in the workplace. (The **Media Resource Guide** contains a summary of the Video and suggested discussion questions.)

Student Assessment and Learning Guide: Contains matching key term and definition questions, write-in retention questions, write-in critical thinking questions, and practice test of multiple choice and true/false questions.

Technology:

Zapitalism CD-ROM - Simulation program.

Concept Mastery Exam Preparation Disk - Practice test and tutorial.

Business Essentials Disk - Hyperlinks Understanding Business with seven other leading business texts.

Presentation CD-ROM - Contains PowerPoint slides of acetates and transparency masters, video clips, lecture materials. This tool allows you to customize your lecture presentations.

Business Week **Web Site Access with the** *Business Week* **edition.**

Understanding Business **Home Page – http:/www.mhhe.com/ub5e.**

Audiotape: Abridged chapter (Text minus profile, boxes, and end-of-chapter material.

Associated Web Sites

These sites are provided to students for the purpose of analysis and critical thinking of the issues. Students are encouraged to explore other sites. As with any Web site, some may be inactive now.

Integrity:

5 basic points:

http://www.glasscity.net/~rimm/toledo/fivestar.html

Personal integrity - by L. Ron Hubbard (Scientology)

http://www.scientology.org/wis/wiseng/wis1-3/wis3_4.htm

The Integrity Center - corporate watchdog of employees

http://www.integetr.com/

Ethics and Why They're Important to a Business:

http://www.swhaz.com/ethics.html

Unethical Companies:

Hall of Shame (You have to be open-minded - note the issues considered unethical or immoral)

http://www/timothyplan.com/hall_of_shame.htm

The Cost of Unethical Behavior:

http://www.navran.com/Prodicts/DTG/part2-c.html

Codes of Ethics:

Examples from various organizations and professional associations

http://www.echotech.com/codemenu.htm

Examples from a large variety of companies:

http://www.ethics.ubc.ca/papers/business.html

Ethical Decision-Making:

Cadbury's Founder Set the Tone for Ethical Decisions

http://ctg.byuh.edu/ctg/staff/JinYip/ethics-2.html

Worksheet for Ethical Decision Making

http://jcomm.uoregon.edu/~tbivins/j495/worksheet.html

The Six Step Decision Making Model

http://www.navran.com/Newsletter/94-04/04-94a.html

International Business:

Corporate Ethics - for underdeveloped countries (look under corporate ethics)

http://foundation.novartis.com/topix.htm

Ethics Affecting Hazardous Waste:

http://atsdrl.atsdr.cdc.gov:8080/

Ethics Involving Public Service:

School board member ethics:

http://www.prs.k12.nj.us/Board Policies/9000Group/9271.html

Corporate Philanthropy:

Patterns in corporate philanthropy (follow the Table of Contents)

http://www.townhall.com/crc/patterns/

Examples of Corporate Philanthropy:

Edy's Grand Ice Cream Great Expectations Program:

http://www.edys.com/pages/textonly/gndexpct.html

Articles citing many examples of corporate philanthropy

http://www.rpbooks.com/visitors/newsroom/jul15-96.htm

Future:

Towards a new global ethics:

(Look at each of the issues listed in the left side of the screen)

http://www.kit.nl/kvc/boekteksten/chapter1_1/html

***Understanding Business* Home Page:**

http:/www.mhhe.com/ub5e.

What's New in This Edition/Conversion Notes

Additions:

- Profile of Nancy Bierk, Ad Impressions and Logo Masters
- Section "Responsibility to Customers"
- Section "Responsibility to Investors"
- Section "Responsibility to Employees"
- Section "Responsibility to Society"
- Spotlight On Small Business :Myths About Small Business Philanthropy
- Reaching Beyond Our Borders: Far From Giving Them the Shirt Off Your Back
- Taking It to the Net exercises
- Case "Gotta Deadline? Click Here!"
- Video Case Ethics in the Workplace
- Figure 4-1 Overview of Lockheed Martin's Code of Ethics

Revisions:

Statistical data and examples throughout the chapter were updated to reflect current information. In addition:

- Chapter was reorganized to look at ethical behavior from a personal perspective before moving to organizational ethical behavior.
- Definitions of ethics, morality, and integrity was replaced with a more general definition and discussion of ethics.
- Section "Personal Ethics Begins at Home" was revised to include discussion of ethical dilemmas.
- Section "Corporate Social Responsibility" was revised by deleting the discussion of strategic, socialist, and pluralist approaches to corporate responsibility and adding a discussion of the trend toward volunteerism.
- Section "Social Audits" was expanded to include discussions of "watch dog" groups that monitor how well companies enforce their ethical and social responsibility policies.
- Section "International Ethics and Social Responsibility" was revised to emphasize the complexity of imposing one's own ethical and social standards upon a company in another country.

Deletions:

- Profile of Janell Grayson, Co-Owner of Food From the 'Hood
- Case "Ethics in Hollywood and the Entertainment Industry"
- All boxes except Making Ethical Decisions

Brief Chapter Outline/Learning Goals

CHAPTER 4

DEMONSTRATING ETHICAL BEHAVIOR AND SOCIAL RESPONSIBILITY

PROFILE: Nancy Bierk, Ad Impressions and Logo Masters

I. MANAGING BUSINESS ETHICALLY AND RESPONSIBLY.

LEARNING GOAL 1. Explain why legality is only the first step in behaving ethically.

II. LEGALITY IS ONLY THE FIRST ETHICAL STANDARD.

A. Personal Ethics Begin at Home.

LEARNING GOAL 2. Ask the three questions one should answer when faced with a potentially unethical action.

B. Ethics Is More than an Individual Concern.

C. Organizational Ethics Begins at the Top.

LEARNING GOAL 3. Describe management's role in setting ethical standards.

III. SETTING CORPORATE ETHICAL STANDARDS.

LEARNING GOAL 4. Distinguish between compliance-based and integrity-based ethics codes and list the six-steps in setting up a corporate ethics code.

IV. CORPORATE SOCIAL RESPONSIBILITY.

LEARNING GOAL 5. Define social responsibility and examine corporate responsibility to various stakeholders.

A. Responsibility to Customers.

B. Responsibility to Investors.

C. Responsibility to Employees.

D. Responsibility to Society.

E. Social Auditing.

V. INTERNATIONAL ETHICS AND SOCIAL RESPONSIBILITY.

LEARNING GOAL 6. Analyze the role of American businesses in influencing ethical and social responsibility in global markets.

VI. SUMMARY AND REVIEW.

(Learning Objectives are also referenced in the expanded lecture outline later in this chapter)

Key Terms

compliance-based ethics codes *(text page 106)*

corporate philanthropy *(text page 107)*

corporate policy *(text page 107)*

corporate responsibility *(text page 107)*

ethics *(text page 102)*

integrity-based ethics codes *(text page 106)*

social audit *(text page 111)*

social responsibility *(text page 101)*

Lecture Outline

The **PROFILE** at the beginning of this chapter focuses on **NANCY BIERK**, owner of **AD IMPRESSIONS** and **LOGO MASTERS**. Nancy hires people few managers would even consider hiring: ex-convicts, former alcoholics, immigrants.

I. MANAGING BUSINESS ETHICALLY AND RESPONSIBLY.

A. Ethical behavior can influence your success in business.

B. **SOCIAL RESPONSIBILITY** means that a business shows concern for the welfare of society as a whole.

II. LEGALITY IS ONLY THE FIRST ETHICAL STANDARD.

▶ **LEARNING GOAL 1.** Explain why legality is only the first step in behaving ethically.

A. **MORAL AND ETHICAL BEHAVIOR ARE NOT THE SAME AS FOLLOWING THE DICTATES OF THE LAW.**

1. Social responsibility and moral and ethical behavior go **BEYOND** the law.

   a. Ethics deals with the proper relations with and responsibilities toward other people.

   b. Legality deals with much smaller issues.

Lecture Notes

TRANSPARENCY MASTER 27 Chapter Outline	**TM 27** Transparency Masters begin on page 4.73.
LECTURE ENHANCER 4-1 Experiment or Exploitation?	Many homeless men have participated in an Eli Lilly Phase I drug trial. The trials determine whether the drugs are safe and how to adjust the dosages. (See complete lecture enhancer on page 4.40.)
SUPPLEMENTAL CASE 4-1 Ethics in Hollywood and the Entertainment Industry	See complete case on page 4.64.

c. It only refers to laws we have written to protect ourselves—many immoral acts fall within our laws.

2. The term "ethics" can be defined many ways.

   a. Some philosophers distinguish between ethics and morals.

   b. The terms "ethical" and "moral" are used interchangeably in this text.

   c. **ETHICS** refers to the standards of moral behavior; that is, behavior that is accepted by society as right or wrong.

B. **PERSONAL ETHICS BEGIN AT HOME.**

▶ **LEARNING GOAL 2.** Ask the three questions one should answer when faced with a potentially unethical action.

1. Society as a whole is not too socially minded.

   a. A recent book revealed that most Americans have few moral absolutes.

   b. Nearly one-third said they never contributed to a charity.

   c. Two-thirds of U.S. high school seniors said they would lie to achieve a business objective.

2. **ETHICAL BEHAVIOR BEGINS WITH YOU AND ME.**

Lecture Notes

LECTURE ENHANCER 4-2
Is It Possible to Teach Ethics?

When John Schad, former chairman of the Securities & Exchange Commission, pledged $20 million to Harvard University to advance the cause of ethics, the university was more than happy to accommodate his wishes. However, as Thomas Piper, senior associate dean chosen to head the initiative would attest, teaching ethics is not the simplest curriculum to implement. (See complete lecture enhancer on page 4.41.)

OT ACETATE 4-1
Classifying Business Decisions According to Ethical and Legal Relationships

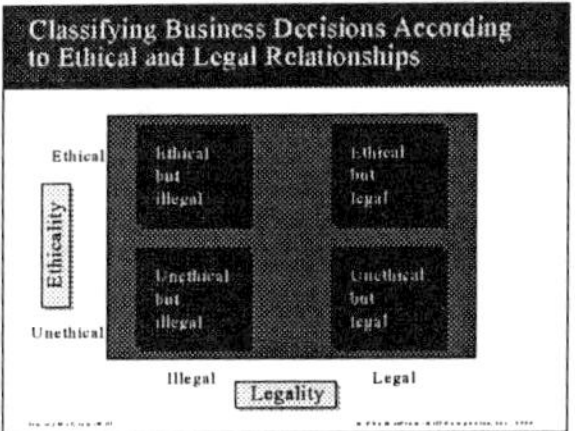

Comments:

1. This acetate is a good starting point in distinguishing between ethical and legal distinctions. Through the use of the matrix, it offers some situations where judgments cannot adequately fit into both categories, legal and ethical, perfectly. For example:
2. In Maricopa County (Arizona), the medical society agreed to establish a maximum fee schedule for health services to curb rising costs. All doctors had to adhere this schedule. The U.S. Supreme Court ruled the agreement to set prices violated the Sherman Act and was illegal. Ethical but illegal.
3. A California company agreed to provide auto dealers a computer program that convinced buyers they should finance a car rather than paying cash. The program omitted the effect of income taxes and misstated the interest earned on the lost savings. The company agreed to provide the program as is as long as it did not violate any laws. Legal but not perhaps ethical.
4. Cigarette manufacturer, R.J. Reynolds targeted African-American customers for a new brand of cigarette called Uptown even though African-Americans have a high incidence of lung cancer and smoking-related illnesses. The Surgeon General criticized this practice but the company cited targeting was legal.

a. We cannot expect "society" to become more moral and ethical unless we as individuals commit to becoming more moral and ethical ourselves.

3. It is important to **KEEP ETHICS IN MIND** when making a business decision.

   a. There is not always an easy choice.

   b. Sometimes the obvious solution from an ethical point of view has drawbacks from a personal or professional point of view.

   c. Sometimes there is no desirable alternative.

4. Three **"ETHICS CHECK QUESTIONS"** can help individuals and organizations be sure their decisions are ethical:

   a. **IS IT LEGAL**

   b. **IS IT BALANCED?**

      (i) (Will I win everything at the expense of another party?)

      (ii) An ethics-based manager tries to make decisions that benefit all parties involved.

   c. **HOW WILL IT MAKE ME FEEL ABOUT MYSELF?**

Lecture Notes

LECTURE ENHANCER 4-3
Social Responsibility Reality Check at Levis

The experiences of Levi Strauss Associates define the ethical minefield in which a huge, socially aware global company has to tread. Levi's social conscience has a long history: after the San Francisco earthquake of 1906, the company placed newspaper ads to tell employees their jobs survived, even if their workplace had not. The company early and forcefully advocated integration in the early 1960s and established ambitious minority-hiring goals in 1967. (See complete lecture enhancer on page 4.42.)

LECTURE ENHANCER 4-4
Ethical Decisions Involve a Moral Choice

There seems to be no direct correlation between acting ethically and success and profit. (See complete lecture enhancer on page 4.43.)

Lecture Outline

5. Individuals and companies that develop a strong ethics code and have a better chance than most of behaving ethically.

C. **ETHICS IS MORE THAN AN INDIVIDUAL CONCERN.**

1. Some managers think ethics is a personal matter—that they are not responsible for an individual's misdeeds.

2. Individuals do not usually act alone—they need the implied, if not the direct, cooperation of others to behave unethically in a corporation.

3. After the disastrous 1992 experience of Sears Automotive Services, Sears replaced 23,000 pages of policies and procedures with a simple booklet called "Freedoms & Obligations."

D. **ORGANIZATIONAL ETHICS BEGINS AT THE TOP.**

▶ **LEARNING GOAL 3.** Describe management's role in setting ethical standards.

1. People learn their standards and values from **OBSERVING WHAT OTHERS DO,** not what they say.

2. Corporate values are **INSTILLED BY THE LEADERSHIP** and example of strong top managers.

Lecture Notes

CRITICAL THINKING
(page 103 in text)

Think of a situation you were involved in recently that tested your ethical behavior. For example, maybe your best friend "forgot" about a term paper due the next day and asked you if he could copy and hand in a paper you wrote for another instructor last semester. What are the consequences of each of your alternatives? Would it have been easier to resolve this dilemma if you had asked yourself the three questions listed above? Try answering them now and see if you would have made a different choice.

LECTURE ENHANCER 4-5
Management Philosophy at Philly Coca-Cola

It's said the best social program in the work is a job. J. Bruce Llewellyn is putting that philosophy to work. (See complete lecture enhancer on page 4.44.)

MAKING ETHICAL DECISIONS
(Box in text, page 105)

"Psst, Kid, Look at This!"

Joe Camel took a lot of heat from people who said his ads appealed to adolescents and encouraged them to smoke. Converse is on the run from people who say the name of its basketball shoe, Run 'N Gun, might encourage adolescent violence, especially in inner cities where handguns are as common as basketballs. The offending companies respond that they are not encouraging adolescent misbehavior. What do you think? Do you think the companies are trying to make adolescents their new customers? If so, is such luring ethical? What are the companies' responsibilities to the well being of the young members of society?

OT ACETATE 4-2
Factors that Influence Managerial Ethics

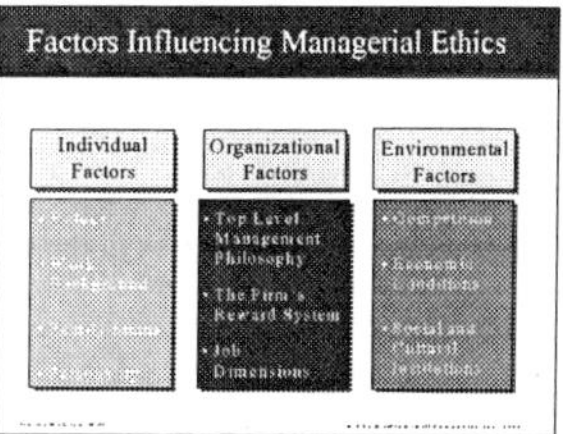

Comments:

1. Factors that influence business ethics are analyzed from three different perspectives: individual factors, organizational factors, and environmental factors. If you work through the acetate factor-by-factor, this should allow for maximum participation and full coverage.
2. Students could be questioned about which of these factors tends to predominate in terms of overall managerial behavior. Also, students can be queried if these factors change noticeably over time.
3. An interesting question to pose to students is what factors most dominate their attitudes concerning ethical behavior. We tried this in our classes last year and got some very interesting responses. Let us know by e-mail what your students have to say.

Lecture Outline

3. In companies such as IBM and Xerox a high value system has become pervasive, and employees feel part of a corporate mission that is socially beneficial.

4. There are many **REASONS WHY A BUSINESS SHOULD BE MANAGED ETHICALLY**:

   a. To maintain a good reputation, keep existing customers, attract new customers, or avoid lawsuits.

   b. To reduce turnover or avoid government intervention.

   c. To please customers, employees, and society.

   d. Because it is the right thing to do.

III. SETTING CORPORATE ETHICAL STANDARDS.

▶ **LEARNING GOAL 4**. Distinguish between compliance-based and integrity-based ethics codes and list the six-steps in setting up a corporate ethics code.

A. Although ethics codes vary greatly, they can be classified into two major categories: compliance-based and integrity-based.

   1. **COMPLIANCE-BASED ETHICS CODES**—emphasize preventing unlawful behavior by increasing control and by penalizing wrongdoers.

Lecture Notes

OT ACETATE 4-3
Who Are the Most Generous Business Tycoons?

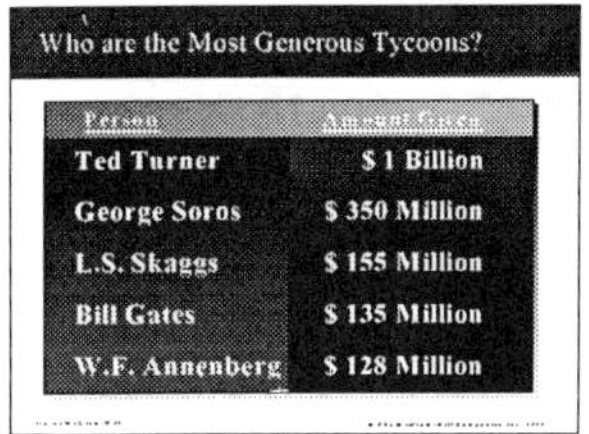

Comments:

1. Business people are often considered to resemble the Scrooge character in Charles Dicken's *A Christmas Carol.* This acetate points out that this characterization is not true.
2. Ted Turner shocked the business community and challenged other business leaders to respond to his massive $1 billion pledge to the United Nations. George Soros has pledged up to $100 million to set up university Internet centers in Russia. Other big time givers include:
   - Bill Gates who provided $100 million into his foundation. He also pledged $15 million to Harvard University.
   - Walter Annenberg agreed to donate up to $500 million into public school systems until the year 2000
   - William Hewlett has donated over $100 to a public policy institute her founded in 1994
   - Ted Arison of Carnival Cruise Lines gave 1.3 million shares of his company's stock to the New World Symphony in Miami.
3. It would be interesting to ask students if they think business and business leaders do their fair share to help their communities.

TRANSPARENCY MASTER 28
Overview of Lockheed Martin's Code of Ethics
(Figure 4.1 on text page 106)

Transparency Masters begin on page 4.73.

OT ACETATE 4-4
Why People Volunteer

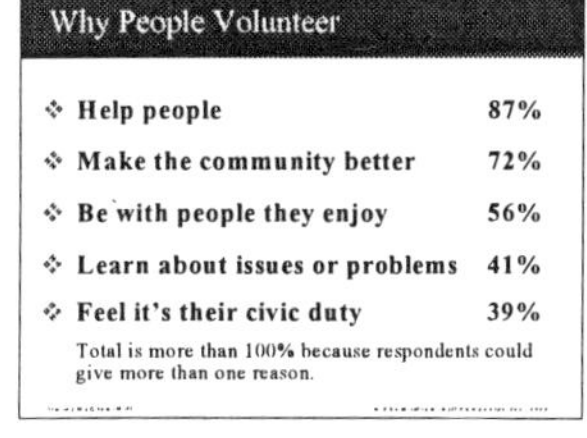

Comments:

1. It might be useful to ask students if they volunteer their time to various organizations in the community. A quick follow up question is "why do they do it?"
2. This acetate includes the primary reasons people volunteer their time to various organizations and groups. It will be interesting to see how the student's answers matched up.
3. A broader reaching discussion could be generated concerning the whole issue of volunteering. President Clinton held a conference in 1997 to encourage more volunteerism from Americans. A question for students to consider, "should government involve itself less in particularly local matters and let volunteers take on more responsibility for their communities?

Lecture Outline

2. **INTEGRITY-BASED ETHICS CODES** define the organization's guiding values, create an environment that supports ethically sound behavior, and stress a shared accountability among employees.

B. A long-term improvement of America's business ethics calls for a six-step approach to **ENFORCING ETHICS CODES:**

1. **TOP MANAGEMENT** must adopt and unconditionally support an explicit corporate code of conduct.

2. **EMPLOYEES** must understand that expectations for ethical behavior begin at the top and that senior management expects all employees to act accordingly.

3. **MANAGERS** and others must be trained to consider the ethical implications of all business decisions.

4. **AN ETHICS OFFICE MUST BE SET UP**—phone lines should be established so that employees who don't want to be seen with an ethics officer can inquire about ethical matters anonymously.

5. **OUTSIDERS** such as suppliers, subcontractors, distributors, and customers must be told about the ethics program.

TRANSPARENCY MASTER 29
Strategies for Ethics Management *(Figure 4.2 on text page 106)*

Transparency Masters begin on page 4.73.

CRITICAL THINKING EXERCISE 4-1
Ethical Dilemmas

See complete exercise on page 4.57.

LECTURE ENHANCER 4-6
J. C. Penney's Landmark Ethics Code

James Cash Penney opened his first Golden Rule Store—later known as J. C. Penney Company—to provide top-quality customer service, treat his employees fairly, and apply ethical standards to business. (See complete lecture enhancer on page 4.45.)

a. Often pressure to put aside ethical considerations comes from the outside.

b. It helps employees resist such pressure when everyone knows what the ethical standards are.

6. **THE ETHICS CODE MUST BE ENFORCED.**

a. If rules are broken, **CONSEQUENCES** should follow quickly.

b. This will communicate to employees that the code is serious and cannot be broken.

IV. CORPORATE SOCIAL RESPONSIBILITY.

▶ **LEARNING GOAL 5.** Define social responsibility and examine corporate responsibility to various stakeholders.

A. **SOCIAL PERFORMANCE** of a company has several dimensions:

1. **CORPORATE PHILANTHROPY** includes charitable donations to nonprofit organizations.

2. **CORPORATE RESPONSIBILITY** includes everything from minority hiring to the making of safe products, and more.

3. **CORPORATE POLICY** refers to the position a firm takes on issues that affect the firm and society.

B. **IMPACT OF CORPORATIONS ON SOCIETY**

OT ACETATE 4-5
Factors That Cause Workers to Act Unethically

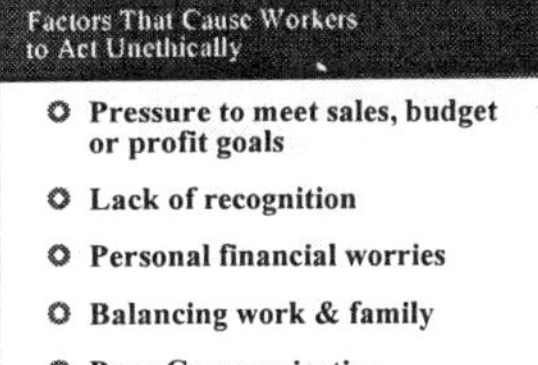

Comments:

1. If workers behave unethically on the job, what's the probable cause? That is the question addressed in this acetate.
2. As you go over the acetate with students, it's important to note that many factors can be handled by closer attention by managers. This is particularly true of the first two statements and the last one.
3. A question students can be asked to discuss involves statements three and four. Where does the responsibility of business lie in regard to private issues such as finances and family issues? Should businesses offer financial planning seminars to its workers? Should businesses grant family leave or time off for important family matters? How far should business go to relieve personal stress related to finances or family?

PROGRESS CHECK (page 107 in text)

- ➤ What are the six steps to follow in establishing an effective ethics program in a business?
- ➤ When faced with ethical dilemmas, what questions can you ask yourself that might help you make ethical decisions?

LECTURE ENHANCER 4-7
Putting His Money Where His Mouth Is

Putting his money where his mouth is, Ted Turner pledged $1 billion to the U.N. and urged the rich to give more to charity. (See complete lecture enhancer on page 4.46.)

LECTURE ENHANCER 4-8
Different Views of Corporate Responsibility

What should be the guiding philosophy for business in the 21st century? Three different views of corporate responsibility have been presented. (See complete lecture enhancer on page 4.47.)

CRITICAL THINKING EXERCISE 4-2
Surveying Public Interest Organizations

See complete exercise on page 4.60.

LECTURE ENHANCER 4-9
Newman's Own Philanthropy

"It's pretty kicky." That's how philanthropist and Oscar-winning actor Paul Newman describes the feeling he gets from giving all after-tax profits from his food company, Newman's Own, to charity. He's been feeling "kicky" to the tune of $80 million since the nation first tasted his salad dressing 15 years ago. (See complete lecture enhancer on page 4.48.)

Lecture Outline

1. Many people get a one-sided view of the impact that companies have on society.
2. Few people see the positive impacts, such as the commitments of many companies to volunteerism.
3. In a recent survey, two-thirds of the MBA students surveyed said that they would take a lower salary to work for a socially responsible company.
4. Social responsibility is seen differently through the eyes of various stakeholders to whom businesses are responsible.

C. **RESPONSIBILITY TO CUSTOMERS.**

1. Business is responsible to satisfy customers with goods and services of real value.
2. Pleasing the customer is not as easy as it seems.
3. Three out of five new businesses fail—perhaps because their owners failed to please their customers.

D. **RESPONSIBILITY TO INVESTORS.**

1. Milton Friedman has said that corporate social responsibility means making money for stockholders.

Lecture Notes

LECTURE ENHANCER 4-10
Volunteerism Is Growing

Many companies are seeing the benefits of encouraging employees to volunteer on company time. (See complete lecture enhancer on page 4.49.)

SUPPLEMENTAL CASE 4-2
The Profit Objective and Social Responsibility

See complete case on page 4.67.

SPOTLIGHT ON SMALL BUSINESS
(Box in text, page 109)

"Myths About Small Business Philanthropy"

Many entrepreneurs have a hard time figuring out how to start a charitable-giving program in their businesses. Often this is because of misconceptions. Three myths are presented.

OT ACETATE 4-6
Top Five Unethical/Illegal Behaviors of Workers

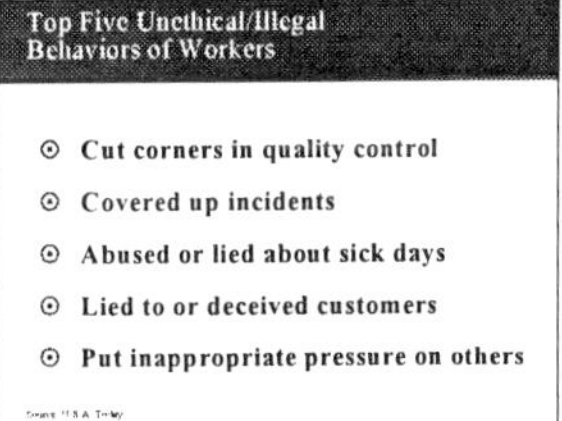

Comments:

1. This acetate is one that businesses should look over carefully. If workers behave unethically, or even illegally, these tend to be the most common behaviors.
2. Students can be asked if any of these behaviors are ever justified on the job. They could also address what they are the most serious violations.
3. Another question can raise the issue of which of these transgressions is the most serious in the eyes of students.

Lecture Outline

2. Some believe that before you can do good you must do well; others believe that by doing good, you can also do well.

3. Many people believe that it makes financial as well as moral sense to invest in companies that are planning ahead to create a better environment.

E. **RESPONSIBILITY TO EMPLOYEES.**

1. Businesses have a responsibility to **CREATE JOBS.**

2. Business has an obligation to see to it that **HARD WORK AND TALENT ARE FAIRLY REWARDED.**

3. Business also has a responsibility to **MAINTAIN JOB SECURITY** or, if layoffs are impossible to avoid, give employees warning.

F. **RESPONSIBILITY TO SOCIETY.**

1. A major responsibility of business to society is to **CREATE NEW WEALTH**.

   a. Most nonprofits own shares of publicly-held companies

   b. As those share prices increase, funds are available to benefit society.

2. Businesses are responsible for **PROMOTING SOCIAL JUSTICE.**

LECTURE ENHANCER 4-11
Clean Hands Investing

Socially responsible investing, which for nearly two decades has involved funds that promote a mix of liberal ideals, is taking a turn toward more custom-tailored investing. Faced with more clients who insist on putting their scruples above returns, money managers have created funds that address specific moral, ethical, and religious issues. (See complete lecture enhancer on page 4.51.)

OT ACETATE 4-7
Where Employers Lose the Most

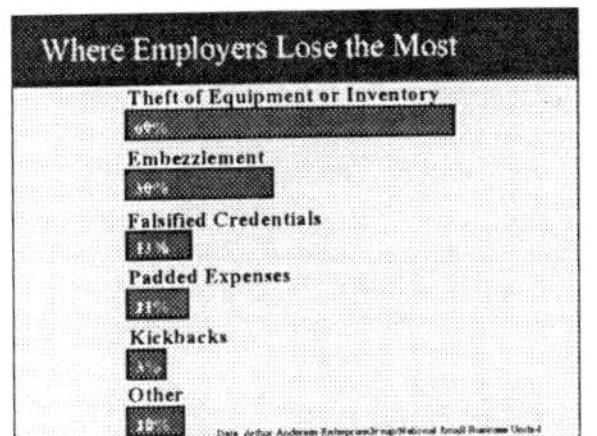

Comments:

1. Unethical or illegal behaviors can cost business a great deal. This acetate deals with the question of where businesses lose the most from such behaviors.
2. Students can be questioned regarding how businesses can stop such problems from starting. Issues of proactive v/s reactive management actions can be addressed in dealing with problems such as the ones listed on the acetate.

OT ACETATE 4-8
What Concerns Workers Most on the Job?

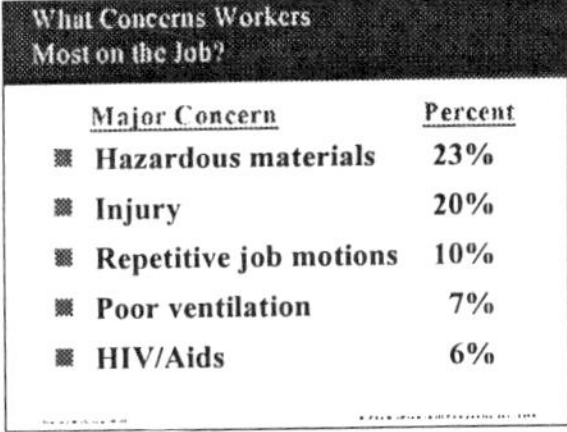

Comments:

1. Employers are not the only ones concerned about problems on the job. Workers also have concerns that can clearly affect performance and attitudes. This acetate lists the concerns workers identified as bothering or affecting their job performance.
2. See if students can add to the list. Also ask if they concur with the ranking done by workers in the study listed on the acetate.
3. Ask students what may be some future concerns of workers on the job. Studies are showing that high-tech workers are experiencing problems due to extended time spent at computers and other equipment.

LECTURE ENHANCER 4-12
How Far We've Come

April 22, 1970, the first Earth Day, marked the beginning of an environmental movement that has grown and waned during the succeeding years. Since 1970 there have been vast changes in the environment and the ways human affect it. (See complete lecture enhancer on page 4.52.)

Lecture Outline

a. For its own well-being, business depends on its employees being active in civil society such as politics, law, churches, arts and charities.

b. Many companies use group volunteer projects to encourage team building while improving their communities.

3. Business is responsible for **CONTRIBUTING TO MAKING ITS OWN ENVIRONMENT A BETTER PLACE.**

4. Many corporations are publishing reports that document their net social contribution.

G. **SOCIAL AUDITING.**

1. How can you know hoe well organizations are making social responsiveness an integral part of top management's decision making?

2. A **SOCIAL AUDIT** is a systematic evaluation of an organization's progress toward implementing programs that are socially responsible and responsive.

3. **PROBLEMS** related to social auditing:

a. It is **DIFFICULT TO DEFINE** what "socially responsible and responsive."

b. Business activities and their effects on society are **DIFFICULT TO MEASURE.**

Lecture Notes

CRITICAL THINKING EXERCISE 4-3
Social Responsibility Successes and Failures

See complete exercise on page 4.62.

OT ACETATE 4-9
Three Concepts of Social Responsibility

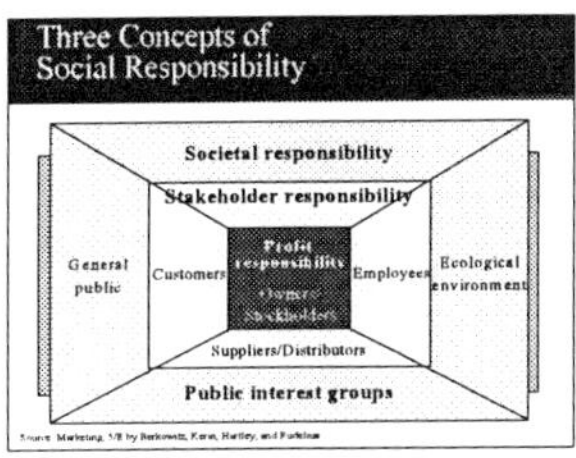

Comments:

1. This acetate investigates differing concepts of the social responsibility of an organization. Students can see how different perspectives have grown from the pure profit motive.
2. For your discussion, ***profit responsibility*** holds that businesses have one simple duty, to maximize profits for its owners and stockholders.
    - ***Stakeholder responsibility*** focuses on the obligations of an organization to those that can affect its achievements and overall objectives. Groups involved in stakeholder responsibility include customers, employees, suppliers, and distributors.
    - ***Societal responsibility*** refers to the obligations that organizations have to the general public and ecological and environmental conditions.
3. Students can easily be encouraged to comment on these three concepts and offer their opinions concerning what direction business should be headed.

TRANSPARENCY MASTER 30
Socially Responsible Business Activities
(Figure 4.3 on text page 111)

Transparency Masters begin on page 4.73.

4. Some suggest that positive actions be added up and **NEGATIVE EFFECTS SUBTRACTED** to get a **NET SOCIAL CONTRIBUTION**.

5. Four groups serve as "watchdogs" regarding how well companies enforce their ethical and social responsibility policies:

   a. **SOCIALLY CONSCIOUS INVESTORS**, who insist that companies extent the company's own high standards to all their suppliers.

   b. **ENVIRONMENTALISTS**, who apply pressure by naming names of companies that don't abide by the environmentalists' standards.

   c. **UNION OFFICIALS**, who hunt down violations and force companies to comply to avoid negative publicity.

   d. **CUSTOMERS**, who take their business elsewhere if a company demonstrates socially irresponsible practices.

V. INTERNATIONAL ETHICS AND RESPONSIBILITY.

▶ **LEARNING GOAL 6.** Analyze the role of American businesses in influencing ethical and social responsibility in global markets.

A. ETHICAL PROBLEMS ARE NOT UNIQUE TO THE UNITED STATES.

Lecture Notes

OT ACETATE 4-10
Most Admired Companies by Industry

Comments:

1. Who's the most admired in various phases of business activity? That's the issue covered in this acetate.
2. Try uncovering the industries without showing the companies and see which companies the students pick as their most admired.
3. In case you are interested or think the students might be curious, the following companies ranked at the bottom of their industries:
   - *Apparel* — Fruit of the Loom
   - *Airlines* — TWA
   - *Food Services* — Flagstar (Denny's)
   - *Food Products* — Archer Daniels Midland
   - *Beverages* — Canandaigua Wine
   - *Electronics* — Westinghouse Electric

LECTURE ENHANCER 4-13
The CEP's Corporate Conscience Awards

Each year the Council on Economic Priorities presents the "Corporate Conscience Awards," recognizing corporations that have taken bold actions in social and/or environmental responsibility. (See complete lecture enhancer on page 4.53.)

Lecture Outline

1. The text gives the examples of recent "influence peddling" in Japan, South Korea, and China.
2. **WHAT IS NEW IS THAT LEADERS ARE BEING HELD TO NEW, HIGHER STANDARDS.**

B. Many American businesses are demanding socially responsible behavior from international suppliers.

1. They make sure their suppliers do not violate U.S. human rights and environmental standards.
2. In contrast there are companies such Nike that have often been criticized for the low pay and long hours of factory workers in Asia.
3. Should international suppliers be required to adhere to American ethical standards? What about countries where child labor is an accepted part of society? What about multinational corporations?
   a. None of these questions are easy to answer.
   b. They show how complex social responsibility issues are in international markets.

LECTURE ENHANCER 4-14
Blackmail Japanese Style

Ryuzaburo Tamenaga was amazed at how easy it was to shake down Japanese companies. Japanese companies were so terrified of tarnished reputations they would hand Tamenaga envelopes filled with cash to keep him quiet. (See complete lecture enhancer on page 4.55.)

LECTURE ENHANCER 4-15
Where Bribery Is Business As Usual

Transparency International, an anticorruption pressure group founded by a former World Bank official, ranks nations on the basis of the prevalence of bribery, as perceived by businessmen. (See complete lecture enhancer on page 4.56.)

SUPPLEMENTAL CASE 4-3
France's AIDS Scandal

See complete case on page 4.70.

REACHING BEYOND OUR BORDERS

(Box in text, page 113)

"Far From Giving Them the Shirt Off your Back"

Lecture Outline

c. It isn't enough for a company to be right when it comes to ethics and social responsibility—it also has to convince its customers it's right.

IV. SUMMARY AND REVIEW.

Lecture Notes

PROGRESS CHECK
(page 113 in text)

- What is corporate social responsibility and how does it relate to each of business's major stakeholders?
- What is a social audit, and what kinds of activities are monitored in such a program?

Answers to Practicing Management Decisions

CASE ONE

GOTTA DEADLINE? CLICK HERE

1. *Would you consider submitting a paper from one of these Web sites as your own? Why or why not?*

   This is clearly an unethical thing to do, but students may present several conditions under which they may feel forced to do this. They were sick, or their father died, or whatever. The idea is to show that ethics do not vary with circumstances.

2. *Do you agree with the Web site owner who said he is "improving" education by exposing these papers as the mediocre results of mediocre assignments? Justify your answer.*

   There are no excuses for unethical or illegal behavior. Only explanations or defenses. Students learn by trying and making mistakes. Taking that away from them destroys education and the right to learn by doing.

3. *View this issue through the eyes of your professor. The Web sites are out there and your students have access to them. What would you do to discourage your students from plagiarism?*

   There are many ways to plagiarize. Getting papers from the Internet is only one. Plagiarism results in failure and dismissal at many schools. Such rules should be clear. But students may have some creative ways of presenting such information and getting conformance.

CASE TWO

VIDEO CASE: ETHICS IN THE WORKPLACE

1. *What are other difficult ethical issues you may face on the job?*

There are a thousand answers to this question. They may bring up sexual harassment, stealing, deceiving customers, lying, and much more. Allow a free flow of idea.

2. *What do you think happens to people that follow their ethical standards completely, when such standards go against the wishes of their supervisors? Would you advise such people to compromise.*

There are many ramifications from being totally honest. You may be fired even. But sticking to your ethical standards will usually be best for you in the long run. Compromise is always possible as long as you don't lose your reputation or go against your ethical standards completely. It is very useful to go over various situations to see just where students stand when it comes to compromising their ethical standards.

3. *How would you personally handle all the situations presented above? Why would you behave in the manner you chose?*

This question gives students a chance to rethink situation after situation and at least explore the ethical and unethical responses. Are there lots of gray areas? What do you do in such situations?

Lecture Enhancers

LECTURE ENHANCER 4-1

EXPERIMENT OR EXPLOITATION?

John Carter spent eight weeks cooped up in a research lab as a human guinea pig for an Eli Lilly & Co. drug experiment. When the test was over, he got a $4,200 check for his trouble, which included having his blood drawn repeatedly but no side effects from a drug he knew only as EZZB.

Two days later, decked out in new clothes, Carter bought some liquor and invited a woman to his newly rented apartment. When he awoke from a drunken stupor, the woman—and his money—were gone, he said. "I had a lot of plans for that money," said Carter, recalling his dashed hopes of attending bartending school. "It was easy money for just being a guinea pig, but it's gone."

Carter is among many homeless men who have participated in the pharmaceutical company's Phase I clinical trials over the years. The trials determine whether drugs are safe and how to adjust doses before they are given to actual patients in Phase II trials.

While some in the research industry have questioned the accuracy of trials on homeless people—a group more prone to alcoholism and drug abuse—Lilly maintains that using the homeless doesn't threaten the trials integrity. In 1997 *The Wall Street Journal* reported that some homeless alcoholics said they participated in Lilly's trials shortly after drinking binges.

Prospective volunteers, however, undergo a series of tests that weed out alcoholics and drug abusers, and those who suffer from chronic conditions such as heart, lung, or liver disease, said Lilly spokesman Ed West. The goal is to select only healthy volunteers. "Any individual that has a severe medical condition or liver disease related to drinking is going to be detected . . . and eliminated," West said. "They'll have no impact on the data."

Some critics say that because homeless or impoverished volunteers are desperate for money, they sometimes don't mention side effects from the drugs for fear of being ejected from the trials. "There's always the concern that they might not necessarily be telling the truth . . . They basically tell you what you want to hear," said Philip Brown, a physician at Pharmaceutical Research Associates, based in Charlottesville, Virginia.

He also said Lilly's screening process, which includes urine tests and physical exams, might not be sophisticated enough to detect alcoholics suffering from the early stages of liver disease. Determining which volunteers have the disease is important because most drugs are metabolized by the liver.

Many local homeless shelters post the names and numbers of drug companies seeking volunteers. Among them is Horizon House, whose executive director said she has no qualms about providing the information. "The point is that they're legally earning the money. Some people use it to buy cars, get an apartment or set themselves straight," Lena Hackett said. "I don't think it's my place or anyone else's place to tell a homeless person, 'You can't earn this money because you might spend it on something illegal'."

LECTURE ENHANCER 4-2

IS IT POSSIBLE TO TEACH ETHICS?

When John Schad, former chairman of the Securities & Exchange Commission, pledged $20 million to Harvard University to advance the cause of ethics, the university was more than happy to accommodate his wishes. However, as Thomas Piper, senior associate dean chosen to head the initiative would attest, teaching ethics is not the simplest curriculum to implement. In fact many rival deans argued that ethics could not be taught in the classroom, a debate that lingers in academic circles.

What has Harvard done to extend the study of ethics? As part of its ethics program, Harvard:

- Asks applicants to write an essay on how they managed and resolved an ethical dilemma.
- Requires all MBAs to take a nongraded, nine-session course on ethics.
- Works with faculty to integrate ethics into the core courses in such subjects as accounting, marketing, and operations.
- Encourages mainstream faculty to do case studies on ethical questions.
- Offers three ethics electives.

Some schools such as the University of Virginia believe ethics should be treated like any other mainstream course, with a full-semester graded course. Piper of Harvard does not necessarily agree but admits the university is considering a fourth elective in ethics and is doing more research on how the issue affects such business areas as international competition. The ethical dilemma lingers on.

LECTURE ENHANCER 4-3

SOCIAL RESPONSIBILITY REALITY CHECK AT LEVI'S

The experiences of Levi Strauss Associates define the ethical minefield in which a huge, socially aware global company has to tread. Levi's social conscience has a long history: after the San Francisco earthquake of 1906, the company placed newspaper ads to tell employees their jobs survived, even if their workplace had not. The company early and forcefully advocated integration in the early 1960s and established ambitious minority-hiring goals in 1967.

When the company went public in 1971, Levi's advised potential investors that it would not sell its conscience with its stock. After the Haas family took the company private again in 1985, Levi's once more spelled out its beliefs in mission and aspiration statements. Among them was a promise to provide all employees with the chance to grow and advance in an open corporation.

But reality caught up with the company in the 1980s. Sales and cost pressures prompted Levi's to take some manufacturing outside the U.S. The company shut down a plant in San Antonio, Texas, amid criticism that the dedication to its work force had faded like its jeans.

Levi's is still high on the list of socially responsible companies. Says chief operating officer Robert Haas: "It's really important to be clear about what your values are. People tend to respond more strongly to values the agree with. And when you do take difficult actions, do it in a way that is most sensitive to the needs of the stakeholders and reduces both the reputational damage and the disruption that is a consequence of whatever action you have to take."

The Council on Economic Priorities, which tracks the corporate social and environmental performance of hundreds of companies, gave Levi's a Corporate Conscience Award for International Commitment in 1994 for "unprecedented commitment to nonexploitive work practices in developing countries."

LECTURE ENHANCER 4-4

ETHICAL DECISIONS INVOLVE A MORAL CHOICE

Often the business literature focuses on the benefits from making ethical decisions in a company. For example, a recent survey of business schools and members of Congress found that 63 percent believed that businesses actually strengthen their competitive positions by maintaining high ethical standards. The Business Roundtable is made up of top executives. They too felt that there is no conflict between ethical practices and profits.

The problem with such surveys and reports is that it makes ethical behavior look easy and profitable. In other words, one would be foolish not to act ethically because it is always in the company's best interest, including profit interests.

It doesn't take much reflection to see that such conclusions are misleading. There are thousands of people out in the real world who are making millions of dollars selling illegal drugs and pornography or who are making huge profits by misleading the government or consumers. On the other hand, there are even more people who are not making much money even though they are acting ethically and providing the best products they can at reasonable prices. In short, there is no direct correlation between acting ethically and profits. Some ethical companies make profits and some do not.

The ethical question, therefore, is not one of profit or loss. It is one of morals. Sometimes it will cost an executive to be honest, fair, socially responsive and responsible. That is a sign of moral and business maturity. It is important to be a moral and ethical person regardless of the economic outcome. It is equally important for a firm to act responsibly and ethically regardless of the economic outcome. On the other hand, it is not "right and just" to act unethically to increase economic gain or to further a "cause" you believe in. For example, it is not necessarily the moral and ethical thing to do to close down or destroy a plant that is making sugar or something else you believe is harmful to people or the environment.

Moral issues are almost always difficult ones to make. There are no easy solutions. That is why there are no "answers" to the ethical boxes in the text. There are no right and wrong answers. One can only take a moral and ethical position based on spiritual and moral beliefs and do what one thinks best given the circumstances. Always there are consequences to one's actions. The question then becomes: Are the consequences best for everyone concerned or not. If not, could they be?

LECTURE ENHANCER 4-5

MANAGEMENT PHILOSOPHY AT PHILLY COCA-COLA

Bruce Llewellyn has a lot on his mind, which you might expect from the chairman and chief executive officer of a large bottling operation, in this case The Philadelphia Coca-Cola Bottling Company. He would like to see greater price elasticity in soft drinks. He wants greater efficiency in distribution. He craves customer satisfaction.

What J. Bruce Llewellyn thinks about, too, is changing the world.

"This country has got to come to some fundamental conclusions," he has decided. One option, says this most accomplished of businessmen—African-American or otherwise—is "to continue to build prisons, continue to have welfare payments, continue to have people with dysfunctional families and children with babies out of wedlock."

The other? "Accept people who do the right thing, get an education, are wiling to work hard and are willing to aspire to the America dream." Choose Door No. 2, and "I guarantee I can solve all the problems with all the quote, unquote disenfranchised people in America . . . "Here's how you solve the problem," he says. "You get a fella married, with 2.2 children. I don't know how you get that other two-tenths of a child, but you get him. You get him a house mortgage. You get him a car note. Then you get these 2.2 kids that he hopefully feels will be most successful at one point, so he's helping with their education." In Llewellyn's view a potential menace to society has been disarmed: "You'll never bear from him. He's too busy trying to sustain his dream and his aspirations."

It's been said the best social program in the world is a job. Count Llewellyn as a true believer in that philosophy, and one who practices what he preaches. Philadelphia Coca-Cola is not only the seventh largest bottler in the Coke system, it is the second-largest minority-owned business in the country. Not only does the company serve a marketplace that is one-quarter non-white, but a like proportion of its workforce and its management team can be classified the same.

An equal opportunity employer if ever there was one, Philly Coke spans the globe in search of personnel. There are internships and summer jobs offered locally as well as recruitment at traditionally black colleges in the South. Coke folk from Africa, Asia, and Europe have come to learn in the House of Llewellyn, and in turn, Philly Coke feeds the Coke system with new talent.

"We'd like to think we've created a lot of career opportunities here for a lot of different people," appraises Wilson, "and this is like a little UN here. I think that's good for our people, to expose the to that diversity. We've had Chinese people here, French people. We've had Russians, Ukrainians who've spent some time. There are people in Croatia who want to come over. We like those things."

"Besides being an excellent businessman," says one admiring top manager at the plant, "Bruce is an ass-kicker. You have to do your job and do it well."

"We don't carry anybody," agrees Wilson. "I've got a boss who's color blind. The only color he likes is green."

LECTURE ENHANCER 4-6

J. C. PENNY'S LANDMARK ETHICS CODE

James Cash Penney opened his first Golden Rule Store—later known as J. C. Penney Company—to provide top-quality customer service, treat his employees fairly, and apply ethical standards to business. In 1914, he formalized his beliefs into the "Penney Principles:"

- To serve the public, as nearly as we can, to its complete satisfaction.
- To offer the best possible dollar's worth of quality and value.
- To strive constantly for a high level of intelligent and helpful service.
- To charge a fair profit for what we offer—and not all the traffic will bear.
- To apply this test to everything we do: "Does it square with what is right and just."

LECTURE ENHANCER 4-7

PUTTING HIS MONEY WHERE HIS MOUTH IS

Ted Turner was on a plane headed for New York City to address a 1997 U.N. Association dinner when he decided to give away $1 billion. Looking over statements prepared by his financial advisers, he noticed that his net worth had shot up from $2.2 billion to $3.2 billion between the beginning of the year and the time of the donation, largely on the strength of a 50 percent rise in Time Warner stock. "Hey, not bad," Turner recalls thinking at the time. "Why not go for the billion? Let's go for the big one." After bouncing the idea off his wife, Jane Fonda, over dinner at the Waldorf-Astoria, Turner stunned an audience that included U.N. Secretary-General Kofi Annan by announcing from the podium that he will give $1 billion over ten years to fund U.N. programs.

While others have given more over the course of their lives, Turner's is the largest donation ever made to a single organization. Turner, founder of CNN and vice chairman of Time Warner, says he did not realize its rank at the time he chose the billion-dollar figure. He prefers to focus on how important it is for wealthy people to share their bounty when the world is awash in money because of rising stock markets. And Turner says he hopes his gift will encourage others to support the U.N. and the programs it operates worldwide, which range from removing land mines to providing inoculations for children.

Turner has long cultivated a reputation for brashness in support of causes lie believes in, many of them involving the environment and the stresses of overpopulation. Turner has called it a "pretty pathetic thing" that many wealthy people give little to charity. His role models range from billionaire philanthropist George Soros to octogenarian Oseola McCarty, the Mississippi washerwoman who gave $150,000 to pay for scholarships at a local college. And, says Turner, he draws inspiration from "A Christmas Carol" and the joy Scrooge finds when be finally adopts a more charitable attitude toward the Cratchit family.

His gift is earmarked for nonadministrative programs, and Turner says he hopes it will boost popular support for the U.N. "It's the organization that has the most reach and the most influence and is doing the most good," he notes. The U.N. has been going through hard times, battling bankruptcy and contemplating layoffs, in part because the U.S. is as much as $1.5 billion behind in its dues—more than the organization's entire annual budget. Turner has promised to help raise more money for the organization through the U.N. Foundation, a new charitable organization he intends to set up as a conduit for his gift.

Rather than giving the $1 billion in a lump sum, Turner is setting aside that amount in Time Warner stock to support ten gifts of $100 million each over the course of a decade. Many of the details of the donation, including its tax benefits to Turner, have yet to be worked out. "I don't even know what the tax breaks are," says Turner. "I haven't considered them." His casual style of giving has not made things easy for his financial advisers. "They haven't really had time to do much more than say, 'Please don't say too much until we can work this out'," he adds. But even though they may have wanted him to move more cautiously, Turner says he was intent on making the announcement immediately. "I couldn't wait, because I had the whole United Nations there and all their supporters. I was kind of winging it a little bit."

LECTURE ENHANCER 4-8

DIFFERENT VIEWS OF CORPORATE RESPONSIBILITY

What should be the guiding philosophy for business in the 21st century? For most of the 20th century there has been uncertainty regarding the position top managers should take. The question revolves around the treatment of stakeholders. Remember stakeholders are those people who can affect or are affected by the achievement of an organization's objectives; they include stockholders, employees, customers, suppliers, distributors, competitor's, and the general public. Three different views of corporate responsibility to these stakeholders have been presented.

1. **The strategic approach.** The strategic approach requires that management's primary orientation be toward the economic interests of stockholders. The rationale is this: As owners, the stockholders have the right to expect management to work in their best interests (to optimize profits). Furthermore, Adam Smith's invisible hand says that the maximum social gain is realized when managers attend only to their shareholder's interests. For example, IBM's John Akers said that if IBM would decide whether to cease operations in a country, it would be a business decision. He said, "We are not in business to conduct moral activity; we are not in business to conduct socially responsible action. We are in business to conduct business." The strategic approach encourages managers to consider actions' effects on stakeholders other than owners, but others' interests are secondary. Often those interests are considered only when they would adversely affect profits if ignored.
2. **The socialist approach.** Using the socialist approach, management gives equal attention to all stakeholders: owners, employees, the local community and so forth. A recent law' in Pennsylvania is based on this approach. The law seeks to protect companies from hostile takeovers. The idea is to protect customers, employees, and the public at large from decisions that may benefit owners, but harm the others. The argument against such an approach is that it turns private organizations into public institutions with ho special responsibility to their owners. Special-interest groups could lobby managers to take all kinds of actions that may cut into profits and damage the success or life of the firm.
3. **The pluralist approach.** This approach recognizes the special responsibility of management to optimize profits, but not at the expense of employees, suppliers, and members of the community. This approach recognizes the moral responsibilities of management that apply to all human beings. Managers don't have moral immunity when making managerial decisions. This view says that corporations can maintain their economic viability only when they fulfill their moral responsibilities to society as a whole. When stockholders' interests compete with the interests of the community, as they often do, managers must decide using ethical and moral principles.

The guiding philosophy for the 21st century will be some version of the pluralist approach. Managerial decision making won't be easy, and new ethical guidelines may have to be drawn. But the process toward such guidelines has been started, and a new era of more responsible and responsive management is beginning.

LECTURE ENHANCER 4-9

NEWMAN'S OWN PHILANTHROPY

"It's pretty kicky." That's how philanthropist and Oscar-winning actor Paul Newman describes the feeling he gets from giving all after-tax profits from his food company, Newman's Own, to charity. He's been feeling "kicky" to the tune of $80 million since the nation first tasted his salad dressing 15 years ago.

Though Newman says his company began as a joke when he and a writer friend, A.E. Hotchner, teamed up to market the vinaigrette they gave to friends for Christmas, its good works couldn't be more serious.

Sales of Newman's Own salad dressing, spaghetti sauce, popcorn, lemonade and salsa served up $10 million in 1996 to those in need. Among them: children with grave illnesses who went to six special summer camps that Newman founded for them, and 50 charitable causes.

Most companies give away 2 percent of profits. Newman gives 100 percent. "Giving the profits away was a philosophy that evolved with the company," Newman says. 'Everyone said, 'If you're going to sell [the salad dressing], you've got to put your face on the label.' I said, Are you nuts?' With that, it would be tacky not to give the money away."

LECTURE ENHANCER 4-10

VOLUNTEERISM IS GROWING

On a recent weekday, lawyer Nela Brown got paid by Shell Oil for skipping work. Instead she volunteered, one of 70 lawyers and staff from Shell's legal department who built box gardens for low-income seniors at Houston apartment. Before Noah's New York Bagels opens new stores, employees of each store will spend a day together on a volunteer project such as painting a crisis center or shelter. Discount brokerage Charles Schwab spent $1 million in January 1997 to bring 900 executives to San Francisco so they could bond while building hours and renovating schools in low-income neighborhoods.

These scenarios are suddenly common. One-third of large companies now have a formal policy to pay workers or give them time off for volunteer work. And the number is growing so fast that you might expect more praise from social activists or alarm from shareholders concerned about such use of company resources. But since the 1997 volunteer summit in Philadelphia under the chairmanship of Colin Powell, companies are making little secret that they have an agenda beyond being helpful. They are helping themselves.

A 1997 Cone/Roper survey of 2,000 consumers shows 76 percent will switch to brands or stores that seem concerned about the community, up 14 percentage points from three years before. Other studies confirm what managers have noticed: Workers who volunteer at something they find meaningful return to work more fulfilled and motivated, and with ties to the community, which stunts turnover and helps recruitment.

Companies are especially latching onto the idea of having groups of employees volunteer on the same project so that they can get to know each other better outside the office. They call it team building, and underlings often blossom with leadership qualities.

Shell CEO Philip Carroll, who must justify the diversion of resources, thinks that he can actually squeeze more real work out of those who volunteer, even on their own time. Day-to-day business can leave people feeling sorry for themselves he says. "You spend a day at a place that faces problems infinitely more difficult, and you come back and say, 'Maybe life isn't so tough.'"

LensCrafters has pledged volunteers to give eye care to one million needy people by 2003, but CEO Dave Brown says his employees have been "under direct orders not to actively seek publicity. I don't want anyone thinking the company is doing this for any reason other than it's the right thing to do."

Brown says LensCrafters regularly surveys employees and customers on their satisfaction. Workers who volunteer are noticeably more satisfied with their jobs, and customers of those stores are noticeably more satisfied with the service, he says.

He says LensCrafters workers could volunteer to build wheelchair ramps, but it makes more sense for them to leverage their skills by providing eye care. More companies are striving to align volunteerism with skills inherent to their workforce. More than 150 employees from five Home Depot stores in Los Angeles renovated a women's shelter in nearby Long Beach.

When customers ask about a product, Home Depot workers can often tell them they personally used the product on a recent volunteer project and "offer tips not on the box," says Joel Pollock, district manager of the Los Angeles store.

Yet, employees must perceive their volunteer work as worthwhile for the company to win their respect. For that reason, many companies let employees help choose projects. For example, gay employees might find it more rewarding to volunteer on AIDS projects, Hispanic employees on bilingual education projects.

Large institutional investors seldom challenge corporate philanthropy and volunteerism, although they say they would like it better if it were fully disclosed. The shareholders know that good deeds are remembered not just by consumers but by legislators and regulators. When a company is being sued for, say, racial discrimination, it doesn't hurt to mention to the jury employee volunteer efforts aimed at say, literacy programs for minority children.

"Many companies subscribe to the unofficial idea that you have to make deposits in the bank of goodwill in order to make withdrawals when the company is faced with a difficult situation," says Bob Goodwin, CEO of the Points of Light Foundation.

LECTURE ENHANCER 4-11

CLEAN HANDS INVESTING

Socially responsible investing, which for nearly two decades has involved funds that promote a mix of liberal ideals, is taking a turn toward more custom-tailored investing. Faced with more clients who insist on putting their scruples above returns, money managers have created funds that address specific moral, ethical, and religious issues.

Until recently, backers of gay rights would have been led to several established funds—Domini Social Equity, Calvert Social Equity, and Dreyfus Third Century, to name a few—that screen out companies with discriminatory practices, as well as those that promote tobacco and alcohol use or cause pollution. But what about investors who feel strongly that homosexual workers should be treated fairly but aren't' interested in campaigns against smoking and drinking? The Meyers Pride Value Fund picks only companies with policies against discrimination on the basis of sexual orientation. Started in June 1996, it has nearly matched the S&P 500's performance in 1997.

On the other end of the spectrum, fundamentalist Christians have found most socially responsible funds to be at odds with their view that homosexuality is morally wrong. So the Timothy Plan, founding in 1994, avoids companies that offer health benefits to workers' gay partners. It also screens out companies that profit from abortions or produce violent or sexually exploit TV shows or films.

The overall track record for socially responsible funds is lackluster. Chicago-based Morningstar Inc. tracks 17 of these funds with records dating back at least five years. Only five show returns in the top half of funds in their categories. Two of the five are in the top quarter. Three-year records show much the same result. Liberal funds are no more likely to underperform the market that funds based on religious principles.

Big brokerages have generally steered clear of socially responsible funds. But in February 1997 Greenwich Street Advisors, Smith Barney's in-house money management firm., converted a $380 million fund into the liberal-leaning Concert Social Awareness Fund. Like other socially responsible funds, Concert screens out polluters and producers of tobacco, weapons, and nuclear power. It adds companies that have programs to help workers, their communities, or the environment. Since the conversion, it has returned 8.82 percent.

LECTURE ENHANCER 4-12

HOW FAR WE'VE COME

April 22, 1970, the first Earth Day, marked the beginning of an environmental movement that has grown and waned during the succeeding years. Since 1970 there have been vast changes in the environment and the ways human affect it. A sample:

- **Air pollution:** From 1970 to 1993, emissions of major pollutants were reduced:

  lead - *down 98 percent*

  sulfur dioxide - *down 30 percent*

  carbon monoxide - *down 24 percent*

  volatile organic compounds - *down 24 percent*

- **Water pollution:** In 1972 only 36 percent of rivers and lakes were considered fishable and swimmable. In 1993, the figure had increased to 62 percent.
- **Natural Resources:** During the same time period, the nation's inventory of hardwood and softwood trees has grown by 94 million cubic feet.
- **Recycling:** The amount of municipal solid waste recovered through recycling increased by five-fold.

  However, some figures are not so positive:

- **Solid waste:** Municipal solid waste increased by 70 percent.
- **Energy:** In 1970 the U.S. imported seven percent of the petroleum it used. In 1993, we imported over 15 percent.

LECTURE ENHANCER 4-13

THE CEP'S CORPORATE CONSCIENCE AWARDS

Each year the Council on Economic Priorities, a non-profit, public interest research organization based in New York, presents the "Corporate Conscience Awards," recognizing corporations that have taken bold actions in social and/or environmental responsibility. The **1976 Corporate Conscience Awards** winners:

For Community Involvement.

- **W.K. Kellogg Foundation** and **Kellogg Company** (joint winners.) The W.K. Kellogg Foundation has invested more than $11 million over the last four years to establish the necessary infrastructure to engage African-American men and boys across the country as active partners in affirming traditional values and reviving their communities. To encourage support from other corporations, the Kellogg Company announced its own investment of $1 million in the long-term project, called the African-American Men and Boys Initiative (AAMBI). Over the last few years, the foundation has made grants to 32 community-based organizations focusing on cultural development, capacity building, mentoring, education, health, and entrepreneurship.
- **Community Pride Food Stores** a small company that ensures the availability of quality products and services to their customers in the inner city communities of Richmond, Virginia. Community Pride's business practice is based on the concept of community involvement. Services provided by Community Pride involve van rides for tired or elderly shoppers; health awareness activities such as monthly in-store blood pressure checks, cholesterol screenings, and immunization fairs; and help for customers seeking to learn about healthy eating.

For Employee Relations

- **Cooperative Home Care Associates (CHCA)** is a worker-owned home health care company that got its start nine years ago with 20 employees. It recruits and trains former welfare recipients to provide high quality home care services to elderly and disabled patients in the Bronx and Manhattan. Workers can become owners by committing $1,000 over five years, through small payroll deductions. CHCA offers twice as much training as the government requires and pays employees a higher wage than most competitors. Individual health benefits are provided (100 percent) to all full- and part-time workers, who are predominantly Hispanic and African-American women. These progressive policies have resulted in a turnover rate half the industry average.

  Eight of ten CHCA board members are women (two of whom are black), and six of seven officers are women. Three African-American women hold posts as division directors and one is a corporate officer. Two Hispanic men also serve on the board. Two-thirds of officials and managers are minorities; 87 percent are women. Literacy programs are available to all; tuition reimbursement and in-house skills-building and career courses are offered to salaried employees.

For Environmental Stewardship

- **Novo Nordisk**, the world's leading producer of insulin and industrial enzymes, is based in Denmark and operates in 53 countries. Proactive on environmental disclosure, Novo Nordisk initiated annual dialogue with key environmental stakeholders in 1991.

Its first environmental report (1994) goes far beyond what is included in many such documents. Unlike U.S. companies, which primarily track emissions in the waste stream, Novo follows an input-output model of reporting. Discharged liquid wastes are declining as the recycling of such waste increases. Novo also reports on releases of several pollutants on a company-wide basis, serving as a model for other companies.

- **J. Sainsbury plc**. numbers among the world's largest retailers, operating four separate chains in the UK and the US which together serve more than 12 million customers per week. Sainsbury is recognized for issuing standards for all of its suppliers of fresh fruits and vegetables, asking them to implement Integrated Crop Management Strategies (ICMS) in the UK and abroad. Rather than relying primarily on pesticides, the ICMS strategy involves the introduction of beneficial insects such as ladybugs, which prey on the pests that attack crops. ICMS also uses forecasting and monitoring techniques, crop rotation, resistant varieties, and staff training to reduce the need for pesticides.
- **Wilkhahn Wilkening**. In 1989, the company's Administrative Board Management and Work Council committed Wilkhahn to a fundamental ecological transformation of the entire company. This German furniture company created a business division—Innovation and Ecology—to ensure that both products and production continuously become more environmentally compatible. Thus, the company employs a cradle-to-grave approach to all of its product lines.

  Since 1971, all employees have had a 50 percent share in operating profits. A new organizational structure went into effect in January 1994; there is now only one management level below the two main business divisions.

For Global Ethics/Human Rights

- The **Co-operative Bank plc** has 130 outlets and operates the largest telephone banking service in the UK. Founded in 1872, Co-op is considered one of the most innovative banks in the UK. It was the first to introduce free banking, interest paid on current accounts, and a commitment to customer confidentiality.

  The bank is well known for its ethical policy, first introduced in 1992. A major tenet is to forego financing arms deals to oppressive governments (all major UK banks do finance such deals—with Nigeria, Iraq, and Indonesia). Its policy disqualifies investments in companies that deal in tobacco, weapons, or fur; conduct animal testing or exploitive factory farming; or promote blood sports, such as hunting. The bank encourages companies to take a proactive stance on the environment and invests in companies that avoid continued damage to the environment.

LECTURE ENHANCER 4-14

BLACKMAIL JAPANESE STYLE

Ryuzaburo Tamenaga is amazed at how easy it was to shake down Japanese companies. The former racketeer would first become a token shareholder of a major company. Then he would dig up some dirt, such as an executive's extramarital affair. All Tamenaga had to do was hint to officials that he might bring up that issue at a shareholder meeting. Japanese companies are so terrified of tarnished reputations they would hand Tamenaga envelopes filled with cash or shower him with expensive gifts to keep him quiet.

While Japan attempts to clean up such extortion, racketeers—known as "sokaiya"—are still a big factor in problems with corruption. The government is preparing reforms of its financial sector in an effort to attract more foreign investment. But investors may have second thoughts about putting their money in companies suspected of dealing with hoodlums. Many top managers are becoming aware that if they don't clean house, their companies are not going to be able to compete in a global marketplace.

In 1997, America's largest pension fund, the California Public Employees Retirement System, said it would stop dealing with Nomura Securities Co., Japan's top brokerage company. The brokerage company and Kangyo Bank, a major commercial bank, were embroiled in a huge scandal involving sokaiya. Fourteen senior officials at the two companies, including a former president, have been arrested on suspicion of arranging a loan totaling $102 million or of funneling $435,000 in payoffs to the sokaiya.

Most sokaiya have links with gangs, and that gives them powerful leverage. At least three business officials have been killed in suspected sokaiya attacks in the past decade. But sokaiya rarely need to resort to violence: Japanese companies are so obsessed with appearances, that they offer cash several times a year to the nation's estimated 1,000 sokaiya.

One trick sokaiya use is approaching companies to buy advertising space in their magazines that only contain the front and back covers, with blank pages in between. Sometimes officials pay to make sure their ads do not appear in the magazines. Some companies subscribe to hundreds of these publications, which cost about $90 a copy. Others even assign officials to deal with sokaiya and entrust these workers with special sokaiya funds. These officials rarely turn down sokaiya demands or call the police.

In Japan, nearly all shareholder meetings, of "sokai," are held on the same day—June 27 in 1997—to thin out sokaiya ranks. Some 10,000 police officers are mobilized. But skilled sokaiya manage to collect several million dollars a year without even showing up at the share holder meetings. Accepted as a necessary evil, sokaiya activities weren't even made illegal in Japan until 1982.

Today sokaiya still face little chance of being caught, with only about 30 arrested each year. Even if they are convicted, the maximum penalty is only six months in jail or a fine of about $2,600.

LECTURE ENHANCER 4-15

WHERE BRIBERY IS BUSINESS AS USUAL

Transparency International, an anticorruption pressure group founded by a former World Bank official, ranks nations on the basis of the prevalence of bribery, as perceived by businessmen. The best and worst on the 1996 list:

Most Corrupt:

1. Nigeria
2. Pakistan
3. Kenya
4. Bangladesh
5. China
6. Cameroon
7. Venezuela
8. Russia
9. India
10. Indonesia

Least Corrupt:

1. New Zealand
2. Denmark
3. Sweden
4. Finland
5. Canada
6. Norway
7. Singapore
8. Switzerland
9. Netherlands
10. Austria

Critical Thinking Exercises

Name: ____________________

Date: ____________________

CRITICAL THINKING EXERCISE 4-1

ETHICAL DILEMMAS

Below are several situations that present ethical questions in a business. Discuss each situation: (a) from the strictly legal viewpoint, (b) from a moral and ethical viewpoint, and (c) from the point of view of what is best in the long run for the company. Be sure to consider both short- and long-range consequences. Also look at each situation from the perspective of all groups concerned: customers, stockholders, employees, government, community.

1. A disgruntled employee of your major competitor mails top-secret information or new product samples to you. Do you begin to do a dance on your desktop or do you immediately mail the information back to your competitor? What would you do?
   a. Throw the plans or secrets away.
   b. Send them to your research department for analysis.
   c. Notify your competitor about what is going on.
   d. Call the FBI.

2. You are the general manager of a regional chemical company. In the course of producing your bulk chemicals, large amounts of particles and smoke are emitted through your plant's smokestack. The level of pollutants is below current EPA regulations, and you are violating no laws, but neighborhood groups are complaining about minor health problems caused by the smoke. After investigating numerous alternatives, you find the most effective solution would be to install a "scrubber" system which will remove 90 percent of the pollutants and ash. Cost: $1 million. Do you install the system?

3. You are a general manager in a cosmetics firm. The results of a study show that your major brand may cause skin cancer. What do you do?

4. You are the vice president of a beer company in a state which sets the legal drinking age at twenty-one. Your boss asks you to organize a lobbying effort to have the drinking age reduced to eighteen.

5. Because of a loophole in federal laws you find that you could legally pay your workers less than the minimum wage. The cost savings may mean your getting a choice promotion.

6. You are an accountant in a large firm. Your boss tells you to use a controversial accounting practice which will make the company's profits seem higher. She tells you it is only to impress stock-holders and will not be used in statements submitted to the IRS.

7. A worker is repeatedly late for work. You know she has family problems and is going through a difficult period with an alcoholic husband. Her work is inconsistent sometimes average, often excellent. She has been with the company for nine years. On Monday she was two hours late for work.

ANSWERS TO CRITICAL THINKING EXERCISE 4-1

Each of these situations may have several possible solutions. The best solution from the company's point of view may be quite different from one's own philosophical point of view. Below are some discussion points.

1. This actual situation is at the heart of a dispute between supersized rivals 3M Corporation and Johnson & Johnson. It seems a 3M employee named Philip Stegora mailed samples he stole of a new casting tape to J&J and three other competitors. He offered to meet and explain the technology for a fee of $20,000.

   Here's what happened in the 3M and J&J case: None of the contacted companies reported his scheme to 3M. Instead an outside source contacted 3M who then turned the case over to the FBI. The case could have ended there but in patent-infringement proceedings, 3M found that J&J had done chemical tests on the sample Stegora had sent. 3M sued and was awarded $116.3 million from J&J for infringing on its patent and misappropriating trade secrets. Sounds like someone should have sent the tape back to J&J in the first place.

2. In considering whether to install the scrubber, both the short and long-term consequences should be addressed. While the level of pollution is legal today, is it likely to be regulated tomorrow? What would be the public relations impact for the company if it installed the system? If it did not?

3. The key word in this question is "could." The evidence is inconclusive. How would the company be affected if the product were pulled prematurely? How would it be affected if the product causes dozens of cancers and results in huge lawsuits?

4. Eighteen- to 21-year-olds represent a huge market for liquor. But, again, the public reaction should be considered.

5. Many smaller companies are exempt from minimum wage laws but still pay the prevailing wage. The supply and demand for workers is a more important price factor. A company that pays less that minimum wage will not be able to attract as many qualified workers as one that does.

6. This is the only black and white dilemma. To use dual accounting practices to deceive investors is illegal.

7. This worker is going through a difficult time. Her work is, however, "often excellent." The costs of training a replacement worker must be weighed against the possibly temporary reduction in productivity.

Name: ____________________

Date: ____________________

CRITICAL THINKING EXERCISE 4-2

SURVEYING PUBLIC INTEREST ORGANIZATIONS

Newspapers and magazines are full of stories about individuals and organizations that are not socially responsible. What about those individuals and organizations that do take social responsibility seriously? We don't read about them as often. Do a little investigative reporting of your own. List two of the public interest power groups in your community and identify their officers, their objectives, their sources and amount of financial support, the size and characteristics of their membership and examples of their recent actions and/or accomplishments.

1. **ORGANIZATION** SOURCES OF FUNDS ANNUAL BUDGET

   ____________ ____________ ____________

   OFFICERS ____________________

   SIZE AND CHARACTERISTICS OF MEMBERSHIP ____________________

   OBJECTIVES ____________________

   RECENT ACTIONS AND/OR ACCOMPLISHMENTS ____________________

2. **ORGANIZATION** SOURCES OF FUNDS ANNUAL BUDGET

   ____________ ____________ ____________

   OFFICERS ____________________

   SIZE AND CHARACTERISTICS OF MEMBERSHIP ____________________

   OBJECTIVES ____________________

   RECENT ACTIONS AND/OR ACCOMPLISHMENTS ____________________

ANSWERS TO CRITICAL THINKING EXERCISE 4-2

Call the local Chamber of Commerce or Better Business Bureau for help. Also, call local government agencies and see what private firms are operating in your area that have the public interest in mind. For example, there are likely to be environmental groups, animal protection groups, and political action committees.

Name: ____________________

Date: ____________________

CRITICAL THINKING EXERCISE 4-3

SOCIAL RESPONSIBILITY SUCCESSES AND FAILURES

Name at least one example of a company that succeeded or failed to be socially responsible in each of the categories below.

CATEGORY	SUCCESS	FAILURE
Corporate Philanthropy		
Employee Health and Safety		
Environmental Stewardship		
Minority and Women's Employment and Advancement		

ANSWERS TO CRITICAL THINKING EXERCISE 4-3

The Council on Economic Priorities published an annual book, "Shopping for a Better World," that rates hundreds of companies in ten categories of social responsibility. This publication is a good resource for this question.

CATEGORY	SUCCESS	FAILURE
Corporate Philanthropy	**Pfizer, Inc.**'s "Sharing the Care" program serves people who might not otherwise receive needed medicines. The program has provided nearly 700,000 prescriptions to low income, uninsured patients nationwide.	Marketing companies hired to raise funds for charities but keeps 955% of the donations for "administrative costs."
Employee Health and Safety	**Cooperative Home Care Associates**. CHCA offers twice as much training as the government requires. Individual health benefits are provided (100%) to all full- and part-time workers.	Chemical companies in which unborn children of workers suffer genetic damage.
Environmental Stewardship	**Natural Cotton Colours, Inc.** organically grows naturally colored cotton sold under the brand name Fox Fibre. This cotton does not require bleaching and dying, thereby avoiding large amounts of pollution and toxic releases.	**Occidental**, the country's third largest chemical company and the second largest producer of chlorine in the U.S. has total toxic releases three times the average for oil companies.
Minority and Women's Employment and Advancement	The **Federal National Mortgage Association**, a federally chartered and stockholder owned corporation, provides diversity awareness training to all employees and integrates diversity issues into every aspect of its in-house training and development courses.	**Texaco** executives are audiotaped making racist remarks about employees.

Supplemental Cases

CASE 4-1

ETHICS IN HOLLYWOOD AND THE ENTERTAINMENT INDUSTRY

Many people say that the foundation for ethical behavior begins with the family and what the family says. and does. Family values seem to persist into adulthood. Part of what influences a child is the kind of movies and TV shows the family watches. Nobody has to tell you how low the moral and ethical standards for some TV shows and movies have become.

A Hollywood film producer sends 10 copies of a script to 10 different directors, saying "You're my first choice" to all 10. A major studio agrees to the pay demands of a big star but insists on paying some of the money "on the side" so that agents and other stars won't insist on a similar amount. A scene in a script calls for a tennis court, so the producer volunteers his yard, has a court built there, and charges the cost of the court to the film's budget. Creative accounting in the costing of movies means that most movies make no money That way, some investors in films get no money even though the film brought in huge revenues. The industry thinks such accounting practices are ethical because they're legal.

The corruption of youth doesn't stop in Hollywood, though. The singing group 2 Live Crew says things in their songs that professors may be fired for saying in front of their classes. The "proof" that such songs aren't too bad is that the courts haven't forbidden them. Madonna's videos are shown repeatedly on cable TV in the middle of the day They aren't illegal. Neither are shows like "Beavis and Butthead" even though they show dangerous behavior (like saying that playing with fire is fun) that can be and has been copied by young children.

Children watch such shows-sometimes with their parents in the room. Often the parents are busy doing something else and don't carefully monitor what their children watch. Many shows feature businesspeople who are greedy, mean, and dangerous. Often, businesspeople on TV and in the movies lie, cheat, and kill to get what they want. This happens on TV every night of the year That's the ethical foundation being established in some of the children of America in the 1990s. Value-free education is widespread in U.S. public schools. This creates a greater need for parents to instill values in the home, but TV and other influences make that task difficult.

DISCUSSION QUESTIONS FOR CASE 4-1:

1. In recent survey of college students by the Josephson Institute of Ethics in Los Angeles, 75 percent of the undergraduates said they cheated at least once last year A similar survey by the Higher Education Research Institute at UCLA found that 37 percent of students admitted to cheating on exams, while 57 percent said they copied homework. Such figures are higher than they were in the past. How much of such cheating do you feel is influenced by the amount of cheating students see on TV and in the movies?

2. Hollywood movie studios and other businesses are careful not to break the law. That's their standard of morality these days. If Hollywood suffers few social sanctions for its behavior, why should other businesses maintain a higher standard of ethics and morality? After all, they often can make more money as Hollywood can, by pushing the ethical boundary' as far out as possible.

3. What influences have helped shape your personal code of ethics and morality? What influences, if any, have pressured you to compromise those standards in recent years?

4. At one time, there were many words that performers weren't allowed to say on TV and in movies, and they were restricted as to what they could do as well What benefits and disadvantages would occur if America were to return to those standards?

ANSWERS TO DISCUSSION QUESTIONS FOR CASE 4-1:

1. *A recent survey of college students by the Josephson Institute of Ethics in Los Angeles found that 75 percent of all undergraduates say they cheated at least once last year. A similar survey by the Higher Education Research Institute at UCLA found that 37 percent of students admitted to cheating on exams, while 57 percent said they copied homework. Such figures are higher than they were in the past. How much of such cheating do you feel is influenced by the amount of cheating students see on TV and in the movies?*

Television is only one of many influences on today's students. As important or more so are the influences of parents, school, and peers. Who we are is shaped by these things and the experiences we have. Even current events and the news media affect our ethics. Few Americans over the age of 40 feel the same trust in government they did before Watergate.

2. *Hollywood movie studios and other businesses are very careful not to break the law. That is their standard of morality these days. If Hollywood suffers so few social sanctions for their behavior, why should other businesses maintain a higher standard of ethics and morality? After all, they often can make more money, as Hollywood can, by pushing the ethical boundary as far out as possible.*

This question could be an interesting, if heated, debate topic. The ultimate judge of what is profitable is the American consumer and how he or she chooses to spend the entertainment dollar. We seem to be fairly tolerant of Hollywood products, viewing the industry almost as a foreign country strange and not truly representative of the mainstream. Consumer boycotts, however, have occasionally forced changes in televisions programs.

3. *What influences have helped shape your personal code of ethics and morality? What influences, if any, have pressured you to compromise those standards in recent years?*

This question will be answered individually. It could be interesting to note if there are any generalizations that can be reached based on students' ages or sex.

4. *At one time, there were many words that performers were not allowed to say on TV and in the movies, and they were restricted as to what they could do as well. What benefits and disadvantages would occur if America were to return to those standards?*

One possible benefit could be a return to a greater sense of discipline, which could lead to increased responsibility. Stronger sense of moral values, greater awareness of inappropriate behavior, and more positive role models could also result.

Arguments against such restrictions revolve around reduced personal freedom, first amendment rights, and possible censorship.

CASE 4-2

THE PROFIT OBJECTIVE AND SOCIAL RESPONSIBILITY

Milton Friedman, an economist from the University of Chicago, has argued, "Few trends could thoroughly undermine the very foundation of our free society as the acceptance by corporate officials of a social responsibility other than to make as much money for stockholders as possible."

Basically, Friedman's argument for this position goes like this:

1. Business exists to make a profit.
2. When a business makes a profit, it uses scarce resources efficiently, provides desired products and services, creates jobs, and serves society.
3. Business involvement in the social/political process will only increase the political influence of business. Because big business has more to spend, influence will be concentrated in big business.
4. The business of business is business.
5. Business profits belong to stockholders, not the public. On the other hand, there is a sizable body of literature which says that business has a social responsibility beyond profit.

Some points of this argument include the following:

1. As part of society, business should be involved in solving society's problems.
2. It is in the self-interest of business to help solve society's problems.
3. Results have not come from leaving social problems to government.
4. Everyone has a responsibility to help his fellow citizen, including businesspeople.
5. Business has plenty of money to spend on social programs if it wanted.

DISCUSSION QUESTIONS FOR CASE 4-2:

1. Does the president of a firm have a right and obligation to use corporate profits for social programs? To whom do the profits belong?

2. Does a business executive have the same social responsibility as any other citizen, or is his or her responsibility greater or less? Why?

3. What socially responsible behavior could be profitable as well as socially beneficial?

ANSWERS TO DISCUSSION QUESTIONS FOR CASE 4-2:

1. *Does the president of a firm have a right and obligation to use corporate profits for social programs? To whom do the profits belong?*

Profits of a firm belong to stockholders. Whether or not a president should use those profits for social programs is a matter of discussion among the board of directors who represent the stockholders in the firm. Many good arguments could be made for supporting social causes, including good publicity, improving the community, and a general social obligation. Arguments against such expenditures include the fact that stockholders may have causes of their own that they could support if they received more income. Is it better for individuals to support social causes or corporations or both? Open this up to discussion.

2. *Does a business executive have the same social responsibility as any other citizen, or is his or her responsibility greater or less? Why?*

A businessperson has two responsibilities to uphold: one as a citizen like everyone else and one as a corporate leader. One's social obligations can be fulfilled in either role or both. There is no special obligation of a business executive to improve society more than, say, a school teacher or plumber. People often expect more from business leaders. Is that a reasonable expectation, given that businesspeople often make much more money? Would basketball players and football players have the same obligation for the same reason? Why or why not?

3. *What socially responsible behavior could be profitable as well as socially beneficial?*

Virtually anything that benefits society could benefit a business in the long run. Hiring the handicapped may lower the welfare roles and lower government spending. Keeping the environment clean may pay off in healthier and happier workers. Supporting the community may attract more and better workers to the area. In short, it is often in the best interest of a firm to be quite active in social causes.

CASE 4-3

FRANCE'S AIDS SCANDAL

In 1991 doctors and government officials in France were hurling questions and accusations at each other after it was revealed that the country's National Center of Blood Transfusions (CNTS) had knowingly distributed AIDS-contaminated blood to hemophiliacs in 1985. The scandal prompted the center's director to resign, and resulted in several government officials being tried.

The furor began when L'Evenèment du Jeudi, a weekly magazine, published minutes of a 1985 CNTS meeting during which agency officials concluded that 100 percent of the concentrated blood-clotting factors used to treat French hemophiliacs were contaminated with the AIDS virus. The agency, which has a monopoly on blood for transfusions, not only kept its suspicions secret, but it also ignored a 1984 recommendation from the U.S. Centers for Disease Control that blood products be heated in order to kill the deadly virus.

In July 1985 the CNTS finally decided to heat treat all blood products. But for the next three months the agency continued to sell the tainted stock to hemophiliacs without warning them of the risk. That policy was reportedly intended to ward off a blood shortage.

Whatever the reasons, the secrecy and delays produced catastrophic results. Because of the tainted transfusions, nearly half of France's 3,000 hemophiliacs were infected with the AIDS virus; 200 of them subsequently developed the disease, and at least 180 have died.

DISCUSSION QUESTIONS FOR CASE 4-3:

1. Realizing that in 1985 very little was known with certainty about AIDS and its impact on society, how would you have voted at the 1985 CNTS meeting?

2. Why do you think the French agency resisted heat-treating blood products?

3. Could this tragedy have happened in the U.S.?

ANSWERS TO DISCUSSION QUESTIONS FOR CASE 4-3

1. *Realizing that in 1985 very little was known with certainty about AIDS and its impact on society, how would you have voted at the 1985 CNTS meeting?*

This will be an individual decision. It is hoped that the majority of students would have voted to stop distributing the blood products.

2. *Why do you think the French agency resisted heat-treating blood products?*

Even if a blood shortage had not been a possibility, there were powerful incentives to do nothing. The clotting factor makes the difference between life and dead for many hemophiliacs. Many could have died without the clotting factor if it were unavailable. Critics allege that the CNTS was trying to avoid the cost of purchasing heat-treated blood from foreign labs. Others point to the bitter rivalry between French and American researchers over who discovered the AIDS virus. The French may have been unwilling to buy American-developed heat-treatment equipment.

3. *Could this tragedy have happened in the U.S.?*

Unfortunately, it could and did. Today over fifty percent of American hemophiliacs are also HIV positive, and isolated reports still surface of contaminated blood transfusions.

Transparency Masters

TRANSPARENCY MASTER 27	Chapter Outline
TRANSPARENCY MASTER 28	Overview of Lockheed Martin's Code of Ethics *(Figure 4.1 on text page 106)*
TRANSPARENCY MASTER 29	Strategies for Ethics Management *(Figure 4.2 on text page 106)*
TRANSPARENCY MASTER 30	Socially Responsible Business Activities *(Figure 4.3 on text page 111)*

Chapter Outline

CHAPTER 4
DEMONSTRATING ETHICAL BEHAVIOR AND SOCIAL RESPONSIBILITY

PROFILE: Nancy Bierk, Ad Impressions and Logo Masters

I. MANAGING BUSINESS ETHICALLY AND RESPONSIBLY.

II. LEGALITY IS ONLY THE FIRST ETHICAL STANDARD.

A. Personal Ethics Begin at Home.

B. Ethics Is More than an Individual Concern.

C. Organizational Ethics Begins at the Top.

III. SETTING CORPORATE ETHICAL STANDARDS.

IV. CORPORATE SOCIAL RESPONSIBILITY.

A. Responsibility to Customers.

B. Responsibility to Investors.

C. Responsibility to Employees.

D. Responsibility to Society.

E. Social Auditing.

V. INTERNATIONAL ETHICS AND SOCIAL RESPONSIBILITY.

VI. SUMMARY AND REVIEW.

Overview of Lockheed Martin's Code of Ethics

(Figure 4.1 on text page 106)

TREAT IN AN ETHICAL MANNER THOSE TO WHOM LOCKHEED MARTIN HAS AN OBLIGATION

We are committed to the ethical treatment of those to whom we have an obligation.

For our employees we are committed to honesty, just management, and fairness, providing a safe and healthy environment, and respecting the dignity due everyone.

For our customers we are committed to produce reliable products and services, delivered on time, at a fair price.

For the communities in which we live and work we are committed to acting as concerned and responsible neighbors, reflecting all aspects of good citizenship.

For our shareholders we are committed to pursuing sound growth and earnings objectives and to exercising prudence in the use of our assets and resources.

For our suppliers we are committed to fair competition and the sense of responsibility required of a good customer.

This excerpt from Lockheed Martin's Web page is an overview of the stakeholders to whom Lockheed Martin has an obligation to treat in an ethical manner. To see the company's complete code of ethics go to their Web site at http://www.lmco.com/exeth/ethset.html.

Strategies for Ethics Management
(Figure 4.2 on text page 106)

FEATURES OF COMPLIANCE-BASED ETHICS CODES

Ideal:	Conform to outside standards (laws and regulations)
Objective:	Avoid criminal misconduct
Leaders:	Lawyers
Methods:	Education, reduced employee discretion, controls, penalties

FEATURES OF INTEGRITY-BASED ETHICS CODES

Ideal:	Conform to outside standards (laws and regulations) and chosen internal standards
Objective:	Enable responsible employee conduct
Leaders:	Managers with aid of lawyers and others
Methods:	Education, leadership, accountability, decision processes, controls, and penalties

Integrity-based ethics codes are similar to compliance-based ethics codes in that both have a concern for the law and use penalties as enforcement. Integrity-based ethics codes move beyond legal compliance to create a "do-it-right" climate that emphasizes core values such as honesty, fair play, good service to customers, a commitment to diversity, and involvement in the community. These values are ethically desirable, but not necessarily legally.

Socially Responsible Business Activities
(Figure 4.3 on text page 111)

SOCIALLY RESPONSIBLE BUSINESS ACTIVITIES

- **Community-related activities** such as participating in local fund-raising campaigns, donating executive time to various nonprofit organizations (including local government), and participating in urban planning and development.
- **Employee-related activities** such as equal opportunity programs, flextime, improved benefits, job enrichment, job safety, and employee development programs. (You'll learn more about these activities in Chapters 11 and 12.)
- **Political activities** such as taking a position on issues such as nuclear safety, gun control, pollution control, and consumer protection; and working more closely with local, state, and federal government officials.
- **Support for higher education, the arts, and other nonprofit social agencies.**
- **Consumer activities** such as product safety, honest advertising, prompt complaint handling, honest pricing policies, and extensive consumer education programs.

Appendix
Working Within the Legal Environment of Business

Folder Contents

Transparency Masters

B.40

TM 31 Appendix Outline

TM 32 Federal Regulatory Agencies *(Figure A.1 on text page 120)*

TM 33 Patent Law *(Figure A.2 on text page 121)*

TM 34 Consumer Protection Laws *(Figure A.3 on text page 127)*

TM 35 Types of Taxes *(Figure A.4 on text page 128)*

TM 36 How Assets Are Divided in Bankruptcy *(Figure A.5 on text page 129)*

TM 37 Hamburger Regulations *(Figure A.6 on text page 131)*

Overhead Transparency Acetates

ACETATE LE-1 Sources of U.S. Law

ACETATE LE-2 Categories of Business Law

ACETATE LE-3 Criteria for a Valid Contract

ACETATE LE-4 Leaders in Patents in the U.S.

ACETATE LE-5 Types of Patents Issued

ACETATE LE-6 The Average Person Who Files Bankruptcy

(Acetates and Transparency Masters are also available as PowerPoint slides on disk and on the Presentation CD-ROM.)

(Resources Available are also referenced in the expanded lecture outline later in this chapter.)

Other Resources Available

Student Assessment and Learning Guide: Contains matching key term and definition questions, write-in retention questions, write-in critical thinking questions, and practice test of multiple choice and true/false questions.

Technology:

Zapitalism CD-ROM - Simulation program.

Concept Mastery Exam Preparation Disk - Practice test and tutorial.

Business Essentials Disk - Hyperlinks Understanding Business with seven other leading business texts.

Presentation CD-ROM - Contains PowerPoint slides of acetates and transparency masters, video clips, lecture materials. This tool allows you to customize your lecture presentations.

***Business Week* Web Site Access with the *Business Week* edition.**

Understanding Business **Home Page - http:/www.mhhe.com/ub5e.**

Audiotape: Abridged chapter (Text minus profile, boxes, and end-of-chapter material.

What's New in This Edition

Revisions:

Statistical data and examples throughout the chapter were updated to reflect current information. In addition:

- Discussion of forms of competition in the section "Laws to Promote Fair and Competitive Practices" was moved to Chapter 2.
- Figure A2.2 was updated to reflect new length of patent enforceability.

Brief Chapter Outline/Learning Goals

APPENDIX

WORKING WITHIN THE LEGAL ENVIRONMENT OF BUSINESS

I. THE NEED FOR LAWS.

II. BUSINESS LAW.

A. Statuary and Common Laws.

B. Administrative Agencies.

III. TORT LAW.

A. Product Liability.

IV. LAWS PROTECTING IDEAS: PATENTS, COPYRIGHTS, AND TRADEMARKS.

V. SALES LAW: THE UNIFORM COMMERCIAL CODE.

A. Warranties.

B. Negotiable Instruments.

VI. CONTRACT LAW.

A. Breach of Contract.

VII. LAWS TO PROMOTE FAIR AND COMPETITIVE PRACTICES.

A. The Interstate Commerce Act of 1887.

B. The Sherman Antitrust Act of 1890.

VIII. LAWS TO PROTECT CONSUMERS.

IX. TAX LAWS.

X. BANKRUPTCY LAWS.

XI. DEREGULATION.

XII. SUMMARY AND REVIEW.

(Learning Objectives are also referenced in the expanded lecture outline later in this chapter)

Key Terms

administrative agencies *(text page 110)*
bankruptcy *(text page 128)*
breach of contract *(text page 124)*
business law *(text page 119)*
common law *(text page 119)*
consideration *(text page 123)*
consumerism *(text page 126)*
contract *(text page 123)*
contract law *(text page 123)*
copyright *(text page 122)*
damages *(text page 124)*
deregulation *(text page 130)*
express warranties *(text page 122)*
implied warranties *(text page 122)*
involuntary bankruptcy *(text page 128)*
judiciary *(text page 118)*
negotiable instruments *(text page 123)*
patent *(text page 121)*
product liability *(text page 120)*
statutory law *(text page 119)*
taxes *(text page 126)*
tort *(text page 119)*
trademark *(text page 122)*
Uniform Commercial Code (UCC) *(text page 122)*
voluntary bankruptcy *(text page 128)*

Lecture Outline

I. THE NEED FOR LAWS.

A. Laws are an essential part of a civilized nation.

B. The **JUDICIARY** is the branch of government chosen to oversee the legal system.

C. Government has stepped in to make **LAWS** governing behavior because businesspeople have not take sufficient steps to make more and ethical decisions on their own.

II. BUSINESS LAW.

A. **BUSINESS LAW** refers to the rules, statutes, codes, and regulations established to provide a legal framework within which business may be conducted and that is enforceable in court.

B. A businessperson should be familiar with the laws regarding product liability, sales, contracts, fair competition, consumer protection, taxes, and bankruptcy.

C. **STATUTORY AND COMMON LAW.**

1. **STATUTORY LAW** includes state and federal constitutions, legislative enactments, treaties, and ordinances (written laws).

2. **COMMON LAW** is the body of the law that comes from judges' decisions.

a. Also known as **UNWRITTEN LAW.**

Lecture Notes

TRANSPARENCY MASTER 31
Appendix Outline

TM 31 Transparency Masters begin on page B.40.

OT ACETATE LE-1
Sources of U.S. Law

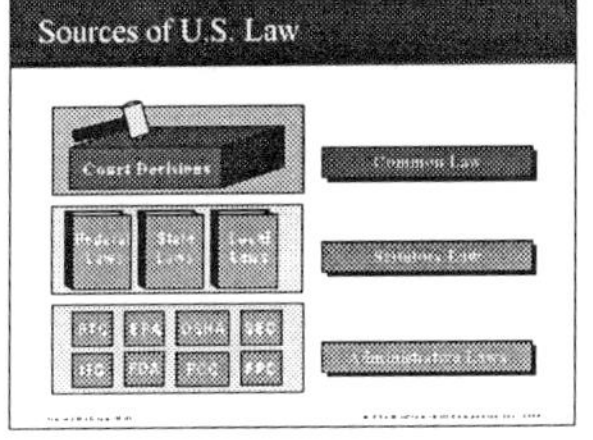

Comments:

1. This acetate highlights for students the key sources of U.S. law. You might want to distinguish how the systems are different in process and authority, but most importantly how they impact on the operation of business.
2. Administrative law will most likely cause the most consternation for students. It may take an explanation to clarify the power of administrative agencies and their purpose in the legal system. Items such as cease-and-desist orders, regulatory law, and administrative hearings could be covered here.
3. You may choose not to take the time but this would be an opportune point to explain the basis of the court system in the U.S. ranging from the U.S. Supreme Court on down.

OT ACETATE LE-2
The Categories of Business Law

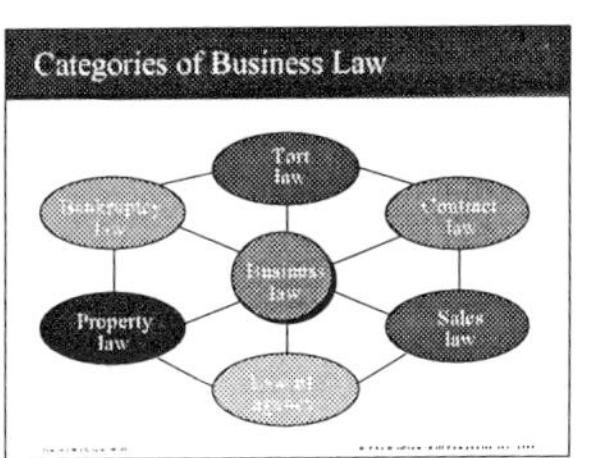

Comments:

1. The major categories of business law are detailed in this acetate. Contract law, tort law, sales law, and bankruptcy law are discussed in the appendix. You may want to check student understanding of these topics by working through this acetate.
2. This acetate also can be used to enhance the brief discussion of torts in the text by highlighting the concepts of intentional torts and contributory negligence.
   - **Intentional torts** are actions that are carried out by the wrongdoer. A firm intentionally slandering another is an example of an intentional tort. For instance, "Bronco Billy Burgers use soy protein instead of real beef." If the condemning firm is aware that this statement is false, the grieving firm may sue under tort law.
   - **Contributory negligence** involves harm caused by carelessness rather than intention. For example, an employee of a beauty salon forgets a customer under a hair dryer and that person's hair is damaged. The owner of the salon could be liable due to the negligence of the employee.
3. Contract law will be covered in depth in the next acetate. You could also expand the brief discussion of sales law in the chapter with additional coverage and examples.
4. Bankruptcy issues will be discussed in **OT ACETATE 1-6.**

Lecture Outline

b. Such decisions are called **PRECEDENTS** and guide judges in their handling of new cases.

D. **ADMINISTRATIVE AGENCIES**.

1. Branches of government called administrative agencies issue rules, regulations, and orders.

2. **ADMINISTRATIVE AGENCIES** are institutions created by Congress with delegated power to pass rules and regulations within its mandated area of authority.

3. Administrative agencies hold quasi-legislative, quasi-executive, and quasi-judicial powers.

   a. The agency is allowed to pass rules and regulations within its area of authority, conduct investigations, and hold hearings when rules and regulations have been violated.

   b. They issue more rulings and settle more disputes than courts.

III. TORT LAW.

A. A **TORT** is a wrongful conduct that causes injury to another person's body, property, or reputation.

Lecture Notes

TRANSPARENCY MASTER 32
Federal Regulatory Agencies *(Figure A.1 on text page 120)*

Transparency Masters begin on page B.40.

OT ACETATE LE-3
Criteria for a Valid Contract

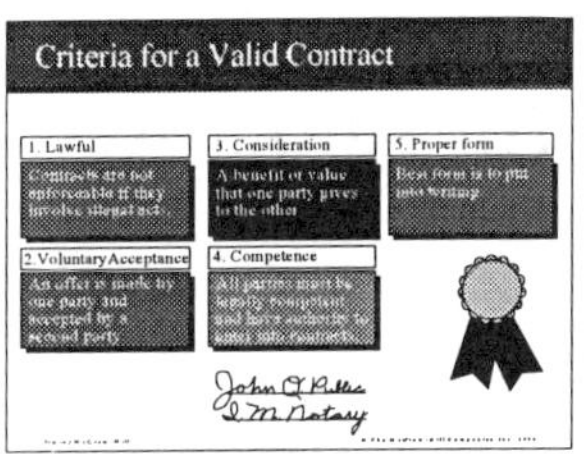

Comments:

1. This information is presented in the text, but a quick review through the acetate will highlight the significance of each step.
2. Some points to bring out to stimulate the discussion:
   - **Lawful:** In most states if two people enter into a contract that involves a gambling wager, that contract would not be enforceable. Contracts entered into with minors are not legal therefore not enforceable.
   - **Voluntary acceptance:** Voluntary acceptance means the decision must be under each party's free will. You can mention to students the three day cancellation option on consumer contracts involving products such as encyclopedias as an example of assuring the voluntary nature of a contract.
   - **Consideration:** Consideration can be a dollar, but that dollar is very important in deciding validity in a contract. That's why some parents choose to charge their children one dollar for a car, house, etc., they wish to give them.
   - **Competence:** Both parties must be legally competent to enter into the contract. People of unsound mind cannot be held liable for voluntary agreements made. Persons under the influence of alcohol or drugs are also not legally competent to enter contracts.
   - **Proper form:** Even though many contracts do not have to be in writing to be legal, it is always best to put the contract in writing.

Lecture Outline

1. An **INTENTIONAL TORT** is a willful act purposely inflicted that results in injury.
2. **NEGLIGENCE** deals with questionable but unintentional behavior that causes harm or injury.
3. Such product liability is one of the more controversial areas of tort law,

B. **PRODUCT LIABILITY**.

1. **PRODUCT LIABILITY** is covered under tort law and holds businesses liable for negligence in the production, design, sale, or use of products it markets.
2. **STRICT LIABILITY** means without regard to fault; that is, a company could be liable for damages caused by placing a product on the market with an unknown defect.
3. The rule of strict liability has caused serious problems for some manufacturers.
4. Manufacturers of chemicals and drugs are lobbying Congress to set damage limits.

IV. **LAWS PROTECTING IDEAS: PATENTS, COPYRIGHTS, AND TRADEMARKS**.

A. A **PATENT** gives inventors **EXCLUSIVE RIGHTS to** their inventions for **20 YEARS**.

Lecture Notes

OT ACETATE LE-4
Leaders in Patents in the U.S.

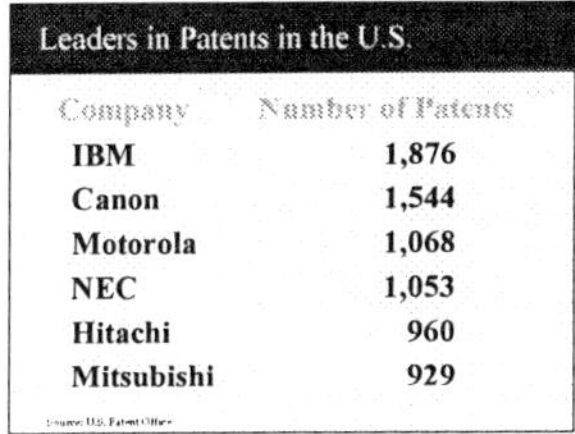

Leaders in Patents in the U.S.

Company	Number of Patents
IBM	1,876
Canon	1,544
Motorola	1,068
NEC	1,053
Hitachi	960
Mitsubishi	929

Source: U.S. Patent Office

Comments:

1. Patents are often an interesting topic to students. Listed in this acetate are the leading companies by the number of patents filed in the U.S.
2. Students may be surprised to see that Canon, a Japanese company, ranks right behind IBM in the number of patents filed. NEC and Hitachi, also Japanese firms are ranked four and five. The data refers to the number of patents filed in 1997. Stay in touch with information on the UB5E web site that will update information such as this on a yearly basis.
3. In case students are interested in finding out more about patents, copyrights, or trademarks, the Small Business Administration and the U.S. Patent and Trademark Office in Washington provide useful information. The SBA can be reached at (800)-634-0245 and the Patent & Trademark Office at (800) 786-9199.

TRANSPARENCY MASTER 33
Patent Law
(Figure A.2 on text page 121)

Transparency Masters begin on page B.40.

Lecture Outline

1. Patents owners may **SELL OR LICENSE** the use of the patent to others.
2. Filing a patent with the U.S. Patent Office requires a **SEARCH** to ensure the patent is truly unique, followed by the **FILING OF FORMS.**
3. Penalties for violating a patent can be severe—Kodak lost millions of dollars for infringing on a Polaroid patent.
4. Some 65% of patent applications are approved, costing the inventory a minimum of $6,000.
5. Critics argue that some inventors use a submarine patent, intentionally delaying a patent application and waiting for others to develop the technology.

B. A **COPYRIGHT** protects an individual's rights to materials such as books, articles, photos, and cartoons.

1. Copyrights are filed with the Library of Congress and involve a minimum of paperwork.
2. They last for the lifetime of the author or artist plus 50 years.

C. A **TRADEMARK** gives exclusive legal protection to a name, symbol, or design (or combination

LECTURE ENHANCER LE-1
Lloyd's of London Offering Patent Insurance

Lloyd's of London is providing insurance to help David take on Goliath in the courtroom. Several U.S. insurance agents have designed an insurance program, backed by Lloyd's of London, that will provide small businesses up to $1 million to sue companies that infringe on their patents. (See complete lecture enhancer on page B.34.)

LECTURE ENHANCER LE-2
Rumble at the Patent Office

Patents provide the fuel of interest to the fire of genius, as Abraham Lincoln said. But these days, patent law is providing fuel for something else—a pitched battle over intellectual property. (See complete lecture enhancer on page B.35.)

OT ACETATE LE-5
Types of Patents Issued

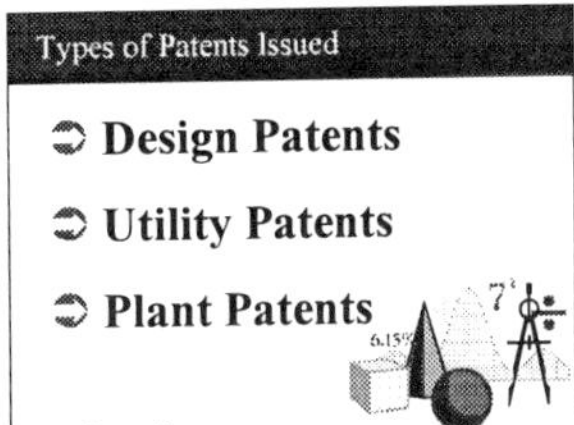

Comments:

1. Students probably do not know that there are differences in patents issued. This acetate lists the three major categories of patents.
2. The three major types of patents are:
   - **Design Patents** - protect the appearance or ornamental design of your invention. This type of patent is most effective for products such as jewelry, clothing, and furniture because it protects the way your idea looks. A design patent is good for 14 years and no maintenance fees are required to keep it in force.
   - **Utility Patents** - protect the function or method of your invention. This type is more complicated than a design patent because it requires you to explain how your invention is used. It is also generally more expensive to file. A utility patent has a term of 20 years from the date you file and requires payments of maintenance fees that can range from $500 to $3,000 depending on your company's size about every four years to keep the patent in force.
   - **Plant Patents** - protect the invention or discovery of a new or distinct plant variety. Special rules are in force for this type of patent including the requirement that you send a copy of your application to the Agricultural Research Service and Department of Agriculture for a plant variety report. The term of this type patent is 20 years and it does require maintenance fees.

of them) that identifies one seller's goods or services from those of competitors.

1. Trademarks generally belong to the owner forever.

V. SALES LAW: THE UNIFORM COMMERCIAL CODE.

A. The **UNIFORM COMMERCIAL CODE (UCC)** is a comprehensive commercial law adopted by all states; it covers **SALES LAWS** and other **COMMERCIAL LAW.**

1. The **11 ARTICLES OF THE UCC** cover sales; commercial paper; bank deposits and collections; letters of credit; bulk transfers; warehouse receipts, bills of lading, and other documents of title; investment securities; and secured transactions.

2. The text discusses two of these articles: **ARTICLE 2 (WARRANTIES)** and **ARTICLE 3 (NEGOTIABLE INSTRUMENTS).**

B. **WARRANTIES.**

1. **EXPRESS WARRANTIES** are specific representations by the seller regarding the goods.

2. **IMPLIED WARRANTIES** are guarantees legally imposed on the seller.

LECTURE ENHANCER LE-3
Is Your Product Warranty Complete?

You probably don't give much thought to warranties until your VCR refuses to tape Seinfeld or your vacuum cleaner starts spewing dust. Unfortunately, if you wait until technical difficulties strike before perusing the small print, you may discover the manufacturer won't take care of repairs. (See complete lecture enhancer on page B.37.)

Lecture Outline

3. A full warranty requires a seller to replace or repair a product at no charge if the product is defective.
4. Limited warranties typically limit the problems that are covered.

C. **NEGOTIABLE INSTRUMENTS**.

1. **NEGOTIABLE INSTRUMENTS** are forms of commercial paper (such as checks) that are transferable among businesses and individuals.
2. **NEGOTIABLE INSTRUMENTS** must be
   a. **WRITTEN** and **SIGNED** by the maker.
   b. **MADE PAYABLE ON DEMAND** at a certain time.
   c. **MADE PAYABLE TO THE BEARER OR TO ORDER**.
   d. **CONTAIN AN UNCONDITIONAL PROMISE TO PAY A SPECIFIED AMOUNT** of money.
3. Checks or other forms of negotiable instruments are transferred when the payee **ENDORSES**, signs the back of the check.

VI. **CONTRACT LAW**.

A. **TERMS**.

Lecture Notes

LECTURE ENHANCER LE-4 Negotiable Instrument Forgery and the UCC	A *Business Week* study concluded that $12.6 billion is lost annually to check forgery. Disputes over who is liable for bad checks often end up in court. These matters are governed by the Uniform Commercial Code, or UCC. (See complete lecture enhancer on page B.38.)

Lecture Outline

1. A **CONTRACT** is a legally enforceable agreement between two or more parties.
2. **CONTRACT LAW** specifies what a legally enforceable agreement is.

B. A contract is **LEGALLY BINDING** if the **FOLLOWING CONDITIONS** are met:

1. An **OFFER** is made.
2. There must be **VOLUNTARY ACCEPTANCE** of the offer.
3. Both parties must give **CONSIDERATION** (something of value).
4. Both parties must be **COMPETENT**.
5. The contract must be **LEGAL**.
6. The contract must be in a **PROPER FORM.**

C. **BREACH OF CONTRACT**.

1. **BREACH OF CONTRACT** means that one party fails to follow the terms of the contract.
2. **CONSEQUENCES** of a breached contract are:
   a. **SPECIFIC PERFORMANCE**—The person violating contract may be required to live up to the agreement if no monetary award is adequate.

Lecture Notes

b. **PAYMENT OF DAMAGES**—The monetary settlement, or **DAMAGES**, is awarded to a person who is injured by a breach of contract.

c. **DISCHARGE OF OBLIGATION.**

3. It is best to have a contract in **WRITING**. A contract should: (1) be in writing, (2) specify the consideration, and (3) be clearly offered and accepted.

VII. LAWS TO PROMOTE FAIR AND COMPETITIVE PRACTICES.

A. Businesses once operated under relatively free market conditions and were able to drive smaller competitors out of business with little recourse.

B. **THE INTERSTATE COMMERCE ACT OF 1887.**

1. The Act stipulated that:

   a. The railroad rates must be "reasonable."

   b. prohibited discriminatory rates, rebates, and other forms of favoritism

   c. outlawed price-fixing agreement between railroads.

2. It established the **INTERSTATE COMMERCE COMMISSION** to enforce these provisions.

Lecture Notes

Lecture Outline

3. An Act was passed in 1995 that abolished the ICC, transferring the responsibilities to other agencies.

C. **THE SHERMAN ANTITRUST ACT OF 1890.** forbids contracts, combinations, or conspiracies in restraint of trade and actual monopolies or attempts to monopolize any part of trade or commerce.

1. **THE CLAYTON ACT OF 1914** prohibits exclusive dealing, tying contracts, interlocking directorates, and buying large amounts of stock in competing corporations.

2. **THE FEDERAL TRADE COMMISSION ACT OF 1914** prohibits unfair methods of competition in commerce and created the Federal Trade Commission.

3. **THE ROBINSON-PATMAN ACT OF 1936** prohibits price discrimination.

4. **THE WHEELER-LEA AMENDMENT OF 1938** gave the FTC additional jurisdiction over false or misleading advertising.

VIII. LAWS TO PROTECT CONSUMERS.

A. **PRESIDENT JOHN F. KENNEDY** identified four **BASIC RIGHTS OF CONSUMERS:**

1. The right to **SAFETY.**

Lecture Notes

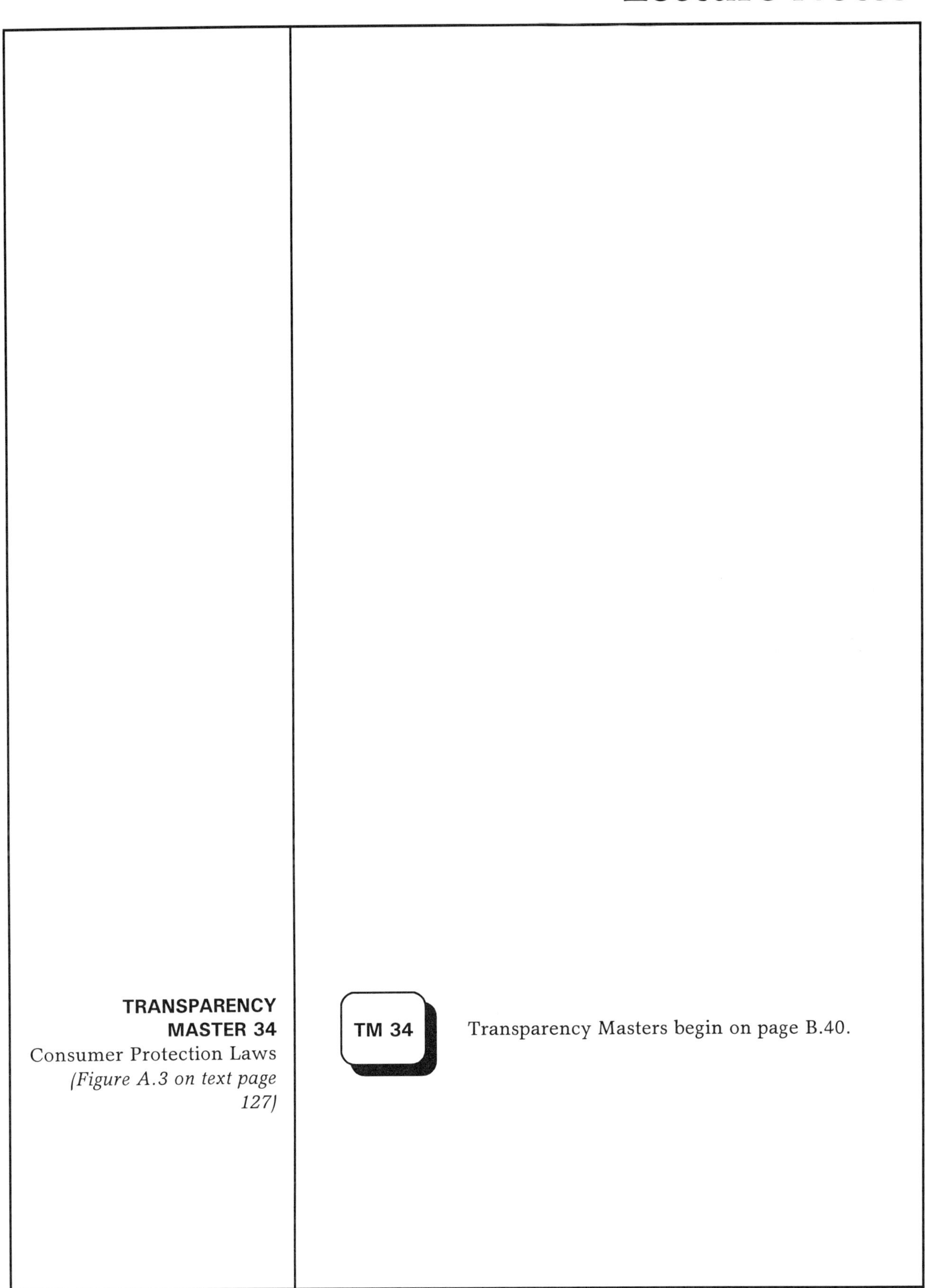

TRANSPARENCY MASTER 34
Consumer Protection Laws
(Figure A.3 on text page 127)

Transparency Masters begin on page B.40.

Lecture Outline

2. The right to be **INFORMED**.
3. The right to **CHOOSE.**
4. THE right to be **HEARD**.

B. **CONSUMERISM** is the people's way of getting their fair share in marketing exchanges.

IX. TAX LAW.

A. Taxes are government's way of raising money.

B. Taxes are also government's way of discouraging citizens from doing what it considers harmful (for example, sin taxes on cigarettes and alcohol.)

C. Government encourage businesses to hire new employees or purchase new equipment by offering a tax credit.

D. Taxes are levied from a variety of **SOURCES.**

1. Income, sales, and property are the major bases of tax revenue.
2. The tax policies of states and cities are taken into consideration when businesses seek to locate operations.

X. BANKRUPTCY LAW.

A. **BANKRUPTCY** is the legal process by which a person or business, unable to meet financial

TRANSPARENCY MASTER 35
Types of Taxes *(Figure A.4 on text page 128)*

Transparency Masters begin on page B.40.

OT ACETATE LE-6
The Average Person Who Files Bankruptcy

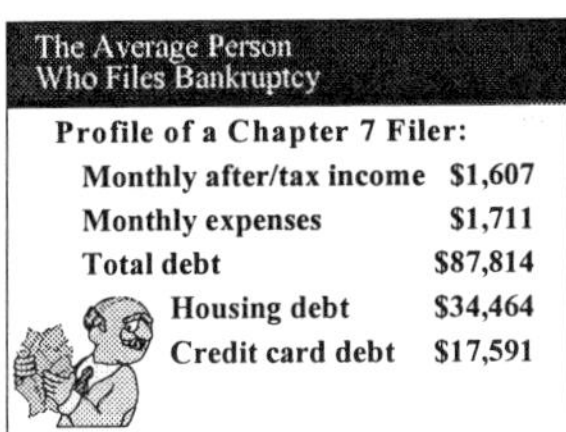

Comments:

1. Consumer bankruptcies hit an all time high in 1997. Many argue that the law has made it somewhat easy to discharge debts through favorable bankruptcy treatment. Consumer advocates say that over-easy credit standards have pushed many Americans to the financial edge. The U.S. Congress is debating the issue of bankruptcy reform and the issue promises to be a hot one throughout the remainder of the 1990s.
2. This acetate profiles a typical chapter 7 bankruptcy filer. You might want to walk the student through each component of the filer's profile and particularly note the heavy incidence of debt.
3. This might also be a good place to explain and clarify the ramifications of bankruptcy. Distinction between voluntary versus involuntary bankruptcy will help. Some students don't realize the long-term effects of bankruptcy. Media and uninformed sources often make it sound like a simple, non-entangled process. This is far from the truth since consumers often play havoc obtaining credit or getting any type of loan long after declaring bankruptcy. This may also be an appropriate time to discuss Chapter 11. Students should be able to note several major companies who have filed under Chapter 11, perhaps some in your own community.

obligations, is relieved of those debts by having the court divide any assets among creditors, freeing the debtor to begin anew.

B. **AMENDMENTS TO THE BANKRUPTCY LAW.**

   1. The Bankruptcy Amendments of 1984 allow a person who is bankrupt to keep part of the equity in a house.

   2. The Bankruptcy Reform Act of 1994 creates reforms that speed up and simplify the process.

C. In 1996 over 1 million Americans filed for bankruptcy—over 90% of filings each year are by individuals.

D. Bankruptcy can be either **VOLUNTARY** or **INVOLUNTARY**.

   1. **VOLUNTARY BANKRUPTCY**—involves legal procedures filed by a debtor.

   2. **INVOLUNTARY BANKRUPTCY**—involves bankruptcy procedures initiated by a debtor's creditors.

E. Bankruptcy procedures are filed under one of the following **SECTIONS OF THE BANKRUPTCY CODE:**

   1. **CHAPTER 7**—Straight bankruptcy or liquidation; used by businesses and individuals.

Lecture Notes

Lecture Outline

2. **CHAPTER 11**—Reorganization; used by businesses and some individuals.

3. **CHAPTER 13**—Repayment; used by individuals.

F. **CHAPTER 7** calls for **"STRAIGHT BANKRUPTCY,"** which requires the sale of nonexempt assets of debts.

1. Cash from the sale is divided among creditors.

2. First, creditors with secured claims are paid and they the unsecured claims are paid.

3. The text lists the order that unsecured claims are paid.

G. **CHAPTER 11**.

1. Chapter 11 allows a company to **REORGANIZE AND CONTINUE OPERATIONS** while paying only a limited proportion of its debts.

2. The Bankruptcy Reform Act of 1994 extends a "fast track" procedure for small businesses filing under Chapter 11.

3. Under Chapter 11 a company **CONTINUES TO OPERATE**, but has court protection against creditors' lawsuits while it tries to work out a debt repayment plan.

Lecture Notes

TRANSPARENCY MASTER 36
How Assets Are Divided in Bankruptcy *(Figure A.5 on text page 129)*

TM 36

Transparency Masters begin on page B.40.

4. Less than 25% of Chapter 11 companies emerge healthy.

5. In 1991 the U.S. Supreme Court ruled that individuals have the right to file bankruptcy under Chapter 11.

H. **CHAPTER 13** permits individuals, including small-business owners, to **PAY BACK CREDITORS OVER A THREE- TO FIVE-YEAR PERIOD.**

XI. DEREGULATION.

A. **DEREGULATION** means that the government withdraws certain laws and regulations that seem to hinder competition.

B. Business and government need to continue to work together to create a competitive environment that is fair and open.

C. There have recently been calls for **NEW REGULATIONS** in some industries—it seems some regulation of business is necessary to assure fair and honest dealings with the public.

D. If businesses do not want additional regulation, they must accept and respond to the responsibilities they have to society.

XII. SUMMARY AND REVIEW.

Lecture Notes

TRANSPARENCY MASTER 37
Hamburger Regulations
(Figure A.6 on text page 131)

TM 37

Transparency Masters begin on page B.40.

Lecture Enhancers

LECTURE ENHANCER LE-1

LLOYD'S OF LONDON OFFERING PATENT INSURANCE

Lloyd's of London is providing insurance to help David take on Goliath in the courtroom. Several U.S. insurance agents have designed an insurance program, backed by Lloyd's of London, that will provide small businesses up to $1 million to sue companies that infringe on their patents. "A patent doesn't mean a lot unless you have the money to enforce it," says Joby A. Hughes. As a patent attorney, Hughes says he's seen many small business owners who "think of their patents as shields, only to find out they could become weights around their neck."

The cost of the average patent-infringement case—more than $1 million—is more than most small companies can handle. That leaves those companies unable to protect their largest assets, according to Don Fancher, an intellectual property specialist at Deloitte & Touche L.L.P., one of the accounting firms that help evaluate the needs and risks of potential clients. "A high percentage of today's fastest growing companies have the vast majority of their assets tied up not in bricks and mortar, but in patents and copyrights," he says. "Up until today, they have had no way to insure themselves and their investors against misuse or theft."

Hughes says the insurance is aimed at companies with $5 million to $100 million in annual revenues. He also expects the coverage to attract venture capitalists, university licensing programs, banks, mergers and acquisitions, and initial public offerings.

Agents will offer both pursuit and defensive insurance. Pursuit coverage pays for the legal expenses in suing a patent infringer; defensive protects companies accused of infringement. Even if a policy holder never takes an infringing competitor to court, the coverage gives them a bankroll that allows them to threaten a law suit. That acts as a deterrent to companies that might risk knocking off a competitor's patents. Lloyd's is the first major insurance company to offer pursuit coverage.

LECTURE ENHANCER LE-2

RUMBLE AT THE PATENT OFFICE

Patents provide the fuel of interest to the fire of genius, as Abraham Lincoln said. But these days, patent law is providing fuel for something else—a pitched battle over intellectual property. Congress is in the midst of altering U.S. patent law, and depending on whom you ask, the changes will either bolster the U.S. industry's technological edge or kill off innovation. The likely outcome is a compromise that will change the U.S. patent system in a way that helps most companies. The new bills "will create a more efficient patent system," says Senate Judiciary Committee Chairman Orrin G. Hatch.

In one corner is a small band of independent inventors and their congressional supporters. In their view, American corporations once habitually stole outside innovators' ideas and infringed their patents, safe in the knowledge that many courts wouldn't uphold the patents. That began to change after the U.S. Court of Appeals for the Federal Circuit was created in 1982 for patent cases. Now, companies are being hit with major damages. Early in 1997 an appeals court upheld $103 million in awards to magnetic resonance imaging pioneer Raymond V. Damadian and his company Fonar Corp. in a suit against General Electric Co. In 1996 Haworth Inc., a Michigan office-furniture maker, won $211.5 million in damages from industry giant Steelcase Inc. over patents dating back to the 1970s.

Large companies are fighting back by trying to change the patent laws, small inventors charge. "They want to return to the good old days of stealing everything," complains Grand Blanc, Michigan inventor Ronald J. Riley. He and other small inventors claim that two industry-backed bills introduced in the 1997 Congress would do just that. The bills propose to turn the U.S. Patent & Trademark Office (PTO) into a semi-autonomous government corporation still linked to the Commerce Department but freed from some bureaucratic rules. But less government oversight would allow big companies to exert undue influence over patent decisions, small inventors argue. Another provision would require that all patent applications be published 18 months after filing instead of keeping them secret until the patents are actually granted—a process that sometimes takes years. The change, small inventors fear, would enable companies to steal their ideas or develop alternative technologies that circumvent the patents.

A third proposal would give anyone the right to challenge patents. Companies could ask the patent office to reexamine patents it granted to others—and then participate in the review. Beverly Selby, executive director of an alliance of independent inventors, warns that the provision will allow Big Business to quash small inventors.

PTO Commissioner Bruce A. Lehman says the changes are vital. Turning the patent office into a government corporation would free it from government rules on everything from hiring to printing. Michael Kirk, head of the American Intellectual Property Law Association, says the change would enable the office to issue better patents faster. And allowing third parties to participate in patent reexaminations would be a cheap, effective way to weed out bad patents.

Even more important, Lehman argues, is the requirement that patents be published 18 months after they're filed. That would solve the problem of "submarine patents," applications that lurk submerged in the patent office for years. When these patents are finally issued, the inventors can use them to sue companies that unknowingly infringed. "It's a method to extort money out of people who got there before you did and who don't know about your patent," charges Lehman. Publishing applications after 18 months would force these patents to the surface far earlier.

Submarine patents are rare, however. And the 1994 General Agreement on Tariffs & Trade (GATT) largely solved the problem by changing the term of patents from 17 years after they are granted to 20 years after filing. So while the submarine patent controversy inspires the most overheated rhetoric, the real question surrounding the 18-month publication term is more subtle. Europe and Japan already have 18-month publication, and U.S. companies want reciprocity. If they have to publish applications elsewhere within 18 months, then foreign companies should meet the same requirement when filing in the U.S., the argument goes. In addition, companies want to avoid sudden surprises from domestic inventors with newly issued patents. Biotech powerhouse Genentech Inc. recently found it had wasted considerable time and money on a research project after a competitor was awarded a patent on the idea. Much of that waste would have been avoided if the patent application had been published earlier.

LECTURE ENHANCER LE-3

IS YOUR PRODUCT WARRANTY COMPLETE?

You probably don't give much thought to warranties until your VCR refuses to tape Seinfeld or your vacuum cleaner starts spewing dust. Unfortunately, if you wait until technical difficulties strike before perusing the small print, you may discover the manufacturer won't take care of repairs.

The right time to check a warranty is before you make a purchase. Look for "full" warranties, which cover the cost of repair or replacement of the entire item, rather than "limited" warranties, which may only cover fixes for certain parts.

By law, any product bought by the fortunate residents of Connecticut, Kansas, Maine, Maryland, Massachusetts, Mississippi, Vermont, West Virginia, or Washington, D.C., is covered by a four-year "implied" warranty, which can't be restricted by the manufacturer. But those who live in other states must pay attention to a warranty's time limit as well.

Finally, when opening your new package, read all paperwork diligently. Those flyaway registration cards are usually for the manufacturer's consumer information files, but they may also serve as a way to establish proof of purchase.

LECTURE ENHANCER LE-4

NEGOTIABLE INSTRUMENT FORGERY AND THE UCC

Frank W. Abagnale was the main speaker at a recent seminar on document fraud. He is an unlikely expert, having spent time in French, Swedish, and U.S. prisons 30 years ago for creating and passing millions of dollars of bad checks. Interpol, Abagnale said, dubbed him a "master forger," a badge of honor of sorts, as Abagnale began his career when he was 16 years old and concluded it at age 21 with a stint in a French lockup. After serving his time there, he was extradited to Sweden and finally to the United States, doing 12 years. He was released early on the condition that he assist the U.S. government in its battle against forgers.

Now he's a "senior advisor" to the FBI's Financial Crimes Unit. In that role, he assisted in designing the new $100 bill. He also provides consulting services to financial institutions and companies worldwide.

Abagnale cited a *Business Week* study which concluded that $12.6 billion is lost annually to check forgery. Bank robbers may grab the headlines, but they only net about $68 million yearly, he said. That's $50 for every man, woman and child nationwide lost to check fraud compared to 27 cents per American taken at gun point. Many frauds are not reported by embarrassed companies, so the $12.6 billion figure is conservative, Abagnale said.

Lack of publicity about the problem has helped put the document fraud industry where it is today, Abagnale said. Politicians, prosecutors and judges don't concentrate on stopping fraud. Consequently, punishments are lower for forgery, assuming someone is arrested, which is rare. "Nobody ever ran for office promising 'I'll clear the streets of check writers if you elect me,'" he said.

Advances in modern technology also have made the forger's job easier. When Abagnale was practicing his former trade, a four-color printer was the size of a large room and cost $250,000. Now, he said, $5,000 worth of computer equipment provides a superior and portable alternative.

Disputes over who is liable for bad checks often end up in court. These matters are governed by the Uniform Commercial Code, or UCC, a set of model statutes designed by legal experts to be used by all states in order to provide a level playing field for commerce. It is not an all-encompassing federal law, but rather a guideline for laws to be adopted by the states individually.

States can adopt a provision of the UCC or not. For example, the portion of the UCC concerning liability in document frauds was amended in 1990. Connecticut adopted the amendment in 1991, but New York state has not yet done so.

What can a company do to make itself less vulnerable? One powerful weapon is known as "positive pay." A customer keeps an electronic list of all checks written and downloads it into the bank's computer at the end of the day. If a check shows up that is not on the list, it is flagged as a forgery and the bank doesn't honor it. Most banks have positive pay programs, said Abagnale.

An alternative for smaller businesses that may lack the sophisticated computer software necessary to create a daily list is "reverse positive pay." In this case, a bank sends a list to the business owner of checks drawn upon the company's account each day. The owner then compares his or her records with the bank's list and notifies the bank if there are any discrepancies.

Companies should stay up to date in reconciling bank statements since the UCC allows only 30 days to report a fraudulent instrument.

Banking procedures are not the only defense. Corporate officers who proudly affix their John Hancocks to annual reports or Security and Exchange Commission filings are a forger's delight. For a signature that will pass muster, the forger can just scan it off the report. Abagnale recommends that the lawyers who draft these reports sign them as opposed to officers whose signatures may appear on checks.

Checks turned out by high-speed laser printers allow forgers to lift the toner off the check with tools as sophisticated as scotch tape and substitute dollar numbers—usually with several extra zeros. Abagnale said that "toner anchorage," a chemical injected into the paper, causes the toner and the paper to fuse, preventing the writing from being lifted and changed. Also, chemicals can be added to checks so they change color upon being exposed to materials, such as bleach, which are used to erase the original writing.

The dollar amounts printed on checks should be in a unique font, or type style. Additionally, the numbers themselves should have writing incorporated into the them. This prevents adding, say, three zeroes to a $20 check and turning it into $20,000.

Because blank check paper is readily available through mail order vendors, prudent companies should arrange with their printer for a unique type of paper with security features built in. One such feature involves micro printing, used in the new $100 bill. Those lines along Bert Franklin's collar actually say something when held under a magnifying glass. Scanners and copiers are not sufficiently sensitive, so they can't reproduce the microprinting. The signature line of the check is a good place to use microprinting.

What scanners and copiers will catch is a "void pantograph." Scanners reproduce patterns of large dots before they reproduce patterns of small ones. A series of large dots spelling out the word "void" should be hidden in a secure check. This pattern may not be visible to the naked eye, but should the document be scanned or copied, up pops "void," thereby ruining the forger's work.

Warning labels should indicate other security features, such as watermarks, and state clearly that if the check does not have a watermark, "do not cash," Abagnale said.

Generally, the more difficult a company makes forgery, the less likely it is to be a victim. Forgers, Abagnale said, look for easy targets, of which there are too many. "We make it so easy for people to steal from us, that people do. People steal from us because we let them," Abagnale said.

Transparency Masters

TRANSPARENCY MASTER 31	Appendix Outline
TRANSPARENCY MASTER 32	Federal Regulatory Agencies *(Figure A.1 on text page 120)*
TRANSPARENCY MASTER 33	Patent Law *(Figure A.2 on text page 121)*
TRANSPARENCY MASTER 34	Consumer Protection Laws *(Figure A.3 on text page 127)*
TRANSPARENCY MASTER 35	Types of Taxes *(Figure A.4 on text page 128)*
TRANSPARENCY MASTER 36	How Assets Are Divided in Bankruptcy *(Figure A.5 on text page 129)*
TRANSPARENCY MASTER 37	Hamburger Regulations *(Figure A.6 on text page 131)*

Appendix Outline

APPENDIX
WORKING WITHIN THE LEGAL ENVIRONMENT OF BUSINESS

I. **THE NEED FOR LAWS.**

II. **BUSINESS LAW.**
   A. Statuary and Common Laws.
   B. Administrative Agencies.

III. **TORT LAW.**
   A. Product Liability.

IV. **LAWS PROTECTING IDEAS: PATENTS, COPYRIGHTS, AND TRADEMARKS.**

V. **SALES LAW: THE UNIFORM COMMERCIAL CODE.**
   A. Warranties.
   B. Negotiable Instruments.

VI. **CONTRACT LAW.**
   A. Breach of Contract.

VII. **LAWS TO PROMOTE FAIR AND COMPETITIVE PRACTICES.**
   A. The Interstate Commerce Act of 1887.
   B. The Sherman Antitrust Act of 1890.

VIII. **LAWS TO PROTECT CONSUMERS.**

IX. **TAX LAWS.**

X. **BANKRUPTCY LAWS.**

XI. **DEREGULATION.**

XII. **SUMMARY AND REVIEW.**

TM-32

Federal Regulatory Agencies
(Figure A.1 on text page 120)

AGENCY	FUNCTION
Federal Trade Commission (FTC)	Enforces laws and guidelines regarding unfair business practices and acts to stop false and deceptive advertising and labeling.
Food and Drug Administration (FDA)	Enforces laws and regulations to prevent distribution of adulterated or misbranded foods, drugs, medical devices, cosmetics, veterinary products, and hazardous consumer products.
Consumer Products Safety Commission	Ensures compliance with the Consumer Product Safety Act and seeks to protect the public from unreasonable risk of injury from any consumer product not covered by other regulatory agencies.
Federal Communications Commission (FCC)	Regulates wire, radio, and TV communication in interstate and foreign commerce.
Environmental Protection Agency (EPA)	Develops and enforces environmental protection standards and researches the effects of pollution.
Federal Power Commision (FPC)	Regulates rates and sales of natural gas producers, wholesale rates for electricity and gas, pipeline construction, and imports and exports of natural gas and electricity to and from the United States.

TM-33

Patent Law

(Figure A.2 on text page 121)

PATENT LAW

- A U.S. patent is enforceable for 20 years from its issue date. An issued patent excludes others from making, using, or selling a patented product or using a patented process.
- A patent defines its protected product or process in claims that set forth the required elements and features of that product or process. An unauthorized product or process that incorporates all of the claimed elements and features typically infringes the patent—even if the product or process utilizes additional elements or features not set forth in the claims.
- A patent must be issued before it can be infringed, which means that a patent pending has no legal effect—it serves only as an advance warning.
- A patent application general takes twenty months to be processed, and is kept secret by the Patent & Trademark Office up until the time the patent is issued.
- If the Patent & Trademark Office or a court determines that a claimed invention has been marketed for more than a year before a patent application is filed, the patent will be rejected or declared invalid.

Consumer Protection Laws

(Figure A.3 on text page 127)

LEGISLATION	PURPOSE
Pure Food and Drug Act (1906)	Protects against the adulteration and misbranding of foods and drugs sold in interstate commerce.
Food, Drug, and Cosmetic Act (1938)	Protects against the adulteration and sale of foods, drugs, cosmetics, or therapeutic devices and allows the Food and Drug Administration to set minimum standards and guidelines for food products.
Wool Products Labeling Act (1940)	Protects manufacturers, distributors, and consumers from undisclosed substitutes and mixtures in manufactured wool products.
Fur Products Labeling Act (1951)	Protects consumers from misbranding, false advertising, and false invoicing of furs and fur products.
Flammable Fabrics Act (1953)	Prohibits the interstate transportation of dangerously flammable wearing apparel and fabrics.
Automobile Information Disclosure Act (1958)	Requires auto manufacturers to put suggested retail prices on all new passenger vehicles.
Textile Fiber Products Identification Act (1958)	Protects producers and consumers against mis branding and false advertising of fiber content of textile fiber products.
Cigarette Labeling Act (1965)	Requires cigarette manufacturers to label cigarettes as hazardous to health.
Fair Packaging and Labeling Act (1966)	Makes unfair or deceptive packaging or labeling of certain consumer commodities illegal.

Consumer Protection Laws *(continued)*

LEGISLATION	PURPOSE
Child Protection Act (1966)	Removes from sale potentially harmful toys and allows the FDA to pull dangerous products from the market.
Truth-in-Lending Act (1968)	Requires full disclosure of all finance charges on consumer credit agreements and in advertisements of credit plans.
Child Protection and Toy Safety Act (1969)	Protects children from toys and other products that contain thermal, electrical, or mechanical hazards.
Fair Credit Reporting Act (1970)	Requires that consumer credit reports contain only accurate, relevant, and recent information and are confidential unless a proper party requests them for an appropriate reason.
Consumer Product Safety Act (1972)	Created an independent agency to protect consumers from unreasonable risk of injury arising from consumer products and to set safety standards.
Magnuson–Moss Warranty–Federal Trade	Provides for minimum disclosure standards for written consumer product.
Commission Improvement Act (1975)	warranties and allows the FTC to prescribe interpretive rules and policy statements regarding unfair or deceptive practices.
Alcohol Labeling Legislation (1988)	Provides for warning labels on liquor saying that women shouldn't drink when pregnant and that alcohol impairs our abilities.
Nutrition Labeling and Education Act (1990)	Requires truthful and uniform labeling on every food the FDA regulates .

TM-35

Types of Taxes

(Figure A.4 on text page 128)

TYPE	PURPOSE
INCOME TAXES	Taxes paid on the income received by businesses and individuals. Income taxes are the largest source of tax income received by the federal government.
PROPERTY TAXES	Taxes paid on real and personal property. Real property is real estate owned by individuals and businesses. Personal property is a broader category that includes any movable property such as tangible items (wedding rings, equipment, etc.) or intangible items (stocks, checks, mortgages, etc.). Taxes are based on their assessed value.
SALES TAXES	Taxes paid on merchandise when it's sold at the retail level.
EXCISE TAXES	Taxes paid on selected items such as tobacco, alcoholic beverages, airline travel, gasoline, and firearms. These are often referred to as sin taxes. Income generated from the tax goes toward a specfifically designated purpose. For example, gasoline taxes often help the federal government and state governments pay for highway construction or improvements.

TM-36

How Assets Are Divided in Bankruptcy

(Figure A.5 on text page 129)

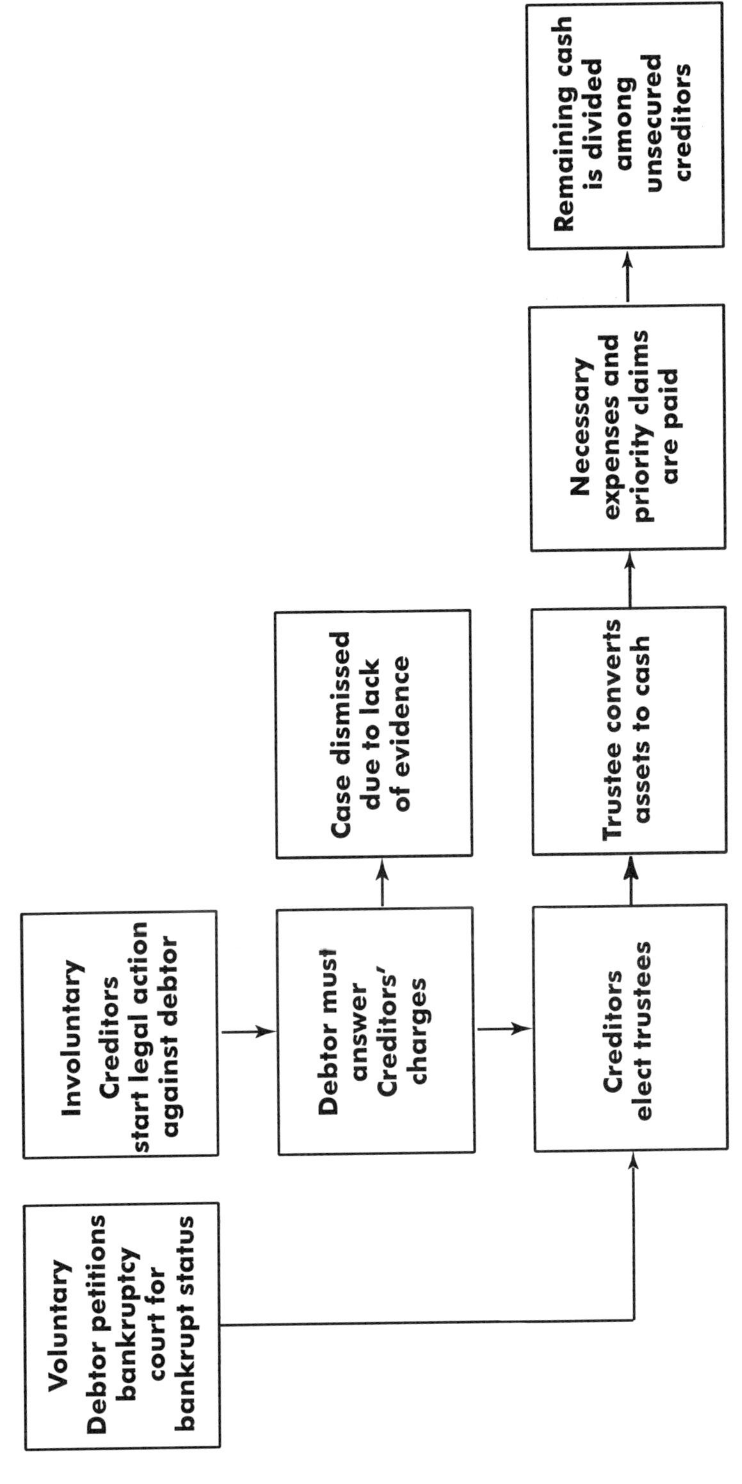

TM-37

Hamburger Regulations

(Figure A.6 on text page 131)

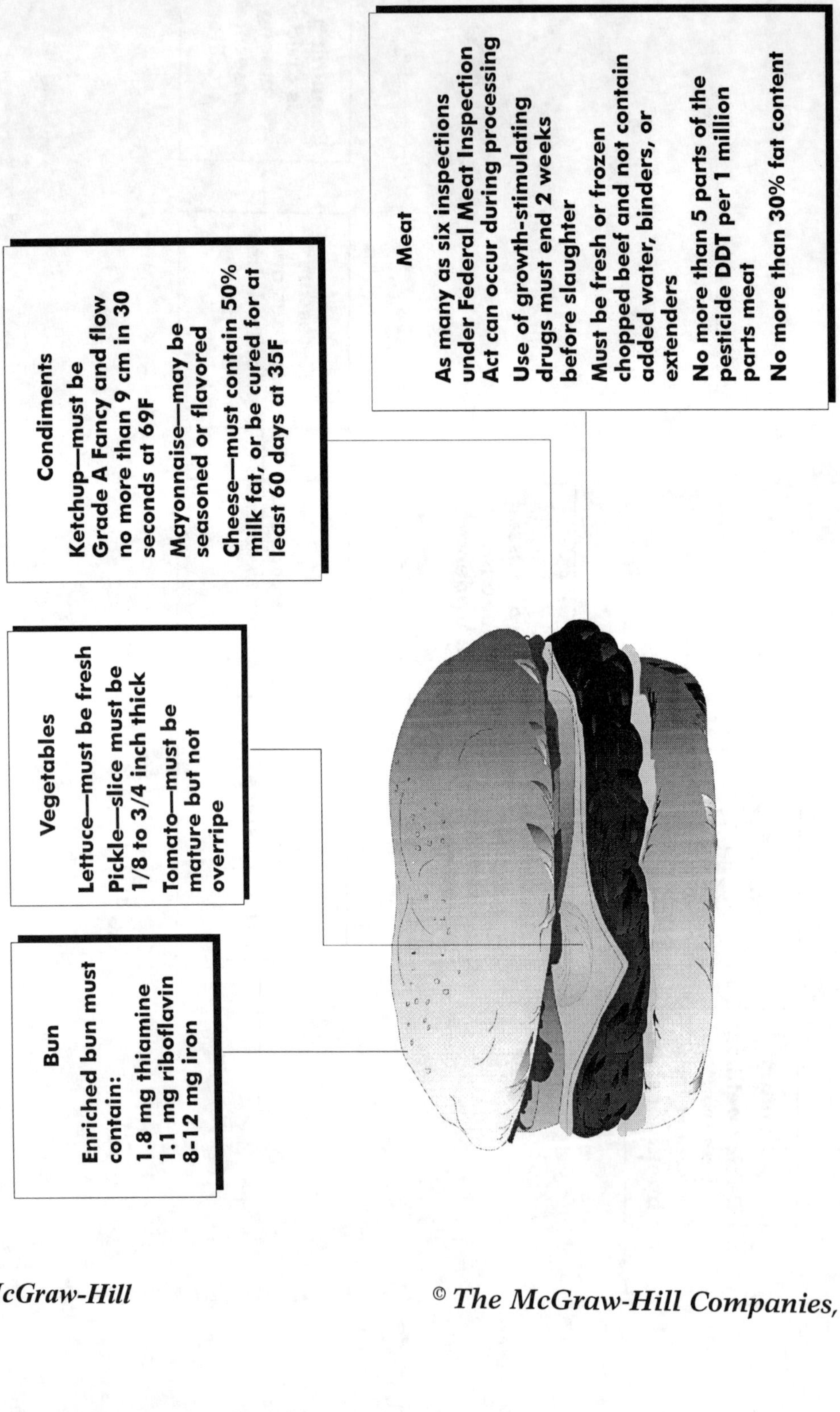

Bun

Enriched bun must contain:
1.8 mg thiamine
1.1 mg riboflavin
8-12 mg iron

Vegetables

Lettuce—must be fresh

Pickle—slice must be 1/8 to 3/4 inch thick

Tomato—must be mature but not overripe

Condiments

Ketchup—must be Grade A Fancy and flow no more than 9 cm in 30 seconds at 69F

Mayonnaise—may be seasoned or flavored

Cheese—must contain 50% milk fat, or be cured for at least 60 days at 35F

Meat

As many as six inspections under Federal Meat Inspection Act can occur during processing

Use of growth-stimulating drugs must end 2 weeks before slaughter

Must be fresh or frozen chopped beef and not contain added water, binders, or extenders

No more than 5 parts of the pesticide DDT per 1 million parts meat

No more than 30% fat content

Forms of Business Ownership

Chapter 5

Folder Contents

ACETATE 5-5 World's Largest Public Companies

ACETATE 5-6 America's Oldest Companies

ACETATE 5-7 Top Mergers in the U.S.

ACETATE 5-8 Franchises Success Versus Independent Business Success

ACETATE 5-9 The Franchise Agreement

ACETATE 5-10 Where Franchisees Get Their Financing

ACETATE 5-11 How to Avoid a Franchise Lemon

ACETATE 5-12 Benefits of Home-Based Businesses

(Acetates and Transparency Masters are also available as PowerPoint slides on disk and on the Presentation CD-ROM.)

(Resources Available are also referenced in the expanded lecture outline later in this chapter.)

Other Resources Available

Video Case - "La-Van Hawkins of Urban City Foods." This updated version of the popular video from the fourth edition of *Understanding Business* shows how La-Van Hawkins has continued to make new inroads into inner-city markets with his creative approach to fast-food franchising. Hawkins is now among the fastest growing and most successful of all Burger King franchisees. (The **Media Resource Guide** contains a summary of the Video and suggested discussion questions.)

Student Assessment and Learning Guide: Contains matching key term and definition questions, write-in retention questions, write-in critical thinking questions, and practice test of multiple choice and true/false questions.

Technology:

Zapitalism CD-ROM – Simulation program.

Concept Mastery Exam Preparation Disk – Practice test and tutorial.

Business Essentials Disk – Hyperlinks Understanding Business with seven other leading business texts.

Presentation CD-ROM – Contains PowerPoint slides of acetates and transparency masters, video clips, lecture materials. This tool allows you to customize your lecture presentations.

Business Week **Web Site Access with the** ***Business Week*** **edition.**

Understanding Business **Home Page – http:/www.mhhe.com/ub5e.**

Audiotape: Abridged chapter (Text minus profile, boxes, and end-of-chapter material.

Associated Web Sites

These sites are provided to students for the purpose of analysis and critical thinking of the issues. The sample sites listed in this chapter are for Ohio. Students are encouraged to explore other sites. As with any Web site, some may be inactive now.

Ohio Secretary of State (controls the formation of corporations in Ohio)

http://www.state.oh.us/sos/info.html

Other Important State of Ohio Agencies for Business:

Ohio Department of Development

http://www.odod.ohio.gov/business.htm

Ohio Attorney General's Office

http://www.ag.ohio.gov/

Ohio Department of Taxation

http://www.state.oh.us/tax/

Ohio State Treasurer's Office

http://www.state.oh.us/treasurer/

Small Business in the State of Ohio

Ohio Small Business Development Center

http://www.seorf.ohiou.edu/~osbdc/

U.s. Government Agencies to Assist Business and Commerce:

U.S. Department of Commerce

http://www.doc.gov/

U.S. Small Business Administration (SBA)

Government services to small business owner

http://www.sbaonline.sba.gov/

Columbus Business Supersite

http://www.columbus.org/busi/index.html

Columbus Small Business Development Center

http://www.columbus.org/busi/sbdc/index.htm

Business Incubator:

http://www.spie.org/web/oer/april/biz_incubat.html

Business Services Available over the Internet:

Tax service for sole proprietorships (note the type of businesses and the required tax forms):

http://unix.worldpath.net/~lrts/

Forming a Corporation in Alaska (note the procedures)

http://www.state.ak.us/local/akpages/COMMERCE/bsc/corpdoc.htm

Understanding Business **Home Page** :

http:/www.mhhe.com/ub5e.

What's New in This Edition

Additions:

- Section "Using Technology in Franchising"
- Reaching Beyond Our Borders: Would You Like Fries With That?
- Figure 5.1 How owners affect management
- Taking It to the Net exercises

Revisions:

Statistical data and examples throughout the chapter were updated to reflect current information. In addition:

- The Blimpie's Tony Conza profile was updated to include a discussion of the franchise's new co-branded outlets.
- The section "S Corporations" was revised with a discussion of the changes to S Corporations created by the Small Business Jobs Protection Act of 1996.
- The section "Limited Liability Companies" was revised to include a discussion of the Uniform Limited Liability Company Act approved by the National Conference of Commissioners on Uniform State Laws in 1995.
- Video case on LaVan Hawkins of Urban City Foods was revised and moved from Chapter 1.

Deletions:

- Boxes Reaching Beyond Our Borders, From the Pages of Entrepreneur
- Figure "Forms of Business Ownership"
- Figure "Examples of Home-Based Franchises"

Brief Chapter Outline/Learning Goals

CHAPTER 5
FORMS OF BUSINESS OWNERSHIP

PROFILE: Tony Conza of Blimpie International Sandwich Shops

I. BASIC FORMS OF BUSINESS OWNERSHIP.

LEARNING GOAL 1. Compare the advantages and disadvantages of sole proprietorships.

II. SOLE PROPRIETORSHIPS.

A. Advantages of Sole Proprietorships.

B. Disadvantages of Sole Proprietorships.

III. PARTNERSHIPS.

LEARNING GOAL 2. Describe the differences between general and limited partnerships and compare the advantages and disadvantages of partnerships.

A. Categories of Partners.

B. Advantages of Partnerships.

C. Disadvantages of Partnerships.

IV. CORPORATIONS.

LEARNING GOAL 3. Compare the advantages and disadvantages of corporations and summarize the differences between C corporations, S corporations and limited liability companies.

A. Advantages of Corporations.

B. Disadvantages of Corporations.

C. Individuals Can Incorporate.

D. S Corporations.

E. Limited Liability Companies.

V. CORPORATE EXPANSION: MERGERS AND ACQUISITIONS.

LEARNING GOAL 4. Define and give examples of three types of corporate mergers and explain the role of leveraged buyouts and taking a firm private.

VI. SPECIAL FORMS OF BUSINESS OWNERSHIP

LEARNING GOAL 5. Outline the advantages and disadvantages of franchises and discuss the opportunities for diversity in franchising and the challenges of international franchising.

VII. FRANCHISES.

A. Advantages of Franchises.

B. Disadvantages of Franchises.

C. Diversity in Franchising.

D. Home-Based Franchises.

E. Franchising in International Markets.

F. Using Technology in Franchising.

VIII. COOPERATIVES.

LEARNING GOAL 6. Explain the role of cooperatives.

IX. WHICH FORM OF OWNERSHIP IS FOR YOU?

X. SUMMARY AND REVIEW.

(Learning Objectives are also referenced in the expanded lecture outline later in this chapter.)

Key Terms

acquisition *(text page 147)*
conglomerate merger *(text page 147)*
conventional (C) corporation *(text page 139)*
cooperative *(text page 155)*
corporation *(text page 134)*
franchise *(text page 149)*
franchise agreement *(text page 149)*
franchisee *(text page 149)*
franchisor *(text page 149)*
general partner *(text page 136)*
general partnership *(text page 136)*
horizontal merger *(text page 147)*
leveraged buyout *(text page 147)*
limited liability *(text page 136)*
limited-liability company *(text page 145)*
limited partner *(text page 136)*
limited partnership *(text page 136)*
master limited partnership *(text page 136)*
merger *(text page 147)*
partnership *(text page 134)*
S corporation *(text page 143)*
sole proprietorship *(text page 134)*
unlimited liability *(text page 135)*
vertical merger *(text page 147)*

Lecture Outline

The **PROFILE** at the beginning of this chapter focuses on **TONY CONZA** of **BLIMPIE INTERNATIONAL SANDWICH SHOPS.** Conza's business started as a partnership, changed to a sole proprietorship, changed again to a franchise operation, and finally changed to a franchise corporation.

I. BASIC FORMS OF BUSINESS OWNERSHIP.

▶ **LEARNING GOAL 1.** Compare the advantages and disadvantages of sole proprietorships.

A. How you form your business can make a difference in your long-term success.

B. The **THREE MAJOR FORMS OF BUSINESS OWNERSHIP** are:

1. A **SOLE PROPRIETORSHIP** is an organization that is owned, and usually managed, by one person; it is the most common form.

2. A **PARTNERSHIP** is a legal form of business co-owned by two or more owners.

3. A **CORPORATION** is a legal entity with authority to act and have liability separate from its owners.

C. Each form of business ownership has its advantages and its disadvantages.

Lecture Notes

TRANSPARENCY MASTER 38
Chapter Outline

TM 38

(Transparency Masters begin on page 5.78.)

LECTURE ENHANCER 5-1
Why Government Ownership

The chapter deals primarily with forms of private business ownership. Public ownership, ownership and/or management by government, may be used for any number of reasons. (See complete lecture enhancer on page 5.50.)

Lecture Outline

II. SOLE PROPRIETORSHIPS.

A. ADVANTAGES OF SOLE PROPRIETORSHIPS.

1. Ease of starting and ending the business.
2. Being your own boss.
3. Pride of ownership.
4. Retention of profit.
5. No special taxes.

B. DISADVANTAGES OF SOLE PROPRIETORSHIPS.

1. **UNLIMITED LIABILITY** means that any debts or damages incurred by the business are your debts and you must pay them.
2. Limited financial resources.
3. Difficulty in management.
4. Overwhelming time commitment.
5. Few fringe benefits.
6. Limited growth.
7. Limited life span.

III. PARTNERSHIPS.

▶ **LEARNING GOAL 2.** Describe the differences between general and limited partnerships and compare the advantages and disadvantages of partnerships.

A. UNIFORM PARTNERSHIP ACT (UPA).

Lecture Notes

LEARNING GOAL 1.
Compare the advantages and disadvantages of sole proprietorships.

OT ACETATE 5-1
Advantages and Disadvantages of Sole Proprietorships

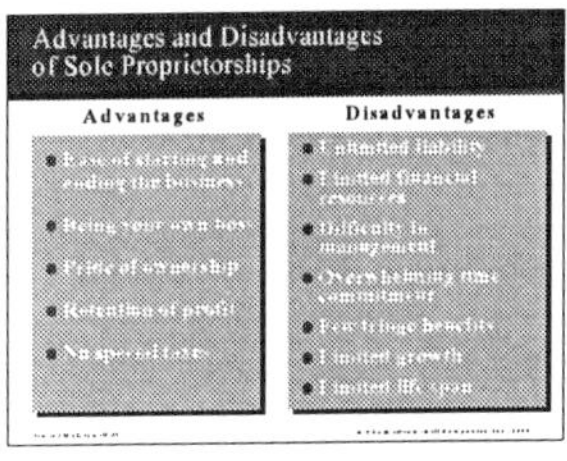

Comments:

1. This acetate compliments information contained in the chapter. The acetate should reinforce the importance of the material to students.
2. It's best to use the acetate to reinforce information students should have already read. You may want to specifically focus on particular advantages and disadvantages such as unlimited liability. If students have questions or comments this is a good time to discuss them.

CRITICAL THINKING
(page 136 in text)

Have you ever dreamed of opening your own business? If you did, what would it be? What talents or skills do you have that you could use? Could you start a business in your own home? How much would it cost to start? Could you begin part-time while you worked elsewhere? What satisfaction and profit could you get from owning your own business? What would you lose?

LECTURE ENHANCER 5-2
The Development of Sears and Roebuck

Sears and Roebuck Company began with an ad in the Help Wanted section of the Chicago *Daily News*. It quickly grew from a sole proprietorship to a partnership to a corporate conglomerate. (See complete lecture enhancer on page 5.51.)

Lecture Outline

1. All states except Louisiana have adopted the Uniform Partnership Act to replace laws relating to partnerships.
2. The UPA defines the **THREE KEY ELEMENTS** of any general partnership:
   a. Common ownership.
   b. Shared profits and losses.
   c. The right to participate in managing the operations of the business.

B. **TYPES OF PARTNERSHIPS.**

1. **GENERAL PARTNERSHIP:** a partnership in which all owners share in operating the business and in assuming liability for the business's debts.
2. **LIMITED PARTNERSHIP:** a partnership with one or more general partners and one or more limited partners.
   a. A **GENERAL PARTNER** is an owner who has unlimited liability and is active in managing the firm.
   b. A **LIMITED PARTNER** risks an investment in the firm, but enjoys limited liability and cannot legally help manage the company.
   c. **LIMITED LIABILITY** means that limited partners are not responsible for the debts

Lecture Notes

LECTURE ENHANCER 5-3
Are Partners Bad for Business?

Inc. Magazine recently polled its subscribers on this question. Most saw some good in partnerships, but the majority felt the personal costs ultimately outweighed all benefits. (See complete lecture enhancer on page 5.53.)

OT ACETATE 5-2
Advantages and Disadvantages of Partnerships

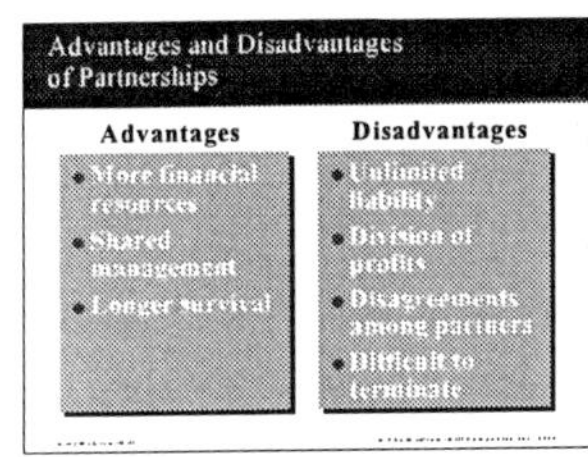

Comments:

1. The advice offered in the previous acetate is also applicable here.
2. Students are often interested in the discussion of partnerships. It's important to note that often the killer of many partnerships is the lack of planning and the failure to fully talk things out. This acetate offers some helpful hints.
3. You might note to students that the questions involved in partnership formation are simple in context yet often difficult in application. It's important to get to the feelings of partners before considering the risk of entering a partnership. Some things to contemplate:
   a. How do the partners differ on how the business should be run? Does one feel participative management would be best? How about the other?
   b. Will each partner be an equal owner, in other words a 50/50 split? If so, how will disagreements be settled? Arbitration might be something discussed at this point.
   c. How can we help each other is certainly a cogent question? Partners should be added for a reason.
   d. Is one of the partners single and the other a family-person? How may this affect their needs? Will one partner need access to capital more often than the other? These questions if handled up-front can help to avoid problems in the future.

of the business beyond the amount of their investment.

3. **MASTER LIMITED PARTNERSHIP** is a new form of partnership that acts like a corporation and is traded on the stock exchange, but is taxed like a partnership avoiding the corporate income tax.

C. **ADVANTAGES OF PARTNERSHIPS.**

1. More financial resources.
2. Shared management.
3. Longer survival.

D. **DISADVANTAGES OF PARTNERSHIPS.**

1. **UNLIMITED LIABILITY.**

   a. Each general partner is liable for the debts of the firm, no matter who was responsible for causing those debts.

   b. You are liable for your partners' mistakes as well as your own.

2. **DIVISION OF PROFITS.**

3. **DISAGREEMENTS AMONG PARTNERS.**

   a. Disagreements can arise over division of authority, purchasing decisions, and division of profit.

Lecture Notes

CRITICAL THINKING EXERCISE 5-1
Picking Partners

See complete exercise on page 5.67.

LECTURE ENHANCER 5-4
Put Partnership Agreements in Writing

One problem with partnerships is that you usually form them with friends. (See complete lecture enhancer on page 5.54.)

PROGRESS CHECK
(page 138 in text)

- Most people who start a business in the United States are sole proprietors. What are the advantages and disadvantages of this form of business?
- What are some of the advantages of partnerships over sole proprietorships?
- Why would unlimited liability be considered one of the biggest drawbacks to sole proprietorships and general partnerships?
- What is the difference between a limited partner and a general partner?

HOW TO FORM A PARTNERSHIP
(Box in text, page 139)

SPOTLIGHT ON SMALL BUSINESS

(Box in text, page 138)
"Choose Your Partner"

Lecture Outline

b. Because of such potential conflicts, all terms of partnership should be spelled out in writing to protect all parties.

4. **DIFFICULT TO TERMINATE.**

E. Many businesspeople try to avoid the disadvantages of the sole proprietorship and partnership by forming corporations.

IV. CORPORATIONS.

▶ **LEARNING GOAL 3.** Compare the advantages and disadvantages of corporations and summarize the differences between C corporations, S corporations and limited liability companies.

A. A **CONVENTIONAL C CORPORATION** is a state-chartered legal entity with authority to act and have **LIABILITY SEPARATE FROM ITS OWNERS.**

1. The corporation's owners (stockholders) are not liable for the debts of the corporation beyond the money they invest.

2. A corporation also enables many people to share in the ownership of a business without working there.

3. A **CORPORATION** is an artificial being, an entity that exists only in the eyes of the law.

B. **ADVANTAGES OF CORPORATIONS.**

1. **MORE MONEY FOR INVESTMENT.**

Lecture Notes

MAKING ETHICAL DECISIONS
(Box in text, page 140)

"Are You Your Brothers' Keeper?"

Imagine that you and your partner own a construction company. You receive a bid from a subcontractor that you know is 20 percent too low. Such a loss to the subcontractor could put him out of business. Accepting the bid will certainly improve your chances of winning the contract for a big shopping center project. Your partner wants to take the bid and let the sub suffer the consequences of his bad estimate. What do you think you should do? What will be the consequences of your decision?

OT ACETATE 5-3
Advantages and Disadvantages of Corporations

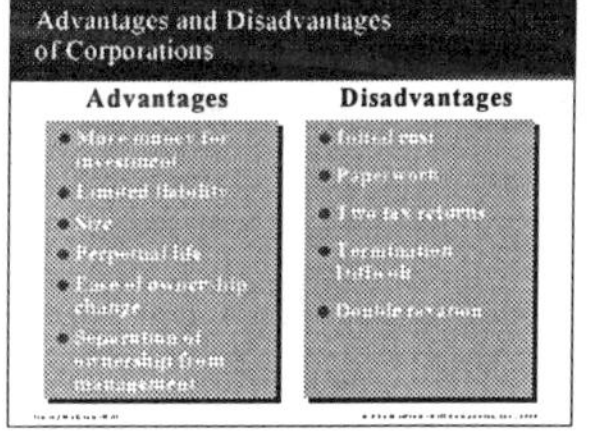

Comments:

1. Once again, a good time to handle any questions or comments students might have concerning corporate advantages and disadvantages.
2. It's also helpful to note to students that the vast majority of corporations in the United States are small. In the introductory course, quite often students have this perception of corporations all being massive. They also assume that forming a corporation is a mind boggling and expensive task that smaller companies cannot handle or afford.

CORPORATE TYPES
(Box in text, page 140)

Lecture Outline

a. To raise money, a corporation sells ownership (stock) to anyone interested.

b. Corporations may also find it easier to obtain loans.

2. **LIMITED LIABILITY.**

a. Limited liability is probably the most significant advantage of corporations.

b. Limited liability means that the owners of a business are responsible for losses only up to the amount they invest.

3. **SIZE.**

a. Corporations have the ability to raise large amounts of money.

b. They can also hire experts in all areas of operation.

c. They can buy other corporations in other fields to diversity their risk.

d. Corporations have the size and resources to take advantage of opportunities anywhere in the world.

4. **PERPETUAL LIFE.**

a. The death of one or more owners does not terminate the corporation.

5. **EASE OF OWNERSHIP CHANGE.**

Lecture Notes

LECTURE ENHANCER 5-5
The *Fortune* List of Most Admired Corporations

Fortune's annual survey of corporate reputations shows what elevates companies above their peers is a lot of honest hard work. (See complete lecture enhancer on page 5.55.)

TRANSPARENCY MASTER 39
How Owners Affect Management
(Figure 5.1 on text page 142)

(Transparency Masters begin on page 5.78.)

Lecture Outline

6. **EASE OF DRAWING TALENTED EMPLOYEES.**
7. **SEPARATION OF OWNERSHIP FROM MANAGEMENT.**
   a. Owners/shareholders are separate from the managers and employers.
   b. The owners thus have some say in who runs the corporation, but no control.

C. **DISADVANTAGES OF CORPORATIONS.**

1. **INITIAL COST.**
   a. Incorporation may cost thousands of dollars and involve expensive lawyers and accountants.
   b. There are less expensive ways of incorporating in certain states.
2. **PAPERWORK.**
   a. A corporation must prove all its expenses and deductions are legitimate.
   b. A corporation must keep detailed records.
3. **TWO TAX RETURNS**—both a corporate tax return and an individual tax return.
4. **SIZE.**
   a. Large corporations sometimes become inflexible and too tied down in red tape.

LECTURE ENHANCER 5-6
Going Public

When small, privately held corporations reach the stage in their development when large amounts of new capital are required, they often choose the option of selling stock to outsiders. This process is called "going public." (See complete lecture enhancer on page 5.56.)

OT ACETATE 5-4
Who Makes Up Corporate Boards?

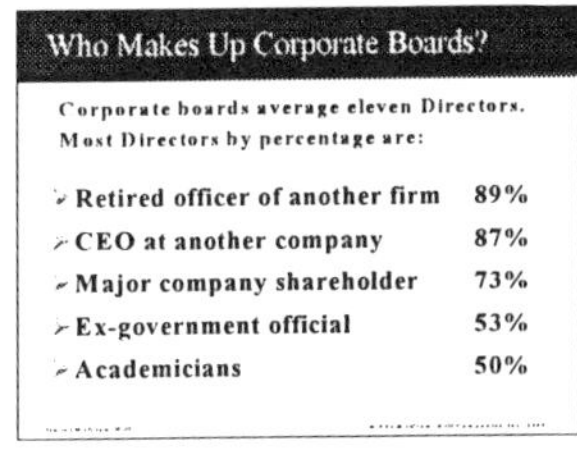

Comments:

1. Students are often a bit confused by corporate boards and the directors that serve on them. For example, students often feel that boards are nothing more than managers from the company. The concept of outside director often has to be explained. This acetate should assist with that task.
2. In case students are curious about compensation for outside directors, here are some numbers you can provide:

Firms under $1 billion	$27,805
$1 billion to $2.99 billion	$30,548
$3 billion to $4.99 billion	$34,775
$5 billion and over	$35,620

3. Compensation also includes other perks such as office space, use of company vacation facilities and corporate jets, and in some instances stock options. In simple words, a pretty decent position if you can get it. Consultants Korn/Ferry report that the average director in the U.S. works approximately 103 hours per year (that's about two hours a week.) Also, directors are often awarded stock options, and hefty fees for chairing committees. Directors are often even paid for attending meetings. In fact, some directors even earn pension benefits after just a few years of service.
4. One last question students may ask, "is it required that a corporation have a board of directors?" No legal requirement whatsoever.

OT ACETATE 5-5
The World's Largest Public Companies

Comments:

1. Please note to students that these companies are ranked by market value. This information is from the Dow Jones Global Index and marks market value as of June 30, 1997. Check the UB5E web page for updates.
2. In case students would like to know what the estimated market value is for the top six listed in the acetate, here is the data from Dow Jones:

General Electric	$214 billion
Royal Dutch Shell	$177 billion
Coca-Cola	$167 billion
Nippon Telegraph & Telephone	$152 billion
Exxon	$151 billion
Microsoft	$151 billion

Lecture Outline

5. **DIFFICULTY OF TERMINATION.**

6. **DOUBLE TAXATION.**

   a. Corporate income is taxed twice.

   b. The corporation pays tax on income before it can distribute any to stockholders.

   c. The stockholders pay tax on the income they receive from the corporation.

   d. States often tax corporations more harshly than other enterprises.

7. **POSSIBLE CONFLICT WITH BOARD OF DIRECTORS.**

   a. Since the board chooses the company's officers, an entrepreneur can be forced out of the very company he founded.

D. **INDIVIDUALS CAN INCORPORATE** By incorporating, individuals such as doctors and lawyers can save on taxes and receive other benefits of incorporation.

E. **S CORPORATIONS.**

1. An **S CORPORATION** is a unique government creation that looks like a corporation, but is taxed like sole proprietorships and partnerships.

   a. S corporations have shareholders, directors, and employees, but the profits are

Lecture Notes

HOW TO INCORPORATE
(Box in text, page 144)

taxed as the personal income of the shareholders.

b. The benefits of S corporations change every time the law changes.

2. **S CORPORATIONS MUST:**

   a. Have no more than 75 shareholders.

   b. Have shareholders who are individuals or estates and are citizens or permanent residents of the U.S.

   c. Have only one class of outstanding stock.

   d. Not have more than 25% of income derived from passive sources (rents, royalties, interest, etc.)

3. Changes in the Small Business Jobs Protection Act of 1996 have made the formation of operation of a S corporation easier.

   a. The law increased the maximum number of shareholders from 35 to 75.

   b. It allows tax-exempt organizations to own shares in S corporations after January 1, 1998.

   c. S corporations can now own subsidiaries.

4. **DISADVANTAGES OF S CORPORATIONS.**

Lecture Notes

Lecture Outline

a. The top tax rate for S corporations is almost five points higher than the highest corporation rate.

b. Fast-growing small businesses that don't intend to pay dividends to owners are switching to C corporation status to avoid the higher taxes.

c. Many businesses are changing to limited liability companies (LLC) that have much the same appeal.

F. **LIMITED LIABILITY COMPANIES.**

1. **A LIMITED-LIABILITY COMPANY** is similar to an S corporation without the special eligibility requirements.

   a. Limited liability companies are so new that many states have just recently passed legislation regarding them.

   b. By the fall of 1996, all fifty states and the District of Columbia recognized LLCs.

2. **THE UNIFORM LIMITED LIABILITY COMPANY ACT** was prepared for the National Conference of Commissioners on Uniform State Laws in an effort to provide uniform legislation regarding limited liability companies.

Lecture Notes

LECTURE ENHANCER 5-7
Lloyd's of London Goes Limited

One of the oldest insurers in the world is Lloyd's of London. For centuries Lloyd's "names", or individuals who pledge assets to underwrite insurance risk, have agreed to unlimited liability. That unique structure changed in 1994. (See complete lecture enhancer on page 5.57.)

OT ACETATE 5-6
America's Oldest Companies

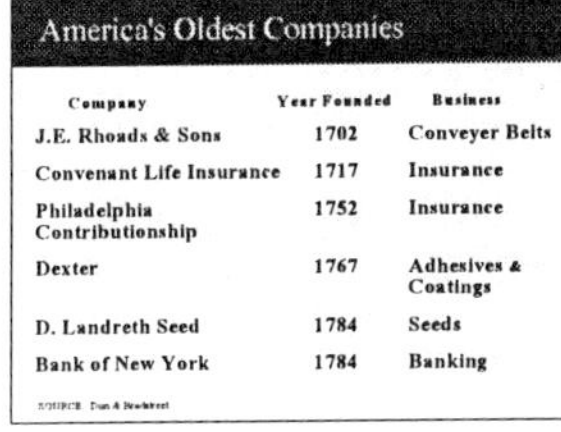

America's Oldest Companies

Company	Year Founded	Business
J.E. Rhoads & Sons	1702	Conveyer Belts
Convenant Life Insurance	1717	Insurance
Philadelphia Contributionship	1752	Insurance
Dexter	1767	Adhesives & Coatings
D. Landreth Seed	1784	Seeds
Bank of New York	1784	Banking

SOURCE: Dun & Bradstreet

Comments:

1. This should be an interesting acetate to students. It lists the oldest companies in America. As students can see, several of these companies predate the American Revolution.
2. A few facts you may wish to point out, the oldest company in the U.S., J.E. Rhoads & Sons starting off tanning leather for buggy whips. We all know which way that business went. Fortunately for the company, when the Industrial Revolution started its steamroller effect, the company shifted to making conveyor belts.
   - D. Landreth Seed is the only company that has not changed. It sold vegetable seeds to Thomas Jefferson (whose estate by the way still buys from Landreth) and George Washington (who got 30-day credit terms.)
   - Dexter originally started as a gristmill. As demand fell off, the company began producing specialty papers for stationery and later for tea bags. Today, the firm makes among other things, adhesives and coatings for aircraft. It was a $1 billion company last year.
3. To lighten things up a bit, see if students will volunteer choices for companies that will still be around 100, 200 years from now. Tough call.

PROGRESS CHECK
(page 145 in text)

- ➤ What are the major advantages and disadvantages of incorporating a business?
- ➤ Could you be sued if you were a general partner in a partnership?
- ➤ What is the role of owners (stockholders) in the corporate hierarchy?
- ➤ If you buy stock in a corporation and someone gets injured by one of the corporation's products, can you be sued? Why or why not?

TRANSPARENCY MASTER 40
Comparison of Forms of Business Ownership
(Figure 5.2 on text page 146)

(Transparency Masters begin on page 5.78.)

Lecture Outline

3. LLCs are best for many new businesses for the following reasons:
   a. Personal-asset protection.
   b. Choice to be taxed as partnership or as corporation.
   c. Flexible ownership rules.

V. CORPORATION EXPANSION: MERGERS AND ACQUISITIONS.

▶ **LEARNING GOAL 4.** Define and give examples of three types of corporate mergers and explain the role of leveraged buyouts and taking a firm private.

A. Merger activity in 1996 hit an all time high of more than $660 billion.
   1. Many were mega mergers—the result of major changes in the entertainment, drug, and telecommunications industries.
   2. A **MERGER** is the result of two firms forming one company.
   3. An **ACQUISITION** is when one company buys another company.

B. There are three major types of corporate mergers: vertical, horizontal, and conglomerate.
   1. **VERTICAL MERGER** is the joining of two firms involved in different stages of related businesses.

CRITICAL THINKING
(page 145 in text)

In the past, forming a corporation was the only way to achieve limited liability. Why would most sole proprietors and partners be expected to form limited liability companies in the future rather than corporations?

SUPPLEMENTAL CASE 5-1
Mergers

See complete case on page 5.71.

OT ACETATE 5-7
The Top Mergers in the U.S.

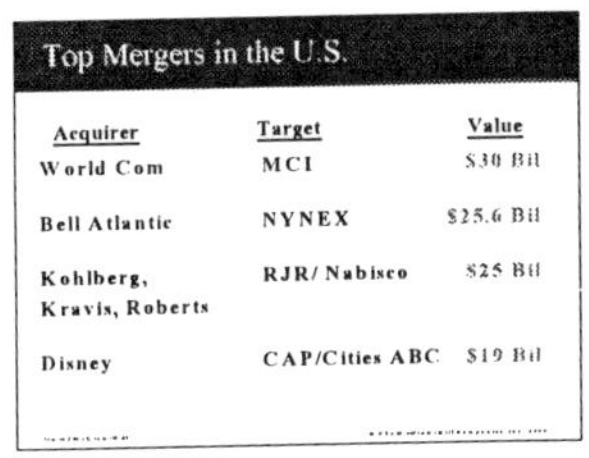

Top Mergers in the U.S.

Acquirer	Target	Value
World Com	MCI	$30 Bil
Bell Atlantic	NYNEX	$25.6 Bil
Kohlberg, Kravis, Roberts	RJR/Nabisco	$25 Bil
Disney	CAP/Cities ABC	$19 Bil

Comments:

1. The top four mergers among companies in the U.S. are identified in this acetate. Students may be surprised by the amount of money involved in these deals.
2. This is an opportune time to discuss the issue of mergers and acquisitions with students. It's also helpful they fully comprehend the different types of mergers (vertical, horizontal, and conglomerate) that are covered in the chapter.
3. A useful out-of-class assignment is to have students find examples of the different types of mergers that have occurred in the U.S. economy. They should have no problem with conglomerate examples, but vertical and horizontal can be a bit trickier.
4 A natural discussion question from this acetate is "why do merger occur?" Students should be able to offer several suggestions ranging from growth in international competition, to need for growth, to outright corporate greed.

TRANSPARENCY MASTER 41
Types of Mergers
(Figure 5.3 on text page 148)

(Transparency Masters begin on page 5.78.)

Lecture Outline

2. **HORIZONTAL MERGER** joins two firms in the same industry and allows them to diversify or expand their products.

3. **CONGLOMERATE MERGER** unites completely unrelated firms.

C. Rather than merge or sell to another company, some corporations decide to maintain control of the firm internally.

1. Taking a firm private involves the efforts of a group of stockholders or management to obtain all the firm's stock for themselves.

2. A **LEVERAGED BUYOUT** is an attempt by employees, management, or a group of investors to purchase an organization primarily through borrowing.

   a. The funds borrowed are used to buy out the stockholders in the company.

   b. Employees, managers, or group of investors now become the owners of the firm.

3. Merger mania has also involved foreign companies purchasing U.S. companies.

VI. SPECIAL FORMS OF BUSINESS OWNERSHIP.

Lecture Notes

LECTURE ENHANCER 5-8
Pepsi Pulls Back from Diversification

PepsiCo Inc. has decided the combination of Pepsi, Pizza Hut, Taco Bell, and Kentucky Fried Chicken is indigestible. (See complete lecture enhancer on page 5.58.)

LECTURE ENHANCER 5-9
The Price of Freedom

In the experience of Ted Waitt, founder of Gateway 200, the price of independence may be $3 billion. (See complete lecture enhancer on page 5.60.)

LECTURE ENHANCER 5-10
Employee Owners at Garden State Brickface

Employees of Garden State Brickface are enthusiastic participants in an ESOP. (See complete lecture enhancer on page 5.61.)

Lecture Outline

A, In addition to the three basic forms of business ownership, we shall discuss two special forms of ownership.

B. A **FRANCHISE AGREEMENT** is an arrangement whereby someone with a good idea for a business (the **FRANCHISOR**) sells the rights to use the business name and to sell a product or service (the **FRANCHISE**) to others (the **FRANCHISEE**) in a given territory.

C. A **COOPERATIVE** is an organization that is owned by members/customers who pay an annual membership fee and share in any profits (if it is a profit-making organization).

VII. FRANCHISES.

▶ **LEARNING GOAL 5.** Outline the advantages and disadvantages of franchises and discuss the opportunities for diversity in franchising and the challenges of international franchising.

A. Some people would like to own their own businesses but want more assurance of success—Franchising may be an alternative for such people.

1. Franchising accounts for 40% of the national retail sales.

2. The most popular businesses for franchising are restaurants, retail stores, hotels and

SUPPLEMENTAL CASE 5-2
Opportunities in Franchising

See complete case on page 5.75.

OT ACETATE 5-8
Franchise Success Versus Independent Business Success

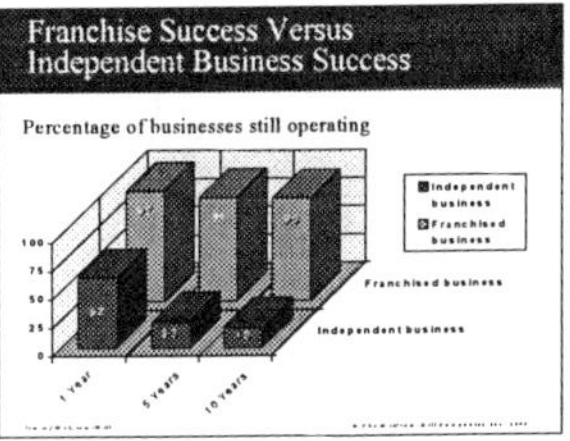

Comments:

1. The information in this acetate is very helpful in highlighting the lower degree of risk associated with most franchised businesses.
2. You might note that three-fourths of the independently-owned businesses are no longer operating after just five years. This number is highly debated but the simple reality is a good many independent businesses do not survive. Chapter five will offer further information concerning the high failure rates of independent businesses.
3. This could be a good place to stimulate discussion as to WHY students think franchised businesses have higher success rates than independently owned businesses. Information in the text should strengthen their arguments.
4. It's also a good point to stress why franchisors are often intent on seeing franchisees succeed. Remember the domino effect discussed in the text.

Lecture Outline

motels, and automotive parts and service centers.

3. Some entrepreneurs have had great success taking American franchises overseas.

B. **ADVANTAGES OF FRANCHISES:**

1. **MANAGEMENT AND MARKETING ASSISTANCE** including an established product, help in choosing a location, and assistance in all phases of operation.

2. **PERSONAL OWNERSHIP**—You are still your own boss, although you must follow the rules, regulations, and procedures of the franchise.

3. **NATIONALLY RECOGNIZED NAME**—You get instant recognition and support.

4. **FINANCIAL ADVICE AND ASSISTANCE**.

   a. Franchisees get assistance arranging financing and learning to keep records.

   b. Some franchisors will even provide financing to potential franchisees.

5. **LOWER FAILURE RATE**.

   a. Historically, the failure rate for franchises has been lower than that of other business ventures.

Lecture Notes

Lecture Outline

b. Studies show that you should carefully research any franchise before buying.

C. **DISADVANTAGES OF FRANCHISES.**

1. **LARGE START-UP COSTS.**

a. Most franchises will demand a fee to obtain the rights to the franchise.

b. Start-up costs can be as high as $600,000 for a McDonald's restaurant.

2. **SHARED PROFIT**—The franchisor often demands a large share of the profits, or royalty, based on sales not profit.

3. **MANAGEMENT REGULATION.**

a. Some franchisees may feel burdened by the company's rules and regulations.

b. In recent years franchisees have been banding together to resolve their grievances with franchisors.

4. **COATTAIL EFFECTS.**

a. The actions of other franchisees have an impact on the franchise's future growth and level of profitability.

b. Franchisees must also look out for competition from fellow franchisees.

5. **RESTRICTIONS ON SELLING.**

TRANSPARENCY MASTER 42
Additional Benefits and Drawbacks of Franchising
(Figure 5.4 on text page 152)

(Transparency Masters begin on page 5.78.)

QT ACETATE 5-9
The Franchise Agreement

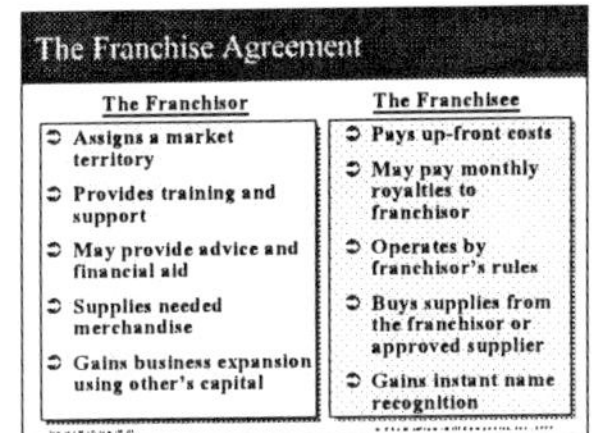

Comments:

1. This acetate highlights roughly what's involved in a basic franchise agreement. The acetate should help to reinforce information the students can read in the chapter.
2. It's helpful to reinforce the principles of contract law with this acetate. Students should be aware that a franchise agreement is a legal binding contract in which both parties agree to perform specific obligations. They also need to know that the conditions in franchise agreements are not always the same. In our classes we have found that students sometimes assume that a franchise agreement is a simple, standard legal document.
3. What's very helpful is to bring an example of a franchise agreement to class. Even better is to bring two, to highlight to students the differences that can exist. Students are often very surprised by the size and the scope of the agreements.

Lecture Outline

a. Many franchisees face restrictions in the reselling of their franchises.

b. Franchisors often insist on approving the new owner, who must meet their standards.

6. **FRAUDULENT FRANCHISORS.**

a. Most franchisors are not large systems.

b. There has been an increase in complaints to the FTC about franchisors that delivered little or nothing that they promised.

D. **DIVERSITY IN FRANCHISING.**

1. A survey by Women in Franchising indicates that **WOMEN** own 30% of the country's franchised businesses. They are becoming franchisors as well.

2. When women find it difficult to obtain financing to expanding their businesses, they often turn to finding franchisees to sidestep expansion costs.

3. Franchising opportunities fit the needs of many aspiring minority businesspersons.

4. The Commerce Department's Federal Minority Business Development Agency provides **MINORITIES** with training in how to run franchises.

Lecture Notes

OT ACETATE 5-10
Where Franchisees Get Financing

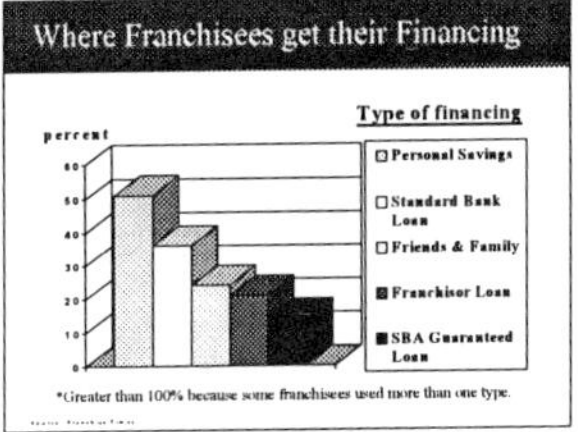

Comments:

1. A question that virtually always surfaces in class is "where do franchisees get the money to start their franchises?" This acetate should help with that query.
2. Students should be apprised of the fact that standard bank loans and franchisor loans are often dependent on the type of franchise involved and the reputation of the franchisor. Banks and franchisors often want the franchisee to come up with some money out of their own pocket. In some instances as much as 33%. Today, many large franchisors are actively seeking minority and female franchisees and provide a form of financial assistance.
3. The buying a franchise boxed insert in the text is an excellent resource for students to refer to get a good overview of what you need to know about a franchise before risking any of your capital.

BUYING A FRANCHISE
(Box in text, page 153)

Lecture Outline

E. **HOME-BASED FRANCHISES.**

1. Home-based businesses offer advantages but leave owners with a feeling of isolations.

2. Home-based franchisees feel less isolated.

F. **FRANCHISING IN INTERNATIONAL MARKETS.**

1. More than 450 of the 3,000 franchisors have outlets overseas. Canada is by far the most popular target because of proximity and language.

2. Franchisors find the costs of franchising high in these markets, but the costs are counterbalanced by less competition and rapidly expanding consumer base.

3. Franchisors must be careful to adapt to the region.

G. **USING TECHNOLOGY IN FRANCHISING.**

1. Franchisors are using technology to meet the needs of customers and franchisees.

2. Franchise Web sites can streamline communication with employees, customers, and vendors.

Lecture Notes

LECTURE ENHANCER 5-11
Home is Where the Money Is

Buying a home-based franchise lets you try out a business without much risk. (See complete lecture enhancer on page 5.63.)

OT ACETATE 5-11
How to Avoid a Franchise Lemon

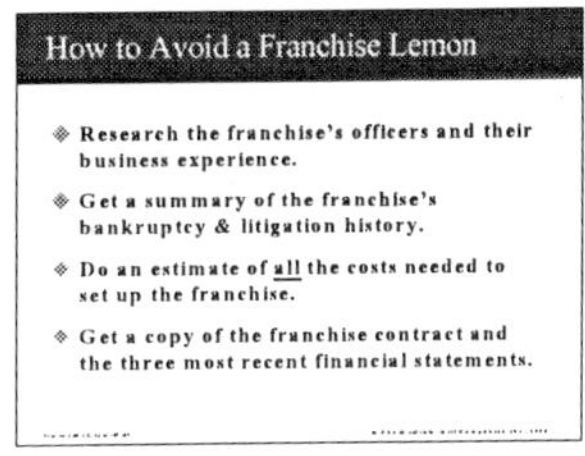

Comments:

1. This is valuable information for anyone that has ever given thought to purchasing a franchise. Students should be able to relate the advice in the acetate to the coverage of franchises in the chapter.
2. Students may question that OT 5-8 illustrates that percentage wise, franchises tend to stay in business long term. True, but not all franchises. Therefore the importance of knowing what you are getting involved in.
3. You might point out to students that a good deal of the information they will cover in this course will prepare them to handle the advice given in the acetate. This is particularly true in dealing with the financial information that's covered in the last section of the text.

REACHING BEYOND OUR BORDERS
(Box in text, page 155)
"Would You Like Fries With That?"

You've been studying all night and your stomach is growling so loud that it's scaring your dog. How does a nice hot McDonald's mutton burger sound? Well if you were in India right now, you could zip on down to the Golden Arches for a Maharaja Mac. That's two all mutton patties, special sauce, lettuce, cheese, pickle and onions, all on a sesame-seed bun. Don't bother asking, "Where's the beef?" in India. The large Hindu population in India believe cows are sacred.

OT ACETATE 5-12
Benefits of Home-Based Businesses

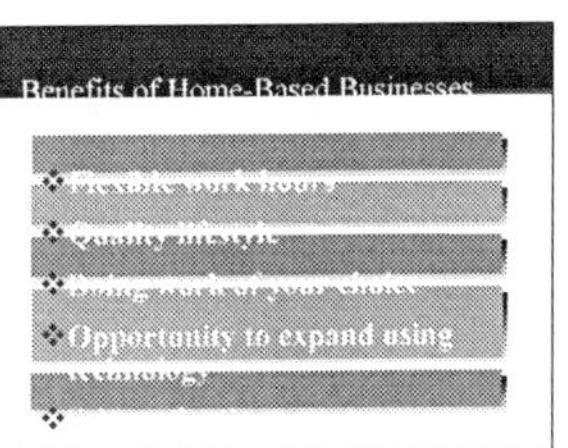

Comments:

1. Home-based businesses are growing at an enormous rate. This acetate helps to clarify some of the reasons why.
2. You can ask the class if any of them currently are involved in a home-based business. By going down the acetate's points one-by-one it will be interesting to see how students react to the various benefits listed. It's also interesting to ask what are the downsides of a home-based business.

3. Using the Internet every franchisee has immediate access to every subject that involves the franchise operation.

VIII. COOPERATIVES.

▶ **LEARNING GOAL 6.** Explain the role of cooperatives.

A. **COOPERATIVES** are organizations that are owned by members/customers who pay an annual membership fee and share in any profit-making organization.

   1. There are 47,000 cooperatives in the U.S.

   2. Members democratically control these businesses by electing a board of directors that hires professional management.

B. Some cooperatives give the group **MORE ECONOMIC POWER** than they would have as individuals (i.e. farm cooperatives.)

   1. The farm cooperative started with farmers joining together to get better prices for their food products.

   2. The organization expanded so that farm cooperatives now buy and sell other products needed on the farm.

   3. In spite of debt and mergers, cooperatives are still a major force in agriculture today.

LECTURE ENHANCER 5-12 Joining Hands Across the Waters: Strategic Alliances	With Europe, Asia, and the Third World buying a wide range of products and services, American companies find the opportunities almost unlimited. (See complete lecture enhancer on page 5.65.)
LECTURE ENHANCER 5-13 Coops Allow Small Businesses to Compete Against Big Ones	As word spreads, the idea of business cooperatives (member-owned organizations established by a large groups of small business owners) is spreading. (See complete lecture enhancer on page 5.66.)

Lecture Outline

IX. WHICH FORM OF OWNERSHIP IS FOR YOU?

There are **RISKS TO EVERY FORM** of business ownership. The miracle of free enterprise is that the freedom and incentives of capitalism make risks acceptable to many people.

X. SUMMARY AND REVIEW.

CRITICAL THINKING EXERCISE 5-2
Choosing a Form of Business Ownership

See complete exercise on page 5.68.

PROGRESS CHECK
(page 157 in text)

- What opportunities are available for starting an global franchise?
- What is a cooperative?

Answers to Practicing Management Decisions

CASE ONE

SHOULD COOPERATIVES GO CORPORATE?

1. *What are some of the advantages and disadvantages of a cooperative's changing to a corporation? What would be the major reason for them to do so?*

The largest benefit is to get limited liability. There is also the opportunity to raise more money, to get more investors, to bring in professional managers, and more. It is interesting to let students explore these ideas in their own minds.

2. *What is the future of cooperatives that provide housing and other services to the elderly? What are some of the differences you would expect to see at a cooperative housing development versus a corporate one?*

The future is great. The fastest growing part of the population is people over 65 and the fastest part of that segment is people over 85, so the future is bright. You would expect a cooperative to have fewer managers and more of the elderly involved in administration and other managerial and worker tasks: cooking, cleaning, etc.

3. *What advantages do you see in the fact that members of a cooperative often volunteer their time to help in the running of the organization?*

Not only are costs of operation lower, but the people take more pride (and thus better care) of what they have. People feel more needed and more motivated to do a good job. Esprit de corps develops among the volunteers and that builds morale and teamwork.

4. *Might farmers lose some control over the production and marketing of their goods if farm cooperatives were to begin going corporate?*

Yes, that is one of the main reasons cooperatives are so popular now. Furthermore, farmers get to share in the profits with cooperatives, and they would lose that benefit.

CASE TWO

VIDEO CASE: LA-VAN HAWKINS OF URBAN CITY FOODS

1. *Why do you think entrepreneurs like Jay Goltz succeed when so many others fail?*

First of all, Goltz got the necessary education. Second, he saved his money, showing he has the discipline needed to run such a business. Finally, he focused on customer satisfaction, the number one reason that smaller businesses succeed or fail. Like other entrepreneurs, he could have failed, but he had the preparation and determination to make it work.

2. *Can a person develop the personality traits necessary to be a successful entrepreneur? How?*

It is very difficult to alter ones basic personality. For example, an entrepreneur needs to take risks. Not all people are wired to do that. Entrepreneurs also need to be self-directed, self-nurturing, and energetic. Some people need stroking by others and don't have the energy to work as hard as necessary. In short, entrepreneurs are a different breed, and they are not easily made; they are pretty much born that way.

3. *How important is a business plan in getting started in a business such as Artists' Frame Service?*

A business plan is not always necessary for entrepreneurship. You can, for example, start a lawn-mowing business or a window-washing business without an elaborate plan. But when you intend to become a large business that calls for much money, you have to have a great plan to use for investors and bankers. A business plan is not only good for investors, it is a road map to follow for marketing and other functions as well.

Lecture Enhancers

LECTURE ENHANCER 5-1

WHY GOVERNMENT OWNERSHIP

The chapter deals primarily with forms of private business ownership. Public ownership, ownership and/or management by government, may be used for any number of reasons including the following:

- *The investment needed may be too steep for private investors, or the potential returns may be so small or intangible that private investors are unwilling to take the risk.* In the 1930's the rural electrification program (REA) was government-financed because private utilities found the profit potential too low for their taste. Another example is the space program. Private investors lacked the enormous capital necessary to finance our exploration of space and saw the payoff as being years down the road. In fact, although we have benefited in many nonmonetary ways, NASA still has not earned a "profit."
- *Public ownership may be the only option left when privately owned firms fail.* For instance, the federal government set up the National Railroad Passenger Corporation (Amtrak) and the Consolidated Rail Corporation (Conrail) when Penn Central and other private railroads were unable to provide needed services profitably.
- *Some widespread services are too important to society's welfare to be left to the frequently warring world of private businesses.* Regardless of how you view it, the U.S. Postal Service is needed to see that mail service is provided to isolated areas at an affordable rate, not just to the denser, more profitable urban areas. Social Security and education are other examples.
- *There are services for which there is no rational alternative other than public ownership.* Services such as police protection and national security could not be handled by a private firm as it would be impossible to separate the paying "users" from the nonpaying "outsiders." Some experts also argue that public ownership way be desirable to stimulate competition with privately owned firms.

Instances such as the above are the exception rather than the rule. The vast majority of our nation's productive activity is channeled private sector.

LECTURE ENHANCER 5-2

THE DEVELOPMENT OF SEARS AND ROEBUCK

WATCHMAKER WANTED
with references
who can furnish tools.
State age, experience, and salary
required.
T39, Daily News

The above ad appeared in the Help Wanted section of the Chicago Daily News of April 11, 1887. It was placed by Richard W. Sears of Chicago and was answered by Alvah Roebuck, a watch assembler and repairman from Indiana.

Sears was a railroad stationmaster and telegraph operator in Redwood, Minnesota, where a shipment of watches remained unclaimed by the owner. Sears sold the watches to nearby farmers. This effort was so successful and rewarding that he started ordering and "peddling" watches. He soon quit his railroad job and moved to Minneapolis, where he founded the R. W. Sears Watch Company.

In 1887, Sears moved to Chicago, placed the above ad, and he and Roebuck formed a partnership. Sears was the hyperactive, brilliant advertiser, promoter, and salesman, while Roebuck was the quiet, reserved organizer. As their business boomed, they expanded into diamonds and general jewelry, general household and farm goods, musical instruments, and anything else the customers ordered. The main business was done by catalog and mail orders, which required extensive advertising, low prices, and a "money-back guarantee."

Sears would take the orders and then rush around to find the goods to fill them. This pressure caused Roebuck to sell out to Sears in 1895 for $25,000. Sears then required an organizer and manager. He hired Julius Rosenwald, who played a key role in the firm's development. Rosenwald, who was noted for his business skills, became president in 1908 when Sears resigned after a disagreement with him. Rosenwald brought in General Robert E. Wood, the quartermaster who had masterminded the Panama Canal construction, to lead the firm into a new era.

After Roebuck went broke in the 1929 crash, his old company, now a thriving mail-order firm, put him on the publicity department payroll to make goodwill tours.

Largely as a result of the automobile and the mobility created by World War I, there was a migration from the farms to the cities in the 1920's. Sensing that this shift would vitally affect them, Rosenwald shifted the firm's emphasis from mail-order business to urban merchandising. Later, the firm opened up stores outside the cities where there was plenty of parking space.

Realizing the effects of World War II's "G.I. Bill" on U.S. business, General Wood started a modernization and expansion program in the late 1940's that put Sears out in front of Montgomery Ward and other competitors for over two decades.

Wood also got Sears into auto service, operations in Latin America, home and auto insurance, auto rental, pest control, gardening, and house decorating.

By the mid-1980s, Sears had become prominent in real estate and securities investing through acquiring Dean Witter Reynolds, the nation's seventh-largest securities brokerage firm, and Coldwell Banker and Co., the largest independent real estate services company. It already was a force in the insurance field through its Allstate Insurance subsidiary.

The 1990s saw another crisis for Sears. In 1990 it slipped to the nation's number three retailer from number two the years before. Shareholder groups pressured Sears' board to spin-off some businesses and undertake a makeover of the retail operations. The restructuring eventually resulted in the closure of Sears' huge catalog operations and closing 113 stores.

LECTURE ENHANCER 5-3

ARE PARTNERS BAD FOR BUSINESS?

Inc. Magazine recently polled its subscribers on this question. Most saw some good in partnerships, but the majority felt the personal costs ultimately outweighed all benefits. (See complete lecture enhancer on page 5.56.)

When asked whether partnership is a bad way to run a business, over half, 59 percent, said yes.

Reasons why partnership were bad included:

- Personal conflicts outweigh the benefits 60 percent
- Partners never live up to one another's expectations 59 percent
- Companies function better with one clear leader 53 percent
- Partnerships dilute equity too much 6 percent
- Partners can't call their own shots 6 percent

Reasons why partnership were good included:

- Partnership spreads the workload 55 percent
- Partnership spreads to emotional burden 41 percent
- Partners provide executive talent not otherwise affordable 40 percent
- Partners spread the financial budget 33 percent
- Makes company building less lonely 26 percent

When asked who really runs the company, *Inc.* partners answered:

- Myself 52 percent
- Equal partnership 39 percent
- My partner 9 percent

Of those partners who characterized partnerships as good, the majority (60 percent) said they were or are involved in "equal partnerships."

LECTURE ENHANCER 5-4

PUT PARTNERSHIP AGREEMENTS IN WRITING

One problem with partnerships is that you usually form them with friends. It is difficult to force friends to spell out a partnership agreement. It is like forcing your potential spouse to sign a marriage agreement. It is possible, but seems too formal for such an intimate arrangement. Nonetheless, it is important to put partnership agreements in writing.

What will happen if one of the partners wants to drop out? Who is responsible for hiring and firing workers? What if you want to remodel who is in charge? Clarifying such questions while the partners are on good terms is very important.

For most small companies, such agreements cost between $1,000 and $4,000. You should use a lawyer and be quite open about questions that need to be discussed and issues that must be raised. You are not likely to think of all the contingencies that might arise, so hiring someone with lots of experience in this area can be a real help. The money is well worth it when you think of the battles that can arise when there is no such agreement. By the way, working on such an agreement is one test of the compatibility of partners. If you can't agree on an agreement, maybe you shouldn't be partners in the first place.

LECTURE ENHANCER 5-5

THE *FORTUNE* LIST OF MOST ADMIRED CORPORATIONS

Each year *Fortune* magazine asks top executives, outside directors, and securities analysts to evaluate the companies in their industry on each of eight criteria. These criteria are added together to obtain an overall "admired" score. Below are the top ten and bottom ten companies for 1995, 1996, and 1997.

THE MOST ADMIRED COMPANIES IN AMERICA

THE TOP TEN

	1997	1996	1995
1	General Electric	Coca-Cola	Coca-Cola
2	Microsoft	Procter & Gamble	Mirage Resorts
3	Coca-Cola	Rubbermaid	Merck
4	Intel	Johnson & Johnson	UPS
5	Hewlett-Packard	Intel	Microsoft
6	Southwest Airlines	Merck	Johnson & Johnson
7	Berkshire Hathaway	Microsoft	Intel
8	Disney	Mirage Resorts	Pfizer
9	Johnson & Johnson	Hewlett-Packard	Procter & Gamble
10	Merck	Motorola	Berkshire Hathaway

THE BOTTOM TEN

1997	1996	1995
Flagstar	TWA	Cal Fed Bancorp
TWA	Morrison Knudsen	Amerco
Apple Computer	Kmart	Beverly Enterprises
Standard Commercial	USAir Group	USAir Group
Woolworth	A&P	Flagstar
Advanta	Continental Airlines	Morrison Knudsen
Outboard Marine	Amerco	Canandaigua Wine
Amerco	Salomon	Kmart
Great Western	Woolworth	Standard Commercial
DIMON	Standard Commercial	TWA

LECTURE ENHANCER 5-6

GOING PUBLIC

When small, privately held corporations reach the stage in their development when large amounts of new capital are required, they often choose the option of selling stock to outsiders. This process is called "going public."

For the corporation this means a welcome influx of funds which never have to be repaid. Firms can use this capital to finance new products, fuel expansion, or retire old long-term debt. As equity doesn't require fixed interest payments, the company's bottom line profit, may improve. And simply being listed on a public exchange enhances the corporation's reputation with investors and, indirectly, its credit rating.

On the other hand, going public greatly complicates the company's operations. The initial stock offering underwriting costs and legal fees are often over $100,000. Corporate officers may find their valuable time eaten up by meetings with investment brokers and other Wall Street denizens to "sell" the newly public corporation.

Some company executives complain of the loss of independence. Business decisions, once made informally or on instinct, must now be explained to thousands of stockholders. Business operations and financial records are open to inspection by any of the owner-stockholders. As one executive noted, "My wife thinks it's terrible that everyone knows my salary."

In addition to the required annual report to stockholders, there's the additional burden of SEC reporting requirements for corporations with more than 300 stockholders. The Securities and Exchange Commission requires publicly traded corporations to file quarterly reports, called 10-K's, disclosing pertinent business information which may affect investors.

The newly public firm also faces the challenge of communicating with perhaps ten thousand new owners for good news and bad. Companies which never had a public relations department soon find it essential. A small drop in stock prices may bring a flood of telephone calls inquiring about the company's future.

The worst nightmare of all corporate officers, however, is that outside stockholders will disapprove of corporate operations enough to gather the votes necessary to unseat the firm's management. For this reason firms going public usually offer less than 50 percent of their shares to outside investors.

LECTURE ENHANCER 5-7

LLOYD'S OF LONDON GOES LIMITED

One of the oldest insurers in the world is Lloyd's of London. For centuries Lloyd's "names", or individuals who pledge assets to underwrite insurance risk, have agreed to unlimited liability. That unique structure changed in 1994 when institutional investors, assured by offers of limited liability, were admitted into Lloyds.

Lloyd's has taken a pounding in recent years. Battered by claims from an array of disasters, including the Exxon oil spill, the number of individual investors has dropped to 19,537 from 31,329 since 1989, and underwriting capacity has shrunk by 19 percent. While Lloyd's once controlled half of the world's insurance, its share now hovers at two percent.

Members felt they had little choice but to vote to admit corporate capital, recognizing that the steady loss of members and underwriting capacity threatened Lloyd's survival. The entrance of corporate capital also signals the end of Lloyd's outdated capital structure. "No one in their right mind would continue to accept unlimited liability if they could avoid it," says a former Lloyd's "name".

LECTURE ENHANCER 5-8

PEPSI PULLS BACK FROM DIVERSIFICATION

When the combination of Pepsi, Pizza Hut, Taco Bell, and Kentucky Fried Chicken proved indigestible, PepsiCo Inc. decided to spin off the fast-food franchises into a stand-alone, publicly-traded entity. Pepsi's spinoff plans, announced in January 1997, begin the breakup of what once seemed a brilliant combination of pop and pizza. But some believe a stand-alone company, in this case an $11 billion business, has a better shot at tackling the tricky problems bedeviling the fast-food business-too many restaurants, big capital costs, higher food prices, competition from jazzed-up supermarkets, and picky consumers looking for new, tasty products. And Pepsi, free of these headaches, could concentrate on its core businesses—soft drinks and snacks.

Pepsi's restaurant acquisitions in the 1970s and 1980s appeared then to offer a way to compensate for Coca-Cola Co.'s seemingly insurmountable lead in the beverage business, particularly overseas. While Coke had geographic diversity, Pepsi boasted business diversity.

It seemed to work, at first. Rather than thrusting itself into the competitive world of burgers, PepsiCo's restaurant business aimed at three fast-growing fast-food niches: pizza, chicken, and tacos. Furthermore, owning three of the biggest fast-food chains offered a chance to sell Pepsi-Cola syrup to the soda fountains at the stores, not to mention massive advertising and sampling opportunities of Pepsi drinks.

But by the early 1990s, it was becoming evident that fast food wasn't necessarily a path for big bucks. Trickier to manage than packaged-goods businesses, fast food is a capital-intensive business that sucks cash and is vulnerable to changes in consumer preferences. In 1994, PepsiCo allocated 48 percent of its capital to the restaurant business, according to one analyst. At the same time, the growth started to slow.

"When you started to have a store at every corner, it wasn't such a good business anymore," notes Emanuel Goldman, an analyst at PaineWebber. "The business slowed at the same time they were mismanaging it."

Pepsi's restaurants, known for their innovation, seemed to falter. And new products are crucial in the restaurant business, driving the same-store sales that are a key indicator for restaurant profitability. "In the beverage and snacks businesses, you can be a genius every couple of years, but in the restaurant business you have to be a genius every year," Mr. Goldman says. To attract fickle customers, he says, "you have to have a new product or 'Jurassic Park' promotions."

New products at Pepsi's fast-food chains have been a hit-or-miss affair. Pizza Hut personal-pan pizza, introduced in the early 1980s, was a huge success. Still, he says, a decade later, Bigfoot pizza (so-called because of its super size) "stubbed its toe." Stuffed-crust pizza, introduced in 1995, was successful but could have been more so if the company had followed it up with variations. Taco Bell's "Border Lights" menu quickly showed that people don't go to fast-food restaurants to count calories.

Trends in the industry haven't helped. Because of the relatively low investment needed to open a fast-food store, restaurants are popping up everywhere. From 1980 to 1995, the number of fast-food stores increased 74 percent to 190,877. By overexpanding, fast-food chains have become their own worst enemy, says one analyst. This is a classic game of prisoner's dilemma: No one wants to fold because they're afraid the other guy will take the pot.

To make matters worse, many grocery stores have spruced up their delis and transformed them into takeout restaurants, offering everything from chicken wings to chicken fajitas. Food stores have been fighting back and that's been taking its toll on fast-food chains.

All this means that a stand-alone, publicly traded entity consisting of three fast-food chains in a highly competitive field isn't likely to be a Wall Street star. But more optimistic observers believe such a company will be better equipped to tackle the vagaries of the restaurant industry—particularly because the three chains won't have to compete with beverages and snacks for the attention for senior management.

LECTURE ENHANCER 5-9

THE PRICE OF FREEDOM

Inflation may be at a historic low, but the price of independence is climbing. What better evidence than Ted Waitt, founder and 46 percent owner of South Dakota's mail-order computer retailer Gateway 2000? Waitt, the son of a fourth-generation cattle broker, walked away from a monumental deal with Compaq Computer that would have left him with a personal fortune of more than $3 billion. No, he did not get kicked in the head by a cow.

In 1997 there were persistent rumors that growth-obsessed Compaq was stalking Gateway. Compaq CEO Eckhard Pfeiffer has said he wants to more than double his company's revenues, to $40 billion, by the end of the decade. Compaq, an outstanding performer in a difficult-to-manage industry, amassed $4 billion in cash at the end of 1996 so Pfeiffer could go shopping. Earlier in 1997 he talked with Micron Technology about buying its mail order computer company, Micron Electronics. No sale.

But Pfeiffer figured he had reeled in one of the computer industry's prize catches in Gateway, the off-beat Sioux City outfit whose packaging bears the black-and-white markings of a cow's hide but whose revenues more resemble filet mignon. Few know or even suspect just how close Pfeiffer came. The contracts were ready, and Waitt had the proverbial pen in hand before he evidently had a mental flash and rejected a nearly $7 billion takeover by Compaq. Gateway's current market value is $4.8 billion

Waitt, a college dropout who founded Gateway in his father's Iowa farmhouse, put a stop to the deal only days, possibly hours, before it was to be announced. The exact details aren't clear, but at one point Pfeiffer and Waitt met at Waitt's estate on the Missouri River. Gateway's public relations firm had begun preparing a press release. Waitt had even dispatched a courier to foreign offices to deliver the news to key executives. But ultimately Waitt couldn't sign on the dotted line.

The deal appears to have fallen apart when Compaq started to project some corporate muscle, as in, "You work for us now." Waitt bristled at his executives' being treated as subordinates, not equals. Both Compaq and Gateway declined to comment. But a source close to Waitt says, "Anyone who really knows Ted Waitt knows that there are things more important to him than money. Two of those things are Gateway and its people."

And ultimately the $3 billion windfall for Waitt may not have been much of an incentive anyway: though he needed to borrow $10,000 from his grandmother to start Gateway in 1985, his 36 million shares in the company are worth more than $2 billion. What's an extra billion for a man who loves running the company he founded and has nurtured from such humble roots? It seems that Waitt's vision of the future told him the Compaq offer wasn't worth it—not to a billionaire free spirit who values his independence.

LECTURE ENHANCER 5-10

EMPLOYEE OWNERSHIP AT GARDEN STATE BRICKFACE

If you happen to be visiting the offices of Garden State Brickface, Windows & Siding in Roselle, New Jersey chances are you'll see a lot of Post-it notes printed with the message: Memo from the Owner. That's because the 110 employees of the residential and commercial remodeling firm, from vinyl-siding managers to middle managers, are all part-owners in the company. "I thought it would be a good investment to have my employees as partners," explains David Moore, president.

Employees of Garden State Brickface are participants in an Employee Stock Ownership Plan, commonly known as an ESOP. Toward the end of 1996, all employees received the first annual statement of their ESOP holdings, which ranged in value from several hundred dollars to several thousand, depending on a person's salary and length of service.

The Employee Stock Ownership Plan is a federal program that was started in 1974, and there are currently about 10,000 privately held companies with ESOPs. The plans operate through a trust to which a participating company sells part or all of its stock, and the employees are the beneficiaries of the trust. When an employee leaves the company for whatever reason, he receives the accumulated value of his ESOP, while the trust retains control of the stock. The stock is paid for over a five-year term from company profits, after which employees are fully vested in the ESOP.

Menke & Associates is a specialist in the design and installation of ESOPs. "Employees are sharing equity ownership," explains Glenn Laury, a Menke & Associates vice president. "They are encouraged to work harder and smarter and make the company even more successful. The ESOP trust also creates a marketplace for the stock. The owner is basically creating a succession plan for his business because the trust, as an entity, can buy his stock." Laury adds that in order to qualify for an ESOP, a company should be a profitable, taxpaying corporation with at least 15 employees—and with principals who are willing to share ownership.

David Moore sold 33.33 percent of Garden State Brickface's stock to the ESOP in 1996. He made that decision after watching many employees weather years of ups and downs at the family-owned operation.

The company was founded in 1953 by Moore's grandfather, father, and two uncles. Moore came aboard in 1980 after graduating from Harvard Business School with plans of expanding the company beyond a small contracting business. By 1988, Garden State Brickface had 500 employees and handled 3,000 projects per year.

Tragedy struck, though, in December of that year. Moore's uncle, Larry Goldberger, the company president, died suddenly of a brain aneurism. Moore and other managers were not prepared with a succession plan; the company ended up being sold to an outside investor in a 1989 leveraged buyout. By March 1991, a debt-laden Garden State Brickface filed for Chapter 11 bankruptcy.

When Moore bought the company back from the bank in May 1992, he espoused a philosophy of controlled growth. And he vowed to take care of the employees—with everything from a suggestion box that pays $2 to $10 for every idea, to an ESOP. "Many key employees have been here through it all," says Moore. "Plus, there is a lot of evidence that companies with employees that have stakes in the business do better than those that don't."

Cindy Wilson, vice president of Human Resources and Administration, says that employees were initially confused and skeptical about the ESOP. But excitement and involvement grew. Garden State Brickface just organized an ESOP Advisory Committee of 11 people, each representing a different part of the company. "Everyone is so much more aware of things," Wilson explains. "From ordering pens to cement, they realize it is coming out of their pockets."

LECTURE ENHANCER 5-11

HOME IS WHERE THE MONEY IS

For 15 years, Lillian Larson, 40, of Marietta, Ga., put on a suit and pumps and commuted 45 minutes each way to a corporate job. Now she works in shorts or jeans in an office that's a few steps from her bedroom. "If I'm really busy," says Larson, "I can be at my desk at 5:30 a.m. in my jammies. I feel you can get so much more work accomplished by working from home."

When Larson purchased her ProForma printing and promotions franchise, she joined the millions of Americans who now run businesses from their homes. According to the International Franchise Association, 10 percent of the half-million-plus franchisees are home-based. Low-cost franchises—those that cost $50,000 or less to start—are the fastest-growing segment in franchising. They are also the most risky, says Rob Bond, publisher of Source Book Publications, of Oakland, Calif., who has been publishing "Bond's Franchise Guide" for 11 years.

Approximately 15 percent to 20 percent of the companies listed in the International Franchise Association's "Franchise Opportunities Guide" fall into the $50,000 and under category. Low cost, home-based businesses have become a $427 billion industry, and franchisors are rushing to offer opportunities that fit the niche. But as fast as new franchise systems open, others disappear. Historically, it's the lower-cost, very new concepts that fold more quickly than securely financed concepts.

The safest route into the low-cost franchise world is to select a franchisor who is financially secure, says Mr. Bond. "Look for a system with a critical mass of franchisees large enough to sustain itself." After years of analysis, Mr. Bond pegs that number at 30. "When a system has 30 or more franchisees, it usually has a positive cash flow from royalties and doesn't need to worry about getting new franchise fees to pay administrative salaries and company overhead," he says.

In a recent survey of 266 franchises with an average total investment of $50,000 or less, only half had 30 units or more. The greatest number of these are in the home improvement and repair category, including carpet and blind cleaning; bathroom, kitchen and furniture restoration; pest extermination; lawn care; and home security system sales and installation.

The advantages of home-based franchises are legion. The investment often is minimal. Most franchisees convert an extra bedroom or basement work space into an office and store supplies in their garages.

Lee Oppenheim, 40, and his wife, Linda, 39, of Calabasas Hills, California, operate a successful Elephant House greeting-card business from half a spare bedroom; the other half is a play area for their children. For Lee Oppenheim, who ran retail pet stores for 20 years before shifting to his Elephant House franchise, the greatest advantage of the home-based business is flexibility.

Buying a home-based franchise lets you try out a business without much risk, says Joe Howard, 48, of Poolesville, Maryland. He and his wife, who both have full-time jobs, bought an Elephant House franchise last year. They do all the bookkeeping on the same computer their young children use to play games, and they have hired a college student to help service their 60 customers.

Other advantages to running a franchise from home include everything from being able to do a load of laundry between phone calls to being available for a sick child (although experts advise not mixing family business with a franchise business except in extreme emergency).

But the easy entry to such low-cost franchises can be a double-edged sword, warns Mr. Bond. A franchise that's simple and inexpensive will soon have competition. Franchisors of low-cost systems often can't afford to give the same level of training and support as their higher-priced colleagues. Low-cost franchises can also fall apart because franchisees are not committed enough to them.

LECTURE ENHANCER 5-12

JOINING HANDS ACROSS THE WATERS: STRATEGIC ALLIANCES

With Europe, Asia, and the Third World buying a wide range of products and services, American companies find the opportunities almost unlimited. Joint ventures and mergers with companies native to these global markets provide businesses a chance to enter those markets less warily. Joint venturing involves both participants in sales, distribution, or manufacturing.

For example, an American company with a design for a high-efficiency boiler decided to sell the technology internationally., Rather than take on a foreign market single-handedly, the company entered a joint venture with a German business that produced a similarly designed high-efficiency burner that could be fitted to the boiler.

Since the products fit together, both companies decided to produce each other's design in their own markets. This gave the German company an immediate outlet in the U.S. and gave the American company an entry into the vigorous German economy. Joint ventures and mergers aren't always easy to pull off. Even a large company such as McDonald's had its problems when it opened its first restaurant in Moscow. After ensuring a steady supply of quality meat and potatoes from its partner (the Moscow municipal authorities), McDonald's officials were told the price for beef would increase from 2.4 rubles per kilogram to 14 rules and that rent would increase by 10 times. The increases forced McDonald's to double its prices soon after opening.

Joint ventures and mergers with foreign firms will continue to dominate the headlines throughout the 1990s.

LECTURE ENHANCER 5-13

COOPS ALLOW SMALL BUSINESSES TO COMPETE AGAINST BIG ONES

As word spreads, the idea of business cooperatives (member-owned organizations established by a large groups of small business owners) is spreading. According to the National Cooperative Bank, 2 million businesses belong to 20,000 co-ops nationwide. Franchises, for example, are starting their own co-ops to lower costs. The Employers' Health Purchasing Co-Op in Seattle negotiates for favorable health plans for small businesses.

Contract Sheet is a cooperative public relations firm. Aldus, the manufacturer of PageMaker, invited more than 140 independent software writers to develop complementary software for its company. In short, "Cooperation allows the entrepreneur to tap much larger resources for purchasing, marketing, or accessing technology."

Critical Thinking Exercises

Name: ______________________

Date: ______________________

CRITICAL THINKING EXERCISE 5-1

PICKING PARTNERS

Did you ever think you might like to go into business for yourself? What kind of business would you like to start? What resources (both personal skills and capital) would you need to make your business a success? Sometimes it helps to have a partner to share the burdens of starting a business what skills would you need to look for in your partner?

Use the space below to list the personal skills and capital needed for your proposed business. Put your initials next to the skills and capital you would bring to the business. Think of a friend who might be interested in joining you as a partner. Put your friends initials next to the skills and capital he or she can offer. What capital or skills are missing?

Type of Business: ______________________

Proposed Partner: ______________________

Personal Skills Needed:	**Capital Needed:**
______________________	______________________
______________________	______________________
______________________	______________________
______________________	______________________
______________________	______________________

What skills and/or capital are missing? ______________________

____

What can you do to get what is needed? ______________________

____

____

____

Name: ____________________

Date: ____________________

CRITICAL THINKING EXERCISE 5-2

CHOOSING A FORM OF BUSINESS OWNERSHIP

The needs of the businessperson starting a new business is a major consideration when deciding the best form of business ownership. The kind of business being started is also important to consider when deciding to make your new business a sole proprietorship, partnership, or corporation. Look at the list of new businesses below. Indicate the form of ownership you think would be best for each business. Give the reason for your selection.

BUSINESS	FORM	REASON
Swimming pool repair		
Flower shop		
Mexican		
Termite control service		
Textbook publishing company		
Law firm		
Underwear manufacturer		
Child care center		

ANSWERS TO CRITICAL THINKING EXERCISE 5-2

SWIMMING POOL REPAIR

A swimming pool repair company would probably operate best as a sole proprietorship or partnership at first. There is no great need for capital at first, so a partner may not be needed. A good way to start would be to hire a few good people and begin work. If many jobs came in, you could hire more workers. If the managerial task became too much, you could hire an accountant or office manager. A partner would be good if you wanted an expert in marketing or some other assistant. Also, it is often fun to have a partner to share ideas and successes with.

FLOWER SHOP

A flower shop would likely do best as a partnership. The reason for that is that retail stores demand that someone be there all the time. Since stores are open as much as seven days a week, 12 hours a day, it helps to have a partner to share the managerial responsibilities. A partner is also helpful in raising the initial capital. A sole proprietor could succeed if he or she found an excellent manager or two to help.

MEXICAN RESTAURANT

A Mexican restaurant, like a flower shop, may do best as a partnership for the same reasons. All retail stores demand long hours and it is good to have a partner when you are sick or need a vacation. The capital required also calls for a partner in most cases. Again, it is possible to run such a restaurant as a sole proprietor if you can find good managers and workers.

TERMITE CONTROL

A termite control service is much like the swimming pool company, a consumer service. One can start out small with little capital and build as the business builds. A sole proprietor can do fine with some good employees. A partner can be of much assistance in marketing and sharing the burden if the business grows rapidly. A partner is good for sharing thoughts and worries and joys, but not necessary.

TEXTBOOK PUBLISHING

A textbook publishing company calls for a corporate-type of structure because the costs of publishing a text are so high. The cost of publishing this text plus all the supplements teachers manual, study guide, test bank, videos, computer projects, and so on, comes to a million dollars or so. It is very difficult for a sole proprietor or a partnership to raise such funds. The production facilities and other physical spaces are subject to accidents that could lead to lawsuits. A corporation protects its owners from losses beyond what they invest. All in all, a corporate form is probably best in this situation.

LAW FIRM

Law firms can be sole proprietorships, but the growth would be severely limited. Besides, there would be no one to cover when the owner gets sick or goes on vacations. In this case, it is best to have a partner or several partners. In fact, that is what most law firms do. Whether or not the partners decide to incorporate has much to do with taxes and liability. The need for capital is not that great.

UNDERWEAR MANUFACTURER

An underwear manufacturer would likely need buildings and equipment that could not be obtained without much capital. That calls for incorporating and raising those funds through the sale of stock. This is much like the publishing case.

CHILD CARE

A child care center could very well be a sole proprietorship if it was small enough. Employees could be hired to do all that was necessary. On the other hand, a partner may be needed to help finance the building, if the building is not rented. A partner could help in many other ways as well being there when you can't be, sharing ideas, etc. Incorporation would only be necessary to protect against liability, which can be important, or for tax purposes if the center expands to make lots of money. An S corporation may be a good idea in that case. Of course, a child care center could also be a cooperative if the parents are willing.

S corporations could be used for the swimming pool company, the flower shop, and the Mexican restaurant as well. The basic goal is to minimize taxes. Such a decision is best left to a small business expert who is also a lawyer or accountant or both.

Supplemental Cases

CASE 5-1

MERGERS

In spite of the fact that the text talks about the idea that "Small is beautiful," the fact is that many corporations merge with other corporations to become huge corporations. You may have read the headlines when Pepsi bought Beatrice or when two "Big Eight" accounting firms merged to become the largest accounting firm in the United States. What's behind these corporate marriages, known as mergers and acquisitions, and what impact do they have on employees, consumers, and competition?

What Are Mergers and Acquisitions and Why Do They Happen?

When two companies find that they have mutual interests in each other, they may decide to form one company. This is known as a merger. One company buying another is called an acquisition.

One cause of acquisitions is that some large companies prefer to be "vertically integrated." That is, rather than buying materials from another company, they prefer to make them so that they have control during periods of shortages, for example. However, it is often easier and more profitable for them to buy a smaller company that already has the expertise required to manufacture the materials than to learn from scratch.

Furthermore, merging with or acquiring a company can improve a firm's competitive position by giving them capability they did not have before. For example, the merger of two accounting firms Peat Marwick and Klynveld Goerdeler, expanded Peat Marwick's impact on the international market, where KMG is a major competitor.

Also, mergers and acquisitions were occurred in the late 1980s in such great numbers, especially among larger firms, because the economic climate was right. That is, interest rates were low, making borrowing to acquire other firms less expensive. In addition, the stock market was strong, so that a company could issue stock more easily to raise the necessary capital to buy another company. Before the new tax bill went into effect, there was a particular flurry to buy new companies because the economic climate was expected to be more uncertain after the changes in the tax bill.

Implications for Employees

When both companies agree to a merger, the overtaking company generally realizes if the two are to work together, they will have to allow the smaller company to have a fair amount of autonomy to continue to run the business.

In a hostile takeover, however, one company attempts to acquire another without the consent or agreement of the other company. They can do this by trying to acquire a majority of the stock. Such a situation can have far reaching consequences for employees. During a friendly merger, the top executives usually become the top executives of the newly formed company. But the company will no longer need two manufacturing or human resource managers, making the corporate staff vulnerable to layoffs.

In fact, layoffs are a concern for employees at all levels. Top management had learned to protect itself with golden parachutes, but there weren't enough to provide a soft landing for the 10,000 employees who lost their jobs when Chevron took over Gulf.

Some mergers and acquisitions have been unsuccessful. One survey showed that half the executives of the acquired company left within the first year after the takeover, and another quarter planned to leave in the next two years. In a service industry where the people are the business, it is unlikely that a merger will succeed without the cooperation of the acquired firm's employees.

Implications for Competition and Consumers

In the cases of Coca-Cola attempting to buy Dr. Pepper and Pepsi Co. trying to take over Seven Up, the smaller companies successfully filed anti-trust suits. The courts ruled that both Pepsi and Coke would have virtual monopolies in the soft drink market if they were allowed to acquire the smaller companies. What this means for the consumer is that there may be fewer choices of where to buy in the future.

In the extreme case, if all larger companies merge, there would be three or four huge conglomerates in each market, which could have a negative effect on competition and give the few remaining companies greater control over price.

Implications for Stockholders

In some cases, the stockholders themselves will initiate a takeover. They are hoping, some say, to make a killing when the price of the stock shoots up, either because of takeover rumors or because the company is purchased for a higher price.

DISCUSSION QUESTIONS FOR CASE 5-1:

1. What positive effects can a merger or acquisition have on the companies involved? What are some negative effects?

2. Do you see mergers and acquisitions as a benefit or a drawback to the economy as a whole in the long run? Why?

3. Find articles in the paper that discuss the mergers and see what the authors have to say about the impact on the economy.

ANSWERS TO DISCUSSION QUESTIONS FOR CASE 5-1:

1. *What positive effects can a merger or acquisition have on the companies involved? What are some negative effects?*

   The positive effects include the removal of managers who are not productive and who are not making the maximum use of resources. Acquisitions also free capital that may be tied up in buildings and other areas which are not as productive as the money could be in other areas of the business. All in all, mergers and acquisitions usually strengthen the firm. After all, that is one purpose of doing them. The negative effects are that managers and employees may be fired. The union may lose its power. New managers may be less ethical and may treat workers less kindly.

2. *Do you see mergers and acquisitions as a benefit or a drawback to the economy as a whole in the long run? Why?*

   Mergers and acquisitions are a benefit in the long run, although the short-term consequences of lost jobs, etc. may be painful. The United States must learn to compete with foreign businesses. That means having the most efficient and effective firms possible. Some organizations have grown fat and lazy in the United States and mergers and acquisitions get rid of much of the fat. The process of making firms more efficient would go much, much slower without such pressures.

3. *Find articles in the paper that discuss the mergers and see what the authors have to say about the impact on the economy.*

   Pay attention to the fact that the question asks for impact on the economy, not impact on the managers or workers. Most articles will say the impact is favorable, with some firms as exceptions. But have the students look for themselves. Learning means doing research as well as listening in class. You can't always trust what you read and hear. You have to learn someday to dig out the facts on your own. There is no better time to start than in school.

CASE 5-2

OPPORTUNITIES IN FRANCHISING

In 1990, there were over 500,000 franchised businesses in the United States. Projections show that nearly 50 percent of all retail sales in the 1990s will be through franchises, which employ over 7 million people. Franchise sales grew 114 percent during the 1980s, compared to only 81 percent for retail sales. Fewer than 4 percent of the franchise outlets go out of business each year. Compare that with the failure rate of sole proprietorship (25 percent to 33 1/3 percent in the first year), and franchises start to look rather attractive.

Hot franchises in the 1990s include business services, nonfood retailing, automotive services, and personal/home services. Some 20 or 30 years ago, you could get a McDonald's or AAMCO transmission franchise for about $10,000. Today, a McDonald's franchise will cost an average of $610,000. Nonetheless, McDonald's is still a good investment. An average McDonald's brings in $1.6 million in sales, and an operator may net $150,000 or more. Newer franchises cost less, but involve more risk. You can, for example, get a Jazzercise franchise for $2,000.

The success stories are many. MAACO Enterprises was founded in 1972. It specializes in auto body repair and painting. By 1988, it had over 400 units in 42 states and Canada selling close to $200 million worth of services per year. Fantastic Sam's began franchising its hair-cutting services in 1976. In a two-year period from 1985 to 1987, the company opened 450 new franchised stores. In 1987, Donald Ervin and a group of investors bought Precision Tune. They doubled sales to $160 million in 1989 and now have over 500 outlets.

Maybe you would enjoy running a Big Daddy's Lounge and Package Liquor Stores or perhaps Packy the Shipper franchises might catch your eye. If you are not sure about franchising, maybe you should contact the International Franchise Association for more information. The address is 1350 New York Avenue, N.W. (Suite 900), Washington, D.C., 20005. The phone number is (202) 628-8000. You can get the names, addresses, phone numbers, cash investment, and qualifications needed, and other data on members. The association offers several interesting publications, including Is Franchising for You? and How to Be a Franchisor.

DISCUSSION QUESTIONS FOR CASE 5-2:

1. What kinds of questions might you ask before buying a franchise?

2. Are the lower risks of franchise organizations worth giving up the freedom of ownership and control? How would you find information to answer such questions?

3. Look around your town and see which franchises seem successful. Is it true that the three most important promotional elements for a franchise are location, location, and location? Is there evidence of this around you?

ANSWERS TO DISCUSSION QUESTIONS FOR CASE 5-2:

1. *What kinds of questions might you ask before buying a franchise?*

The "Checklist for Evaluate a Franchise" box has several clues. You would want to know what the sales and profit potential is, what the competition is like, what the investment cost would be and how it could be financed, what the experience of other comparable franchises has been, and what kinds of assistance are available.

2. *Are the lower risks of franchise organizations worth giving up the freedom of ownership and control? How would you find information to answer such questions?*

A franchise is worth giving up some freedoms if the returns are more assured and if there is less risk involved. Naturally, the answer varies by franchise. The best way to find out such answers is to talk to several franchisees of the same company in different parts of the country. What have their experiences been? What advice do they have? What would they have written into the contract if they could start all over again?

3. *Look around your town and see which franchises seem successful. Is it true that the three most important promotional elements for a franchise are location, location, and location? Is there evidence of this around you?*

In my town, there are several franchises that are the biggest sellers in the region. Almost always the main reason is location. The most successful franchises seem to be the old established ones plus a few new hot ideas. McDonalds', Burger King, and the fast-food restaurants in general seem to do well. Computer stores come and go as do video outlet stores. In general, franchises do better than independent businesses.

Transparency Masters

TRANSPARENCY MASTER 38	Chapter Outline
TRANSPARENCY MASTER 39	How Owners Affect Management *(Figure 5.1 on text page 142)*
TRANSPARENCY MASTER 40	Comparison of Forms of Business Ownership *(Figure 5.2 on text page 146)*
TRANSPARENCY MASTER 41	Types of Mergers *(Figure 5.3 on text page 148)*
TRANSPARENCY MASTER 42	Additional Benefits and Drawbacks of Franchising *(Figure 5.4 on text page 152)*

Chapter Outline

CHAPTER 5
FORMS OF BUSINESS OWNERSHIP

PROFILE: Tony Conza of Blimpie International Sandwich Shops

I. BASIC FORMS OF BUSINESS OWNERSHIP.

II. SOLE PROPRIETORSHIPS.

A. Advantages of Sole Proprietorships.

B. Disadvantages of Sole Proprietorships.

III. PARTNERSHIPS.

A. Categories of Partners.

B. Advantages of Partnerships.

C. Disadvantages of Partnerships.

IV. CORPORATIONS.

A. Advantages of Corporations.

B. Disadvantages of Corporations.

C. Individuals Can Incorporate.

D. S Corporations.

E. Limited Liability Companies.

V. CORPORATE EXPANSION: MERGERS AND ACQUISITIONS.

VI. SPECIAL FORMS OF BUSINESS OWNERSHIP

VII. FRANCHISES.

A. Advantages of Franchises.

Chapter Outline *(continued)*

B. Disadvantages of Franchises.
C. Diversity in Franchising.
D. Home-Based Franchises.
E. Franchising in International Markets.
F. Using Technology in Franchising.

VIII. COOPERATIVES.

IX. WHICH FORM OF OWNERSHIP IS FOR YOU?

X. SUMMARY AND REVIEW.

TM-39

How Owners Affect Management

(Figure 5.1 on text page 142)

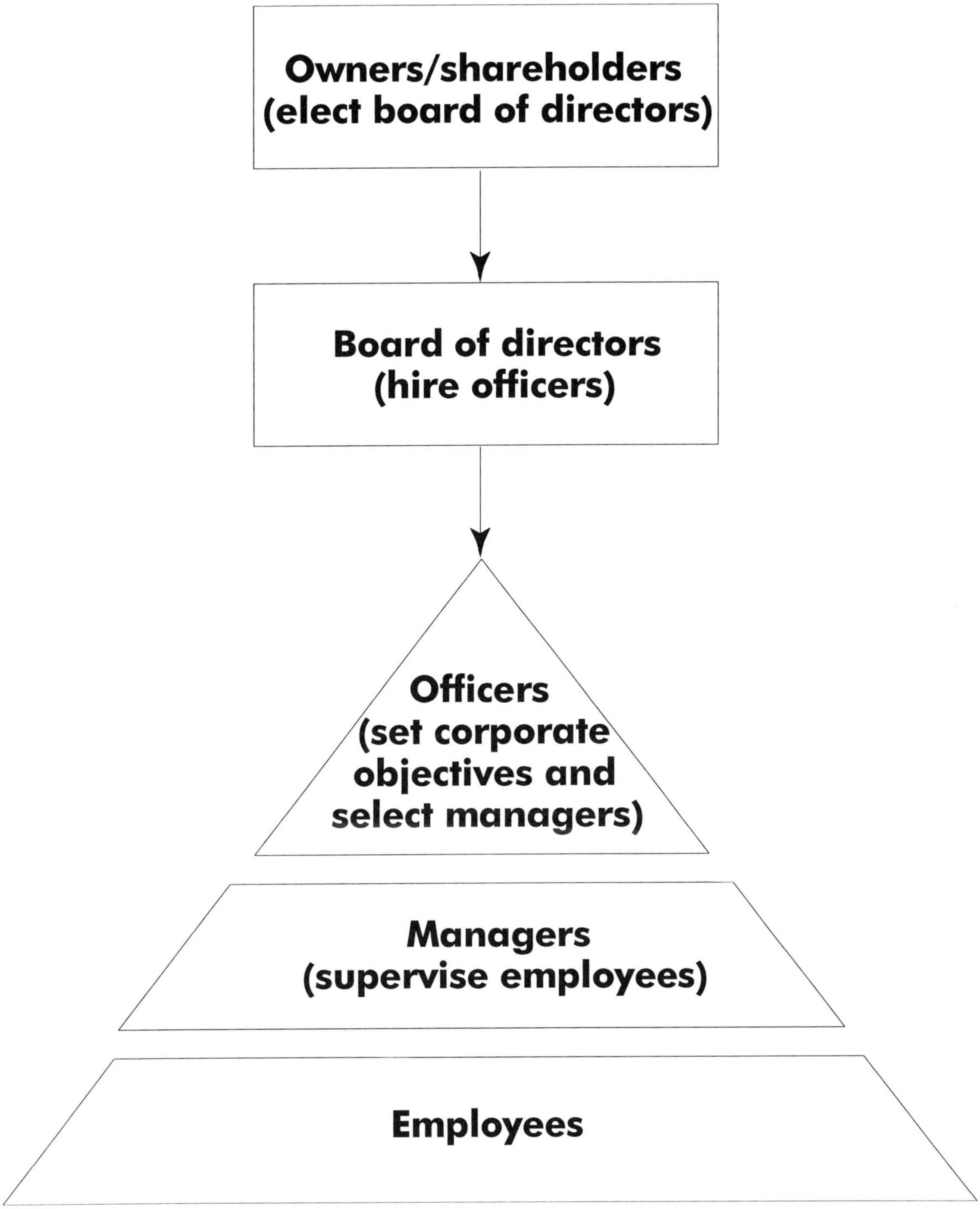
Owners/shareholders
(elect board of directors)
Board of directors
(hire officers)
Officers
(set corporate
objectives and
select managers)
Managers
(supervise employees)
Employees

Comparison of Forms of Business Ownership

(Figure 5.2 on text page 146)

		PARTNERSHIPS		CORPORATIONS		
	Sole Proprietorship	**General Partnership**	**Limited Partnership**	**Conventional Corporation**	**S Corporation**	**Limited Liability Company**
Documents needed to start business	None, may need permit or license	Partnership agreement (oral or written)	Written agreement. Must file certificate of limited partnership	Articles of incorporation, bylaws	Articles of incorporation, bylaws, must meet criteria	Articles of organization and operating agreement; no eligibility requirements
Ease of termination	Easy to terminate: just pay debts and quit	May be hard to terminate, depending on the partnership agreement	Same as general partnership	Hard and expensive to terminate	Same as conventional corporation	May be difficult, depending upon operating agreement
Length of life	Terminates on the death of owner	Terminates on the death or withdrawal of partner	Same as general partnership	Perpetual life	Same as conventional corporation	Same as partnership
Transfer of ownership	Business can be sold to quali?ed buyer	Must have other partner(s)' agreement	Same as general partnership	Easy to change owners; just sell stock	Can sell stock, but with restrictions	Can't sell stock

Comparison of Forms of Business Ownership *(continued)*

		PARTNERSHIPS		CORPORATIONS		
	Sole Proprietorship	**General Partnership**	**Limited Partnership**	**Conventional Corporation**	**S Corporation**	**Limited Liability Company**
Financial resources	Limited to owner's capital and loans	Limited to partners' capital and loans	Same as general partnership	More money to start and operate; may sell stocks and bonds	Same as conventional corporation	Same as partnership
Risk of losses	Unlimited liability	Unlimited liability	Limited liability	Limited liability	Limited liability	Limited liability
Taxes	Taxed as personal income	Taxed as personal income	Same as general partnership	Corporate, double taxation	Taxed as personal income	Taxed as personal income
Management responsibilities	Owner manages all areas of the business	Partners share management	Can't participate in management	Separate management from ownership	Same as conventional corporation	Varies
Employee benefits	Usually fewer benefits and lower wages	Often fewer benefits and lower wages; promising employee could become a partner	Same as general partnership	Usually better benefits and wages, advancement opportunities	Same as conventional corporation	Varies

Types of Mergers
(Figure 5.3 on text page 148)

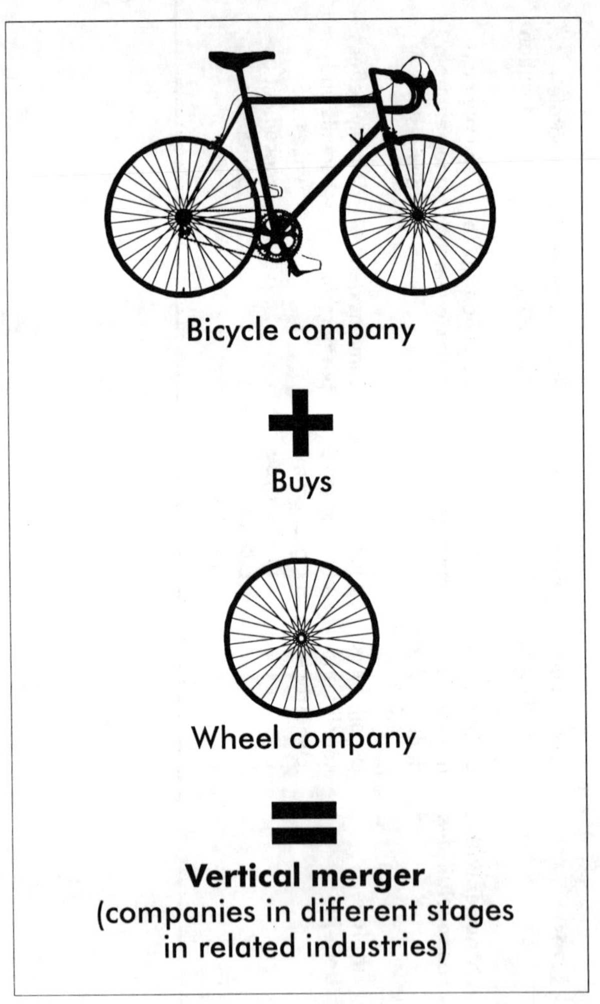

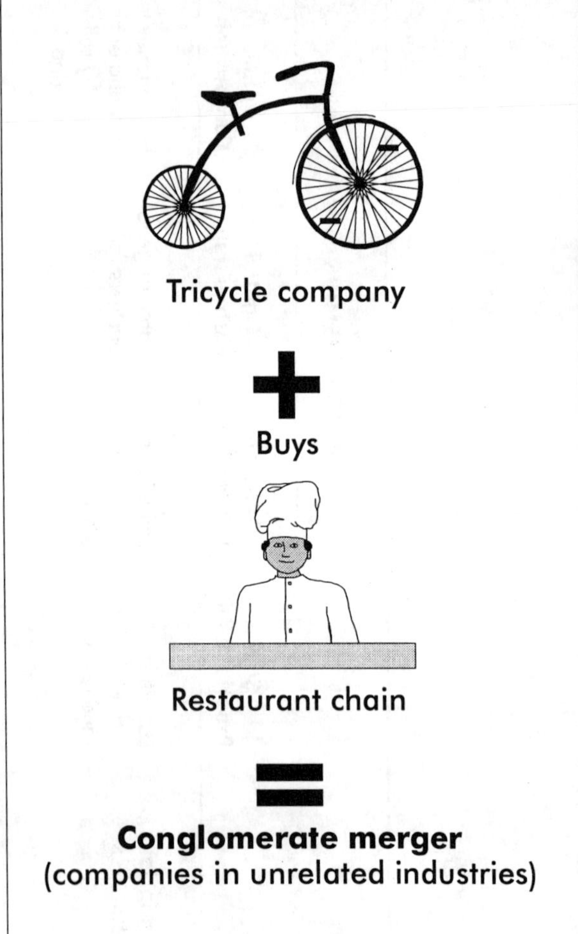

TM-42

Additional Benefits and Drawbacks of Franchising

(Figure 5.4 on text page 152)

BENEFITS	DRAWBACKS
• Nationally recognized name and established reputation	• High initial franchise fee
• Help with finding a good location	• Additional fees may be charged for marketing
• A proven management system	• A monthly percentage of gross sales may go to the franchisor
• Tested methods for inventory and operations management	• Possible competition from other nearby franchisees
• Financial advice and assistance	• No freedom to select decor or other design features
• Training in all phases of operation	• Little freedom to determine management procedures
• Promotional assistance	• Many rules and regulations to follow
• Periodic management counseling	
• Proven record of success	
• It's your business!	

Entrepreneurship and Starting a Small Business

Chapter 6

Folder Contents

OT ACETATE 6-3 Who Starts New Businesses?

OT ACETATE 6-4 Most Common Type of Home-Based Businesses

OT ACETATE 6-5 Take the Intrapreneur Quiz

OT ACETATE 6-6 Take the Intrapreneur Quiz

OT ACETATE 6-7 How Much Capital Do Entrepreneurs Have to Start Their Businesses?

OT ACETATE 6-8 What Sources Did You Use to Get Start-Up Capital?

OT ACETATE 6-9 Hours Worked Per Week the First Year in Business

OT ACETATE 6-10 How to Get a Yes From a Banker

OT ACETATE 6-11 Top Priorities of Small Business Owners

OT ACETATE 6-12 Major Concerns of Small Business Owners

OT ACETATE 6-13 Eight Ways to Improve Your Company Profit

(Acetates and Transparency Masters are also available as PowerPoint slides on disk and on the Presentation CD-ROM.)

(Resources Available are also referenced in the expanded lecture outline later in this chapter.)

Other Resources Available

Video Case - "Jay Goltz, Entrepreneurial Wizard." Named one of Forbes Magazine's "Biz Kids" shortly after beginning his service-oriented business, Artists' Frame Service, Jay Goltz is a dynamic and energetic businessman who united his passion for art with the mission of sound business. This video profiles Goltz's unique formula for success. (The **Media Resource Guide** contains a summary of the Video and suggested discussion questions.)

Student Assessment and Learning Guide: Contains matching key term and definition questions, write-in retention questions, write-in critical thinking questions, and practice test of multiple choice and true/false questions.

Technology:

Zapitalism CD-ROM - Simulation program.

Concept Mastery Exam Preparation Disk - Practice test and tutorial.

Business Essentials Disk - Hyperlinks Understanding Business with seven other leading business texts.

Presentation CD-ROM - Contains PowerPoint slides of acetates and transparency masters, video clips, lecture materials. This tool allows you to customize your lecture presentations.

***Business Week* Web Site Access with the *Business Week* edition.**

***Understanding Business* Home Page - http:/www.mhhe.com/ub5e.**

Audiotape: Abridged chapter (Text minus profile, boxes, and end-of-chapter material.

Associated Web Sites

These sites are provided to students for the purpose of analysis and critical thinking of the issues. Students are encouraged to explore other sites. As with any Web site, some may be inactive now.

Publications and Organizations:

Inc. Magazine

http://www.inc.com/

Entrepreneur Magazine

http://entrepreneurmag.com/

World Entrepreneur Association

http://www.wrldea.com/

Liraz Publishing:

Take the Entrepreneur Test (also take the test on Page 205 of your textbook)

http://www.liraz.com/

The Entrepreneur's Mind

http://www.benlore.com/

Top 75 entrepreneurs (listed by states)

http://entrepreneurmag.com/entmag/50states4.hts

Many Personal Examples

Use any of the web browsers under NET SEARCH and enter the term "Entrepreneur of the Year"

Companies Demand IDEA PEOPLE:

The five people of innovation

http://www.pinchot.com/pinweb/intramgt/innouniv/5peoplin.html

Are You an Intrapreneur? - take the test (Results will be e-mailed back to you)

http://www.pinchot.com/pinweb/instruments/areintra.html

Being Incompetent in Business (observe and avoid these characteristics)

http://www.hardatwork.com/Stump/DWPP/Incompetent.html

Organizations That Can Help Get a Business Started:

U.S. Small Business Administrations (SBA)

http://www.sbaonline.sba.gov/

Service Corps of Retired Executives (SCORE)

http://www.sbaonline.sba.gov/SCORE/

Understanding Business **Home Page:**

http:/www.mhhe.com/ub5e.

What's New in This Edition

Additions:

- Profile of David Marcheschi of Water Concepts LLC
- Section "Age of the Entrepreneur"
- Section "Micropreneurs and Home-Based Businesses"
- Taking It to the Net exercises
- Video case on Jay Goltz of Artists' Frame Service
- From the Pages of Business Week: If I Had Only Known Then...
- Reaching Beyond Our Borders: Make Money Exporting, But It's a Work-out

Revisions:

Statistical data and examples throughout the chapter were updated to reflect current information. In addition:

- Section "What Does It Take to be an Entrepreneur?" was revised to include a discussion of the sources of innovation based on Sam Walton's theory of "flashlighting".
- Section "The Small Business Administration (SBA)" was expanded.

Deletions:

- Profile
- Boxes Legal Briefcase, Reaching Beyond our Borders
- Figures "Classification of Small Businesses," "Areas in Which Small Companies Believe They Have an Advantage over Big Company Competitors," and "Information Sources for Small Businesses"

Brief Chapter Outline/Learning Goals

CHAPTER 6
ENTREPRENEURSHIP AND STARTING A SMALL BUSINESS

PROFILE: David Marcheschi of Water Concepts LLC

I. THE AGE OF THE ENTREPRENEUR.

II. THE JOB-CREATING POWER OF ENTREPRENEURS IN THE UNITED STATES.

III. WHY PEOPLE TAKE THE ENTREPRENEURIAL CHALLENGE.

LEARNING GOAL 1. Explain why people are willing to take the risks of entrepreneurship; list the attributes of successful entrepreneurs; and describe the benefits of entrepreneurial teams and intrapreneurs.

A. What Does It Take to Be an Entrepreneur?

B. Entrepreneurial Teams.

C. Micropreneurs and Home-Based Businesses.

D. Encouraging Entrepreneurship—What Government Can Do.

E. Entrepreneurship Within Firms.

IV. GETTING STARTED IN SMALL BUSINESS.

LEARNING GOAL 2. Discuss the importance of small business to the American economy and summarize the major causes of small-business failure.

A. Small Versus Big Business.

B. Importance of Small Business.

C. Small-Business Success and Failure.

V. LEARNING ABOUT SMALL-BUSINESS OPERATIONS.

LEARNING GOAL 3. Summarize ways to learn about how small businesses operate.

A. Learn from Others.

B. Get Some Experience.

C. Take Over a Successful Firm.

VI. MANAGING A SMALL BUSINESS.

LEARNING GOAL 4. Analyze what it takes to start and run a small business.

A. Begin with Planning.

   1. Writing a Business Plan.

B. Getting Money to Fund a Small Business.

   1. The Small Business Administration (SBA).

C. Knowing Your Customers.

D. Managing Employees.

E. Keeping Records.

F. Looking for Help.

VII. GOING INTERNATIONAL: SMALL-BUSINESS PROSPECTS.

LEARNING GOAL 5. Outline the advantages and disadvantages of small businesses entering global markets.

VIII. SUMMARY AND REVIEW

(Learning Objectives are also referenced in the expanded lecture outline later in this chapter)

Key Terms

Active Corps of Executives (ACE) *(text page 182)*

business plan *(text page 175)*

entrepreneurial team *(text page 166)*

entrepreneurship *(text page 163)*

incubators *(text page 176)*

intrapreneur *(text page 169)*

market *(text page 180)*

micropreneur *(text page 167)*

Service Corps of Retired Executives (SCORE) *(text page 182)*

small business *(text page 170)*

Small Business Investment Companies (SBIC) *(text page 179)*

venture capitalist *(text page 178)*

Lecture Outline

The **PROFILE** at the beginning of this chapter focuses on **DAVID MARCHESCHI**, an entrepreneur who took a risk and started **WATER CONCEPTS LLC.** to distribute Water Joe, spring water laced with caffeine.

I. THE AGE OF THE ENTREPRENEUR.

A. One poll of college seniors showed that 515 of the men and 31% of the women were attracted to **STARTING THEIR OWN BUSINESSES** rather than joining a corporation.

B. One study revealed that the average respondent had already started 2.3 businesses.

C. Colleges are responding by offering more courses on the subject of entrepreneurship.

D. An **ENTREPRENEUR** is an innovator who assumes the risks of starting and managing a business.

II. THE JOB-CREATING POWER OF ENTREPRENEURS IN THE UNITED STATES.

A. One of the major issues in the U.S. today is the need to **CREATE MORE JOBS.**

B. You can get some idea about the **JOB-CREATING POWER** of entrepreneurs when you look at some of the great American entrepreneurs from the past and the present.

Lecture Notes

TRANSPARENCY MASTER 43
Chapter Outline

TM 43

LECTURE ENHANCER 6-1
Jennie Bettles of SameSky Inc.

Jennie Bettles is an entrepreneur who used her zest for adventure to start an Internet-based adventure travel company, SameSky Inc. (See complete lecture enhancer on page 6.50.)

LECTURE ENHANCER 6-2
Who Is the Most Admired Entrepreneur?

Attendees at the 1997 Inc. 500 Conference were asked to list the three active entrepreneurs whom they most admire. (See complete lecture enhancer on page 6.51.)

OT ACETATE 6-1
How Did They Begin?

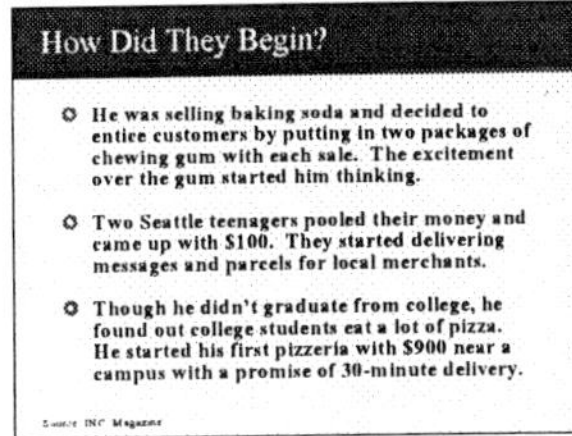

Comments:

1. This acetate will help in starting the chapter discussion. Students enjoy stories of how things began and these short vignettes will supplement additional information about the history of successful entrepreneurs in the chapter.
2. See if the students can guess the companies in the short descriptions provided on the acetate. The answers are:

   Wrigley's Chewing Gum (William Wrigley, Jr.)

   United Parcel Service

   Domino's Pizza (Tom Monaghan)

Lecture Outline

C. The text lists a number of examples including past entrepreneurs George Eastman of Kodak and Henry Ford of Ford Motor Company and contemporary entrepreneurs Steve Jobs, Michael Dell, and Craig McCaw.

III. WHY PEOPLE TAKE THE ENTREPRENEURIAL CHALLENGE.

▶ **LEARNING GOAL 1.** Explain why people are willing to take the risks of entrepreneurship; list the attributes of successful entrepreneurs; and describe the benefits of entrepreneurial teams and intrapreneurs.

A. Reasons why people are **WILLING TO TAKE THE RISKS** of business ownership include:

1. **OPPORTUNITY**.
2. **PROFIT**.
3. **INDEPENDENCE**.
   a. Many entrepreneurs do not enjoy working for someone else.
   b. Some have found more self-satisfaction in starting their own businesses.
4. **CHALLENGE**.
   a. Some believe that entrepreneurs are excitement junkies who flourish on taking risks.
   b. Many content that entrepreneurs take moderate, calculated risks.

Lecture Notes

LECTURE ENHANCER 6-3
For These Entrepreneurs, Business Is Kids' Stuff

Teen entrepreneurship may be one of the hottest trends of the 1990s. (See complete lecture enhancer on page 6.52.)

OT ACETATE 6-2
Why People Start Their Own Businesses

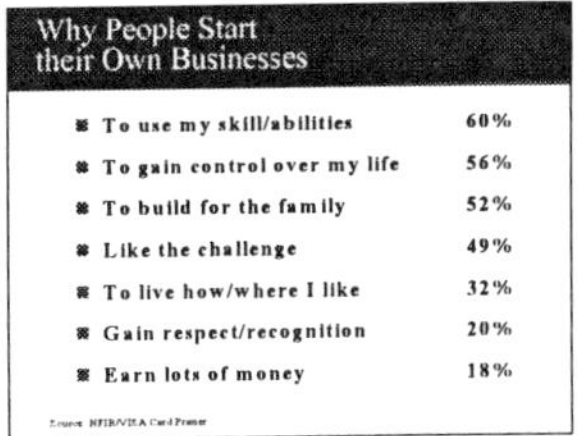

Comments:

1. This acetate lists (in order of importance) the primary reasons why people start their own businesses.
2. Before showing students the acetate, you could ask them to comprise their own list of why they want to be in their own businesses. After viewing the list, some students might be a bit surprised that money does not top the list of why people start their own businesses.
3. You may wish to ask the class what would be important to them in making the decision to start their own business and what would be their greatest fear.

LECTURE ENHANCER 6-4
Tomima Edmark: Inventor and Entrepreneur

With the proceeds from a kissing book, Edmark created a multimillion dollar entrepreneurial enterprise. (See complete lecture enhancer on page 6.53.)

Lecture Outline

c. In general, entrepreneurs seek achievement more than power.

B. **WHAT DOES IT TAKE TO BE AN ENTREPRENEUR?**

1. The list of **ENTREPRENEURIAL ATTRIBUTES** includes:

   a. **SELF-DIRECTED.**

   b. **SELF-NURTURING.**

   c. **ACTION-ORIENTED.**

   d. **HIGH ENERGY LEVEL.**

   e. **TOLERANT OF UNCERTAINTY.**

2. More entrepreneurs don't get the ideas for their products and services from some **FLASH** of inspiration—often the source of innovation is more like a **FLASHLIGHT**.

3. An entrepreneurial test to determine if you have the entrepreneurial spirit is provided at the end of the chapter.

C. **ENTREPRENEURIAL TEAMS.**

1. An **ENTREPRENEURIAL TEAM** is a group of experienced people from different areas of business who join together to form a managerial team with the skills needed to develop, make, and market a new product.

OT ACETATE 6-3
Who Starts Businesses?

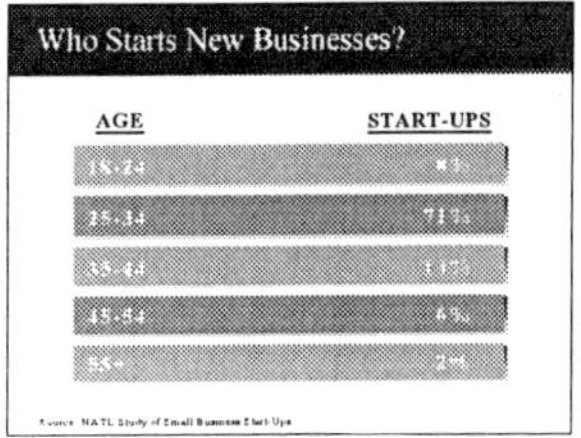

Comments:

1. This acetate identifies by age category "who" starts businesses. Students may be interesting in knowing that the "average" age of budding entrepreneurs is 29.
2. A good discussion question is "why do so many people start businesses between the ages of 25-34?" Students should be able to provide a good many reasons why including, work experience, capital accumulated, maturity, education completed, etc.
3. A follow-up question is "why do so few people start new businesses between the ages of 45-54?" Again, students should offer a bevy of suggestions.

CRITICAL THINKING EXERCISE 6-1
What Does It Take to Be an Entrepreneur?

See complete exercise on page 6.68.

LECTURE ENHANCER 6-5
Charles Babbage: 19th Century Entrepreneur

Nineteenth century England was not ready for Charles Babbage. (See complete lecture enhancer on page 6.55)

TRANSPARENCY MASTER 44
Advice for Potential Entrepreneurs
(Figure 6.1 on text page 166)

(Transparency Masters begin on page 6.78.)

CRITICAL THINKING
(page 166 in text)

Do you know anyone who seems to have the entrepreneurial spirit? What about him or her makes you say that? Are there any similarities between the characteristics demanded of an entrepreneur and those of a professional athlete? Would an athlete be a good prospect for entrepreneurship? Why or why not? Could teamwork be important in an entrepreneurial effort?

Lecture Outline

2. This gives the company the **COMBINATION OF SKILLS** need to get the new company off to a great start.

D. **MICROPRENEURS AND HOME-BASED BUSINESSES.**

1. Some business owners are **MICROPRENEURS**, owners interested in simply enjoying a better lifestyle and doing what they want.
2. While entrepreneurs are committed to the quest for growth, micropreneurs can be happy with little expansion.
3. Many micropreneurs are **HOME-BASED BUSINESS OWNERS,** and many are owned by people who are trying to combine career and family.
4. **ADVICE FOR POTENTIAL HOME-BASED ENTREPRENEURS**. Focus on:
   a. Opportunity instead of security.
   b. Getting results instead of following routines.
   c. Earning a profit not earning a paycheck.
   d. Trying new ideas instead of avoiding mistakes.
   e. Long-term vision not short-term payoff.

Lecture Notes

SUPPLEMENTAL CASE 6-1
3M Company,
Intrapreneurial Leader

See complete case on page 6.72.

OT ACETATE 6-4
The Most Common Type of
Home-Based Businesses

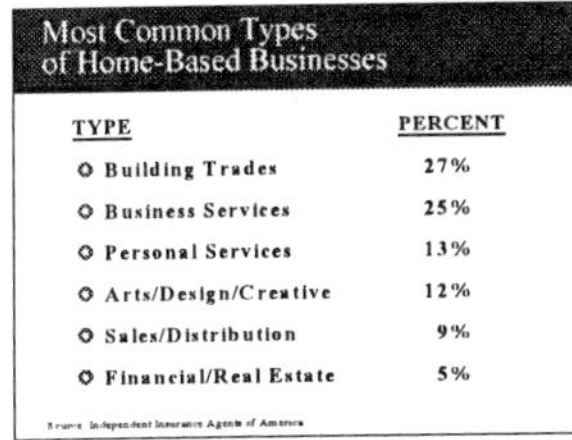

Comments:

1. This acetate also explores the growing area of home-based businesses. Referring to **OT ACETATE 5-12** might be useful here.
2. Students can be asked what types of business and personal services are most appropriate for home-based businesses. Multiple answers and suggestions can be expected here.
3. It may be interesting to combine the topics of home-based businesses with telecommuting to get a contemporary perspective about the workplace of the future. Student opinions can be solicited and discussed by the entire class.

Lecture Outline

E. **ENCOURAGING ENTREPRENEURSHIP—WHAT GOVERNMENT CAN DO.**

1. The government passed the **IMMIGRATION ACT OF 1990** to encourage more entrepreneurs to come to the United States.

    a. It created a category of **"INVESTOR VISAS"** that allows 10,000 people to come to the United States each year if they invest $1 million in an enterprise that creates or preserves 10 jobs.

    b. Some believe that the more entrepreneurs that can be lured to the U.S., the more jobs will be created.

2. One way to encourage entrepreneurship is through **ENTERPRISE ZONES** that feature low taxes and government support.

    a. The government could encourage entrepreneurship by offering investment **TAX CREDITS** to businesses that invest in creating jobs.

    b. The government could also institute a plan of public investment to **REBUILD THE NATIONAL'S INFRASTRUCTURE.**

F. **ENTREPRENEURSHIP WITHIN FIRMS.**

1. **INTRAPRENEURS** are creative people who work as entrepreneurs within corporations.

Lecture Notes

MAKING ETHICAL DECISIONS
(Box in text, page 169)

"Going Down with the Ship"

Suppose you have worked for two years in a company and you see signs that the business is beginning to falter. You and a co-worker have ideas about how to make a company like your boss's succeed. You are considering quitting your job and starting your own company with your friend. Should you approach other co-workers about working for your new venture? Will you try to lure your old boss's customers to your own business? What are your alternatives? What are the consequences of each alternative? What is the most ethical choice?

LECTURE ENHANCER 6-6
Listen To Your Entrepreneur

In 1975 Stephen Wozniak approached his employer, Hewlett-Packard, with an idea for a new computer. (See complete lecture enhancer on page 6.56)

LECTURE ENHANCER 6-7
Breeding Entrepreneurship on the Net

In just 13 months Bill Gross hatched 23 Internet startups. (See complete lecture enhancer on page 6.?.)

OT ACETATE 6-5 and **OT ACETATE 6-6**
Take the Intrapreneur Quiz

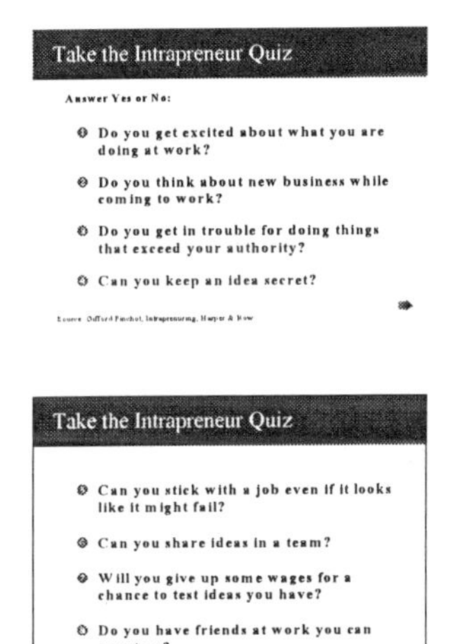

Comments:

1. These two acetates test student aptitudes for intrapreneurship. Students are often fascinated by the work of Intrapreneurs. It's especially interesting for them to know that products such as the Ford Mustang and Post-It Notes were created by intrapreneurs.
2. You can work through the acetate by discussing it question-by-question or by having students take the quiz and then offering suggestions regarding their responses.
3. Students can consider themselves as potential intrapreneurs if they answered yes to all the questions on the quiz. Intrapreneurs need to exude confidence, self direction, ambition, and a need for success.

PROGRESS CHECK
(page 169 in text)

- ➤ Can you name some of the famous entrepreneurs from the past and some from the present?
- ➤ Why are people willing to take the risks of entrepreneurship?
- ➤ What are the advantages of entrepreneurial teams?

2. By using company's existing resources—human, financial, and physical, they launch new products and generate new profits.

3. Examples in the text focus on 3M, Hewlett-Packard, and Lockheed Corp.

IV. GETTING STARTED IN SMALL BUSINESS.

▶ **LEARNING GOAL 2.** Discuss the importance of small business to the American economy and summarize the major causes of small-business failure.

A. The purpose of this part of the chapter is to explore small businesses, their role in the economy, and how they are started and managed.

1. You will learn that, in general, the same principles apply to both small and large companies.

2. All organizations demand capital, good ideas, planning, information management, budgets, accounting, marketing, employee relations, and good overall management.

B. **SMALL VERSUS BIG BUSINESS.**

1. **SMALL BUSINESS** is defined by the SBA as **A BUSINESS THAT IS:**

   a. **INDEPENDENTLY OWNED AND OPERATED.**

   b. **NOT DOMINANT IN ITS FIELD OF OPERATION.**

Lecture Notes

LECTURE ENHANCER 6-8 Intrapreneur Versus Entrepreneur	The major differences noted between intrapreneurs and entrepreneurs are that intrapreneurs are more group-oriented, capable of working better within bureaucracies, and have more flexibility in dealing with others. (See complete lecture enhancer on page 6.59.)
LECTURE ENHANCER 6-9 The Small Advantage	How does a small company—long on potential but short on cash—hire and keep the right people? (See complete lecture enhancer on page 6.60)

Lecture Outline

c. **MEETS CERTAIN STANDARDS IN TERMS OF EMPLOYEES OR ANNUAL RECEIPTS** (for example, less than $2 million a year for service companies).

2. Small businesses account for over **40% OF THE GROSS NATIONAL PRODUCT**.

3. The first jobs of about 80% of all Americans are in small business.

C. **IMPORTANCE OF SMALL BUSINESS.**

1. Ninety percent of the **NATION'S NEW JOBS** in the private sector are in small businesses.

   a. Dun & Bradstreet reports that the biggest employment increases in 1994 were in services, manufacturing, retail, and construction.

   b. The smallest job increases were in transportation, public utilities, mining, and government.

   c. As a result of the declining value of the dollar, small manufacturers that supply exporting industries are the winners in the 1990s.

2. **ADVANTAGES SMALL BUSINESSES HAVE** over big companies are their more personal customer service and their ability to respond quickly to opportunities.

LECTURE ENHANCER 6-10
The Emotional Challenges of Starting a Business

Starting a business isn't a job or a career. Its a way of life. (See complete lecture enhancer on page 6.61.)

OT ACETATE 6-7
How Much Capital Do Entrepreneurs Have to Start Their Businesses?

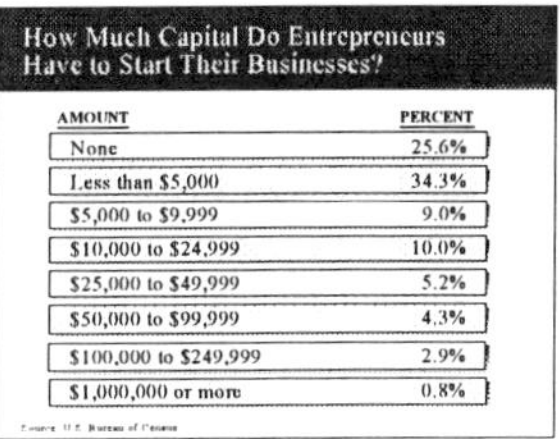

Comments:

1. Students should find this acetate quite interesting. As the information shows, 60% of entrepreneurs start their businesses with less than $5,000. As opportunities increase for home-based businesses and specialty service businesses, entrepreneurs find that often they can get started with minimal investments.
2. Ask students what types of businesses can be started with minimal amounts of capital? It will be interesting to hear some of the ideas they come up with. See if how many students in the class are currently have their own business or work in a family business.
3. Students could be assigned an out-of-class project to find five successful businesses nationally or in their market area that started operations with less than $5,000. They might be surprised with what they find.

OT ACETATE 6-8
What Sources Did You Use to Get Start-up Capital?

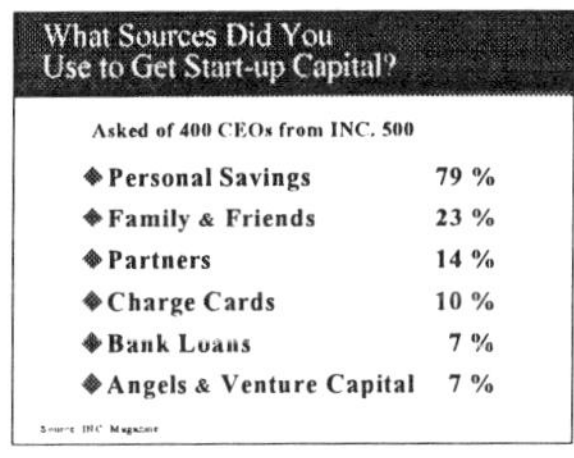

Comments:

1. Getting start-up capital is the key to any emerging business. The information here however, might surprise students. It's doubtful many believe that the vast majority of entrepreneurs financed their businesses with money out of their own pockets. Well, facts are facts.
2. Ask students why entrepreneurs seem to have so much difficulty getting start-up capital from a lending institution like a bank. You can expand the discussion to include venture capitalists as a source of financing. What are the good points/bad points of dealing with a venture capitalist?
3. Many entrepreneurs are turning to using credit cards as a source of financing for their businesses. What's the danger of doing this? What are the advantages of using credit cards as a source of financing?

Lecture Outline

3. Big businesses don't serve all the needs of the market—there is plenty of room for small businesses in niches.

D. **SMALL-BUSINESS SUCCESS AND FAILURE.**

1. **FAILURE RATE.**
   a. There is some debate about how many new small businesses fail each year.
   b. Conventional wisdom says that four out of five businesses (80%) fail in their first five years.
   c. Yet the SBA reports a 62% death rate within six years.
   d. However, a recent study by economist Bruce Kirchhoff shows that the failure rate is only 18% over the first eight years.
   e. It now seems that business failures are much lower than traditionally reported.
2. Still nearly one out of five businesses that fails is left owing money to creditors.
3. Many small businesses fail because of **MANAGERIAL INCOMPETENCE** and **INADEQUATE FINANCIAL PLANNING.**
4. Choosing the **RIGHT TYPE OF BUSINESS** is critical to success.

SPOTLIGHT ON SMALL BUSINESS
(Box in text, page 172)

"Causes of Small Business Failure"

SCORE, the Service Corps of Retired Executives, part of the Small Business Administration, complied 18 reasons why small businesses fail.

SPOTLIGHT ON SMALL BUSINESS
(Box in text, page 173)

"Situations of Small Business Success"

Small businesses are more likely to succeed when . . .

a. Many businesses with the lowest failure rates require advanced training to start.

b. In general it seems that the easiest businesses to start are the ones that tend to have the least growth and the greatest failure rate.

V. LEARNING ABOUT SMALL-BUSINESS OPERATIONS.

▶ **LEARNING GOAL 3.** Summarize ways to learn about how small businesses operate.

A. LEARN FROM OTHERS.

1. Investigate local community colleges for small business classes.
2. Talk to others who have already done it.

B. GET SOME EXPERIENCE.

1. Go to work for others and learn all you can.
2. Forty-two percent of small-business owners got the idea for their business from their prior jobs.
3. The general rule is: 3 years of experience in a comparable business.

C. TAKE OVER A SUCCESSFUL FIRM.

1. After many years, some small business owners feel stuck in their businesses.

Lecture Notes

CRITICAL THINKING
(page 173 in text)

Imagine yourself starting a small business. What kind of business would it be? How much competition is there? What could you do to make your business more attractive than competitors'? Would you be willing to work 60 to 70 hours per week?

OT ACETATE 6-9
Hours Worked Per Week the First Year in Business

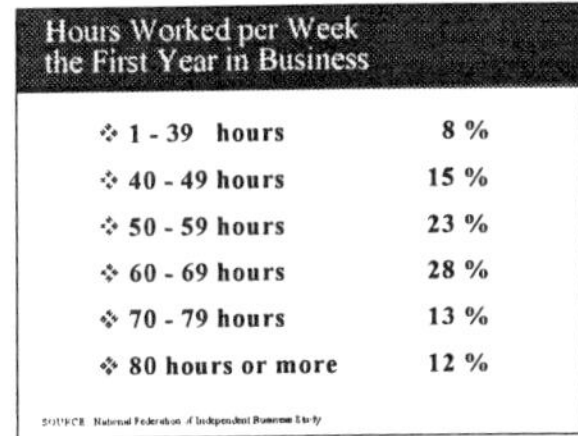

Hours Worked per Week the First Year in Business

Hours	Percent
1 - 39 hours	8 %
40 - 49 hours	15 %
50 - 59 hours	23 %
60 - 69 hours	28 %
70 - 79 hours	13 %
80 hours or more	12 %

Comments:

1. This acetate should be interesting to students. It's interesting primarily because students often have the attitude that going into your own business means less hours on the job and more flexibility. You might note to them that over 50% of the new business owners reported that they worked over 60 hours per week the first year they were in business.
2. Discussion could be stimulating if someone in the class has experience in a small business or was raised in a family that operated a small business. These persons can often easily verify to the class the validity of the information in this acetate.
3. By the way, you might want to inform them that the average number of hours worked by employees in a corporation is 41.5 hours per week. Big difference!

Lecture Outline

2. The text describes a method of becoming successful small business managers.
    a. The first step is to find a businessperson running a successful small business.
    b. For another year or so, work hard to learn all about the business.
    c. At the end of two years, offer to become assistant manager.
    d. At the end of two years, offer to manage the business when the owner retires.
    e. You can establish a profit-sharing plan for yourself plus a salary.
    f. The owner benefits by keeping ownership and earning profits without working.
3. If profit sharing doesn't appeal to the owner, you may want to buy the business outright.

VI. MANAGING A SMALL BUSINESS.

▶ **LEARNING GOAL 4.** Analyze what it takes to start and run a small business.

A. Ninety percent of all failures are a result of **"POOR MANAGEMENT."**

1. This could mean poor planning, poor record keeping, poor inventory control, poor promotion, or poor employee relations.

Lecture Notes

LECTURE ENHANCER 6-11
On-Line@
BUREAUCRACY.CA

What's in a name when it comes to establishing a marketing presence on the Internet? Way more than necessary if you're a small, proud Canadian company that wants a quick, snappy Canadian address. (See complete lecture enhancer on page 6.62.)

Lecture Outline

2. It could likely include poor capitalization.

3. This section explores the major functions of business as they pertain to small business:

   a. **PLANNING** your business (business plan.)

   b. **FUNDING** your business (finance.)

   c. **KNOWING** your customers (marketing,)

   d. **MANAGING** your employees (human resource development.)

   e. **KEEPING RECORDS** (accounting).

B. **BEGIN WITH PLANNING.**

1. A **BUSINESS PLAN** is a detailed written statement that describes the nature of the business, the target market, the advantages the business will have in relation to competition, and the resources and qualifications of the owner(s)

   a. A business plan is mandatory for talking with bankers or other investors.

   b. Michael Celello, president of the People's Commercial Bank, says that fewer than 10% of prospective borrowers come to a bank adequately prepared and offers several tips.

2. **WRITING A BUSINESS PLAN.**

Lecture Notes

LECTURE ENHANCER 6-12
There's No Substitute for a Business Plan (I)

If there is one thing that small-business experts agree on is the need for a well-thought-out business plan no matter how well-financed and experienced the prospective business owner is. (See complete lecture enhancer on page 6.63.)

LECTURE ENHANCER 6-13
There's No Substitute for a Business Plan (II)

Once the plans are written and the business begins operation, how many managers use them on a daily basis. *Inc.* magazine contacted 50 companies and asked them about their business plans. (See complete lecture enhancer on page 6.64.)

SPOTLIGHT ON SMALL BUSINESS
(Box in text, page 177)

"Outline of a Comprehensive Business Plan"

A good business plan is between 25 and 50 pages long and takes at least six months to write.

CRITICAL THINKING EXERCISE 6-2
Writing a Business Plan

See complete exercise on page 6.69.

Lecture Outline

a. One of the most important parts of the business plan is the executive summary, which has to catch the reader's interest.

b. There are computer software programs now to help you get organized.

c. Getting the completed business plan in the right hands is almost as important as getting the right information in.

C. **GETTING MONEY TO FUND A SMALL BUSINESS.**

1. Entrepreneurs often are not highly skilled at obtaining, managing, and using money.

   a. Inadequate capitalization or poor financial management can destroy a business, even when the basic idea is good.

   b. One of the secrets of finding the money is knowing where to look for it.

2. New entrepreneurs have several **SOURCES OF CAPITAL:** personal savings, relatives, former employers, banks, finance companies, venture capital organizations, government agencies, and more.

   a. **STATES ALSO PROVIDE SUPPORT FOR ENTREPRENEURS.**

      (i) State commerce departments serve as clearinghouses for these programs.

OT ACETATE 6-10
How to Get a Yes From a Banker

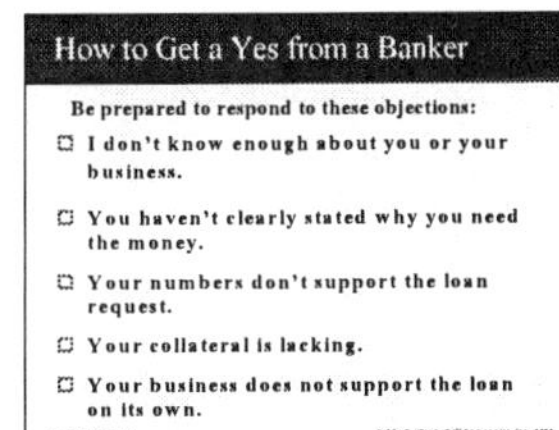

Comments:

1. The information here should support a good deal of the information provided in the chapter concerning the business plan. As was noted, financial problems are one of the key reasons why so many small businesses are forced from operation. Financing is a primary source of stress for small businesspeople. This acetate describes what banks look for before okaying financing. How many firms fall into the financial trap waiting for them?
2. It's important to inform students that bankers want businesses to survive. Students often have the perception that bankers look for businesses to fail. As the acetate notes, bankers are very interested in how will the loan be paid back and when the loan will be paid back. But remember, the more your business grows, the higher the probability the bank will grow as well.
3. The acetate also clearly points out that the key to dealing with bankers is, to be prepared and have a sound business plan. It's important for students to remember that bankers do not finance dreams.
4. It's important to note here that relationships with a banker can be vital at any stage of a business. The chapter offers considerable advice in building relations and the search for financing.

Lecture Outline

(ii) States also create incubators and technology centers to reduce startup capital needs.

b. **INCUBATORS** provide **LOW-COST OFFICES** with **BASIC BUSINESS SERVICES** such as accounting, legal advice and secretarial help.

c. Technology-minded entrepreneurs often have the best shot at attracting start-up capital.

d. Other than personal savings, individual investors are the primary source of capital for most entrepreneurs.

e. **VENTURE CAPITALISTS** may ask for a hefty stake (as much as 60%) in your company in exchange for the cash to start your business.

3. **THE SMALL BUSINESS ADMINISTRATION (SBA)**

   a. The SBA may provide the following types of **FINANCIAL ASSISTANCE:**

      (i) Direct loans.

      (ii) Guaranteed loans.

      (iii) Participation loans.

LECTURE ENHANCER 6-14
Angels On-Line

An on-line federal matchmaking service is set to match wealthy individuals looking to invest with small companies in need of funds. (See complete lecture enhancer on page 6.65.)

Lecture Outline

(iv) Loans from Minority Enterprise Small Business Investment Companies (MESBICS).

(v) Loans from the women's financing section.

(vi) Microloans.

b. The SBA's **MICROLOAN PROGRAM** awards loans on the basis of belief in the borrowers' integrity and the soundness of their business idea.

c. You may also want to consider requesting funds from **SMALL BUSINESS INVESTMENT COMPANIES (SBICS).** SBICs are private investment companies which the Small Business Administration licenses to lend money to small businesses.

d. **SMALL BUSINESS DEVELOPMENT CENTERS** (SBDCs), funded jointly by the federal government and individual states, can help evaluate the feasibility of your idea, develop your business plan, and complete your funding application.

4. Obtaining money from banks, venture capitalists, and government sources is very difficult for most small businesses.

OT ACETATE 6-11
Top Priorities of Small Business Owners

Top Priorities of Small Business Owners

- Generating more sales
- Better marketing
- Understanding the financial condition of the business
- Starting a retirement plan
- Setting personal & business goals

Comments:

1. Priorities come and go at different stages of a business. This acetate lists the key overall priorities of small businesses in addressing the needs of their market in the future.
2. All of these topics and concerns will be covered throughout in the textbook.
3. This acetate is sort of a "gripe list" for small business owners. It may be effective in using this information to first question students about what they think are the factors that bother small business owners most often. This acetate provides some basic facts concerning entrepreneurship. You might preface this acetate by asking how many students in the class hope to become entrepreneurs? As students can see from **OT ACETATE 6-9** that 80% of the entrepreneurs questioned worked over 40 hours per week. Going through this acetate fact-by-fact, should generate good discussion and comments by students.
4. You may recall from chapter two, how government regulations and laws are crowding more into business operations. Even though this is not listed in this acetate, It seems small business owners find this encroachment to be particularly distasteful.
5. To alleviate the stress of starting a small business, her are some simple notes to go over with students:
   a. **Read**. Especially if you receive a disclosure document or are asked to sign a binding contract. This may be the time to call an attorney for expert advice.
   b. **Stay calm.** Don't lose your temper or dream about easy money. There are no easy profits. You might want to contact some current owners in similar businesses and see what they think. Ask if thcy would go into their venture again.
   c. **Contact reliable sources** to check out the business. Sources such as the Better Business Bureau can be excellent resources.
   d. Even though not all contracts have to be in writing to be valid, it's important to **get everything in writing.** If you order supplies or inventory, have the company sign a letter of confirmation.

D. **KNOWING YOUR CUSTOMERS.**

1. A **MARKET CONSISTS OF PEOPLE WITH:** (1) unsatisfied **WANTS AND NEEDS**, (2) with the **RESOURCES**, and (3) the **WILLINGNESS** to buy.

2. The goal of a businessperson is to **FIND A NEED AND FILL IT.**

3. In order to fill these needs, one must **FIRST IDENTIFY** the **WANTS AND NEEDS** of potential customers.

4. You will gain more insights about markets in Chapters 13 and 14.

E. **MANAGING EMPLOYEES.**

1. If you talk to small business owners, you will find that one of their Most difficult chores is to **FIND, HIRE, TRAIN, AND KEEP GOOD EMPLOYEES.**

   a. Nonetheless, employees of small companies are often **MORE SATISFIED WITH THEIR JOBS** than their counterparts in large companies.

   b. They find they are **MORE CHALLENGED**, their ideas are **MORE ACCEPTED**, and their **BOSSES TREAT THEM WITH MORE RESPECT.**

PROGRESS CHECK
(page 180 in text)

- There were nine sections in the business plan on pp. 177. This is probably the most important document a small-business owner will ever make. Can you describe at least five of those sections now?
- The U.S. Small Business Administration gives reasons why small businesses fail financially. Can you name three?

SUPPLEMENTAL CASE 6-2
Can Small Farms Be Profitable?

See complete case on page 6.75.

LECTURE ENHANCER 6-15
FedEx Targets Its Customers

In order to reach its goals, an organization must define who its customers are. (See complete lecture enhancer on page 6.66.)

CRITICAL THINKING EXERCISE 6-3
What If?

See complete exercise on page 6.71.

Lecture Outline

2. As the business grows, it becomes necessary to **DELEGATE AUTHORITY**.
   a. This is touchy especially in businesses with employees who have been with the company since its start.
   b. These long-term employees may not have the necessary managerial skills.
3. Attitudes such as you **"CAN'T FIRE FAMILY"** or you must promote someone because "They're family" can hinder growth.
4. You'll learn more about managing employees in Chapters 7 through 12.

F. **KEEPING RECORDS.**

1. A businessperson who sets up an **ACCOUNTING SYSTEM** early will save much grief later.
2. **COMPUTERS** make record keeping easier and let the business owner follow the progress of the business.
3. A good accountant is invaluable in setting up record keeping systems and providing tax planning, financial forecasting, and choosing sources of financing.
4. You will learn more about accounting in Chapter 18 focuses on accounting.

Lecture Notes

LECTURE ENHANCER 6-16
Relinquishing the Reins

It may seem early to talk about turning over the reins of your company to someone else when this chapter's topic is "starting" a small business. Let's just consider this as an early warning. (See complete lecture enhancer on page 6.67.)

OT ACETATE 6-12
Major Concerns of Small Business Owners

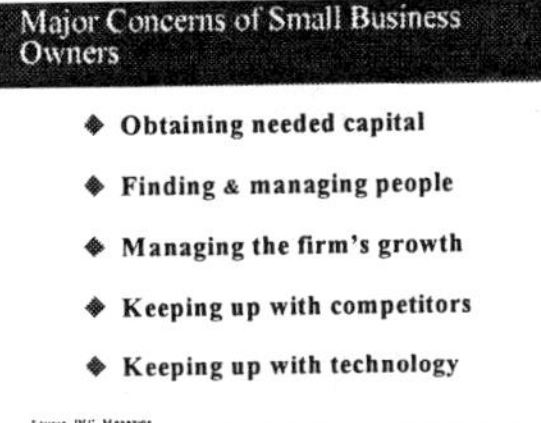

Comments:

1. This acetate complements the previous one. Here the major concerns of small businesses are listed. It's easy to see that the job of a small businessperson never gets any easier.
2. Ask students which concern they consider the most critical. After the class decides, group the students that picked number 1, 2, etc. and have them work as a group to come up with reasons and rationales for their particular selection. Also see if anyone has any other concern they feel should be listed.

Lecture Outline

G. **LOOKING FOR HELP.**

1. Small businesspeople **NEED HELP** setting up their businesses early in the process.
2. A necessary aide is a competent, experienced **LAWYER** who knows and understands small businesses.
3. A **MARKETING CONSULTANT** with small-business experience can help with marketing decisions.
4. Two other valuable experts are a commercial loan officer and an insurance agent.
5. The **SERVICE CORPS OF RETIRED EXECUTIVES (SCORE)** consists of 13,000 volunteers who provide consulting services for small businesses free.
6. The SBA also sponsors the **ACTIVE CORPS OF EXECUTIVES (ACE)**, volunteers who counsel small businesses.
7. Other helpful contacts: other small business owners, chambers of commerce, the Better Business Bureau, and trade associations.

VII. GOING INTERNATIONAL: SMALL-BUSINESS PROSPECTS.

▶ **LEARNING GOAL 5.** Outline the advantages and disadvantages of small businesses entering global markets.

From the Pages of
BusinessWeek
(Box in Text, page 182)
"If I'd Only Known Then . . ."

If friends and family are offering business advice, cover your ears. Comprehensive Business Services Inc., a national accounting franchise, asked 250 small-business owners who they consulted for advice when they launched their companies—and who they'd recommend now. The consensus: Go with the pros.

OT ACETATE 6-13
Eight Ways to Improve Your Company Profit

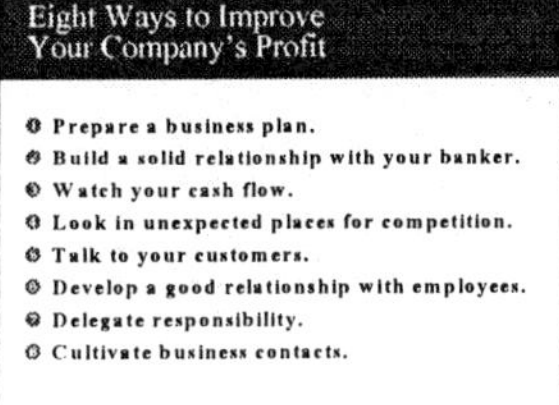

Comments:

1. This acetate effectively synopsizes the information contained in the chapter. Students should be able to comprehend these eight points even this early in the course. If they have questions concerning cash flow, you can note that this topic will be covered in depth in chapters 18 and 19.
2. The acetate note Issues involving planning and delegating as a means of increasing profits. These topics are covered fully in the next section of the textbook. Therefore the acetate can be used as a lead into the next section of the text dealing with management.

Lecture Outline

A. The **WORLD MARKET** is potentially a more lucrative market for small businesses that the U.S. alone.

1. However, most small businesses still do not think internationally.

2. Only 20% of small businesses executives say they export.

B. Many potential international businesspeople **DO NOT** enter the global market **BECAUSE:**

1. **FINANCING IS MORE DIFFICULT** to arrange.

2. They **DON'T KNOW HOW** to get started.

3. They **DON'T UNDERSTAND THE CULTURAL DIFFERENCES.**

4. The **BUREAUCRATIC PAPERWORK** is overwhelming.

C. There are many good **REASONS FOR SMALL BUSINESS PEOPLE TO CONSIDER GOING INTERNATIONAL:**

1. **TWO-THIRDS OF THE WORLD'S MARKET** lies **OUTSIDE THE U.S.**

2. Exporting can **ABSORB EXCESS INVENTORY.**

3. It can **SOFTEN DOWNTURNS IN THE U.S. MARKET.**

4. It can **EXTEND THE LIFE OF PRODUCTS.**

TRANSPARENCY MASTER 45
U.S. Industries with the Highest Potential in International Markets
(Figure 6.2 on text page 183)

(Transparency Masters begin on page 6.78.)

REACHING BEYOND OUR BORDERS
(Box in text, page 184)
"Yes, You Can Make Money Exporting, But It's a Workout"

When Krescenthia David finally got her exercise video onto Wal-Mart and Kmart shelves she thought she had it made. But the shoppers were already saturated with thousands of different workout tapes ranging from Cindy Crawford to Richard Simmons. When David found out that there were only about 10 exercise videos in the Japanese market, she recast her video and began exporting. In 1996 about 90% of her sales were in Japan.

D. Small businesses have several **ADVANTAGES OVER LARGE BUSINESSES**:

1. Overseas buyers enjoy dealing with individuals rather than with large corporate bureaucracies.
2. Small companies can usually begin shipping much faster.
3. Small companies provide a wide variety of suppliers.
4. Small companies can give more personal service and more attention.

E. **SOURCES OF INFORMATION** about international business can be obtained from the Commerce Department, SBA, banks, local freight forwarders, export management companies, and export trading companies.

VIII. SUMMARY AND REVIEW.

IX. APPENDIX: ENTREPRENEUR READINESS QUESTIONNAIRE.

PROGRESS CHECK (page 185 in text)

- ➤ Why do many small businesses avoid doing business overseas?
- ➤ What are some of the advantages small businesses have over large businesses in selling in global markets?

APPENDIX: ENTREPRENEUR READINESS QUESTIONNAIRE

Due to the nature of this appendix, no lecture material is provided.

TRANSPARENCY MASTER 46
Entrepreneur Readiness Questionnaire
(Figure on text page 191)

(Transparency Masters begin on page 6.78.)

Answers to Practicing Management Decisions

CASE ONE

BMOC: STARTING A SMALL BUSINESS AT SCHOOL

1. *What are the advantages and potential problems of starting a business while in school?*

The advantage is that you can learn and earn while you are going to school. You can find other students to help in the business and can make many mistakes that will prevent you from making similar mistakes later. You will develop good work habits and have four or more years of experience when you graduate.

On the other hand, a small business takes so much time that your grades may suffer. You may feel stressed and too tired to study. In other words, you should try to start a business that does not demand full-time work.

2. *What kinds of entrepreneurs are operating around your school? Talk to them and learn from their experiences.*

Be sure to look for pizza parlors, copy shops, dry cleaners and other stores that cater to students. See if the owners were not students at your school at one time. Now is the time to learn some hints before you graduate.

3. *What opportunities exist for satisfying student needs at your school? Pick one idea, write a business plan, and discuss it in class. Pick one idea, write a business plan, and discuss it in class (unless it's so good you don't want to share it; in that case, good luck.)*

Be sure to consider the need for dating services, entertainment services, dances, food services, tutoring, typing services, rides home and other transportation and escort services, and more.

CASE TWO

VIDEO CASE: JAY GOLTZ, ENTREPRENEURIAL WIZARD

1. *Why do you think entrepreneurs like Jay Goltz succeed when so many others fail?*

First of all, Goltz got the necessary education. Second, he saved his money, showing he has the discipline needed to run such a business. Finally, he focused on customer satisfaction, the number one reason that smaller businesses succeed or fail. Like other entrepreneurs, he could have failed, but he had the preparation and determination to make it work.

2. *Can a person develop the personality traits necessary to be a successful entrepreneur? How?*

It is very difficult to alter ones basic personality. For example, an entrepreneur needs to take risks. Not all people are wired to do that. Entrepreneurs also need to be self-directed, self-nurturing, and energetic. Some people need stroking by others and don't have the energy to work as hard as necessary. In short, entrepreneurs are a different breed, and they are not easily made; they are pretty much born that way.

3. *How important is a business plan in getting started in a business such as Artists' Frame Service?*

A business plan is not always necessary for entrepreneurship. You can, for example, start a lawn-mowing business or a window-washing business without an elaborate plan. But when you intend to become a large business that calls for much money, you have to have a great plan to use for investors and bankers. A business plan is not only good for investors, it is a road map to follow for marketing and other functions as well.

Lecture Enhancers

LECTURE ENHANCER 6-1

JENNIE BETTLES OF SAMESKY INC.

Do you dream of a life of adventure, of traveling the globe and experiencing first-hand the fascinating cultures of the world? You're not alone. According to the Travel Industry Association of America, tourism is such a growing industry that employment directly generated by travel will grow more than 18 percent (more than a million jobs) by 2005. Adventure travel is a particularly fast growing segment of the tourism market. In fact, *Entrepreneur Magazine* listed adventure tourism as one of the top ten businesses of 1998.

Jennie Bettles is an entrepreneur who used her zest for adventure to start an Internet-based adventure travel company, SameSky Inc. "Our company was established to support a community of explorers," says Bettles. SameSky's Web site is a one-stop resource for travelers looking for out-of-the-ordinary vacations. SameSky's unique tours include adventures such as climbing Mount Kilimanjaro to the top of Africa (19,340 ft.), traveling a rarely used trail, and staying in tents as you go. If you are a more pampered adventurer, how about learning to cook gourmet dishes in a magnificent Italian palace?

Bettles consults individually with customers to find the specific tours they're looking for. "Adventure means different things to different people. Sometimes clients are in the mood for a trip that's athletically challenging, and sometimes they want something more educational." If you prefer to search for your dream adventure on your own, you can use SameSky's Adventure Bureau to enter your interests, your favorite activities, and what part of the world you would like to explore. The tool will suggest tours based on your responses.

"We wanted to serve both ends of the marketplace," says Bettles. "It's difficult for consumers to learn about all the travel options available, so we wanted to provide a central resource to help them. Our service is also beneficial to tour operators because we offer them a channel to the marketplace." Bettles created a database of more than 200 adventure tours and plans to add another 200. She earns a commission from the tour operators on each booking she makes.

SameSky also provides an online marketplace for travel gear, travel books and international language tapes, as well as a place for chatting about travel and world cultures. The Web site also caters to virtual travelers, those who prefer to read books or watch videos about world adventures.

Bettles took a risk and it paid off. Stories about people taking risks by starting their own businesses are commonplace in this age of the entrepreneur. We'll discuss such risk takers in this chapter and maybe you'll be inspired to become an entrepreneur yourself.

LECTURE ENHANCER 6-2

WHO IS THE MOST ADMIRED ENTREPRENEUR?

Attendees at the 1997 *INC.* 500 Conference were asked to list the three active entrepreneurs whom they most admire. Their choices:

1. Bill Gates 59%
2. Ted Turner 8%
3. Steve Jobs 5%
4. Ross Perot 4%
5. Wayne Huizenga 3%

LECTURE ENHANCER 6-3

FOR THESE ENTREPRENEURS, BUSINESS IS KID'S STUFF

Seventeen-year-old Larry Adler expects to make $2 million with his promotions and business-consulting firm this year. Seventeen-year-old Morris Beyda's computer instruction company earned $15,000 in 1991. David Eilers, 15, mowed down $50,000 last year with his David's Mowing Service.

Teen entrepreneurship may be one of the hottest trends of the 1990s. Membership in Future Business Leaders of America hit 300,000 in the 1990s, compared to 204,000 in 1980. Wharton School of Business processed 500 applications for 45 slots in its two-program in the basics of entrepreneurship for kids. That was 66 percent more applicants than the year before. Business-minded kids are buying books on marketing and management. Adler released his own manual, *Corporate Kids*. Neale Godfrey, founder of The First Children's Bank in New York, released *The Kids' Money Book.* Other selections include: *Fast Cash for Kids* by Bonnie and Noel Drew and *The Lemonade Stand: A Guide to Encouraging the Entrepreneur in Your Child* by Emmanuel Modu, founder of the Center for Teen Entrepreneurs.

Why the early interest in business? "Money," admits Adler. Teenagers spent $79 billion in 1991. Parents don't want to pay for all those Nikes and Nintendos so kids are finding their own income. Money isn't the only reason. Only 33 percent of the teens surveyed by Teenage Research Unlimited agreed that success means making a lot of money, compared with 54 percent only two years earlier. Kids are spending more, but they are also saving more. Teen savings rose 26 percent in 1990 to $22.9 billion from $18.2 billion the year before. Just like their parents, kids say the unfriendly economy including layoffs and light summer job market plus the desire for greater financial security are tempting kids to start their own businesses.

Most kid entrepreneurs agree that one of the biggest reasons for getting into business is that it's fun. "I wouldn't do this if it wasn't," confirms David Leopold, 17, of D&L Collectibles, a sportscard sales and trading business. Leopold finds it thrilling to sell high-priced cards like Ricky Henderson ($180), Johnny Bench ($310), and Nolan Ryan ($950.) But what he really enjoys is "to sell a baseball card to a 5-year-old with a big, oversized baseball hat on and watch him smile. If the fun stopped, I wouldn't do this any more."

LECTURE ENHANCER 6-4

TOMIMA EDMARK: INVENTORY AND ENTREPRENEUR

In 1989 Tomima Edmark was a mid-level sales manager for IBM. Acutely aware that she had hit the corporate ceiling, Edmark was looking to invent something. "I was always thinking of other things I could do," she said. She wrote a book on the art of kissing, inspired by "a really bad date" she had while in graduate school.

Later that year, at a movie with her mother, Jean, the hair-turning idea began to take shape. "I saw a woman in the theater with an elegant French twist in her hair and it just dawned on me: I wonder if I can turn a ponytail inside out," Edmark said.

Edmark suffers from dyslexia, a condition where letters and words are seen backwards or upside down. She considers this a gift rather than a handicap. "Would a normal person ever think to turn a ponytail inside out? Think about it, that's a really dyslexic concept."

Early versions of the tool included a toothbrush with a rubber band and a pencil with a paper clip stuck in the end. Finally, she took a circular knitting needle, cut it in half, made a loop—and a multi-million dollar idea was born.

After several failed attempts to interest companies in her product, Edmark turned to direct marketing. Within weeks of placing a $500 ad in a hair magazine in 1991, orders started pouring in at the rate of about 200 a month. Edmark and her cleaning lady stuffed envelopes with TopsyTails at her kitchen table.

Then in February 1992 came a blurb in *Glamour* magazine. Suddenly Edmark was staying up until 2 or 3 in the morning, stuffing, stuffing, and stuffing. Orders jumped to 10,000 a month.

"It was extraordinary. My mailbox was overflowing. I had envelopes in every corner of the house," she said. "That's when I decided to jump off the cliff to see if I could fly." Edmark took a $25,000 buyout from IBM and became her own boss.

Edmark is proud of the fact that she succeeded without financial help from either family or an institution. The first TopsyTail mold was paid for by proceeds from the kissing book, and her IBM buyout paid for a patent.

No shy violet, Edmark has turned herself into a kind of one-woman rooting section for would-be do-it-yourself entrepreneurs. "After all," Edmark points out, "the Pilgrims didn't come over to America and say, 'Hey, I want to work for a big corporation.'" In this spirit she has written eight slim pamphlets and a resource guide containing her accumulated wisdom on starting a business. A financing tip: "You should be very careful about how you approach a relative or friend."

She's aiming at finding a few more TopsyTails. "I want to do this a couple more times," says Edmark. "It's a personal goal to prove I wasn't just lucky."

She next came up with a set of six plastic rings that, when threaded with a scarf, become a hair bow. "I thought this would be bigger than Topsy, but I didn't realize that women had quit wearing hair bows." So she's trotting out two more products.

Edmark was cruising the Seychelles in 1994, wearing a banana-husk hat she had bought in the port of Mahe to protect her skin from the sun. The hat, Edmark admits, was hideous. But when her shipmates kept asking where they could buy one, it got her thinking seriously.

Edmark's "Halo" hat neatly sidesteps the two basic millinery problems: hot head and hat hair. The Halo has a series of grommets for ventilation and a set of eight "fingers" set inside an oversized crown that holds the hat on the head without shmushing up your hair. And it folds up. Just $29.95. "This is not a chapeau," she concedes. Given that the hats will probably cost less than $7 each to make, that would allow for a very fat profit.

Edmark figures if the hat doesn't grab you, the kissing machine will. The what? The kissing machine. Before she got married a year and a half ago, Tomima was dating this guy. A really fun guy. "He would call me up in the middle of the night and say, 'Hey, a couple of friends and I are going to jump off this skyscraper with parachutes, wanna watch?'" There's only so many dates like that any woman can take, but before love fled, the fun boyfriend told Tomima that people can hold wires attached to a transformer and stereo speakers and, when they complete the circuit by touching, a low-level tingle will pulse through them to the beat of the music.

The old Tomima lightbulb went off. Could touching be kissing? The Kissing Machine—patent pending—does the tingle thing with fancier packaging. The 9-volt charge is so low, says Edmark, it does not require UL approval for safety. Look for it priced at around $49.95. We know what you're thinking, but this is strictly good clean fun. "I'm only going to market it from the neck up," says Edmark.

LECTURE ENHANCER 6-5

CHARLES BABBAGE: 19TH CENTURY ENTREPRENEUR

Nineteenth century England was not ready for Charles Babbage. The mathematician had already proven his ingenuity by inventing the speedometer, the cow catcher, and the first reliable life-expectancy tables when his enthusiasm turned to the problem of calculations. His first machine, which was designed to calculate logarithms, was an intricate system of gears and cogs which he called the Differential Engine.

No sooner had the Differential Engine been completed than Babbage proposed an expanded machine: one with a central "mill" for performing logical operations, a "store" or memory to hold information, and means to put information in and retrieve it. In short, all the elements of a modern computer. The Analytical Engine became his obsession. Along with his patron, Ada, the Countess of Lovelace, he worked for nearly forty years to perfect it. Ada, Lord Byron's mathematically gifted daughter, wrote the initial set of instructions for the Engine, the world's first computer program.

When Babbage died in 1871, all he had to show of his machine were thousands of sketches—the machine was never built. In order to perform the intricate calculations he developed, the Engine's parts had to be machined to precise tolerances. No craftsman of the age could do so. If it had been built, it would have been as big as a football field and would have required half a dozen locomotive engines to power it.

LECTURE ENHANCER 6-6

LISTEN TO YOUR ENTREPRENEUR

In 1975 Stephen Wozniak approached his employer, Hewlett-Packard, with an idea for a new computer. Wozniak and a friend had used existing components to build a prototype small computer that could be hooked up to a television set.

Hewlett-Packard was not interested in the novel, but unproven, idea that the average person would want, or know how to use, a computer in his or her home. Instead, Wozniak and his partner, Steven Jobs, quit their jobs and started an assembly line in their basement and later their own company. The enterprise: Apple Computer, with annual sales approaching $2 billion.

LECTURE ENHANCER 6-7

BREEDING ENTREPRENEURSHIP ON THE NET

Bill Gross has stuffed a lot of creativity—and commerce—into his 38 years. As a kid he rigged up homemade electric games and sold candy (at a markup) to friends. To help pay his way through Cal Tech he built and sold plans for a solar heating device, started a successful stereo equipment company, then sold a major software upgrade to Lotus. In 1991 he started Knowledge Adventure—a maker of educational software—and sold it six months later to CUC International for close to $100 million. Phew.

What's next? Idealab!, a Pasadena-based enterprise designed to breed Internet companies. Gross started Idealab! in 1997; it has already hatched 23 Internet startups. Most of them are just past the concept stage—five to ten employees, scant revenues, big plans. The biggest by far is CitySearch, an on-line listing service for community information covering five cities so far. Selling advertising on its Web pages, CitySearch employs 400 people and was recently valued at just over $100 million in a Morgan Stanley private placement. Investors in the deal included AT&T.

Microsoft started developing a CitySearch competitor, called Cityscape, 18 months ago, but the names were so similar and CitySearch so well-established that Gross believes the software giant had to change its service's name. It's now known as Sidewalk.

None of Gross' other companies has yet come close to matching CitySearch's success. CareerLink matches people with jobs by letting companies pick through prescreened applicants. Both employers and job seekers pay. **EVENTS.COM** aims to assemble a complete list of every major event in the U.S., from a New York Philharmonic performance to a Chicago Bulls game to a rock concert in Los Angeles. HomeLink lets potential homebuyers take virtual tours of neighborhoods and individual homes. **WEDDINGPLANNER.COM** promises a complete schematic for planning a wedding on-line; the site is to be supported by advertising from dressmakers, event planners and caterers. **ANSWERS.COM** has assembled 65 experts ready to answer any question within 24 hours. It charges $1.79 for easy questions, ranging to $11.99 for hard ones.

One of Gross' most interesting hatchlings is Data Mining Co., from which companies can download algorithms that identify patterns in their data. Giant corporations like American Express use expensive data-mining technology to target specific customers with promotions. Idealab!'s Data Mining Co. will charge one-time download fees—say, $50 per computer—making the technology available to small-scale firms and entrepreneurs.

Another Idealab! progeny, IntraNetics, sells pre-configured intranets. Companies often spend $250,000 or more to customize their intranet systems. IntraNetics has packaged turnkey intranet software it hopes will fit the needs of most small businesses. Price? Around $5,000.

Why so many ventures? Because no one knows what will or will not work on the Internet. "Some companies will be stillborn; others will get somewhere," says Charles Conn, CitySearch's chief executive and an old friend of Gross.

Gross says the design of his incubator for companies was partly inspired by George Hatsopoulos, 70, founder of Thermo Electron Corp. in Waltham, Mass. Thermo Electron has started and taken public 19 corporate offspring while keeping a controlling interest in each. Thermo Electron's startups are not equally successful. Their present market capitalizations range all the way from $93 million to $3.2 billion.

"I felt if someone else [Hatsopoulos] could make this work with physical processes, it would work way better on the Internet," says Gross. Why better on the Internet? Because capital costs are relatively low for Internet startups. "I'm doing this as fast as ideas can be blended," Gross says.

Idealab!'s $5 million in seed money came in part from Compaq Computer Chairman Benjamin Rosen, AT&T'S former chief financial officer, Robert Kavner, and Hollywood's Steven Spielberg, who tracked Gross down after Spielberg's son was captivated by a Gross game.

Most of the programmers for Idealab!'s Web startups are entrepreneurial hotshots from nearby Cal Tech. Gross maintains a pool of 20 programmers and Web site graphic designers to be on call for the startup companies. Like so many off-the-shelf components, the members of this talent pool can be quickly assembled into what Gross calls "Internet startups in a box." This setup enables Gross to move very fast from idea to execution. It also gives very young people a shot at running their own shows. "I think people are motivated the most when they have unbelievable control of their destiny," Gross says.

Can this idea lab spawn successful companies? Thermo Electron's George Hatsopoulos isn't convinced Gross' variation on the Thermo model will work. He points out that Thermo started with a profitable parent company that was 27 years old before it hatched its first startup. By then it had plenty of cash flow to fund the new ventures. By contrast, only half of Idealab!'s startups have revenues. None have profits.

But Gross seems convinced he needn't wait for a positive cash flow before launching additional companies. He knows that there is plenty of capital available for Internet start- ups with impressive sponsorship and plans to take advantage of that with public offerings ahead of a positive cash flow.

He also hopes to sell some of them to larger companies. "I don't hold on to anything for nostalgia's sake," he says. With estimated revenues of up to $20 million in 1997, CitySearch may try to sell some stock in 1998.

LECTURE ENHANCER 6-8

INTRAPRENEUR VERSUS ENTREPRENEUR

The major differences noted between intrapreneurs and entrepreneurs are that intrapreneurs are more group-oriented, capable of working better within bureaucracies, and have more flexibility in dealing with others.

Some specific characteristics of intrapreneurs have been identified:

1. A vision.
2. The ability to be a corporate hybrid.
3. The need to act.
4. The ability to pursue mundane tasks.
5. The ability to combine vision and action.
6. Dedication.
7. The power to put internal priorities first.
8. The ability to set self-determined goals.
9. The need to set high standards.
10. The power to overcome, and not to avoid mistakes and failures.
11. Risk managing ability.
12. Loyalty to long-term business objectives.

Are intrapreneurs born or can they be developed? Anyone can become an intrapreneur. The critical point in being an intrapreneur is the "state of mind." If people believe they can be intrapreneurs, have intrapreneurial material, and work long and hard toward their goals, they can succeed as intrapreneurs. The most important factor is desire.

LECTURE ENHANCER 6-9

THE SMALL ADVANTAGE

How does a small company—long on potential but short on cash—hire and keep the right people? According to Al Croft, president of A.C. Croft management consulting firm, the best strategy may be to accentuate on their smallness. "Compensation and benefits are important standards, but they only go so far," says Croft. As money loses ground to things like personal satisfaction and helping others as sources of job gratification, small business gains on the corporate personnel department.

"The best thing any small-business owner can do is make sure employees understand the important part they play in the organization, and create an atmosphere that encourages employees to be conscious and proud of the contribution they make to the company," says Croft. "Giving employees a sense of self-worth is a very important aspect of staying in business."

LECTURE ENHANCER 6-10

THE EMOTIONAL CHALLENGES OF STARTING A BUSINESS

The text discusses the long hours small business owners spend starting and managing their new ventures. Let's consider another challenge that starting a new business creates: the emotional challenge. Most company founders struggle with a very vulnerable sense of self. Starting a business isn't a job or a career. It is a way of life. Many people start a business to achieve a sense of accomplishment, but that sense of accomplishment is a long time in coming. The lack of this feeling of accomplishment can crush confidence and create doubt that no founder can afford.

Most new business owners have experienced some success in their prior jobs. They start with confidence in their skills. Keeping this emotional balance without the support of a workplace is difficult. There are no more helpful, motivating fellow workers; no more confirmations of worth from supervisors (bonuses, promotions, etc.); no more idea that work is a job that you do only at the office.

Tim DeMello, founder of Wall Street Games Inc., puts it this way, "When I started Wall Street Games, that was the loneliest period of my entire life. Those months I worked at home, I used to attack my wife in the driveway when she'd pull in, because I needed some form of companionship. Plus, you're focusing on something no one can truly appreciate. It's one of the scariest things in the world to sit there with an empty yellow legal pad and understand that nothing's going to happen unless I initiate it, so what in God's name do I do now? You don't want to try out your ideas on everyone, because you don't want a lot of people to say, 'This is crazy,' You are going through so much self-doubt as it is, you don't need anyone else's. You end up waiting until the idea is totally together before you start presenting it. I think you've got to go through that stage, but it's tough."

DeMello's company now has 10 full-time and 125 part-time employees. His self-worth got a booster shot when the success of his business was profiled in *Inc.* magazine. How does DeMello maintain balance now that he's no longer alone and he's proved the wisdom of this business idea? DeMello says, "I revisit the vision constantly." He doesn't look back on past victories. "I read the *Inc.* story only once. I remember saying to people, 'It doesn't meant anything.' Hopefully it gives you a little boost of self-esteem, and you use it in you business if you can, but you go on...I know how much work it was to get where I am—and I don't mean I think I'm at the top; as soon as I say something like that I'll crash in two seconds. But I feel I've done something that isn't that simple."

LECTURE ENHANCER 6-11

ON-LINE @ BUREAUCRACY.CA

What's in a name when it comes to establishing a marketing presence on the Internet? Way more than necessary if you're a small, proud Canadian company that wants a quick, snappy Canadian address.

Saul Rothbart, a Toronto entrepreneur, attempted to secure an Internet domain (one of those snazzy new media creations that usually go "**www-dot-something-dot...**") for his "cyber-lot," an on-line car-listing service. Rothbart wanted a domain name that ended with **.CA**, the official Canadian designation on the Internet, "to let the Web community know that I am a Canadian company." But after taking one look at the stiff and wordy regulations from the **CA** domain committee, which has authority over such matters, he decided not to bother—choosing instead a non-Canadian name (**Goodcar.com**) in the more accessible, U.S.-based **.COM** domain. "In the U.S., it's first-come, first-served," says Rothbart. "Individuals, companies it doesn't matter. You pay your $50 and it's done."

Not so in Canada. To get the short-and-spiffy name of **autosellers.ca** (his first choice), Rothbart would have to federally incorporate a company called Autosellers, since addresses are limited to company names or trademarks, and only those with a national presence. Rothbart found the alternative unpalatable: the much longer, nonmnemonic domain of **www.autosellers.toronto.on.ca.** Says Rothbart: "The names have to be simple. These things are important marketing tools. They are call letters, like CFNY [a Toronto-area radio station]."

CA domain registrar John Demco defends the system. He says his committee decided in 1987 to hand out names strictly according to geopolitical boundaries and legally registered names. "We were after the best name space usable by all Canadian organizations for many years to come," he says.

But, as Rothbart points out, the tidy hierarchical system of handing out Internet addresses is actually stifling and anti-democratic—a particularly repugnant characteristic to those used to the Net's free-for-all spirit. "**.CA** belongs to Canada," says Rothbart. "It doesn't belong to the CA registry. If I want to call my site '**ABC**' and it's not taken, who are they to say I can't?"

LECTURE ENHANCER 6-12

THERE'S NO SUBSTITUTE FOR A BUSINESS PLAN (I)

When Ned Densmore bought a small bookstore in 1975, he already had a lot of experience working for other bookstores on the East Coast. Even though he thought he knew all he needed to know about book retailing, he sat down and wrote a business plan to be sure his goals matched the need for a bookstore in his particular location. He looked at the inventory and the location and put it all down on paper to help him understand what he was getting into. Today, Densmore's Village Book Store has been enlarged to more than 7,000 square feet and 10 employees and has expanded its inventory to include music cassettes, compact discs, and toys.

If there is one thing that small-business experts agree on, it is the need for a well-thought-out business plan—no matter how well-financed and experienced the prospective business owner is. Harriet Fox, founder of a small-business consulting firm in Florida, says, "Your business plan is like a road map. It describes the direction the company is going in and how it's going to get there... I see a direct relationship between the absence of a business plan and the failure of a business."

The text describes what should be included in a business plan. Fox adds that the plan should cover at least three years and include what she calls the five M's: market, methodology, management, money, and menaces. The most common mistake made by small-business owners is failure to plan for the worst-case scenario. Imagine yourself as a potential investor and be wary of a plan that "can't fail."

There are computer software programs that can help you through every step of the process of writing a business plan. Most of the programs help you write your narrative and create your spreadsheets. Some are more comprehensive than others, so compare programs before choosing the one that's right for you. Here are a few available programs:

- The American Institute of Small Business in Minneapolis takes the user through every step of the business plan: (800)328-2906.
- Tim Berry's Business Plan Toolkit offers step-by-step business plan building: (800)336-5544.
- BizPlanBuilder includes a step-by-step guide that gives tips for getting loans and basics of management: (800)442-7373.

LECTURE ENHANCER 6-13

THERE'S NO SUBSTITUTE FOR A BUSINESS PLAN (II)

When Sun Microsystems developed its first business plan, founder Scott McNealy estimated that their first years sales would be $4 million and $10 million during the second. When first year sales reached $9 million, followed by $39 million, most assumptions in the business plan went out the window, and McNealy hasn't looked at the plan since. Sun Microsystems is not alone. A company called Gateway Technology forecast in its business plan that it would sell $35 million in IBM-compatible machines its first year. The company changed its name to Compaq, and sold $111 million, followed by $329 million in its second year. Lotus Development Corporation set its first year sales revenue forecast at $3 million. The company, which developed the 1-2-3 software tool, posted first-year sales of $53 million.

According to venture capitalists, who read hundreds of business plans a year, sales forecasts are the weakest parts of the plans. The benefit of writing a plan, they say, is not in the actual details and numbers, but in getting the founders to think through their strategies. Fleshing out the basic idea forces starry-eyed entrepreneurs to face nuts-and-bolts realities such as staffing requirements, direct and indirect competition, and distribution logistics.

Once the plans are written and the business begins operation, how many managers use them on a daily basis? *Inc.* magazine contacted 50 companies and asked them about their business plans. FedEx, Nike, and ASK Computer couldn't find theirs. Rolm Corporation thought its plan might be in the hands of a division it sold off a few years ago. And Hewlett-Packard didn't know if it ever had a formal plan. Only ten companies were willing and able to turn their plans over.

LECTURE ENHANCER 6-14

ANGELS ON-LINE

Rich individuals looking to invest in small companies soon will be able to access an on-line federal matchmaking service. The service sponsored by the U.S. Small Business Administration's Office of Advocacy and the Defense Department, is the federal government's first major effort to organize the informal, multibillion-dollar world of so-called angel investors, officials said. Angels are private investors who help finance growing companies.

Would-be angels who sign up for the Angel Capital Electronic Network, or Ace-Net, will receive a password allowing them to view the names and financial reports of money-seeking enterprises. The businesses pay a fee, which will vary by state, for a listing on the private Internet site.

The SBA decided to spearhead the project as part of its mandate to improve small business access to capital. The idea is to create a whole new generation of angels and a whole new generation of businesses. The SBA estimated that 300,000 businesses are candidates for angel money: They are big enough that they have outgrown traditional capital sources including the SBA's own loan-guarantee program. But they aren't ready to go public, or even attract venture capital.

Because small companies using the network are essentially soliciting money from the public, they will need to complete a small corporate offering registration, or SCOR. But neither the nonprofit organizations nor the federal government will screen the companies' information for accuracy.

To protect amateur investors, who don't always perform due diligence on a company before handing over their money, the network is limiting access to investors whose net worth exceeds $1 million. The Securities and Exchange Commission raised no objection to the network, the SBA said.

While potential investors praised the network concept, some worried that it will attract many marginal companies seeking capital. This will make it too time-consuming to find that one promising company. But the SBA said the system will allow investors to search for companies using a variety of criteria, including industry, size and age, and—if an entrepreneur chooses—the owner's gender and race.

Meanwhile, the network could prove to be a real time saver for entrepreneurs. While entrepreneurs generally know where to look to find bank financing, or even venture capital, there are no directories of angels. It takes entrepreneurs a lot of time to find potentially interested investors.

Although nobody has exact figures, angels invest an estimated $10 billion to $10 billion annually in almost 40,000 different businesses. In contrast. venture capital funds invested $7.4 billion last year.

The SBA is spending about $200,000 and the Defense Department is chipping in $50,000 to get the network started. The agencies said that, through fees, the network will pay for itself.

LECTURE ENHANCER 6-15

FEDEX TARGETS ITS CUSTOMERS

In order to reach its goals, an organization must define who its customers are. The result is often a broad general statement about "buyers of consumer products" or "our valued customers." Realizing who buys the company's products and why is vital to long-term success.

Consider the case of FedEx, an air package company that guarantees overnight shipment of packages coast to coast. The company was begun by Frederick Smith, who dreamed up the idea of combining a squadron of planes with a fleet of delivery vans for a term paper in an economics course at Yale. (The paper earned Smith a "C".) FedEx got off to a rocky start before settling into a steady stream of increasing profits.

The majority of Federal's customers were large businesses shipping important packages from one office to another or from plant to plant. The big break came when the company identified that its true customers were not professional shipping agents, but rather the secretaries and executives who knew very little about air freight. Federal initiated a catchy advertising campaign featuring terrified underlings facing the reality that the package that "absolutely, positively, had to be there tomorrow" wasn't, while FedEx would have gotten it there. The result: FedEx saw a compound growth rate of over 40 percent from 1982 to 1987.

LECTURE ENHANCER 6-16

RELINQUISHING THE REINS

It may seem early to talk about turning over the reins of your company to someone else when this chapter's topic is "starting" a small business. Let's just consider this as an early warning. One of the major killers of a successful business is known as "CEO disease." You know the type: the boss that has all the answers and doesn't delegate authority to others or train someone to take his place. For example, William Norris, founder of Control Data Corporation, wouldn't turn over the reins even though his company was falling apart around him. What happened? A computer power turned into a computer wimp.

Not all companies, of course, succumb to the disease. The Gap avoided it when founder Donald Fisher recognized that he knew little about merchandising. In the early 1980s the company was headed for trouble. Fisher lured Millard "Mickey" Drexler away from Ann Taylor Stores and made him president. Fisher gave Drexler complete say-so in creating a new image for The Gap. The company is now the envy of the retail industry. It has generated $2.7 billion in equities for the Fisher family. Drexler got the credit for the turnaround. But Fisher, who is still chairman and CEO, gets credit for making it happen by realizing his own limitations and not letting ego get in the way of his company's future.

Critical Thinking Exercises

Name: ____________________

Date: ____________________

CRITICAL THINKING EXERCISE 6-1

WHAT DOES IT TAKE TO BE AN ENTREPRENEUR?

Entrepreneurship is risky business. Thousands of new businesses are started and thousands of others fail each year. Why would someone give up the security of working for others to assume the risk of business ownership? Find out by interviewing two or three small businesspeople in your area. Ask them the questions listed below.

1. Did you ever work for someone else? If so, why did you stop?

2. Why did you want to go into business for yourself?

3. What expectations did you have when you started the business?

4. Which of these expectations were fulfilled?

5. Which of your expectations were not fulfilled?

6. What advice do you have for an entrepreneur thinking of starting a new business today?

Name: ______________________

Date: ______________________

CRITICAL THINKING EXERCISE 6-2

WRITING A BUSINESS PLAN

One of Mike McNeely's favorite pastimes as a teenager was taking his old car apart and putting it back together again. After graduation, Mike started working as a mechanic for his Uncle Larry's auto repair shop. Many of the customers specifically ask for Mike to work on their cars because they know that he knows what he's doing and that he's honest.

It's been ten years since Mike started his job. Now he thinks that he would like to open his own auto repair shop. He saved up some money and he thinks his rich Uncle Buck will lend him the rest. He started writing a business plan and so far has: (1) a description and appraisal of the market area, (2) an analysis of the competition, (3) a list of potential suppliers, (4) a list of purchasing and pricing procedures, and (5) a list of personnel needed and their job descriptions.

1. What important items are missing from Mike's plans?

2. What steps can Mike take to insure success if he starts his own business?

ANSWERS TO CRITICAL THINKING EXERCISE 6-2

1. *What important items are missing from Mike's plans?*

The business plan should start with a brief overview stating the goals and objectives of the firm. How big does Mike want to get? How many employees? In what locations? Using what kind of financing?

It is nice to think that a "rich uncle" will provide financing, but even rich uncles need to know how much money will be needed, how it will be spent, and what risks are involved. He may also have some interest in how the money is going to be paid back. You need a cash-flow analysis just to get some short-term money from a bank. You simply cannot be casual about funding and succeed in a small business.

If Mike intends to have others on his managerial team, he should describe them and their backgrounds and who will be responsible for what. In addition, he should mention any outside experts, such as accountants and lawyers he may use.

A more complete marketing program will show potential investors, including Uncle Buck, how Mike intends to promote the business. Many mistakes are made at this stage, such as not doing promotions early enough and then sitting around waiting for customers. A sales forecast needs to be made to show whether or not the goals of the firm are being met right from the start.

In short, a business plan cannot be some casual thrown-together proposal. It takes time and effort. But the time is well spent because the business can then get off on the right foot.

2. *What steps can Mike take to insure success if he starts his own business?*

No one can be sure of success with a small business. That is why so many of them fail within five years. The best way to protect against failure is to have a very complete business plan at the start, to hire the best advice possible, and to set up measures along the way to show if the business is getting off track. One of the most critical areas of concern is financing. But marketing and personnel are important as well, especially in this era when there are serious shortages in the labor market.

Name: ______________________

Date: ______________________

CRITICAL THINKING EXERCISE 6-3

WHAT IF?

What if you wanted to go into business for yourself? What kind of business would you like to own and operate? After you choose a business, answer the following questions.

1. What product or service would you provide?

2. What kinds of skills do you have that will help you get the business up and running?

3. What resources do you need to start the business?

4. How would your business be different from your competitors? Will you offer something different? Will you offer the same type of product or service, but of a better quality or a lower price? Just what will make your business "special"?

Supplemental Cases

CASE 6-1

3M COMPANY, INTRAPRENEURIAL LEADER

Each year the 3M Company will produce about 60,000 different products from 45 separate divisions employing more than 5,000 engineers and scientists making $12 billion in sales. A $12 billion company hardly sounds like an entrepreneurial hideout, but it is.

Employees are encouraged to spend some 15 percent of their work time on new ideas without having to account for that time in any short-term way. In the long term, of course, the company expects results, and results they get. That's where the 60,000 products come from. Not all the discoveries are planned, however.

Patsy Sherman, for example, accidentally spilled a test chemical on her tennis shoe (people dress informally at 3M). She discovered that chemicals and dirt could not remove or stain the spot. This discovery led to the profitable Scotchgard fabric protector.

Remember those yellow Post-it notes that Art Fry developed for marking his Sunday hymnal? Well, Art started at the University of Minnesota and worked as an intern at 3M. It was 20 years later that Fry developed Post-it notes.

To give you some idea of how wide the product line is at 3M, let's look at some products they are working on. One hot item is a programmable optical disk; others include bioelectronic ears and space shuttle insulation. There is an Electronic and Information Technologies Sector, a Graphics Sector, an Industrial and Consumer Sector, and a Life Sciences Sector. The company started out as Minnesota Mining and Manufacturing (3M) company. It has come a long way from the mining days. Most of its success is due to intrapreneuring.

DISCUSSION QUESTIONS FOR CASE 6-1:

1. Why is it important for laboratory people to follow their new product ideas through production and marketing?

2. How can a multibillion dollar corporation keep its entrepreneurial spirit alive?

3. Is it healthy for a corporation to be involved in such widely diverse industries as Scotch tape and bioelectronic ears? Doesn't that prevent the corporation from having expertise in all those areas?

4. Could 3M survive without intrapreneuring?

ANSWERS TO DISCUSSION QUESTIONS FOR CASE 6-1:

1. *Why is it important for laboratory people to follow their new product ideas through production and marketing?*

   Because no one else in the company is as committed to that product and willing to fight for it to get the attention it deserves. The person who invents a product is able to generate excitement among others because his or her excitement is so high. Furthermore, following one's creation to completion gives one incentive to do it again.

2. *How can a multibillion dollar corporation keep its entrepreneurial spirit alive?*

   One way is to give in-house entrepreneurial types free reign to create new ideas and to support the development of those ideas. Another way is to break the larger firm down into smaller divisions with relative freedom to create new product ideas and to compete as a separate unit. A combination of the two would allow even the largest firms to remain entrepreneurial.

3. *Is it healthy for a corporation to be involved in such widely diverse industries as Scotch tape and bioelectronic ears? Doesn't that prevent the corporation from having expertise in all those areas?*

   It is healthy to have a diversity of products so that the failure of some will not hurt the whole firm. Expertise can be maintained in several different areas by creating specialized divisions like those at the 3M company.

4. *Could 3M survive without intrapreneuring?*

   3M could survive, but it could not grow as rapidly as it has nor come up with so many new and helpful products. Intrapreneuring keeps the product line fresh and the company personnel on their toes. It creates excitement inside and outside the firm.

CASE 6-2

SMALL FARMS BE PROFITABLE?

The newspapers are full of stories about the decline of the small farm. The government spends billions of dollars each year trying to save the farmer. Clearly, farming is not a business to be entering today, especially a small farm. That is what most people think. But not Booker T. Whatley.

Booker thinks he has a formula for successful small farming. His slogan: "Stay small, but get smart." Here is the formula. Find a small farm on a paved road within 50 miles of a city of at least 50,000 people. Grow about 10 different crops such as sweet potatoes, berries, and sweet corn. If one crop fails, you see, you will have nine others to sell. Completely irrigate the farm with a drip irrigation system to ensure against drought. The farm doesn't have to be much bigger than 25 acres. (The average American farm is 456 acres, which is nearly double the 1953 acreage.) The idea is to gross about $100,000 a year. You'll need a medium-size tractor, but not much else in the form of equipment.

The secret to success is not the production, but the marketing function. The idea is to make this a "pick-your-own" farm products place. People in town would pay you a nominal membership fee for the right to pick fresh vegetables at a cost of about 40 percent below supermarket prices. The theme is, "Eliminate the middleman for cheap, farm-fresh produce." That is why the farm is located relatively close to town. You save the time and money of harvesting; your customers do it for you.

For year-round income, you might add a place to raise rabbits, quail, or bees. Building and stocking a pond with fish provides a source of entertainment for customers and another cash crop. You may also want to lease out a nut tree or grapevine. You see the possibilities. The details depend on the location, local tastes, and competition.

Mr. Whatley's model was designed using a $250,000 grant from the Rockefeller Foundation (at Tuskegee Institute). One farmer in Alabama followed these ideas and has a 45-acre farm with 1,000 beehives that produce 17,000 pounds of honey. There are also pick-your-own blueberry patches and a plot of grapevines. Some land is leased for sheep grazing. The owner is now planning a fish pond.

One variation on Whatley's theme is growing specialty foods such as alfalfa sprouts. Since sprouts are grown indoors, you avoid the problem of weather changes. In a 1,500-square-foot shed, Bob Peer grows about 2,200 pounds of sprouts a week. The sprouts mature in just a few days and sell for about $1.00 per six-ounce container. Indoor farming may be the future for small farmers.

DISCUSSION QUESTIONS FOR CASE 6-2:

1. Is a business plan as necessary for starting a small farm as for starting a small retail store? What are the differences, if any?

2. Could a farmer use the concepts of learning from others and taking over from others, as described in this chapter?

3. Can you anticipate any special problems a farmer might have in starting a business versus other small-business owners?

4. Evaluate the Whatley formula.

ANSWERS TO DISCUSSION QUESTIONS FOR CASE 6-2:

1. *Is a business plan as necessary for starting a small farm as for starting a small retail store? What are the differences, if any?*

   A business plan for a small retailer and a small farm are very similar. You still need a financial plan, a marketing plan, the capital required, a location analysis, and some information about you and your experience, expertise, etc. The difference today is that most small farms are failing and banks may be reluctant to lend money to someone to start a farm. Therefore, your business plan may have to be more elaborate to explain why your farm will be different.

2. *Could a farmer use the concepts of learning from others and taking over from others, as described in this chapter?*

   Definitely. A young farmer could learn much from men like Booker Whatley. In fact, Mr. Whatley conducts seminars to teach his principles to prospective farmers. Farmers get old too and often cannot pass on the farm to children who would prefer to work in the city. This is an excellent opportunity to take over some very large farms, manage them, and earn much more than you would by buying and running your own smaller farm.

3. *Can you anticipate any special problems a farmer might have in starting a business versus other small-business owners?*

   A farmer may have more difficulty getting financing from a bank because so many farms are failing, especially smaller farms. Farmers need an especially good business plan to show potential lenders why this business will be a success. The success of this particular strategy depends much on a good marketing plan to get local people to buy into the system. An important part of the business plan, is a step by step outline of the marketing plan, including target markets, market potential, and so forth.

4. *Evaluate the Whatley formula.*

   This plan has proven successful for a number of people in a variety of cities. Naturally, the plan depends a lot on the area, the weather, and the economic conditions of the region. Nonetheless, the principles can be applied effectively if adapted to the market and the conditions of the region. The idea of varying your crops and sharing in the harvest are good ones as are the irrigation and the marketing strategies.

Transparency Masters

TRANSPARENCY MASTER 43	Chapter Outline
TRANSPARENCY MASTER 44	Advice for Potential Entrepreneurs *(Figure 6.1 on text page 166)*
TRANSPARENCY MASTER 45	U.S. Industries with the Highest Potential in International Markets *(Figure 6.2 on text page 183)*
TRANSPARENCY MASTER 46	Entrepreneur Readiness Questionnaire *(Figure on text page 191)*

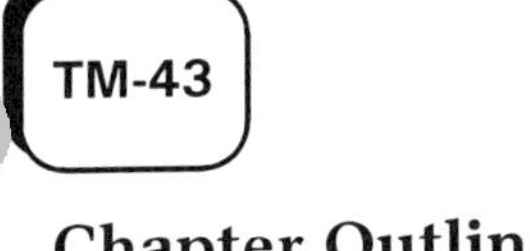

Chapter Outline

CHAPTER 6
ENTREPRENEURSHIP AND STARTING A SMALL BUSINESS

PROFILE: David Marcheschi of Water Concepts LLC

I. THE AGE OF THE ENTREPRENEUR.

II. THE JOB-CREATING POWER OF ENTREPRENEURS IN THE UNITED STATES.

III. WHY PEOPLE TAKE THE ENTREPRENEURIAL CHALLENGE.

A. What Does It Take to Be an Entrepreneur?

B. Entrepreneurial Teams.

C. Micropreneurs and Home-Based Businesses.

D. Encouraging Entrepreneurship—What Government Can Do.

E. Entrepreneurship Within Firms.

IV. GETTING STARTED IN SMALL BUSINESS.

A. Small Versus Big Business.

B. Importance of Small Business.

C. Small-Business Success and Failure.

V. LEARNING ABOUT SMALL-BUSINESS OPERATIONS.

A. Learn from Others.

B. Get Some Experience.

C. Take Over a Successful Firm.

VI. MANAGING A SMALL BUSINESS.

A. Begin with Planning.
   1. Writing a Business Plan.

B. Getting Money to Fund a Small Business.
   1. The Small Business Administration (SBA).

C. Knowing Your Customers.

D. Managing Employees.

E. Keeping Records.

F. Looking for Help.

VII. GOING INTERNATIONAL: SMALL-BUSINESS PROSPECTS.

VIII. SUMMARY AND REVIEW

Advice for Potential Entrepreneurs
(Figure 6.1 on text page 166)

ADVICE FOR POTENTIAL ENTREPRENEURS

- Research your market, but don't take too long to act.
- Work for other people first and learn on their money
- Start out slowly. Start your business when you have a customer. Maybe try your venture as a sideline at first.
- Set specific objectives, but don't set your goals too high. Remember, there's no easy money.
- Plan your objectives within specific time frames.
- Surround yourself with people who are smarter than you—including an accountant and an outside board of directors who are interested in your well-being and who'll give you straight answers.
- Don't be afraid to fail. Former football coach Vince Lombardi summarized the entrepreneurial philosophy when he said, "We didn't lose any games this season, we just ran out of time twice." New entrepreneurs must be ready to run out of time a few times before they succeed.

Source: Joseph Mancuso, "The Right Stuff: Do You Have What It Takes to Start Your Own Business?" *The Wall Street Journal's Managing Your Career,* Spring 1991 pp. 15–19.

U.S. Industries with the Highest Potential in International Markets
(Figure 6.2 on text page 183)

U.S. INDUSTRIES WITH THE HIGHEST POTENTIAL IN INTERNATIONAL MARKETS

1. Computers and peripherals (hardware)
2. Telecommunications equipment and systems
3. Computer software and services
4. Medical instruments, equipment, and supplies
5. Electronic parts
6. Analytical and scientific laboratory instruments
7. Industrial process control instruments
8. Aircraft and parts and avionics and ground support equipment
9. Automotive parts and service equipment and accessories
10. Electronic production and test equipment
11. Electronic power generation and distribution systems and transmission equipment
12. Food processing and packaging equipment and machinery
13. Safety and security equipment
14. Printing and graphic arts equipment
15. Water resources equipment

TM-46A

Entrepreneur Readiness Questionnaire

(Figure on text page 191)

Looking at my overall philosophy of life and typical behavior, I would say that . . .	Agree Completely (1)	Mostly Agree (2)	Partially Agree (3)	Mostly Disagree (4)	Disagree Completely (5)
	Response				
1. I am generally optimistic.	1	2	3	4	5
2. I enjoy competing and doing things better than someone else.	1	2	3	4	5
3. When solving a problem, I try to arrive at the best solution first without worrying about other possibilities.	1	2	3	4	5
4. I enjoy associating with co-workers after working hours.	1	2	3	4	5
5. If betting on a horse race I would prefer to take a chance on a high-payoff "long shot."	1	2	3	4	5
6. I like setting my own goals and working hard to achieve them.	1	2	3	4	5
7. I am generally casual and easy-going with others.	1	2	3	4	5
8. I like to know what is going on and take action to find out.	1	2	3	4	5
9. I work best when someone else is guiding me along the way.	1	2	3	4	5
10. When I am right I can convince others.	1	2	3	4	5
11. I find that other people frequently waste my valuable time.	1	2	3	4	5
12. I enjoy watching football, baseball, and similar sports events.	1	2	3	4	5
13. I tend to communicate about myself very openly with other people.	1	2	3	4	5

Source: Kenneth R. Van Voorhis, *Entrepreneurship and Small Business Management* (New York: Allyn & Bacon, 1980).

Entrepreneur Readiness Questionnaire *(continued)*

Looking at my overall philosophy of life and typical behavior, I would say that . . .	Agree Completely (1)	Mostly Agree (2)	Partially Agree (3)	Mostly Disagree (4)	Disagree Completely (5)
	Response				
14. I don't mind following orders from superiors who have legitimate authority.	1	2	3	4	5
15. I enjoy planning things more than actually carrying out the plans.	1	2	3	4	5
16. I don't think it's much fun to bet on a "sure thing."	1	2	3	4	5
17. If faced with failure, I would shift quickly to something else rather than sticking to my guns.	1	2	3	4	5
18. Part of being successful in business is reserving adequate time for family.	1	2	3	4	5
19. Once I have earned something, I feel that keeping it secure is important.	1	2	3	4	5
20. Making a lot of money is largely a matter of getting the right breaks.	1	2	3	4	5
21. Problem solving is usually more effective when a number of alternatives are considered.	1	2	3	4	5
22. I enjoy impressing others with the things I can do.	1	2	3	4	5
23. I enjoy playing games like tennis and handball with someone who is slightly better than I am.	1	2	3	4	5
24. Sometimes moral ethics must be bent a little in business dealings.	1	2	3	4	5
25. I think that good friends would make the best subordinates in an organization.	1	2	3	4	5

Management, Leadership, and Employee Empowerment

Chapter 7

Folder Contents

Overhead Transparency Acetates

OT ACETATE 7-1	The Process of Management
OT ACETATE 7-2	Sources of Management Information
OT ACETATE 7-3	Why the Cuts in Middle Management?
OT ACETATE 7-4	Management Planning Levels and Time Spans
OT ACETATE 7-5	Manager's Empowerment Checklist
OT ACETATE 7-6	Take the Empowerment Quiz
OT ACETATE 7-7	Take the Empowerment Quiz
OT ACETATE 7-8	Required Skills of a "Quality" Manager
OT ACETATE 7-9	Tips for the New Manager
OT ACETATE 7-10	Key Management Challenges in the Future

(Acetates and Transparency Masters are also available as PowerPoint slides on disk and on the Presentation CD-ROM.)

(Resources Available are also referenced in the expanded lecture outline later in this chapter.)

Other Resources Available

Video Case - "Lou Gerstner and the IBM Turnaround" demonstrates how IBM CEO Lou Gerstner's strong leadership in the areas of team building, sound fiscal oversight, risk management, and creating a culture of service have brought about a change in fortunes for the corporate giant. (The **Media Resource Guide** contains a summary of the Video and suggested discussion questions.)

Student Assessment and Learning Guide: Contains matching key term and definition questions, write-in retention questions, write-in critical thinking questions, and practice test of multiple choice and true/false questions.

Technology:

Zapitalism CD-ROM - Simulation program.

Concept Mastery Exam Preparation Disk - Practice test and tutorial.

Business Essentials Disk - Hyperlinks Understanding Business with seven other leading business texts.

Presentation CD-ROM - Contains PowerPoint slides of acetates and transparency masters, video clips, lecture materials. This tool allows you to customize your lecture presentations.

***Business Week* Web Site Access with the *Business Week* edition.**

***Understanding Business* Home Page - http:/www.mhhe.com/ub5e.**

Audiotape: Abridged chapter (Text minus profile, boxes, and end-of-chapter material.

Associated Web Sites

These sites are provided to students for the purpose of analysis and critical thinking of the issues. Students are encouraged to explore other sites. As with any Web site, some may be inactive now.

American Management Association (AMA):

http://www.amanet.org/

General Leadership Principles That Can Be Applied to Politics and Business:

http://www.ssu.missouri.edu/faculty/RCampbell/Leadership/chapter2b.htm

Responsibility of supervisors - note the many legal implications of actions taken by supervisors

http://www.safetyonline.net/coastal/htrain/superv.htm

Leadership Versus Management:

http://www.forerunner.com/forerunner/X0364_Leadership.html

Women as Leaders - short but interesting perspective

http://www.cowan.edu.au/wil/lect96.htm

Leaders and Teams:

http://www.sna.com/switp/lead.html

Empowerment

http://www.afpc.af.mil/quality/covey.htm

Management and the Manager's Job - broad overview of management - this lecture goes beyond our textbook

http://www.ee.uwa.edu.au/~ccroft/em333/leca.html

Bonuses for Executives - Is it fair??

http://www.tcac.com/~steveb/ceo.html

Autocratic Power - a social perspective

http://www.bravenewweb.com/idea/02AutoPower.html

Decision-Making

Useful Tips

http://www.liraz.com/tdecision.htm

Decisions affecting ethics

http://jcomm.uoregon.edu/~tbivins/j495/Worksheet.html

Customer service
Many nice comments - note the level of service given to each customer

http://www.tradeshop.com/~raylc/master/referals.html

Customer service manager - note the role this persons wants to serve

http://www.biosystems.com/biobull/vol2iss3/sawka.htm

Good telephone answering skills

***Understanding Business* Home Page:**

http:/www.mhhe.com/ub5e.

What's New in This Edition

Additions:

- Profile of Lynn Mercer of Lucent Technologies
- Section "A Corporate Scorecard"
- Section "Creating a Learning Organization"
- Section "Leadership Teams"
- Video case Lou Gerstner and IBM Turnaround
- Making Ethical Decisions: Leading By Example
- Taking It to the Net exercises

Revisions:

Statistical data and examples throughout the chapter were updated to reflect current information. In addition:

- The theme of managing organizations to please customers was woven throughout the chapter.
- The traditional management function of directing was presented from the more contemporary view of leading.
- The section "Planning: Creating a Vision for the Organization" was expanded to include discussion of mission statements, SWOT analysis, and operational planning.
- Two sections on empowering were combined into the section "Empowering." Section was expanded to include the term enabling.
- The section "New Criteria for Measurement: Customer Satisfaction" was expanded to include a discussion of internal and external customers.

Deletions:

- Profile
- Making Ethical Decisions box
- Case: Changing the Paradigm
- Tellabs video case

Brief Chapter Outline/Learning Goals

CHAPTER 7

MANAGEMENT, LEADERSHIP, AND EMPLOYEE EMPOWERMENT

PROFILE: Lynn Mercer of Lucent Technologies

I. THE NEW APPROACH TO CORPORATE MANAGEMENT.

LEARNING GOAL 1. Explain the four functions of management and why the role of managers is changing.

A. Managers Are No Longer Just Bosses.

B. The Definition and Functions of Customer-Oriented Management.

II. PLANNING: CREATING A VISION FOR THE ORGANIZATION.

LEARNING GOAL 2. Relate the planning process to the accomplishment of corporate goals.

III. ORGANIZING: CREATING A UNIFIED SYSTEM OUT OF MULTIPLE ORGANIZATIONS.

LEARNING GOAL 3. Describe the organizing function of management and illustrate how the function differs at various management levels.

A. The Customer-Oriented Organization.

B. Organization Involves Multiple Firms.

C. Empowering Workers.

IV. CONTROLLING.

LEARNING GOAL 4. Summarize the five steps of the control function of management.

A. New Criteria for Measurement: Customer Satisfaction.

B. A Corporate Scorecard.

V. LEADERSHIP: VISION AND VALUES.

LEARNING GOAL 5. Explain the differences between managers and leaders, and compare the characteristics and uses of the various leadership styles.

A. Creating a Learning Organization.

B. Leadership Styles.

C. The Trend Toward Self-Managed Teams.

D. Leadership Teams.

VI. TASKS AND SKILLS AT DIFFERENT LEVELS OF MANAGEMENT.

LEARNING GOAL 6. Describe the three general categories of skills needed by top, middle, and first-line managers.

A. Delegating: Becoming a Team Leader.

B. Decision Making: Finding the Best Ethical Alternative.

VII. LEARNING MANAGEMENT SKILLS.

LEARNING GOAL 7. Illustrate the skills aspiring managers need to develop to be successful in the future.

A. Verbal Skills.

B. Writing Skills.

C. Computer Skills.

D. Human Relations Skills.

E. Managing Diversity.

F. Time Management Skills.

G. Technical Skills.

VIII. MANAGERS AND LEADERS ARE NEEDED EVERYWHERE.

IX. SUMMARY AND REVIEW.

(Learning Objectives are also referenced in the expanded lecture outline later in this chapter)

Key Terms

autocratic leadership *(text page 213)*
conceptual skills *(text page 217)*
contingency planning *(text page 203)*
controlling *(text page 200)*
decision making *(text page 218)*
delegating *(text page 218)*
empowerment *(text page 207)*
enabling *(text page 207)*
external customers *(text page 209)*
goals *(text page 201)*
human relations skills *(text page 217)*
internal customers *(text page 209)*
laissez-faire (free-reign) leadership *(text page 213)*
leadership *(text page 210)*
leading *(text page 200)*
learning organization *(text page 212)*
management *(text page 199)*
managing diversity *(text page 221)*
middle management *(text page 203)*
mission statement *(text page 200)*
objectives *(text page 201)*
operational planning *(text page 203)*
organizing *(text page 200)*
participative (democratic) leadership *(text page 213)*
planning *(text page 199)*
strategic (long-range) planning *(text page 202)*
supervisory (first-line) management *(text page 204)*
SWOT *(text page 201)*
tactical (short-range) planning *(text page 202)*
technical skills *(text page 217)*
top management *(text page 203)*
vision *(text page 200)*

Lecture Outline

The **PROFILE** at the beginning of this chapter focuses on **LYNN MERCER**, a plant manager at **LUCENT TECHNOLOGIES**, who recognizes that rapid change requires new management approaches.

I. THE NEW APPROACH TO CORPORATE MANAGEMENT.

▶ **LEARNING GOAL 1.** Explain the four functions of management and why the role of managers is changing.

A. A number of changes have prompted managers to reorganize their organizations and their approaches to management.

1. Changes are necessary because of **GLOBAL COMPETITION, TECHNOLOGICAL CHANGE,** and the growing **IMPORTANCE OF PLEASING CUSTOMERS.**

2. The **NEED TO RESPOND BETTER TO CUSTOMERS** is motivating businesses to reorganize to give more authority and responsibility to lower-level managers.

3. In response to foreign competition, American firms have restructured and changed their management styles to become more responsive.

4. Accelerating technological change increases the need for a new breed of worker, one who is more educated and has higher skill levels. **HIGHER EDUCATED WORKERS**

Lecture Notes

TRANSPARENCY MASTER 47
Chapter Outline

Transparency masters begin on page 7.80.

LECTURE ENHANCER 7-1
The Mother of Management

Mary Parker Follett believed very strongly that the person doing the job was the person most likely to know how to do the lob better. She felt that it was human nature to want to be self-managed. (See complete lecture enhancer on page 7.53.)

OT ACETATE 7-1
The Process of Management

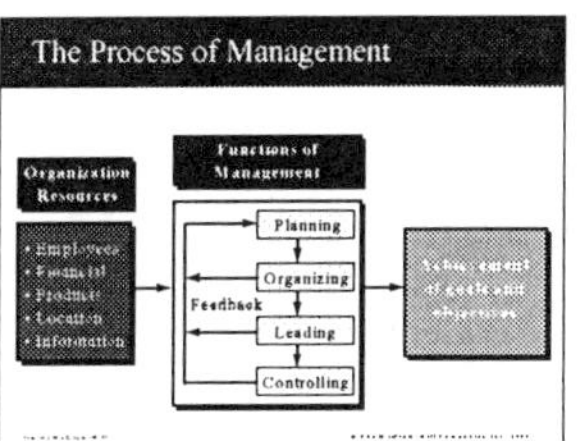

Comments:

1. This acetate acquaints students with the four key functions of management and the importance of using these functions and other resources to achieve the organization's goals and objectives.
2. It's important students note that managers are delegated authority over organizational resources for the purpose of accomplishing something. Effectively learning and using the functions of management helps managers make the most efficient use of these resources.
3. Ask students which of the organizational resources is most important to managers. We would agree that all are very important, students however will likely focus on the role of employees in organizational effectiveness.
4. You might want to cite the importance of feedback in applying managerial functions. Students should understand that the management process is a continuous challenge.

Lecture Outline

demand more freedom of operation and different managerial styles.

5. The start of the next century is shaping up as a time to get rid of old management styles and introduce a new way of operating.
6. Hundreds of firms have gone through sweeping organizational and managerial changes, becoming leaner and ready to take on world competition.

B. **MANAGERS ARE NO LONGER JUST BOSSES.**

1. Management has been defined as "the art of getting things done through people."
2. Bosses are changing from "bossy" behavior to leading, guiding and coaching employees.
3. Managers in the future are much more likely to be working in teams.
4. This approach to management will demand that a manager be a skilled communicator and team player as well as a planner, coordinator, organizer, and supervisor.

C. **THE DEFINITION AND FUNCTIONS OF CUSTOMER-ORIENTED MANAGEMENT.**

1. **MANAGEMENT** is the process used to accomplish organizational goals through planning, organizing, directing, and controlling people and other organizational resources.

LECTURE ENHANCER 7-2
The Function of A Manager

As nearly everyone knows, an executive has practically nothing to do except . . . (See complete lecture enhancer on page 7.54.)

OT ACETATE 7-2
Sources of Management Information

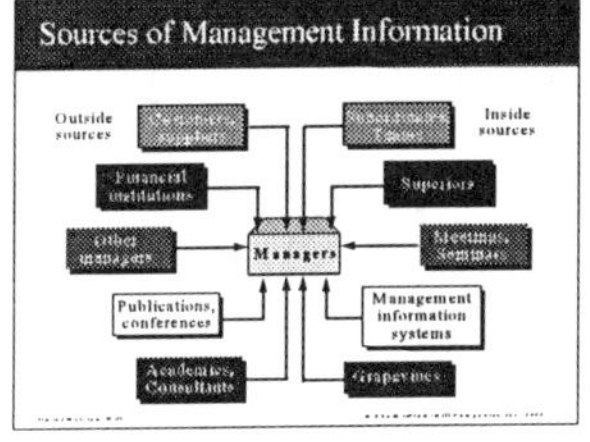

Comments:

1. External and internal sources of management information are provided here.
2. It's helpful to point out that managing is a distinct process that can be learned and perfected. Therefore, sources of information can be invaluable to the manager in successfully performing his/her job.
3. You could go over each of the outside and inside sources and have students site examples of how the manager can utilize information from this source. For example, what kind of information could customers or suppliers provide that would help the manager? Obviously, such factors as expected demand, market trends, customer expectations, product quality, etc., could be provided to the manager as feedback concerning his/her organizational performance.
4. Ask students to think of additional sources of information managers might use. They may respond with additional sources such as computer simulations, and hopefully college coursework.

Lecture Outline

2. The **FUNCTIONS OF MANAGEMENT** are:

   a. **PLANNING** includes anticipating future trends and determining the best strategies and tactics to achieve organizational goals and objectives

   b. **ORGANIZING** includes designing the organization structure, attracting people to the organization, and creating conditions that ensure that everyone works together to achieve the organization's goals.

   c. **LEADING** means creating a vision for the organization and guiding, training, coaching, and motivating others to work effectively to achieve the organization's goals and objectives.

   d. **CONTROLLING** is determining whether an organization is progressing toward its goals and objectives, and taking corrective action if it's not.

II. PLANNING: CREATING A VISION.

▶ **LEARNING GOAL 2.** Relate the planning process to the accomplishment of corporate goals.

A. Planning is the management function that involves anticipating future trends and determining the best strategies and tactics to achieve organizational objectives.

Lecture Notes

TRANSPARENCY MASTER 48
What Managers Do
(Figure 7.1 on text page 199)

TM 48 Transparency masters begin on page 7.80.

CRITICAL THINKING EXERCISE 7-1
Management Functions

See complete exercise on page 7.71.

PROGRESS CHECK
(page 200 in text)

- What were some of the factors that have forced managers to change their organizations and managerial styles?
- What's the definition of management used in this chapter, and what are the four functions in that definition?

Lecture Outline

1. **PLANNING** involves the setting of the organizational vision, goals, and objectives.

2. A **VISION** is more than a goal; it is the larger explanation of why the organization exists and where it is trying to head.

3. A **MISSION STATEMENT** outlines the fundamental purposes of the organization.

4. **GOALS** are the broad, long-term accomplishments an organization wishes to attain.

5. **OBJECTIVES** are specific, short-term statements detailing how to achieve the organizational goals.

6. Planning is a continuous process.

B. Planning answers **THREE FUNDAMENTAL QUESTIONS:**

1. **WHAT IS THE SITUATION NOW?**

2. **WHERE DO WE WANT TO GO?**

3. **HOW CAN WE GET THERE FROM HERE?**

C. **TYPES OF PLANNING.**

1. **STRATEGIC (LONG-TERM) PLANNING** determines the major goals of the organization and the policies and strategies for obtaining and using resources to achieve those goals.

LECTURE ENHANCER 7-3
Apple Computer Defines Itself

The once mighty Apple Computers has fallen on rough times lately. The company started with products that had a huge technological lead over the competition. (See complete lecture enhancer on page 7.55.)

TRANSPARENCY MASTER 49
Planning Functions
(Figure 7.2 on text page 202)

Transparency masters begin on page 7.80.

Lecture Outline

a. Long-range planning is becoming more difficult because changes are occurring too fast for long-range thinking.

b. The long-range goal is to be flexible and responsive to the market.

c. Strategic planning is usually done by top management.

2. **TACTICAL (SHORT-RANGE) PLANNING** is the process of developing detailed, short-term decisions about what is to be done, who is to do it, and how it is to be done.

   a. Tactical planning is normally done by managers or teams of managers at lower levels of the organization.

   b. **OPERATIONAL PLANNING** is setting of work standards and schedules necessary to implement the tactical objectives.

3. **CONTINGENCY PLANNING** is the preparation of alternative courses of action that may be used if the primary plans do not achieve the objectives of the organization.

   a. It is wise to have alternative plans of action ready in anticipation of environmental changes.

Lecture Notes

LECTURE ENHANCER 7-4
Planning Failure

One side of planning that is rarely discussed is failure. (See complete lecture enhancer on page 7.56.)

PROGRESS CHECK
(page 203 in text)

- What's the difference between strategic, tactical, and contingency planning?
- Why would organizations today be less concerned about strategic planning than they once were? What has become of even greater concern? Could strategic planning get in the way of an organization being flexible enough to respond to market changes?

b. The leaders of market-based companies stay flexible, listen for opportunities, and seize opportunities when they come.

III. ORGANIZING: CREATING A UNIFIED SYSTEM.

▶ **LEARNING GOAL 3.** Describe the organizing function of management and illustrate how the function differs at various management levels.

A. After planning a course of action, managers must organize the firm to accomplish their goals.

1. When organizing, a manager develops a structure that relates all workers, tasks, and resources to each other called the **ORGANIZATION STRUCTURE.**

2. The **ORGANIZATION CHART** pictures who reports to whom and who is responsible for each task.

3. The corporate hierarchy illustrated on the organization chart includes top, middle, and first-line managers.

B. **LEVELS OF MANAGEMENT**.

1. **TOP MANAGEMENT** is the highest level of management and consists of the president and other key company executives who develop **STRATEGIC PLANS.**

Lecture Notes

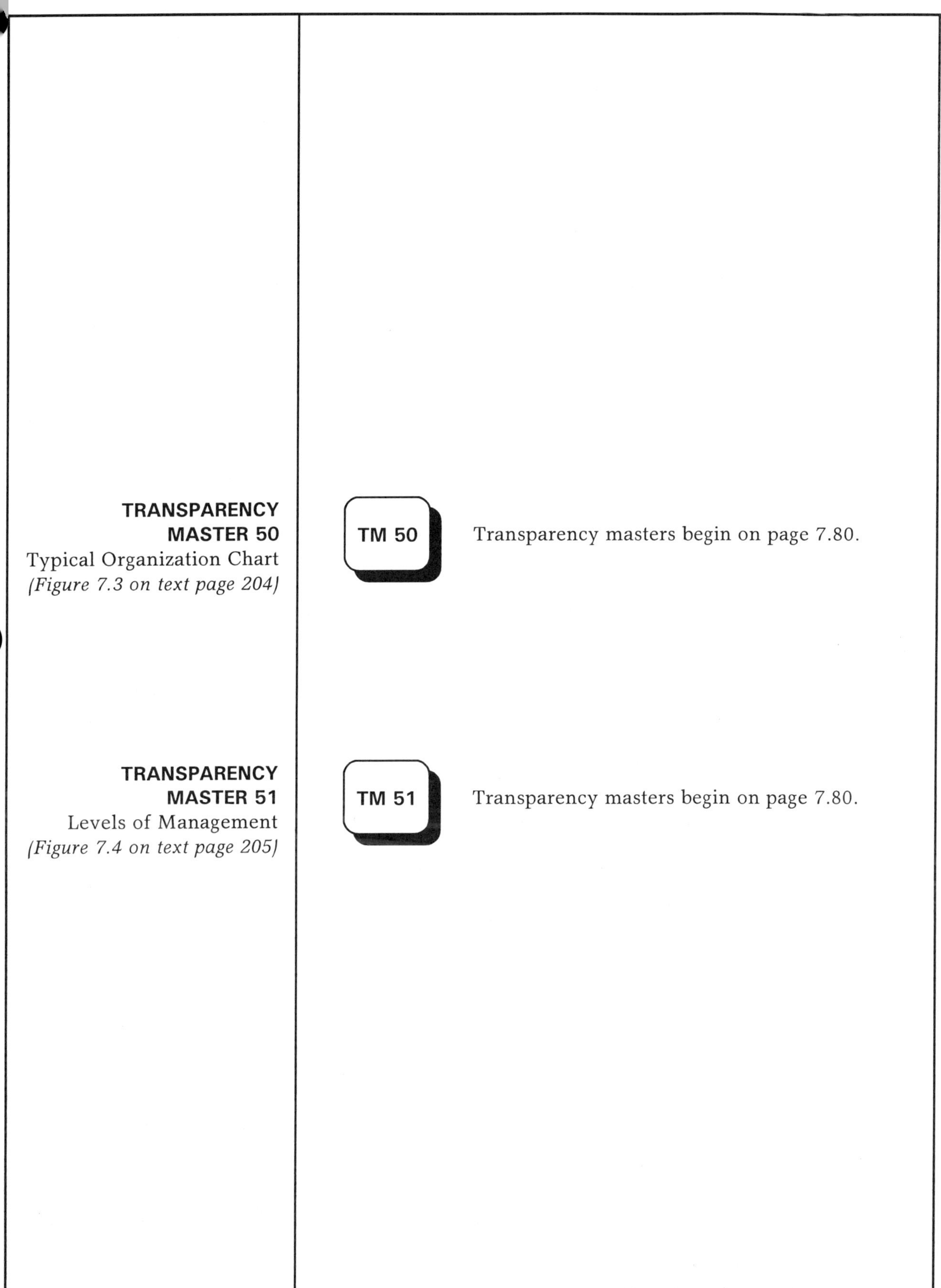

TRANSPARENCY MASTER 50
Typical Organization Chart
(Figure 7.3 on text page 204)

TM 50

Transparency masters begin on page 7.80.

TRANSPARENCY MASTER 51
Levels of Management
(Figure 7.4 on text page 205)

TM 51

Transparency masters begin on page 7.80.

Lecture Outline

a. Titles include **CHIEF EXECUTIVE OFFICER (CEO), CHIEF OPERATING OFFICER (COO),** and **CHIEF FINANCIAL OFFICER (CFO.)**

2. **MIDDLE MANAGEMENT** includes branch and plant managers, deans, and department heads who are responsible for **TACTICAL PLANS.**

3. **SUPERVISORY (FIRST-LINE) MANAGEMENT** includes people directly responsible for assigning specific jobs to workers and evaluating their daily performance.

C. **THE CUSTOMER-ORIENTED ORGANIZATION.**

1. The firm must find the best way to organize to respond to the needs of customers and other stakeholders.

   a. **STAKEHOLDERS** include anyone who is affected by the organization and its policies and products.

   b. Most large firms are being restructured into smaller, more customer-focused units to become more responsive.

2. Companies are no longer organizing to make it easy for managers to have control. Instead, they are organizing so that **CUSTOMERS** have control.

LECTURE ENHANCER 7-5
Attributes of Excellent Companies

In the 1980s the authors of *In Search of Excellence* visited many of the top firms in the United States to find out what made them different, better than the other firms. (See complete lecture enhancer on page 7.57.)

OT ACETATE 7-3
Why the Cuts in Middle Management?

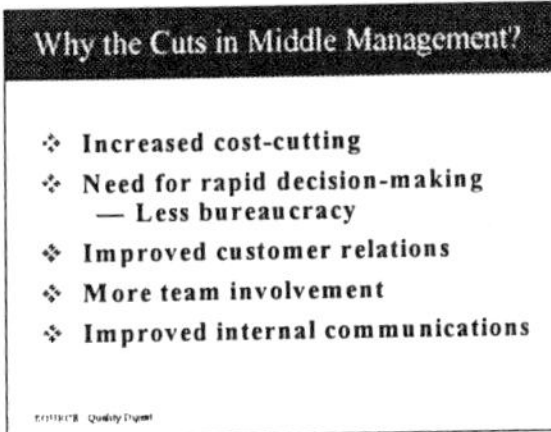

Comments:

1. Many students will be aware that middle managers have been decimated during the 1990s. Some suggest that middle managers may cease to exist as a key organizational component in the future. You might want to ask students if they know anyone personally (family, friend, etc.) that has been subject to cuts in middle management.
2. This acetate gets into some of the reasons why we have seen such reduction in the ranks of middle managers during the 1990s. A logical question for discussion is will this trend continue on or is the worst for middle management over?
3. It is interesting to see where the students fall on this issue. Do they think such reductions are a good idea or have middle managers fallen prey to greedy top executives or an unlimited quest to please stockholders? The issue of empowerment looms heavily here. Empowerment is the topic in the next two acetates.

SPOTLIGHT ON SMALL BUSINESS

(Box in text, page 206)
"Customer Focus on the Internet"

Companies now do about $1.4 billion worth of business on the Internet, and that is expected to reach $3.3 billion by the year 2000.

Lecture Outline

D. **ORGANIZATION INVOLVES MULTIPLE FIRMS.**

1. Today, the organization task is more complex because firms are forming partnerships, joint ventures, and other arrangements that make it necessary to organize the **WHOLE SYSTEM.**
2. In order for an organization to provide quality goods and services, it must develop close relationships with suppliers to provide world-class parts and materials.
3. Today firms throughout the world are linked by computers so that they operate as one.
4. **SMALL BUSINESSES** are key forces in shaping American business in this time of interfirm relationships.

E. **EMPOWERING WORKERS.**

1. For traditional organizations, directing involves giving assignments, explaining routines, clarifying policies, and providing feedback on performance.
2. In **TRADITIONAL ORGANIZATIONS**, all managers, from top managers to first-line supervisors, direct employees.
   a. **TOP MANAGERS** are concerned with the broad overview of where the company is headed.

SUPPLEMENTAL CASE 7-1
Team Concepts in a Small Service Firm

See complete case on page 7.74.

OT ACETATE 7-4
Management Planning Levels and Time Spans

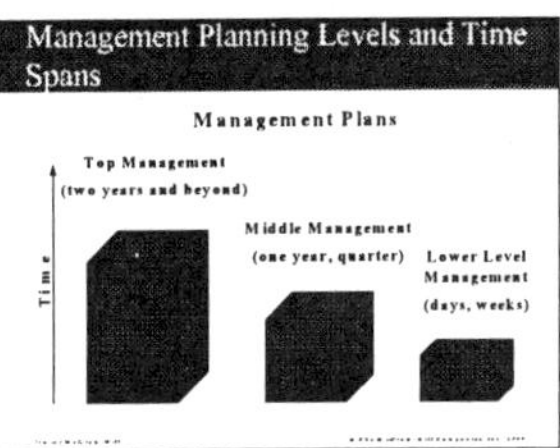

Comments:

1. The purpose of this acetate is to communicate the different planning responsibilities associated with the three levels of management.
2. This acetate assists students in understanding that planning is a responsibility of all managers. Nonetheless, the acetate shows how the responsibilities change at different levels of management. Differentiation in job requirements at various levels of management can easily be addressed here. Also, again the use of teams in contemporary organizations brings more players into the planning function.
3. This is also a good time to reinforce the concepts in the text dealing with strategic, tactical, and contingency planning.
4. Your students might want to discuss their involvement in strategic, tactical, and contingency. You could ask how many have set long-term goals and objectives in their careers? Is personal planning really important? A good many possibilities here!

SUPPLEMENTAL CASE 7-2
Changing the Paradigm

See complete case on page 7.77.

   b. **MIDDLE MANAGERS** are responsible for directing employees to meet company objectives.

   c. **FIRST-LINE MANAGERS** spend much of their time giving specific, detailed instructions to employees.

3. **PROGRESSIVE MANAGERS** in the future are less likely to be giving specific instructions to employees.

   a. They are more likely to **EMPOWER** them to make decisions on their own.

   b. **EMPOWERMENT** is a total quality term that means giving employees the authority and responsibility to respond quickly to customer requests.

   c. **ENABLING** is the term used to describe giving workers the education and tools needed to assume their new decision-making roles.

4. **SELF-MANAGED, CROSS-FUNCTIONAL TEAMS** are groups of employees from various departments such as purchasing, marketing, and engineering.

IV. CONTROLLING.

▶ **LEARNING GOAL 4.** Summarize the five steps of the control function of management.

Lecture Notes

Lecture Outline

A. The **CONTROL FUNCTION** is the heart of the management system because it provides the feedback that enables managers to adjust to any deviations from plans.

B. **CONTROLLING CONSISTS OF THE FOLLOWING STEPS:**

1. **SETTING CLEAR PERFORMANCE STANDARDS**
2. **MONITORING AND RECORDING ACTUAL PERFORMANCE.**
3. **COMPARING RESULTS AGAINST PLANS AND STANDARDS**
4. **COMMUNICATING RESULTS AND DEVIATIONS TO THE EMPLOYEES INVOLVED.**
5. **TAKING CORRECTIVE ACTION WHEN NEEDED.**

C. **SETTING STANDARDS.**

1. To measure results against standards, the standards must be **SPECIFIC, ATTAINABLE,** and **MEASURABLE.**
2. Clear **PROCEDURES FOR MONITORING** performance should be established.

D. **NEW CRITERIA FOR MEASUREMENT: CUSTOMER SATISFACTION.**

Lecture Notes

TRANSPARENCY MASTER 52
The Control Process
(Figure 7.5 on text page 208)

TM 52

Transparency masters begin on page 7.80.

Lecture Outline

1. The criteria for measuring success in a customer-oriented firm is **CUSTOMER SATISFACTION OF BOTH INTERNAL AND EXTERNAL CUSTOMERS.**
   a. **INTERNAL CUSTOMERS** are units within the firm that receive services from other units.
   b. **EXTERNAL CUSTOMERS** include dealers and ultimate customers who buy products for their own personal use.
2. Other **CRITERIA** of organizational effectiveness may include the firm's **CONTRIBUTION TO SOCIETY** or the **ENVIRONMENT.**

E. **A CORPORATE SCORECARD.**

1. A **CORPORATE SCORECARD** measures financial progress, return on investment, and profits, in addition to customer satisfaction.
2. No company can prosper in the long run without a balanced approach that measures both financial growth and employee and customer satisfaction.
3. Better controls make the company stronger.

V. LEADERSHIP: VISION AND VALUES.

▶ **LEARNING GOAL 5.** Explain the differences between managers and leaders, and compare the characteristics and uses of the various leadership styles.

MAKING ETHICAL DECISIONS
(Box in text, page 211)
"Leading by Example"

The popular press does not report it much, but many business leaders are quite generous when it comes to giving away the money they earn.

Lecture Outline

A. **LEADERSHIP** involves creating vision for others to follow, establishing corporate values and ethics, and transforming the way the organization does business so it is more effective and efficient.

B. **LEADERS:**

1. Have a **VISION** and **RALLY OTHERS** around that vision.
2. Establish **CORPORATE VALUES.**
3. Emphasize **CORPORATE ETHICS.**
4. **DON'T FEAR CHANGE**, but embrace it and create it.

C. **CREATING A LEARNING ORGANIZATION.**

1. A **LEARNING ORGANIZATION** is one skilled at crating, acquiring, interpreting, retaining, and transferring knowledge; and at purposefully modifying its behavior based on new technologies.
2. Most companies are good at acquiring information but weaker at interpreting, retaining, and transferring knowledge—that's where leadership comes in.
3. Some firms have added a **CIO (CHIEF INFORMATION OFFICER)** to their staffs.

D. **LEADERSHIP STYLES.**

LECTURE ENHANCER 7-6
Servant Leaders

We've talked of visionary leaders who communicate their vision to his subordinates. Given the current changes in organizational structure, it may be time to come up with a more downsized, restructured concept of leadership: the leader exists to serve those he leads, those who follow him. (See complete lecture enhancer on page 7.59.)

TRANSPARENCY MASTER 53
Managers Versus Leaders
(Figure on text page 211)

Transparency masters begin on page 7.80.

REACHING BEYOND OUR BORDERS
(Box in text, page 211)
"Global Management"

As students read about countries that make up the former Soviet Union going to a market economy and Eastern Europeans opening their doors to Western businesses, they're demanding to know more about global business management.

LECTURE ENHANCER 7-7
Coping With an Intolerable Boss

Millions of workers have them—intolerable bosses. (See complete lecture enhancer on page 7.60.)

Lecture Outline

1. Research studies have not been able to identify one set of **TRAITS** that are common to all leaders.
2. There are also **DIFFERENT LEADERSHIP STYLES:**
   a. **AUTOCRATIC LEADERSHIP** involves making managerial decisions without consulting other, and implies power over others.
   b. **PARTICIPATIVE** or **DEMOCRATIC LEADERSHIP** consists of managers and employees working together to make decisions.
   c. **LAISSEZ-FAIRE** or **FREE-REIN LEADERSHIP** involves managers setting objectives and employees being relatively free to do whatever it takes to accomplish those objectives.
   d. Individual leaders rarely fit neatly into just one category.
3. **WHEN TO USE VARIOUS LEADERSHIP STYLES.**
   a. The best leadership style to use depends on **WHO IS BEING LED AND IN WHAT SITUATIONS.**
   b. Any **ONE MANAGER CAN USE A VARIETY OF LEADERSHIP STYLES** depending

Lecture Notes

CRITICAL THINKING EXERCISE 7-2
Leadership Styles

See complete exercise on page 7.72.

TRANSPARENCY MASTER 54
Various Leadership Styles
(Figure 7.6 on text page 214)

Transparency masters begin on page 7.80.

OT ACETATE 7-5
Manager's Empowerment Checklist

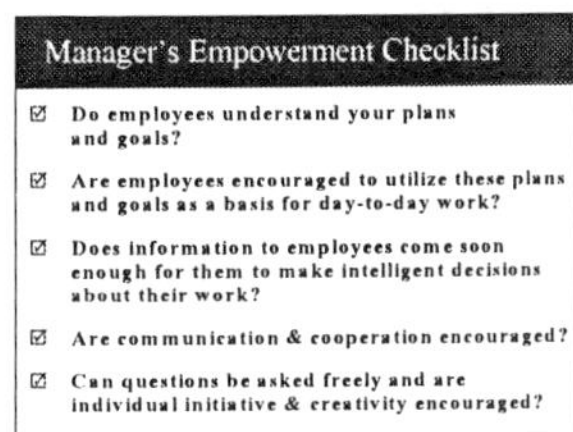

Comments:

1. Empowerment is a key term for managers and non-managerial employees to remember today. As workers become better educated and able to use modern technology, it is likely organizations will rely less and less on managers and more on the workers themselves. This acetate provides a clear step-by-step path to effectively empowering employees.
2. It may be interesting to question students concerning managers they have worked under. Did the manager "empower" them in performing their job? Could they have performed the job better if the manager had empowered them? How could the organization have helped the manager in his/her job?
3. A very relevant question to pose to students came from one of our textbook users in Florida. She said to question students if their college empowered them? An interesting thought to explore.

OT ACETATE 7-6 and **OT ACETATE 7-7**
Take the Empowerment Quiz

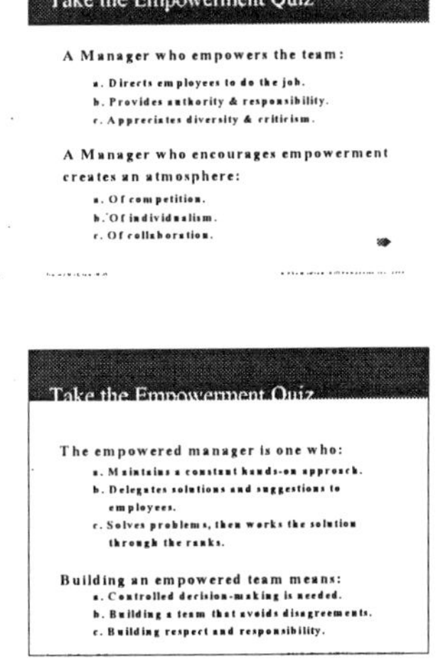

Comments:

1. This acetate tests student's knowledge of empowerment by using four short multiple choice questions. Students should answer these questions openly and honestly.
2. The answers to the empowerment quiz are as follows:

   B

   C

   B

   C
3. The key points to focus on in the acetate quiz are responsibility, collaboration, decision-making, and respect.

on whom he or she is dealing with and the situation.

E. **THE TREND TOWARD SELF-MANAGED TEAMS.**

1. The trend in the United States is toward self-managed teams and away from management, with its emphasis on planning, organizing, directing, and controlling.
2. More planning, organizing, and controlling is being delegated to lower-level managers.
3. This means that the trend will continue away from autocratic leadership toward laissez-faire leadership.
4. It also means developing and training employees to assume greater responsibility.

F. **LEADERSHIP TEAMS.**

1. Intensified competition and globalization are making the present style of leadership obsolete.
2. According to one study, within ten years only 14% of companies will be run by one leader—the majority will be run by **TEAMS OF LEADERS.**

LECTURE ENHANCER 7-8
A Manager's Expectations: The Self-Fulfilling Prophecy

Supervisors may have an extraordinary influence on employees—an effect they may be often unaware of. Psychologists have demonstrated that the power of one's expectations alone can influence the behavior of others. This phenomenon has been called the "self-fulfilling prophesy": people sometimes become what others expect them to become. (See complete lecture enhancer on page 7.61.)

From the Pages of BusinessWeek
(Box in Text, page 216)
"Teaming from Anywhere"

The trend toward teams has led companies to completely alter their office arrangements so that individuals can have separate offices and still meet in teams when needed.

PROGRESS CHECK
(page 216 in text)

- What are some characteristics of leadership today that make leaders different from traditional managers?
- Explain the differences between autocratic and democratic leadership styles.
- What is a self-managed team and how does it operate?

CRITICAL THINKING
(page 216 in text)

Do you see any problems with a democratic managerial style? Can you see a manager getting frustrated when he or she can't be bossy? Can someone who's trained to give orders (for example, a military sergeant) be retrained to be a democratic manager? What problems may emerge? What kind of boss would you be? Do you have evidence to show that?

Lecture Outline

VI. TASKS AND SKILLS AT DIFFERENT LEVELS OF MANAGEMENT.

▶ **LEARNING GOAL 6.** Describe the three general categories of skills needed by top, middle, and first-line managers.

A. The further up the managerial ladder a person moves, the greater the need for people who are visionaries, good planners, organizers, coordinators, communicators, morale builders, and motivators.

B. Managers must have **THREE CATEGORIES OF SKILLS:**

1. **TECHNICAL SKILLS** involve the ability to perform tasks of a specific department such as selling (marketing) or bookkeeping (accounting).

2. **CONCEPTUAL SKILLS** refer to a manager's ability to picture the organization as a whole and the relationship of various parts to perform tasks such as planning, organizing, controlling, systems development, problem-analysis, decision-making, coordinating, and delegating.

3. **HUMAN RELATIONS SKILLS** include leadership, motivation, coaching, communication, morale-building, training and development, help and supportiveness, and delegating.

Lecture Notes

Lecture Outline

4. **FIRST-LEVEL MANAGERS** need **MORE TECHNICAL AND HUMAN RELATIONS SKILLS**; whereas, **TOP MANAGERS**, need **FEW TECHNICAL SKILLS AND GREATER CONCEPTUAL SKILLS**.

C. **DELEGATING: BECOMING A TEAM LEADER.**

1. The most difficult task for most managers to learn is **DELEGATING**, assigning authority and accountability to others while retaining responsibility for results.

2. **TO DELEGATE EFFECTIVELY, A MANAGER MUST:**

   a. **SELECT THE APPROPRIATE PERSON TO DO THE JOB.**

   b. **ASSIGN THE TASK.**

   c. **GIVE THE AUTHORITY TO COMPLETE THE JOB.**

   d. **MAKE THOSE PEOPLE WHO ASSUME THE TASK RESPONSIBLE FOR GETTING IT COMPLETED ON TIME.**

3. Most progressive managers of the 21st century will be team leaders.

   a. They will set specific goals in cooperation with teams of workers and set up feedback and communication procedures.

TRANSPARENCY MASTER 55
Skills Needed at Various Levels of Management
(Figure 7.8 on text page 217)

TM 55

Transparency masters begin on page 7.80.

Lecture Outline

b. Employees will be given the freedom to decide how to complete specific tasks.

D. **DECISION MAKING: FINDING THE BEST ETHICAL ALTERNATIVE.**

1. **DEFINE THE PROBLEM.**
2. **DESCRIBE AND COLLECT NEEDED INFORMATION.**
3. **DEVELOP ALTERNATIVES.**
4. **DECIDE WHICH ALTERNATIVE IS BEST.**
5. **DEVELOP AGREEMENT AMONG THOSE INVOLVED.**
6. **DO WHAT IS INDICATED.**
7. **DETERMINE WHETHER THE DECISION WAS A GOOD ONE AND FOLLOW UP.**

VII. LEARNING MANAGERIAL SKILLS.

▶ **LEARNING GOAL 7.** Illustrate the skills aspiring managers need to develop to be successful in the future.

A. In all managerial jobs, oral communication, writing, computers, and human relations, are the skills in greatest demand.

B. **VERBAL SKILLS.**

1. The majority of a manager's job involves **COMMUNICATING**: talking, conducting meetings, making presentations, etc.

LECTURE ENHANCER 7-9
World Class Bad Decisions

In the Decision Making Hall of Fame, one room should be reserved for truly bad decisions. (See complete lecture enhancer on page 7.63.)

TRANSPARENCY MASTER 56
The Decision-Making Process
(Figure 7.9 on text page 219)

Transparency masters begin on page 7.80.

LECTURE ENHANCER 7-10
Problem Solving for Decision Makers

In the age of teams, managers don't solve problems alone. They must operate from a business discipline that will enable a group of workers to frame a problem and agree on the most efficient way to solve it. (See complete lecture enhancer on page 7.64.)

Lecture Outline

2. One of the most important parts of communicating is **LISTENING.**

C. **WRITING SKILLS.**

1. Managers must communicate through memos, reports, letters, etc. To learn to write, you must practice writing.

2. Today most E-mail and fax messages are set by the managers themselves.

3. **GOOD WRITING SKILLS** are becoming increasingly important.

D. **COMPUTER SKILLS.**

1. Computers are as much a part of modern offices as typewriters were twenty years ago.

2. The efficient manager must be able to **SURF THE INTERNET** to find needed facts and figures quickly.

E. **HUMAN RELATIONS SKILLS**.

1. Managers must not only get along with people, they must inspire and motivate them. Assume leadership positions in campus groups to gain experience.

2. Managers have to know how to deal effectively with people from many different cultures.

F. **MANAGING DIVERSITY.**

Lecture Notes

TRANSPARENCY MASTER 57
Evaluating Your Management Potential
(Figure 7.10 on text page 220)

Transparency masters begin on page 7.80.

OT ACETATE 7-8
Required Skills of a "Quality" Manager

Comments:

1. This acetate lists three skills for the quality manager of the new millennium. The inventory of these skills includes three key factors:
   - **Interpersonal skills** - the ability to communicate, be a good listener, diplomat, and be believable and sincere with workers.
   - **Management skills** - the ability to handle administrative tasks and responsibilities, coach employees, and motivate the workers.
   - **Change agent skills** - the ability to facilitate change within the organization, resolve any conflicts, sell new concepts and ideas to workers.
2. Managers in the contemporary organization need qualities different from past managerial requirements. This acetate helps to identify characteristics of innovative managers.
3. It's helpful to point out to students that flexibility in the work place is not a way to pacify or accommodate disgruntled employees, it's a competitive advantage. Remember, the key to empowering employees is to free them to perform at their full potential. The next acetate provides an empowerment checklist that managers can use.
4. Managers must also remember that serious challenges face employees in meeting obligations to work and family. As the text noted in previous chapters, we have experienced a significant growth in the number of single person households and dual-income families. The added responsibility the average worker takes on today makes finding a workable balance between work and family all the more critical. Managers must be innovative in recognizing and implementing a reasonable balance between work and family.

Lecture Outline

1. **MANAGING DIVERSITY** means building systems and a culture that unites different people in a common pursuit without undermining their diversity.

2. If people are to work on teams, they have to **LEARN TO DEAL WITH PEOPLE WHO HAVE DIFFERENT PERSONALITIES, PRIORITIES, AND LIFESTYLES.**

3. **HETEROGENEOUS (MIXED) GROUPS** are more productive than **HOMOGENOUS (SIMILAR) GROUPS** in the workplace.

4. It is often quite profitable to have employees who match the diversity of customers.

G. **TIME MANAGEMENT SKILLS**.

1. Managers must learn to control the many demands made upon their time.

2. Time management skills learned now will help increase productivity at school and home as well as on the job.

H. **TECHNICAL SKILLS.**

1. You must choose some area of specialization.

2. The most common areas among top managers are marketing, finance, production, law, and engineering.

Lecture Notes

LECTURE ENHANCER 7-11
Why Good Employees Can Be Bad Managers

You have a good employee, a hard worker, technically proficient. You promote him and it turns out to be a bad decision. You have promoted your best technical employee, and in the process, lose a good employee and gain a poor manager. How does this happen? (See complete lecture enhancer on page 7.67.)

LECTURE ENHANCER 7-12
Time Management Tips

Entrepreneur magazine asked a group of businesspeople to divulge some of their favorite techniques for managing time. (See complete lecture enhancer on page 7.68.)

LECTURE ENHANCER 7-13
Leadership Advantage: A Boss With Daughters

Looking for a male boss who wants to promote women? See if he has a daughter. (See complete lecture enhancer on page 7.69.)

OT ACETATE 7-9
Tips for the New Manager

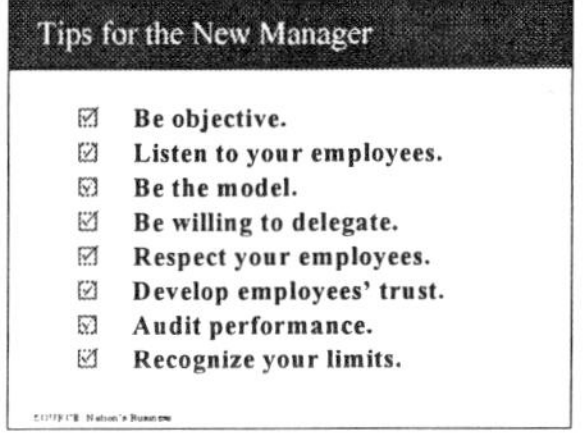

Comments:

1. New managers are often in need of a tip sheet on how to perform their new tasks. This acetate offers ten steps that can assist the new manager in his/her job.
2. It's important to point out to students such important factors as listening, delegating, and appraising performance, in dealing with employees. These are all covered in the sections on management and human resource management. However, the new manager must remember that personally they have to keep a close watch on such things as being a role model for employees, being objective, and recognizing their own limitations.
3. It's also critical for many new managers to be able to deal effectively in a team setting. Self-managed teams are being adapted at many organizations. As managers empower employees through self-managed, cross-functional teams, the role and responsibility of managers takes on new perspectives.

Lecture Outline

VIII. MANAGERS AND LEADERS ARE NEEDED EVERYWHERE.

A. Studying management and leadership prepared people for a career in any organization.

B. When selecting a career in management, a student has several decisions to make:

1. What kind of organization is most desirable?
2. What type of managerial position seems most interesting?
3. What type of industry is most appealing?

IX. SUMMARY AND REVIEW.

Lecture Notes

OT ACETATE 7-10
Key Management Challenges in the Future

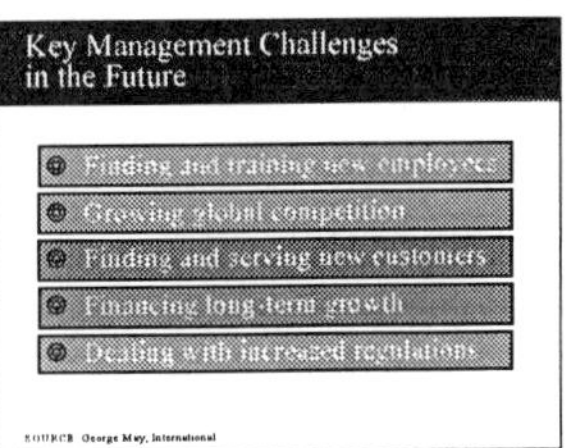

Comments:

1. This last acetate for the chapter sums up relevant challenges managers will face in the future. Expectations are these challenges will last well into the new millennium.
2. Ask students which of the five challenges facing management is the most crucial. Make sure students can defend their choice.
3. See how students feel about a career in management after discussing this acetate. The next several chapters deal specifically with developing management skills.

LECTURE ENHANCER 7-14
Management Lessons from Revolutionary Companies

Revolutionary companies don't just adjust to a changing world with evolutionary adaptations. When the business world shakes things up, revolutionary companies shake it up right back with their own shape on circumstances. (See complete lecture enhancer on page 7.70.)

CRITICAL THINKING
(page 222 in text)

What kind of management are you best suited for: human resource, marketing, finance, accounting, production, credit, or what? Why do you feel this area is most appropriate? Would you like to work for a large firm or a small business? Private or government? In an office or out in the field? Would you like being a manager? If you aren't sure, read on and see what's involved.

PROGRESS CHECK
(page 222 in text)

- Which managerial skills are used more by supervisors than by top managers and vice versa?
- What are the seven Ds of decision making?

Answers to Practicing Management Decisions

CASE ONE

MARKET-BASED MANAGEMENT AT KOCH INDUSTRIES

1. *Giving employees the freedom to own their own jobs creates all kinds of incentives for the employee to work hard as long as the rewards match the effort. What is your reaction to paying employees based on their output rather than their job assignment? That is, an employee could assume many jobs or work with many people as will cooperate with them to make as large a contribution as possible to the firm.*

The advantages for the employees, clearly, are many. They can do more things, make more money, and have more fun. By working hard, you can make more. The problem is that employees are not all the same. Some don't like to work so hard and put pressure on others not to work too hard and make them look bad. But if all workers are motivated and willing, paying them by output results in more output, happier workers, and more profit. You have to be careful that people don't overwork and get burnout, however.

2. *Under communist economies, there is a saying, "We pretend to work and they pretend to pay us." This means that workers in such societies do not put forth their best effort and are not paid well either. Do you believe that most workers would work harder and better if given more freedom and if they were paid according to what they produce rather than what their job description was?*

Experience in many businesses has shown that workers will work harder when they are paid by what they produce. Many field workers are paid that way, and they work from early morning to late at night trying to make as much as possible. Obviously, therefore, the system can be abused, but many companies motivate employees this way and everyone benefits.

3. *The University of Virginia has a program for selected students that has no majors and no requirements. Each student in the program is free to choose his or her own curriculum. What would prevent the University from giving the same freedom to all students? What would be the advantages and disadvantages for both students and the University?*

Many students have no idea what they want or need to take in college. Others tend to choose the courses that are easiest. But some students prosper under a program where they can choose their own courses. The advantage to students is that they can focus on their careers and design curricula that will help them. For example, an English teacher can take many English courses and fewer math. Colleges tend to produce well-rounded graduates with less proficiency in any one area. This question tends to produce lots of reactions and comments. It would benefit many schools to have such a debate among top administrators.

4. *A "learning organization" is one where each employee is encouraged to seek more education and then share that learning with others so that changes can be made*

continuously. Do most managers seem to encourage or discourage such a procedure? Discuss.

Managers often discourage such a procedure because it leaves them out of the loop and, therefore, not as important. Today, however, managers are learning to empower employees to do all kinds of things, including educate themselves and others. The office of the future will be very different from the office of the past. There will be fewer managers with lots of education and employees with little. Instead, almost everyone will be highly educated, and managers will be more team members than bosses.

CASE TWO

VIDEO CASE: LOU GERSTNER AND THE IBM TURNAROUND

1. *To make IBM into a more responsive organization, Gerstner had to dismiss many long-term managers and employees. The corporate culture at IBM had been that no one was forced to leave. What can Gerstner to do maintain morale and motivation among the remaining managers and employees under the new culture where jobs are less secure?*

It will not be easy to maintain morale and motivation, especially among older workers who worry whether they are the next ones to be let go. Gerstner must maintain his open communications with these workers and show them that his vision will lead to the growth and profits that are necessary to preclude any more dismissals.

2. *What were some of the conditions at IBM before Gerstner took over that made management and leadership difficult?*

IBM was a huge corporation whose focus was on manufacturing and on tradition. The lack of a customer and stockholder focus was a disaster. IBM was also too big to be flexible and responsive to a rapidly changing marketplace. The company was divided into customer-oriented areas that were smaller, more self-directed, and profitable.

3. *IBM, like many other U.S. firms, is partnering with previous competitors to make the best products possible for consumers. What environmental circumstances led to such cooperation? Do you see any danger to the economy and competition from corporations getting bigger and bigger and uniting with other large corporations?*

The government is concerned that organizations like Microsoft have gotten so big and powerful that they are no longer maintaining a competitive atmosphere. This may or may not be true, but that belief will affect all companies as they merge and cooperate to take on world competition. The solution to the problem is for government and business leaders to open better communications and decide the best policies for the future. Usually that means minimal government interference.

Lecture Enhancers

LECTURE ENHANCER 7-1

THE MOTHER OF MANAGEMENT

Mary Parker Follett graduated from Thayer College and Radcliffe. While she was in college, Follett taught political science at a nearby secondary school. She was a part of Boston high society and participated on committees that set minimum wages for women and children. The management theorist of that time (the early 1900s) was Frederick Taylor, the "father of scientific management." His writings favored command-style, hierarchical organizations. Employees were treated much like robots or computers; things to be manipulated and directed. Taylor did not believe in participative management. Managers acted more like dictators.

Mary Parker Follett, on the other hand, believed very strongly that the person doing the lob was the person most likely to know how to do the lob better. She felt that it was human nature to want to be self-managed. Furthermore, Follett believed in the concept of cross-functional rather than vertical authority. Her idea was for people in various departments to share information with one another to the benefit of all.

Follett believed that managers should be leaders rather than dictators. They were to provide a "vision" and help focus all the resources of the firm on meeting that vision. Follett also felt that knowledge and experience, not titles and seniority, should decide who should lead.

Follett's concepts, written in the 1920s and 1930s, were way ahead of her time. She was relatively ignored while Frederick Taylor grew in importance. But times change and innovative ideas from the past suddenly take on new meaning. That is exactly what has happened to Follett's writings A new book titled *Mary Parker Follett-Prophet of Management: A Celebration of Writings* from the 1920s was recently released by the Harvard Business School Press (1995).

London School of Economics Chairman Sir Peter Parker says that he is not sure who the father of management is, but he is sure who the mother is: Mary Parker Follett. Her ideas about empowerment, self-management, cross-functional cooperation, and conflict resolution are now being implemented in leading firms throughout the world. In this chapter, we shall explore both traditional and new management concepts. Much of it is based on the fundamentals that Mary Parker Follett established 70 years ago.

LECTURE ENHANCER 7-2

THE FUNCTION OF A MANAGER

As nearly everyone knows, an executive has practically nothing to do except:

to decide what is to be done;

to tell somebody to do it;

to listen to reasons why it should not be done, why it should be done by someone else, or why it should be done in a different way;

to follow up to see if the thing has been done;

to discover that it has not;

to inquire why;

to listen to excuses from the person who should have done it;

to follow up again to see if the thing has been done, only to discover that it has been done incorrectly;

to point out how it should have been done;

to conclude that as long as it has been done, it may as well be left where it is;

to wonder if it is not time to get rid of a person who cannot do a thing right;

to reflect that he probably has a wife and a large family, and that certainly any successor would be just as bad, and maybe worse;

to consider how much simpler and better the thing would have been done if one had done it oneself in the first place;

to reflect sadly that one could have done it right in 20 minutes, and, as things turned out, one has had to spend two days to find out why it has taken three weeks for somebody else to do it wrong.

(Anonymous)

LECTURE ENHANCER 7-3

APPLE COMPUTER DEFINES ITSELF

The once mighty Apple Computers has fallen on rough times lately. The company started with products that had a huge technological lead over the competition. They were the first low-cost computers with built-in color, graphics, sound, and programming languages. Co-founders Steven Jobs and Steve Wozniak built a company that created the personal computer market. At its peak, Apple commanded over fifteen percent of the market.

By 1996, however, the company was in serious trouble. Its first quarter financial results showed huge losses ($69 million.) Its computers were outsold by Windows-based machines by nine to one. Steve Wozniak discussed what he thinks happened:

> "The computer was never the problem. The company's strategy was. Apple saw itself as a hardware company; in order to protect our hardware profits, we didn't license our operating system. We had the most beautiful operating system, but to get it you had to buy our hardware at twice the price. That was a mistake. What we should have done was calculate an appropriate price to license the operating system.
>
> "We were also naive to think that the best technology would prevail. It often doesn't."

LECTURE ENHANCER 7-4

PLANNING FAILURE

One side of planning that is rarely discussed is failure. Sometimes key components are unavailable. Sometimes competitors' reactions are grossly underestimated. Often a plan is undertaken based on assumptions that don't pan out—it could even be one single assumption.

An example: Gavilan Computer Company. Gavilan was founded in the early 1980s to develop a portable personal computer and raised $31.7 million to do so. But its executives couldn't convince Lotus Development Corp. to sell them the code that would allow Gavilan to run the popular Lotus 1-2-3 software program. Jan Lewis, former Gavilan vice president, explains. "It became evident that the benchmark (for success) would be whether a machine ran Lotus, and ours didn't. There were many, many visits to Lotus in Boston, begging and pleading for the code. We offered $1 million for it and were turned down. They never gave in and we never gave up. It was a desperate situation. We just clung to our dreams."

In 1984 Gavilan introduced the computer without Lotus. Only a few hundred sold and within months the company sank into bankruptcy proceedings. Its assets were sold at auction shortly after.

LECTURE ENHANCER 7-5

ATTRIBUTES OF EXCELLENT COMPANIES

In the 1980s, the most popular book on management was called *In Search of Excellence*. It was on the best-seller list for over a year. Clearly, managers saw in it some advice worth taking. The authors visited many of the top firms in the United States to find out what made them different, better than the other firms. They were searching for excellence. Their findings support what you have read in the text thus far. Basically, excellent organizations insisted on top quality. They cared for their customers. They listened to their employees and treated them like adults. They emphasized human creativity over analysis and high-tech tools. The eight attributes of successful firms were as follows:

1. **A bias for action**. "Do it, fix it, try it" was one slogan. The idea is to get on with it and not try to analyze decisions to death. If someone has a new idea, try it and see what happens. Remain flexible. "Ready. Fire. Aim. Learn from your tries. That's enough."
2. **Close to the customer.** Excellent companies listen to their customers intently and regularly. They then provide unparalleled quality, service, and reliability. "Probably the most important management function . . . is staying close to the customer to satisfy his needs and anticipate his wants." In this text, that was called "Find a need and fill it."
3. **Autonomy and entrepreneurship.** Excellent companies encourage risk taking and support good tries. "Make sure you generate a reasonable number of mistakes." The key to remaining competitive is innovation, and the way to assure innovation is to support the creative thinkers in the firm. "No support systems, no champions. No champions, no innovations."
4. **Productivity through people.** Basically, this was support for participative management. Treat employees like adults. Seek their input. Treat them as the primary source of productivity gains. "Many of the best companies really do view themselves as an extended family."
5. **Hands on, value driven.** A belief in doing the best, in the importance of details, in superior quality and service, in the importance of informality to enhance communication, and in economic growth and profits.
6. **Stick to your knitting.** Do what you are good at. That is, don't acquire businesses that you don't know how to run. Do one thing well rather than many things in a mediocre way.
7. **Simple form, lean staff.** Keep the organization form simple. Keep staff positions to a minimum. This is the KISS formula: Keep it simple, Sam!
8. **Simultaneous loose-tight properties.** Establish a strong corporate culture emphasizing quality, service, and excellence and then delegate authority to let the people do it.

Soon after the book came out, Tom Peters wrote a new book called *Thriving on Chaos*. It emphasized the point that there is no such thing as an excellent company—there are only companies that maintain their excellence by adapting quickly to market changes. The secret to staying excellent is to:

1. Become a niche-oriented market creator, finding new, small markets and meeting their needs with short production runs. This comes very close to making custom-designed products for individual buyers.
2. Change the structure of the organization to have fewer layers of management. This allows the firm to adapt to consumer needs more quickly.
3. Be responsive and adaptive and be fast in making such changes.
4. Be internationalist, even if you are a small firm. The big markets are in other countries.
5. Keep the organization small so it can be flexible and if the organization is large, keep individual units small and semiautonomous so they can be flexible and adapt quickly.
6. Involve employees in managerial decision making, and let them share in the profits.

LECTURE ENHANCER 7-6

SERVANT LEADERS

We've talked of visionary leaders who communicate their vision to his subordinates. Given the current changes in organizational structure, it may be time to come up with a more downsized, restructured concept of leadership. Actually the new concept of leadership isn't all that new. Twenty years ago Robert Greenleaf described the leadership style that is quietly working in some nonprofits and a few businesses across the country. He called it servant leadership. This combination of two opposites offers a new insight: the leader exists to serve those he leads, those who follow him. Their fulfillment is his aim. Some of the aspects of servant leaders include:

- **They take their subordinates and their work very, very seriously.** We're talking more than empowerment here. Servant leaders see human beings as having value in their own right, not just for the value they add to the organization. In their minds, the business exists as much to provide meaningful work for people as it exists to provide products and services to the customers.
- **They listen and then take their lead from the troops.** They figure out the will of the group, express that will, and then further it however they can.
- **They heal.** Servant leaders have an openness to share in mistakes and pain. Even though it sounds sappy, the hottest new management buzzword of restructuring companies is "grief work." That is, dealing with the rage, resentment, and fear among survivors.
- **They are self-effacing.** They don't draw a lot of attention or glorify leadership, that would be self-defeating.
- **They see themselves as stewards.** They must have a long-term perspective in order to be a steward of institutional vitality.

TD Industries, a $75-million-a-year mechanical contracting company has used servant leadership as the focal point of its supervisor training for twenty years. CEO Jack Lowe Jr, compares it to a different current management concept: "It sounds a little like the quality movement, doesn't it?"

LECTURE ENHANCER 7-7

COPING WITH AN INTOLERABLE BOSS

Millions of workers have them—intolerable bosses—variously described as Snakes in the Grass, Attilas, Heel-Grinders, Egotists, Dodgers, Business Incompetents, Detail Drones, Slobs, and the like. Some bosses were deemed doubly intolerable—Snake and Slob together. All these descriptions are based on interviews with successful executives of very large companies by researchers at the Center for Creative Leadership, a nonprofit research and executive training institution in Greensboro, N.C. Researchers Michael Lombardo and Morgan McCall, Jr. interviewed 73 managers as part of a study of how executives grow and change in their careers. Of the 73, only 19 said they had never worked for an intolerable boss.

"The most frequently mentioned failing in our catalogue of sins was lack of basic integrity," said the authors. Those with this failing they called Snakes, and ten of the executives said they had worked under them. The Snakes, said the authors, "lied, failed to keep their word, used their authority to extract confidential information, created compromising situations for their subordinates, or otherwise couldn't be trusted."

Dictators, nine of them, made up the next largest group of intolerables, variously described by executives as Little Napoleons, martinets, and ex-Marine types. For convenience, Lombardo and McCall call them Attilas. "They were both the easiest to spot and hardest to cope with," according to their report. "They simply sat on people." One executive related that his boss told him, "You have too much freedom and I will curtail it."

Heel-Grinders, of which there were eight, are described as having not even a modicum of human respect for those who report to them. Unforgiving and intolerant, they demean, humiliate, and emasculate. The authors called seven bosses Egotists "who already knew everything, wouldn't listen, and paraded their pomposity." Another seven rated the Dodger designation because they were unwilling or unable to make decisions.

"Just plain incompetent" was the tag awarded to six bosses who "didn't know what they were doing and apparently were afraid to admit it." Six more were found to be Detail Drones, who made big issues out of little ones. And finally, five Slobs were uncovered whose "personal habits, appearance, or prejudices were intolerable to others." One was a drunk, another slept on the job.

Still the underlings learned to cope and survive. Four of them finally quit. Some switched to other jobs within their companies. One man resigned and simultaneously reapplied to the same company, getting a new job and a better boss. Seven responded with outright defiance, openly resisting the boss. Some of this group simply "dealt him out—worked around him." In all seven instances they worked to remove the boss from his job, but succeeded only twice.

Whatever explains the behavior, say the authors, the rarity of open resistance reflects a theme in the interviews: "Even an intolerable boss is still the boss," and a majority of the executives kept right on working for him. A few of the managers tried to change the boss, but few succeeded. The more productive strategy, said the authors, was "to change one's own response or, as a last resort, to get out of the situation."

LECTURE ENHANCER 7-8

A MANAGER'S EXPECTATIONS: THE SELF-FULFILLING PROPHECY

Supervisors may have an extraordinary influence on employees—an effect they may be often unaware of. Psychologists have demonstrated that the power of one's expectations alone can influence the behavior of others. This phenomenon has been called the "self-fulfilling prophesy": people sometimes become what others expect them to become.

Expectations or assumptions are at the root of most business problems and successes. Some managers treat their employees in a way that leads to superior performance; others unintentionally treat their people in a way that leads to lower performance than the employees are capable of achieving. If a manager's expectations are high, productivity is likely to be excellent. If expectations are low, productivity is likely to be poor.

What managers expect of employees and the way managers treat them largely determines employees' performance and career progress. In other words, subordinates, more often than not, meet their superior's expectations. A unique characteristic of superior managers is their ability to create high performance expectations that subordinates fulfill.

Managers can communicate their expectations to employees in both verbal and non-verbal ways. Non-verbal messages are communicated unintentionally, making it impossible for managers to hide their expectations from their subordinates. For instance, their concern or lack of it can be shown in tone of voice, eye contact, physical touch, body posture, facial expressions, and other mannerisms. Non-verbal messages can hinder as well as help.

What seems to be important in the manager's communication with employees is not what the supervisor says as much as how he or she behaves. Indifferent and noncommittal treatment communicates low expectations and leads to poor performance.

Managers who expect good things from their employees and others appear to provide the following:

1. **Climate** The manager sets an accepting, encouraging social and emotional mood, or climate, for employees with more "potential." This includes warmth, attention, smiling, nodding the head appreciatively—all positive non-verbal messages.
2. **Feedback** The manager gives these employees more verbal clues about their performance, more reaction, more praise, and sometimes even more criticism—all of which help to teach the person what is needed for improvement.
3. **Input** The manager will literally teach a larger quantity of and more difficult material to employees who supposedly have more potential.
4. **Output** The manager encourages the chosen employees to ask more questions, urges them to respond to the manager's instructions,

allows more time to do a job correctly, and gives them the benefit of the doubt.

The employee also influences the manager by his or her own verbal and non-verbal messages. These, in turn, can lead to the manager's acting in such a way that the worker's own prophecy is fulfilled.

Young employees, or those who are new to their jobs, are most affected by the supervisor's expectations. From the moment they enter the organization, new employees are given cues about the quality of performance that is expected and rewarded. As outsiders, they are motivated to make sense out of the ambiguous surroundings and to be accepted by this new social system. They are more receptive to cues from their environment than they will ever be again.

A young person's first supervisor is likely to be the most influential person in his or her career. If this manager is unable or unwilling to help the young trainee develop skills necessary to perform effectively, the trainee will set lower standards than he or she is capable of achieving. The self-image will be impaired, negative attitudes will be developed, and performance will be less than desired. If, on the other hand, the supervisor helps the new employee to achieve maximum potential, that person will build the foundation for a successful career.

LECTURE ENHANCER 7-9

WORLD CLASS BAD DECISIONS

In the Decision Making Hall of Fame, one room should be reserved for truly bad decisions. One of the classics, already mentioned in an earlier chapter, was Hewlett-Packard's decision not to develop a product created by an employee: Steve Wozniak went off with his device to co-found Apple Computer.

Some rejected ideas have involved whole industries. When Alexander Graham Bell invented the telephone in 1876, he had a hard time attracting backers. President Rutherford B. Hayes used a prototype telephone and remarked "That's an amazing invention, but who would ever want to use one of them?" Bell approached Western Union Telegraph Company and offered to sell them the patents. Their decision: they had no use for an electrical toy.

A young inventor, Chester Carlson, took his idea to twenty corporations, all of whom turned him down. He finally got a small New York company named Haloid Co. to purchase the rights to his electrostatic paper-copying process. Haloid became Xerox Corporation, and Carlson's process made both Xerox and Carlson very rich.

In 1962 four musicians played for executives of Decca Recording Company. One executive later explained that they just didn't like the group's sound, noting that guitar groups were on their way out. Four other record companies turned them down. The Decision Making Hall of Fame will have a special place for Decca, which turned down the Beatles.

LECTURE ENHANCER 7-10

PROBLEM SOLVING FOR DECISION MAKERS

Suppose you're a brand manager in your company's gourmet snack foods division. After a number of successful years on the market, your sesame snack product has matured, and sales have begun to soften. A brand extension has been proposed. How do you decide if this is the right course of action?

Or perhaps you work for a computer superstore chain that wants to expand. You've been assigned the task of choosing where to locate new stores. Your team is generating lots of ideas for sites. How do you know when to call a halt to the research and select from among the various alternatives?

These situations underscore the extent to which solving problems is central to the work of the manager. And in the age of teams, managers don't solve problems alone. They must operate from a business discipline that will enable a group of workers to frame a problem and agree on the most efficient way to solve it. Yet as basic as this task is, many organizations don't solve problems using processes that result in optimal solutions. The signs of this are too much with us, from the frequent fizzling of comprehensive change-management efforts, to the stalling of "solutions" to more routine, business problems such as the creation and marketing of new products and the expansion of a brand or business.

Deficits in basic thinking skills are, in fact. felt at all levels of organizations. Chrysler, for example, has begun screening applicants for assembly-line jobs to see if they can demonstrate problem-solving skills. In the schools, the question "Why can't Johnny think?" has been added to the question "Why can't Johnny read?" Universities have been designing curricula to teach both basic and so-called higher-order thinking.

But companies can't wait for such reforms in education to percolate down into their work force. So what follows is a six-step guide for making basic business decisions, and some insights from a top tackler of management problems, General Electric.

The six-step model is taken from *Judgment in Managerial Decision Making* by Max Bazerman, J. Jay Gerber Distinguished Professor of Dispute Resolution and Organization at Northwestern's Kellogg Graduate School of Management. It is a "prescriptive" model in the sense that it lays out an optimal approach to making decisions in a fully rational manner. Of course, real-world decision making regularly falls short of this purely rational ideal. But given the fog that can cloud critical thinking and problem solving in the workplace, a refresher on (or introduction to) some ideal problem-solving methods can only help.

Define the Problem.

Defining, or framing, the problem is perhaps the most important step—if for no other reason than it's where most managers and teams first go astray. "We know less about problem definition than we do about decision-making errors and biases," acknowledges Bazerman. Nevertheless, there are some obvious mistakes that can be identified. For instance, defining the problem in terms of a proposed solution. In the gourmet brand example, focusing too quickly on the proposed brand extension can interfere with a more fundamental and broad-based analysis of the factors contributing to the brand's current health. Another example: diagnosing the problem in terms of its symptoms. Prematurely addressing the symptom of sluggish brand sales can lead to a misguided attempt to launch a new ad campaign. If the symptom is actually being caused by distribution snarls, those advertising dollars will be wasted. "So often we simply respond to the problems that come to us, when they aren't the right problems to be focusing on," cautions Bazerman. So don't let the symptoms or the proposed solution impede your effort to uncover the underlying problem.

Identify the Criteria.

Most managers need to accomplish more than one objective when making a decision. In the computer superstore situation, the choice of new store locations will depend upon such factors as cheap commercial rental space, the existence of an adequately trained labor pool, proximity to existing distribution centers, ease of access for customers, and market research about sales potential in a given city or neighborhood.

Weight the Criteria.

The relevant criteria will vary in importance, so once they have all been identified, they should be weighted—as signed a numerical value according to their relative importance. In the above example, if sales forecasts and rental costs are deemed five times more important than proximity to an existing distribution center, these differentials should be quantified by the numerical weight assigned to each criterion.

Generate Alternatives.

"An inappropriate amount of search time is often spent seeking alternatives," writes Bazerman. "An optimal search continues only until the cost of search outweighs the value of the added information." Sometimes, of course, you can't know the value of the added information until after the fact; that is, until after it's been collected and analyzed. Still, your search for alternatives should be guided by the relative weights you've assigned to the relevant criteria. Returning to the superstore location, for example, allocate your time so that you're concentrating on alternatives that maximize sales potential and minimize rental costs.

Rate Each Alternative on Each Criterion.

Determining how well each alternative solution satisfies each of the identified criteria usually involves forecasting future conditions, nèver an easy prospect. But in this purely rational model, the potential consequences of choosing each possible alternative are carefully assessed and assigned a numerical value.

Compute the Optimal Decision.

If the first five steps have been done right. this last one is a straightforward matter. For each alternative, multiply the expected effectiveness of the alternative for each criterion by the weight assigned to each criterion. Adding up the totals for each criterion yields an overall score for the alternative. The alternative with the highest score is the rational choice.

Problem Solving for Teams.

We've described a six-step model for individual decision making, but it's perfectly appropriate for teams as well, notes Bazerman, with some modifications. For example, he explains "In a group setting you often have multiple definitions of the problem. Even though it may require spending more time on this step, it's important to agree on the problem definition before trying to generate alternatives." Moreover, a political dimension enters into the team context in a much more forceful way: Skillful political operators often try to manipulate the agenda by the way they frame a problem. Weighing the evidence for a particular problem definition—assessing it in light of the perspective of and potential benefit to the person offering the definition—thus takes on added importance.

Implementation and evaluation procedures become more crucial in a team context as well. "All the problem-solving approaches we use end up with these two components," says Steve Mercer, manager of executive education at General Electric's offices in Crotonville, New York. He outlines one approach that includes defining the problem, initiating immediate action to contain the problem (or minimize its harm) while its causes are being studied, verifying the cause of the problem, verifying the corrective action necessary, implementing the corrective action, and then doubling back to ensure that the problem doesn't occur again.

GE is adamantly opposed to the notion that one approach to problem solving will fit all situations, Mercer says. "At the corporate level, we try to avoid edicting processes to our constituent businesses, because then you create clones. A process that works for one of our manufacturing businesses may not be the best one for GE Capital. So we may expose people to five or six different approaches to problem solving in our executive education classes, but we don't promote any one particular model. Rather, we delegate the problem- solving courses to the training and development departments of the respective businesses. We tell each department to come up with the processes that make the most sense for its business."

In the real world of managerial decision making, where (research indicates) the average manager engages in a different activity every nine minutes, managers seldom have the luxury of the time it takes for such careful processes. Nobel laureate Herbert Simon has shown that in such settings purely rational judgment is "bounded" by time and cost constraints that limit the quality and quantity of available information, and also by the misperceptions and motivational biases to which decision makers fall prey. In other words, instead of making the optimal decisions prescribed by the rational model, managers "satisfice." As Bazerman writes, "They search until they find a solution that meets a certain acceptable level of performance."

In the real world, managers must make decisions amid uncertainty and the ever-pressing demands of time and tasks. The purely rational, prescriptive approach to decision making outlined here can, however, provide a framework for understanding how judgment can be optimized, when we have the will, and the time.

LECTURE ENHANCER 7-11

WHY GOOD EMPLOYEES CAN BE BAD MANAGERS

You have a good employee, a hard worker, technically proficient. You promote him and it turns out to be a bad decision. You have promoted your best technical employee, and in the process, lose a good employee and gain a poor manager. How does this happen? Good technical employees can make good managers, of course, but many do not. Good technical specialists—engineers, accountants, computer gurus, financial analysts, statistical experts—are more likely to have introvert personalities. Introverts prefer to work alone. They revel in painstaking details, meaningful paperwork, tedious activities, precision. They can focus for hours on extracting meaningful data from mounds of information. The presence of ambiguity and clutter motivates them to find the "perfect solution."

The traits that make technical experts successful actually get in the way of managing others. The world of the worker encourages them to seek precision and order. By contract, the management role is messy, complicated, and ambiguous. Additionally, the sense of pride and reward for completing a task is missing.

Relationship complexities are more dynamic than task complexities. Management analysis must account for distasteful political elements, egos, pride, insecurities, envy, hurt feelings, and petty conflicts.

To make the successful transition to leadership, technical experts learn to rely more upon their instincts, insights, intuitions, tolerance for human equations, underlying values, and their "feel" for things. Rational analysis is still important; it just is not sufficient.

LECTURE ENHANCER 7-12

TIME MANAGEMENT TIPS

Entrepreneur magazine asked a group of businesspeople to divulge some of their favorite techniques for managing time. Here are a few of their comments:

- **Keep an appointment book—the two-page type**. Write all your incoming calls on one side so you can follow-up without worrying that things fell through the cracks.
- **Keep a "to do" list.** If tomorrow's list is longer than a few lines, you're operating on the "hope" method. That is, "I hope I get it done."
- **Constantly reassess your priorities.** The key is to realize that you're never going to get everything done that you want to get done. Just keep writing off things at the bottom of the list until you can write the list off altogether.
- **Get the critical things done.** Don't step over a dollar to get to a nickel. You can get A, B, and C done when it would have been better to finish D.
- **Delegate**. Get rid of things that other people can do for you.
- **Manage phone calls.** Learn to cut off calls without alienating callers. Only return those calls in which you are truly interested in what the callers have to say.
- **Plan your time, but leave time open for opportunistic objectives**. Things change. Make sure your calendar isn't too full to take advantage of new opportunities.
- **Carry a tape recorder** to record fleeting thoughts that could be gone in two traffic lights.
- **Set aside an hour a day for your own personal time** to replenish your mind and body. It will help keep you from burning out and make you able to tackle the other tasks that demand your time.

LECTURE ENHANCER 7-13

LEADERSHIP ADVANTAGE: A BOSS WITH DAUGHTERS

Looking for a male boss who wants to promote women? See if he has a daughter. "In the very early days," says Felice Schwartz, founder of Catalyst, a research firm that promotes women in business, "I used to feel way ahead if I saw a couple of pictures of daughters on a [chief executive's] desk." Now, she says, it can be even more meaningful, because grown daughters of a man in his 50s are likely to be pursuing careers. Having daughters is a "sensitizer," says Ms. Schwartz, "He gets intimate exposure, [learning] that women [in business] experience more stress and why."

American Brands Chairman William Alley was recently honored by the National Women's Economic Alliance for his corporate support of women. He gives some of the credit to his four daughters, who have called him with such questions as: "I'm working as hard as he is and making less. What do I do?" In his own dealings with women employees, Mr. Alley often asks himself, "Now how would I want her treated if she were my daughter?"

LECTURE ENHANCER 7-14

MANAGEMENT LESSONS FROM REVOLUTIONARY COMPANIES

Revolutionary companies don't just adjust to a changing world with evolutionary adaptations. When the business world shakes things up, revolutionary companies shake it up right back with their own shape on circumstances. They seem to rewrite the rules. Fortune looked at five of these companies to see what they had in common and here is what they came up with:

- Revolutionary companies are very sensitive to the technological or market forces that create change. They don't just listen to what the customers say they want today. They figure out what they will need tomorrow.
- They have a clear mission defined by the top brass. They know what they are trying to do and which activities will fit their strategic focus and which will not.
- They use computer technology, but don't go on technology binges and buy a bunch of gizmos with an undefined hope that they will make the company high-tech.
- Their organization is dedicated to accomplishing their sharply focused goals. Getting It Done is more important than Following The System.
- They encourage teamwork, while they promote individual enterprise.
- They emphasize the importance of their organizational culture: the shared outlook that gets them to achieve.
- They are in partnership with their customers and make it their business to know the customers as well as they know themselves. They stress the importance of service.

Critical Thinking Exercises

Name: ______________________

Date: ______________________

CRITICAL THINKING EXERCISE 7-1

MANAGEMENT FUNCTIONS

Remember the four management functions? They are: planning, organizing, controlling, and directing. Think of a job you have now or one you've had in the past. List the managerial activities you have done or observed. If you have never had a paid job remember it takes management skills to manage a home, run a baseball team, and lead a church group. Classify each activity of your job according to whether it involved planning, organizing, directing, or controlling.

PLANNING	ORGANIZING	LEADING	CONTROLLING

Name: ____________________

Date: ____________________

CRITICAL THINKING EXERCISE 7-2

LEADERSHIP STYLES

Congratulations! You have just been made manager of Fred Fiedler's Fantasy Haven, a specialty candy store. The text tells us that any manager can have a variety of leadership styles. The appropriate style to use depends on whom is being led and the specific situation. Consider each of the following employees and situations. Which leadership style will you use? (Remember the leadership styles are: autocratic, democratic, and laissez-faire.) Give the rationale for your choice.

1. Pops Sickle has worked at Fred Fiedler's Fantasy Haven since it opened 37 years ago. Even though Pops can handle anything that comes up in the store, he continuously passed up the chance to be manager because he doesn't want the responsibility. Everyone else is out sick today so you and Pops are the only ones able to cover the store during the Valentine's Day rush. What leadership style will you use? Why?

2. Randy Rancid is doing a rotten job! He's gotten the chocolate-covered caramels stuck in with the soft creams for the fifth time this week. Your older customers are not amused. Randy has been with the store three years and was hoping to get the manager's post. Randy has a new idea for developing a line of flavored popcorn. What leadership style will you use with Randy? Why?

3. Bubbles Gumm is about to blow it! This is Bubbles' first job and she's a little nervous. She doesn't know a cashew from a hazelnut and panics when a customer asks for the All-American Triple Decker Hot Fudge Sundae. You don't want to chew Bubbles out, so what leadership style will you use with Bubbles? Why?

ANSWERS TO CRITICAL THINKING EXERCISE 7-2

1. *Pops Sickle has worked at Fred Fiedler's Fantasy Haven since it opened 37 years ago. Even though Pops can handle anything that comes up in the store, he continuously passed up the chance to be manager because he doesn't want the responsibility. Everyone else is out sick today so you and Pops are the only ones able to cover the store during the Valentine's Day rush. What leadership style will you use? Why?*

We would probably use a democratic management style in this situation. Do you agree? The reason for such a style is that the man is quite capable of managing on his own, but does not feel comfortable doing so. A democratic style enables him to work with you, asking questions, and generally feeling part of a team. He probably doesn't need the rules and regulations of a bureaucratic style because he knows them all by now, and he doesn't need to be bossed around as often happens in an autocratic style.

2. *Randy Rancid is doing a rotten job! He's gotten the chocolate-covered caramels stuck in with the soft creams for the fifth time this week. Your older customers are not amused. Randy has been with the store three years and was hoping to get the manager's post. Randy has a new idea for developing a line of flavored popcorn. What leadership style will you use with Randy? Why?*

We know you are tempted to use an autocratic style in this situation, but obviously such a style has not been successful in the past. It usually is not in such situations. It is probably best to sit down with Randy and discuss the problem and then listen to his ideas. He may become much more motivated under a democratic system where he feels he has some input. If that doesn't work out, Randy may have to find work elsewhere.

3. *Bubbles Gumm is about to blow it! This is Bubbles' first job and she's a little nervous. She doesn't know a cashew from a hazelnut and panics when a customer asks for the All-American Triple Decker Hot Fudge Sundae. You don't want to chew Bubbles out, so what leadership style will you use with Bubbles? Why?*

It is clear that Bubbles needs some guidance here, but not just bossing around. She needs rules and regulations to follow. She needs to feel comfortable with procedures. That calls for an autocratic style of management where everything is laid out for Bubbles to do. Later she may move up to the place where a more democratic style is called for. Do you agree? Why or why not?

Supplemental Cases

CASE 7-1

CHANGING THE PARADIGM

Noel Tichy, a business professor at the University of Michigan, advises you not to try this at home. Consider the two ways to boil a live frog. The first way is to drop little Kermit into boiling water. He'll hop right out according to those acquainted with the classic physiological phenomenon. But try placing Kermit in a pot of cold water and gradually raising the temperature. He'll sit there and boil to death. This is meant to be a parable for business leadership in the 1990s, not a lesson in animal torture. Kermit failed to adjust to a shifting paradigm. He ignored a critical, though gradual, change in his environment. Before coming to a full boil, he should have remembered the words of American patriot Thomas Paine, "A long habit of not thinking a thing wrong gives it the superficial appearance of being right."

Used in business, the word paradigm (pronounced as in "Brother, can you paradigm?") simply refers to the accepted view of how things have always been done and should continue to be done. A paradigm shifter is someone who throws out the rules of the game and starts radical change. Tichy, who worked with General Electric's ultimate paradigm shifter, Jack Welch, adds, "It's not just quantum ideas, but the guts to stick with them. In industry after industry, a lot of frogs are waking up and finding it's too late to jump. Banking is there. Auto has had two chances and may not get a third. And now the computer industry is feeling the heat."

Jack Welch's restructuring of GE meant far fewer middle managers and more power to those who remained. John Trani (the Welch lieutenant who overhauled and runs GE Medical Systems) says, "People come to me and ask, 'Why was I good enough yesterday, but not today?' It's simple. In 1954, Roger Bannister won world acclaim for breaking 'the four-minute mile. Today high schoolers can do that. The standard is always changing, but there's always a top 10 and a bottom 10." As a matter of policy, Welch demands that all GE businesses be number one or number two in their industry.

DISCUSSION QUESTIONS FOR CASE 7-1:

1. How is the business environment changing from what it was 10 or 20 years ago? What can managers do to adapt to these changes?

2. Noel Tichy suggests that companies that don't adjust to shifting paradigms face death. As an example, he points to buggy makers who turned up their noses at Henry Ford's smelly exhaust. Can you think of other victims of shifting paradigms?

3. Experts say that in order for a paradigm shift to occur within a corporation, top management has to have a strong commitment to change. Says Ram Charan, a consultant to many Fortune 500 companies, "There has to be divine discontent within the status quo at the very top, and courage to do something about it." Explain why commitment to change on the part of top management is crucial to change within a corporation.

ANSWERS TO DISCUSSION QUESTIONS FOR CASE 7-1:

1. *How is the business environment changing from what it was 10 or 20 years ago? What can managers do to adapt to these changes?*

The most significant change in the business environment is new competition from overseas. First the Japanese took away much of our TV, VCR, steel, and electronics industries. Now the Germans are threatening to do the same with other industries. The new European Community (EC) has ISO 9000 standards that are based on total quality management, meaning total customer satisfaction. Managers can prepare for these changes by restructuring to eliminate many middle managers (bureaucracy). They can also empower employees to be more responsive to customers. Managers must create the vision a world class competitor. Management must also set the corporate culture—hard working but friendly; quality oriented and flexible; and willing to adapt to change as needed (good listening skills). The old management principles simply won't work in tomorrow's competitive environment.

2. *Noel Tichy suggests that companies that don't adjust to shifting paradigms face death. As an example, he points to buggy makers who turned up their noses at Henry Ford's smelly exhaust. Can you think of other victims of shifting paradigms?*

Steel industry leaders who didn't incorporate the latest equipment, auto makers who didn't adopt total quality until late in the game, electronic manufacturers who wouldn't risk trying the latest things (e.g., VCRs, Handycams), elementary schools who haven't adopted the latest teaching technology and now may lose to private schools, the health care insurance system that may lose out to national health care, and more. Your students will have fun with this one.

3. *Experts say that in order for a paradigm shift to occur within a corporation, top management has to have a strong commitment to change. Says Ram Charan, a consultant to many Fortune 500 companies, "There has to be divine discontent within the status quo at the very top, and courage to do something about it." Explain why commitment to change on the part of top management is crucial to change within a corporation.*

It is nearly impossible for someone at a lower-level position in a firm to attempt radical change without the blessing of top management. Radical change takes time, money, and commitment. Only top management can convince lower-level managers to help create self-managed teams, cross-functional teams, and other restructuring changes that will ultimately result in the loss of many managerial jobs.

CASE 7-2
TEAM CONCEPTS IN A SMALL SERVICE FIRM

Litel Communications is a Columbus, Ohio communications firm. Order time for a new service was taking 14 days. Management decided to adopt the idea of work teams to restructure the firm. As a consequence the order time was cut from 14 days to one day. The old process was to have a salesperson take the order on a form, have someone else keyboard the form into a computer, and someone else check the credit application, all from different departments. The new process is to bring people from all the departments together into a cross-functional team to shepherd applications through. The team is responsible for the process from start to finish. Both speed and quality were improved as a result.

Teamwork has made working at Litel more interesting because everyone is trained to do all the jobs on the team. Furthermore, compensation is tied to the success of the team, not to individual accomplishment. Therefore, everyone learns to work as a team member. The only people to lose out are middle managers. The teams are self-managed, so there is little need for middle managers.

Middle managers are still needed to train the workers, to motivate them, to support them with needed technology and other materials, and to coach them when needed.

DISCUSSION QUESTIONS FOR CASE 7-2:

1. Self-managed teams still need the support of managers because they need training, coaching, and support. Can you see, then, why GE and other companies have workers grade management performance? How do you think traditional managers will react to having employees grade them rather than the other way around?

2. How long will service firms be able to say in their ads, "Allow six weeks for delivery," when self-managed teams are cutting such turnaround times to two days or less?

3. What are some of the consequences of self-managed teams for business school students studying to be managers?

4. How would you react to being paid as a member of a team rather than for your individual accomplishments? Would you be inclined to work harder or less hard as a result?

ANSWERS TO DISCUSSION QUESTIONS FOR CASE 7-2:

1. *Self-managed teams still need the support of managers because they need training, coaching, and support. Can you see, then, why GE and other companies have workers grade management performance? How do you think traditional managers will react to having employees grade them rather than the other way around?*

Traditional managers of the old school will resist being evaluated by employees. Younger, more progressive managers should have fewer problems with the concept. In order for the self-managed team concept to work, there must be support from top management and adequate training for everyone, including managers, to be able to handle their new roles.

2. *How long will service firms be able to say in their ads, "Allow six weeks for delivery," when self-managed teams are cutting such turnaround times to two days or less?*

This concept is already eroding. Most mail order firms now have on-line computer systems so that a telephone order can be filled immediately. Next day delivery is routinely offered through Federal Express or UPS. In order to stay competitive, service firms will have to shorten their delivery time. Those that don't will soon be out of business.

3. *What are some of the consequences of self-managed teams for business school students studying to be managers?*

The traditional business school education stresses individual decision making, often referred to as the "lone ranger" approach to management. In firms that use self-managed teams, a more democratic decision making style is needed.

4. *How would you react to being paid as a member of a team rather than for your individual accomplishments? Would you be inclined to work harder or less hard as a result?*

This will be an individual answer. Many individuals are comfortable working with others, but some are not. Those individualists will have a more difficult time being evaluated, and paid, as part of a group.

Transparency Masters

Chapter Outline

CHAPTER 7
MANAGEMENT, LEADERSHIP, AND EMPLOYEE EMPOWERMENT

PROFILE: Lynn Mercer of Lucent Technologies

I. THE NEW APPROACH TO CORPORATE MANAGEMENT.

A. Managers Are No Longer Just Bosses.

B. The Definition and Functions of Customer-Oriented Management.

II. PLANNING: CREATING A VISION FOR THE ORGANIZATION.

III. ORGANIZING: CREATING A UNIFIED SYSTEM OUT OF MULTIPLE ORGANIZATIONS.

A. The Customer-Oriented Organization.

B. Organization Involves Multiple Firms.

C. Empowering Workers.

IV. CONTROLLING.

A. New Criteria for Measurement: Customer Satisfaction.

B. A Corporate Scorecard.

V. LEADERSHIP: VISION AND VALUES.

A. Creating a Learning Organization.

B. Leadership Styles.

C. The Trend Toward Self-Managed Teams.

D. Leadership Teams.

Chapter Outline

VI. TASKS AND SKILLS AT DIFFERENT LEVELS OF MANAGEMENT.

A. Delegating: Becoming a Team Leader.

B. Decision Making: Finding the Best Ethical Alternative.

VII. LEARNING MANAGEMENT SKILLS.

A. Verbal Skills.

B. Writing Skills.

C. Computer Skills.

D. Human Relations Skills.

E. Managing Diversity.

F. Time Management Skills.

G. Technical Skills.

VIII. MANAGERS AND LEADERS ARE NEEDED EVERYWHERE.

IX. SUMMARY AND REVIEW.

TM-48

What Managers Do

(Figure 7.1 on text page 199)

WHAT MANAGERS DO

Planning

- Setting organizational goals.
- Developing strategies to reach those goals.
- Determining resources needed.
- Setting standards.

Organizing (staffing)

- Allocating resources, assigning tasks, and establishing procedures for accomplishing goals.
- Preparing a structure (organization chart) showing lines of authority and responsibility.
- Recruiting, selecting, training, and developing employees.
- Placing employees where they'll be most effective.

Leading (directing)

- Guiding and motivating employees to work effectively to accomplish organizational goals and objectives.
- Giving assignments.
- Explaining routines.
- Clarifying policies.
- Providing feedback on performance.

Controlling

- Measuring results against corporate objectives.
- Monitoring performance relative to standards.
- Taking corrective action.

Some modern managers perform all of these tasks with the full cooperation and participation of workers. Empowering employees means allowing them to participate more fully in decision making.

Planning Functions

(Figure 7.2 on text page 202)

FORMS OF PLANNING	EXAMPLES OF PLANNING FOR FIBERRIFIC
STRATEGIC PLANNING Broad long-range goal-setting by top managers	**STRATEGIC PLAN** Goal set by president: to make Fiberrific the preferred breakfast of health-conscious consumers
↓	↓
TACTICAL PLANNING Specific short-range objectives/identification by lower managers	**TACTICAL PLAN** Objective set by director of research and development: To develop a dry cereal that provides 100% of the adult RDA of vitamins, minerals, and fiber by the end of the year
↓	↓
CONTINGENCY PLANNING Backup plans in case primary plans fail	**CONTINGENCY PLAN** Objective set by director of research and development: If dry cereal doesn't meet the market needs, develop a comparable breakfast bar by the end of the year

Typical Organization Chart

(Figure 7.3 on text page 204)

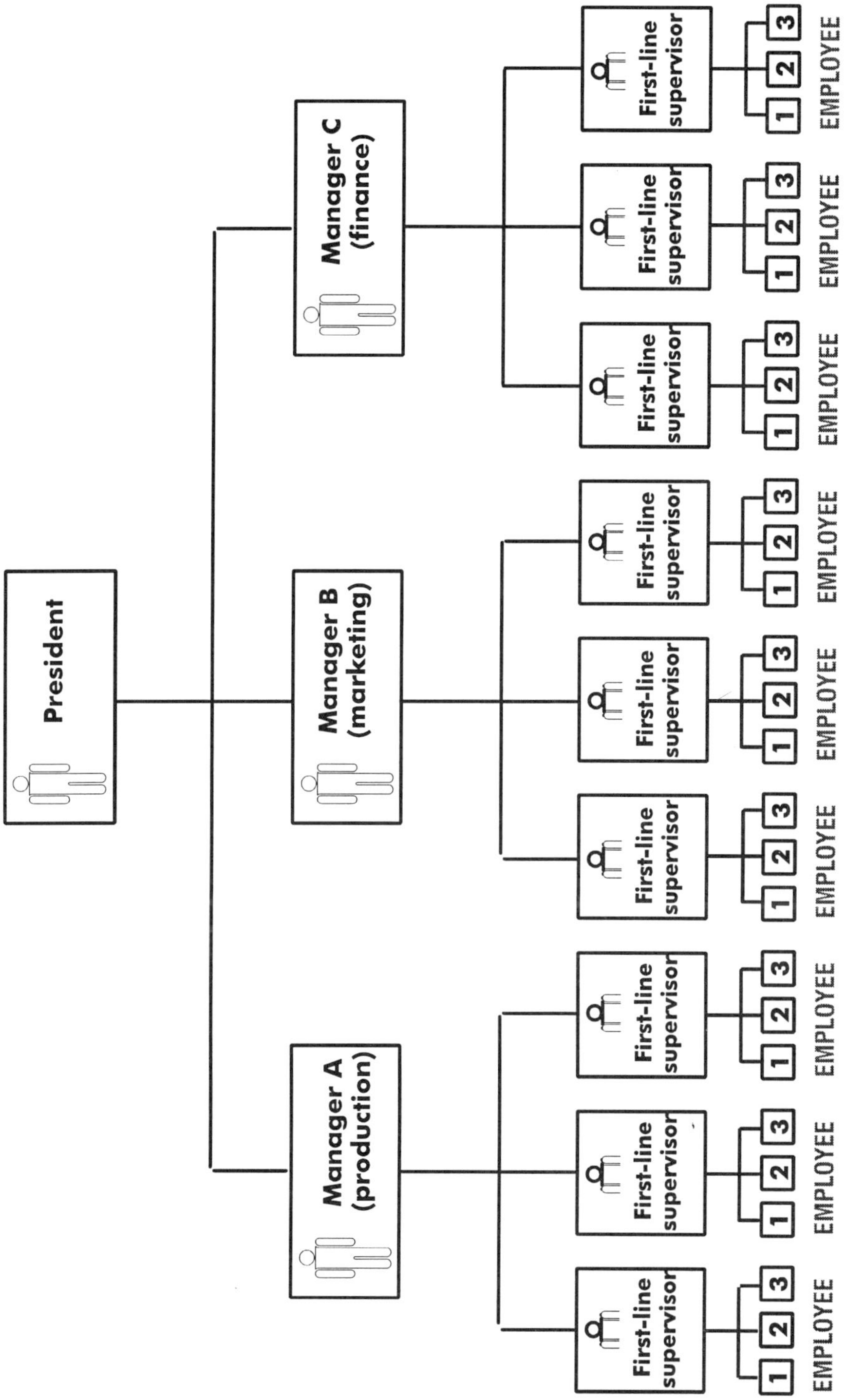

President

Manager A (production)

Manager B (marketing)

Manager C (finance)

First-line supervisor | First-line supervisor | First-line supervisor (under each manager)

1 2 3 EMPLOYEE (under each first-line supervisor)

TM-51

Levels of Management
(Figure 7.4 on text page 205)

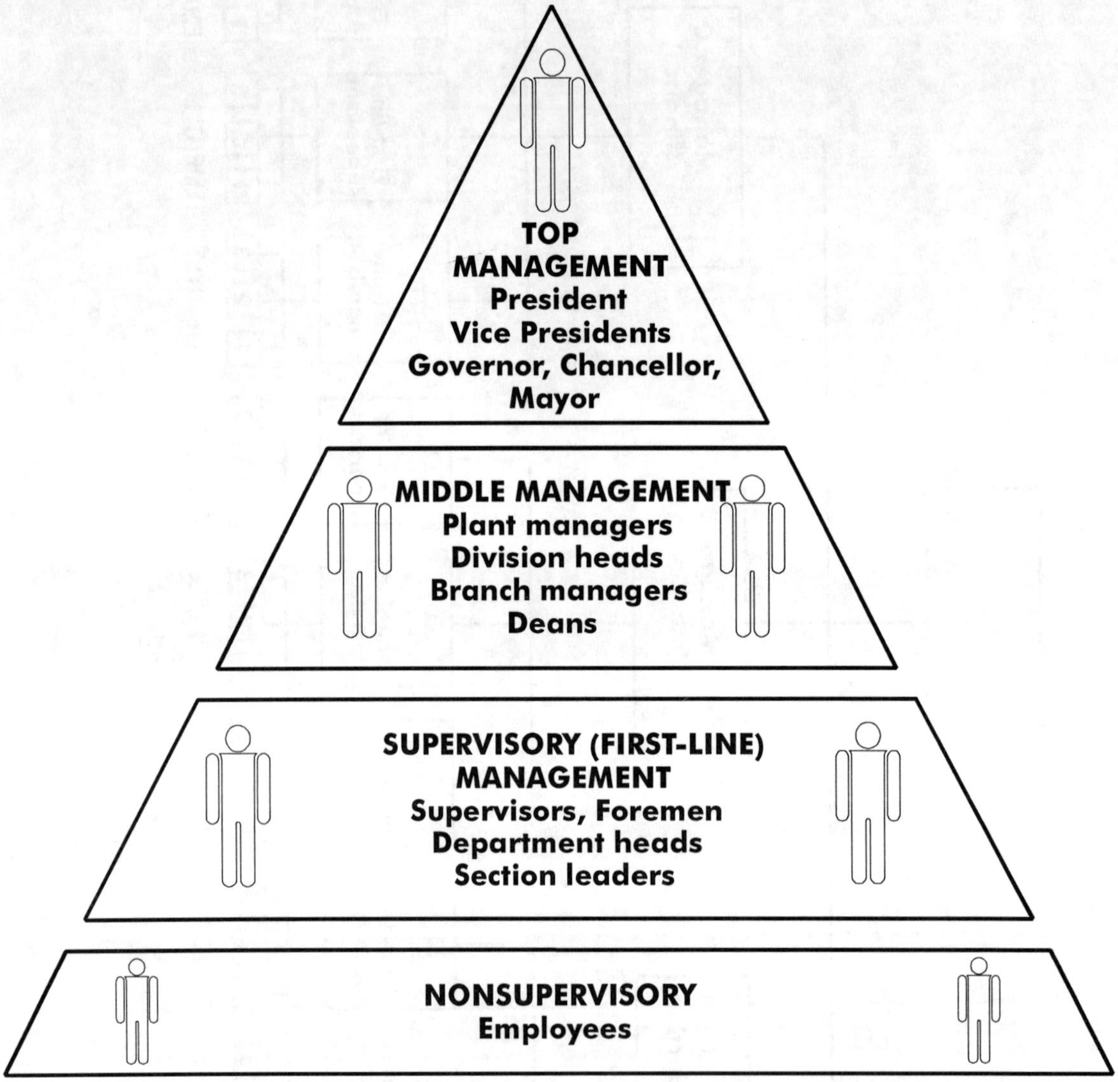
TOP
MANAGEMENT
President
Vice Presidents
Governor, Chancellor,
Mayor
MIDDLE MANAGEMENT
Plant managers
Division heads
Branch managers
Deans
SUPERVISORY (FIRST-LINE)
MANAGEMENT
Supervisors, Foremen
Department heads
Section leaders
NONSUPERVISORY
Employees

TM-52

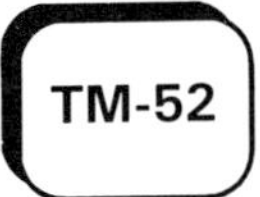

The Control Process

(Figure 7.5 on text page 208)

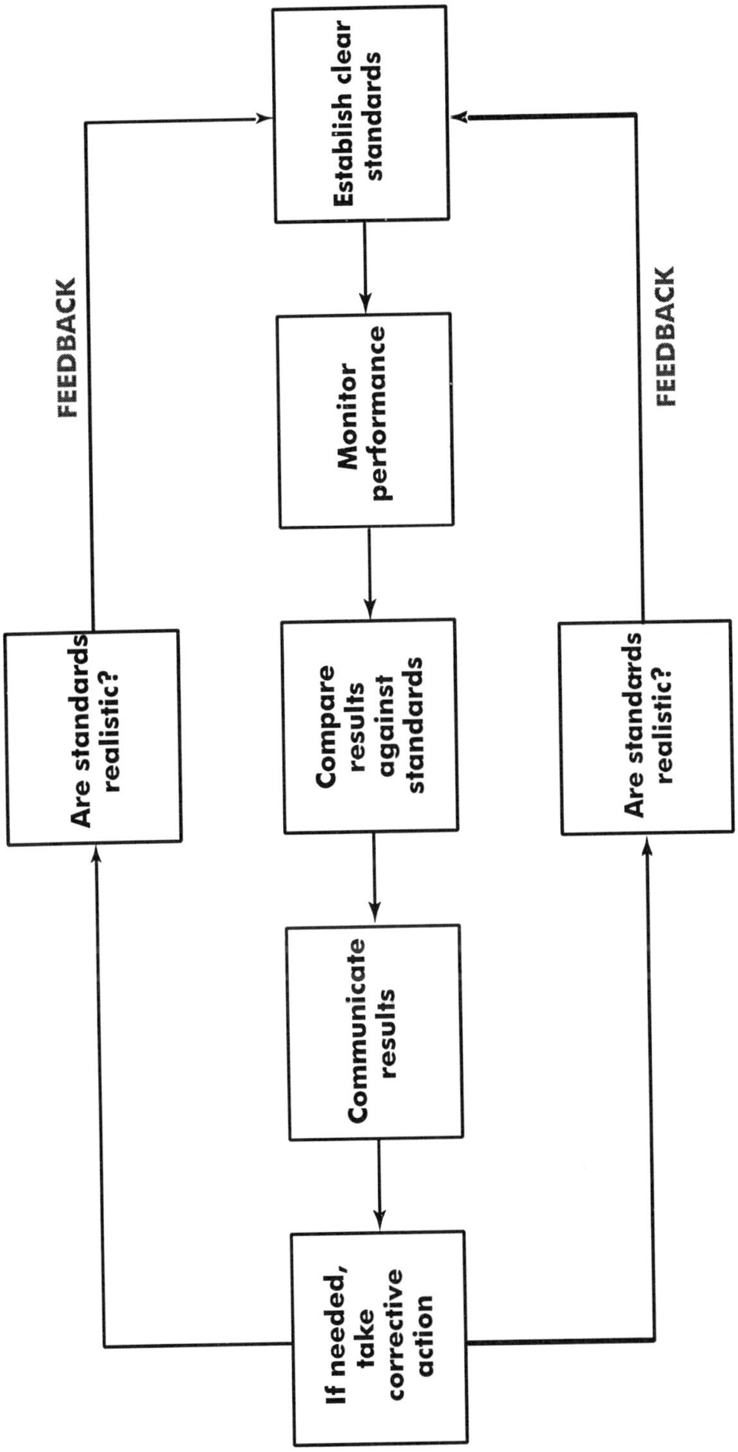
Establish clear standards
Monitor performance
Compare results against standards
Communicate results
If needed, take corrective action
Are standards realistic?
Are standards realistic?
FEEDBACK
FEEDBACK

Managers Versus Leaders
(Figure on text page 211)

MANAGERS	LEADERS
Do things right	Do the right thing
Command and control	Inspire and empower
Seek stability and predictability	Seek flexibility and change
Are internally focused	Are externally oriented
Work within the firm	Coordinate the whole system
Are locally oriented	Are globally oriented
Think mostly of workers	Think mostly of customers and other stakeholders

Various Leadership Styles

(Figure 7.6 on text page 214)

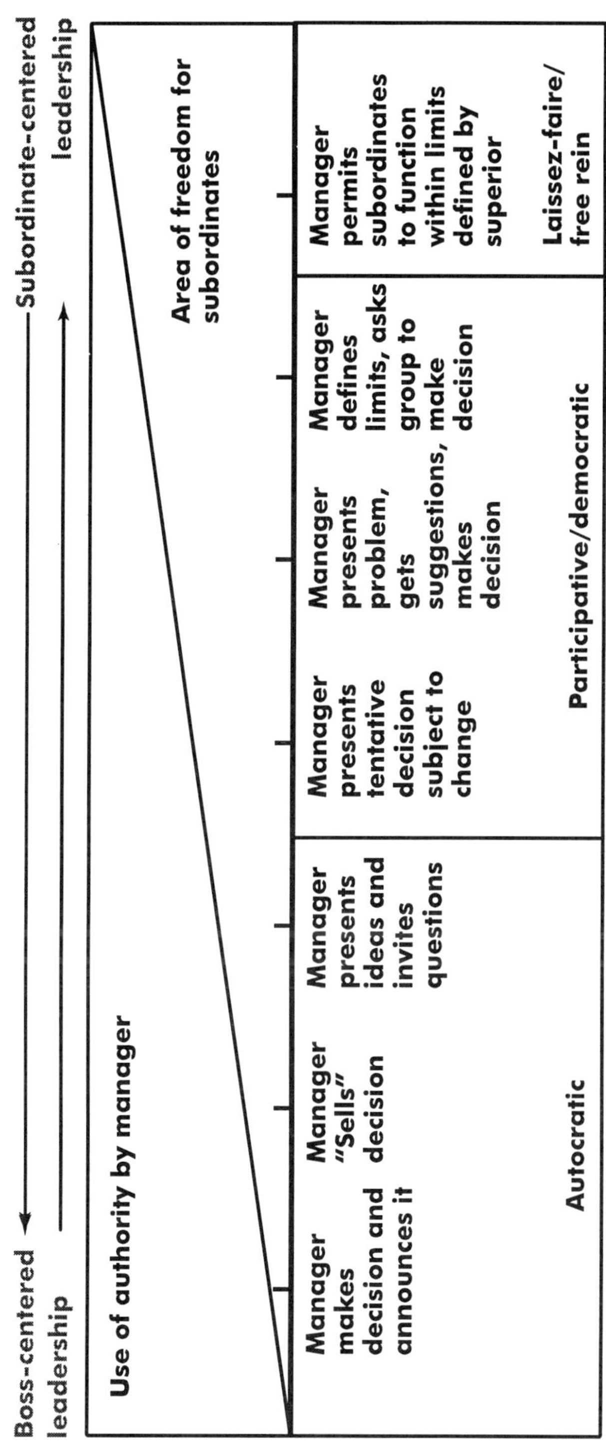

Skills Needed at Various Levels of Management
(Figure 7.8 on text page 217)

SKILLS NEEDED AT VARIOUS LEVELS OF MANAGEMENT

Top managers	Technical skills	Human relations skills	Conceptual skills
Middle managers	Technical skills	Human relations skills	Conceptual skills
First-line managers	Technical skills	Human relations skills	Conceptual skills

All managers need human relations skills. At the top, managers need strong conceptual skills. First-line managers need strong technical skills. Middle managers need to have a balance between technical and conceptual skills.

The Decision-Making Process

(Figure 7.9 on text page 219)

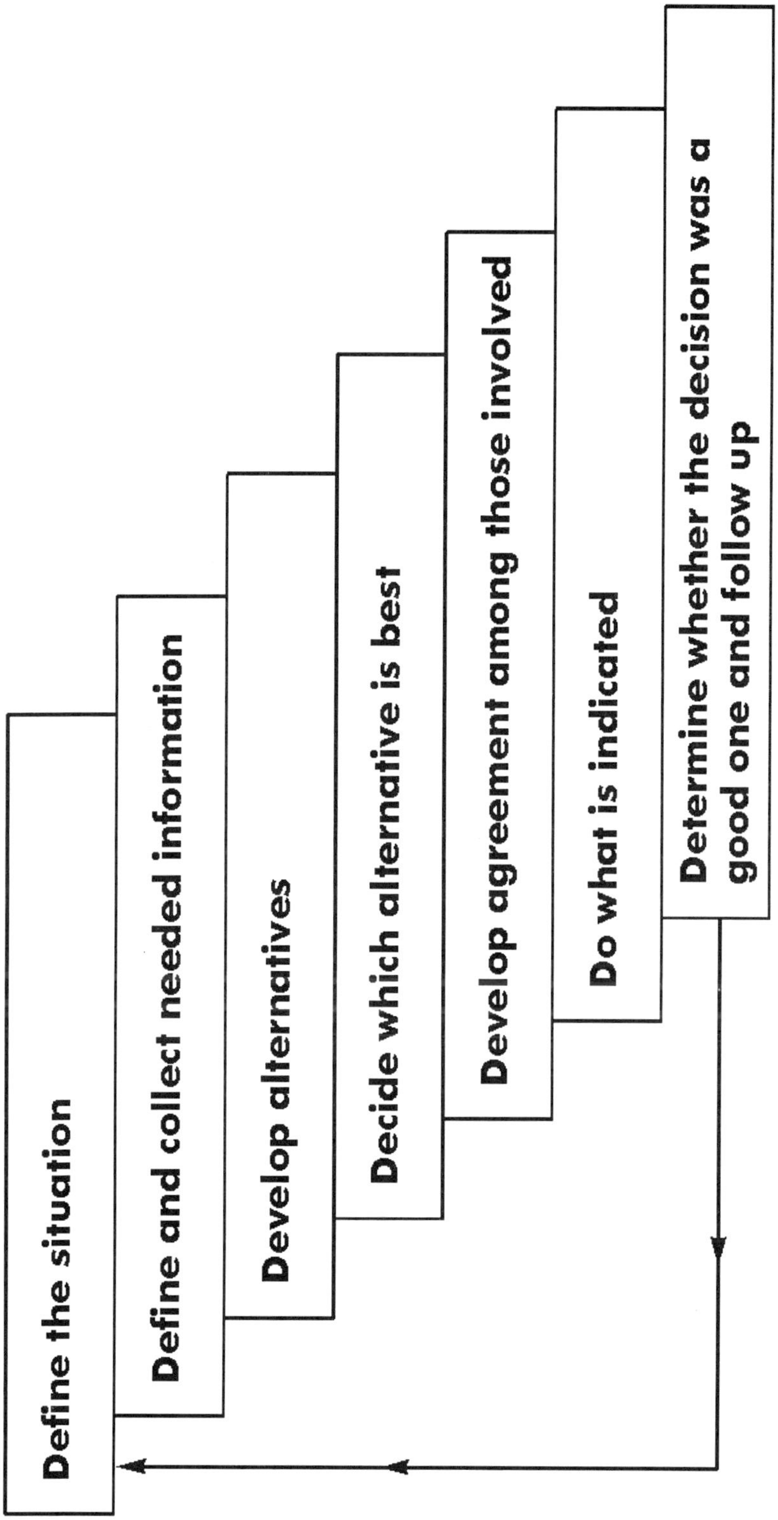

1. Define the situation
2. Define and collect needed information
3. Develop alternatives
4. Decide which alternative is best
5. Develop agreement among those involved
6. Do what is indicated
7. Determine whether the decision was a good one and follow up

Evaluating Your Management Potential
(Figure 7.10 on text page 220)

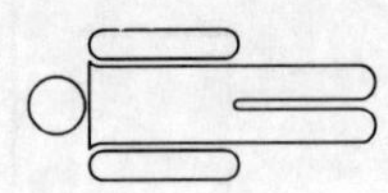

Evaluating your management potential

Skill needed	Personal evaluation			
	Excellent	Good	Fair	Need work
Verbal skills				
Writing skills				
Computer skills				
Human relations skills				
Time management skills				
Other technical skills				

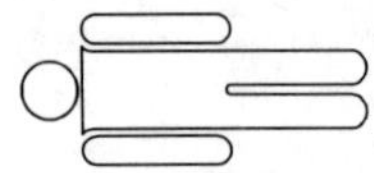

Organizing a Customer-Driven Business

Chapter 8

Folder Contents

TM 64 Different Types of Teams *(Figure 8.6 on text page 244)*

TM 65 Traditional Organizational Chart *(Figure 8.7 on text page 246)*

TM 66 An Inverted Organization Structure *(Figure 8.8 on text page 246)*

TM 67 Bureaucratic Versus Customer-Focused Organization Structure *(Figure 8.9 on text page 249)*

Overhead Transparency Acetates

OT ACETATE 8-1 Purpose of an Organizational Chart

OT ACETATE 8-2 Is A Bureaucratic Organization for You?

OT ACETATE 8-3 Is A Bureaucratic Organization for You?

OT ACETATE 8-4 Steps in Implementing Change in Organizations

OT ACETATE 8-5 How to Improve Organizational Structure

OT ACETATE 8-6 Tips for Team Leaders

OT ACETATE 8-7 Ways to Destroy Team Efforts

OT ACETATE 8-8 Ways to Destroy Team Efforts

OT ACETATE 8-9 The Four "R's" of Organizational Transformation

OT ACETATE 8-10 The Trend Toward Outsourcing

OT ACETATE 8-11 Downsizing Marches On

OT ACETATE 8-12 What Are the Effects of Downsizing?

OT ACETATE 8-13 Examples of Informal Group Norms

(Acetates and Transparency Masters are also available as PowerPoint slides on disk and on the Presentation CD-ROM.)

(Resources Available are also referenced in the expanded lecture outline later in this chapter.)

Other Resources Available

Video Case - Big Apple Bagel and the Saint Louis Bread Company. Big Apple Bagel and the Saint Louis Bread Company are examples of smaller organizations that have been restructured to meet the needs of today's marketplace. (The **Media Resource Guide** contains a summary of the Video and suggested discussion questions.)

Student Assessment and Learning Guide: Contains matching key term and definition questions, write-in retention questions, write-in critical thinking questions, and practice test of multiple choice and true/false questions.

Technology:

Zapitalism CD-ROM – Simulation program.

Concept Mastery Exam Preparation Disk – Practice test and tutorial.

Business Essentials Disk – Hyperlinks Understanding Business with seven other leading business texts.

Presentation CD-ROM – Contains PowerPoint slides of acetates and transparency masters, video clips, lecture materials. This tool allows you to customize your lecture presentations.

***Business Week* Web Site Access with the *Business Week* edition.**

Understanding Business **Home Page – http:/www.mhhe.com/ub5e.**

Audiotape: Abridged chapter (Text minus profile, boxes, and end-of-chapter material.

Associated Web Sites

These sites are provided to students for the purpose of analysis and critical thinking of the issues. Students are encouraged to explore other sites. As with any Web site, some may be inactive now.

Organization Structure

World Food Program - a real customer-driven business

http://www.wfp.org/Info_Org_Home.html

Organization Structure - Read MIT's Human Resources Principle

http://www.itd.umich.edu/itd-hr/matrix.html

Cross-Functional Team - for increased sales

http://www.ktic.com/topic6/12_ktcas.htm

Role of the team/management accountant

http://www.nan.shh.fi/raw/ima/splink2.htm

Principles of Organizational Design and Change - good ideas and links to other references

http://choo.fis.utoronto.ca/FIS/Courses/LIS1230/LIS1230sharma/od1.htm

Total Quality Management (TQM) - taken from Professor Giuliani's course in Operations Management

many examples and relevant sites

http://cs.franklin.edu/Faculty/Giuliani/pcmt150/omu3ln.htm

Reengineering - taken from Professor Giuliani's course in Operations Management

many examples and relevant sites

http://cs.franklin.edu/Faculty/Giuliani/pcmt150/omu12ln.htm

Understanding Business **Home Page**:

http:/www.mhhe.com/ub5e.

What's New in This Edition

Additions:

- Profile Mei-Lin Cheng and Julie Anderson, managers at Hewlett Packard
- Section "Extranets Link Company Intranets"
- Taking It to the Net exercises
- Case: IBM Outsources The Manufacturing Of PCS
- Spotlight on Small Business: Fun Night at the Ice Cream Parlor
- Making Ethical Decisions: When Does Benchmarking Become Unethical?
- From the Pages of Business Week

Revisions:

Statistical data and examples throughout the chapter were updated to reflect current information. In addition:

- Section "The Changing Organizational Hierarchy" was expanded to include additional discussion of downsizing.

Deletions:

- Profile
- Discussion of group norms and group cohesiveness from section "The Informal Organization Helps Create Teamwork"
- Case: Creating Cross-Functional Teams in Service Organizations
- Boxes From the Pages of Entrepreneur, Spotlight on Small Business, Making Ethical Decisions

Brief Chapter Outline/Learning Goals

CHAPTER 8

ORGANIZING A CUSTOMER-DRIVEN BUSINESS

PROFILE: Mei-Lin Cheng and Julie Anderson of Hewlett-Packard

I. THE CHANGING ORGANIZATIONAL HIERARCHY.

LEARNING GOAL 1. Describe the traditional hierarchical, bureaucratic organization structure and how it is being restructured.

A. The Fundamentals of Bureaucracy.

II. HOW ORGANIZATIONS HAVE EVOLVED.

LEARNING GOAL 2. Explain the organizational theories of Fayol and Weber.

A. The Background of Organizational Theory.

B. Fayol's Principles of Organization.

C. Max Weber and Organizational Theory.

III. DESIGNING MORE RESPONSIVE ORGANIZATIONS.

LEARNING GOAL 3. Discuss the various issues connected with organizational design.

A. Tall Versus Flat Organization Structure.

B. Choosing the Appropriate Span of Control.

C. Advantages and Disadvantages of Departmentalization.

D. Different Ways to Departmentalize.

E. Centralization Versus Decentralization of Authority.

IV. ORGANIZATION MODELS.

LEARNING GOAL 4. Describe the differences between line, line and staff, matrix, and cross-functional organizations.

A. Line Organizations.

B. Line-and-Staff Organizations.

C. Matrix Organizations.

V. CROSS-FUNCTIONAL, SELF-MANAGED TEAMS.

A. Limitations of Cross-Functional Teams.

B. Cross-Functional Teams Lead to Networking.

C. Extranets Link Company Intranets.

VI. THE RESTRUCTURING PROCESS AND TOTAL QUALITY.

LEARNING GOAL 5. Explain the benefits of turning organizations upside down and inside out.

A. Turning the Organization Upside Down to Empower Employees.

B. Turning the Organization Inside Out (Outsourcing).

C. Creating Internal Customers.

VII. ESTABLISHING A SERVICE-ORIENTED CULTURE.

LEARNING GOAL 6. Give examples to show how organizational culture and the informal organization can hinder or assist organizational change.

A. The Informal Organization Helps Create Teamwork.

VIII. SUMMARY AND REVIEW.

(Learning Objectives are also referenced in the expanded lecture outline later in this chapter)

Key Terms

bureaucracy *(text page 230)*
centralized authority *(text page 239)*
competitive benchmarking *(text page 246)*
continuous improvement *(text page 245)*
core competencies *(text page 246)*
cross-functional teams *(text page 242)*
decentralized authority *(text page 239)*
departmentalization organization *(text page 236)*
extranet *(text page 243)*
formal organization *(text page 250)*
hierarchy *(text page 230)*
informal organization *(text page 250)*
intranets *(text page 243)*
inverted organization *(text page 245)*
line personnel *(text page 240)*
matrix organization *(text page 241)*
networking *(text page 243)*
organizational culture *(text page 249)*
organizational design *(text page 230)*
outsourcing *(text page 246)*
reengineering *(text page 245)*
restructuring *(text page 231)*
span of control *(text page 235)*
staff personnel *(text page 240)*
total quality management (TQM) *(text page 245)*

Lecture Outline

The **PROFILE** at the beginning of this chapter focuses on **MEI-LIN CHENG** and **JULIE ANDERSON**, both managers at **HEWLETT PACKARD**, one of America's most admired companies.

I. THE CHANGING ORGANIZATIONAL HIERARCHY.

▶ **LEARNING GOAL 1.** Describe the traditional hierarchical, bureaucratic organization structure and how it is being restructured.

A. Moving from a boss-driven to an employee-driven company isn't easy.

1. American companies are trying to develop an organizational design that best serves the needs of customers, stockholders, employees, and the community.
2. **ORGANIZATIONAL DESIGN** is the structuring of workers so that they can best accomplish all the goals of the firm.
   a. In the past, many organizations were designed so that managers could control workers, using a hierarchy.
   b. A hierarchy means that there's one person at the top and many levels of managers responsible to that person.
   c. Some organizations have as many as 10 to 14 layers of management between

Lecture Notes

TRANSPARENCY MASTER 58
Chapter Outline

Transparency masters begin on page 8.87.

LECTURE ENHANCER 8-1
Get Organized

Could there be a society with all its CDS in order? Its videotapes categorized? Its food recipes databased? Its holiday card lists on floppy disks? Its income-tax returns ready to file on the way to bed after the big New Year's Eve party? (See complete lecture enhancer on page 8.56.)

OT ACETATE 8-1
Purpose of an Organization Chart

Purpose of an Organization Chart

- Show the activities of the organization.
- Highlight subdivisions of the organization.
- Identify different types of work performed.
- Provide information about different management levels.
- Show the lines of authority in the organization and the flow of organizational communications.

Comments:

1. This acetate identifies the major purposes of an organizational chart.
2. You may wish to discuss each of the five purposes in relation to the principles of Henri Fayol and Max Weber. Discussion could include: unity of command (no employee has more than one immediate boss), chain-of-command (highlighting the flow of information and reporting procedures), and parity of authority and responsibility (authority must equal responsibility).
3. Ask the students if your college has an organization chart. If possible get a copy to show to them the same principles at work.

TRANSPARENCY MASTER 59
A Typical Organizational Structure *(Figure 8.1 on text page 230)*

Transparency masters begin on page 8.87.

Lecture Outline

the chief executive officer and the lowest-level employee.

3. **BUREAUCRACY** is the term used in organizations to describe having many layers of management who set rules and regulations and participate in all decisions.
4. Organizations are eliminating managers and giving more power to lower-level employees, called **DOWNSIZING**.
5. Recent research has shown that downsizing has little positive affect on earnings or stock market performance in the long run.

B. **THE FUNDAMENTALS OF BUREAUCRACY.**

1. In a bureaucracy:
   a. **CHAIN OF COMMAND** goes from the top down.
   b. There are **RULES AND REGULATIONS.**
   c. Organizations are **SET UP BY FUNCTION.**
   d. **COMMUNICATION** among departments **IS MINIMAL.**
2. The typical career is to move up within a function.
3. Today's workforce is better educated and fewer firms are using a traditional bureaucratic style of organization.

Lecture Notes

LECTURE ENHANCER 8-2 A Dilbert View of Downsizing	Scott Adams, the creator and heart of the cartoon character Dilbert, knows about corporate organization. (See complete lecture enhancer on page 8.58.)
SUPPLEMENTAL CASE 8-1 Restructuring Hits Management Positions	See complete case on page 8.78.
LECTURE ENHANCER 8-3 Bureaucracy Strangles Intrapreneurship	In the 1980s "intrapreneurship" became a buzzword among managers who wanted to introduce small-business fervor into lumbering corporations. (See complete lecture enhancer on page 8.59.)

4. The problem is that such organizations aren't responsible to customers—Employees tend to follow the rules and aren't very flexible.

5. To be able to respond to customer demands more quickly, organizations are restructuring.

    a. **RESTRUCTURING** means redesigning an organization so that it can more effectively and efficiently service customers.

    b. Organizations that have made such changes have regained market leadership.

6. There are still remnants of bureaucracy among today's organizations, such as universities and government agencies.

II. HOW ORGANIZATIONS HAVE EVOLVED.

▶ **LEARNING GOAL 2.** Explain the organizational theories of Fayol and Weber.

A. THE BACKGROUND OF ORGANIZATIONAL THEORY.

1. Not until the 20th century and introduction of mass production did business organizations grow complex and difficult to manage.

2. The bigger the plant, the more efficient production became, a concept called **ECONOMY OF SCALE**.

CRITICAL THINKING (page 231 in text)

Start noticing how many clerks and other customer-contact people say things like, "That's not our policy" or "We don't do things that way" when you request some unusual service. Such answers are the result of bureaucratic rules and regulations that employees are forced to follow. Imagine a day when employees are free to adjust to the wants and needs of customers. What organizational changes would have to be made? Would the results be worth the effort?

LECTURE ENHANCER 8-4
Bob Felton Hates Bureaucracy

According to Bob Felton, only two rules would exist, he declared: 1. "Delight your internal and external customer," and 2. "Use your best judgment." (See complete lecture enhancer on page 8.60.)

Lecture Outline

3. The text discusses two major organization theorists:

   a. **HENRI FAYOL** *(Administration Industrielle et Generale* in France in 1919)

   b. **MAX WEBER** (*The Theory of Social and Economic Organizations* in Germany about the same time.)

B. **FAYOL'S PRINCIPLES OF ORGANIZATION.**

1. Fayol introduced principles such as:

   a. **UNITY OF COMMAND. E**ach worker is to report to only one boss.

   b. **HIERARCHY OF AUTHORITY.** One should know to whom to report.

   c. **DIVISION OF LABOR.** Functions were divided into areas of specialization.

   d. **SUBORDINATION OF INDIVIDUAL INTERESTS TO THE GENERAL INTERESTS.** Goals of the organization were to be considered more important then personal goals.

   e. **AUTHORITY.** Managers should give orders and expect them to be carried out.

   f. **DEGREE OF CENTRALIZATION.** The decisions needed to be made by top

Lecture Notes

management depends upon the size of the organization.

g. **CLEAR DEFINITION OF COMMUNICATION CHANNELS.**

h. **ORDER**. "A place for everything and everything in its place."

i. **EQUITY**. Employees should be treated fairly and justly.

j. **ESPRIT DE CORPS.** Employees should be proud of and loyal to the organization.

2. These principles have been taught for years, becoming synonymous with the concept of management.

3. These principles led to rigid organizations.

C. **MAX WEBER AND ORGANIZATION THEORY.**

1. Max Weber used the term bureaucrats to describe middle managers whose function was to implement top management's orders.

2. Weber identified three **LAYERS OF AUTHORITY**:

a. **TOP MANAGERS** who were the decision makers.

b. **MIDDLE MANAGERS** who developed the rules and procedures for **SUPPORTING THE DECISIONS.**

Lecture Notes

CRITICAL THINKING EXERCISE 8-1
Organization Chart

See complete exercise on page 8.74.

OT ACETATE 8-2 and **OT ACETATE 8-3**
Is a Bureaucratic Organization for You?

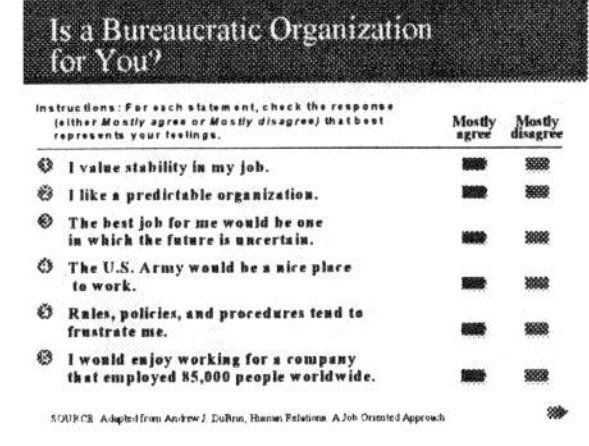

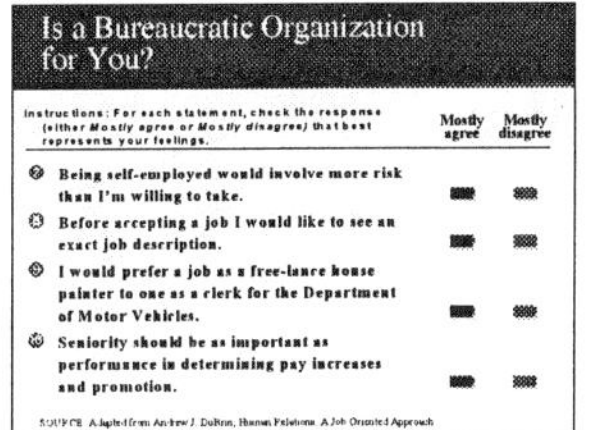

Comments:

1. Ask students to respond to each of the statements on the acetate. It's best to uncover them one-by-one and seek answers.
2. Ask the students to track what statements they mostly agreed with or mostly disagreed with. This provides insight into their attitudes concerning bureaucratic organizations.
3. Scoring directions: ask students to compare their responses to the answers below. If students agree with 9-10 of the answers, they would enjoy working in a bureaucracy; 6-8 responses agree they might survive; less than 4 they would not like a bureaucratic system.

1. Mostly agree	6. Mostly disagree
2. Mostly agree	7. Mostly agree
3. Mostly disagree	8. Mostly agree
4. Mostly agree	9. Mostly disagree
5. Mostly disagree	10. Mostly agree

TRANSPARENCY MASTER 60
Bureaucratic Organization Structure *(Figure 8.2 on text page 234)*

Transparency masters begin on page 8.87.

Lecture Outline

c. **WORKERS AND SUPERVISORS** who did the work.

3. Weber promoted the pyramid-shaped organization structure.
   a. Weber put great trust in managers and felt the less decision making employees had to do, the better.
   b. Today, however, many firms believe that workers are the best source of ideas, and managers are there to support workers.

4. **WEBER'S PRINCIPLES** were similar to Fayol's with the addition of:
   a. **JOB DESCRIPTIONS.**
   b. **WRITTEN RULES.**
   c. **CONSISTENT PROCEDURES, REGULATIONS, AND POLICIES.**
   d. **STAFFING AND PROMOTIONS BASED ON QUALIFICATIONS.**

III. DESIGNING MORE RESPONSIVE ORGANIZATIONS.

▶ **LEARNING GOAL 3.** Discuss the various issues connected with organizational design.

Lecture Notes

Lecture Outline

A. In the late 1970s management began the process of reorganizing firms, making them smaller, less complex, and more efficient.

B. **TALL VERSUS FLAT ORGANIZATION STRUCTURES.**

1. **TALL ORGANIZATIONS** have many layers of management.

   a. The organization chart becomes very tall because of the levels of management.

   b. Organizations are divided into regions, divisions, centers, and plants—each with several layers of management.

   c. The cost of all these managers and support people was high.

2. **FLAT ORGANIZATIONS** cut out management layers and expand sideways instead.

   a. The trend is toward more flat organization structures.

   b. Organizations that cut management are tending to create teams.

C. **CHOOSING THE APPROPRIATE SPAN OF CONTROL.**

1. **SPAN OF CONTROL** refers to the optimum number of subordinates a manager supervises or should supervise.

LECTURE ENHANCER 8-5
Horizontal Structure: The Organization of the 1990s

Self-managing teams are a major tenet of the flat organization structure. The structure is based on one basic idea: The people who do the work should have the means to change to meet the needs of the customer. (See complete lecture enhancer on page 8.62.)

LECTURE ENHANCER 8-6
The Return of the Middle Manager

After years of being disrespected, devalued and discarded by corporate America, middle managers are emerging as prized players once again. (See complete lecture enhancer on page 8.63.)

OT ACETATE 8-4
Steps in Implementing Change in Organizations

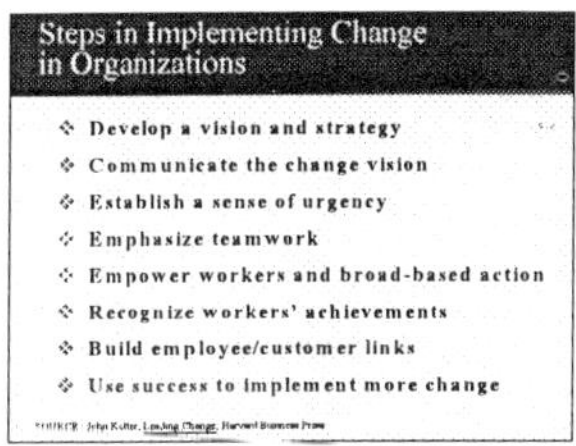

Comments:

1. Implementing change in an organization is no easy task by any means. This acetate addresses the question of how to implement change within an organization with the minimal amount of impact.
2. Students should make note of terms and concepts such as teamwork, empowerment, customer focus, etc. that have been continuous themes thus far in the text.
3. Ask students why people are often adverse to change. See if they can name companies or industries that have been particularly adept at implementing change into the organizational structure.

Lecture Outline

a. At lower levels, it is possible to implement a wide span of control.

b. The number narrows at higher levels of the organization.

2. Variables in span of control include:

   a. The more experienced, the broader the span of control.

   b. **CAPABILITIES OF THE SUBORDINATES.** The more need for supervision, the narrower the span of control.

   c. **COMPLEXITY OF THE JOB.**

      (i) **GEOGRAPHICAL CLOSENESS.** The more concentrated the work area, the broader the span of control.

      (ii) **FUNCTIONAL SIMILARITY.** The more similar the employees' functions are, the broader the span of control.

      (iii) **NEED FOR COORDINATION.** The greater the need for coordination, the narrower the span of control.

      (iv) **PLANNING DEMANDS.** The more planning required, the narrower the span of control.

LECTURE ENHANCER 8-7
Decentralization, Span of Control

In the past two decades the hierarchical model has begun to change. One trend: managers have increased the number of people reporting to them. (See complete lecture enhancer on page 8.65.)

(v) **FUNCTIONAL COMPLEXITY.** The more complex, the narrower the span of control.

d. Other factors to consider include professionalism of superiors and subordinates and the number of new problems that occur in a day.

3. The trend is to expand the span of control as organizations get rid of middle managers.

D. **ADVANTAGES AND DISADVANTAGES OF DEPARTMENTALIZATION.**

1. **DEPARTMENTALIZATION** is dividing organizational functions into separate units.

   a. **FUNCTIONAL STRUCTURE,** the traditional technique for departmentalizing, is the grouping of workers into departments based on similar skills, expertise, or resource use.

2. The **ADVANTAGES** of functional departmentalization are:

   a. **SKILLS CAN BE DEVELOPED IN DEPTH.**

   b. It allows for **ECONOMIES OF SCALE** as resources can be centralized.

   c. There is **GOOD COORDINATION** within the function.

Lecture Notes

CRITICAL THINKING EXERCISE 8-2
You, The Manager

See complete exercise on page 8.75.

Lecture Outline

3. The **DISADVANTAGES** of departmentalization are:
   a. **LACK OF COMMUNICATION** between departments.
   b. **EMPLOYEES IDENTIFY WITH THE DEPARTMENT** rather than the total organization.
   c. **RESPONSE TO EXTERNAL CHANGE IS SLOW.**
   d. Employees become **NARROW SPECIALISTS.**
4. Businesses are now trying to **REDESIGN THEIR STRUCTURES** to increase communication among employees.

E. **DIFFERENT WAYS TO DEPARTMENTALIZE.**

1. By **PRODUCT** (an automobile manufacturer may have separate divisions for trucks, passenger automobiles, vans, etc.)
2. By **FUNCTION** (production, marketing, finance, personnel, and accounting are common.)
3. By **CUSTOMER GROUP** (a food producer may have one department focus on home products and another that services restaurants, etc.)

Lecture Notes

OT ACETATE 8-5
How to Improve Organizational Structure

How to Improve Organizational Structure

- Break the business into smaller units
- Build teamwork
- Impose autonomy
- Create meaningful incentives
- Outsource non-operating activities
- Share business capabilities across units

Comments:

1. This acetate focuses on organizational structure. It's important for students to understand that as an organization grows or diversifies, structure and organization become increasingly important.
2. Once again, many of the concepts of the current chapter as well as previous chapters are presented to students. Understanding the basics of organization is often very difficult for students. It's doubtful at this stage of their careers they would have much experience or exposure to organizational principles. Working through this acetate slowly and precisely will help build their awareness and understanding.

TRANSPARENCY MASTER 61
Ways to Departmentalize
(Figure 8.3 on text page 238)

Transparency masters begin on page 8.89.

Lecture Outline

4. By **GEOGRAPHIC LOCATIONS**.
5. By **PROCESS** (a dress manufacturer may have a department for dress designing, another department to make the patterns, another to cut out the material, another to sew, etc.)

F. **CENTRALIZATION VERSUS DECENTRALIZATION OF AUTHORITY**.

1. The degree to which an organization allows managers at lower levels to make decisions determines the degree of decentralization.
2. **CENTRALIZED AUTHORITY** means decision-making remains in the upper layers of management.
3. **DECENTRALIZED AUTHORITY** means decision-making is delegated to lower level managers.
4. Most organizations have some form of both centralized and decentralized authority.
5. The trend is toward **MORE DECENTRALIZED AUTHORITY**.

IV. ORGANIZATION MODELS.

▶ **LEARNING GOAL 4.** Describe the differences between line, line and staff, matrix, and cross-functional organizations.

LECTURE ENHANCER 8-8
Delegation and Mistakes

Kenneth H. Olsen, founder and CEO of Digital Equipment Corporation, is known for his autocratic style. However, at the same time he strongly believes in delegating responsibility, something other computer entrepreneurs have found difficult to do. (See complete lecture enhancer on page 8.66.)

LECTURE ENHANCER 8-9
A Japanese Manager Interprets Responsibility

In his sixth week as managing director of the Hanshin Tigers baseball team, Shingo Furuya called his wife to say goodbye and jumped out of an eighth-floor window to the ground 92 feet below. (See complete lecture enhancer on page 8.67.)

PROGRESS CHECK
(page 239 in text)

- What is bureaucracy and why has it led to the need for restructuring organizations?
- How many of Fayol's 10 principles can you name?
- What principles did Weber add?
- What are the trends in tall versus flat organizations, a narrow versus wide span of control, departmentalization, and the centralization versus decentralization of authority?

Lecture Outline

A. There are several ways to structure an organization to accomplish their goals.

B. **LINE ORGANIZATIONS.**

1. A **LINE ORGANIZATION** has direct two-way lines of responsibility, authority, and communication running from top to bottom, with all employees reporting to only one boss (i.e. Army.)

2. **ADVANTAGES:**

   a. **CLEARLY DEFINED RESPONSIBILITY AND AUTHORITY.**

   b. **EASY TO UNDERSTAND.**

   c. **ONLY ONE SUPERVISOR FOR EACH PERSON.**

3. **DISADVANTAGES:**

   a. **TOO INFLEXIBLE.**

   b. **FEW SPECIALIST TO ADVISE EMPLOYEES ALONG THE LINE.**

   c. **TOO LONG LINES OF COMMUNICATION.**

   d. **UNABLE TO HANDLE COMPLEX DECISIONS.**

C. **LINE-AND-STAFF SYSTEMS ORGANIZATIONS.**

LECTURE ENHANCER 8-10
The First American Organization Chart

Henry Varnum Poor was perhaps the first American to draw an organization chart, during his study of railroad management in the 1860s. (See complete lecture enhancer on page 8.68.)

TRANSPARENCY MASTER 62
Organization Types *(Figure 8.4 on text page 240)*

Transparency masters begin on page 8.87.

Lecture Outline

1. **LINE PERSONNEL** perform functions that contribute directly to the goals of the organization.

2. **STAFF PERSONNEL** advise and assist line personnel.

3. Advantage: **HAVING EXPERT CONSULTANTS CONTINUOUSLY AVAILABLE.**

D. **MATRIX ORGANIZATIONS.**

1. Both line, and line and staff organization structures suffer from a certain inflexibility.

   a. Both have established lines of authority and communication and work well in organizations with relatively unchanging environments and slow product development.

   b. The economic, technological, and competitive environments are rapidly changing.

   c. In such organizations, emphasis is on new product development, creativity, and interdepartmental teamwork.

2. **MATRIX ORGANIZATIONS** bring specialists from different parts of the organization together to work on specific projects, but still remain part of a line and staff structure.

Lecture Notes

LECTURE ENHANCER 8-11
Managing the Boss

Managing the boss is fairly simple—often simpler than managing subordinates. (See complete lecture on page 8.69.)

TRANSPARENCY MASTER 63
A Matrix Organization
(Figure 8.5 on text page 242)

TM 63

Transparency masters begin on page 8.87.

Lecture Outline

a. Matrix organization structures were developed in the aerospace industry.

b. The structure is now used in banking, management consulting firms, ad agencies, and school systems.

3. **ADVANTAGES OF MATRIX ORGANIZATIONS:**

   a. **FLEXIBILITY.**

   b. **INTERORGANIZATIONAL COOPERATION AND TEAMWORK.**

   c. **CREATIVITY.**

   d. **MORE EFFICIENT USE OF ORGANIZATIONAL RESOURCES.**

4. **DISADVANTAGES OF MATRIX ORGANIZATIONS:**

   a. **COSTLY AND COMPLEX.**

   b. **CONFUSION IN LOYALTIES.**

   c. **REQUIRES GOOD INTERPERSONAL SKILLS AND COOPERATIVE EMPLOYEES AND MANAGERS.**

5. Matrix organizations seem to violate some traditional managerial principles, but the system functions relatively effectively.

Lecture Notes

Lecture Outline

V. CROSS-FUNCTIONAL, SELF-MANAGED TEAMS.

A. **CROSS-FUNCTIONAL TEAMS** are groups of employees from different departments who work together on a semi-permanent basis (as opposed to the temporary teams established in matrix-style organizations).

1. Often the teams are empowered to make decisions on their own without seeking the approval of management.
2. Self-managed teams reduce the barriers between design, engineering, marketing, and other functions.
3. Technology is increasing the trend toward cross-functional teams in that employees from different departments can work simultaneously on the same project using computers.

B. **LIMITATIONS OF CROSS-FUNCTIONAL TEAMS.**

1. Managers of functional areas often **RESIST CHANGE.**
2. Members of the team are often **UNSURE** of what is expected of them.

Lecture Notes

SUPPLEMENTAL CASE 8-2
Creating Cross-Functional Teams

See complete case on page 8.81.

OT ACETATE 8-6
Tips for Team Leaders

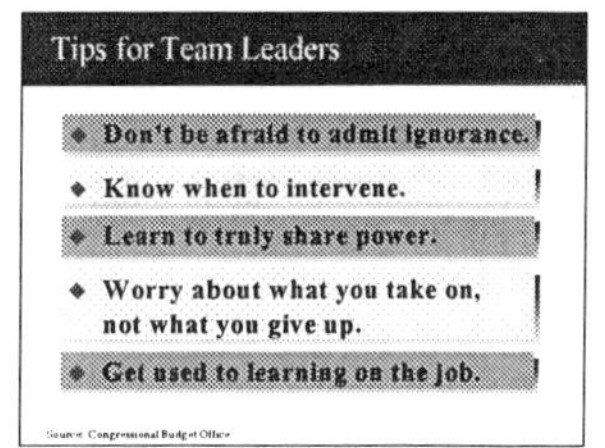

Comments:

1. This acetate offers tips for team leaders. It provides insight into the challenge and opportunities provided from work teams in organizations. In dealing with the workplace of the future, managers will need to work with and through teams of workers.
2. It's important for students to remember that learning on the job is a key to success. Each work team can be different in operational structure as well as in the responsibilities associated with different teams.

TRANSPARENCY MASTER 64
Different Types of Teams
(Figure 8.6 on text page 244)

Transparency masters begin on page 8.87.

OT ACETATE 8-7 and **OT ACETATE 8-8**
Ways to Destroy Team Efforts

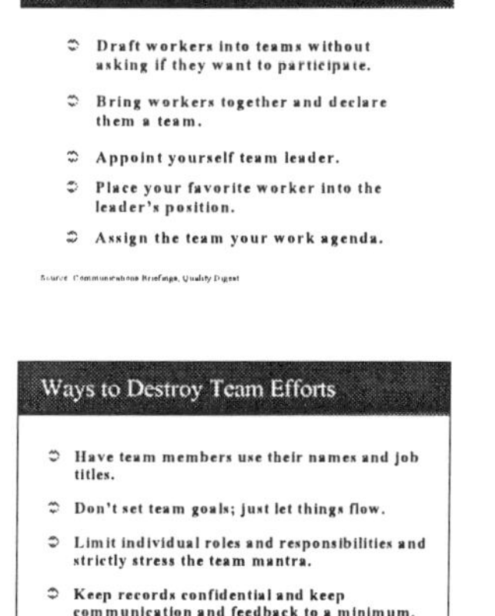

Comments:

1. These two acetates offer ten suggestions of how "not" to deal with teams in the organization.
2. Some of the recommendations of what "not" to do are quite obvious, some are not so obvious. For example, it doesn't help to have team members lose their individuality all for the sake of the team. They can come to resent the team structure and often even disrupt its operations.
3. Ask if any students are currently members of work teams at their jobs. Check with the students and ask how they feel about working under a team structure. It's true that some management analysts believe that American workers are not well suited for team structures because of our cultural influences fostering individual achievement and rewards. Question students if they think teams will continue to be an integral part of the workplace.

Lecture Outline

3. Requires **DIFFERENT SKILLS** from working alone .

4. **ADDITIONAL TRAINING** is necessary.

5. The most common problem with teams is that companies rush out and form the **WRONG KIND OF TEAM FOR THE WRONG KIND OF JOB.**

C. **CROSS-FUNCTIONAL TEAMS LEAD TO NET-WORKING.**

1. It is a good idea to include customers, suppliers, and distributors on cross-functional product development teams.

2. Cross-functional teams may cross national boundaries.

3. **NETWORKING**, in this context, means the linking of organizations with communications technology and other means to work together on common objectives.

D. **EXTRANETS LINK COMPANY INTRANETS.**

1. An **EXTRANET** is an extended Internet that connects suppliers, customers, and other organizations.

2. It is made up of linked **INTRANETS**, communication links within companies that travel over the Internet.

Lecture Notes

LECTURE ENHANCER 8-12
Cross-Functional Teams for Small Companies

When Betty Wagner had her third child, she found that managing her company by herself was too much. Therefore, she turned her company from a boss-driven firm into a team operation. (See complete lecture enhancer on page 8.70.)

LECTURE ENHANCER 8-13
Self-Organizing: Another Approach to Structure

Recently many management experts have been using the term "self-organization." (See complete lecture enhancer on page 8.71.)

3. Everyone in the firm is electronically linked so they can communicate and work together on projects.

VI. THE RESTRUCTURING PROCESS AND TOTAL QUALITY.

▶ **LEARNING GOAL 5.** Explain the benefits of turning organizations upside down and inside out.

A. **TOTAL QUALITY MANAGEMENT (TQM)** is the practice of striving for maximum internal and external customer satisfaction by developing and providing them with high-quality, high-value, want-satisfying goods, services, and ideas.

1. **CONTINUOUS IMPROVEMENT** means constantly improving the way the organization does things so that customer needs can be better satisfied.

2. When an organization needs dramatic changes, only reengineering will do.

3. **REENGINEERING** is the fundamental rethinking and radical redesign of organizational processes to achieve dramatic improvements in critical measures of performance.

B. **TURNING THE ORGANIZATION UPSIDE DOWN TO EMPOWER EMPLOYEES.**

Lecture Notes

PROGRESS CHECK
(page 244 in text)

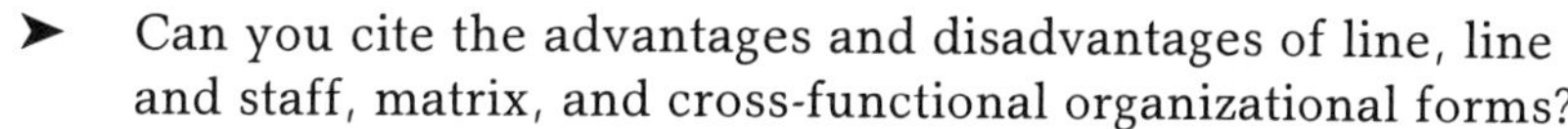

- ➤ Can you cite the advantages and disadvantages of line, line and staff, matrix, and cross-functional organizational forms?
- ➤ Why do cross-functional teams often lead to networking?
- ➤ What are the differences among intranets, internets, and extranets?

OT ACETATE 8-9
The Four "R's" of Organizational Transformation

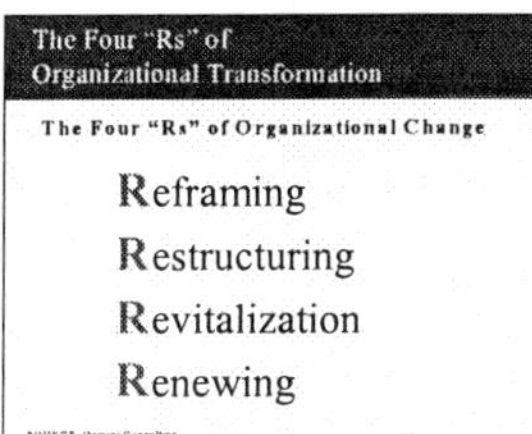

Comments:

1. James Kelly, of Gemini Consulting provided the information for this acetate. Kelly believes that for organizations to promote real, rather than cosmetic change, leaders must first establish a framework for transformation by determining the purpose of the change, its expected benefits, the resources the organization will commit, and the time frame involved. Based on this assumption, Gemini developed the four "R's" of transformation.
2. To better explain this information to students, the four "R's" can be interpreted as such:
   - A. **Reframing** - Adopting a strategic vision, making it an integral part of the cultural mind-set, and mobilizing the organization for change.
   - B. **Restructuring** - Continuously adjusting the business portfolio to keep resources strategically deployed, and reengineering business processes to ensure maximum efficiency and continuous improvement.
   - C. **Revitalization** - Inventing and growing new businesses and leaders.
   - D. **Renewing** - Renewing the organization through strategic alliances, partnerships, joint ventures and other collaborative movements. Growing the organization's people through reskilling, redeploying and leveraging technology to accelerate their rate of learning.
3. The Gemini Consulting Group is located at 25 Airport Road, Morristown, NJ 07960. You might want to contact them for further information or visit the companies web site.

CRITICAL THINKING
(page 245 in text)

Given the dramatic changes that occur when companies adopt cross-functional, self-managed teams, what would prevent the majority of companies from adopting such an organization structure? Given the flexibility and high education requirements of empowered employees, what changes must occur in U.S. schools to prepare students for such jobs?

Lecture Outline

1. Many firms are discovering that the key to long-term success in a competitive market is to empower front-line people to respond quickly to customer wants and needs.
2. The most advanced service organizations have turned the traditional organizational structure upside down.
3. These **INVERTED ORGANIZATIONS** have contact people at the top and the chief executive officer at the bottom.
   a. There are few layers of management, and their job is to assist and support front-line people.
   b. Companies based on this structure support front-line personnel with internal and external databanks, advances communication systems, and professional assistance.
4. **FRONT-LINE PEOPLE HAVE TO BE BETTER EDUCATED, BETTER TRAINED, AND BETTER PAID** than in the past.

C. **TURNING THE ORGANIZATION INSIDE OUT (OUTSOURCING.)**

1. In the past, each organization had a separate department for each function such as accounting, marketing, and production.

Lecture Notes

TRANSPARENCY MASTER 65
Traditional Organizational Chart *(Figure 8.7 on text page 246)*

Transparency masters begin on page 8.87.

TRANSPARENCY MASTER 66
An Inverted Organization *(Figure 8.8 on text page 246)*

Transparency masters begin on page 8.87.

SUPPLEMENTAL CASE 8-3
Empowering Employees at Frito-Lay

See complete case on page 8.84.

MAKING ETHICAL DECISIONS
(Box in text, page 247)

"When Does Benchmarking Become Unethical?"

There is nothing illegal or unethical about researching your competitors and other companies to learn their best practices and then using those best practices in your own firm. But when does such research become unethical?

OT ACETATE 8-10
The Trend Toward Outsourcing

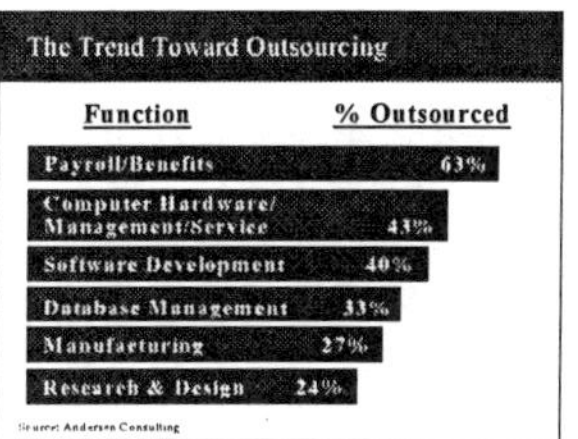

Comments:

1. A growing trend in organizations in the late 1990s has been the shift to outsourcing many functions and business operations. This acetate lists key business functions that are outsourced by organizations as they attempt to cut costs and work more intently on core competencies.
2. Ask students what they feel the results of outsourcing have been on jobs. Some will argue that outsourcing has cost jobs, while others will defend businesses outsourcing specific services and functions and claim it actually creates new jobs.
3. Some question if outsourcing is just another business fad and will not last. This is very doubtful given the competitiveness of today's businesses. See what students think about this and see how many have seen the effects of outsourcing on their jobs.

Lecture Outline

a. Today's organizations are benchmarking each function against the best in the world.

b. **COMPETITIVE BENCHMARKING** is rating an organization's practices, processes, and products against the world's best.

2. If the organization can't do as well as the best, the idea is to outsource the function to an organization that is the best.

    a. **OUTSOURCING** is assigning various functions, such as accounting and legal work, to outside organizations.

    b. Some functions, such as information management and marketing, may be too important to outsource.

3. **CORE COMPETENCIES** are those functions that the organization can do as well or better than anyone else in the world.

D. **CREATING INTERNAL CUSTOMERS.**

1. Some departments would rather function the old way where each department had its own agenda.

2. To improve internal services, management sets up **BUY-SELL RELATIONSHIPS AMONG TEAMS AND BUSINESS UNITS** in the organization.

From the Pages of BusinessWeek
(Box in Text, page 249)
"Strategic Outsourcing"

Larger companies are outsourcing some operations to smaller, more specialized companies that can perform the function more efficiently and faster. That enables companies to compete globally and stay current with the latest changes in markets and technology.

TRANSPARENCY MASTER 67
Bureaucratic Versus Customer-Focused Organization Structure
(Figure 8.9 on text page 249)

TM 67

Transparency masters begin on page 8.89.

3. This creates a **COMPETITIVE SITUATION** between an internal department and an outside firm, forcing internal units to become more internally customer oriented.

VI. ESTABLISHING A SERVICE-ORIENTED CULTURE.

▶ **LEARNING GOAL 6.** Give examples to show how organizational culture and the informal organization can hinder or assist organizational change.

A. Organizational change is bound to cause some **RESISTANCE**, and should be accompanied by the establishment of an **ORGANIZATIONAL CULTURE THAT FACILITATES SUCH CHANGE.**

1. **ORGANIZATIONAL CULTURE** is the widely shared values within an organization that provide coherence and cooperation to achieve common goals.

a. The culture of an organization is reflected in stories, traditions, and myths.

b. An organizational culture can also be negative.

2. Good organizational culture emphasizes **SERVICE TO CUSTOMERS.**

a. The atmosphere is one of friendly, caring people who enjoy working together.

SPOTLIGHT ON SMALL BUSINESS
(Box in text, page 250)

"Fun Night at the Ice Cream Parlor"

Amy's ice cream parlors in Austin and Houston Texas attract a lot of customers because of the off-beat corporate culture that makes her stores special. Employees might be wearing pajamas (Sleep-Over Night) or masks (Star-Wars Night). Lighting may be provided by candles (Romance Night) or strobe lights (Disco Night). It's fun at Amy's—for the employees and for the customers. Corporate culture can go a long way toward making a small company a success or a failure. Ask Amy Miller.

LECTURE ENHANCER 8-14
Effects of Corporate Culture on Performance

John Kotter and James Heskett, Harvard business school professors, extensively surveyed 207 major American companies to analyze their corporate cultures and to quantify the impact of corporate culture on the companies' financial results. (See complete lecture enhancer on page 8.72.)

LECTURE ENHANCER 8-15
The Informal Organization Is Very Important

The informal organization of a firm may be more important than you realize. (See complete lecture enhancer on page 8.73.)

b. Those companies have **LESS NEED FOR CLOSE SUPERVISION** of employees.

c. Within that atmosphere, **SELF-MANAGED TEAMS CAN DEVELOP AND FLOURISH.**

d. The key to productive culture is **MUTUAL TRUST.**

e. The best organizational cultures stress **HIGH MORAL AND ETHICAL VALUES.**

B. **THE INFORMAL ORGANIZATION HELPS CREATE TEAMWORK.**

1. All organizations have two systems.

   a. The **FORMAL ORGANIZATION** appears on the organization chart.

   b. The **INFORMAL ORGANIZATION** is the system of relationships among employees that develop outside the formal organization.

   c. The **FORMAL ORGANIZATION** is the structure that details lines of responsibility, authority, and position.

   d. The **INFORMAL ORGANIZATION** is the system of relationships that develop spontaneously as employees meet and form power centers.

Lecture Notes

LECTURE ENHANCER 8-15
The Informal Organization Is Very Important

The informal organization of a firm may be more important than you realize. (See complete lecture enhancer on page 8.73.)

OT ACETATE 8-11
Downsizing Marches On

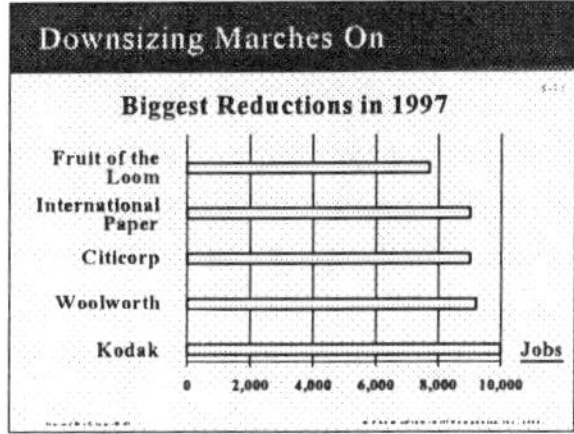

Comments:

1. This acetate complements the previous one in addressing the effects of corporate downsizing in the 1990s.
2. It's easy for students to see here that downsizing has not been universally embraced by workers. In fact it appears that a good deal of job stress is related to insecurities on the job
3. See if students agree with the conclusion of workers on the acetate. Do they feel they will have to work harder in the future to earn a living? In job stability a thing of the past? Good discussion points.
4. Students and workers often construe downsizing as just another form of corporate insensitivity to its employees. The challenge of global markets and advances in production could be a key points to note concerning corporate downsizing
5. The concept of tall versus flat organization structures discussed in the textbook can be easily analyzed here and applied to corporate decisions to downsize.

OT ACETATE 8-12
What Are the Effects of Downsizing?

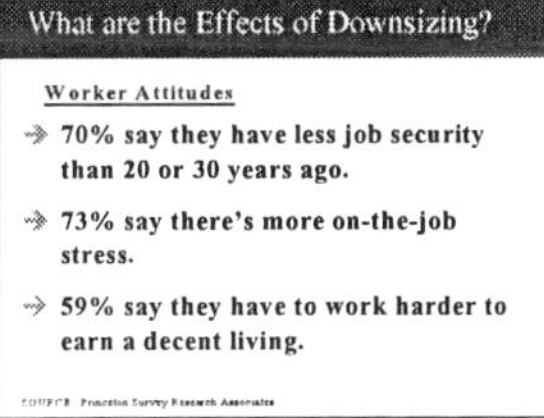

Comments:

1. This acetate complements the previous one in addressing the effects of corporate downsizing in the 1990s.
2. It's easy for students to see here that downsizing has not been universally embraced by workers. In fact it appears that a good deal of job stress is related to insecurities on the job
3. See if students agree with the conclusion of workers on the acetate. Do they feel they will have to work harder in the future to earn a living? In job stability a thing of the past? Good discussion points.
4. Students and workers often construe downsizing as just another form of corporate insensitivity to its employees. The challenge of global markets and advances in production could be a key points to note concerning corporate downsizing
5. The concept of tall versus flat organization structures discussed in the textbook can be easily analyzed here and applied to corporate decisions to downsize.

2. No organization can operate effectively without both types of organization.

   a. The **FORMAL ORGANIZATION** can be **SLOW** and **BUREAUCRATIC**, while the **INFORMAL ORGANIZATION CAN ADAPT QUICKLY.**

   b. The **INFORMAL ORGANIZATION** is **TOO UNSTRUCTURED AND EMOTIONAL** for decision-making, while the **FORMAL ORGANIZATION PROVIDES GUIDELINES AND LINES OF AUTHORITY.**

3. It is wise to learn quickly who the important people are in the informal organization.

4. The center of the informal organization is the **GRAPEVINE**.

5. Successful managers learn to **WORK WITH THE INFORMAL ORGANIZATION** and use it to the organization's advantage.

VII. SUMMARY AND REVIEW.

PROGRESS CHECK
(page 252 in text)

- ➤ What's the difference between continuous improvement and reengineering?
- ➤ What does it mean to turn an organization chart upside down?
- ➤ Inside out?
- ➤ What's an internal customer?
- ➤ How important is the informal organization to the success of organizational change?

OT ACETATE 8-13
Examples of Informal Group Norms

Examples of Informal Group Norms

- ➤ Do your job, but don't produce more than the rest of the group.
- ➤ Don't tell off-color jokes or use profane language among group members.
- ➤ Listen to the boss and use his/her expertise, but don't trust him/her.
- ➤ Everyone is to be clean and organized at their work stations.
- ➤ Never side with managers in a dispute involving group members.
- ➤ Respect and help your fellow group members on the job.
- ➤ Criticize the organization only among group members. Never among strangers.
- ➤ Drinking is done off-the-job. Never at work!

SOURCE: St. Louis Post Dispatch

Comments:

1. Group norms are an interesting topic to discuss in teaching organizational structure. Students have a difficult time relating to many of the formal principles but have not problem identifying the presence and influence of informal groups. This acetate illustrates some examples of group norms that are set in the workplace.
2. You may ask students if they can identify norms in the informal groups in which they are members. Does the group have dress codes? Are there taboo topics in the group? These are just a few possibilities.
3. A discussion could involve the importance of informal groups in the company such as unions and the importance they exert in work situations. You can note to students that unions will be fully covered in chapter 12.

Answers to Practicing Management Decisions

CASE ONE

IBM OUTSOURCES THE MANUFACTURING OF PCS

1. *What technological changes in the world have forced companies to outsource various functions, and what technological innovations allow them to do so with little inconvenience?*

Communications technology makes it possible to find the best products anywhere in the world. If a company cannot make some part of a product better than others, it will go out of business. Therefore, companies have learned to outsource functions such as accounting and, often, production. Communications technology also makes it easy to keep in touch with the other companies. Computers, modems, fax machines, and the like link companies together as closely as departments were once held together.

2. *What affect will outsourcing have on trade relationships among countries?*

Trade relationships should improve as company after company form partnerships of all kinds with companies in other countries. The intrafirm trade will be so great that international trade will naturally follow. In fact, there is so much intrafirm international trade now that international trade figures are inaccurate because they don't always reflect such transfers.

3. *Would it be true to describe the business environment today as a global environment? What words would you use to describe the linkages among companies in many different countries?*

Yes, companies today truly operate in a global environment. McDonald's is as big overseas as in the United States. Honda is as important in the United States as in Japan. International travel and international trade is so open today that most businesses feel the international competition. That is not to say that there aren't a lot of small, local businesses like barber shops and the like. But they may soon face international competition just as other small businesses have in the past. For example, local hamburger places have been replaced by McDonald's and other global companies like Burger King. The same is true of ice cream parlors, stationery shops, hardware stores, and the like.

4. *How much influence will the Internet have on world trade and outsourcing among countries? What does the Internet provide that wasn't available before?*

The Internet is proving to be much more important to world trade than once projected. Not all the glitches have been worked out, but the potential is there. You can now search the Internet for autos, CDS, clothes, and all kinds of goods and services. More are being added by the minute. The Internet provides information, ease of ordering, fast comparison of prices, global access to products, and more. Let your students guide you on this because many of them are way ahead of the faculty when it comes to searching the Web.

CASE TWO

VIDEO CASE: BIG APPLE BAGELS AND THE SAINT LOUIS BREAD COMPANY

1. *Which of Fayol's principles of organization still appear to be used at Big Apple Bagels and the Saint Louis Bread Company and which do not? Why do you suppose this has happened?*

The companies maintain order, equity, and an esprit de corps. However, they don't have unity of command because they use cross-functional teams. Many people can make demands of the team, including customers and other team members. There is no clear hierarchy of authority either. Most people are on the same level: team members. The division of labor is broken down as team members do multiple tasks. Are there dangers in cross-functional teams that could be reduced by going back to the old principles? Should these companies go back? Whey or why not?

2. *Weber was the founder of concepts such as written rules, job descriptions, and consistent procedures. Why are these principles no longer as effective in meeting the needs of customers? To what extent has information technology changed the way organizations can be and are structured?*

Because employees need to respond quickly to customer requests. You can't do that when you have to seek approval for everything.

3. *To what extent has information technology changed the way organizations can be, and are, structured?*

Information technology has everything to do with how organizations are now structured. Computer systems have enabled everyone in the firm to have the same data when making decisions. Customer data is also available to everyone. Therefore, everyone can participate in decision making and often everyone does. That is what self-managed cross-functional teams do. Bonus: Compare cross-functional teams to the old line and staff type organizations and matrix-style organizations.

People on cross-functional teams operate as their own consulting staff and work much the same as in matrix-style organizations, only more permanently.

Lecture Enhancers

LECTURE ENHANCER 8-1

GET ORGANIZED

Life would seem to be getting better in a world where bringing order out of personal chaos is a multimillion-dollar industry. A computer subnotebook, replacing the old packet of paper scraps, can send e-mail, tell time, and beep before a meeting or a big date. A personal digital assistant has built-in software for scheduling, sketching, and note taking—and can even understand your handwriting.

Whole stores bulge with handy tools—boxes, shelving, filing systems, and software—for the badly closeted, the ill-desked, and the overthinged. There is even a national organization for these organizers, the National Association of Professional Organizers, which has created National Get Organized Week.

Could there be a society with all its CDS in order? Its videotapes categorized? Its food recipes databased? Its holiday card lists on floppy disks? Its income-tax returns ready to file on the way to bed after the big New Year's Eve party?

The word, coming directly from Don McCullough, the executive director of the association, is "no." In fact, he confessed, his desk is cluttered and he would need a moment to find the number for the head of a subgroup that deals with "chronic personal disorganization."

Organization is not always desirable. The world would lose some of its unpredictable charm if everyone suddenly shaped up. But since there's no danger of that, you can file this notion away for future reference.

"We say GO, or 'Get Organized,' a motto we hope will encourage people to look at what they do and determine ways to do it more efficiently," said McCullough, whose group, based in Austin, Texas, has 780 members, ranging from people who organize desks to those who manage time to others who help with such problems as out-of-control garages and attics.

"I tell people, 'Throw away everything on top of your desk except for a single yellow legal pad with things you want to do written in a single neat list,"' says Jeffrey Mayer, author of *Time Management for Dummies.* "Use software to remind you to do future things."

"When you type in names, addresses, and phone numbers," notes Mayer, sniffing at what he finds in many a client's drawers, "you are building a powerful source bank, not accumulating thousands of unsortable business cards, bits of paper, and torn-off letterheads."

Other organizers propose solutions that range from tips for the mildly cluttered to the serious strategies needed to rescue the nearly buried. Among them is an Atlanta writer who filled his house with research materials on AIDS, leaving only a narrow path from his front door to his back-room office.

About three to five percent of the U.S. population appears to have some sort of personal organization disorder, Kolberg said. As with many problems, the goal in handling it is progress, not perfection.

One Texas man started to turn his life around when he donated, at the behest of his organization adviser, much of his extensive collection of National Geographic magazines to a woodcarving club that needed wildlife pictures.

The husband of an Atlanta woman became alarmed after his wife saved 634 plastic margarine tubs, saying she intended "to use them for something" but never did. A counselor persuaded her to donate many of them to a charity, where they would find a second life.

People who keep clutter on their desks often do so as a form of security blanket. It's mess, they admit, but a mess they know, control and, in a strange way, have come to love, Kolberg observed.

Life, organizers noted, is often a matter of choices.

Clean desk versus messy desk. E-mail versus paper. Save versus toss. Yet just as people cart home exotic exercise machines, then fail to lose weight because they ignore them, they also purchase schedulers, phone indexers, and other esoteric software programs, yet plunge deeper and deeper into dither.

Good systems follow previous human thought that reflect patterns and humans know. Quicken, a personal accounting software system, has been successful, because it is built around a screen image of a check and a checkbook, two familiar images.

Are there a few words to be said in favor of mess? Yes, said Norman, author of *The Psychology of Everyday things* and vice president of research for Apple Computers. "If you're writing the great American novel, all these organizers aren't going to help you," he said, suggesting that writers and artists might need to go with the flow, accept chaos, revel in its many flavors, and reflect it.

But for most, the cluttered life is more hindrance than inspiration. "We may laugh about being messy and disorganized," Kolberg said, "but for some people, it gets near gridlock."

LECTURE ENHANCER 8-2

A DILBERT VIEW OF DOWNSIZING

Scott Adams, the creator and heart of the cartoon character Dilbert, knows about corporate organization. An M.B.A. from Berkeley, he did time in cubicle 4S700R at Pacific Bell. He claims he is "the first cartoonist to write about business from the inside, from the perspectives of 17 years in cubicle hell."

His take on corporate downsizing? "After all the bright people fled, companies realized they had to make downsizing sound like more of a positive development in order to keep morale high. This was accomplished through a creative process of inventing happier-sounding phrases that meant essentially the same thing. 'You're fired' (1980); 'You're laid off' (1985); 'You're downsized (1990); "You're rightsized" (1995). I expect the trend to continue. You'll see the following phrases used during the next five years. 'You're happysized!'; 'You're spendidsized'; 'You're orgasmsizided!'"

LECTURE ENHANCER 8-3

BUREAUCRACY STRANGLES INTRAPRENEURSHIP

In the 1980s "intrapreneurship" became a buzzword among managers who wanted to introduce small-business fervor into lumbering corporations. The idea was that the parent company would provide seed money to employees, who would gain the satisfaction of running their own shop while producing products that benefitted their corporate sponsor.

The ventures did produce some successes. IBM developed its IBM Personal Computer through such a venture. At Xerox Corporation about half dozen successful companies have been created. Most, though, have fallen flat. Companies like Control Data Corporation and Northwestern Bell Telephone Co. have ended their programs. So did IBM, which says the program was unnecessary after the company decentralized. Of the 14 ventures Eastman Kodak created, six have been shut down, three have been sold, four have been merged into the company, and only one still operates independently. One of Kodak's projects was canceled because the company didn't like the unit's logo, a Cheshire cat, considering it too frivolous for a serious organization.

The problem, management experts say, is that a go-go small business culture can't easily be grafted onto a deliberate corporate giant. The practices that make corporations successful—training procedures, personnel policies, hierarchical management structures—are incompatible with risk-taking entrepreneurs. In addition, employees-turned-entrepreneurs are often ill-prepared for their new roles. Researchers, for example, who have spent their careers in the Lab are unfamiliar with the rigors of the marketplace.

LECTURE ENHANCER 8-4

BOB FELTON HATES BUREAUCRACY

Bob Felton was walking past a conference room at Indus Group headquarters when he noticed the company's technical writers were settling in. "What's going on?" he asked. "We're having our Friday afternoon staff meeting," came the reply.

"It's over," he declared.

"We just started!"

"It's over." he said again. "We don't have staff meetings here."

Mr. Felton has no problems with meetings per se, just with regularly scheduled meetings. "People should talk to each other every day," he says. "They shouldn't save up what they have to say to try to look good in front of everyone else."

Bob Felton is compulsive about communication because he considers isolation the worst affliction in any organization. Indeed, it was through the collaboration and spontaneity of employees that his software-development company grew to nearly $100 million in sales in seven years. Such free communication can also expose the trouble spots in a company.

Felton learned the stultifying effects of bureaucracy in the Navy, where he was a commander in the nuclear-submarine fleet. Later, he witnessed the perils of haughty management at an engineering company that nearly failed. "Part of the way we run this company," he says today, referring to Indus Group, "is from the scar that's still there" from that debacle.

He formed Indus in 1990 with $2 million in real-estate and stock-market earnings to develop software for operating utility' plants, refineries and other huge processing operations. He and his partners didn't particularly need the work; they were in it to build something and have fun. So they vowed to create a culture in which people came to work eagerly and left with a sense of satisfaction. That, in turn, meant battling against fiefs.

Felton was not opposed to hierarchy, or chains of command. Employees need bosses, he says, and bosses needed bosses. Ultimately someone has to make a decision. But he resolved never to publish a policy manual; doing so, he reasoned, would only seed a bureaucracy of enforcement. He vowed never to create a personnel department; putting people in charge of other people and nothing else risked the creation of too much process overhead.

Only two rules would exist, he declared: 1. "Delight your internal and external customer," and 2. "Use your best judgment."

Early on, with just 20 people in the company, two key software developers had personal reasons to leave San Francisco—one for Pittsburgh, the other for Portland, Oregon. Felton suggested that each of them file a memo to let everyone else know what they were doing—a way of combating isolation. Today, all of Indus's 400 employees regularly file these personal-action reports, identifying, among other things, obstacles to their work. Everyone's report is electronically posted for everyone else's inspection.

Felton responds to enough of them that everyone in the company, especially the bosses, knows that he is watching closely. One project manager insisted on exercising prior approval over the reports posted by his subordinates. "He's no longer with us," Felton says.

After taking the company public in 1997, Felton divided Indus into regions and created additional management—all of which sounds like the very creeping bureaucracy he vowed never to allow. But Indus, he says, has an antidote to prevent structure from becoming bureaucracy. "Anybody," he says, "can communicate with anybody at any time."

LECTURE ENHANCER 8-5

HORIZONTAL STRUCTURE: THE ORGANIZATION OF THE 1990S

Self-managing teams are a major tenet of the flat organization structure. The structure is based on one basic idea: The people who do the work should have the means to change to meet the needs of the customer.

The text discusses the trend away from tall organization structure and toward flat or horizontal organization structure. Some analysts believe organizations should follow the example set by law firms and have only three hierarchial levels: associate, partner, and senior partner. The career path would be a progression to more complex work and more important clients. Titles don't change, but everyone knows each others' status.

Self-managing teams are a major tenet of the flat organization structure. The structure is based on one basic idea: The people who do the work should have the means to change to meet the needs of the customer. Marvin Weisbord, an expert on organizational development, notes that self-management typically delivers 40 percent increases in output per man-hour.

How does an organization adopt this horizontal structure? Doug Smith and Frank Ostroff of McKinsey Smith, a blue-chip consulting firm on organization, offers these ten keys for a horizontal company:

1. **Organize around process, not task.** Identify the process that meet customer needs. For example, low cost or fast service can be addressed by order generation and new-product development processes.
2. **Flatten the hierarchy by minimizing subdivisions of processes**. Arrange teams that do lots of steps in a process rather than just a few steps.
3. **Give senior leaders charge of processes and process performance.**
4. **Link performance objectives and evaluation to customer satisfaction.**
5. **Make teams, not individuals, the focus of organization performance and design.**
6. **Combine managerial and non-managerial activities** as often as possible.
7. **Encourage each employee** to develop several competencies.
8. **Train people on a just-in-time, need-to-perform basis.**
9. **Maximize supplier and customer contact** with everyone in the organization.
10. **Reward individual skill development and team performance** rather than individual performance alone.

LECTURE ENHANCER 8-6

THE RETURN OF THE MIDDLE MANAGER

After years of being disrespected, devalued and discarded by corporate America, middle managers are emerging as prized players once again.

"There has been an incredible turnaround," said John A. Challenger, executive vice president of Chicago-based outplacement firm Challenger, Gray & Christmas. "Middle managers have gone from being pilloried, cast out as bureaucrats to being among the most highly prized, skilled, and knowledgeable people in the marketplace." In fact, companies across the country plan to add to managerial and professional staffs at "unprecedented rates" in the first half of this year, said Alan R. Schonberg, president of Management Recruiters International Inc.

An MRI survey of 4,300 executives indicated 56 percent plan to increase their managerial and professional staffing levels in the first half of this year, the highest rate recorded since the survey began 16 years ago. Another 37.3 percent plan to maintain current levels and only 6.7 percent plan decreases. The survey found demand will be strongest in such high-growth fields as telecommunications and information technology.

With the national unemployment rate for managers and professionals at 1.7 percent in December, shortages will be "extreme," Schonberg said. "The market for those in the segment . . . has never, ever been hotter."

Schonberg's assessment falls at the most bullish end of the spectrum—other observers are more cautiously optimistic—but clearly the picture has brightened. At the more careful end is the American Management Association (AMA), which tracks job creation by category, separating middle managers from salaried professionals and technical workers.

Of the jobs created by the association's member firms from July 1996 through June of 1997, "Nine percent went to middle managers compared with 22 percent to salaried professionals and technical workers."

Also, massive corporate layoffs are not exactly a thing of the past, and if history is any indicator, this is bad news for middle managers. Middle managers make up five to eight percent of the work force, but every year, they are between 16 and 20 percent of those losing jobs. (The AMA defines middle managers as those above the frontline supervisors but below the senior managers who report directly to CEOs.)

There are still major downsizings, so there is a weird dynamic going on. One piece of that dynamic is a decline in loyalty to any individual employer—a factor that is costing companies big bucks as they try to attract, and retain, quality employees.

For the last few years, the message has been "Employees need to learn to take care of themselves. . . . This is not employment for life." The employee who hears it is working on his or her own career and personal development, so companies, particularly in go-go sectors like technology, need to make special efforts to attract and retain high-quality managers.

The lures include signing bonuses; so-called "golden handcuffs," such as bonuses that are not payable until the end of a year or stock options that vest over time; and generous relocation packages. Indeed, a broad survey by Right Management last summer found 44 percent of responding firms had made use of retention bonuses.

Still, for those who are in the job market, things never feel exactly rosy until a job is landed. The difficulty of an individual job search varies, and often, age is a factor.

A recent study by American Management Association found the younger the person who lost a job through involuntary termination, the quicker he or she found a new job and the greater his or her chances of improving his or her salary.

Laid-off workers under age 35 took an average of 3.4 months to find a new job and on average, their new jobs paid 110.7 percent of what their previous job paid. In contrast, those ages 45 to 54 took an average of 5.6 months to find a new job, and those jobs on average paid 95.5 percent of what the previous job paid.

Things were especially difficult for middle managers laid off in the '80s, noted Charles W. Sweet, president of A.T. Kearney Executive Search in Chicago.

"Very frankly, the people who were in middle management . . . were blown out of the labor markets," he said. "They bought franchises, or retired, but they have not found their way back into the traditional corporate economy."

And because imaginative managers are difficult to find and costly to recruit, many firms are investing heavily in training and development—both through in-house programs and by reimbursement for outside schooling.

LECTURE ENHANCER 8-7

DECENTRALIZATION, SPAN OF CONTROL

In the past two decades the hierarchical model has begun to change. One trend: managers have increased the number of people reporting to them. After taking over Franklin Mint in 1985, Stewart Resnick cut management layers from six to four while nearly doubling sales. He has also doubled the number of people reporting to him to twelve.

Many experts, such as J. Brian Quinn of Darthmouth, believe the number could be much larger than that. He argues that spans of control—the number of subordinates one executive can effectively command—are giving way to "spans of communications," the number of people an executive can reach through a good information system. Ultimately, he says, one manager could have as many as 200 people reporting to him.

These trimmed companies will occasionally find themselves short-handed. Instead of rebuilding staffs, they can create temporary task forces to address particular problems, such as a quality glitch. Or they can hire consultants or outside specialists. IBM signed up a new Pitney Bowes service to run mail rooms, stockrooms, and reproduction operations in two locations on a trial basis.

LECTURE ENHANCER 8-8

DELEGATION AND MISTAKES

Kenneth H. Olsen, founder of Digital Equipment Corporation, was known for his autocratic style. However, at the same time he strongly believed in delegating responsibility, something other computer entrepreneurs have found difficult to do.

In delegating responsibility, Mr. Olsen was always willing to forgive worker mistakes. John F. Smith, Digital's twelfth employee and now the vice president for engineering and manufacturing, recalls buying a $7,000 soldering machine, a huge investment at the time, that proved unreliable. He says he came in nights and weekends to adjust it so Mr. Olsen wouldn't realize his error.

Ultimately, Mr. Smith bought a replacement machine, moved the lemon to a vacant storeroom, covered it with a canvas, and thought he had gotten away with it. Several years later he came across the machine and idly lifted the covering. He found a hand-lettered sign that read "Smith's folly. (signed) Ken Olsen."

LECTURE ENHANCER 8-9

A JAPANESE MANAGER INTERPRETS RESPONSIBILITY

In his sixth week as managing director of the Hanshin Tigers baseball team, Shingo Furuya called his wife to say goodbye and jumped out of an eighth-floor window to the ground 92 feet below. His suicide was both the act of a deeply despondent individual no longer able to cope and a lesson in how seriously many Japanese managers view responsibility. While many Americans feel little company loyalty and switch easily between companies, Japanese tend to regard a job as a lifetime position and judge themselves in the light of how well they do it.

Individually assuming corporate blame is a deeply rooted practice in Japan, even when the person in charge may not have made the mistake. In 1985, for example, the president of Japan Air Lines stepped down after one of his company's jets crashed into a mountainside, killing 520 people.

Baseball managing directors in Japan, unlike general managers of U.S. teams, seldom arrange trades or put together rosters. Yet they are held responsible if the team fares badly. Furuya's title was managing director, but, says sports commentator Shinya Sasaki, "He was just another middle-class manager forced to shoulder heavy responsibility without being given authority to make a decision."

LECTURE ENHANCER 8-10

THE FIRST AMERICAN ORGANIZATION CHART

Henry Varnum Poor was perhaps the first American to draw an organization chart, during his study of railroad management in the 1860s. Poor's chart was in the form of a tree, with the president and board of directors as the roots, the operating divisions and service departments as the branches, and the lesser superintendents and employees as the leaves.

LECTURE ENHANCER 8-11

MANAGING THE BOSS

Most managers have a boss. Few people are as important to the success of a manager as the boss. Yet management books and courses give plenty of advice on how to manage subordinates, few even mention managing the boss. Few employees believe that the boss can be managed at all. They complain about the boss but do little to manage him (or her). Yet managing the boss is fairly simple—often simpler than managing subordinates.

Peter Drucker offers us a few Do's and Don'ts in boss management. These include:

1. DO realize it is both your duty and in your self interest to make the boss as effective and as achieving as possible.
2. DO learn what your boss's idiosyncrasies are, what are his or her strengths and weaknesses, likes and pet peeves. The key is to respond to them in a manner that helps the supervisor be effective and efficient. Your goal is to make the boss's strengths effective and the weaknesses irrelevant. For example, if the boss is good at marketing but uncomfortable with financial figures and analysis, bring him into the marketing decision but prepare the financial analysis beforehand.
3. DO create a relationship of trust. This means making sure your boss has confidence you will play to his or her strengths and safeguard the boss against his or her limitations and weaknesses.
4. DO keep the boss aware. Make sure the boss understands what you are up to, what to expect, and what not to expect.
5. DON'T expose the boss to surprises—even pleasant ones. To be surprised in the organization one is responsible for is humiliating and usually publicly humiliating.
6. DON'T underrate the boss! The boss may look stupid—and looks are not always deceiving but there is no risk at all in overrating a boss. The worst that can happen is the boss may feel flattered. But if you underrate the boss he could see it and resent it. Or the boss could attribute to you the same brain deficiency you attributed to the boss and will consider you ignorant, dumb, or lacking in imagination.

LECTURE ENHANCER 8-12

CROSS-FUNCTIONAL TEAMS FOR SMALL COMPANIES

Betty Wagner graduated from a community college and went to work for a small metal fabricator called Cavalier Gage & Electronic. She began as a secretary, but moved up through the ranks, eventually buying the company from its owner.

When Betty had her third child (the second still being a toddler), she found that managing the company by herself was too much. Therefore, she turned her company from a boss-driven firm into a team operation. She began by opening her books and sharing the information with her managers. Together they developed the company's first business plan—decided to target small medical equipment manufacturers.

Working together, a cross-functional team was able to cut bidding time on new contracts from two days to less than an hour. Using total quality concepts such as continuous improvement, the company eventually became one of only 2,500 U.S. companies to be certified for ISO 9000 international standards. It's quite possibly the smallest company to be so certified. The company was in trouble when Betty decided to go to cross-functional teams. Now it's thriving and she's rehiring many of the workers she had to let go when times were tough.

Betty Wagner is just one of thousands of managers throughout the world who've restructured their organizations to stay competitive in global markets. Many leading U.S. firms—including Motorola, American Express, Bell Atlantic, General Motors, AT&T, IBM. Kodak, Taco Bell, and Mack Trucks—have gone through drastic organizational changes in the past few years. Ms. Wagner shows, however, that such changes are equally important in smaller firms. Few developments in business have more far-reaching implications for today's students than the organizational changes now taking place.

LECTURE ENHANCER 8-13

SELF-ORGANIZING: ANOTHER APPROACH TO STRUCTURE

Recently many management experts have been using the term "self-organization." The business world has seen many experiments with empowerment, teaming, listening to the voice of the customer, and organizational learning. These are movements toward self organization.

The Unshackled Organization by Jeffrey Goldstein offers one definition of a self-organizing enterprise: "Self-organization is not hierarchically driven. Instead, it is a process of system transformation that is self-generating. Self organization happens when a work group or an organization is facing a challenge and is allowed to respond to that challenge in a spontaneous, unshackled manner. . . [A] work group or organization as a natural system will spontaneously know how to reorganize in the face of a challenge, if the obstacles hindering its capacity to self-organize are removed."

Goldstein also talks about teams, another popular subject. He warns, however, that trying to impose a structure over a culture that isn't oriented toward collaborative behavior won't succeed. That may create teams, but not necessarily teams that are effective. Rather, it is better to create real teams, which are the result of self-organization, as people begin to work together to work through problems and difficulties.

LECTURE ENHANCER 8-14

EFFECTS OF CORPORATE CULTURE ON PERFORMANCE

John Kotter and James Heskett, Harvard business school professors, extensively surveyed 207 major American companies to analyze their corporate cultures and to quantify the impact of corporate culture on the companies' financial results. What they found is that the cultures of the most successful companies serve the interest of three groups of stakeholders: customers, employees, and stockholders.

Companies that satisfied only one or two of these groups showed an average increase of sales of 166 percent vs. 682 percent for those that satisfied all three. For example, Citicorp is a financial giant that has a strong culture, but is a relatively poor performer. Citicorp had a high survey score for customer service, but low scores for satisfying stockholders and employees.

LECTURE ENHANCER 8-15

THE INFORMAL ORGANIZATION IS VERY IMPORTANT

The informal organization of a firm may be more important than you realize. When you read the text, you may get the idea that the informal organization is nothing more than a bunch of rumors and hearsay that is spread among the employees. But, in reality, such rumors and gossip are very important in maintaining company-wide information flows. Results of a study by CPA\Administrative Reports show that the office grapevine is 75 percent to 90 percent accurate and provides managers and staff with better information than formal communications.

The rumor mill is busier than ever in corporations because of all the restructuring and takeovers that are happening. People wonder whether or not they are going to be laid off or forced to move. This makes them more eager to believe and start rumors.

Rather than ignore or try to suppress the "grapevine," managers should tune in to it. In fact, they should identify the people in the organization who are key to the information flow and feed them information that they can spread to others. Managers should make as big an effort to know who their internal disseminator of information is as they do to find the proper person to send a press release. Then, like the California raisins, the employees can be sure of what they hear because they "heard it through the grapevine!"

Critical Thinking Exercises

Name: ____________________

Date: ____________________

CRITICAL THINKING EXERCISE 8-1

YOU, THE MANAGER

Think of a job you have performed alone. It can be a paid job or a job you have done around the house such as cleaning or doing laundry. You have done the work alone in the past, but help is on the way! Imagine we are giving you three people to help you do the work and are making you their manager. Write down how you will divide up the duties. For each duty describe the authority that goes with the responsibility. (For example, the person who mops the floor must have the authority to take the mop and bucket from the broom closet.)

EMPLOYEE 1

DUTIES (RESPONSIBILITIES)	AUTHORITY
______________________	______________________
______________________	______________________
______________________	______________________
______________________	______________________
______________________	______________________

EMPLOYEE 2

DUTIES (RESPONSIBILITIES)	AUTHORITY
______________________	______________________
______________________	______________________
______________________	______________________
______________________	______________________
______________________	______________________

EMPLOYEE 3

DUTIES (RESPONSIBILITIES)	AUTHORITY
______________________	______________________
______________________	______________________
______________________	______________________
______________________	______________________
______________________	______________________

Name: ______________________

Date: ______________________

CRITICAL THINKING EXERCISE 8-2

ORGANIZATION CHART

Dr. Rea Searge is president of Peabody Researchers, Inc, a pharmaceutical company. Peabody uses a line and staff structure to organize its employees. On a separate sheet of paper, draw an organization chart of Peabody Researchers, Inc. In addition to Dr. Searge, Peabody has the following employees:

A quality control officer

A vice-president of production

A research and development department of 150 people

A sales force of 100 people

A vice-president of finance

Marketing managers for three regions

A vice-president of marketing

A director of personnel

A vice-president of research and development

Production managers for three product lines

An administrative assistant to the president

A production force of 500 people

ANSWERS TO CRITICAL THINKING EXERCISE 8-2

The following people are **staff**:

director of personnel

vice-president for research and development

administrative assistant to the president

research and development department

quality control officer

The rest have **line** positions.

Let the students draw the chart on the board with as little assistance as possible so they can think it through.

Supplemental Cases

CASE 8-1

RESTRUCTURING HITS MANAGEMENT POSITIONS

AT&T trimmed 9,000 people from its work force in 1990. The company had already cut 24,000 jobs in 1986. Du Pont announced a cut of some 10,000 jobs in 1991. The list of companies with similar stories is quite long. In fact, 66 percent of the companies with more than 5,000 employees have recently downsized their organizations. Half of the smaller companies let workers go as well. Job cuts in 1992 reached 2,700 per business day! Even top-flight managers with good work records are not immune to the budget ax. A recent study indicated that typical 40-year-old white-collar workers will change jobs two or three times in the rest of their careers at least once voluntarily. This includes a vast group of real estate managers, central purchasing agents, human resources specialists, futurologists, economists, planners, and analysts of all kinds.

Such a restructuring is inevitable in a period when competition from foreign firms is intensifying. American firms had grown fat around the middle and needed to become "lean and mean" to be more efficient and productive. Once lower-level employees were eliminated, managers logically followed.

Tom Peters, coauthor of *In Search of Excellence,* believes the staffs of the Fortune 500 companies are still hopelessly bloated. Peters feels that many of those managers got their M.B.A. degree and got to top positions without ever getting real-world experience in designing, making, selling, and servicing products. They tend to rely on technology rather than people for their answers and ignore the retraining and redeployment of the work force.

Peters recommends that managers get out of their offices and ask their workers how to make the firm more productive. Then they should visit customers to learn what they would like to see changed. Management is no longer viewed as an intellectual position involving planning, organizing, leading, and controlling. Rather, it is a hands-on job where managers and employees work as a team to make the firm productive. Those who used to sit and ponder are out of there. More cuts will be coming.

Once they are out the company doors, unemployed managers are finding a hard reality. There are more professionals fighting for fewer jobs than in the past. The average laid-off manager took eight months to find a new job in 1990. That's two months longer than in 1989. Outplacement firms report that more laid-off managers than ever are becoming seriously depressed. In fact, one counseling program identified nineteen who appeared suicidal, up from only three the year before.

What is being done to help these displaced managers? One growing business is outplacement services, which grew from a small industry twenty years ago to a $500 million industry in 1991. Ninety percent of downsizing large companies offer such help to their laid-off managers. Social institutions, such as churches, are also forming counseling groups of out-of-work members.

Some laid-off managers find themselves halfway back at their old companies. In fact, 38 percent of restructuring companies continue to use former employees as independent contractors. IBM had three of its ex-managers set up an executive placement company that sends former IBM managers back to Big Blue temporarily, though not in their previous jobs.

Other out-of-work managers use being laid off as a chance to escape the corporate world completely. About one quarter of them seriously consider becoming entrepreneurs; twelve percent actually did so in 1990. Although being laid off can represent an opportunity for a better career, it will never be an easy experience, no matter how common it becomes.

DISCUSSION QUESTIONS FOR CASE 8-1:

1. What does the reduction in middle management jobs mean for tomorrow's undergraduate and graduate business students?

2. How could you, as the president of a firm, decide which managers to let go?

3. What are the advantages and disadvantages of cutting staff personnel in areas like personnel, quality control, planning, and auditing? Could there be serious consequences of rapid cutbacks in management?

4. What alternatives does a company have when it seems top-heavy with staff, other than firing them all and becoming leaner and meaner in one swift action?

ANSWERS TO DISCUSSION QUESTIONS FOR CASE 8-1:

1. *What does the reduction in middle management jobs mean for tomorrow's undergraduate and graduate business students?*

   When they are moving up the corporate ladder, there will be fewer positions available, and competition for those positions will be stiffer.

2. *How could you, as the president of a firm, decide which managers to let go?*

   Some managers could be encouraged to take early retirement; others may leave if given incentives and help in finding new jobs. After that, you would have to carefully evaluate the effectiveness of each manager and dismiss those who are not contributing enough. (You may want to discuss the whole issue of firing people here and the difficulties involved, including psychological difficulties.)

3. *What are the advantages and disadvantages of cutting staff personnel in areas like personnel, quality control, planning, and auditing? Could there be serious consequences of rapid cutbacks in management?*

   The best answer to this question is one that emerges from a class discussion of the value of staff managers to an organization and the cost of losing them. Quality control, for example, may seem too costly to have, but may be absolutely necessary in the long run because of lost customers caused by product defects. The same is true of the need for planning and auditing. Such functions may seem easy to cut until mistakes occur and the company had not planned for change or the IRS calls top managers in to audit the books. Naturally, a firm can have too many staff positions, but that does not mean that staff positions are not necessary.

4. *What alternatives does a company have when it seems top-heavy with staff, other than firing them all and becoming leaner and meaner in one swift action?*

   IBM retrained its staff members and made them members of the marketing team. Moving people from staff to line positions is one way of getting rid of staff. Another is to simply not replace staff members when they quit or retire. Another strategy is to hire an outplacement manager to help staff members find positions in other firms.

CASE 8-2

CREATING CROSS-FUNCTIONAL TEAMS

The Direct Response Group (DRG) at Capital Holding is a direct marketer of life, health, property, and casualty insurance. In the past, it sold a mass-produced product to a mass market. Over time, however; sales slowed, profits eroded, and the company decided it had to refocus its efforts. That meant, for one thing, selling to particular, identifiable customers and giving those customers a customized product/service package that was world class, enabling the company to compete globally.

Organizational change began with a vision statement that emphasized caring, listening to, and satisfying customers-one on one. To accomplish that goal, the company formed a cross-functional team to study the sales, service. and marketing processes and completely redesign those functional areas. The idea was to have a world-class customer-driven company. That meant gathering as much information as possible about customers.

Front-line customer-contact people were empowered with user-friendly information systems that made it possible for one contact person, working with a support team, to handle any question that customers had. Management used external databases to get detailed information on some 15 million consumers. The combined internal and external databases were used to develop custom-made products for specific customer groups.

The whole company was focused on satisfying customer wants and needs. That meant changing processes within the firm so that they were geared toward the customer. For example, one case worker is now attached to each customer, and that case worker is responsible for following an application through the entire approval and product design process. Previously, many people handled the application and no one person was responsible for it.

An analysis of the corporate culture showed that people were more concerned with pleasing their bosses than pleasing the customer. People hoarded information instead of sharing information because the people with information had power. The information system had to be changed to encourage sharing.

A pilot program was started whereby a customer-management team was formed to serve 40,000 customers. The team consisted of 10 customer service representatives and their support team (a marketer, an expert in company operations, and an information systems person). Employees are now rewarded for performance, and merit raises are based on team performance to encourage team participation.

DISCUSSION QUESTIONS FOR CASE 8-2:

1. Are traditional bureaucracies set up to provide custom-made products to individual consumers? Could they be, or is it always better to have customer-oriented teams design such products?

2. Anyone who has worked in team situations has discovered that some members of the team work harder than others; nonetheless, the whole team is often rewarded based on the overall results, not individual effort. How could team evaluations be made so that individual efforts could be recognized and rewarded?

3. What service organizations, private or public, would you like to see become more customer-oriented? How could this case be used as a model for that organization?

4. What are some major impediments to implementing customer-oriented teams in service organizations?

ANSWERS TO DISCUSSION QUESTIONS FOR CASE 8-2:

1. *Are traditional bureaucracies set up to provide custom-made products to individual consumers? Could they be, or is it always better to have customer-oriented teams design such products?*

   Traditional bureaucracies are organizations that have many layers of management who set rules and regulations and participate in all decisions. Such an organization, by definition, would be unable to swiftly respond to customer needs. Decision making needs to be placed close to the customer, not in successive layers of management.

2. *Anyone who has worked in team situations has discovered that some members of the team work harder than others; nonetheless the whole team is often rewarded based on the overall results, not individual effort. How could team evaluations be made so that individual efforts could be recognized and rewarded?*

   Team contributions are team contributions and difficult to isolate as individual efforts. In fact, the purpose of team organization is to combine the best efforts of many individuals rather than relying on only one. Team members exercise informal pressure to ensure continued quality effort. Such informal pressure is much more effective than organizational efforts.

3. *What service organizations, private or public, would your like to see become more customer oriented? How could this case be used as a model for that organization?*

   The chances are that almost every students' list will contain (1) the U.S. Postal Service and (2) your school. This case shows that the entire organization must be committed to the customer-oriented team approach for it to be effective. Such an approach would be difficult in a public organization such as the Post Office. The potential for creating a customer-oriented school should be interesting to pursue.

4. *What are some of the major impediments to implementing customer-oriented teams in service organizations?*

   Service organizations are quite different from product-producing organizations in that there is no distance between the production of the service and the customer. The service is created when the customer receives it. Most service-organizations already have a customer-oriented focus. This case shows, however, that much improvement can be made in the delivery of that service.

CASE 8-3

EMPOWERING EMPLOYEES AT FRITO-LAY

Frito-Lay's sales force under a traditional management structure was doing about $700 million in sales per year. Now, annual sales are closer to $2 billion. What made the difference? Frito-Lay decided that its salespeople were entrepreneurs who needed support and guidance to quickly and efficiently respond to the wants and needs of commercial customers. They call on commercial accounts over 100,000 times a day. Old-fashioned management was simply not designed to handle such conditions. Instead, Frito-Lay had to empower its salespeople to make decisions on the spot. That meant finding good people and giving them as much responsibility as possible. Then the entire company was organized to support the people on the front line.

Everyone in product development, distribution, and human resources tries to create an environment that encourages and supports involvement with customers. Frito-Lay sells directly to commercial customers. That makes the product fresher. Managers support the people in the field. They provide them information and do everything they can to make the field salesperson's job easier.

One way Frito-Lay made the salesperson's job easier was to give each of them a hand-held computer to track orders and to reduce paperwork. The computers calculate totals (including sales tax and discounts), print out sales tickets (using printers in the truck), and send data back to the company for analysis. Salespeople can also receive data from the company about the status of an order. The goal at Frito-Lay is to never have inventory on hand that is more than two-days old. Thus its Doritos, Lay's potato chips, Ruffles, and Fritos corn chips are fresh and crisp when you buy them.

DISCUSSION QUESTIONS FOR CASE 8-3:

1. Why is it better to have research reports go directly to salespeople rather than to managers who then tell salespeople what the managers feel that salespeople need to know?

2. How will training of managers differ from traditional training now that managers are no longer considered bosses, but are servants, supporters, coaches, and cheer leaders?

3. Managers may still do planning, organization, and some controlling of operations, but much more of such planning is done with other departments such as distribution and production. What kinds of companies would be more efficient by having cross-departmental teams doing planning, organizing, and controlling? What firms may be better off keeping the traditional functional structure?

4. How would you compare a sales job at Frito Lay with other sales jobs you have known? Can you see the advantages to salespeople of empowerment? Are there any disadvantages?

ANSWERS TO DISCUSSION QUESTIONS FOR CASE 8-3:

1. *Why is it better to have research reports go directly to salespeople rather than to managers who then tell salespeople what the managers feel that salespeople need to know?*

Salespeople interact with customers on a daily basis. They are better able to interpret research data than managers in distant offices. They can also obtain feedback from customers on product ideas and acceptance, giving research reports an additional dimension.

2. *How will training of managers differ from traditional training now that managers are no longer considered bosses, but are servants, supporters, coaches, and cheer leaders?*

Managers must learn different skills than before. Technical skills will be needed less and human relations skills more. Cooperative decision making must be stressed, likewise motivation strategies and techniques. Above all, communication must be improved upward and downward.

3. *Managers may still do planning, organization, and some controlling of operations, but much more of such planning is done with other departments such as distribution and production. What kinds of companies would be more efficient by having cross-departmental teams doing planning, organizing, and controlling? What firms may be better off keeping the traditional functional structure?*

Firms with similar products or services could benefit by having cross-departmental teams doing planning. For organizations with many different types of products and services, planning, organizing, and controlling may also need to be handled very differently.

4. *How would you compare a sales job at Frito Lay with other sales jobs you have known? Can you see the advantages to salespeople of empowerment? Are there any disadvantages?*

Salespeople at Frito Lay have much greater freedom than traditional sales positions do. They also have more decision making authority and control of their activities. This type job will be attractive to people who are organized, self-motivated, and technically skilled. There is a large proportion of the work force who are able workers, but lack this self-drive. They would be miserable in this type position.

Transparency Masters

TRANSPARENCY MASTER 58	Chapter Outline
TRANSPARENCY MASTER 59	A Typical Organizational Structure *(Figure 8.1 on text page 230)*
TRANSPARENCY MASTER 60	Bureaucratic Organization Structure *(Figure 8.2 on text page 234)*
TRANSPARENCY MASTER 61	Ways to Departmentalize *(Figure 8.3 on text page 238)*
TRANSPARENCY MASTER 62	Organization Types *(Figure 8.4 on text page 240)*
TRANSPARENCY MASTER 63	A Matrix Organization *(Figure 8.5 on text page 242)*
TRANSPARENCY MASTER 64	Different Types of Teams *(Figure 8.6 on text page 244)*
TRANSPARENCY MASTER 65	Traditional Organizational Chart *(Figure 8.7 on text page 246)*
TRANSPARENCY MASTER 66	An Inverted Organization *(Figure 8.8 on text page 246)*
TRANSPARENCY MASTER 67	Bureaucratic Versus Customer-Focused Organization Structure *(Figure 8.9 on text page 249)*

Chapter Outline

CHAPTER 8
ORGANIZING A CUSTOMER-DRIVEN BUSINESS

PROFILE: Mei-Lin Cheng and Julie Anderson of Hewlett-Packard

I. THE CHANGING ORGANIZATIONAL HIERARCHY.

A. The Fundamentals of Bureaucracy.

II. HOW ORGANIZATIONS HAVE EVOLVED.

A. The Background of Organizational Theory.

B. Fayol's Principles of Organization.

C. Max Weber and Organizational Theory.

III. DESIGNING MORE RESPONSIVE ORGANIZATIONS.

A. Tall Versus Flat Organization Structure.

B. Choosing the Appropriate Span of Control.

C. Advantages and Disadvantages of Departmentalization.

D. Different Ways to Departmentalize.

E. Centralization Versus Decentralization of Authority.

IV. ORGANIZATION MODELS.

A. Line Organizations.

B. Line-and-Staff Organizations.

C. Matrix Organizations.

V. CROSS-FUNCTIONAL, SELF-MANAGED TEAMS.

A. Limitations of Cross-Functional Teams.

B. Cross-Functional Teams Lead to Networking.

C. Extranets Link Company Intranets.

VI. THE RESTRUCTURING PROCESS AND TOTAL QUALITY.

A. Turning the Organization Upside Down to Empower Employees.

B. Turning the Organization Inside Out (Outsourcing).

C. Creating Internal Customers.

VII. ESTABLISHING A SERVICE-ORIENTED CULTURE.

A. The Informal Organization Helps Create Teamwork.

VIII. SUMMARY AND REVIEW.

TM-59

A Typical Organizational Structure

(Figure 8.1 on text page 230)

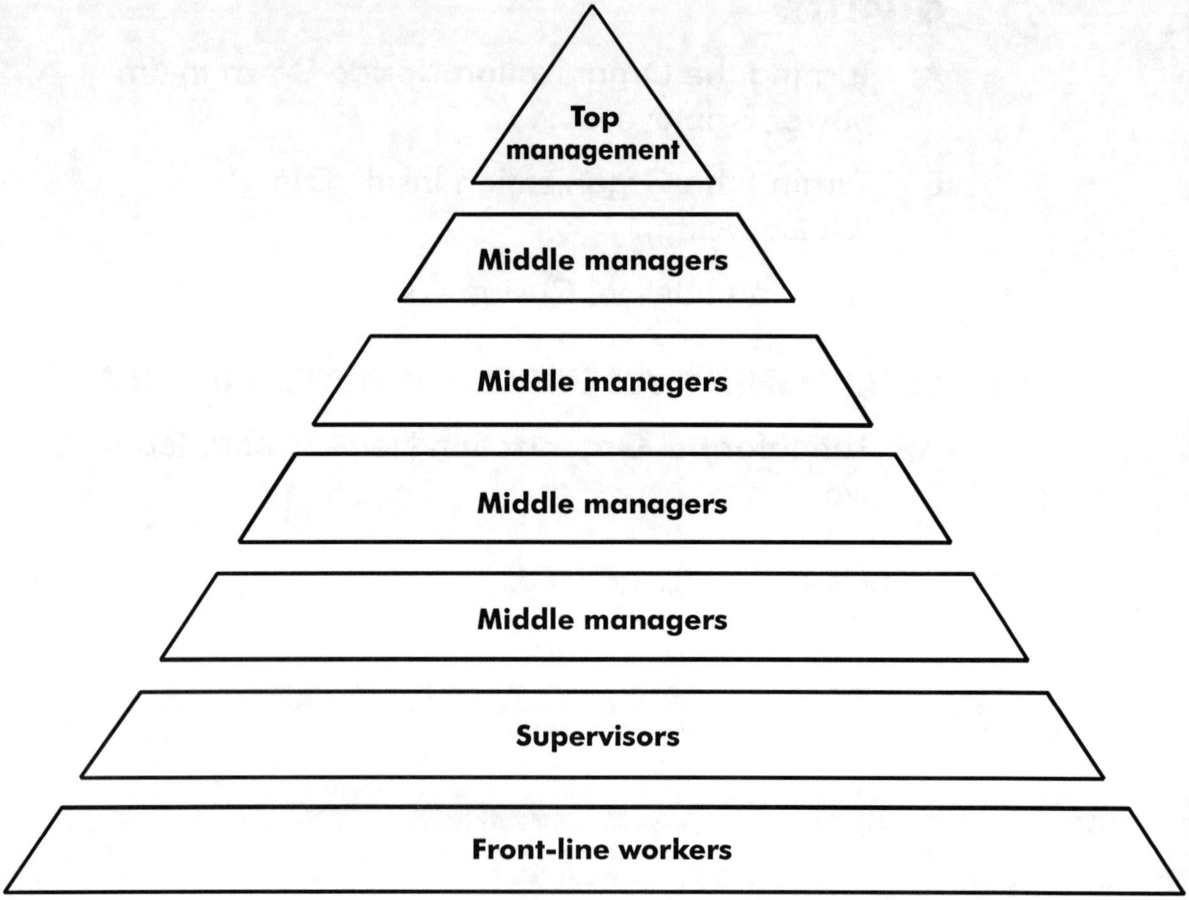
Top management
Middle managers
Middle managers
Middle managers
Middle managers
Supervisors
Front-line workers

TM-60

Bureaucratic Organization Structure

(Figure 8.2 on text page 234)

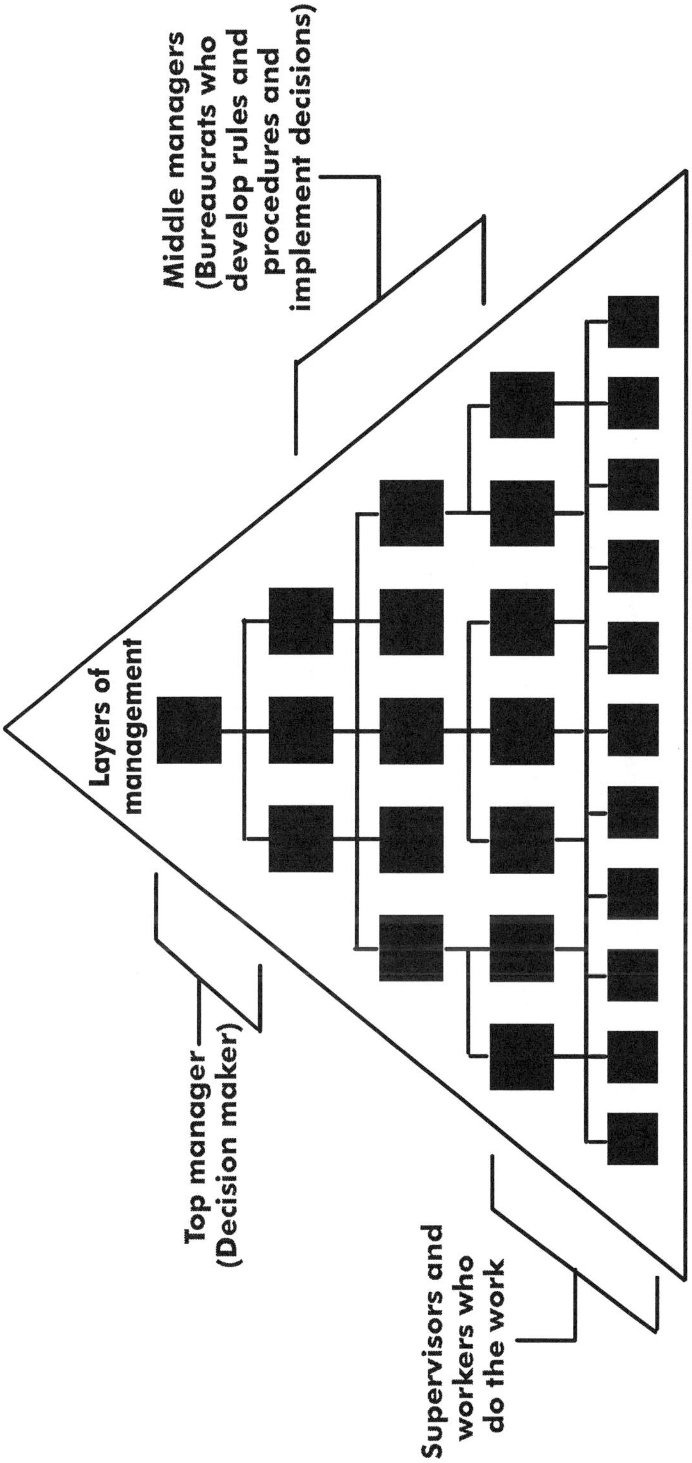
Middle managers (Bureaucrats who develop rules and procedures and implement decisions)
Layers of management
Top manager (Decision maker)
Supervisors and workers who do the work

Ways to Departmentalize

(Figure 8.3 on text page 238)

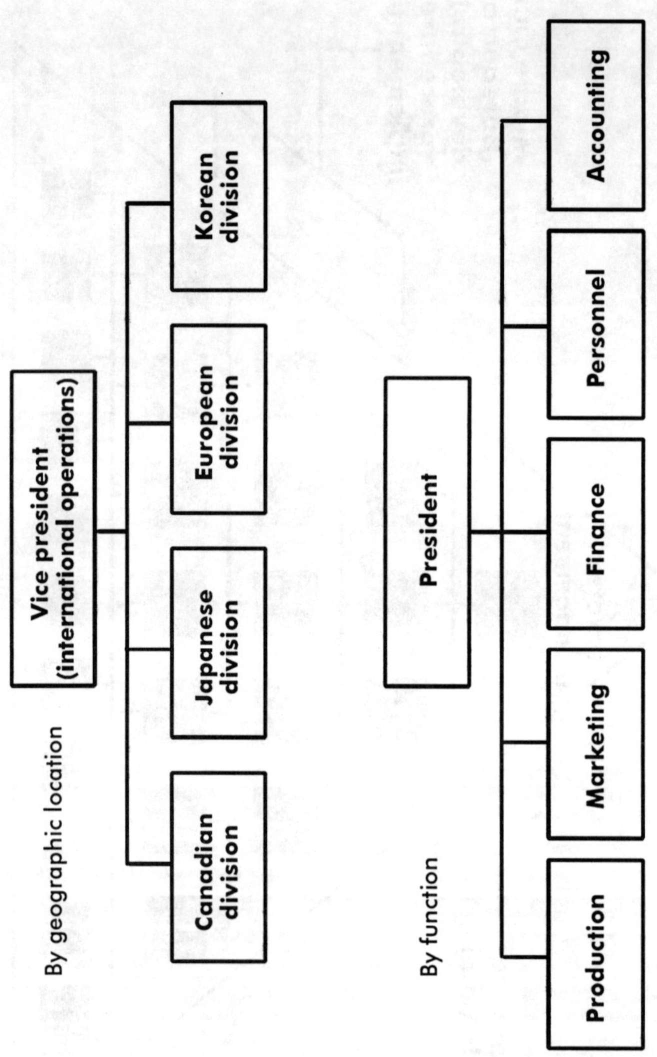

Ways to Departmentalize *(continued)*

By customer group

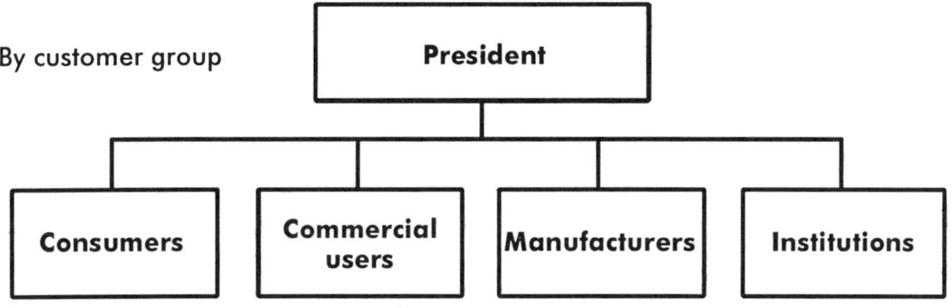

By process

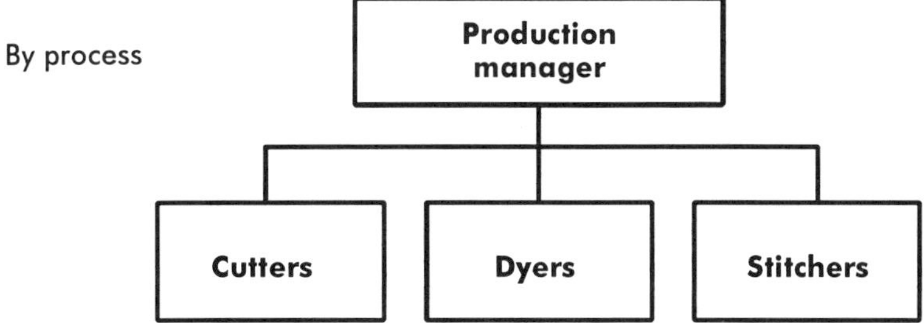

By product

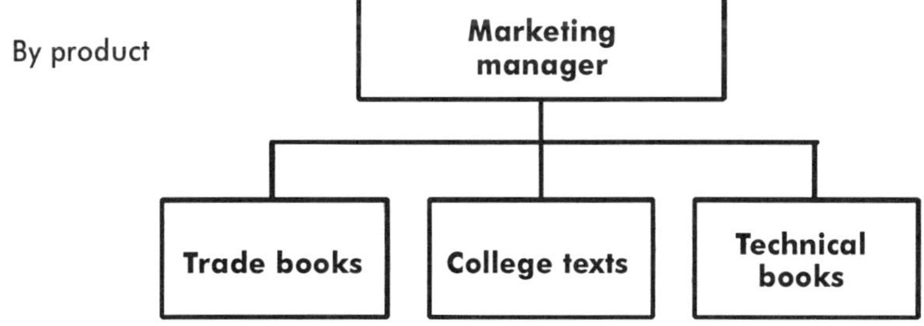

TM-62

Organization Types

(Figure 8.4 on text page 240)

	ADVANTAGES	DISADVANTAGES
LINE	Clearly defined responsibility and authority Easy to understand One supervisor for each group of employees	Too inflexible Few specialists to advise Long lines of communication Unable to handle complex questions quickly
LINE-AND-STAFF	Expert advice from staff to line personnel Establishes lines of authority Encourages cooperation and better communication at all levels	Tons of paperwork Potential overstaffing Potential overanalyzing Lines of communication can be blurred Staff frustrations because of lack of authority
MATRIX	Flexible Encourages cooperation among departments Can produce creative solutions to problems Allows organization to take on new projects without adding to the organization structure	Costly and complex Can confuse employees Requires good interpersonal skills and cooperative managers and employees Difficult to evaluate employees and to set up reward systems
CROSS-FUNCTIONAL, SELF-MANAGED TEAMS	Greatly increases interdepartmental coordination and cooperation Quicker response to customers and market conditions Increased employee motivation and morale	Some confusion over responsibility and authority Perceived loss of control by management Difficult to evaluate employees and set up reward systems Requires self-motivated, highly trained workers

A Matrix Organization

(Figure 8.5 on text page 242)

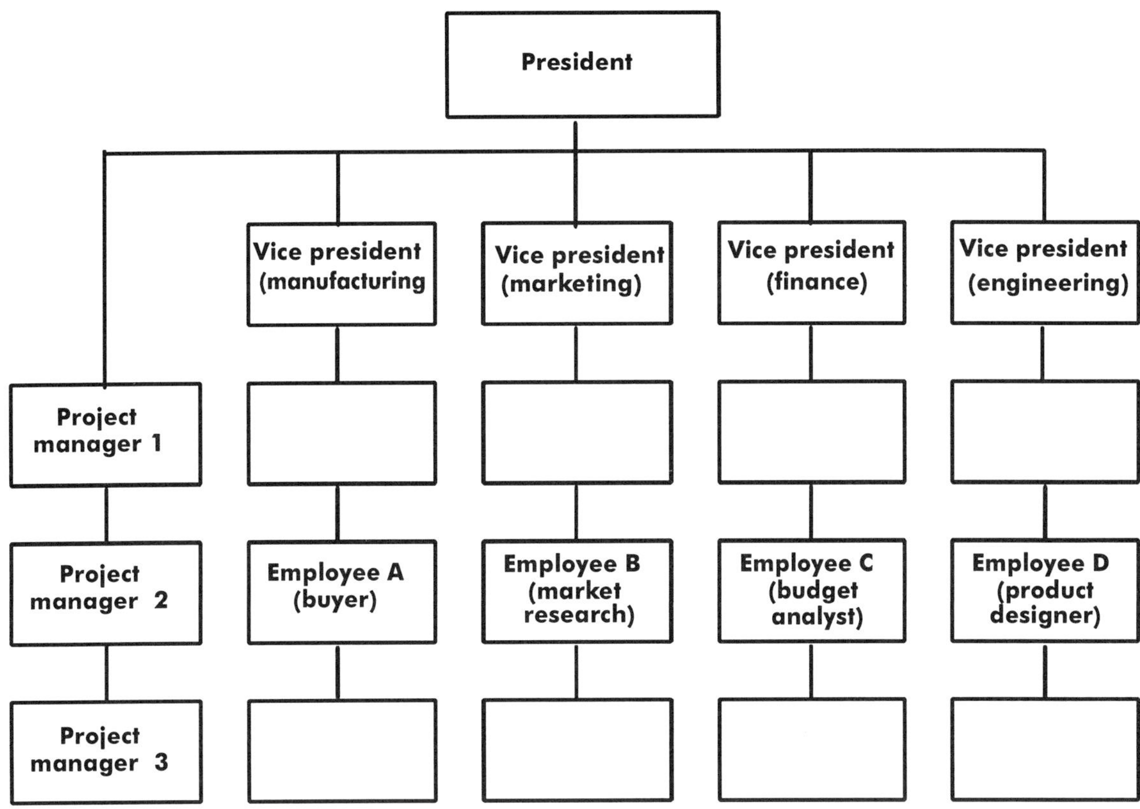

TM-64

Different Types of Teams

(Figure 8.6 on text page 244)

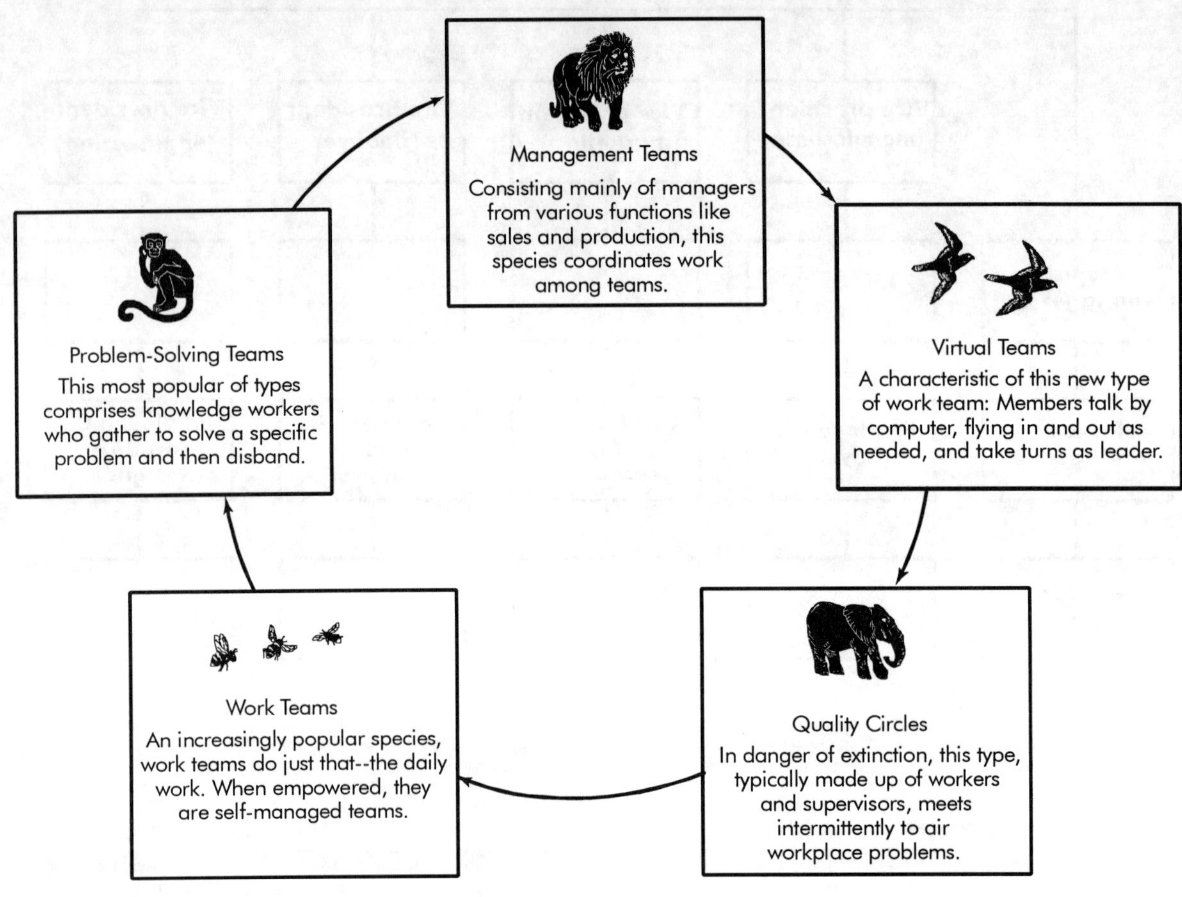

Traditional Organizational Chart
(Figure 8.7 on text page 246)

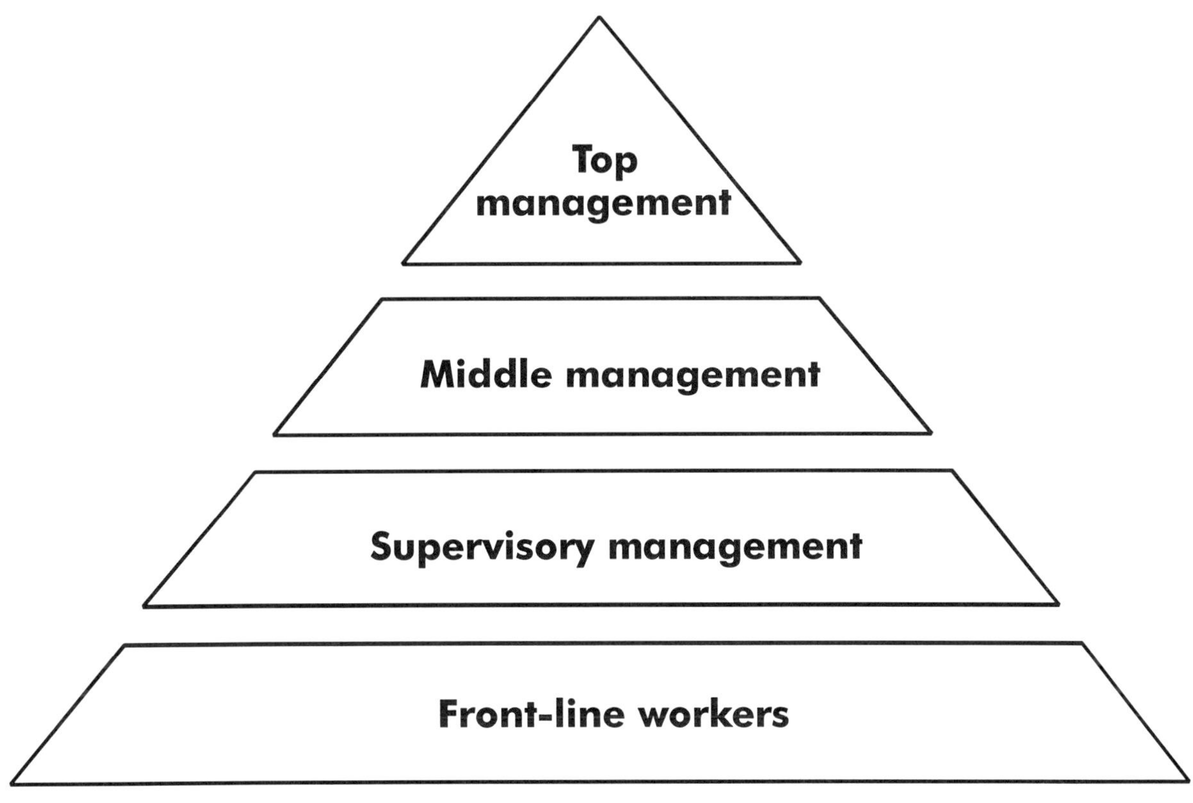

An Inverted Organization Structure
(Figure 8.8 on text page 246)

Empowered front-line workers (often in teams)

Support personnel

Top management

Bureaucratic Versus Customer-Focused Organization Structure
(Figure 8.9 on text page 249)

BUREAUCRATIC	CUSTOMER-FOCUSED
Coordination from the top	Self-management
Top-down chain of command	Bottom-up power relationships
Many rules and regulations	Employees free to make decisions
Departmentalization by function	Cross-functional teams
Specialization	Integration and cooperation
One firm does it all	Outsourcing
Management controls information	Information goes to all
Largely domestic orientation	Global orientation
Focus on external customers	Focus on both internal and external customers

Using the Latest Technology to Produce World-Class Products and Services

Chapter 9

Folder Contents

OT ACETATE 9-4 How Productivity Varies in Automobile Production

OT ACETATE 9-5 What's Had the Biggest Effect on Productivity?

OT ACETATE 9-6 Production and Operations Management: Functions and Tools

OT ACETATE 9-7 How to Increase Team Productivity

OT ACETATE 9-8 Changing Employer Productivity Expectations

OT ACETATE 9-9 Changing Employer Productivity Expectations

(Acetates and Transparency Masters are also available as PowerPoint slides on disk and on the Presentation CD-ROM.)

(Resources Available are also referenced in the expanded lecture outline later in this chapter.)

Other Resources Available

Video Case - "Washburn Guitars." This video shows how Washburn, which makes only a few products each day (about fifteen guitars), stays competitive by using TQM and the latest production techniques, such as flexible manufacturing. (The **Media Resource Guide** contains a summary of the Video and suggested discussion questions.)

Student Assessment and Learning Guide: Contains matching key term and definition questions, write-in retention questions, write-in critical thinking questions, and practice test of multiple choice and true/false questions.

Technology:

Zapitalism CD-ROM - Simulation program.

Concept Mastery Exam Preparation Disk - Practice test and tutorial.

Business Essentials Disk - Hyperlinks Understanding Business with seven other leading business texts.

Presentation CD-ROM - Contains PowerPoint slides of acetates and transparency masters, video clips, lecture materials. This tool allows you to customize your lecture presentations.

***Business Week* Web Site Access with the *Business Week* edition.**

***Understanding Business* Home Page - http:/www.mhhe.com/ub5e.**

Audiotape: Abridged chapter (Text minus profile, boxes, and end-of-chapter material.

Associated Web Sites

These sites are provided to students for the purpose of analysis and critical thinking of the issues. Students are encouraged to explore other sites. As with any Web site, some may be inactive now.

Unit 2 - Review of Operations Management:

http://cs.franklin.edu/Faculty/Giuliani/pcmt310/pmu2ln.htm

Unit 3 - Product Design and Process Selection for Manufacturing:

http://cs.franklin.edu/Faculty/Giuliani/pcmt310/pmu3ln.htm

Unit 4 - Adopting Technology in Manufacturing and Service:

http://cs.franklin.edu/Faculty/Giuliani/pcmt310/pmu4ln.htm

Unit 5 - Product Design and Process Selection for Service:

http://cs.franklin.edu/Faculty/Giuliani/pcmt310/pmu5ln.htm

Unit 9 - Project Planning and Control:

http://cs.franklin.edu/Faculty/Giuliani/pcmt310/pmu9ln.htm

Understanding Business Home Page:

http:/www.mhhe.com/ub5e.

What's New in This Edition

Additions:

- Profile Tom Smith of Tom Smith Industries
- Section "Services Go Interactive"
- Legal Briefcase
- Spotlight on Small Business: Speeding Up Research
- Case: Visualizing the Virtual Factory
- Taking It to the Net exercises

Revisions:

Statistical data and examples throughout the chapter were updated to reflect current information. In addition:

- Section "Site Selection in the Future" was condensed.
- Section "Production Processes" was condensed.
- Section "Mass Customization" was revised to include discussion of mass customization of services.

Deletions:

- Profile
- Section "People Problems on the Plant Floor"
- Section "Improving Productivity"
- Section "Productivity and Quality in Nonprofit Organizations"
- Case Competing in Time at Digital Equipment Corporation"
- Boxes From the Pages of Entrepreneur, Legal Briefcase

Brief Chapter Outline/Learning Goals

CHAPTER 9

USING THE LATEST TECHNOLOGY TO PRODUCE WORLD-CLASS PRODUCTS AND SERVICES

PROFILE: Tom Smith of Tom Smith Industries (TSI)

I. AMERICA'S MANUFACTURING BASE.

LEARNING GOAL 1. Describe the production process and explain the importance of productivity.

A. The Basics of Production Management.

B. Production and Productivity.

II. KEEPING COSTS LOW: SITE SELECTION.

LEARNING GOAL 2. Explain the importance of site selection in keeping down costs and identify the criteria used to evaluate different sites.

A. Locating Close to Markets to Serve Customers Better.

B. Site Selection in the Future.

III. PRODUCTION PROCESSES.

LEARNING GOAL 3. Classify the various production processes and how materials requirement planning links organizations in performing those processes.

A. Materials Requirement Planning: The Right Place at the Right Time.

IV. MODERN PRODUCTION TECHNIQUES.

LEARNING GOAL 4. Describe manufacturing techniques such as just-in-time inventory control, flexible manufacturing, lean manufacturing, and competing in time.

A. Just-In-Time Inventory Control.

B. Flexible Manufacturing.

C. Lean Manufacturing.

D. Mass Customization.

E. Competing in Time.

F. Computer-Aided Design and Manufacturing.

LEARNING GOAL 5. Show how CAD/CAM improves the production process.

V. CONTROL PROCEDURES: PERT AND GANTT CHARTS.

LEARNING GOAL 6. Illustrate the use of PERT, Gantt charts, and TQM in production planning.

A. Total Quality in Production Management.

B. Measuring Productivity in the Service Sector.

LEARNING GOAL 7. Explain the importance of productivity in the service sector.

C. Services Go Interactive.

D. Preparing for the Future.

VI. SUMMARY AND REVIEW.

(Learning Objectives are also referenced in the expanded lecture outline later in this chapter)

Key Terms

analytic system *(text page 265)*

assembly process *(text page 265)*

computer-aided design (CAD) *(text page 271)*

computer-aided manufacturing (CAM) *(text page 272)*

critical path *(text page 273)*

enterprise resource planning *(text page 266)*

flexible manufacturing *(text page 269)*

form utility *(text page 261)*

Gantt chart *(text page 274)*

lean manufacturing *(text page 269)*

mass customization *(text page 270)*

process manufacturing *(text page 265)*

production *(text page 261)*

production and operations management *(text page 261)*

program evaluation and review technique (PERT) *(text page 273)*

purchasing *(text page 269)*

quality control *(text page 274)*

robot *(text page 274)*

synthetic systems *(text page 265)*

telecommuting *(text page 263)*

Lecture Outline

PROFILE: TOM SMITH is the owner of **TOM SMITH INDUSTRIES (TSI)**, one of those companies that will make or break the United States in the 21st century.

I. AMERICA'S MANUFACTURING BASE.

▶ **LEARNING GOAL 1.** Describe the production process and explain the importance of productivity.

A. A NEW ERA IN THE INDUSTRIAL REVOLUTION.

1. The heart of the free enterprise system in the U.S. has always been its manufacturers.
2. American manufacturers implemented a number of things to regain a competitive lead.
   a. Today, however, manufacturing produces less than one-fourth of the U.S. gross domestic product.
   b. Competition from foreign manufacturers forces U.S. companies to alter their production techniques and managerial style.
3. To regain competitive edge, American manufacturers have implemented:
   a. **A CUSTOMER FOCUS.**
   b. **COST SAVINGS THROUGH SITE SELECTION.**
   c. A faster response to the market through **FLEXIBLE MANUFACTURING.**

Lecture Notes

TRANSPARENCY MASTER 68
Chapter Outline

TM 68

(Transparency masters begin on page 9.79.)

LECTURE ENHANCER 9-1
America's New Manufacturing Base

General Motors and almost all other large manufacturers are cutting back dramatically on the number of people they employ. On the surface, it looks like America is losing its manufacturing base. (See complete lecture enhancer on page 9.48.)

LECTURE ENHANCER 9-2
The First Copying Machine

When Thomas Jefferson wanted to preserve his papers, he couldn't wait for Xerox. So he found a way to make copies on is own. (See complete lecture enhancer on page 9.49.)

Lecture Outline

d. More savings on the plant floor through **LEAN MANUFACTURING.**

e. **COMPUTER-AIDED MANUFACTURING** and other modern practices.

f. **TOTAL QUALITY MANAGEMENT.**

g. **BETTER CONTROL PROCEDURES.**

4. Important issues will need to be debated:

   a. The merits of **MOVING PRODUCTION FACILITIES TO FOREIGN COUNTRIES.**

   b. **REPLACING WORKERS WITH ROBOTS AND OTHER MACHINERY.**

   c. **PROTECTING AMERICAN MANUFACTURERS** through quotas and other restrictions of free trade.

5. Tomorrow's college graduates will face tremendous challenges (and career opportunities) in redesigning and rebuilding America's manufacturing base.

B. **THE BASICS OF PRODUCTION MANAGEMENT.**

1. **PRODUCTION AND OPERATIONS MANAGEMENT** is all the activities managers do to create goods and services.

2. The concepts that apply to service organizations apply generally to manufacturing organizations as well.

OT ACETATE 9-1
The Production and Operations Process

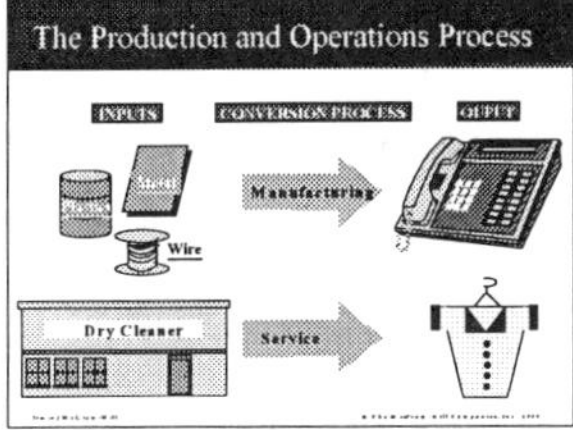

Comments:

1. This acetate views the production process for manufactured goods and services such as dry cleaning. From this acetate you can explain the differences between production and operations management.
2. It's helpful to look at this process from a traditional perspective of input—conversion process—outputs. Some of the inputs in production can be labor, information, energy, equipment, and money. The conversion process involves planning, budgeting, scheduling, distributing, etc. Outputs, as the acetate highlights can be in the form of goods or services.

Lecture Outline

3. New production techniques make it possible to virtually custom-made products for individual industrial buyers.
   a. This requires getting closer to customers to find out what their product needs are.
   b. The future will require effective marketing combined with effective production and management to keep the U.S. competitive.
4. There are **OPPORTUNITIES FOR CAREERS** in production and operations management today.
   a. Few college students are majoring in careers involving manufacturing and mining.
   b. Student entrepreneurs who have the skills to own or work in highly automated factories and mines will have more opportunities.

C. **PRODUCTION AND PRODUCTIVITY.**

1. Production uses basic **INPUTS** to produce **OUTPUTS**.
2. **PRODUCTION** is the creation of finished goods and services using the factors of production: land, labor (machinery), capital, entrepreneurship, and information.

LECTURE ENHANCER 9-3
Harley Davidson Goes with its Strengths

In 1985 Harley-Davidson was the last survivor of some 143 American motorcycle manufacturers. Facing corporate extinction a few years earlier, the company began a drastic renovation of its plant systems in a bid to improve quality and reduce production costs. (See complete lecture enhancer on page 9.51.)

TRANSPARENCY MASTER 69
The Production Process
(Figure 9.1 on text page 261)

(Transparency masters begin on page 9.79.)

Lecture Outline

3. **FORM UTILITY** is the value added by the creation of finished goods and services using raw materials, components, and other inputs.

4. Production is the creative process in all industries that produce goods and services.

5. To be competitive, manufacturers must keep the costs of *inputs* down and the amount of *output* relatively high.

   a. **PRODUCTIVITY** is the term used to describe output per unit of input.

   b. **OUTPUT** could mean goods or services.

II. KEEPING COSTS LOW: SITE SELECTION.

▶ **LEARNING GOAL 2.** Explain the importance of site selection in keeping down costs and identify the criteria used to evaluate different sites.

A. The shift of manufacturing and service organizations sometimes results in pockets of unemployment and tremendous growth in others.

1. Entrepreneurs move their facilities from one location to another for several reasons:

   a. Manufacturers often choose sites that are **CLOSE TO THE RIGHT KIND OF LABOR OR CHEAP LABOR.**

   b. Even though the cost of labor is becoming a smaller chunk of total production

LECTURE ENHANCER 9-4
Gold from Old Computers

Eric Buechel's warehouse is "where mainframes come to die." (See complete lecture enhancer on page 9.52.)

OT ACETATE 9-3
Leading U.S. Manufacturing States

Comments:

1. This acetate identifies the five leading manufacturing states in the U.S. Students from these five states are most likely to be interested in this information.
2. An assignment for students is to find out what company is the leading manufacturer in their state and what is the primary product that's produced. If you want to interject a little controversy and integrate the global market into class, quiz students on what country they feel makes the best products. Have them list the five nations they feel produce the highest quality products and rank the leaders in descending order. It will be interesting to see how students respond. The same assignment can be given related to companies.
3. It might be helpful to probe students why they make the selection they did. The idea of perception could be approached here. It will be covered more in depth in the marketing chapters.

costs, **CHEAP LABOR REMAINS A MAJOR REASON LESS TECHNOLOGICALLY ADVANCED MANUFACTURERS MOVE THEIR PLANTS.**

c. It is important for firms to maintain the **SAME QUALITY STANDARDS AND FAIR LABOR PRACTICES** wherever they produce.

d. Many firms are moving to the souther part of the U.S. because the region has mostly nonunion labor.

2. The survival of U.S. manufacturing depends on its ability to remain competitive, and that means ether cheaper inputs or increased outputs.

3. **CHEAPER RESOURCES** are another major reason for moving production facilities.

4. **REDUCING TIME TO MARKET** critical to successful global competition.

   a. Manufacturers need sites that move their products through the system quickly and at the lowest costs.

   b. One key to reducing time-to-market involves seeking countries with the most advanced information systems.

LEGAL BRIEFCASE
(Box in text, page 263)
"Nike's Indonesian Factory"

In their search for cheap labor, many companies have taken their production facilities to other countries or have outsourced production to foreign firms. One well-known company that does this is Nike.

Lecture Outline

B. LOCATING CLOSE TO MARKETS TO SERVE CUSTOMERS BETTER.

1. Some businesses remain in large metropolitan areas to be near where their customers are.

2. By locating close to their customers, businesses lower transportation costs and can be more responsive to customer needs for service.

3. Many businesses are building factories in foreign countries to get closer to international customers.

   a. When U.S. firms select foreign sites, they also study they quality of life for workers and managers.

   b. Site selection has become a critical issue in production and operations management.

C. SITE SELECTION IN THE FUTURE.

1. New developments in information technology are enabling firms and employees more flexibility in choosing locations.

2. **TELECOMMUTING**, working from home via computer and modem, is a major trend in business.

Lecture Notes

LECTURE ENHANCER 9-5
American Eagle Brick: Competing Across Borders

All other things being equal, you would expect the company with cheaper labor—on average, five times cheaper—to eat its competitor's lunch. But in business things are rarely equal, even if they look that way. (See complete lecture enhancer on page 9.53.)

CRITICAL THINKING EXERCISE 9-1
Site Selection

See complete exercise on page 9.66.

3. Today, a big incentive to locate in a particular location is the **TAX SITUATION AND DEGREE OF GOVERNMENT SUPPORT**.

   a. Some states and local governments have higher taxes, yet many offer tax reductions and other supports to attract new businesses.

   b. Once a location is selected, production can begin.

III. PRODUCTION PROCESSES.

▶ **LEARNING GOAL 3.** Classify the various production processes and how materials requirement planning.

A. THE PRODUCTION PROCESS.

1. Andrew S. Grove, chief executive officer of Intel, defines the **THREE BASIC REQUIREMENTS OF PRODUCTION:**

   a. To build and deliver products in response to the demands of the customer at a scheduled delivery time.

   b. To provide an acceptable quality level.

   c. To provide everything at the lowest possible cost.

B. TYPES OF PRODUCTION OPERATIONS.

1. **SYNTHETIC SYSTEMS** either change raw materials into other products.

MAKING ETHICAL DECISIONS

(Box in text, page 264)

"Stay or Leave"

A company can increase its profits 50 percent by moving its production facilities to Mexico. What would you do?

LECTURE ENHANCER 9-6

The Green Eavesdropper

In a company history Green Giant Company owned up to the fact that in the early days their own management didn't know how canning worked. (See complete lecture enhancer on page 9.55.)

a. **PROCESS MANUFACTURING**, an activity that physically or chemically changes material.

b. **ASSEMBLY PROCESS**, in which components are put together to constitute a new entity.

2. **ANALYTIC SYSTEMS** break down raw materials into components to extract other products.

3. **CONTINUOUS VERSUS INTERMITTENT PROCESSES.**

a. A **CONTINUOUS PROCESS** is one in which long production runs turn out finished goods over time.

b. An **INTERMITTENT PROCESS** is an operation where the production run is short and the machines are changed frequently to produce different products.

c. Today, most new manufacturers use intermittent processes.

C. **MATERIALS REQUIREMENT PLANNING: THE RIGHT PLACE AT THE RIGHT TIME.**

1. The technological changes in manufacturing have resulted in an entirely new terminology for production and operations management.

Lecture Notes

CRITICAL THINKING EXERCISE 9-2
Production Processes

See complete exercise on page 9.68.

OT ACETATE 9-2
Synthetic and Analytic Production Systems

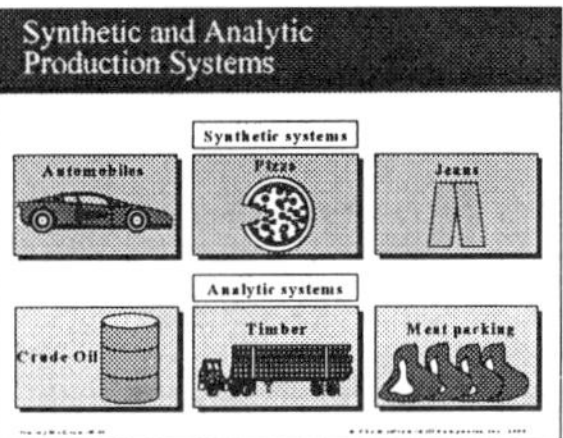

Comments:

1. This acetate reinforces the difference between synthetic and analytic productions systems that's covered in the chapter. Students are generally most confused by the analytic process.
2. By use of the examples in the acetate, you can communicate the differences in the processes rather simply. You might want to take the time to clarify the two forms of synthetic systems, **process manufacturing** and **assembly processes**, for students who may be confused.

Lecture Outline

a. **MATERIALS REQUIREMENT PLANNING (MRP)** is a computer-based operations management system that uses sales forecasts to make sure the needed parts and materials are available at the right place and the right time.

b. MRP was most popular with companies that made products with a lot of different parts.

2. **MRP II** is an advanced version of MRP that involves more than materials planning. It includes planning all the resources involved including projected sales, personnel, plant capacity, and distribution limitations.

3. **ENTERPRISE RESOURCE PLANING** is a computer-based production and operations system that links multiple firms into one, integrated production unit.

   a. The software enables the monitoring of quality and customer satisfaction as it's happening.

   b. **MRP II** monitors processes in **MULTIPLE FIRMS** at the same time.

   c. Eventually, such programs will link suppliers, manufacturers, and retailers in a completely integrated manufacturing and distribution system.

Lecture Notes

OT ACETATE 9-4
How Productivity Varies in Automobile Production

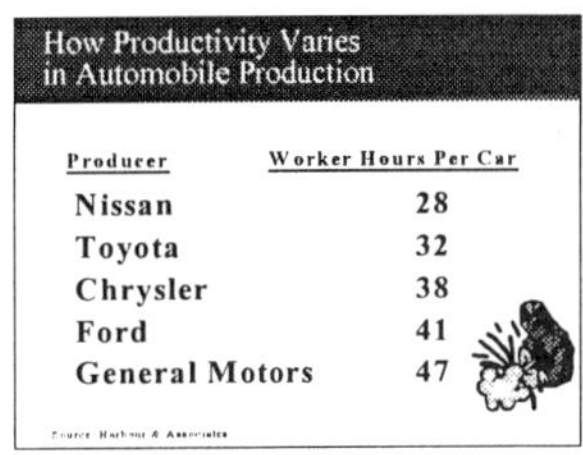
How Productivity Varies in Automobile Production

Producer	Worker Hours Per Car
Nissan	28
Toyota	32
Chrysler	38
Ford	41
General Motors	47

Comments:

1. One of the most competitive industries in the world is the automobile industry. It's also one of the most interesting industries to students. This acetate brings home the question of productivity in a manner that students should be able to relate to.
2. Ask students why such numbers as the ones offered in the acetate are important to companies such as Chrysler, Ford, and especially General Motors. They should be able to identify the cost differences that exist in production.
3. See if students can come up with any ideas how the American companies can improve their productivity numbers. You might want to mention to them that wage differences in auto production are almost non-existent today in countries like the U.S., Japan, and Germany.

PROGRESS CHECK
(page 267 in text)

- ➤ What is production?
- ➤ What are the major factors that determine where a plant locates?
- ➤ Can you explain the differences among the following production processes: process, assembly, analytic, continuous, and intermittent?
- ➤ What is enterprise resource planning?

Lecture Outline

IV. MODERN PRODUCTION TECHNIQUES.

▶ **LEARNING GOAL 4.** Describe manufacturing techniques such as just-in-time inventory control, flexible manufacturing, lean manufacturing, and competing in time.

A. The goal of manufacturing and process management is to provide high-quality goods and services instantaneously in response to customer demand.

1. Traditional organizations were not designed to be so responsive, but to make a limited variety of products at a low cost.
2. Over the years, low cost often came at the expense of quality and flexibility.
3. Such inefficiencies made U.S. companies subject to foreign competition.
4. As a result of this competition, companies today must make a wide variety of high-quality custom-designed products at a very low cost.

B. **JUST-IN-TIME INVENTORY CONTROL.**

1. One major cost of production is holding parts in warehouses.
2. **JUST-IN-TIME INVENTORY CONTROL** is a system which arranges for delivery of the smallest possible quantities at the latest

OT ACETATE 9-5
What's had the Biggest Effect on Productivity?

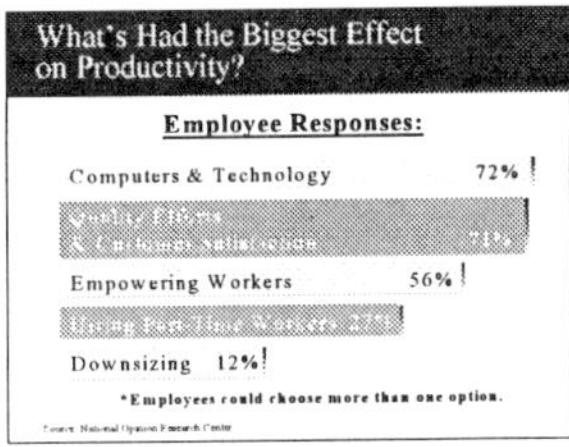

Comments:

1. In working with this acetate, you might want to just show students the top part with the question and then invite their responses. It's likely they will agree that computers and technology have had the biggest effect.
2. The last two categories, hiring part-time workers and downsizing can produce considerable debate depending on the demographics of the class. Last year we almost had a royal battle in some of our evening classes as students debated the benefits and shortcomings of these factors.
3. See by chance if students have anything to add to the responses listed on the acetate. Maybe someone will note the effect of teams or some other pertinent issue.

REACHING BEYOND OUR BORDERS
(Box in text, page 268)
"Benchmarking the Best"

The term globalization means that the world's best manufacturers can enter almost any market almost any time. In other words, if you aren't one of the world's best manufacturers, you're likely to go out of business.

Lecture Outline

possible time to keep inventory as low as possible.

a. Suppliers deliver their products "just in time" to go on the assembly line; a minimum of inventory is kept.

b. Using enterprise requirement planning (ERP) or similar system, the manufacturer determines what parts and supplies will be needed.

c. Efficiency is maintained by having the supplier linked by computer to the producer,

3. The latest version of JIT is called **JIT II,** designed to create more harmony and trust than JIT.

4. ERP and JIT systems make sure: the right materials are at the right place at the right time at the cheapest cost to meet customer needs.

C. **NEW PURCHASE AGREEMENTS.**

1. **PURCHASING** is the function in the firm that searches for quality material resources, finds the best suppliers, and negotiates the best price for quality goods and services.

2. In the past, manufacturers tended to deal with many different suppliers.

Lecture Notes

LECTURE ENHANCER 9-7
The New Reality: Reevaluating Just-In-Time Inventory Techniques

When cooperation between channel members is been lacking, JIT becomes something of a corporate shell game in many industries as companies vie to keep their inventory on some other companies' books. (See complete lecture enhancer on page 9.56.)

OT ACETATE 9-6
Production and Operations Management: Functions and Tools

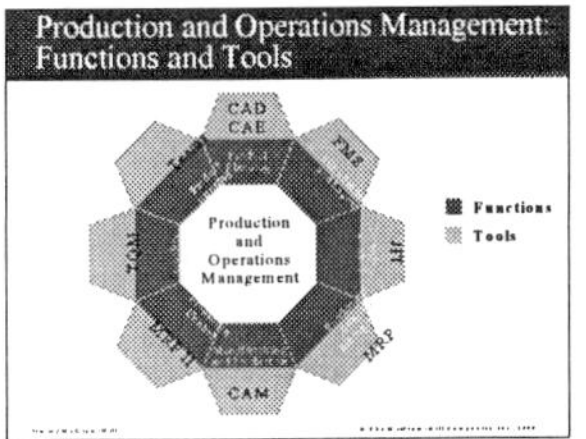

Comments:

1. This acetate covers many key terms from the chapter and divides them according to functions related to production and tools used in POM. This is an excellent time to review terms and concepts such as TQM, Just-In-Time, Material Requirement Planning, CAD/CAM etc.
2. If students question CAE, that stands for computer-aided engineering. This is term is in the chapter but sometimes confuses them.
3. The video case about Washburn Guitars is an excellent example to use in conjunction with this acetate. The production process at Washburn is interesting to students and it highlights many of the key concepts discussed in the chapter.

3. Today, they rely more heavily on one or two—the relationship between suppliers and manufacturers is much closer.
4. The purchasing department is responsible for finding such suppliers, negotiating long-term contracts, and getting the best price possible.

D. **FLEXIBLE MANUFACTURING** is the design of machines to do multiple tasks so that they can produce a variety of products.

E. **LEAN MANUFACTURING.**

1. **LEAN MANUFACTURING** is the production of goods using less of everything compared to mass production: less human effort, less manufacturing space, less investment in tools, less engineering time to develop a new product in half the time.
2. A company becomes lean by **CONTINUOUSLY INCREASING THE CAPACITY TO PRODUCE MORE**, higher quality results with fewer resources.
3. GM redesigned its production processes, abandoning the assembly line, to make the Saturn automobile.
   a. The most dramatic change was to switch to modular construction.

Lecture Notes

CRITICAL THINKING (page 269 in text)

Earlier we talked about continuous processes versus intermittent processes. Can you see how flexible manufacturing makes it possible for intermittent processes to become as fast as continuous processes? What are the implications for saving time on the assembly line, saving money, and cutting back on labor?

OT ACETATE 9-7
How to Increase Team Productivity

How to Increase Team Productivity

- ✓ Teach other members by sharing personal skills & strengths
- ✓ Emphasize by showing concern for teammates
- ✓ Ask and invite questions
- ✓ Motivate teammates through praise and recognition

Comments:

1. Using the letters **TEAM,** students can follow how to make the best use of teams in the production process.
2. The two letters that cause the most consternation for managers is **E** for empathize and **M** for motivate. Managers have to work at showing concern for employees and team members. Ask how students feel their bosses or even their college instructors are doing at this task.

b. GM also expanded use of **ROBOTS**, computer-controlled machines capable of performing many tasks requiring the use of materials and tools.

c. Robots usually are fast, efficient, and accurate, but can never completely replace a creative worker.

E. **MASS CUSTOMIZATION** means tailoring products to meet the needs of individual customers.

1. Flexible manufacturing systems enable manufacturers to custom-make goods as quickly as mass-produced items.

2. Mass customization is also coming to services.

F. **COMPETING IN TIME** means getting your product to market before your competitors.

G. **COMPUTER-AIDED DESIGN AND MANUFACTURING.**

▶ **LEARNING GOAL 5.** Show how CAD/CAM improves the production process.

1. **COMPUTER-AIDED DESIGN (CAD)** is the integration of computers into the design of products.

2. **COMPUTER-AIDED MANUFACTURING (CAM)** is the integration of computers into the manufacturing of products.

SPOTLIGHT ON SMALL BUSINESS

(Box in text, page 271)
"Speeding Up Research"

Since 1988, only 28 firms have won the Malcolm Baldrige National Quality Award. Eight of those honorees were small businesses. But only one small business in the professional services firm has ever won. That firm is Custom Research Inc. (CRI). It won the award in 1996. The company's strategic plan called for cross-functional work teams to deliver customer-focused, quality service.

SUPPLEMENTAL CASE 9-1
Competing in Time at Digital Equipment Corporation

See complete case on page 9.70.

SUPPLEMENTAL CASE 9-2
The Automation of General Motors

See complete case on page 9.73.

LECTURE ENHANCER 9-8
Computer-Integrated Manufacturing for Small Business

Although experts have been saying for over a decade that factory automation will soon be common in small companies, it just hasn't happened yet. (See complete lecture enhancer on page 9.57.)

3. **CAD/CAM**, the combining of computer-aided design with computer-aided manufacturing, mad it possible to custom-design products for small markets.

4. Computer-aided design has **INCREASED PRODUCTIVITY** by 2 to 1.

   a. In the past computer-aided design machines couldn't talk to computer-aided manufacturing machines.

   b. Recently software programs have been designed to unite CAD with CAM: **COMPUTER-INTEGRATED MANUFACTURING (CIM).**

V. CONTROL PROCEDURES: PERT AND GANTT CHARTS.

▶ **LEARNING GOAL 6.** Illustrate the use of PERT, Gantt charts, and TQM in production planning.

A. An important function of a production manager is to be sure that products are manufactured and delivered on time.

B. **PROGRAM EVALUATION AND REVIEW TECHNIQUE (PERT).**

1. **PERT** is a method for analyzing the tasks involved in completing a given project, estimating the time needed to complete each

LECTURE ENHANCER 9-9
People Problems on the Plant Floor

Recent studies indicate that the manufacturing companies that did the best job were those that had a heavy people orientation as well. (See complete lecture enhancer on page 9.58.)

CRITICAL THINKING
(page 272 in text)

Computer-aided design and computer-aided manufacturing (CAD/CAM) have revolutionized the production process. Now, everything from cookies to cars can be designed and manufactured much more cheaply. Furthermore, customized changes can be made with very little increase in cost. What will such changes mean for the clothing industry, the shoe industry, and other fashion-conscious industries? The age of custom-designed consumer and industrial goods has arrived. How will you benefit as a consumer?

PROGRESS CHECK
(page 272 in text)

- What is just-in-time inventory control?
- How does flexible manufacturing differ from lean manufacturing?
- What is meant by competing in time?

task, and identifying the minimum time needed to complete the total project.

2. The **STEPS INVOLVED IN USING PERT** include:

   a. Analyzing tasks that need to be done and sequencing the tasks.

   b. Estimating the time needed to complete each task.

   c. Drawing a PERT network illustrating the information from steps 1 and 2.

   d. Identifying the **CRITICAL PATH**, the sequence of tasks that takes the longest time to complete.

   e. This path is referred to as the critical path, because **A DELAY** in the time needed to complete this path **WOULD CAUSE THE PROJECT OR PRODUCTION RUN TO BE LATE.**

3. A PERT network can be made up of thousands of events over many months, and is usually done by computer.

4. The **GANTT CHART** is a bar graph that clearly shows what projects are being worked on and how much has been completed (on a daily basis).

Lecture Notes

TRANSPARENCY MASTER 70
PERT Chart for a Video
(Figure 9.2 on text page 274)

TM 70

(Transparency masters begin on page 9.79.)

a. The computer is helping the paper Gantt chart becoming obsolete.

b. Using a Gantt-like computer program, a manager can trace the production process minute by minute.

C. **TOTAL QUALITY IN PRODUCTION MANAGEMENT.**

1. **QUALITY CONTROL** is the measurement of products and services against set standards.

   a. Earlier, quality control was often done at the end of the production line by a quality control department.

   b. **TOTAL QUALITY** means satisfying customers by building in and ensuring quality from product planning to production, purchasing, sales, and service.

   c. Emphasis is placed on **CUSTOMER SATISFACTION.**

2. TQM programs begin by analyzing the consumer to see what quality standards need to be established.

3. Quality is then designed into products, and every product must meet those standards.

D. **MEASURING PRODUCTIVITY IN THE SERVICE SECTOR.**

Lecture Notes

TRANSPARENCY MASTER 71
A GANTT Chart for a Doll Manufacturer *(Figure 9.3 on text page 275)*

(Transparency masters begin on page 9.79.)

LECTURE ENHANCER 9-10
How to Improve Total Quality a Little at a Time

Total quality relies upon two tenets: (1) do things a little bit at a time, all the time; this will bring the highest probability of success and (2) leading is better than managing. (See complete lecture enhancer on page 9.59.)

SUPPLEMENTAL CASE 9-3
Quality—America Is Back

See complete case on page 9.76.

Lecture Outline

1. The greatest productivity problem in the U.S. is in the service economy.
2. It is **DIFFICULT TO MEASURE PRODUCTIVITY** in the service sector.
3. Computers are improving service sector productivity; for example, ATMs speed banking transactions.
4. Operations management has led to **PRODUCTIVITY INCREASES IN THE SERVICE SECTOR**, but haven't been reflected in national productivity figures.

▶ **LEARNING GOAL 7.** Explain the importance of productivity in the service sector.

E. **SERVICES GO INTERACTIVE.**

1. The service industry has always taken advantage of new technology to increase customer satisfaction.
2. Now interactive computer networks are revolutionizing services.
3. As computers and modems get faster, the Internet may take over much of traditional retailing.
4. The service sector is experiencing the same kind of revolution as manufacturing has.

F. **PREPARING FOR THE FUTURE.**

Lecture Notes

LECTURE ENHANCER 9-11
Incentives for Quality at GE

GE's quality-control program, Jack Welch says, is "a mammoth undertaking; I mean, I can't even begin to describe the size of this undertaking." A sure sign of top management's determination: 40 percent of GE executive bonuses now will depend on implementation of the program. (See complete lecture enhancer on page 9.60.)

LECTURE ENHANCER 9-12
Productivity Bottleneck in the Office: The Keyboard

The modern office is likely to be equipped with a host of specialized equipment. But within this state-of-the-art system is a turn-of-the-century bottleneck—the computer keyboard. (See complete lecture enhancer on page 9.61.)

LECTURE ENHANCER 9-13
Who's Best at Service?

A recent survey asked respondents to name companies they and others in their firms view as role models for service. (See complete lecture enhancer on page 9.62.)

OT ACETATE 9-8 and **OT ACETATE 9-9**
Changing Employer Productivity Expectations

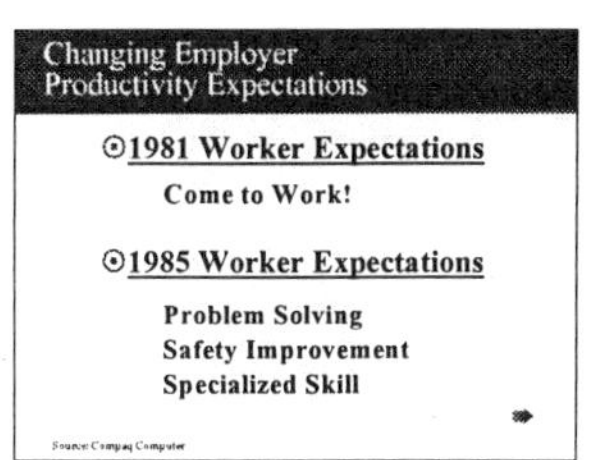

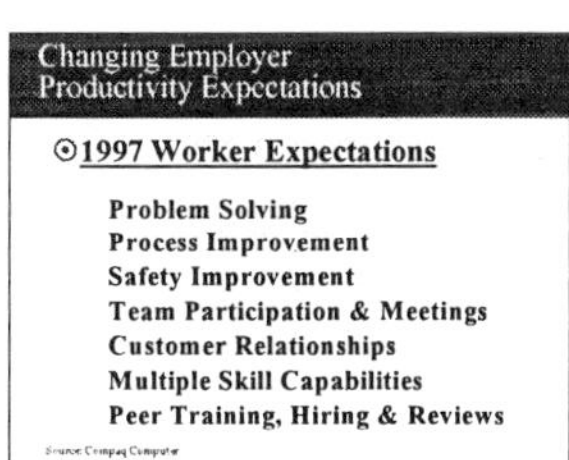

Comments:

1. This is an interesting acetate for students to observe. It measures the expectations of employers concerning workers over a period of approximately 20 years.
2. An obvious question to address from the acetate's information, is "why have expectations changed so dramatically?" Student should be able to offer a wide range of reasons.
3. With **ACETATE 9-9**, it's important to emphasize that this is the type of employee that employers are looking to hire. The more students hone from their college experience, the higher the probability they will be that person.

Lecture Outline

1. Changes in technology mean **NEW OPPORTUNITIES** and **HIGHER STANDARD OF LIVING AND QUALITY OF LIFE**, but it also means preparing for such changes.
2. The new era in manufacturing and service sectors will require **SPECIAL TRAINING** to manage the new high-tech workers.
3. Many universities are adding **COURSES IN MANUFACTURING MANAGEMENT** and robotics to help students prepare.
4. There will be more emphasis on **PARTICIPATIVE MANAGEMENT** and the design of **ATTRACTIVE WORK ENVIRONMENTS.**

VI. SUMMARY AND REVIEW.

Lecture Notes

LECTURE ENHANCER 9-14
Productivity and Quality in Nonprofit Organizations

The United States can't remain competitive with the rest of the world if ineffective government agencies keep draining funds away from businesses. (See complete lecture enhancer on page 9.63.)

LECTURE ENHANCER 9-15
The Virtual Factory

The virtual factory already exists—thanks to one Missouri company and the Internet. (See complete lecture enhancer on page 9.64.)

PROGRESS CHECK
(page 277 in text)

- Could you draw a PERT chart for making a breakfast of three-minute eggs, buttered toast, and coffee? Which process would be the critical path, the longest process? How could you use a Gantt chart to keep track of production?
- Why does service productivity seem to lag behind industrial productivity, and what can be done about it?

Answers to Practicing Management Decisions

CASE ONE

VISUALIZING THE VIRTUAL FACTORY

1. *What skills do you anticipate needing to work in such a virtual environment?*

To work in a virtual environment, one must be very flexible and ready to adapt to constantly changing circumstances. One must also be able to communicate electronically through e-mail and fax. Computer skills are critical as are writing skills.

2. *Since many companies will be virtual, there will be fewer long-term contracts and more subcontracting, and long-term employment may become a thing of the past. How can you learn to prosper in an environment that is looking for part-time experts?*

First of all, you have to develop some expertise that is wanted. Computer skills of all kinds are likely to be included. Also, you must be somewhat of a Jack of all trades; that is, a person who can fit into many different circumstances and thrive in each. A general background is often best. So, one needs to be a specialist in something and a generalist overall.

3. *What affect will the linking of companies have on global politics? Where are companies most likely to locate? What does that mean for future development in the United States? In less-developed countries?*

Companies are already linked globally. This means that trade within a company becomes international trade. Once that happens, borders mean almost nothing and companies will locate where taxes and government regulations are lowest and employee wages are low or where productivity is very high. If the United States lowers taxes and maintains its leadership position in technology, it will be a winner. If taxes and regulations are increased, production may well go to third world counties with lower wages, lower taxes, and fewer regulations. Technology is transferable to any nation.

4. *What problems do you anticipate as companies become more and more reliant on the computer and computer networks?*

Computers can be shut down by cutting off electricity. Whole cities could be brought to a standstill by blowing up the electric plant. Computer viruses could also mess up integrated systems. Note the year 2000 problem and how much it will cost companies. Computers definitely have their advantages and disadvantages, and a paper backup system often proves to be a life saver.

CASE TWO

VIDEO CASE: THE PRODUCTION PROCESS AT WASHBURN GUITARS

1. *What small manufacturing facilities are located in or near your town? Why not visit them and see for yourself what it's like working for a small manufacturer?*

Some students may work in a local production facility. This could lead to a field trip.

2. *Do you think guitars lend themselves well to continuous process manufacturing? Why or why not?*

Some guitars can be mass produced, but those made for professional musicians must be custom made to fit their needs. The idea is to custom make guitars in the fastest time possible.

3. *One of the more important aspects of small-batch manufacturing is scheduling. What kinds of scheduling techniques have you learned in this chapter that you could use?*

Just in time inventory control would help keep down inventory carrying costs. The chapter also discusses Program Evaluation and Review Techniques (PERT) and GANTT charts.

4. *Does a career in production management seem attractive to you? Why or why not?*

The jobs in this video look more attractive than those shown for most assembly-line work.

Lecture Enhancers

LECTURE ENHANCER 9-1

AMERICA'S NEW MANUFACTURING BASE

America's manufacturing base was once anchored by large manufacturers like General Motors and Ford. But General Motors and almost all other large manufacturers are cutting back dramatically on the number of people they employ. On the surface, it looks like America is losing its manufacturing base.

Below the surface, however, you'll find a new manufacturing base being established by thousands of small and medium-sized manufacturing plants. For example, Eaton Corporation (a Cleveland-based auto parts maker) built a 120-employee plant in Hamilton, Indiana. Intel Corporation built a computer chip plant in Santa Clara, California, that created some 250 jobs. Thousands of other examples could be given of small, flexible plants that are changing the nature of manufacturing in the United States.

Thomas Kassouf is president of one of those flexible plants—the Carlyle Compressor Company (a division of The Carrier Corporation) in Arkadelphia, Arkansas. If you visited his plant, you'd see the new face of American manufacturing. The plant makes compressors for air conditioners. The first thing you'd notice is how clean and quiet the factory is. But many of the innovations aren't so apparent. The plant now has 450 workers, and they're very different from their counter-parts in the past. For example, potential employees must take a state test. Only those scoring in the top third may advance. Their references are checked carefully to make sure that the candidates can work well with others, and they're interviewed by fellow workers. Only one in 16 applicants is hired.

Those who get past the interviews must take a six-week course at night to learn blueprint reading, math (*e.g.*, metric calculations), statistical process control methods, computer skills, and human relations skills. All this occurs before the person is hired. Kassouf is careful to hire top people because he then empowers those workers to make decisions on their own. For example, workers can install the machines and may determine their layout. Working in teams, employees are virtually self-managed. Men and women work side by side because the plant was designed so that no heavy lifting is involved.

Recognizing the benefits of such plants, the county underwrote the costs to build a sewer line to the industrial park where Carlyle is located. The state gave the company tax breaks. The plant is competitive with the best in the world because it practices the latest in total quality concepts.

LECTURE ENHANCER 9-2

THE FIRST COPYING MACHINE

It was reported that Thomas Jefferson was devastated in 1770 when his family home, Shadwell, was destroyed by fire while he was away practicing law. The flames consumed his papers, his books, and his other personal possessions Ten years later disaster struck again. Then governor of Virginia, he lost his state papers when the British raided Richmond, the state's capital.

The prolific Jefferson was noted for both the quantity and the quality of his writing. He would carefully record in a pocket notebook the minutiae of his day—how long a ferry took to cross a river, for example. And, of course, he penned the Declaration of Independence. Always concerned with preserving his papers—as well as those of the public record—for posterity, he would spend hours copying by hand his correspondence for his files.

What Jefferson needed was a piece of equipment found in just about every modern-day office: a copying machine. And by the end of the 1780s, he had one. So did several of his contemporaries, including Benjamin Franklin and George Washington.

It was Franklin who in 1780 brought the first copying machine to the attention of his colleagues. The versatile inventor had been toying with his own version of the thing when he learned, while in Paris serving as American minister to France, of one built by James Watt, inventor of the steam engine.

"But as I love to encourage Ingenuity," he wrote to James Woodmason, who sold the presses for James Watt and Co., "You may put me down as a subscriber and send me three of the machines, which are for some Friends." Woodmason wrote back, saying in effect, "Sorry, but I need the cash up front." Franklin reluctantly anted up, though he tartly replied that he did not approve of extending credit (in Franklin's day, credit meant money to allow a seller to produce goods) to a company, "for I think Credit is upon the whole of more Mischief than Benefit to Mankind."

In 1775 Watt was in Birmingham, England, building his steam engines. Overwhelmed by the task of handwriting copies of his voluminous business correspondence for his records, he turned his inventor's prowess toward devising a copying machine. What he came up with consisted of a slow-drying ink made of gum arabic—a sticky, water-soluble gum from the acacia tree—and dampened tissue paper. He used the ink to create the original and then pressed the original and the tissue paper together. Some of the ink from the original would transfer to the tissue, which served as the copy. It was important that the tissue be thin enough to be read through, yet strong enough not to tear. The process could be repeated as long as the ink from the original document had not dried, a period of about 24 hours.

Watt later refined the process by devising two presses that more easily applied the pressure necessary to transfer the ink: a roller press made of lignum vitae (a hardwood from America) and a screw-down press. By 1794 Watt—as well as several competitors—had even built a portable copying machine about the size of a large briefcase.

Franklin sent Jefferson one of Watt's original machines in 1780. Jefferson was so taken with the device that in 1786, while visiting friends in England, he actually designed his own portable version. Using spring-mounted brass rollers, which adjusted to the combined thickness of the tissue and the document being copied, he downsized Watt's invention so that it would fit comfortably on the traveling lap-top desk he had designed for himself in 1776. Later, in Paris, he found a superior grade of paper to replace the flimsy tissue.

Jefferson used his copying press for close to 20 years. Then, in the early 1800s, he switched to a polygraph, a contraption developed by John Isaac Hawkins, an English-born inventor living in Philadelphia. The polygraph comprised as many as five pens, which were linked together by horizontal and vertical rulers, forming a series of parallelograms, and a sheet of paper held taut within a frame for each pen. Every hand movement of a pen—up, down, left, right—was mimicked by the other pens,'so as many as four copies of the original could be produced simultaneously. Hawkins didn't know it, but the device was an expansion of the pantograph, invented in 1631 by Christoph Schemer, a German Jesuit astronomer and educator. Schemer had joined light, rigid rods together and attached two pencils to produce one original and one copy.

Today copying machines in the United States pump out well over 7 trillion copies each year; seventeen vendors sell the machines, including Canon, Ricoh, and of course the biggest copy-daddy of them all, Xerox. All told, in the United States alone, it's an $18.5 billion industry. Jefferson, no doubt, would be pleased.

LECTURE ENHANCER 9-3

HARLEY DAVIDSON GOES WITH ITS STRENGTHS

In 1985 Harley-Davidson was the last survivor of some 143 American motorcycle manufacturers. Facing corporate extinction a few years earlier, the company began a drastic renovation of its plant systems in a bid to improve quality and reduce production costs. The Harley-Davidson name on a heavyweight motorcycle can generate raw emotional appeal—enough to make fans eagerly shell out twice as much for a Harley as for a comparable Honda that is built in the U.S.

Until 1981 Harley was a subsidiary of the sports equipment giant AMF. Roger Lutz is senior manufacturing engineer at Harley-Davidson Motor Co. assembly plant. In the early 1980s, Lutz says, the assembly plant was in "chaos." Not only did it assemble motorcycles, it also made a variety of products for AMF. Harley bikes bumped along the production line, while bowling pins were made nearby.

Image was just about all Harley had left in 1981, when a group of AMF executives led a management buyout and took the firm private. (It went public again in 1986). Simultaneously the new owners had to revise their approaches to every aspect of the business—manufacturing, marketing, and distribution.

Like many other American industries, Harley took a cue from Japanese production methods. Over time it reduced inventory levels, thus freeing up labor and capital and making quality problems easier to spot and correct. "They literally scrapped millions of dollars worth of inventory and started all over again," Lutz said.

Harley also encouraged workers to meet on company time and discuss production issues, and gave them more authority to check the accuracy of work in process. It arranged manufacturing processes into more logical sequences, drawing together production "cells' out of operations that had been spread out around the plant. As one result, material handling declined sharply. Harley found that it only needed about a dozen forklifts to move pats, while 50 to 60 of them used to crowd factory aisles.

While reducing inventory and manufacturing costs, the company has been able to cut assembly defects substantially, Lutz said. Today about 15 percent of bikes reaching the end of the line need some kind of re-work, down from 40 percent a few years ago.

LECTURE ENHANCER 9-4

GOLD FROM OLD COMPUTERS

Eric Buechel's warehouse contains rows of hulking computers, each weighing tons. They once whirred and flashed, but now they rest unplugged and discarded. "This is where mainframes come to die," Buechel declares. His company, Advanced Recovery Inc., is an entrepreneurial response to a looming environmental problem: millions of obsolete computers.

This unwelcome by-product of the computer age is the result of technology's upward spiral—ever lower prices for increasingly powerful machines. With manufacturers introducing upgrades every six months, one research firm estimates that 75 to 100 million PCS will be retired in 1998. Consequently, American businesses and individuals are discarding their old mainframes, personal computers, and work stations at an astonishing rate.

If the pace of discarding continues, about 150 million computer carcasses will reside in the nation's landfills by the year 2005. The disposal costs alone for the machines could be $1 billion, ignoring the landfill space required—an acre of land dug to a depth of 3½ miles, room to stack about fifteen Empire State Buildings end to end.

Which is precisely the opportunity Buechel and other entrepreneurs see. At Advanced Recovery, based in Belleville, New Jersey, the castoff computers are pulled apart and mined for metals from aluminum to gold. The semiconductor chips are plucked out and sold to parts wholesalers and computer-maintenance shops. But what can't be resold is trucked away—and dumped in a nearby landfill.

Electronic Recovery Specialists is another company that has found its fortune in other people's garbage. The Chicago-based company also buys and breaks down old computers—hacking them apart in some cases—for the gold and other precious metals they contain. The result: $7 million in 1996 revenues.

Founded by Davis Gilbert in 1979, the company recovers the gold-bearing bits and pieces, and then sells them to refiners. Mainframes and PCS arrive by the truckload at Gilbert's shop in a warehouse surrounded by scrap yards on Chicago's West Side. Eleven employees dismantle the machines and sort their innards, filling bins and barrels with circuit boards, detached connector pins, and gold foil. Aluminum disc drives are stacked in one corner; in another, plastic computer shells are heaped halfway to the ceiling. Gilbert processes 10 tons of junked computers per week from sources such as modem-maker U.S. Robotics Inc. and other corporations, municipalities, blood banks, and universities.

Gold, an excellent conductor of electricity, has been used in computers and other electronic products for decades. But recovering it wasn't profitable in the United States until the 1970s when, freed from federal price control, gold's value rocketed from $35 an ounce to more than $800. All of a sudden, all the old printed circuit boards and electronic equipment sitting around became a rich gold mine. "There's not a single company in the world I couldn't walk into and show 'em where the gold is," Gilbert says.

LECTURE ENHANCER 9-5

AMERICAN EAGLE BRICK: COMPETING ACROSS BORDERS

All other things being equal, you would expect the company with cheaper labor—on average, five times cheaper—to eat its competitor's lunch. But in business things are rarely equal, even if they look that way. Ask George Cudahy, whose American Eagle Brick plant faces a Mexican rival whose operation is a mirror-image of his own. "We share the same mountain, have the same model kiln, we both have the same extruder, a J.C. Steele model 60E," says Cudahy. "But he pays his people a fraction of what I pay mine."

American Eagle's competition is Productos de Barro Industrializados, right next door in Juarez, Mexico. Two brick makers whose brickyards are divided by a chain-link fence, the only barrier separating them on an international frontier.

Both yards are capable of producing around 65,000 bricks daily, from shale quarried from the same source. But Mexican wages for factory hands top out at $60 a week, while new employees at George Cudahy's yard start at just under $300.

Guess who's eating whose lunch?

American Eagle, with some 60 percent of the local market, can barely keep up with demand. What's more, increasingly that demand is coming from as far away as Houston, Albuquerque, Denver, and Dallas—bold new markets where bricks from the border area seldom ventured before. All told, American Eagle will record sales of $2.5 million in 1998.

Changes brought by NAFTA and Cudahy's strategy, have made his company a fierce competitor. For years, the U.S. brick maker employed heavily armed guards to deter thieves from taking dynamite from its storage sheds. "It was really the Wild West out here," says Cudahy, a graduate of the U.S. Naval Academy who flew 186 combat missions over Laos and Vietnam.

Between the vandals and the competition, the century-old El Paso Brick Co. was on the verge of collapse when Cudahy, a native of Kenosha, Wisconsin, rode into town more than seven years ago. He had just completed a second career in aircraft production and had planned to indulge in his twin passions of fishing and flying in the region he had fallen in love with during a duty assignment at Los Alamos Scientific Laboratories in New Mexico.

Instead, he got into the brick business, almost on a dare. "I wanted to help a friend," he recalls. "But I saw an opportunity to acquire the assets of a dysfunctional company and make something of it."

After assembling a group of investors to recapitalize the operation, he set out to remake the company, which he rechristened American Eagle Brick. The company aimed for a more refined product: "designer" bricks for high-end buyers. "You try different mixes of clay and ore, different colors, different facings, and you try to squeeze pennies out of every batch," Cudahy explains. "I'm big on automation, but I won't buy a machine unless it can pay for itself within a year."

There are other things he won't do, like let his kiln go cold, preferring to run it 24 hours a day, every day. That saves on power and manpower costs—no wasteful starting and stopping—and lets American Eagle purchase energy cheaply.

He also won't permit workers compensation to swell to 22 percent of his payroll costs, as was the case seven years ago. A military-strict safety program reduced those costs to 5 percent. All told, such attention to detail lowered the price of his bricks to around $150 per thousand, cheap enough to compete with his rival in Juarez, who slightly undercuts his price, but with less quality control.

What finally pushed George Cudahy to a victory in the battle of the brickyards is the North American Free Trade Agreement. Although American Eagle sends less than one percent of its product south of the border, it's a beneficiary of booming trade. Since NAFTA boosted trade across the border, hundreds of flatbed trucks from around the U.S. pass through El Paso every week bearing parts and machinery for *maquiladoras*, or low-cost assembly plants, on the Mexican side. Most go back empty, leaving American Eagle to enjoy rock-bottom "back haul" rates out of town.

Cheap freight rates—less than $1 a mile per 48,000 brick load—allow American Eagle to offer just-in-time sales, luring contractors with wholesale orders direct from the brickyard. Derering Co. of Houston, a building-materials distributor, hauls an average of ten truckloads a week out of El Paso.

Productos de Barro manages its U.S. sales through a distributor in El Paso but can't pursue George Cudahy's nimble retail strategy for one simple reason: Juarez traffic bound for the U.S. is often held for hours by custom inspectors looking for drugs and other contraband. Truckers don't like waiting hours to move a shipment as low-margin as bricks.

That suits George Cudahy just fine. "It's phenomenal that we can sell our product this far away," he says with a smile. "We compete on quality and price, but at our prices we can compete to the west even further than we can in Texas."

LECTURE ENHANCER 9-6

THE GREEN EAVESDROPPER

In an official company history Green Giant Company owned up to the fact that in the early days their own management didn't know how canning worked. Small canneries of that time hired plant superintendents who kept canning methods a secret from the company as a form of job insurance.

"George F. Winter solved this problem in 1916," says the company history, "by hiding in the rafters of the plant, watching the superintendent at work and taking notes on his procedures. Winter's feat enabled the company to learn the actual canning process for the first time. George went on to become superintendent of production and a member of the board of directors until his retirement in 1954."

LECTURE ENHANCER 9-7

THE NEW REALITY: REEVALUATING JUST-IN-TIME INVENTORY TECHNIQUES

One of the business techniques imported from Japan in the 1980s was the concept of just-in-time (JIT) inventory—having raw materials and components delivered to the user just at the time they are needed for production. Effective use of JIT requires close coordination between the supplier and the organizational buyer.

The cost of materials and other goods and services needed to produce a product is about half the revenue received for it. Reducing this cost, even a small amount, can create a significant improvement in a company's bottom line. Statistics from the U.S. Department of Commerce show a steady decline in the amount of inventory carried by producers relative to the sales of their products or services. Just-in-time inventory and delivery have become the reality for organizational marketers.

When marketers and customers cooperate as partners, JIT has often worked well. Montreal-based Future Electronics is hooked up by an electronic data interchange system to Bailey Controls, an Ohio-based supplier of control systems. Every week, Bailey electronically sends Future its latest forecasts of what materials the Canadian company will need for the next six months. Future Electronics can then stock up in time.

Wal-Mart Stores Inc. is widely cited as one of the best practitioners of inventory management. And the Bentonville, Arkansas-based discount retailer is constantly trying to better its performance.

Among its current projects is an inventory-reporting system it is developing with W&H Systems Inc. in Carlstadt, New Jersey, and Rank Video Systems of America in Northbrook. Since the bulk of movie videotape sales are on weekends, Wal-Mart will take an electronic inventory of its shelves nationwide every Sunday night and automatically notify the video distributor, which will then place an order with Rank early Monday morning to manufacture the replacement tapes for delivery to stores on Thursday before rentals pick up again.

When cooperation has been lacking, JIT has become something of a corporate shell game in many industries as companies vie to keep their inventory on some other companies' books. And there is evidence that despite all the money companies have spent on computers to track sales and inventory, just-in-time inventory doesn't always work.

"The reality today is that with just-in-time, there are still a lot of empty shelves in the stores," says Perry Caicco, president of Toronto-based Consumers Distributing Inc.

LECTURE ENHANCER 9-8

COMPUTER-INTEGRATED MANUFACTURING FOR SMALL BUSINESS

The bulk of manufacturing automation is in large companies. For instance, 80 percent of the robots used in the United States are in companies like Ford and IBM. Although experts have been saying for over a decade that factory automation will soon be common in small companies, it just hasn't happened yet.

As the gap widens between the skills workers need and the skills they have, small companies' need for sophisticated equipment increases. To attract quality workers, small companies must have the right equipment.

Why are small companies slower to automate? There are lots of reasons. At the top of the list are the high initial equipment costs and the high cost of training. Many small firms simply don't have the money to do it. Whereas large companies have greater resources and can spread the cost of technology over several products, small-business owners spend their own money and can lose the business if the technology doesn't pay for itself. One way to overcome these disadvantages is for several smaller manufacturers to pool their resources and buy or lease equipment.

The software for implementing CAD/CAM often costs $30,000 or more. Small businesses must think of creative ways to finance such an expense or to share the expense with others. Often larger firms will help finance compatible with their own automated systems. Vendors of automated equipment now recognize the problems caused by their customers' skill deficiencies. Their sales pitches now emphasize training and technical support. Small businesses can also work closely with local educational institutions to help train their employees. Community colleges across the country have increased their attention to "manufacturing education." Their aim is to teach current workers basic literacy, critical thinking, and technical skills.

Another problem is that firms are introducing computer manufacturing piecemeal, one step at a time. This sounds like a good idea because of the high cost, but it often results in a system that's not as efficient as it could be. The most successful automation users implement the new technology as a whole, from order entry to moving the product out the door.

As computer integration becomes more popular, the price of CAD/CAM systems should go down Then even the smallest firms should be able to take advantage of the technology.

LECTURE ENHANCER 9-9

PEOPLE PROBLEMS ON THE PLANT FLOOR

With all of this talk of automation and computers, it's easy to get the idea that using machine-centered production like CAD/CAM is the only remedy for improving ailing productivity levels. Recent studies by another consulting firm, Ernst & Young, indicate that the manufacturing companies that did the best job were those that had a heavy people orientation as well. They call it *human-integrated manufacturing (HIM).*

Tracy O'Rourke introduced HIM at Varian Corporation with a communications campaign. He communicated the importance of a customer focus, quality, fast response, flexible factories, time-to-market, and organizational excellence. Before instituting HIM, customer focus was almost nonexistent at Varian. The firm took technology, converted it to products, and then took it to the market. Now it begins with finding out what the customer wants first. How's it working? O'Rourke lets the numbers do the talking. The cost of goods sold dropped from 70 cents per sales dollar to 65 cents in his first 12 months, and O'Rourke expects it to drop another 5 cents in the next two years.

It's important to remember that production is still dependent upon people, and it will be people who determine future systems' success or failure. Several steps must occur before people and machines will be combined to revolutionize manufacturing.

- There's an obvious need to train future production workers in the use and repair of computers, robots, and automatic machinery.
- Today's production workers must be retrained or relocated to adapt to the new high-tech systems.
- Major adjustments must be made in the relationships between suppliers and producers to implement concepts such as just-in-time inventory programs and enterprise networking.
- Production managers must be retrained to deal with more highly skilled workers who demand a much more participative managerial style.
- Employees must be trained to work in teams and to understand the concepts of competing in time, empowerment, total quality and continuous improvement.

LECTURE ENHANCER 9-10

HOW TO IMPROVE TOTAL QUALITY A LITTLE AT A TIME

Total quality relies upon two tenets: (1) do things a little bit at a time, all the time; this will bring the highest probability of success and (2) leading is better than managing. Let's consider the first tenet: doing a little bit at a time. Most of what you do every day is forced upon you as you balance one commitment against another. Your priorities are set by problems. Here are five keys to attacking your problems a little bit at a time:

1. Any effort to solve a problem is worthwhile if it is done all the time.
2. Don't wait for a detailed plan. Learn by doing.
3. No improvement is too small—continuously fine-tune.
4. Start simple—come up with a good idea and run with it.
5. There is no end to the process—you must continuously improve.

Now for the second tenet: leading is better than managing. Your job as leader is to find the best people for the job, tell them what you want them to do, and then let them do it. Let's look closer at each of these three tasks.

1. **Find and keep the best people for the job.** Remember good people are hard to find. It is as important to transfer poor performers as it is to find good ones.
2. **Let subordinates know what is to be done**. Know your customers' needs and develop job measures that lead·to continual improvement in what is done to meet your those needs. Set achievable goals. Ask for constructive complaining. It is your employees' job to tell you when things aren't working. Never assume people have the information they need; inform them regularly and clearly.
3. **Let them do their jobs.** Make sure everyone knows what their responsibilities are. Attach authority to responsibilities.

You can't improve everything at once. Pick the biggest problem and do something. Now. Then do a little more tomorrow. Keep in mind that a journey of a thousand miles begins with a single step.

LECTURE ENHANCER 9-11

INCENTIVES FOR QUALITY AT GE

To keep GE ahead, CEO Jack Welch and his executives have devised on array of corporate strategies. They are putting heavy reliance on the quality-control program that far outstrips run-of-the-mill efforts; shifting GE's sales emphasis from manufacturing products to supplying services; pushing profitable niche acquisitions; and rapidly expanding abroad.

GE's quality program, which was borrowed from Motorola Inc., involves training "Black Belts" for four months in statistical and other quality-enhancing measures. The Black Belts then spend full time roaming GE plants and setting up quality-improvement projects. Welch has told young managers that they haven't much future at GE unless they are selected to become Black Belts. The company already has trained 2,000 of them and plans to increase that number to 4,000 by year end and to 10,000 by the year 2000. In all, it is investing hundreds of millions of dollars in training, in specific projects, and in computer systems to analyze and run the quality-control program.

The program is producing a variety of benefits, Welch says. "Your customers are happy with you, you are not firefighting, you are not running in a reactive mode." GE hopes the program, by preventing costly snafus, will save $7 billion to $10 billion over the next decade and thus bolster profits.

The program probably will help profits, GE watchers say, but only if implemented enthusiastically. "Anytime you've got a top-down program like this, especially in a successful organization like GE, you run into resistance," notes Edward Lawler, a management professor at the University of Southern California.

The quality-control program, Welch says, is "a mammoth undertaking; I mean, I can't even begin to describe the size of this undertaking." A sure sign of top management's determination: 40 percent of GE executive bonuses, which run as high as $1 million, now will depend on implementation of the program. Previously, bonuses were based only on profit and cash flow.

LECTURE ENHANCER 9-12

PRODUCTIVITY BOTTLENECK IN THE OFFICE: THE KEY-BOARD

The modern office is likely to be equipped with personal computers linked through local area networks to each other and to a host of specialized equipment, from laser printers to data bases storing millions of customer records. Within this state-of-the-art system is a turn-of-the-century bottleneck—the computer keyboard.

The computer keyboard is simply a transplanted typewriter keyboard, the same keyboard that has been used since the 1890s. While the arrangement of keys is familiar, it is far from efficient. When the first typewriters were introduced, keys were arranged alphabetically (vestiges of this arrangement can be seen on the second row of keys—D F G H J K L). Printing bars were mechanically pushed against the paper by the pressure on the keys. Typists soon became proficient enough to cause jams as they typed faster than the mechanical bars could move.

Typewriter manufacturers went back to the drawing boards and designed a new keyboard to slow typists down to speeds within the limits of the crude mechanism. The resulting keyboard is referred to as "Qwerty," named for the first six keys of the top row. Keys were placed awkwardly to force slower typing. The "A", for instance, one of the most frequently used keys, was placed under a typist's left-hand little finger, the weakest finger on the hand. "E" requires an awkward reach using the middle finger of the left hand. Results were encouraging—typing speeds declined.

Today mechanical keys have been replaced by electronic ones, but the keyboard arrangement has remained unchanged. In the 1930s August Dvorak designed a better keyboard that groups the most frequently used letters on the home row and eliminates many awkward reaches. The Dvorak system is faster to learn, easier to type, less tiring, and less likely to cause errors than Qwerty. Using it increases typing speed by more than 20 percent. Yet the system never caught on—typists did not want to learn a new system when their typewriters all used Qwerty, and manufacturers did not want to produce Dvorak typewriters as long as typists used Qwerty.

LECTURE ENHANCER 9-13

WHO'S BEST AT SERVICE?

The London Business School and business schools at the University of Southern California and the University of North Carolina asked respondents to name companies they and others in their firms view as role models for service. Only about a third of executives chose non-U.S. companies as global leaders, and half of the top 10 were manufacturers.

Their findings:

1. Toyota Motors
2. Federal Express
3. Disney
4. Ritz-Carlton Hotels
5. Xerox
6. Motorola
7. AT&T
8. Nordstrom
9. Hewlett-Packard
10. Sony

LECTURE ENHANCER 9-14

PRODUCTIVITY AND QUALITY IN NONPROFIT ORGANIZATIONS

The United States can't remain competitive with the rest of the world if ineffective government agencies keep draining funds away from businesses. In the early 1990s, state and local government agencies found themselves with reduced revenues because of a national recession. Some responded with programs as dramatic as those instituted at the most progressive manufacturing firms. A case in point is the city of Madison, Wisconsin.

Mayor Joseph Sensenbrenner went to a seminar given by the late quality expert W. Edwards Deming. He listened to case histories of how organizations like American Express can mail out a new credit card in less than a week. It was taking six weeks to get a driver's license renewed in Madison.

The idea, Deming said, is to institute proven quality techniques. You've learned that quality includes continuous improvement in pleasing customers and reducing the variation in whatever product or service is offered. Mayor Sensenbrenner decided to try the quality process in the city garage, which serviced some 765 vehicles. It took an average of nine days to service a vehicle, so police cars and other important vehicles were off the road for too long.

The problem turned out to be that the city was ordering the cheapest vehicles every year. That meant that there were different models purchased every year and thousands of parts were needed to service all those different vehicles (leading to waste in inventory.) A team of people analyzed the problem and came up with a new purchasing plan that saved an impressive $700,000 a year. Furthermore, turnaround time for repairs fell from nine days to just three.

What's most interesting about the Madison case is that the city adopted many of the most advanced production and operations management concepts. A formal quality and productivity program was established, and a full-time quality and productivity administrator was hired. The city's mission statement includes continuous improvement, customer input, employee involvement, innovation, and trust.

Most government departments aren't designed to work with each other cooperatively. Bureaucracy prevails. That is, it's hard to get anything done because the thousands of rules and procedures normally prohibit a government worker from being flexible in response to citizen complaints and needs. That's all being changed in Madison through the efforts of one educated leader. Market forces are exerting great pressure on businesspeople to make fundamental changes for efficiency and survival. The next decade could well become known as the era of productivity improvement in all organizations.

LECTURE ENHANCER 9-15

THE VIRTUAL FACTORY

AeroTech Service Group, based in St. Louis, Missouri, has built a highly effective virtual factory with McDonnell Douglas Aerospace. The open and flexible network permits members to carry out a wide variety of collaborative tasks and is extremely secure.

Those attributes explain why the number of participants in its computer-linked manufacturing community has soared since mid-1993, when AeroTech, a McDonnell Douglas spin-off, began adding external suppliers to the network. Until then, the network had been limited to 50 or so McDonnell employees who used it to pass data between different computer systems within the organization. When external suppliers joined, they were so impressed with the way the network helped them work with McDonnell that they started to ask their suppliers and partners to join. By the fall of 1994, there were 400 internal and external users. There are now several thousand.

To accommodate a broad range of tasks and users, and to make the system as simple as possible to use, AeroTech employs protocols developed for the Internet, which itself is just an extra-large network that connects millions of dissimilar computers around the world. In addition, AeroTech permits members to choose from a wide assortment of telecommunication methods and speeds. Those members with minimal or sporadic needs access the system with modems, while more permanent participants, such as customers within other large aerospace companies or the U.S. government, use dedicated high-bandwidth links.

The network offers its members enormous advantages. Consider how McDonnell Douglas and UCAR Composites, a $12 million manufacturer of tooling for high-performance composite components based in Irvine, California, use the network to build prototypes of complex new parts rapidly. McDonnell wanted to send UCAR design updates electronically but could not allow UCAR to establish direct link into its computers because of security concerns namely, that an aggressive hacker might tap into such a link to access or modify data within McDonnell computers.

AeroTech provided an alternative. At McDonnell, computer-aided design files are translated into the numerical-control machine code needed to operate UCAR's metal-cutting machines. Using standard Internet protocols over a dedicated high-speed link, McDonnell then transfers the CAD file and the metal-cutting program to AeroTech's secure network node. AeroTech's system then forwards them to UCAR on normal phone lines.

Once information on the job arrives in California, CAD engineers can view it on their own CAD/CAM systems to make last-minute checks on the program. They then transfer the cutting program to their machines and begin manufacturing. The solution was particularly attractive for UCAR, which already had a paperless manufacturing operation. Now it could feed the data directly into its manufacturing and quality-assurance systems. As a result of the AeroTech system, the cost of these transfers has fallen from $400 per file (for tapes and express mail) to $4—and can be carried out in seconds rather than days.

This method of transferring cutting programs also is being used by hundreds of small machine shops, many of whose IT systems and expertise are much less sophisticated than UCAR's. These companies, which include many five- or six-person shops, can dial AeroTech using a regular modem, download a program or a drawing onto their PCs, and use the data to manufacture the parts.

This virtual factory also helps its members find the best suppliers much more quickly than before. In the past, McDonnell Douglas would invite representatives of qualified suppliers to come to St. Louis to view bid-request packages (containing engineering drawings and manufacturing-process specifications) so that they could decide whether and how much to bid for particular jobs. The groups would remain at the bidding table until all jobs were subcontracted—a process that often would take days.

Using the virtual factory's electronic bidding system, a McDonnell buyer now can E-mail qualified suppliers throughout the world that a job is available for bidding and let them access information about the job securely through the Internet. The suppliers then can use the system to return their bids to St. Louis. The system even ranks the bids for the buyer on the basis of cost. McDonnell estimates that the savings from electronic bidding alone pay for the operating costs of the entire system.

AeroTech also helps the electronic manufacturing community coordinate schedules better by allowing remote members to use scheduling software on one another's machines. A Department of Defense project manager in Washington, D.C., might use the system to access a McDonnell Douglas mainframe and run the graphics-based program that maintains a project's schedule. The manager then could get early warnings of time overruns by checking whether subcontractors were completing their subassemblies on time.

One of the most powerful functions that the AeroTech community provides is the ability to operate large, complex software programs securely from afar, without the need for sophisticated equipment on the local site. As a part of its contract with McDonnell Helicopter, for example, the U.S. Army periodically reviews engineering designs for the new Longbow helicopter. The army now can view these drawings by operating a McDonnell computer from a remote location, rather than by downloading the files, which would require the army to have the enormous CAD software systems on its own machines.

It's true that closed groups of technically sophisticated companies with long-standing partnerships carry out many of these same kinds of tasks. But, unlike them, AeroTech has made it possible for both longtime and casual partners to collaborate easily, securely, and cheaply, and without having to invest in new and proprietary information technology.

Critical Thinking Exercises

Name: ____________________

Date: ____________________

CRITICAL THINKING EXERCISE 9-1

SITE SELECTION

As you drive to school or work, you probably pass a number of manufacturing plants. Choose three of these plants and see if you can figure out why the company chose to locate the plant there. The chart below lists the factors that managers consider in site selection that were discussed in your text. Check the factors that seem to apply to the companies you selected.

FACTOR IN SITE SELECTION	Company A:	Company B:	Company C:
INEXPENSIVE LABOR			
PLENTY OF SKILLED LABOR			
ABUNDANT AND INEXPENSIVE RESOURCES (water, electricity, wood, coal, etc.)			
LOCATED CLOSE TO MARKET			
LOW COST OF LAND			

FACTOR IN SITE SELECTION	Company A:	Company B:	Company C:
QUALITY OF LIFE (climate, educational facilities, etc.)			
TAX AND GOVERNMENT SUPPORT			
ACCESS TO TRANSPORTATION			

Name: ____________________

Date: ____________________

CRITICAL THINKING EXERCISE 9-2

PRODUCTION PROCESSES

The text discusses two types of manufacturing systems: synthetic systems which either change raw materials into other products or combine raw materials/parts into a finished product and analytic systems which break down raw material into components to extract other products. Look at each of the products listed below and check whether each was produced using a synthetic or analytic manufacturing system.

PRODUCT	SYNTHETIC SYSTEM	ANALYTIC SYSTEM
Orange juice		
Hair brush		
Tongue oil		
Computer		
Desk		
Textbook		
Milk		
Dress		
Coal		
Newspaper		
Telephone		

ANSWERS TO CRITICAL THINKING EXERCISE 9-2

PRODUCT	SYNTHETIC SYSTEM	ANALYTIC SYSTEM
Orange juice		X
Hair brush	X	
Tongue oil		X
Computer	X	
Desk	X	
Textbook	X	
Milk		X
Dress	X	
Coal		X
Newspaper	X	
Telephone	X	

Supplemental Cases

CASE 9-1

COMPETING IN TIME AT DIGITAL EQUIPMENT CORPORATION

Marketing strategists at Digital Equipment Corporation (DEC) spotted a window of opportunity in the late 1980s for a new minicomputer. The problem was that there were less than two years to design, manufacture, test, market, deliver; and service a highly complex computer. However, 15 months later the company was producing computers in plants in New England, the Caribbean, and Europe. How did DEC do it? It used cross-functional teams from various parts of the world that worked together to create the product. The project, named Calypso, eventually generated huge profits for Digital.

The project began with a vision for the product. A small group took the idea to various parts of the company to find people who'd be interested in working on the project. Some 50 core people from 14 separate company locations joined the team. They were located in New England, California, the Caribbean, and Ireland. They communicated with each other by phone, telephone conferences, electronic mail, and computer conferencing. A common database was created to hold all the information about the project and from time to time certain team members flew to various sites to work with others.

The core team then went to other companies to find key components Digital was surprised to find that one of its customers, Raytheon, shared its vision so it proposed an alliance. Raytheon would do a parallel product for its military market. Thus, teams of workers from Digital and teams from Raytheon worked together and came up with solutions and products at the same time.

The secrets to the success of this project were a shared vision, common purpose, clear goals, and well-articulated tasks. But the methods used didn't look anything like a traditional production process. There was a project manager—Pauline Nist—but not all the engineers reported to her. Some members of the teams reported to their own functional areas in the firm, while others reported to the production teams. It's hard to believe that such a loosely aligned group of people could produce a product so quickly. But that's the benefit of production teams. They follow no set rules. They do not answer to a bureaucracy. They're free to do what's necessary to get done. Empowerment is critical to the project's success. So is "partnering" with another company In short, businesses today are forming cross-functional multifirm teams to create products quickly. This is true in the aircraft, software, computer, and other high-tech industries where fast product development is important.

DISCUSSION QUESTIONS FOR CASE 9-1:

1. What skills will tomorrow's college graduates need to participate in cross-functional multi-firm teams?

2. Note that some of the team members lived in other countries. What maybe the impact of multinational teams working together be on global politics and cooperation?

3. What are some of the technological advances that have made such multinational teams possible?

4. Once every company learns to network with other companies to produce and market products quickly, what can such networks do to make their products more attractive to potential customers?

ANSWERS TO DISCUSSION QUESTIONS FOR CASE 9-1:

1. *What skills will tomorrow's college graduates need to participate in cross-functional multi-firm teams?*

   Tomorrow's college graduates will have to be prepared to work with other workers in ways that we can only imagine. They will need strong communication skills, technical skills, and human relations skills. Imagination, cooperation, and the ability to work within a diverse workforce will be necessary.

2. *Note that some of the team members lived in other countries. What maybe the impact of multinational teams working together be on global politics and cooperation?*

   When people work together, they begin to see each other as individuals, not nationalities. The generalization of "global politics" is much more personal when it is discussed between two co-workers. Multinational teams can only promote greater international understanding.

3. *What are some of the technological advances that have made such multinational teams possible?*

   Such long-distant partnerships can only succeed if dependable instant communication is available. Satellite transmission of telephone calls and fax messages have made this possible. Jet travel has cut the time required to visit international coworkers. But is probably computer technology that done the most to pave the way for such partnerships. Computers allow individuals in different countries to access the same information in a common format.

4. *Once every company learns to network with other companies to produce and market products quickly, what can such networks do to make their products more attractive to potential customers?*

   Each company has its own special competitive advantage. Some companies have strong research and development resources. Others may have an efficient distribution system. Still others may have a respected product brand name. By combining each of these strengths, the network creates synergy.

CASE 9-2

THE AUTOMATION OF GENERAL MOTORS

No firm is more committed to computerizing production than General Motors. GM invested $8 billion in its Saturn plant in Tennessee. Saturn provides 6,000 jobs in the plant and 10,000 more in nearby facilities. Here are some of the impacts of plants such as Saturn.

Soon you will be able to go into a GM dealer and order a car, including colors, optional equipment, financing arrangements, and delivery date—all at a computer terminal. The computer will translate your order into parts orders. Radios, air conditioners, tires, and thousands of other parts will be ordered from suppliers all over the world. Computer designed inventory control will allow just-in-time delivery to the production floor. From order to delivery could take less than two weeks.

Meanwhile, at the factory the car is designed and built using computer-aided design and manufacturing. Robots do much of the assembling and moving of parts. Workers are not on assembly lines; rather, they work in small groups (modules) to build subassemblies. Testing of parts is done in the modules to raise quality control. The robots and computers are able to talk to each other, and control systems catch flaws almost immediately. Productivity in some areas increased over present plants by 800 percent.

Workers are paid a salary, not hourly wages. Workers as a whole have no more than six job categories, and each worker does a wider variety of work. Workers have a much larger say in how jobs are performed and at what pace. Employees don't punch a time clock. They pick their co-workers. If they get tired of doing one job, they can ask their boss for a transfer. The company has frequent morale-boosting programs, and employees can run on an outdoor obstacle course during off hours.

The whole plant is virtually paperless. Everything from order forms to engineering drawings are on computers. Computer specialists linked the system into computer integrated manufacturing. When a car is ordered, computers begin designing an inventory of spark plugs, air filters, and other parts to be sent to automobile dealerships to service the cars for the foreseeable future.

DISCUSSION QUESTIONS FOR CASE 9-2:

1. In 1992, GM said it was laying off 74,000 workers. The majority were not white collar. Do you think automation will lead to similar layoffs among other auto manufacturers?

2. How will such new manufacturing techniques affect the job market in the rest of the 1990s?

3. What will be the impact of such plants on suppliers, competitors, and dealers? What about unions?

4. Can you imagine GM being linked with all of its suppliers, dealers, and salespeople with one computer network that could create instant communications among all these people? What impact might that have on quality control? What other advantages do you see to such a system?

ANSWERS TO DISCUSSION QUESTIONS FOR CASE 9-2:

1. *In 1992, GM said it was laying off 74,000 workers. The majority were not white collar. Do you think automation will lead to similar layoffs among other auto manufacturers?*

   It is likely unless sales growth is way beyond what is now expected. One way to stay competitive in world markets where labor is much cheaper is to eliminate the need for labor on production lines. That is what the auto companies are doing, and that means fewer, but higher paid workers.

2. *How will such new manufacturing techniques affect the job market in the rest of the 1990s?*

   There will be many new jobs available in computer engineering, electrical engineering, systems design, and other related fields. Many of the new jobs have not even been created yet. This is the industrial era all over again with new kinds of jobs being created every day while old skills will become obsolete.

3. *What will be the impact of such plants on suppliers, competitors, and dealers? What about unions?*

   Suppliers will become more attractive if they anticipate changes such as just-in-time inventory control and design their systems to fit such needs. Competitors will simply lose out if they do not adjust to the new technology. One cannot continue to plow by horse and compete with those using huge plows. Similarly one cannot compete with mechanical equipment when competitors are using computer-controlled robots. Dealers will love the flexibility of ordering custom-made goods today and having them delivered in just a few days. Custom design and mass production will merge as machinery changes involve nothing more than a few changes in a computer program. Unions will continue to lose strength among blue collar workers, simply because there will be fewer of them, but white collar workers may seek the protection of union contracts as their jobs are put on the line.

4. *Can you imagine GM being linked with all of its suppliers, dealers, and salespeople with one computer network that could create instant communications among all these people? What impact might that have on quality control? What other advantages do you see to such a system?*

   Quality control would definitely improve if companies were in constant contact with suppliers and could inform them immediately if some part was not quite correct. The opportunity for improving just-in-time inventory control is great. Best of all, relationships between and among firms grow when the firms are in constant contact and easy contact as well. Eventually such a system will lead to making cars to order so that you and I will be able to custom design our cars and have them made to our specifications in as little as a month.

CASE 9-3

QUALITY—AMERICA IS BACK

Ask any production manager in Japan what person has had the greatest influence on their tremendous increase in quality products, and they are sure to answer, "W. Edwards Deming." He taught them the concepts of statistical control of quality, and they applied the principles. Today we call this system total quality management (TQM). Japanese businesses do not need as many quality control people at the end of assembly lines because they test for quality all along the production line. As a consequence, many Japanese products are not only priced well, they are higher in quality as well.

Another American named Philip Crosby wrote a book called Quality Is Free that has had a big impact on the thinking of managers at IBM and other leading firms. He followed that successful book with two others: Quality without Tears and The Art of Getting Your Own Sweet Way. What are all these books saying? "Why not do things right the first time?" or, "Set high standards and meet them every time."

Quality will remain a major focus in the 1990s because America is starting to listen to its experts—as Japan did. American industry, whether it is a manufacturing or service business, recognizes it has got to change the way it does business to compete in global markets. For example, some 35 percent of U.S. factories, offices, and stores now have some quality and productivity initiatives in place. It is no accident that Ford used the theme "Quality Is Job One" for its ad campaign. Not only has Ford adopted a TQM program; it is effectively encouraging its suppliers to focus on quality as well. Ford bestows Total Quality Excellence (TQE) awards to its suppliers that meet its stringent requirements. So far, only 8 have earned the honors, but a few more are in the final phase of qualifying and another 40 are reviewing the guidelines to see if they can make the grade.

Ford's TQE measures product quality, engineering, delivery, overall business relations, the supplier's commitment to Ford, how the company reacts to problems, and the viability of its communication network. Why should suppliers try to pass all these tests? Because Ford plans to decrease its supplier base from 1,400 to 1,000 before the end of the 1990s. Winning a TQE may mean continued business.

TQE winners say that, aside from the brownie points from Ford, their efforts resulted in improved efficiency, employee satisfaction, reduced waste, and better overall reputation and credibility. The first TQE winner, Rohm and Haas Co., claims that the required documentation and record keeping helped the company structure its own business and opened communications with Ford's advanced engineering staff. As you read in this chapter, Ford itself has turned to flexible manufacturing to make its plant more efficient. It has also adopted total quality management throughout its plants.

DISCUSSION QUESTIONS FOR CASE 9-3:

1. How did it happen that American businesses let the quality of their products slip below that of foreign producers?

2. How can computers and robots add to product quality? What effect does that have on labor?

3. Have you seen quality improvements in American cars in the last few years? What other products need more attention to quality?

4. What services need a quality boost? How would you go about implementing that boost?

ANSWERS TO DISCUSSION QUESTIONS FOR CASE 9-3:

1. *How did it happen that American businesses let the quality of their products slip below that of foreign producers?*

Emphasis in the United States was on productivity, not quality control. Meanwhile the Japanese were learning statistical quality control from American consultants. Now companies such as Ford are making quality a number one priority and quality may soon come back to American goods. It is not hard to implement statistical quality control, especially in computer-controlled manufacturing.

2. *How can computers and robots add to product quality? What effect does that have on labor?*

Computers and robots can be programmed to check on quality at various stages of the production process to assure almost perfect parts. Humans tend to be more prone to errors, and computers and robots have another reason for replacing labor on the production line.

3. *Have you seen quality improvements in American cars in the last few years? What other products need more attention to quality?*

There has been a noticeable improvement in auto quality, but foreign producers are getting better too. The United States is in a real economic war, and quality is a major weapon. Quality is needed in products such as clothing, shoes, electronics, cameras, and just about every consumer product from toys to homes.

4. *What services need a quality boost? How would you go about implementing that boost?*

I'm sure your students have their own opinions about this one. Surely some government organizations would be included. Some banks and retail stores would also. This is often a fun discussion as people air their complaints.

Transparency Masters

TRANSPARENCY MASTER 68	Chapter Outline
TRANSPARENCY MASTER 69	The Production Process *(Figure 9.1 on text page 261)*
TRANSPARENCY MASTER 70	PERT Chart for a Video *(Figure 9.2 on text page 274)*
TRANSPARENCY MASTER 71	A GANTT Chart for a Doll Manufacturer *(Figure 9.3 on text page 275)*

Chapter Outline

CHAPTER 9
USING THE LATEST TECHNOLOGY TO PRODUCE WORLD-CLASS PRODUCTS AND SERVICES

PROFILE: Tom Smith of Tom Smith Industries (TSI)

I. AMERICA'S MANUFACTURING BASE.

A. The Basics of Production Management.

B. Production and Productivity.

II. KEEPING COSTS LOW: SITE SELECTION.

A. Locating Close to Markets to Serve Customers Better.

B. Site Selection in the Future.

III. PRODUCTION PROCESSES.

A. Materials Requirement Planning: The Right Place at the Right Time.

IV. MODERN PRODUCTION TECHNIQUES.

A. Just-In-Time Inventory Control.

B. Flexible Manufacturing.

C. Lean Manufacturing.

D. Mass Customization.

E. Competing in Time.

F. Computer-Aided Design and Manufacturing.

V. CONTROL PROCEDURES: PERT AND GANTT CHARTS.

A. Total Quality in Production Management.

B. Measuring Productivity in the Service Sector.

C. Services Go Interactive.

D. Preparing for the Future.

VI. SUMMARY AND REVIEW.

The Production Process

(Figure 9.1 on text page 261)

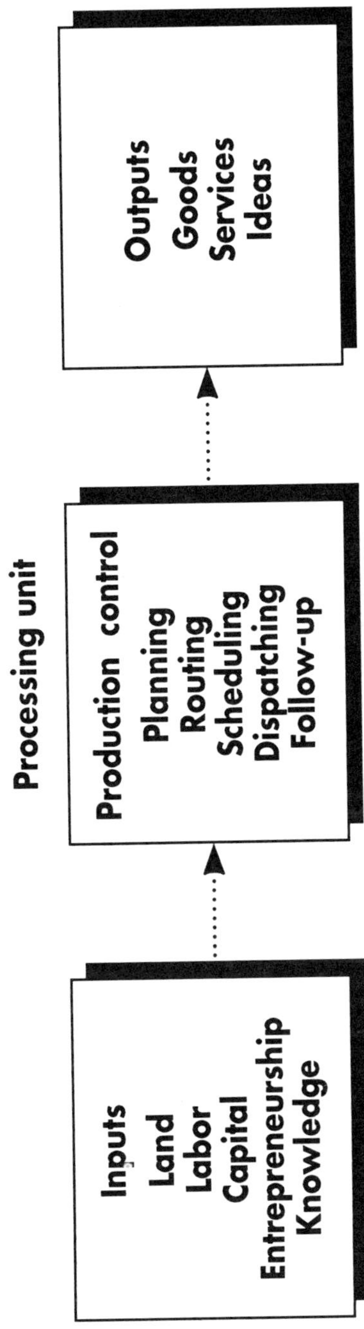

PERT Chart for a Video
(Figure 9.2 on text page 274)

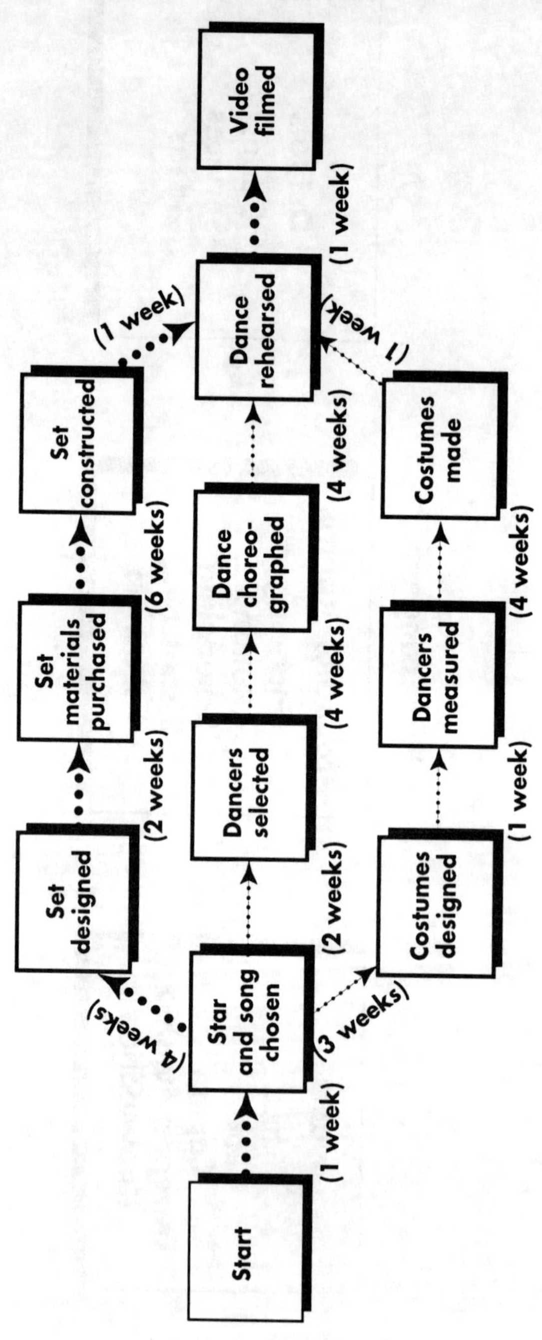

TM-71

A GANTT Chart for a Doll Manufacturer

(Figure 9.3 on text page 275)

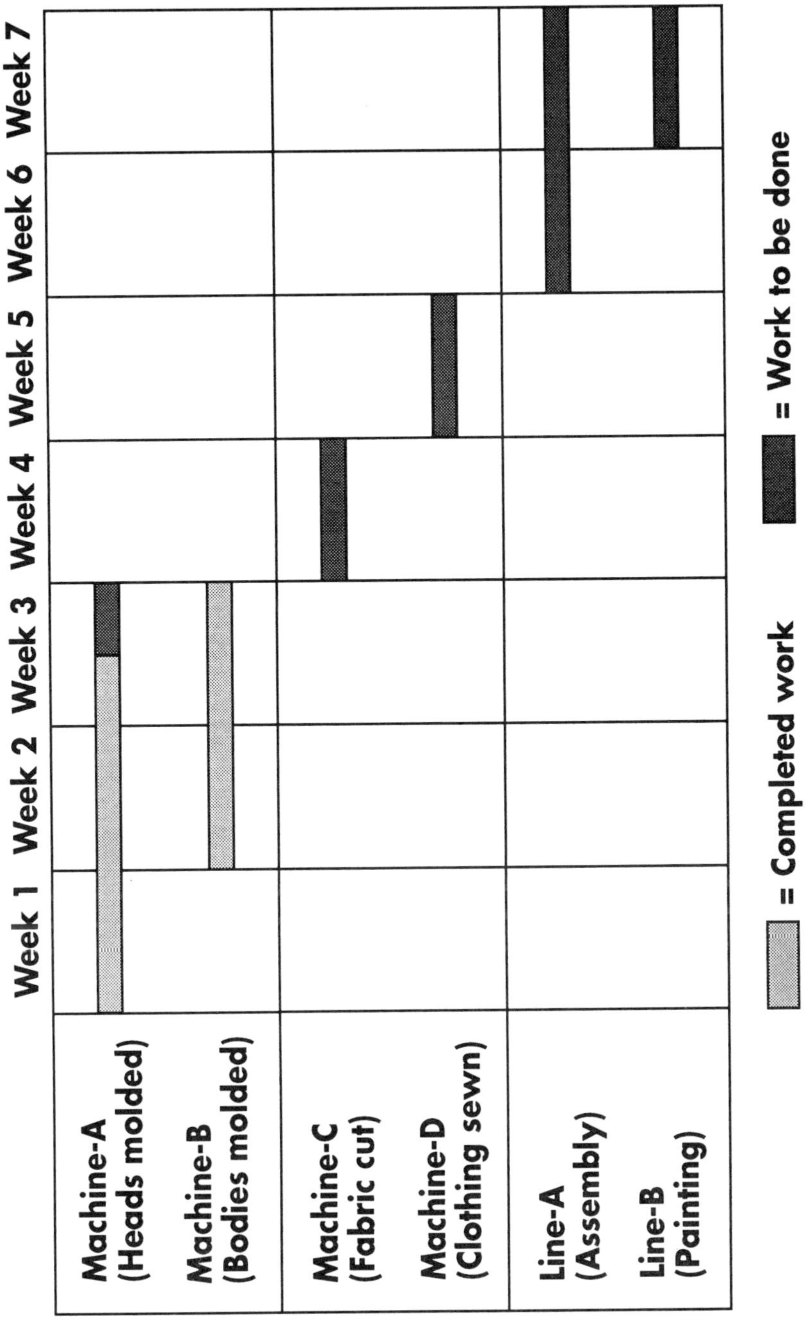
Week 1
Week 2
Week 3
Week 4
Week 5
Week 6
Week 7
Machine-A (Heads molded)
Machine-B (Bodies molded)
Machine-C (Fabric cut)
Machine-D (Clothing sewn)
Line-A (Assembly)
Line-B (Painting)
= Completed work
= Work to be done

Motivating Employees and Building Self-Managed Teams

Chapter 10

Folder Contents

Overhead Transparency Acetates

OT ACETATE 10-1 Intrinsic Versus Extrinsic Rewards

OT ACETATE 10-2 Does Company Morale Affect Motivation?

OT ACETATE 10-3 Five Personal Qualities Related to Job Motivation

OT ACETATE 10-4 Most Common Motivators Used by Businesses in the U.S.

OT ACETATE 10-5 How Do Workers Feel About Reward and Incentive Programs?

OT ACETATE 10-6 How to Use Expectancy Theory

OT ACETATE 10-7 Employee Questions About Expectancy Theory

OT ACETATE 10-8 Six Keys to Motivation

OT ACETATE 10-9 How Often Do Employees Feel Stressed on the Job?

OT ACETATE 10-10 Warning Signs of Employee Stress

OT ACETATE 10-11 Where Are Workers Most Satisfied With Their Jobs?

(Acetates and Transparency Masters are also available as PowerPoint slides on disk and on the Presentation CD-ROM.)

(Resources Available are also referenced in the expanded lecture outline later in this chapter.)

Other Resources Available

Video Case - "Southwest Airlines." How does Southwest maintain its unique cost-effective position? In an industry in which antagonistic labor-management relations are common, how does Southwest build cooperation with a workforce that is 85 percent unionized? This video shows how Kelleher's "fun in the workplace: philosophy fosters a more positive working environment. (The **Media Resource Guide** contains a summary of the Video and suggested discussion questions.)

Student Assessment and Learning Guide: Contains matching key term and definition questions, write-in retention questions, write-in critical thinking questions, and practice test of multiple choice and true/false questions.

Technology:

Zapitalism CD-ROM – Simulation program.

Concept Mastery Exam Preparation Disk – Practice test and tutorial.

Business Essentials Disk – Hyperlinks Understanding Business with seven other leading business texts.

Presentation CD-ROM - Contains PowerPoint slides of acetates and transparency masters, video clips, lecture materials. This tool allows you to customize your lecture presentations.

***Business Week* Web Site Access with the *Business Week* edition.**

Understanding Business **Home Page - http:/www.mhhe.com/ub5e**.

Audiotape: Abridged chapter (Text minus profile, boxes, and end-of-chapter material.

Associated Web Sites

These sites are provided to students for the purpose of analysis and critical thinking of the issues. Students are encouraged to explore other sites. As with any Web site, some may be inactive now.

Organizational Behavior:

Overview and relationship with Human Resources

http://commerce.ubc.ca/PhD/ob.html

Historical Background

http://www.cba.neu.edu/~ewertheim/introd/history.htm

Motivating Employees - Changing Old Habits:

http://www.ciwmb.ca.gov/mrt/wpw/wpbiz/fsmotivt.htm

To wear hearing protection

http://www.cabotsafety.com/tech/earlog/earlog7.html

Incentive Awards - Safety:

http://www.giftcert.com/premchce/premierechoice_safetyprograms.html

Team Building:

http://www.facilitiesnet.com/NS/NS3a96c.html

Several interesting articles - related to management personality traits:

http://www.itstime.com/sep96.htm

Motivating women employees - two important reasons

http://www.info-now.com/html/9300mot1.htm

Companies Save on Healthcare by Motivating Employees to Exercise:

http://www.execreport.com/zine/0796.Healthbeat.html

Job Stress:

Definitions

http://www.express.com/~png/sharing/pete28.html

Overview

http://www.allabouthealth.com/Current/Articles/Cotton--JobStress.htm

Reasons

http://www.prb.com/html/cstress.html

Helpful tips on reducing work-place stress

http://donrichard.com/jobfair/articles/art06.htm

Understanding Business Home Page

http:/www.mhhe.com/ub5e.

What's New in This Edition

Additions

- Section "Meeting Employee Expectations: Vroom's Expectancy Theory"
- Section "Treating Employees Fairly: Equity Theory"
- Section "A Model for the Future: Employee Empowerment"
- Spotlight on Small Business: Motivating Low-Wage Earners
- Reaching Beyond Our Borders: The Challenge of Global Work Teams
- Taking It to the Net exercises
- Figure 10-4 Comparison of Maslow's hierarchy of needs and Herzberg's 2-factor theory
- Case: Making Teams Work in a Changing Market
- Video Case: Southwest Airlines

Revisions

Statistical data and examples throughout the chapter were updated to reflect current information. In addition:

- Profile of Herb Kelleher of Southwest Airlines was updated.
- Section "Theory Z" was condensed.
- The 4th edition section "Management by Objectives" was condensed and blended into the section "Goal-Setting Theory." An update regarding the status of MBO was added.
- Section "Motivation in the Future" was expanded to include discussion of managing diversity in the workplace.
- Legal Briefcase box on UPS was updated to include discussion of 1997 strike.

Deletions

- Section "Rethinking the Corporation"
- Case: Theories X and Y: That's How the Cookie Crumbles
- Boxes: From the Pages of Entrepreneur, Spotlight on Small Business, Reaching Beyond Our Borders, Teamwork Calls for Team Compensation

Brief Chapter Outline/Learning Goals

CHAPTER 10

MOTIVATING EMPLOYEES AND BUILDING SELF-MANAGED TEAMS

PROFILE: Herb Kelleher of Southwest Airlines

I. THE IMPORTANCE OF MOTIVATION.

LEARNING GOAL 1. Explain Taylor's scientific management.

A. Early Management Studies (Taylor).

B. The Hawthorne Studies (Mayo).

LEARNING GOAL 2. Describe the Hawthorne studies and relate their significance to human-based management.

II. MASLOW'S HIERARCHY OF NEEDS.

LEARNING GOAL 3. Identify the levels of Maslow's hierarchy of needs and relate their importance to employee motivation.

A. Applying Maslow's Theory.

III. MCGREGOR'S THEORY X AND THEORY Y.

LEARNING GOAL 4. Differentiate among Theory X, Theory Y, and Theory Z.

A. Theory X.

B. Theory Y.

C. Theory Z.

IV. HERZBERG'S MOTIVATING FACTORS.

LEARNING GOAL 5. Distinguish between motivators and hygiene factors identified by Herzberg.

A. Applying Herzberg's Theories.

V. JOB ENRICHMENT.

LEARNING GOAL 6. Explain how job enrichment affects employee motivation and performance.

VI. GOAL-SETTING THEORY AND MANAGEMENT BY OBJECTIVES.

LEARNING GOAL 7. Identify the steps involved in implementing a management by objectives (MBO) program.

VII. MEETING EMPLOYEE EXPECTATIONS: EXPECTANCY THEORY.

LEARNING GOAL 8. Explain the key factors involved in expectancy theory.

VIII. TREATING EMPLOYEES FAIRLY: EQUITY THEORY.

LEARNING GOAL 9. Examine the key principles of equity theory.

IX. IMPLEMENTING THE NEW CONCEPTS: MOTIVATION THROUGH COMMUNICATION.

A. Open Communication and Self-Managed Teams.

B. Changing Organizations is Not Easy.

C. A Model for the Future.

1. Learning From the Miller Brewing and Mary Kay Experience.

D. Motivation in the Future.

X. SUMMARY AND REVIEW.

(Learning Objectives are also referenced in the expanded lecture outline later in this chapter)

Key Terms

equity theory *(text page 302)*

extrinsic reward *(text page 288)*

expectancy theory *(text page 302)*

goal-setting theory *(text page 300)*

Hawthorne effect *(text page 292)*

hygiene factors *(text page 297)*

intrinsic reward *(text page 288)*

job enlargement *(text page 300)*

job enrichment *(text page 298)*

job rotation *(text page 300)*

job simplification *(text page 300)*

management by objectives (MBO) *(text page 300)*

Maslow's hierarchy of needs *(text page 292)*

motivators *(text page 297)*

principle of motion economy *(text page 298)*

scientific management *(text page 289)*

time-motion studies *(text page 289)*

Lecture Outline

The **PROFILE** at the beginning of this chapter focuses on **HERB KELLEHER** of **SOUTHWEST AIRLINES.** The company now ranks as the 5th largest airline among all global carriers. Analysts credit this achievement to the engaging management style of the company's chairman, **HERB KELLEHER.**

I. THE IMPORTANCE OF MOTIVATION.

A. The key to leadership success is **MOTIVATING OTHERS TO DO THEIR BEST**.

1. People are motivated by a variety of things.
   a. An **INTRINSIC REWARD** is the good feeling you have when you have done a good job.
   b. An **EXTRINSIC REWARD** is something given to you by someone else as recognition for good work and include pay increases, praise, and promotions.
2. **MOTIVATION**, the drive to satisfy a need, ultimately comes from **WITHIN AN INDIVIDUAL.**
3. The purpose of this chapter is to help you learn how to stimulate people and bring out that natural drive to do a good job.
4. The most important person to motivate is **YOURSELF**.

Lecture Notes

TRANSPARENCY MASTER 72
Chapter Outline

(Transparency Masters begin on page 10.86)

LECTURE ENHANCER 10-1
The Secret of Men and Motivation

Marriage makes men more productive employees according to David Neumark of the Federal Reserve Board and Sanders Korenman of Princeton University. (See complete lecture enhancer on page 10.54.)

Lecture Outline

5. The job of a manager is to find each workers' commitment, encourage it, and focus it on some common goal.

B. **EARLY MANAGEMENT STUDIES (TAYLOR)**.

▶ **LEARNING GOAL 1.** Explain Taylor's scientific management.

1. **FREDERICK TAYLOR** is known as the **"FATHER OF SCIENTIFIC MANAGEMENT."**
   a. His book The Principles of Scientific Management was published in 1911.
   b. **TAYLOR'S GOAL** was to **INCREASE PRODUCTIVITY** by studying the most efficient ways of doing things and then teaching workers these methods.
   c. The way to improve productivity was to scientifically study the most efficient way to do things then teach people those methods **(SCIENTIFIC MANAGEMENT.)**
   d. **THREE ELEMENTS** of his approach were: **TIME, METHODS**, and **RULES OF WORK.**
   e. **TIME-MOTION STUDIES** break down the tasks needed to do a job, and measure the time needed to do each task.
2. H. L. Gant, on of Taylor's followers, developed **GANTT CHARTS** by which managers plotted the work of employees a day in advance.

SUPPLEMENTAL CASE 10-1
Using Compensation to Motivate

See complete case on page 10.76.

OT ACETATE 10-1
Intrinsic Versus Extrinsic Rewards

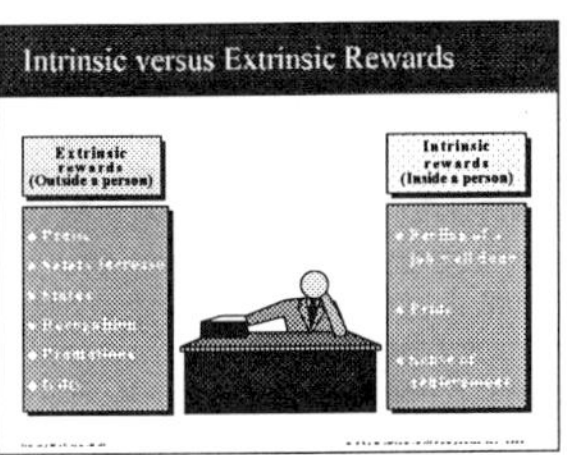

Comments:

1. This acetate illustrates that intrinsic rewards come from within, whereas extrinsic rewards come from outside a person. Ask students which type of reward is most valuable to them and why.
2. Students might like to discuss situations in which they were intrinsically motivated. You can also question, what types of extrinsic rewards do they find most powerful?

Lecture Outline

3. **FRANK AND LILLIAN GILBRETH** used Taylor's ideas in the principle of **MOTION ECONOMY**—breaking down every job into a series of motions (therbligs) and then analyzing each motion to make it more efficient.

4. **SCIENTIFIC MANAGEMENT** viewed people as MACHINES that needed to be properly programmed.

   a. There was little concern for the psychological or human aspects of work.

   b. Much emphasis in some companies is still placed on conformity to work rules rather than on creativity, flexibility, and responsiveness.

C. **THE HAWTHORNE STUDIES (MAYO.)**

▶ **LEARNING GOAL 2.** Describe the Hawthorne studies and relate their significance to human-based management.

1. The **HAWTHORNE STUDIES** were conducted by Elton Mayo at the **WESTERN ELECTRIC COMPANY's** Hawthorne plant in Cicero, Illinois.

   a. Begun in 1927, the studies ended six years later.

   b. The **PURPOSE** of the studies were to **DETERMINE THE BEST LIGHTING** for optimum productivity.

LECTURE ENHANCER 10-2
Gilbreth's Motion Study

Frank Gilbreth began his career as an apprentice bricklayer. His observations of other bricklayers comprised the first motion study. (See complete lecture enhancer on page 10.55.)

LEGAL BRIEFCASE

(Box in text, page 290)

"Scientific Management is Alive and Well at UPS"

United Parcel Service (UPS) is truly a powerhouse of a company. With over $20 billion in revenues and 335,000 employees, UPS is the world's largest package distribution company. The company grew from a small bicycle-messenger service in 1907 to today's mammoth delivery service by dictating every task for its employees. Drivers are required to step out of their trucks with their right foot, fold their money face-up, and carry packages under their left arm. If they are considered slow their supervisor rides with them prodding them with stopwatches and clipboards. Drivers accepted such direction, taking comfort in their $20 per hour wages, generous benefits, and an attractive profit-sharing plan.

OT ACETATE 10-2
Does Company Morale Affect Motivation?

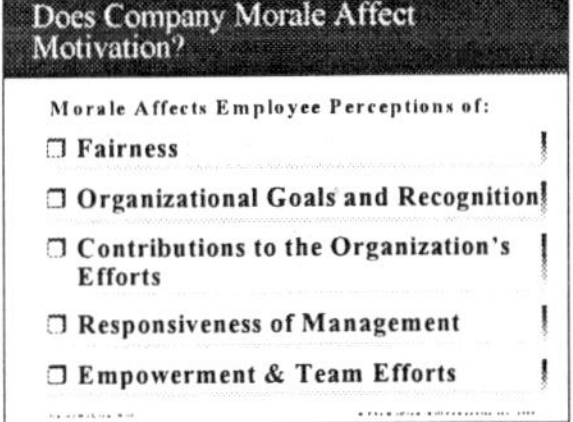

Comments:

1. The straightforward answer to this question is yes. If workers, managers, or others involved within the company do not have a good feeling about the firm, it can and usually will affect motivation. You may want to show students the acetate question first before revealing all the information.
2. The five points listed on the acetate lead effectively into the discussion of motivating employees. A solid case can be made to discuss each of the points thoroughly.
3. A good question to pose to students is, "do they tend to work as hard in a class that they are required to take as part of a degree program as they do in the subjects areas of their major?" A follow up is did the atmosphere and attitude of the instructor make a difference? In other words, if morale was high did it affect your performance?

Lecture Outline

   c. The **PRODUCTIVITY** of the experimental group **INCREASED** compared to the control group whether the lighting was bright or dim.

2. A second series of studies were conducted to see if **OTHER FACTORS** contributed to increased production.

   a. **PRODUCTIVITY INCREASED** during each of the 13 experimental periods.

   b. When conditions were returned to their original status (before the studies were started), **PRODUCTIVITY CONTINUED TO GO UP**. Why?

3. Mayo hypothesized that **HUMAN** or **PSYCHOLOGICAL FACTORS** caused the increases:

   a. The women workers thought of themselves as a **SOCIAL GROUP.**

   b. The women workers were involved in the **PLANNING** of the experiments.

   c. The women workers enjoyed the **SPECIAL ATMOSPHERE** and **ADDITIONAL PAY** for the increased productivity.

4. The term **HAWTHORNE EFFECT** refers to the tendency for people to behave differently when they know they're being studied.

OT ACETATE 10-3
Five Personal Qualities Related to Job Motivation

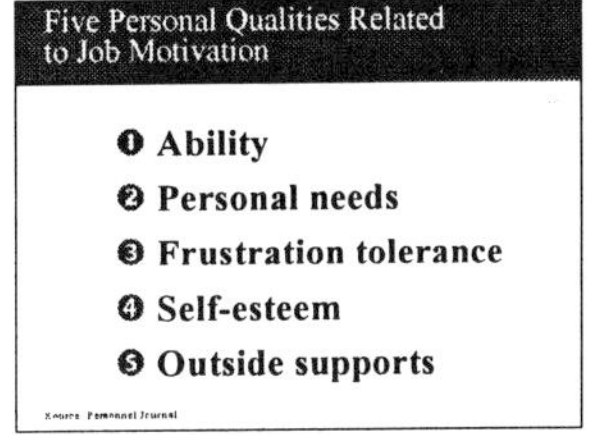

Comments:

1. If we look at each of these qualities separately, several interesting facts can be communicated to students. Intelligence, creativity, energy, and maturity can all be considered factors related to ability. If a person's abilities are congruent with the needs of the job this can serve as a motivating force. However, if an employee's abilities are significantly higher than the job, this can prove to be a contra-motivational factor. This will answer student questions concerning being "over qualified" for a job.
2. If an employee's needs (the need to be secure, liked, appreciated, effective, trusted, autonomous, etc) are reasonably met on the job, internal motivation will incubate and likely grow. The relationship to Maslow can easily be interjected here.
3. Employees that have strong frustration tolerance are capable of being patient in the face of job obstacles or temporary frustrations. Low frustration tolerance can cause severe problems in job situations where at least average frustration tolerance is needed. For example, people that cannot tolerate children not following directions could be easily frustrated, and hence not motivated, as elementary school teachers.
4. An inherent sense of self esteem generally moves workers to perform a job well whether they are closely supervised or not. They appreciate acknowledgement of a job well done, but don't need it to continue to perform effectively.
5. Family, friends, hobbies, interests, and a sense of purpose in life help employees bring energy to the work place. If work is placed in a healthy perspective, a bad workday can be tolerated by a good night with family or friends. Employees whose entire life is work driven tend to overreact to work setbacks and frustrations.

LECTURE ENHANCER 10-3
Recognition: Making Heroes

Companies often make the mistake of equating pay with rewards. Pay is not a reward for outstanding performance, it is compensation for doing the job in the first place. A reward should be a special gain for special achievements. (See complete lecture enhancer on page 10.56.)

a. The Hawthorne studies' results encouraged researchers **TO STUDY HUMAN MOTIVATION** and the **MANAGERIAL STYLES** that lead to more productivity.

b. Mayo's findings led to **NEW ASSUMPTIONS ABOUT EMPLOYEES.**

c. **MONEY** was found to be a relatively **LOW MOTIVATOR.**

II. MASLOW'S HIERARCHY OF NEEDS.

▶ **LEARNING GOAL 3.** Identify the levels of Maslow's hierarchy of needs and relate their importance to employee motivation.

A. **ABRAHAM MASLOW** believed that **MOTIVATION ARISES FROM NEED.**

1. One is motivated to satisfy unmet needs.
2. **SATISFIED NEEDS NO LONGER MOTIVATE.**

B. Maslow placed needs on a **HIERARCHY** of importance:

1. **PHYSIOLOGICAL NEEDS**: Basic survival needs including the need to drink, eat, and be sheltered from heat and cold.
2. **SAFETY NEEDS**: The need to feel secure at work and at home.
3. **SOCIAL NEEDS**: The need to feel loved, accepted, and part of the group.

Lecture Notes

LECTURE ENHANCER 10-4
Maslow's Further Study of Motivation

Anyone who has taken Psychology 101 knows about Abraham Maslow's "hierarchy of needs." People, Maslow found, strive to fulfill progressively higher levels of need, from nourishment, safety, love, and esteem to "self-actualization." It's less well known that Maslow, in the early 1960s, also delved deeply into management and economics. (See complete lecture enhancer on page 10.58.)

TRANSPARENCY MASTER 73
Maslow's Hierarchy of Needs *(Figure 10.1 on text page 292)*

(Transparency Masters begin on page 10.86.)

CRITICAL THINKING EXERCISE 10-1
Maslow's Hierarchy of Needs

See complete exercise on page 10.72.

Lecture Outline

4. **SELF-ESTEEM NEEDS**: The need for recognition and acknowledgment from others, as well as self-respect and a sense of status.

5. **SELF-ACTUALIZATION NEEDS**: The need to develop to your fullest potential.

C. When one need is satisfied, another, higher-level need emerges.

1. The **SATISFIED NEED** is no longer a motivator.

2. Lower-level needs, however, can pop up at any time and take attention away from higher-level needs.

D. **APPLYING MASLOW'S THEORY**.

1. The text relates how Andrew Grove, president of Intel, uses Maslow's concepts to motivate employees in his firm.

2. Once one understands the need level of employees, it is easier to design programs that will trigger self-motivation.

III. MCGREGOR'S THEORY X AND THEORY Y.

▶ **LEARNING GOAL 4.** Differentiate among Theory X, Theory Y, and Theory Z.

A. **DOUGLAS MCGREGOR** categories managers by **THEIR ATTITUDES** which lead to different managerial styles: **THEORY X** and **THEORY Y.**

Lecture Notes

CRITICAL THINKING (page 293 in text)

Your job right now is to finish reading this chapter. How strongly would you be motivated to do that if you were sweating in a 105-degree room? Imagine now that your roommate turns on the air conditioning. Now that you are more comfortable, are you more likely to read? Look at Maslow's hierarchy of needs to see what need would be motivating you at both times. Can you see how helpful Maslow's theory is in understanding motivation by applying it to your own life?

LECTURE ENHANCER 10-5
The Big Thrill Motivation

Another facet of motivation involves the individual's tolerance for risk taking. Some individuals have a kind of psychological urge to reach beyond the status quo and seek out novelty, change, and excitement. (See complete lecture enhancer on page 10.59.)

PROGRESS CHECK (page 294 in text)

- What are the similarities and differences between Taylor's scientific management and Mayo's Hawthorne studies? How did Mayo's findings influence scientific management?
- Can you draw Maslow's hierarchy of needs? Label and describe the parts.
- According to Andrew Grove, what is the ultimate source of all motivation?

Lecture Outline

B. **THEORY X.**

1. The **ASSUMPTIONS** of Theory X management are:

   a. The average person **DISLIKES WORK** and will avoid it if possible.

   b. Because of this dislike, the average person must be **FORCED, CONTROLLED, DIRECTED, OR THREATENED WITH PUNISHMENT TO BE MOTIVATED** to put forth the effort to achieve the organization's goals.

   c. The average worker prefers to be directed, wishes **TO AVOID RESPONSIBILITY**, has relatively **LITTLE AMBITION**, and wants **SECURITY.**

   d. Primary motivators are **FEAR** and **MONEY.**

2. The **CONSEQUENCE OF SUCH ATTITUDES** is a manager who is very "busy."

   a. Motivation is more likely to take the form of **PUNISHMENT** for bad work rather than **REWARD** for good work.

   b. Those were the assumptions behind Taylor's scientific management.

C. **THEORY Y.**

LECTURE ENHANCER 10-6
Personality Traits of CEOs and Army Generals

Researchers at the Center for Creative Leadership have uncovered a coincidence that will not surprise many workers: corporate chief executive officers share a broad range of psychological traits with Army generals. (See complete lecture enhancer on page 10.60.)

SUPPLEMENTAL CASE 10-2
Theories Z and Y: That's How the Cookie Crumbles

See complete case on page 10.79.

Lecture Outline

1. **THEORY Y** makes entirely different **ASSUMPTIONS** about people:

   a. Most people **LIKE WORK**; it is as natural as play or rest.

   b. Most people **NATURALLY WORK TOWARD GOALS** to which he or she is committed.

   c. The depth of a person's commitment to goals depends on the perceived **REWARDS** for achieving them.

   d. Under certain conditions, most people not only accept but **SEEKS RESPONSIBILITY.**

   e. People are capable of using a high degree of **IMAGINATION, CREATIVITY**, and **CLEVERNESS** to solve problems.

   f. In industry, the average person's **INTELLECTUAL POTENTIAL IS ONLY PARTIALLY REALIZED.**

   g. People are **MOTIVATED BY A VARIETY OF REWARDS**. Each worker is stimulated by a reward unique to that worker (time off, money, recognition, etc.)

2. Theory Y emphasizes a relaxed managerial atmosphere in which workers are free to set objectives and be flexible.

Lecture Notes

LECTURE ENHANCER 10-7
Motivation and Creativity

Keeping its artists and writers happy and creative is a top priority at Hallmark, the nation's largest greeting card seller. (See complete lecture enhancer on page 10.61.)

Lecture Outline

3. **EMPOWERMENT** is a key technique in meeting these objectives. To be a real motivator, empowerment requires management to:
   a. Find out what people think the problems in the organization are.
   b. Let them design the solutions.
   c. Get out of the way and let them put those solutions into action.
4. The trend in many U.S. businesses is toward Theory Y management.

D. **OUCHI'S THEORY Z.**

1. Another reason for a more flexible managerial style is to meet competition from foreign firms.
2. In the 1980s **WILLIAM OUCHI** wrote *Theory Z: How American Business Can Meet the Japanese Challenge,* which highlighted how corporations in Japan are run differently from U.S. companies.
3. Out of the Japanese system evolved a concept called **THEORY Z**, which contains the following items:
   a. **VIRTUALLY LIFE-TIME EMPLOYMENT.**
   b. **COLLECTIVE DECISION-MAKING.**

Lecture Notes

TRANSPARENCY MASTER 74
A Comparison of Theories X, Y, and Z *(Figure 10.2 on text page 296)*

TM 74

(Transparency Masters begin on page 10.86.)

Lecture Outline

c. **SLOW EVALUATION AND PROMOTION.**

d. **FEW LEVELS OF MANAGEMENT.**

4. Several U.S. firms attempted to adopt aspects of this style—but, because of cultural differences, Theory Z principles were never widely adopted.

IV. HERZBERG'S MOTIVATING FACTORS.

▶ **LEARNING GOAL 5.** Distinguish between motivators and hygiene factors identified by Herzberg.

A. **THEORIES X, Y, AND Y** are **CONCERNED WITH MANAGEMENT STYLES.**

1. Another theorist looks at what managers can do with the job itself to motivate employees.

2. **HERZBERG** is **CONCERNED IS WITH THE CONTENT OF WORK** rather than style of management.

B. Frederick **HERZBERG** surveyed workers to find out how they **RANK JOB-RELATED FACTORS.** The results were:

1. Sense of achievement.
2. Earned recognition.
3. Interest in the work itself.
4. Opportunity for growth.

Lecture Notes

OT ACETATE 10-4
Most Common Motivators Used by Businesses in the U.S.

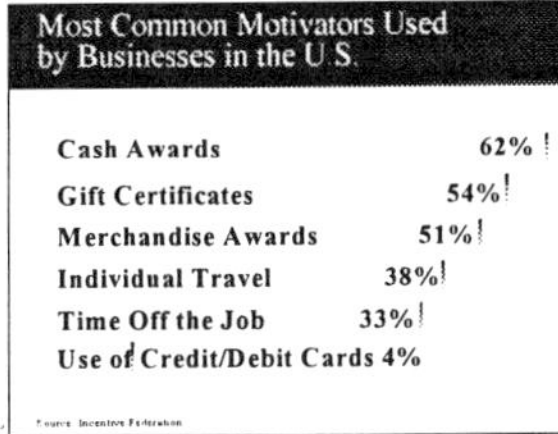

Comments:

1. See if students can guess the leading motivators used by business in the U.S. It's likely they will get the most popular motivator, cash awards, correct. Ask them what particularly motivates them when performing a job? The discussion of Herzberg in the chapter may question business motives in using cash awards as the most popular method of motivation. You could elect to bring that up here.
2. Ask students what managers should use as the basis for motivators. Remind them that often we tend to focus on things that are important to us as being important to others. Can they cite instances where they experienced managers doing exactly that?
3. In the next chapter we will discuss issues such as family leave and other benefits. See how much importance students put to benefit issue such as family leave or child care. Are these motivators to them?

Lecture Outline

5. Opportunity for advancement.
6. Importance of responsibility.
7. Peer and group relationships.
8. Pay.
9. Supervisor's fairness.
10. Company policies and rules.
11. Status.
12. Job security.
13. Supervisor's friendliness.
14. Working conditions.

C. Herzberg noted that the **HIGHEST RANKING FACTORS DEALT WITH JOB CONTENT**.

1. He referred to these as **MOTIVATORS** since they gave employees a great deal of satisfaction.
2. They include the work itself, achievement, and responsibility.

D. The **OTHER FACTORS** had to do with **JOB ENVIRONMENT**.

1. They could **CAUSE DISSATISFACTION** If them were missing but **NOT NECESSARILY MOTIVATION** if they increased.
2. These so called **HYGIENE FACTORS** include working conditions and salary.

CRITICAL THINKING EXERCISE 10-2
The Payoff

See complete exercise on page 10.74.

TRANSPARENCY MASTER 75
Herzberg's Motivators and Hygiene Factors *(Figure 10.3 on text page 297)*

(Transparency Masters begin on page 10.86.)

OT ACETATE 10-5
How Do Workers Feel About Reward and Incentive Programs?

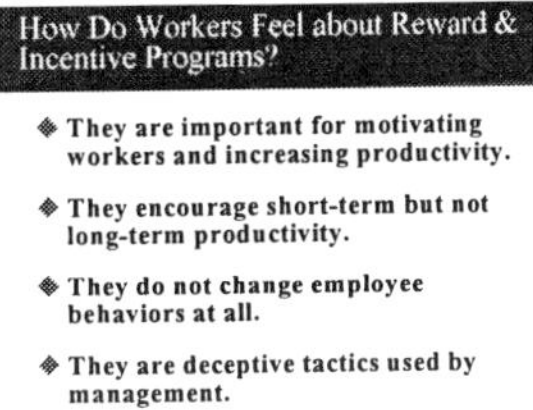

Comments:

1. This acetate shows some interesting opinions employees have concerning reward and incentive programs. The range is virtually from them being important to their being deceptive tactics used to manipulate workers.
2. Why not ask what students think of such programs? Particularly students who work in companies offering such programs. One of the key questions concerning such programs is do they encourage any long-term productivity?
3. If you want to be brave, see if incentives offered in your class (attendance bonuses, extra credit, etc.) motivate students to perform at a higher level of effort. Let use know what you find out.

E. **APPLYING HERZBERG'S THEORIES TO MODERN WORKERS**

1. The text offers several current examples of Herzberg's theories in action.

2. Further surveys support Herzberg's finding that the number one motivator is not money, but a sense of achievement and recognition.

3. There is a good deal of similarity in Maslow's hierarchy and Herzberg's two-factor theory.

V. JOB ENRICHMENT.

▶ **LEARNING GOAL 6.** Explain how job enrichment affects employee motivation and performance.

A. **JOB ENRICHMENT** is a motivational strategy that emphasizes motivating the worker through the job itself.

B. The **FIVE CHARACTERISTICS** of work believed to be **IMPORTANT IN AFFECTING MOTIVATION AND PERFORMANCE** are:

1. **SKILL VARIETY**, the extent to which a job demands different skills of the person.

2. **TASK IDENTITY**, the degree to which the job requires doing a task with a visible outcome from beginning to end.

TRANSPARENCY MASTER 76
Comparison of Maslow's Hierarchy of Needs and Herzberg's Theory of Factors
(Figure 10.4 on text page 298)

(Transparency Masters begin on page 10.86)

SPOTLIGHT ON SMALL BUSINESS

(Box in text, page 299)
"Motivating Low-Wage Workers"

Both large and small companies would agree that attracting and keeping skilled employees is essential for growing a successful business. Most employers however realize this is easier said than done. The situation can even hit crisis proportions in certain service industries such as fast-food where businesses depend on entry-level, low-wage workers and employee turnover can approximate 200 percent in a year. Motivational theorists such as Frederick Herzberg have concluded that money is generally not a good long-term motivator in the workplace but can you possibly motivate a worker to perform who is only earning minimum wage?

Lecture Outline

3. **TASK SIGNIFICANCE,** the degree to which the job has a substantial impact on the lives of others in the company.

4. **AUTONOMY**, the degree of freedom, independence, and discretion in scheduling work and determining procedures.

5. **FEEDBACK**, the amount of direct, clear information received about job performance.

C. The text describes the **JOB ENRICHMENT PROGRAM** at **SHERWIN WILLIAMS.**

D. **OTHER JOB DESIGNS.**

1. **JOB SIMPLIFICATION** produces task efficiency by breaking down the job into simple steps, sometimes necessary with people learning new skills.

2. **JOB ENLARGEMENT** combines a series of tasks into one assignment that is more challenging and motivating.

3. **JOB ROTATION** makes work more interesting by moving employees from one job to another.

VI. GOAL-SETTING THEORY AND MANAGEMENT BY OBJECTIVES.

▶ **LEARNING GOAL 7.** Identify the steps involved in implementing a management by objectives (MBO) program.

Lecture Notes

Lecture Outline

A. **GOAL-SETTING THEORY** is based on setting specific, attainable goals.

1. This will lead to high motivation and performance if the goals are accepted, accompanied by feedback, and facilitated by organizational conditions.
2. Peter Drucker developed such a system in the 1960s called **MANAGEMENT BY OBJECTIVES (MBO.)**

B. **MANAGEMENT BY OBJECTIVES (MBO)** is an example of goal-setting.

1. Management by Objectives was developed to **HELP EMPLOYEES MOTIVATE THEMSELVES.**
2. **MBO** is a system of goal setting and implementation that involves a cycle of discussion, review, and evaluation of objectives among all levels of management and employees.
3. There are six steps in the MBO process.
4. Some critics see MBO as being out of date and inconsistent with contemporary management thought.

C. Management by objectives is most effective in relatively stable situations.

Lecture Notes

TRANSPARENCY MASTER 77
Management by Objectives
(Figure 10.5 on text page 301)

TM 77

(Transparency Masters begin on page 10.86.)

Lecture Outline

1. It is important to understand the difference between helping and coaching subordinates because helping tends to make subordinates weak and dependent while coaching makes them feel capable and part of the team.
2. **HELPING** is working with the subordinate, even doing part of the work if necessary.
3. **COACHING** means acting as a resource—teaching guiding, recommending—but not helping by doing the task.
4. Problems can arise when management uses MBO as a strategy for **FORCING** managers to commit to goals that are not mutually agreed upon.

VII. MEETING EMPLOYEE EXPECTATIONS: EXPECTANCY THEORY.

▶ **LEARNING GOAL 8.** Explain the key factors involved in expectancy theory.

A. According to **VICTOR VROOM's EXPECTANCY THEORY**, employee expectations can affect an individual's motivation.

1. The amount of effort employees exert on a specific task depends on their expectations of the outcome.
2. Expectation varies from individual to individual.

Lecture Notes

OT ACETATE 10-6
How to Use Expectancy Theory

How to Use Expectancy Theory

- Determine the rewards valued by employees.
- Evaluate the desired performance level you seek.
- Make the performance level attainable.
- Make the reward valuable to the employee.

Comments:

1. One key questions in using expectancy theory is setting the right level of expected performance. Attainable performance can be a tricky measure to set. If the level of attainment is set too low, workers will scoff at the ease of the expected task. If set too high, they may not even attempt to try and accomplish the task. You might question students as to what should be the basis that managers work with in setting attainable goals.
2. Another major problem deals with offering a reward the employee considers valuable. This can sometimes be a problem since managers often set rewards in relation to what is important to them. For example, tickets to a St. Louis Rams Football game might be very motivating to me, but may not motivate a co-worker not interested in football. Ask students how managers can find out what will motivate workers toward a higher level of performance. This is one of the key steps in making expectancy theory work.

OT ACETATE 10-7
Employee Questions About Expectancy Theory

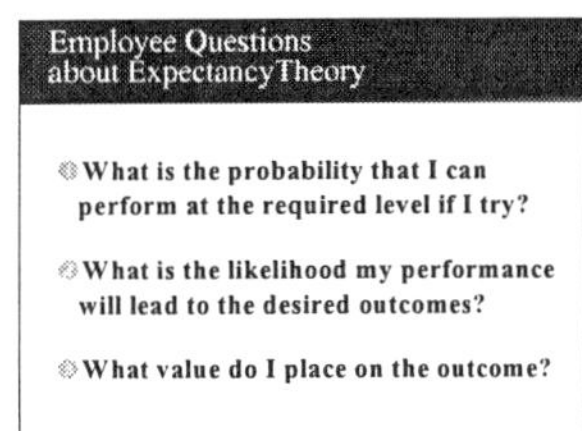

Comments:

1. These are the three key questions workers evaluate in a company's attempt to use expectancy theory.
   a. Probability of success is very important to workers. Think of the following scenario for a moment, if the following grade scale is set for a course, what would be expected student's attitudes?

98 - 100	A
96 - 98	B
95 - 92	C
91 - 89	D
BELOW 89	F

   Students may feel it's virtually impossible to get a good grade.
   b. Likelihood of performance leading to the reward. If I announced to my classes that no one has ever attained a grade of A in my introduction to business class for the past twenty years what would students feel about their chances?
   c. How much value is placed on the outcome? Think of the football tickets mentioned in **OT ACETATE 10-6.** Or consider a student that feels grades mean nothing to future success. Do you think this person would strive hard for an A?
2. Businesses, of course, are faced with the same challenges and questions as described above. Ask students how they could solve some of these problems and still be able to motivate workers?

Lecture Outline

B. **FIVE STEPS TO IMPROVE EMPLOYEE PERFORMANCE:**

1. Determine what rewards are valued by employees.
2. Determine the employee's desired performance standard.
3. Ensure performance standards are attainable.
4. Guarantee rewards are tied to performance.
5. Be certain rewards are considered adequate.

VIII. TREATING EMPLOYEES FAIRLY: EQUITY THEORY.

▶ **LEARNING GOAL 9.** Examine the key principles of equity theory.

A. The basic principle of **EQUITY THEORY** is that workers try to maintain equity between inputs and outputs compared to people in similar positions.

B. When workers do perceive inequity, they will try to reestablish equitable exchanges.

1. They can reduce or increase their efforts or rationalize the situation.
2. In the workplace, inequity leads to lower productivity leads to lower productivity, reduced quality, increased absenteeism, and voluntary resignation.

OT ACETATE 10-8
Six Keys to Motivation

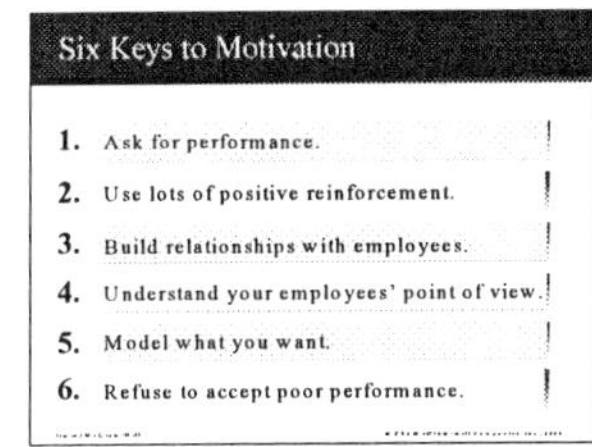

Comments:

1. This acetate highlights six key applications for managers to consider in motivating employees. Remember to stress to students that motivating workers to perform at their highest level of capability is perhaps the most formidable challenge of the manager.
2. Some important considerations to recall for each of the six factors are:

   #1. Describe how the job is being done now, and how you want it to be. Then ask the employee to do it that way.

   #2. Don't take acceptable work for granted. Be sure to thank people and praise them when they improve. Remember that people are different and what motivates one person will not necessarily work with another. Find out what each person likes and then use it.

   #3. You don't have to be buddy-buddy with employees, but you do have to treat them as real, feeling human beings. Employees tend to respond best when you show that you respect them and trust their intentions.

   #4. Get in the habit of listening to your employees and asking for their opinion before you give directions or offer advice. Managers who have an open mind find their employees are more likely to cooperate when it's necessary to do something differently.

   #5. Make good use of time management and be goal-directed in terms of your job. Show your employees that the job really does mean something. It's best to highlight this through your own actions. Employees will learn quality is important and deadlines essential.

   #6 You ultimately will have to tell an employee if his/her work is unacceptable. This could take the form of a reprimand or coaching. Irrespective of which method is used you are demonstrating that standards do matter--which in itself could be motivational. An old saying seems appropriate here, "It's better to aim for 'Excellence' and hit 'Good' than it is to aim for 'Good' and hit 'Average.'"

C. Equity judgements are based on perceptions, and are therefore subject to errors in perception.

1. Organizations can try to deal with this by keeping salaries secret.
2. However, the best remedy, in general, is clear and frequent communication.

IX. IMPLEMENTING THE NEW CONCEPTS: MOTIVATION THROUGH COMMUNICATION.

A. For successful management and motivation, **COMMUNICATION** must flow **TWO WAYS** among **ALL** members of an organization.

1. Communication often flows only one way: from top management down.
2. The flow upward, from workers to managers, is usually severely clogged.
3. To create an atmosphere of "us working together," managers have to become active listeners.

B. **PROCEDURES** for encouraging open communication include:

1. Creating an **ORGANIZATIONAL CULTURE** that rewards listening; creating facilities for dialogues; and showing others that talking with superiors counts.

Lecture Notes

PROGRESS CHECK
(page 303 in text)

- Briefly describe the managerial attitudes behind Theories X, Y, and Z.
- Employees at smaller firms seem relatively happy with their jobs, yet about half plan to leave in a few years. What is lacking in small firms that is causing employees to leave?
- Relate job enrichment to Herzberg's motivating factors.
- What are the six steps in management by objectives?
- Evaluate expectancy theory? Can you think of situations where expectancy theory could apply to your efforts or lack of effort?

LECTURE ENHANCER 10-8
Learning Corporate Language

Despite the best efforts of English professors, business-communication consultants and other horrified bystanders, obfuscation in business lingo appears to be a growing and troublesome phenomenon. Those relatively new to management sometimes fail to comprehend the overstatement, understatement, and evasion that characterize much business talk. (See complete lecture enhancer on page 10.65.)

LECTURE ENHANCER 10-9
Doublespeak

Professor William Lutz is one of this country's foremost authorities on "doublespeak," which is the academic word for double-talk and all forms of deceptive language, including gobbledygook and officialese. (See complete lecture enhancer on page 10.66.)

LECTURE ENHANCER 10-10
Body Language

Your inner feelings and personality are often revealed by the way you move your body, experts are determining. (See complete lecture enhancer on page 10.67.)

SUPPLEMENTAL CASE 10-3
How Corporate Culture Motivates

See complete case on page 10.83.

2. **TRAINING** supervisors and managers in listening skills.

3. **REMOVING BARRIERS** to open communication (separate washrooms, parking lots, etc.) and **PROVIDING WAYS TO FACILITATE COMMUNICATION** (company athletic teams, picnics, etc.)

C. **OPEN COMMUNICATION AND SELF-MANAGED TEAMS.**

1. Companies that have developed highly motivated work forces usually have several things in common, including open communication and self-managed teams.

2. The text offers several examples of communication among members of self-managed teams in such organizations as **FORD MOTOR COMPANY**.

3. For companies to implement such groups, managers must **RE-INVENT WORK.**

D. **CHANGING ORGANIZATIONS IS NOT EASY.**

1. **MANY MANAGERS WERE TRAINED UNDER A DIFFERENT SYSTEM.**

   a. Many are used to telling people what to do rather than consulting them.

   b. It is difficult for such managers to change.

Lecture Notes

LECTURE ENHANCER 10-11
The Myth of Top Management Team

Companies all across the economic spectrum are making use of teams. They go by a variety of names and can be found at all levels. But even in the best of companies, a so-called top team seldom functions as a real team. (See complete lecture enhancer on page 10.68.)

MAKING ETHICAL DECISIONS
(Box in text, page 305)

"Motivating Temporary Employees"

You work as a manager for a Highbrow's, a rather prestigious department store. Each year, in order to handle the large number of buyers at you must hire temporary employees. You lead temporary employees to believe, falsely, that they will become full-time employees. Is this an ethical way to try to motivate these employees? What is the danger of using a tactic such as this?

Lecture Outline

2. Employees often have a difficult time changing as well, and some have trouble getting involved in participative management.

E. **A MODEL FOR THE FUTURE: EMPLOYEE EMPOWERMENT.**

1. The text tells the story of **MILLER BREWING COMPANY** and **MARY KAY COSMETICS** as an example of a company that successfully created an efficient and effective team.

2. Understanding what motivates employees is the key to success in goods-producing companies such as **MILLER BREWING COMPANY** and service-based firms such as **MARK KAY COSMETICS**.

3. The lessons learned from these companies include:

   a. The future growth of industry depends on a motivated, productive work force.

   b. Motivation is largely internally generated by workers themselves.

   c. The first step in any motivational program is to establish open communications.

F. **MOTIVATION IN THE FUTURE.**

1. Employees are not alike—different employees respond to different managerial and motivational styles.

Lecture Notes

OT ACETATE 10-9
How Often Do Employees Feel Stressed on the Job?

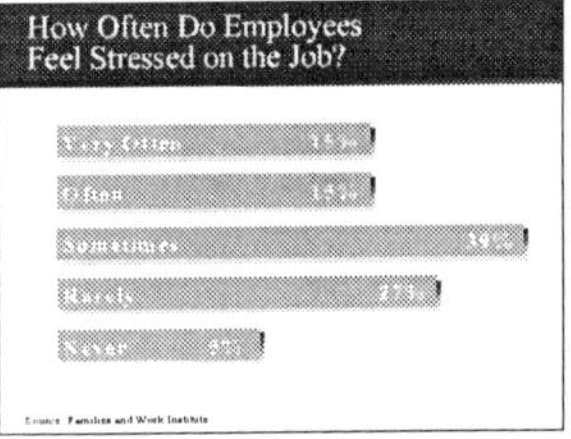

Comments:

1. Employee stress has been a key concern of management in the 1990s. In chapter 12 there's a brief discussion of violence in the workplace, a tragic situation that is often stress related. This acetate evaluates how often employees feel stressed on the job.
2. Students can be asked when they feel most stressed and how they try to deal with it. A good question is how much does stress effect their productivity?
3. Employers often use many of the motivational techniques noted in the chapter to counter employee stress. The chapter discusses job enrichment as one means to alleviate boredom which often leads to stress. You might want to note to students that job enrichment is very closely related to Herzberg's motivational factors. Skill variety, task identity, and task significance are closely related to meaningful work. Autonomy gives employees a feeling of responsibility. Feedback (knowledge of results) actively contributes to a feeling of achievement and recognition. All of these factors can be used to keep the employee active and stress free.

LECTURE ENHANCER 10-12
Employee Control on the Assembly Line

The mere fact that people perceive that they have a modicum of control over their destiny leads to enormous improvements in performance in one study. (See complete lecture enhancer on page 10.69.)

OT ACETATE 10-10
Warning Signs of Employee Stress

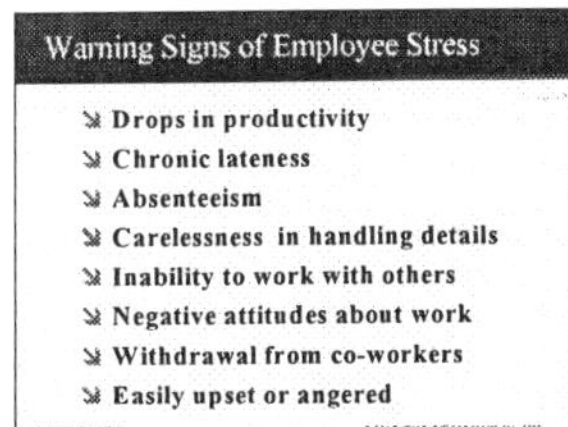

Comments:

1. The information in this acetate fits well with **OT ACETATE 10-9**. Employers can often spot impending stress or on-the-job stress or burnout by looking for the signs listed in the acetate.
2. See which of these signs students see as being the most obvious sign of stress in the worker. Ask why they made this choice and what they would do to counter such a problem if they faced it.
3. As a matter of fact, this acetate is helpful for instructors to look at carefully. It might assist in identifying potential problems with students before they get out of hand. This would be a good topic for a workshop or for a chat session.

LECTURE ENHANCER 10-13
The Consequences of Stress

In an era of corporate bosses who lay off thousands without so much as an attack of indigestion, what makes a CEO kill himself? (See complete lecture enhancer on page 10.70.)

2. Tomorrow's managers will not be able to use any one formula for all employees.

3. They will need to work with each employee as an individual and fit the motivational effort to that individual.

4. Different cultures experience motivational approaches differently.

5. In general, motivation will come from the job itself rather than from external punishments or rewards.

6. Managers need to give workers what they need to do a good job—the right tools, the right information, and the right amount of cooperation.

7. A Gallop survey found that four attitudes correlate strongly with higher profits:

    a. Workers feel they are given the opportunity to do what they do best.

    b. They believe their opinions count.

    c. They sense that their fellow workers are committed to quality.

    d. They've made a direct connection between their work and the company's mission.

X. SUMMARY AND REVIEW.

Lecture Notes

OT ACETATE 10-11
Where Are Workers Most Satisfied With Their Jobs?

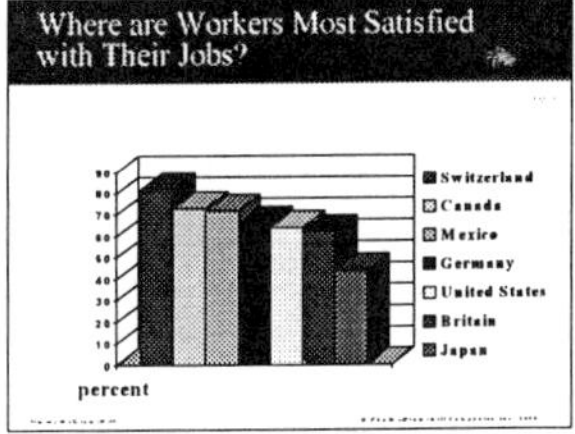

Comments:

1. Where are workers most satisfied with their jobs? Looks like the Swiss win rather handily here. It's interesting to note that Mexico is the only developing nation to finish in the top seven.
2. Factors such as confidence in management, fair evaluation by management, the challenge of the job, and equitable compensation were considered. It's interesting to note the level of satisfaction in Japan. It wasn't long ago that workers in Japan were cast as models for the rest of the world. Today Japanese workers have doubts about their companies. For example, only 33% feel their firms are well managed and only about six in ten workers feel they are evaluated fairly by managers.

REACHING BEYOND OUR BORDERS
(Box in text, page 308)
"The Challenge of Global Work Teams"

The new global economy has altered the world landscape by bringing products and services to every corner of the earth and helping many less-developed countries improve their quality of life. Business globalization has also resulted in the creation of global work teams: a rather formidable task.

PROGRESS CHECK
(page 309 in text)

- ➤ What are several steps firms can use to increase internal communications and thus motivation?
- ➤ What problems may emerge when trying to implement participative management?
- ➤ Why is it important today to adjust motivational styles to individual employees? Are there any general principles of motivation that today's managers should follow?

Answers to Practicing Management Decisions

CASE ONE

MAKING TEAMS WORK IN A CHANGING MARKET

1. *Why do you think worker performance increased so significantly at Custom Research?*

   The teams worked well because the employees felt empowered to do what they needed to do without managerial interference. This new-found freedom gave them the motivation they needed to do a good job. Furthermore, working in a team gave them more resources to do the job.

2. *What principles of motivation seemed to work well for Corzon and Pope in increasing employee productivity?*

   The principle of motivation is to give employees a chance to achieve things on their own. Nothing motivates like the job itself, if the job is done well and the resources are there to help do the job.

3. *Would you like to work in a team-centered organization or more traditional organizational setting? Why did you make the choice you did?*

   Each student must decide this answer on his or her own. But students need to work more often in teams to see how they feel doing that and what the advantages and disadvantages are. Some students feel that not all team members work equally and that is not fair. This is a good time to discuss such issues and how they may be resolved. What would a businessperson do if a team member was not contributing?

CASE TWO

VIDEO CASE: SOUTHWEST AIRLINES

1. *Do Southwest Airlines employees seem more motivated by intrinsic or extrinsic rewards? Explain.*

   The employees seem to be motivated largely by extrinsic rewards. That is, they enjoy the good pay, the free tickets, and so on. But they may also be motivated by the intrinsic reward of doing a good job. Most people like to do a good job; it's just much easier when you are rewarded for doing so.

2. *Herzberg distinguishes between hygiene factors and motivators. Which factors identified by Herzberg as motivators are used at Southwest Airlines?*

   Work itself was Herzberg's number one motivator. Certainly working for an airline can provide such motivation. Achievement, recognition, and responsibility are also motivators. All of them are possible at Southwest. Achievement results in free tickets, for example. Also, success leads to more pay. The last of the motivators, advancement, is not discussed in the case, but is possible at Southwest.

3. *How do the principles of Vroom's expectancy theory relate to Southwest Airlines?*

   Employees don't expect to have as much freedom nor as much compensation as they get at Southwest. Since they expect less, they are more than happy with what they get and are highly motivated as a result.

Lecture Enhancers

LECTURE ENHANCER 10-1

THE SECRET OF MEN AND MOTIVATION

Marriage makes men more productive employees according to David Neumark of the Federal Reserve Board and Sanders Korenman of Princeton University. The two economists cite numerous studies showing that married men get anywhere from 10 percent to 50 percent higher wages than single men of comparable age, race, education, and other variables. They advance three possible explanations: employers discriminate in favor of married men; higher-paid men are desirable marriage partners; or married men are in fact more productive, thus deserving greater reward.

The two analyzed the fifteen-year employment history of a large sample of young men and found that the wages of the married men exceeded those of comparable single men by a gap that steadily widened over the first ten to twenty years after marriage, an indication that simple discrimination is not the cause. They then examined supervisors' performance ratings of managers and professionals in a large manufacturing company. They found that married men consistently had higher performance ratings than comparable single men and were far more likely to be promoted into higher paying jobs.

The two studies, Neumark and Korenman believe, rule out the "discrimination" theory and "selection into marriage" theory, and concluded that marriage wage differences are due to a productivity effect of marriage. They are currently researching just why this should be the case.

LECTURE ENHANCER 10-2

GILBRETH'S MOTION STUDY

Frank Gilbreth began his career as an apprentice bricklayer. He watched other bricklayers and saw that some were slow and inefficient while some were very productive. He discovered that each used a different set of motions to lay bricks. From his observations, he isolated the basic movements necessary to do the job and eliminated wasted ones. His revised method reduced unnecessary motions by 70 percent and tripled bricklayers' productivity.

This was the first "motion study," designed to isolate the best possible method of performing a given job. Later Gilbreth and his wife, Lillian, studied job motions using a motion picture camera and split-second clock. The isolated individual motions they called "therbligs," which is "Gilbreth" spelled backwards with the "th" reversed.

One of Gilbreth's clients in the 1920s was James E. Casey, the founder of UPS. Mr. Casey turned to Gilbreth to develop techniques to measure the time consumed each day by each UPS driver. Later, UPS engineers cut away the sides of a UPS delivery truck and used Gilbreth's techniques to study a driver at work. The changes in package loading that resulted increased efficiency by 30 percent.

LECTURE ENHANCER 10-3

RECOGNITION: MAKING HEROES

Rosabeth Moss Kanter, author of the book *The Change Masters*, has concluded that companies often make the mistake of equating pay with rewards. Pay is not a reward for outstanding performance, it is compensation for doing the job in the first place. A reward should be a special gain for special achievements. Compensation is a right; recognition is a gift.

Recognition—saying thank you in public and perhaps giving a tangible gift along with the words has multiple functions beyond simple courtesy. To the employee, recognition signifies that someone noticed and someone cares. To the rest of the organization, recognition creates role models—heroes—and communicates the standards: these are the kinds of things that constitute great performance. Kanter's management consulting firm has also found a remarkable correlation between recognition and innovation.

Some basic rules should be followed in handing out praise and recognition:

1. **Deliver recognition and reward in an open and publicized way.** If not made public, recognition loses much of its impact and defeats much of the purpose for which it is provided.
2. **Timing is crucial.** Recognize contribution throughout a project. Reward contribution close to the time an achievement is realized. Time delays weaken the impact of most rewards.
3. **Tailor recognition and reward to the unique needs of the people involved.** Have several recognition and reward options to enable managers to acknowledge accomplishment in ways appropriate to the particulars of a given situation.
4. **Deliver recognition in a personal and honest manner**. Avoid providing recognition that is too "slick" or overproduced.
5. **Strive for clear, unambiguous, and well-communicated connection between accomplishments and rewards**. Be sure people understand why they receive awards and the criteria used to determine rewards.
6. **Recognize recognition.** That is, recognize people who recognize others for doing what is best for the company.

Celebrating and publicizing employee achievements need not be expensive. Professor Kanter suggests some simple, low-cost ways to make employees "heroes," such as having coffee with an employee or group of employees that you do not normally see, or letting employees attend important meetings in your place when you're not available.

Others:

1. Send a letter to every team member at the conclusion of their work, thanking them for their contribution.
2. Mention an employee's outstanding work or ideas during your staff meetings or at meetings with your peers and management.

3. Create a "Best Accomplishments of the Year" booklet, and include everyone's picture, name, and statement of their best achievement.
4. Show a personal interest in employees' development and career after a special achievement, asking them how you can help them take the next step.
5. Invite employees to your home for special celebrations, and recognize them in front of their colleagues and spouses.

LECTURE ENHANCER 10-4

MASLOW'S FURTHER STUDY OF MOTIVATION

Anyone who has taken Psychology 101 knows about Abraham Maslow's "hierarchy of needs." People, Maslow found, strive to fulfill progressively higher levels of need, from nourishment, safety, love, and esteem to "self-actualization."

It's less well known that Maslow, in the early 1960s, also delved deeply into management and economics. Setting up shop in a Southern California electronics plant, he produced a journal applying the concept of self-actualization to both the workplace and the marketplace. "This is by far Maslow's best book," says Peter Drucker, perhaps the foremost management authority today. "It had enormous impact on me." Yet after a limited run, Maslow's book slipped into obscurity.

What makes Maslow's book so special—and why did it vanish? In 1962, a few years after postulating the hierarchy of needs, the Brandeis University professor took a summer sabbatical at a company in Del Mar, California, called Non-Linear Systems. The company made voltmeters in a converted blimp hangar. The owner, Andy Kay, had noticed that workers were most productive at the end of the line, where the finality of the assembly provided a sense of accomplishment. So Kay broke his work force into teams, each responsible for an entire product.

Maslow was amazed at the spirit and productivity of the plant and picked up a tape recorder to capture his reactions. The result was a journal, initially called "Summer Notes." In these Maslow coined the phrase "enlightened management" to describe the work conditions leading to self-actualization, or the achievement of one's full potential: trust, teamwork and recognition. Teams, he found, made better workers, and better workers made better teams. Creativity flowed from ambiguity. "Knowledge breeds knowledge."

By 1963, Maslow had given mimeographed copies of "Summer Notes" to several fellow academics. His friend Warren Bennis, a prominent university dean and business theorist, urged him to publish the journal commercially. "It was very radical for the time," Bennis recalls. Yet, he adds, "it never caught on."

The main reason was a new title. Maslow's term for a society of self-actualizing people was "eupsychia," so he gave his book the ghastly title of *Eupsychian Management, A Journal*. Bennis and Drucker tried to dissuade him, but Maslow was proud of his wordsmithing. The book did go through many printings through the early 1970s, but they were small. Only the terms "synergy" and "enlightened management" endured.

LECTURE ENHANCER 10-5

THE BIG THRILL MOTIVATION

Another facet of motivation involves the individual's tolerance for risk taking. Some individuals have a kind of psychological urge to reach beyond the status quo and seek out novelty, change, and excitement. Psychologist Frank Farley, of the University of Wisconsin, has spent twenty years examining what he calls the Type T (thrill-seeking) personality. According to Farley's theory, Big T types are high-profile individuals who seek excitement and stimulation wherever they can find it or create it. For some the thrills are mostly physical. For others they're mental.

The degree of risk that individuals are willing to assume spans a broad continuum. Big T personalities, those who continually live on the edge, are at one end of the scale. Little t's, who cling to certainty and predictability, are at the other. Most people fall somewhere in the middle. But Farley believes it's the Big T segment, a group that makes up an estimated 10 to 30 percent of the American population, that holds the key to America's future. "Type T's are the people who are likely to have enormous impact on society," he says. "They are the great experimenters in life; they break the rules."

Whether male or female, risk-taking individuals tend to be what Farley calls "transmutative thinkers," adept at shifting from one cognitive process to another, and from the abstract to the concrete and vice versa. Thrill seekers are happiest in jobs that provide change, excitement, and an ample outlet for their creativity. They are often drawn to careers in advertising, journalism, or in the brokerage business, where novelty and uncertainty are a given.

Whether individuals seek risks or avoid them affects not only their own job performance but also boss-employee relationships and co-worker production. An organization with too many risk takers can spell trouble. So can one top-heavy with cautious, security-minded individuals. A synergistic mix is best. If it's the thrill-seeking visionaries who drive a company with their ideas, it's their more pragmatic peers who help implement those concepts.

Finally, says Farley, "people who are the most successful realize that if they're going to take risks, they're going to fail once in a while."

LECTURE ENHANCER 10-6

PERSONALITY TRAITS OF CEOs AND ARMY GENERALS

Researchers at the Center for Creative Leadership have uncovered a coincidence that will not surprise many workers: corporate chief executive officers share a broad range of psychological traits with Army generals. In a study of 163 Army brigadier generals and 120 corporate CEOs, the CEOs and generals scored about the same, and much higher than the general population, in such traits as achievement drive, integrity, leadership, willingness to accept norms of society, and self-confidence.

Differences did exist. Some 97 percent of the generals have masters or doctoral degrees, compared to only 33 percent of CEOs. The generals scored an average 124 on an intelligence test, compared with 121 for the CEOs. Both scores rank near the top of the general population. The CEOs had more of an artistic bent than did the generals, although both groups were below the general population.

LECTURE ENHANCER 10-7

MOTIVATION AND CREATIVITY

In a large studio at the headquarters of Hallmark Cards Inc., Robert Hurlburt bent over a potter's wheel. His fingers stained with clay, his face clenched in concentration, Hurlburt was completely out of his element. And in his 17 years at Hallmark, he had never been happier. A metal engraver by trade, Hurlburt was in the midst of a three-month rotation into an artist's heaven—carte blanche to do whatever he wanted to regenerate his creative spirit. After three weeks in the ceramics shop, Hurlburt was producing pots and vases that looked like the work of a professional. His work will probably only end up on a shelf at his home, but if Hurlburt's mood is any indication, Hallmark is likely to see a payoff when he returns to his regular duties. "It's given me an opportunity to get back to thinking wild, crazy things," he said.

Keeping its artists and writers happy and creative is a top priority at Hallmark, the nation's largest greeting card seller with $3.4 billion in sales in 1996.

Sabbaticals like Hurlburt's are only one way Hallmark tries to help workers be creative. Staffers can desert Hallmark's midtown Kansas City headquarters for a downtown loft, where teams of writers and artists get away from phones to exchange ideas. They may spend days in retreat at a farm in nearby Kearney, Missouri, taking part in fun exercises like building birdhouses.

Some go farther afield, sent by the company on trips overseas to soak up atmosphere and culture. Not all the methods are high-budget; for the creators of the irreverent Shoebox line, there are free movie passes and daily screenings of the hippest television shows.

Hallmark isn't the only greeting company that makes a special effort to tweak and coax and nourish its creative staff. Its biggest competitor, American Greetings Corp., operates similar programs. No company, especially one that rely on ideas, can afford to do otherwise, said Calvin Moyer, executive director of the American Creative Association., a nonprofit group in Hockessin, Del., founded six years ago to encourage creativity throughout society.

Hiring talented people isn't enough, Moyer said. "It's like planting blueberries or apple trees in your backyard," Moyer said. "It'll probably grow and produce fruit but if you fertilize it and prune it, you'll have not just fruit but great fruit."

Massaging Hallmark's creative staff of about 700 is the responsibility of Marita Wesley-Clough, a 20-year company veteran who was named director of creative strategy about a year ago. Wesley-Clough sounded like the philosophy major she was in college as she tried to explain her job, describing herself alternately as a shepherd, a midwife and a water bearer. "It's sort of like catching the wind," she said. "The road to creative strategy isn't a clear one."

Nurturing the creative spirit reaches its wackiest heights at the Shoebox Cards division, where a team of seven writers and four editors usually starts its day by watching a tape of the previous night's David Letterman show. They flip through magazines, even work out in the middle of the workday. Sounds like fun, but there are deadlines. The group is expected to turn out 70 cards a week. To do that, they'll generate an average of 150 pieces of writing a day.

At the end of the day, the staff's efforts are sifted at a raucous conference led by chief editor Steve Finken. With a practiced ear for the staff's reaction, Finken reads each card aloud and swiftly separates them into two piles. The reject pile is much larger than the save pile.

Hallmark always ranks high on lists of the best U.S. companies to work for, and despite a massive restructuring to improve efficiency, writers and artists still seem to be having a great time. But there's the same pressure as in any other business. Each card's success is rated through surveys and information gathered by electronic cash registers, and the staff knows exactly how well their work is doing.

The appetite for new products must be fed, and the need to be thoughtful, witty, caring, wise, and a dozen other things every day is unceasing. It can be a grind. Hurlburt said he felt his artistic impulses narrowing after 17 years. When he gets back to work after a few more weeks of puttering, he said, "I don't know if I'll be a better engraver, but I'll be more creatively applied."

LECTURE ENHANCER 10-9

MOTIVATION AND REWARDS

You remember that Herzberg believed that money was not a motivator; that it wouldn't cause people to do a better job. However, the lack of sufficient pay would cause them to perform lower they actually could. He called this a hygiene factor. A recent study by Public Agenda Foundation supports this theory. Some 75 percent of those surveyed said that they deliberately withheld extra effort because they felt excluded from the rewards that top managers and owners enjoyed because of their work. More than 70 percent felt that there was no link between their performance and their rewards.

By not sharing the profits, top managers and investors are unwittingly stifling the growth of profits. Employees have less incentive to learn new techniques and be innovative when they do not share the fruits of these efforts. When employees feel a sense of ownership in the organization, they so their best to make the organization succeed.

In his book *Second to None*, Charles Garfield outlines the steps in creating an effective reward system. He advises managers to:

1. **Reward generously.** Joe Lee, president of General Mills Restaurants says, "You attract and hire people better than the norm, pay them better than the norm, and they perform better than the norm—they produce better meals and service, and more than the extra money that's need to pay them, enough to produce a better return for investors."
2. **Reward everyone.** Dub one person "employee of the month" and you've just dubbed every other employee a loser. Garfield claims that rewarding a select few is probably the single greatest mistake that companies make in developing reward systems. This is particularly true in companies that are striving for teamwork and the full contribution of every employee. Send one superstar to Hawaii and you have an office full of less than enthusiastic employees back at home. We aren't talking big bucks here. Levi Strauss hands out $25 "You're Great" coupons that are popular motivators. Even handwritten notes and thank-yous are appreciated.
3. **Don't just keep upping the ante.** In many companies, the consequence of salespeople reaching their quotas is a pat on the back and a higher quota the next year. Although upping the ante is meant to motivate employees to work harder, it often has the opposite effect. It's demotivating to be praised one moment and then the next moment to be told to "do better next year."
4. **Reward for specialized skills**. Corporate ladders aren't as tall as they used to be. In today's flatter organizations there just aren't that many rungs to climb. A way of rewarding employees in flatter organizations is to give them horizontal rather than vertical promotions. William Wiggenhorn of Motorola comments, "We have slowly changed the attitude that promotion is necessarily up the ladder; it can also be across the organization. A lateral move is much more accepted than before." In fact, Semco employees with specialized skills make more than their supervisors.

5. **Create a rewarding environment.** Generous pay, huge sales commissions, and fat profit sharing bonuses do not guarantee greater productivity, better service, or improved quality. There is one rule to making a reward system work: it must be set in a culture and work environment that is rewarding as a whole. We all know people who have quit a good-paying job because they felt that the organization didn't really value them. Successful organizations in the 1990s must cultivate a rich and rewarding work environment by: (1) encouraging employees to innovate, (2) treating them as fully participating partners, (3) paying them well, (4) promoting a spirit of trust and teamwork, and (5) accommodating their family needs as well as business objectives.

LECTURE ENHANCER 10-8

LEARNING CORPORATE LANGUAGE

Despite the best efforts of English professors, business-communication consultants and other horrified bystanders, obfuscation in business lingo appears to be a growing and troublesome phenomenon. This may mean big trouble for inexperienced or naive employees who take business talk at face value. Those relatively new to management sometimes fail to comprehend the overstatement, understatement, and evasion that characterize much business talk.

"You won't succeed if you don't pick up the language," says Felice Schwartz, president of Catalyst, a New York resource center for career women. Subordinates, the counselors say, should pay especially close attention to management "suggestions." When the boss says, "Please finish that job when you have a chance," more often than not he or she really means, "Do the job now, or else." Analysts of business language say executives often disguise orders as suggestions to avoid seeming tyrannical.

An assistant office manager at an auto-parts manufacturer recently discovered the perils of understatement. She was told by her boss of "an impromptu meeting at 4 o'clock—but it's nothing to worry about." She passed up the meeting to learn afterward that it dealt with the reorganization of her department and the cutting back of her staff and responsibilities.

One consultant says a good rule to follow is that when the boss says, "Don't worry," then do worry. "Management deals with change with studied casualness," she says. "The bigger things are, the more people try to speak of them casually."

Recruits are often misled from the beginning by such observations as, "We don't punch the clock around here." That's probably true. Who needs a time clock when employees always come in early and work late? When employees are told of "challenges" or "opportunities," should they expect high adventure and the heights of achievement? No, the counselors say. They should expect a lot of headaches and no spare Excedrin.

LECTURE ENHANCER 10-9

DOUBLESPEAK

Professor William Lutz is one of this country's foremost authorities on "doublespeak," which is the academic word for double-talk and all forms of deceptive language, including gobbledygook and officialese. He teaches English at Rutgers University and practices law, while also editing the Quarterly Review of Doublespeak.

Doublespeak is pervasive in the field of medicine. Malpractice is described as a "therapeutic misadventure." Euphemisms for "death" abound in hospitals, which do not like to admit that their patients ever "pass away." Thus phrases such as "therapeutic misadventure resulting in a terminal episode," are heard, or "terminal episode." One patient "did not fully achieve his wellness potential."

Despite the claims of medicine, doublespeak seems to be most common in government, particularly in the departments of Defense, State, and Agriculture. According to the Department of Agriculture, acid rain has disappeared. Instead, the Northeast has "atmospheric deposition of anthropogenically derived acidic substances."

The Pentagon has described the Titan 2 missile, with more than 600 times the explosive power of the Hiroshima bomb, as "a very large, potentially disruptive re-entry system." "Radiation-enhancement devices" were well on the way to development before Congress learned what a neutron bomb actually was—and cut the funding.

Military officers have referred to a pencil as a "portable hand-held communications inscriber." A bullet hole has been defined as a "ballistically induced aperture in the subcutaneous environment." A tent is a "frame-supported tension device." To kill is to "terminate with extreme prejudice," and a toothpick is a "wood interdental stimulator."

Even the State Department dislikes simple sentences. Human-rights victims in friendly nations now suffer "unlawful or arbitrary deprivation of life," instead of just dying.

LECTURE ENHANCER 10-10

BODY LANGUAGE

Your inner feelings and personality are often revealed by the way you move your body, experts are determining. Confidence or insecurity is telegraphed very well by nonverbal behavior. Take the simple handshake. If a person's hand is cold and clammy, there's a good chance he or she is very tense and nervous. A confident person moves about with a certain steadiness, while an insecure or nervous person is characterized by quick movements. People who stand erect are probably more confident and more comfortable than people who slouch or shift their body weight from one foot to the other.

Even the position of a person's eyebrows when he or she speaks or looks at another can reveal something about that person's mood or feelings. If you say a perfectly innocuous sentence to someone but you say it without any sign of a smile on your face and with your brows lowered, you will convey a hostile impression. Stares accompanied by lowered brows show anger, aggression or assertiveness, while raised brows show fear, surprise, questioning, or retreat.

Body language is also important in the business world. When a respected executive talks to a subordinate, the lower-ranking person will listen intently with his eyes riveted on the executive's face. To look around would be a sign of disrespect. On the other hand, when the subordinate is speaking, it is considered perfectly appropriate if the boss looks about or glances at his watch.

The high-status person might also take the liberty of patting the low-status person on the back or shoulder, something the subordinate would never do. The high-status person always takes the lead. If he is standing, the other person will stand. If he sits, then perhaps the other will feel free to sit.

And, of course, the high-status person directs the topics of conversation and how long the talk will last. It's the same with office visits. The higher-ranking person can exert his or her status by simply dropping into a subordinate's office without notice. The subordinate, of course, calls for an appointment.

LECTURE ENHANCER 10-11

THE MYTH OF TOP MANAGEMENT TEAM

Companies all across the economic spectrum are making use of teams. They go by a variety of names and can be found at all levels. In fact, you are likely to find the group at the very top of an organization professing to be a team. But even in the best of companies, a so-called top team seldom functions as a real team.

Real teams must follow a well-defined discipline to achieve their performance potential. And performance is the key issue—not the fostering of "team values" such as empowerment, sensitivity, or involvement. In recent years, the focus on performance was lost in many companies. Even today, CEOs and senior executives often see few gains in performance from their attempts to become more teamlike.

Nevertheless, a team effort at the top can be essential to capturing the highest performance results possible—when the conditions are right. Good leadership requires differentiating between team and nonteam opportunities, and then acting accordingly.

Three litmus tests must be passed for a team at the top to be effective. (1) The team must shape collective work products—these are tangible performance results that the group can achieve working together that surpass what the team members could have achieved working on their own. (2) The leadership role must shift, depending on the task at hand. And (3) the team's members must be mutually accountable for the group's results.

When these criteria can be met, senior executives should come together to achieve real team performance. When the criteria cannot be met, they should rely on the individual leadership skills that they have honed over the years.

LECTURE ENHANCER 10-12

EMPLOYEE CONTROL ON THE ASSEMBLY LINE

In Search of Excellence, the Peters and Waterman study of America's excellent corporations, recounted an experiment conducted by an industrial psychologist. The subjects were given some difficult puzzles to solve and some rather dull proofreading to do. While they attempted these chores, a raucous audiotape consisting of one person speaking Spanish, two people speaking Armenian, a mimeograph machine running, a chattering typewriter, and street noise ran in the background. Half the subjects were given a button they could push to suppress the noise. The other half were not. Those with buttons to push solved five times more puzzles and made one-quarter as many proofreading errors as those who had no button. The news was that never once (and the experiment was repeated several times) did anyone ever push his or her button. The mere fact that people perceived that they had a modicum of control over their destiny—the option of pushing the button—led to an enormous improvement in performance.

In the follow-up book, *A Passion for Excellence*, another experiment is described, this one at Edison, New Jersey, site of a Ford Motor assembly plant. They had begun an experiment that parallels the one in the lab. Every person on the line in the huge facility was given access to a button that he or she could push to shut down the line—quite a gutsy move on the part of the plant manager. The results that follow occurred during the first 10 months of the experiment.

To begin with, Edison, New Jersey, is not like an industrial psychology lab. People did push their buttons at Edison. To be precise, they shut the facility down 30 times the first day and about 10 times a day thereafter. The good news is that after the first day the average shutdown lasted only about 10 seconds—just time enough to make a quality adjustment, a tweak, a twist, a turn, to tighten up a nut or bolt.

Productivity in the plant did not change. Three other indicators, however, are worthy of note. The number of defects per car produced dropped during the first months of the experiment from 17.1 per car to 0.8 per car. The number of cars requiring rework after they had come off the line fell by 97 percent. And the backlog of union grievances plummeted. Moreover, the change in attitude was as extreme as the numbers. One old pro on the line commented, "It's like someone opened the window and we can breathe."

LECTURE ENHANCER 10-13

THE CONSEQUENCES OF STRESS

When John E. Curtis Jr. missed his 7 a.m. flight from San Antonio, Texas, to Phoenix, Arizona, on March 13, 1997, colleagues on the same trip had a ready explanation. Curtis, 49, was such a dedicated leader that he must have caught a plane the night before. After all, they reasoned, the board of directors' meeting in Phoenix would be his first as CEO of Luby's, America's biggest cafeteria chain. And everyone knew Curtis, who'd spent 18 years climbing the corporate ladder, as a perfectionist.

Changing planes in El Paso, executive vice president William Robson phoned headquarters, then made an ashen-faced announcement. "Mr. Curtis has passed away," he said. "I don't know any of the particulars." The particulars turned out to be as grisly as they were confounding. Curtis checked into a Motel 6 less than nine hours before flight time. After hacking at his left wrist and upper abdomen, he plunged a kitchen knife three times deep into his neck, severing the right jugular. Police found him the next morning, face down in a puddle of blood.

Suicide by stabbing is rare—one or two percent of the annual U.S. total. But "executive suicide" seems to be growing more common in the 1990s. "Nobody's guarding the guardian," says Ron Maris, head of the Center for the Study of Suicide at the University of South Carolina. Maris coined the term ES for the still largely uncharted phenomenon in the 1970s. But interest in it has been rising in the wake of two prominent victims from the Clinton administration: White House lawyer Vincent Foster and Admiral Michael Boorda.

What defines ES, beyond the fact that even people at or near the top of a hierarchy can kill themselves? There are several markers, but the main one is surprise. Two thirds of all suicides signal their intent in advance, in words or deeds. Executive suicides—Foster, Boorda, Curtis et al.—almost never do. "Most men have a hard time asking for help," says Washington University psychiatrist George E. Murphy. "But if you're an executive, one thing you never let anyone see is your weakness."

Despite the famous line, some men do end up as islands—and that seems to have been the case with John Curtis. Born in Abilene, Curtis graduated with honors from Texas Tech University. Curtis rose swiftly through the ranks at Luby's—chief financial officer in 1988, a Harvard Business School fellowship in 1994, president in 1996, CEO January of 1997. No one in the family seemed to sense anything wrong the night he left for Motel 6 instead of the airport.

Pete Erben, Curtis's mentor at Luby's, saw at least a hint of twilight. Yes, he admits, Curtis did seem anxious about the board meeting in Phoenix. Erben, who resigned as Luby's chairman after Curtis's suicide, remembers their last meeting. Among the worries two days before the suicide: a profit margin of six percent for the quarter, down from the usual nine percent.

And there was more. The week before, Erben had approached to Curtis an idea that, in historic terms for Luby's, was almost unthinkable—closing its nonperforming stores at the rate of one percent a year while continuing to grow in more promising locations. Luby's, which operates 226 stores in 11 states from Florida to Arizona, is the industry leader in the cafeteria business. Nationally that's a shrinking sea, but

Luby's has remained a buoyant ship, posting 26 straight years of increasing sales and earnings per share. It has closed only two stores in its 50-year history.

In an era of corporate bosses who lay off thousands without so much as an attack of indigestion, what makes a CEO kill himself? The answers are usually speculative and probably as diverse as the ES victims themselves. One possibility in Curtis's case: he could not bear the shame, or perhaps the cruelty, of laying off one percent of Luby's 13,000-person work force. His wife, Kathi, reported that her husband had been having trouble sleeping for about two weeks, and that "store closings out of state" were one reason. Another: at the annual shareholders meeting, the new CEO said one of his goals was to bring Luby's profit margin—already twice the industry average—eventually into double digits. In Phoenix, he'd have to tell the company's ten directors the numbers were headed down, not up.

Curtis kept the depths of his despair a secret from his wife, his mentor, his pastor, and everyone else. He was, by all accounts, a courtly but quiet man who did not abuse alcohol, own a gun, see a shrink, or lose his temper. One Luby's research-department employee saw the CEO's hands tremble the Monday before he killed himself—but that was all.

On that Wednesday night, he prayed with his wife and left home. An hour later he drove to the Motel 6 eight miles down the road, past a Luby's, and checked into a room at the back with a view of the Dumpster. Sometime during the night, he slipped home again and left a note saying he planned to kill himself in room 214. Kathi found it the next morning.

The 1997 annual conference of the American Association of Suicidology devoted a two-hour session to the deaths of Foster, Boorda, and Curtis. Experts heard the originator of the term ES argue for better monitoring systems for the uniquely isolated subset at the top of the executive heap. "Nobody's looking now," says Ron Maris, "and if you don't look, you don't find."

Critical Thinking Exercises

Name: ____________________

Date: ____________________

CRITICAL THINKING EXERCISE 10-1

MASLOW'S HIERARCHY OF NEEDS

According to Abraham Maslow, we all have certain needs ranging from physical needs to self-actualization. Maslow believed that when needs are unmet, they motivate us to behave a certain way. When the needs are met they no longer motivate us. He also said that when lower order needs remain unmet, we give them our attention and don't attend to the higher needs.

Let's test Maslow's theory to see if it holds true. Poll your class to see which needs each of you are giving your attention to right now (not for the day, not for the future, but for this minute). Mark the need getting the most attention right now with a "0". Look at each of the other needs; place a check mark next to those that have been met. Each person should do this in private; no need for names on papers.

Tally the results on the blackboard. How many class members are focusing on each need? Have all the lower level needs for each person been met (checked off)? What does this information tell you?

_____ Self-actualization needs (accomplish goals and develop to potential.)

_____ Self-esteem Needs (recognition, acknowledgment, and status.)

_____ Social Needs (feeling loved and part of the group.)

_____ Safety needs (security at work and at home)

_____ Physical Needs (food, drink, warmth, etc.)

ANSWERS TO CRITICAL THINKING EXERCISE 10-1

Are some classmates hungry and concentrating on physical needs? Others may be threatened by this exercise and are sitting quietly tending to their safety needs. Others may be quite loud and eagerly participating, meeting their social needs. Others are claiming that their ideas are best, searching for recognition. Still others are calmly going about their business knowing that they are doing all they can do and are happy with themselves.

The point is that individuals are motivated by different things. In order to effectively motivate their employees, managers must listen to their employees, learn what their needs are, and design motivators to meet those needs. For example, if employees are physically uncomfortable or feel unsafe at work, they will pay little attention to meeting company goals unless they perceive that meeting those goals will make them feel comfortable or safe.

Name: ____________________

Date: ____________________

CRITICAL THINKING EXERCISE 10-2

THE PAYOFF

Great news: you landed a job at Dental Suppliers Inc. You are excited about the salary they offered you because it is above the average your fellow graduates are earning. During your first two years with the company, you earn the highest ratings on your performance reviews and receive two salary increases. You are very happy with your job and hope to be promoted to a supervisory position soon.

Recently, Ginger Vitis joined Dental Suppliers after getting her degree at night from a small college. She is considered a good employee with potential. The firm has been trying to hire more female and minority employees because of the 1964 Civil Rights Act.

Last week, you and Ginger were at a business meeting. Casually, Ginger mentioned during lunch that she felt lucky to land a position with such a great starting salary. The conversation stops abruptly when you find out that her starting salary is $300 a month more than what you are making now.

The next day you go straight into your boss's office and say, "What's the deal? I earned the highest performance reviews for two years, and you're paying a newly hired woman more than me." Getting information from your boss is often like pulling teeth, but he tries to explain that your salary was high compared to other employees. You answer, "Well, if that's what Dental Suppliers thinks of me, it can ...."

1. Why are you unhappy with your salary now while you were happy with it before you talked to Ginger?

2. At which level of Maslow's hierarchy of needs are you operating?

3. According to Herzberg, is salary a motivator or a hygiene factor? Does your attitude about your salary support Herzberg's theory? Explain.

4. If you were in your boss's position, what would you do to solve this problem without creating any additional problems? What can you do to prevent this from happening again?

ANSWERS TO CRITICAL THINKING EXERCISE 10-2

1. *Why are you unhappy with your salary now while you were happy with it before you talked to Ginger?*

Perceptions of whether or not a salary are good are often based on what you feel others are making. If they are making more, you may feel cheated, even when your salary is quite high.

2. *At which level of Maslow's hierarchy of needs are you operating?*

You are no doubt at the self-esteem level where you are searching for recognition.

3. *According to Herzberg, is salary a motivator or a hygiene factor? Does your attitude about your salary support Herzberg's theory? Explain.*

Herzberg found that salary was a hygiene factor. It may be a hygiene factor, but it becomes a motivator when it becomes a symbol of accomplishment and of recognition for a job well done.

4. *If you were in your boss's position, what would you do to solve this problem without creating any additional problems? What can you do to prevent this from happening again?*

These kinds of problems constantly come up in firms. The only way to resolve them is to handle them one by one with open negotiations. Rules and procedures help somewhat, but it is perceptions that you are dealing with. The needs of employees must be addressed when conducting negotiations, including safety needs, self-esteem needs, and social needs. In other words, you wouldn't want to discuss such issues in front of other employees.

Supplemental Cases

CASE 10-1

USING COMPENSATION TO MOTIVATE

Jon Wehrenberg is a businessperson always up to a challenge. Three years ago, a friend called and told Jon he knew of a large building-products company that was looking for a domestic supplier of plumbing assemblies. The firm was currently importing products from Korea and was hoping to improve its turnaround time and quality. The deal was worth about $1 million a year to Jon's firm, Jamestown Advanced Products, if he could commit to producing and delivering the specified quantity of custom-order metal products every week. There was also one other stipulation: Jon's company would have to do the work at the same price the Korean supplier was currently charging.

The challenge inspired Jon, and he carefully compiled the important financial information that was needed. He discovered that a pretax profit margin of 12 percent was possible, but only if he could keep direct labor expenses down to 11 percent of company sales. The problem he faced was obvious. The output per worker estimated was realistic but only if he had a work force that wanted to meet and sustain a high level of quality and productivity. The problem was many workers tend to be cynical about management and often lose their motivation if they see productivity increasing and they don't see any benefit to the gain. He decided the solution was logical and simple. In addition to a competitive base wage, he would pay the workers a quarterly bonus if workers could get the labor costs of the firm under 11 percent.

Wehrenberg also agreed that at the end of each week he would provide information concerning sales totals, gross payroll numbers, or any other information workers needed to verify the efficiency of the system. He believed that it was possible over a period of time to get labor costs down to 9 percent, which would mean a quarterly bonus of $1,500 to each worker.

Workers liked the idea and accepted the challenge. Jamestown Advanced Products agreed to a three-year contract to supply the building-products company.

DISCUSSION QUESTIONS FOR CASE 10-1:

1. What does Jamestown Advanced Products do to motivate people using money that other firms do not do? Can you see how money can be a motivator?

2. Do you think Wehrenberg actually wanted the workers to get the labor costs under 11 percent?

3. What kind of workers would enjoy working at Jamestown Advanced Products, and what kind would not? Can you see how productivity at Jamestown would increase as certain kinds of employees would self-select themselves out of the company and others would come who fit the system better?

4. Would such a revenue-sharing system work at most companies? For what kinds of companies would it work best?

ANSWERS TO DISCUSSION QUESTIONS FOR CASE 10-1:

1. *What does Jamestown Advanced Products do to motivate people using money that other firms do not do? Can you see how money can be a motivator?*

It sounds as if money is the motivator, but it may not be the true motivator. Workers like to feel part of a team (you learned that from the Hawthorne studies). Sharing the goals of the firm with workers and then letting them share in any profits motivates them to work harder. That is what MBO is all about. The fact that the workers make more money as well is just icing on the cake.

2. *Do you think Wehrenberg actually wanted the workers to get the labor costs under 11 percent?*

Absolutely. The best work arrangement is win, win. The company wins when workers keep costs down and workers win by getting bonuses. The only concern of workers is that the game is not rigged. Giving them appropriate information makes employees more sure of the honesty of the program.

3. *What kind of workers would enjoy working at Jamestown Advanced Products, and what kind would not? Can you see how productivity at Jamestown would increase as certain kinds of employees would self-select themselves out of the company and others would come who fit the system better?*

Workers who like a challenge would prosper as would workers who like to make decisions for themselves. Workers who are relatively lazy and like to have others make all the decisions are not likely to do well in this situation. As the lazier workers left, the rest of the workers would form a self-motivated team that is likely to be very productive.

4. *Would such a revenue-sharing system work at most companies? For what kinds of companies would it work best?*

It would work at many companies. In some companies, employees are too far from customers to be paid on the basis of sales. Large companies in general may find this. For example, such a system would not work at most colleges. But companies that repair things and service companies in general—such as airlines, auto repair places, and painters—would prosper under such a system.

CASE 10-2

THEORIES X AND Y: THAT'S HOW THE COOKIE CRUMBLES

No two firms better illustrate Theory X and Theory Y than David's Cookies and Mrs. Fields Cookies stores. You'll see what we mean.

First, let's look at David's Cookies. When owner David Liederman first opened his stores, food reviewers criticized his cookies. However, when the New York Times had a cookie-tasting contest, David's won. Today, even though the market for cookies has softened, David's Cookies operates specialty stores and compact self-contained modular stores (called kiosks), and sells frozen cookie dough and ice cream to 2,000 New York-area supermarkets. David has also entered the restaurant business in New York. His latest venture, Emmi's, is a casual dining restaurant that serves American-style dishes. David's a big success thanks to his cookies.

How much confidence does David have in his employees in the cookie business? Apparently not much. David feels it necessary to minimize employee involvement in cookie making so employees can't mess things up. He does that by making all the dough in a factory and shipping it to the stores. All the employee has to do is put the dough on a tray, put it in an automatic oven, and take it out seven and a half minutes later. David has even admitted he was hesitant to sell brownies because he feels workers can't handle the job of adding eggs. He says, "One of the reasons we do well . . . is that a chimpanzee could take cookies out of that bag and more often than not put them on the tray properly." David has also minimized his own risk by franchising his stores.

In contrast, let's look at one of David's main competitors. Mrs. Fields Cookies. Debbi Fields has about 700 company-owned cookie stores. She also has an agreement with National Convenience Stores Inc. to sell her cookies throughout its convenience stores. Mrs. Fields has even entered into head-to-head competition in the consumer packaged chip market with her Mrs. Fields semisweet chocolate chips. Not bad either.

Does Mrs. Fields have the same attitude about her employees as David Liederman? No way! She feels that people "will do their very best provided that they are getting proper support." Mrs. Fields adds, "It's a people company. That's what it's all about . . . What we really do is . . . we take care of people." This philosophy is reflected in how Mrs. Fields makes cookies. Store employees combine ingredients right in the store (some in proportioned containers). The ovens aren't automatic. Employees put in the raw dough to bake and take out the finished cookies when it feels right. "We tell them that we want them to have fun," Mrs. Fields says. "People come to work because they need to be productive. They need to feel successful in whatever they do." Mrs. Fields's idea is to have her managers out where they can be most useful—with employees and customers. Here's how Debbi sums up her job: "To make people feel important and to create an opportunity for them. That's really my role as cookie president, the cookie person."

To keep this momentum going, Mrs. Fields has expanded into a line of Mrs. Fields Bakery Cakes and has scheduled in a low-calorie dessert line. The firm will offer products such as chocolate mousse cake and lemon meringue pie made with Nutrasweet brand sweetener. As Debbi Fields puts it, "When there's a cookie opportunity, we want to be there. Cookies will always be in our future."

DISCUSSION QUESTIONS FOR CASE 10-2:

1. What motivational philosophies are in use at David's and Mrs. Fields Cookies? How do you support your conclusions?

2. Which store is more likely to build employee honesty and loyalty?

3. In which company would you rather be a manager? Employee? Investor? What are your reasons for making these decisions?

ANSWERS TO DISCUSSION QUESTIONS FOR CASE 10-2:

1. *What motivational philosophies are in use at David's and Mrs. Fields Cookies? How do you support your conclusions?*

   Mrs. Fields is a Theory Y manager and David is a Theory X manager. Neither is the correct way to manage; it all depends on the situation and the employees. In one restaurant, you may want to use Theory Y management with one employee and Theory X with another.

2. *Which store is more likely to build employee honesty and loyalty?*

   The first answer to come to mind is probably Mrs. Fields, but that is not necessarily so. Some employees like to be given lots of direction and little responsibility. Managers cannot adopt one managerial style for everyone. Each person must be treated as an individual. If communication is established and employees are listened to, there can be honesty and loyalty in any firm.

3. *In which company would you rather be a manager? Employee? Investor? What are your reasons for making these decisions?*

   It depends on your personal preferences. Most people seem to prefer a theory Y manager, but often become theory X types when confronted with new employees who seem unmotivated at first.

CASE 10-3

HOW CORPORATE CULTURE MOTIVATES

Corporate culture, basically, is the atmosphere created in an organization by its top managers. What is little discussed in the literature is how such a culture can motivate workers, even when the managers are very authoritarian and strict. It says in the text that motivation comes from within. One of the best motivators, therefore, is to create an atmosphere in which employees feel that they are the best and that their contribution makes a difference. That atmosphere breeds self-motivation. You may have seen such motivation on football teams lead by authoritarian, demanding coaches.

Don Oberg is like a demanding football coach, but he runs a tool and die shop. He is strict about cleanliness because some of the parts made in the shop have tolerances of as small as .00005 of an inch (1/150 the width of a human hair). A speck of dirt can create havoc in such an environment. Mr. Oberg is strict about a lot of other things as well. Start at 7, quit at 5; no chit chat, and 15 minutes for lunch. Only the highest standards of work are tolerated or out you go. Signs everywhere say, "Let's Do The Job Right the First time!" and "If It's Almost Right, It's Wrong." Don Oberg is a perfectionist, and his employees know it and appreciate the dedication to quality work. It pays off in assured work, good pay, overtime, and, perhaps most important of all, in a feeling of pride in doing a job well. That is what leads to self-motivation.

One year some 1,600 people applied for jobs at Oberg's firm, and only 30 were hired. The firm can get away with charging premium prices by out-doing the Japanese at their specialty—quality. Dan Oberg has created a corporate culture that is evident the minute you walk into the plant. The grounds are clean and attractive, the plan is spick and span, and the workers are professionals doing their job right because there is a certain pride that comes from doing a job well.

DISCUSSION QUESTIONS FOR CASE 10-3:

1. Have you seen other organizations in which the management was very strict, but created an atmosphere in which employees were motivated to do well?

2. Have you ever experienced the feeling of doing a job well? How did you feel? Were you motivated?

3. Money and the promise of overtime were considered motivators at this plant. Could money be more of a motivator than the researchers think?

ANSWERS TO DISCUSSION QUESTIONS FOR CASE 10-3:

1. *Have you seen other organizations in which the management was very strict, but created an atmosphere in which employees were motivated to do well?*

That is the condition at many colleges among the faculty. It is also true at firms such as IBM and leading accounting firms. People are proud to work for a firm that does it right the first time and don't mind the pressure to do well.

2. *Have you ever experienced the feeling of doing a job well? How did you feel? Were you motivated?*

Let your students share their own experiences here. Does this sometimes happen in college?

3. *Money and the promise of overtime were considered motivators at this plant. Could money be more of a motivator than the researchers think?*

Many people think so. Some football players seem to play their heart out. That is understandable when you learn that they get incentive pay for doing well. The same is true of boxers and tennis players who suffer pain for big payoffs. Is it winning that motivates them, or the money? Some Soviet players cannot keep the money, but seem to try just as hard. Is money a motivator? The final answer is not in yet.

Transparency Masters

TRANSPARENCY MASTER 72	Chapter Outline
TRANSPARENCY MASTER 73	Maslow's Hierarchy of Needs *(Figure 10.1 on text page 292)*
TRANSPARENCY MASTER 74	A Comparison of Theories X, Y, and Z *(Figure 10.2 on text page 296)*
TRANSPARENCY MASTER 75	Herzberg's Motivators and Hygiene Factors *(Figure 10.3 on text page 297)*
TRANSPARENCY MASTER 76	Comparison of Maslow's Hierarchy of Needs and Herzberg's Theory of Factors *(Figure 10.4 on text page 298)*
TRANSPARENCY MASTER 77	Management by Objectives *(Figure 10.5 on text page 301)*

Chapter Outline

CHAPTER 10
MOTIVATING EMPLOYEES AND BUILDING SELF-MANAGED TEAMS

PROFILE: Herb Kelleher of Southwest Airlines

I. THE IMPORTANCE OF MOTIVATION.

A. Early Management Studies (Taylor).

B. The Hawthorne Studies (Mayo).

II. MASLOW'S HIERARCHY OF NEEDS.

A. Applying Maslow's Theory.

III. MCGREGOR'S THEORY X AND THEORY Y.

A. Theory X.

B. Theory Y.

C. Theory Z.

IV. HERZBERG'S MOTIVATING FACTORS.

A. Applying Herzberg's Theories.

V. JOB ENRICHMENT.

VI. GOAL-SETTING THEORY AND MANAGEMENT BY OBJECTIVES.

VII. MEETING EMPLOYEE EXPECTATIONS: EXPECTANCY THEORY.

VIII. TREATING EMPLOYEES FAIRLY: EQUITY THEORY.

IX. IMPLEMENTING THE NEW CONCEPTS: MOTIVATION THROUGH COMMUNICATION.

A. Open Communication and Self-Managed Teams.

B. Changing Organizations is Not Easy.

C. A Model for the Future.

1. Learning From the Miller Brewing and Mary Kay Experience.

D. Motivation in the Future.

X. SUMMARY AND REVIEW.

TM-73

Maslow's Hierarchy of Needs
(Figure 10.1 on text page 292)

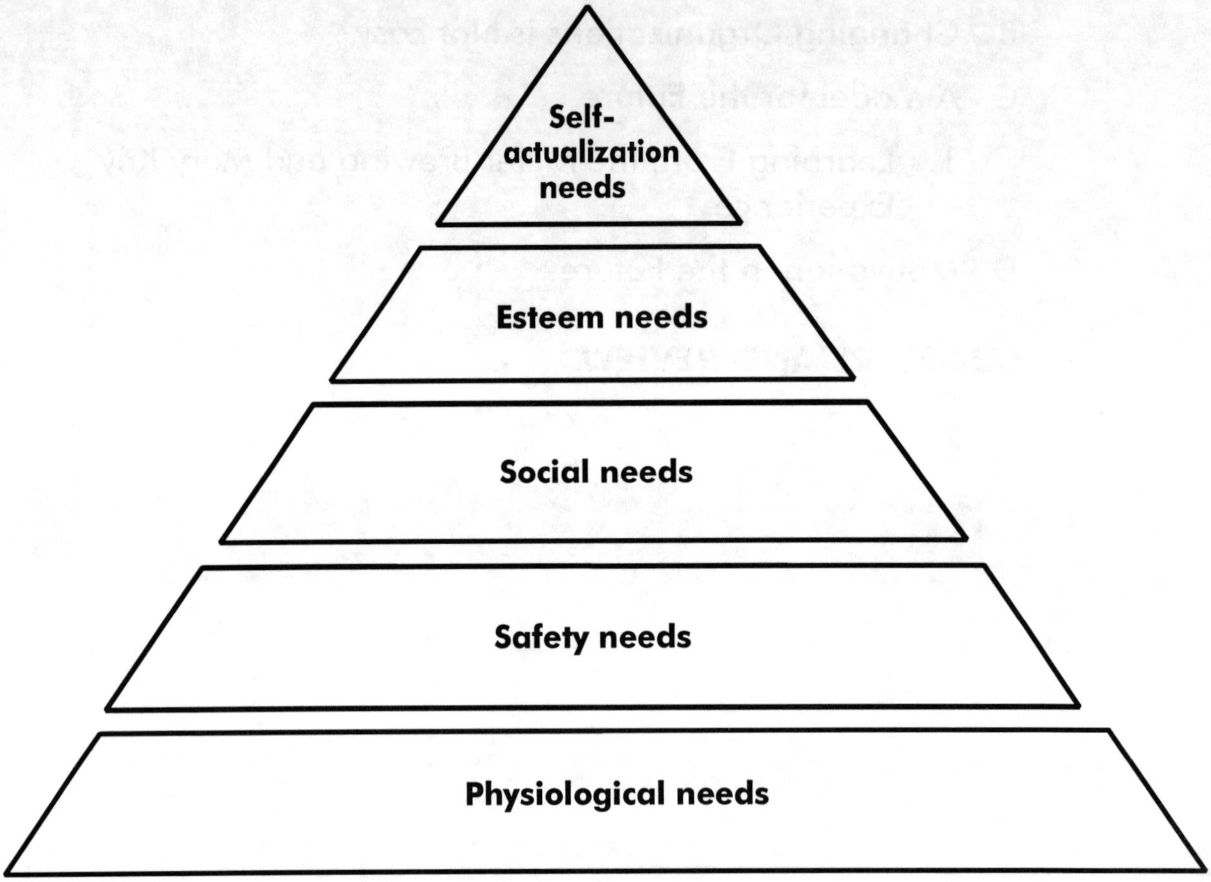
Self-actualization needs
Esteem needs
Social needs
Safety needs
Physiological needs

TM-74

A Comparison of Theories X, Y, and Z

(Figure 10.2 on text page 296)

THEORY X	THEORY Y	THEORY Z
1. Employees dislike work and will try to avoid it.	1. Employees view work as a natural part of life.	1. Employee involvement is the key to increased productivity.
2. Employees prefer to be controlled and directed.	2. Employees prefer limited control and direction.	2. Employee control is implied and informal.
3. Employees seek security, not responsibility.	3. Employees will seek responsibility under proper work conditions.	3. Employees prefer to share responsibility and decision making.
4. Employees must be intimidated by managers to perform.	4. Employees perform better in work environments that are nonintimidating.	4. Employees perform better in environments that foster trust and cooperation.
5. Employees are motivated by financial rewards.	5. Employees are motivated by many different needs.	5. Employees need guaranteed employment and will accept slow evaluations and promotions.

TM-75

Herzberg's Motivators and Hygiene Factors

(Figure 10.3 on text page 297)

MOTIVATORS	HYGIENE MAINTENANCE FACTORS
(These factors can be used to motivate workers.)	(These factors can cause dissatisfaction, but changing them will have little motivational effect.)
Work itself	Company policy and administration
Achievement	Supervision
Recognition	Working conditions
Responsibility	Interpersonal relations (co-workers)
Growth and advancement	Salary, status, and job security

TM-76

Comparison of Maslow's Hierarchy of Needs and Herzberg's Theory of Factors

(Figure 10.4 on text page 298)

Maslow	Herzberg factors	Herzberg
Self-actualization	Work itself Achievement Possibility of growth	Motivational
Esteem or ego	Advancement Recognition Status	Motivational / "Hygiene Maintenance"
Social	Interpersonal relations Superior Subordinates Peers Supervision	"Hygiene Maintenance"
Safety	Company policy and administration Job security Working conditions	"Hygiene Maintenance"
Physiological	Salary Personal life	"Hygiene Maintenance"

TM-77

Management by Objectives

(Figure 10.5 on text page 301)

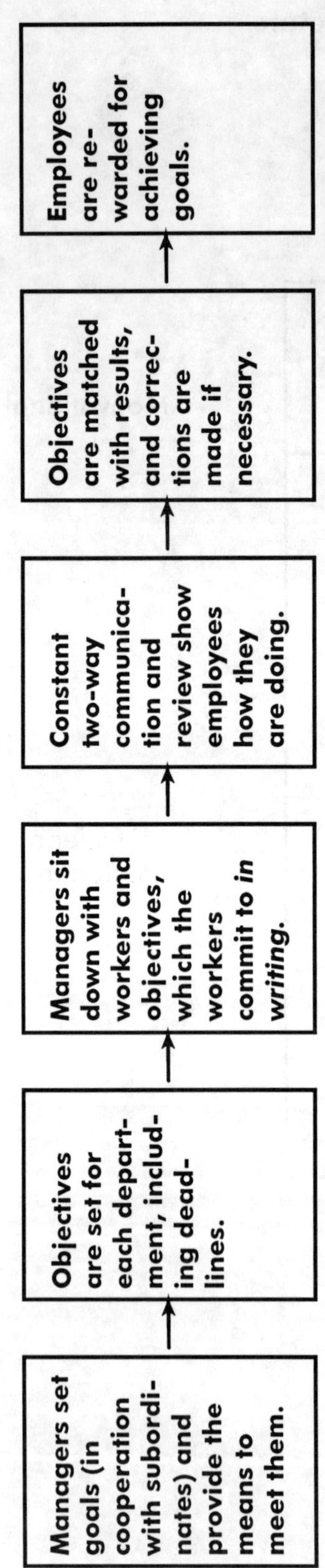

Human Resource Management: Finding and Keeping the Best Employees

Chapter 11

Folder Contents

OT ACETATE 11-5 Why Companies Use Temporary Workers

OT ACETATE 11-6 Do Employers Feel Workers Are "Ready" for Work?

OT ACETATE 11-7 Information Sought on Job Descriptions versus Job Specifications

OT ACETATE 11-8 Major Uses of Performance Appraisals

OT ACETATE 11-9 Employers Offering Family-Friendly Benefits

OT ACETATE 11-10 Unusual Benefits Offered to Workers

OT ACETATE 11-11 Percentage of Employers That Grant Family Leave

OT ACETATE 11-12 Job-Oriented Motivational Techniques

OT ACETATE 11-13 Company's Reasons for Establishing Flexible Work Plans

OT ACETATE 11-14 What Do You Know About Equal Employment Opportunity Law?

OT ACETATE 11-15 What Do You Know About Equal Employment Opportunity Law?

(Acetates and Transparency Masters are also available as PowerPoint slides on disk and on the Presentation CD-ROM.)

(Resources Available are also referenced in the expanded lecture outline later in this chapter.)

Other Resources Available

Video Case - "Workplace Trends: Fighting Stress, Workplace Perks, and More Companies Provide Fitness." With workers today working harder and longer hours, and with less job security, managers are using creative perks to keep employees satisfied and motivated. At CIGNA, employees can place take-home meal orders with the company chef. At Salamon Brothers, employees can visit a physician and get prescription drugs delivered at the office. Andersen Consulting subsidizes a concierge to run errands for employees. Other companies provide on-site dry cleaning, laundry services, and subsidized day care. Managers believe they get a long-term return on their investment in the form of happier, more productive workers. (The **Media Resource Guide** contains a summary of the Video and suggested discussion questions.)

Student Assessment and Learning Guide: Contains matching key term and definition questions, write-in retention questions, write-in critical thinking questions, and practice test of multiple choice and true/false questions.

Technology:

Zapitalism CD-ROM - Simulation program.

Concept Mastery Exam Preparation Disk - Practice test and tutorial.

Business Essentials Disk – Hyperlinks Understanding Business with seven other leading business texts.

Presentation CD-ROM – Contains PowerPoint slides of acetates and transparency masters, video clips, lecture materials. This tool allows you to customize your lecture presentations.

***Business Week* Web Site Access with the *Business Week* edition.**

***Understanding Business* Home Page – http:/www.mhhe.com/ub5e.**

Audiotape: Abridged chapter (Text minus profile, boxes, and end-of-chapter material.

Associated Web Sites

These sites are provided to students for the purpose of analysis and critical thinking of the issues. Students are encouraged to explore other sites. As with any Web site, some may be inactive now.

Human Resources Associations:

Human Resources Associations Of Central Ohio

http://www.hraco.com/

Human Resources Planning:

The Ohio Bureau of Employment Services

http://www.ohio.gov/obes/

Human Resource Planning Society

http://www.hrps.org/html/index1.htm

Managing Change - Layoffs and Downsizing

http://www.radonc.uchicago.edu/~sroa/Newsletter/Managing_Change.htm

Recruiting:

Employee Referral Program - good incentive program for recruiting

http://www.jwtworks.com/hrlive/reports/erprat.html

Temporary Workers, Friend Or Foe?

http://www-gsb.stanford.edu/research/faculty/news%20releases/william.barnett/barnett.htm

Management mobility

http://www.bayer.com/bayer/english/3xxxmita/3200/3200.htm

Recruiting:

Adia Employment Services recently renamed Adecco International

http://www.adia.com/Adia

On-line job listings - using the Internet to post and seek jobs - many links available

http://career333.ucr.edu/JobLst/joblist.html

A personal resume - what do you think??

http://httpsrv.ocs.drexel.edu/undergrad/st95fk25/resumejb.html

List of many HR Issues - interesting reading

http://www.adia.com/Adia/HRIssues.html

Selecting Excellent Employees - great points to consider

http://hr2.hr.arizona.edu/HRInfoSeries1.htm

References and Background Checks:

http://hi-tec.twc.state.tx.us/employer/referenc.htm

http://www.all-biz.com/articles/refer.htm

Typical investigation company who can check backgrounds and references

http://www.bullockco.com/preref.html

Performance Evaluations and Written Warning Notices:

http://www.oada.com/current/archive/sept96/sept4.htm

Sample List of Fringe Benefits Available to Employees of this Company:

http://www.thompson.com/tpg/pen_ben/perk/perktoc.html#A1

Testing of Potential Employees:

Types of tests

http://www.usaor.net/users/mdt/typesoftests.htm

Safety-Related Workplace Drug Testing

http://www.peabodybrown.com/publications/Labor/winter94/labordrug.html

California Court ruling on drug testing - note the responsibilities of the employer

http://employerlaw.com/cgi-shl/dbproc.exe/el/getpage^14

American Society for Training and Development:

http://wwcareers.com/A/0121.html

Understanding Business **Home Page**

http:/www.mhhe.com/ub5e.

What's New in This Edition

Additions:

- Profile of Madye H. Whitehead and Charles Henson of Design Alternatives
- Section "Outsourcing: Common Alternative Staffing Options"
- Section "Diversity in Management Development'
- Section "Compensating Teams"
- Reaching Beyond Our Borders: Working with Employees in Different Countries
- Spotlight On Small Business: Small Businesses Must Compete to Attract Qualified Workers
- Taking It to the Net exercises
- Video case: Workplace Trends

Revisions:

Statistical data and examples throughout the chapter were updated to reflect current information. In addition:

- The 4th edition section "Making New Employees Feel at Home" was condensed and blended into the section "Training and Developing Employees for Optimum Performance."
- Section "Job Simulation" was condensed.
- Section "Flextime Plans" was condensed.
- The discussion about how to minimize the chance of wrongful discharge lawsuits was moved from section "Terminating Employment and Downsizing" to Figure 11-6.
- Section "Laws Protecting the Disabled and Older Employees" was expanded to include discussion of the 1997 EEOC guidelines to the ADA.

Deletions:

- Profile
- Section "Proposed Wages and Benefits Legislation"
- Figures "Steps in Human Resource Planning." "Steps in the Selection Process," "Application Form," and "Government Legislation"
- Video case
- Boxes: Reaching Beyond Our Borders, From the Pages of Entrepreneur

Brief Chapter Outline/Learning Goals

CHAPTER 11

HUMAN RESOURCE MANAGEMENT: FINDING AND KEEPING THE BEST EMPLOYEES

PROFILE: Madye H. Whitehead and Charles Henson of Design Alternatives

I. WORKING WITH PEOPLE IS JUST THE BEGINNING.

LEARNING GOAL 1. Explain the importance of human resource management and describe current issues in managing human resources.

A. Developing the Ultimate Resource.

B. The Human Resource Challenge.

II. DETERMINING YOUR HUMAN RESOURCES NEEDS.

LEARNING GOAL 2. Summarize the six steps in planning human resources.

III. RECRUITING EMPLOYEES FROM A DIVERSE POPULATION.

LEARNING GOAL 3. Describe methods companies use to recruit new employees and explain some of the issues that make recruitment challenging.

IV. SELECTING EMPLOYEES WHO WILL BE PRODUCTIVE.

LEARNING GOAL 4. Outline the six steps in selecting employees.

A. Outsourcing: Common Alternative Staffing Options.

V. TRAINING AND DEVELOPING EMPLOYEES FOR OPTIMUM PERFORMANCE.

LEARNING GOAL 5. Illustrate the use of various types of employee training and development methods.

A. Management Development.

1. Importance of Networking.

B. Diversity in Management Development.

VI. APPRAISING EMPLOYEE PERFORMANCE TO GET OPTIMUM RESULTS.

LEARNING GOAL 6. Trace the six steps in appraising employee performance.

VII. COMPENSATING EMPLOYEES: ATTRACTING AND KEEPING THE BEST.

LEARNING GOAL 7. Summarize the objectives of employee compensation programs and describe various pay systems and fringe benefits.

A. Pay Systems.

B. Compensating Teams.

C. Fringe Benefits.

VIII. SCHEDULING EMPLOYEES THAT MEET ORGANIZATIONAL AND EMPLOYEE NEEDS.

LEARNING GOAL 8. Explain scheduling plans managers use to adjust to workers' needs.

A. Flextime Plans.

B. Home-Based and Other Mobil Work.

C. Job-Sharing Plans.

IX. MOVING EMPLOYEES UP, OVER, AND OUT.

LEARNING GOAL 9. Describe the ways employees can move through a company: promotion, reassignment, termination, and retirement.

A. Promoting and Reassigning Employees.

B. Terminating Employees.

C. Retiring Employees.

X. LAWS AFFECTING HUMAN RESOURCE MANAGEMENT.

LEARNING GOAL 10. Illustrate the effects of legislation on human resource management.

A. Laws Protecting the Disabled and Older Employees.

B. Effects of Legislation.

X. SUMMARY AND REVIEW.

(Learning Objectives are also referenced in the expanded lecture outline later in this chapter)

Key Terms

affirmative action *(text page 338)*

apprenticeship program *(text page 326)*

cafeteria-style fringe benefits *(text page 333)*

compressed workweek *(text page 334)*

contingent workers *(text page 325)*

core time *(text page 334)*

employee orientation *(text page 326)*

flextime plans *(text page 334)*

fringe benefits *(text page 333)*

human resource management *(text page 316)*

job analysis *(text page 320)*

job description *(text page 320)*

job sharing *(text page 335)*

job simulation *(text page 327)*

job specifications *(text page 320)*

management development *(text page 327)*

mentor *(text page 328)*

networking *(text page 328)*

off-the-job training *(text page 327)*

on-the-job training *(text page 326)*

performance appraisal *(text page 329)*

recruitment *(text page 321)*

reverse discrimination *(text page 339)*

selection *(text page 322)*

training and development *(text page 326)*

vestibule training *(text page 327)*

Lecture Outline

PROFILE: MADYE H. WHITEHEAD and **CHARLES HENSON** of **DESIGN ALTERNATIVES** created a business that offers managers the help they need in understanding and managing diversity.

I. WORKING WITH PEOPLE IS JUST THE BEGINNING.

▶ **LEARNING GOAL 1.** Explain the importance of human resource management and describe current issues in managing human resources.

A. **HUMAN RESOURCE MANAGEMENT** is the process of evaluating human resource needs, finding people to fill those needs, and optimizing this important resource by providing the right incentives and job environment, all with the goal of meeting the objectives of the organization.

B. **DEVELOPING THE ULTIMATE RESOURCE.**

1. There is a major shift from traditional manufacturing industries to service industries that require more technical job skills.
2. A major problem is retraining workers for new, more challenging jobs.
3. **EMPLOYEES ARE THE ULTIMATE RESOURCE.**
    a. This resource has always been plentiful, so there was little need to nurture and develop it.

Lecture Notes

TRANSPARENCY MASTER 78
Chapter Outline

(Transparency Masters begin on page 11.90.)

TRANSPARENCY MASTER 79
Human Resource Management
(Figure 11.1 on text page 316)

(Transparency Masters begin on page 11.90.)

OT ACETATE 11-1
The Job of Human Resource Management

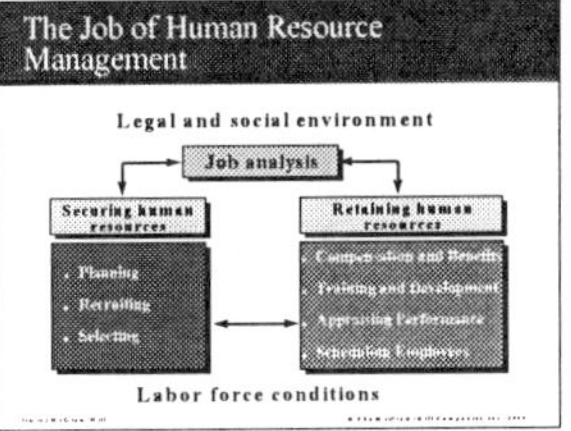

Comments:

1. This acetate highlights the elements involved in the job of the human resource manager. The key components of the job and environmental factors are clearly detailed.
2. You may want to mention that specific laws related to human resource management are covered in the chapter. This could be an appropriate spot to refer back to information covered early in the text related to important trends affecting business.
3. Information pertaining to securing and retaining human resources forms the nucleus of the chapter material. Each activity is discussed in the chapter.

Lecture Outline

b. Qualified labor is more scarce today.

c. The goal of human resource management is to develop this powerful resource to its full potential.

4. Historically, most firms assigned the job of recruiting, selecting, training, motivating, and firing people to functional departments.

5. Today's human resource departments go beyond the clerical functions of the old personnel departments.

a. The role of the human resource management is **A FUNCTION OF ALL MANAGERS**, not just one department's.

b. Most human resource functions are shared between the human resource manager and other managers.

C. **THE HUMAN RESOURCE CHALLENGE.**

1. Changes in the labor force has created problems in the human resource area.

2. Some of the **PROBLEMS** discussed in the text include:

a. Shortages in people trained to work in high tech areas.

b. Abundance of unskilled workers in obsolete fields who need retraining.

Lecture Notes

OT ACETATE 11-2
What Attracts Workers to Specific Employers?

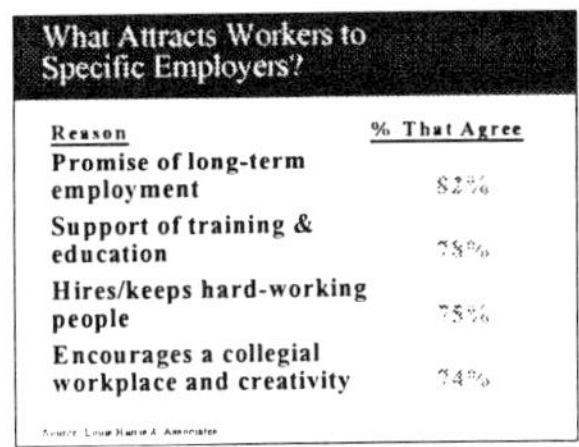

Comments:

1. Why are workers anxious to work for certain companies and somewhat adverse to other? This information is very important for companies in attracting qualified employees. That question is addressed in this acetate.
2. Job security is evidently still important to workers. With threats of outsourcing and downsizing still looming in the workplace, it is not surprising working look for stability. Training and education are not far behind. Workers today realize that staying up on technology and improving skills are critical to continued success in a changing work environment.
3. Ask what is most important to students. See if their answers mirror the responses given on the acetate.

LECTURE ENHANCER 11-1
Wanted: A Global Boss

How does one qualify as a topnotch global boss? (See complete lecture enhancer on page 11.60.)

LECTURE ENHANCER 11-2
The Clerical Evolution

We think of the clerical field as being dominated by women, but in its early years the reverse was true. (See complete lecture enhancer on page 11.62.)

Lecture Outline

c. Growing number of undereducated workers.

d. A shift in age composition in the work force, including many older workers.

e. A complex set of laws and regulations.

f. An increasing number of single parent and two-income families.

g. Shifts in employee attitudes toward work.

h. Continued downsizing.

i. More competition overseas.

j. Increased demand for benefits tailored to the individual.

k. Growing concern over health issues, elder care, child care, etc.

II. DETERMINING YOUR HUMAN RESOURCE NEEDS.

▶ **LEARNING GOAL 2.** Summarize the six steps in planning human resources.

A. **PREPARING FORECASTS OF FUTURE HUMAN RESOURCE NEEDS.**

B. **PREPARING A HUMAN RESOURCE INVENTORY.**

C. **PREPARING A JOB ANALYSIS.**

CRITICAL THINKING
(page 318 in text)

Based on the complex situations you'd be addressing, does human resource management seem like a challenging career? Do you see any other issues, such as the compensation of cross-functional teams, that are likely to affect this function? What have been your experiences in dealing with people who work in human resource management? Would you enjoy working in such an environment?

REACHING BEYOND OUR BORDERS
(Box in text, page 319)
"Working with Employees in Different Countries"

We talked about working with employees from diverse backgrounds in the U.S. How do human resource managers deal with employees in such diverse places as an office in Spain, a service center in Brazil, or a new plant in Korea? How do they cope with hiring employees from other countries for a company's headquarters in the U.S.?

Lecture Outline

1. A **JOB ANALYSIS** is a study of what is done by employees who fill various job titles.

2. The results of the job analysis are two written statements.

   a. A **JOB DESCRIPTION** specifies the objectives of the job, the type of work to be done, the duties, and the relationship of the job to other functions.

   b. **JOB SPECIFICATIONS** specify the minimum qualifications required of a worker to fill specific jobs.

D. **ASSESSING FUTURE DEMAND**—HR managers who are proactive anticipate future needs of their organizations.

E. **ASSESSING FUTURE SUPPLY** in a shifting labor market.

III. RECRUITING EMPLOYEES FROM A DIVERSE POPULATION.

▶ **LEARNING GOAL 3.** Describe methods companies use to recruit new employees and explain some of the issues that make recruitment challenging.

A. **RECRUITMENT** is the set of activities used to obtain a sufficient number of the right people at the right time to select those who best meet the needs of the organization.

Lecture Notes

OT ACETATE 11-7
Information Sought on Job Descriptions versus Job Specifications

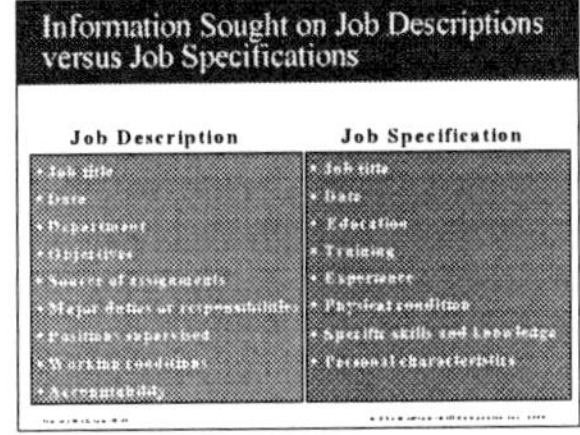

Comments:

1. You can use this acetate to very specifically point out the differences between job descriptions and job specifications. The material is also covered in chapter 11.
2. You can refer back to this acetate when discussing Equal Employment Law since both job descriptions and job specifications are covered under this legislation. Some examples you might want to note include:
   - Courts have ruled employees can only be discharged for deficiencies covered in job descriptions.
   - Job descriptions must include valid information. For example, if a job description requires a worker "be able to lift 200 lbs", that requirement must an actual condition of the job.
   - Conditions set forth in a job specification must hold for **all** prospective employees. For example, if a position requires a college degree you cannot hire a non-degreed person if other applicants have been rejected for lack of a degree. Real opportunity for a class action suit here.
3. Students may ask about job descriptions that include, "and other duties specifically required as part of the position." Courts have been tough on these. For example, making coffee, and picking up laundry are not considered validly covered with such clauses. Again, it's important for companies to present realistic job previews and be specific on job descriptions.

TRANSPARENCY MASTER 80
Job Analysis *(Figure 11.2 on text page 320)*

(Transparency Masters begin on page 11.90.)

SUPPLEMENTAL CASE 11-1
Human Resource Planning and Women Workers

See complete case on page 11.83.

TRANSPARENCY MASTER 81
Employee Sources *(Figure 11.3 on text page 322)*

TM 81

(Transparency Masters begin on page 11.90.)

Lecture Outline

B. **RECRUITING IS DIFFICULT** for several reasons:

1. People with the necessary skills are not available, and must be hired and then trained.
2. The emphasis on corporate culture and teamwork makes it important to hire skilled people who also fit in with the culture.
3. Some organizations have unattractive workplaces or offer low wages.

C. Human resource managers turn to many **SOURCES** for assistance.

1. **INTERNAL SOURCES** include hiring from within the firm and employee recommendations.
   a. Internal sources are less expensive.
   b. Hiring from within helps maintain employee morale.
2. However, it isn't always possible to find qualified workers within the company, so HR managers must use **EXTERNAL RECRUITMENT** sources.

IV. SELECTING EMPLOYEES WHO WILL BE PRODUCTIVE.

▶ **LEARNING GOAL 4.** Outline the six steps in selecting employees.

Lecture Notes

MAKING ETHICAL DECISIONS
(Box in text, page 322)

"Recruiting Employees from Competitors"

You, as the human resource manager at Technocrat, Inc., are considering offering a similar position to a designer who is now with a major competitor. Your thinking is that the new employee will be a source of information about the competition's new products. What are your ethical considerations in this case? Will you lure the employee away from the competition even though you have no need for a designer? What will be the consequences of your decision?

OT ACETATE 11-4
Skills Employers Are Seeking

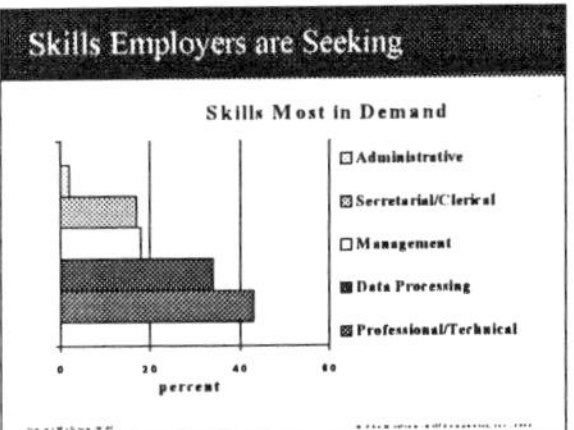

Comments:

1. Conducting a human resource inventory is part of the planning process for organizations. Companies often make use of replacement charts to exactly plot what human resource needs may be over a particular period of time. This acetate lists the skills that are most in demand in contemporary organizations. Students should be very interested in this list.
2. Students should note that professional and technical skills top the list. This edition of Understanding Business focuses on business etiquette and professionalism as a theme. It is also the subject of a video for use in class. Technology is a must in virtually any job situation today. The Taking It To The Net Exercises should help students work with the Internet and find how technology can pay off both in school and in the job market.

OT ACETATE 11-3
What Not to Ask in Job Interviews

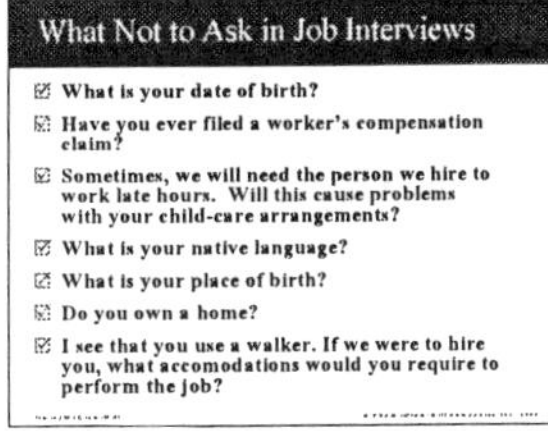

Comments:

1. As the first acetate in the section indicated, the law is an important factor to consider in the human resource management process. Employers need to be careful that they don't even inadvertently violate regulations and laws. This acetate deals with some areas to stay away from in conducting the interview process. Chapter 11 also deals specifically with principles involved in equal employment law. The last two acetates in this section advise specific things to ask and not ask of prospective employees.
2. See if students can explain why the questions listed in this acetate are not permitted in the job interview process. Some are a bit tricky, but with a bit of thought students should be able to discern the proper answer.

Lecture Outline

A. **SELECTION** is the process of gathering information to decide who should be hired, under legal guidelines, for the best interest of the individual and the organization.

B. **STEPS OF THE SELECTION PROCESS:**

1. Completion of an **APPLICATION FORM.**

2. **INITIAL AND FOLLOW-UP INTERVIEWS.**

   a. A member of the human resource department staff often screens applicants in a first interview.

   b. Potential employees are then interviewed by the manager who will supervise the new employee.

3. **EMPLOYMENT TESTS**.

   a. Although testing has been severely criticized, organizations continue to use tests to measure basic competencies.

   b. It is important that the test be directly related to the job.

4. **BACKGROUND INVESTIGATIONS** help weed out candidates least likely to succeed and identify those most likely to succeed.

5. **PHYSICAL EXAMS.**

   a. Medical tests cannot be given just to screen out individuals.

SPOTLIGHT ON SMALL BUSINESS (Box in text, page 323)
"Small Businesses Must Compete to Attract Qualified Workers"

It's harder than ever for businesses to find qualified employees and it is getting more expensive to find new hires. Despite the hurdles, small business management consultants say there are many ways to lure desirable workers.

LECTURE ENHANCER 11-3
Hiring Methods Employers Use Most

A study of 2,300 human resource specialists conducted showed that employers use a number of methods to hire employees. The most frequently used methods are listed. (See complete lecture enhancer on page 11.64.)

LECTURE ENHANCER 11-4
Memorable Job Interview

The world's largest temporary personnel service for accounting, bookkeeping and information systems, Accountemps, recently conducted a nationwide survey of executives about the most unusual job interview they ever conducted. (See complete lecture enhancer on page 11.65.)

LECTURE ENHANCER 11-5
Testing and Diversity

The vast majority of American companies use some form of employment testing, whether through interviews or more formal methods, as a tool for guiding their hiring decisions. But the growing ethnic diversity of the U.S. work force, and the corresponding need to eliminate the potential for discrimination in hiring, have put the efficacy of some of those tests in doubt. (See complete lecture enhancer on page 11.66.)

b. Preemployment testing to detect drug or alcohol abuse or AIDS screening is controversial.

c. Eighty percent of U.S. companies now test their employees and applicants for drug use.

6. **TRIAL PERIODS** allow organizations to hire an employee conditionally.

C. **HIRING CONTINGENT WORKERS.**

1. Sometimes it is more cost-effective to hire contingent workers when a company has a varying need for employees.

2. **CONTINGENT WORKERS** are workers who do not have the expectation of regular, full-time employment.

3. **TEMPORARY STAFFING** is a $40 billion industry.

4. Managers see using **TEMPORARY WORKERS** as a way of weeding out people and finding good hires.

V. TRAINING AND DEVELOPING EMPLOYEES FOR OPTIMUM RESULTS.

▶ **LEARNING GOAL 5.** Illustrate the use of various types of employee training and development methods.

Lecture Notes

OT ACETATE 11-5
Why Companies Use Temporary Workers

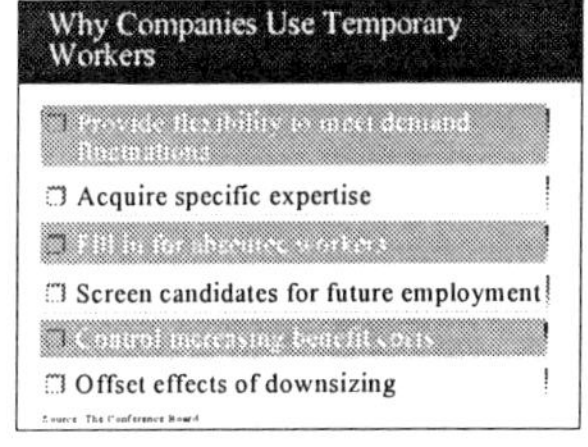

Comments:

1. This acetate highlights emphasizes the growth of temporary workers in U.S. companies. It provides the rationale why companies now use growing numbers of temporary workers.
2. See which of the reasons listed sounds most accurate to students. Ask how many students in the class are employed part-time or as temporary workers. Question how many would like to be full-time. The issue of temporary or contingent workers is a major issue in today's workplace. You might inform them that the UPS strike that is covered in chapter 12 dealt primarily with the issue of hiring temporary workers.
3. This acetate notes that temporary workers can be used to combat the growing cost of fringe benefits in organizations. This problem is a growing concern of most organizations and is addressed in chapter 11.
4. In case they are not aware, students should understand the importance of reviewing fringe benefit packages that firms offer in their employment search. Students tend to focus on salary or per-hour wage as the primary evaluative criteria. The information in the earlier acetate should provide a good background as to why workers want to join certain organizations.

PROGRESS CHECK
(page 326 in text)

- ➤ What is human resource management?
- ➤ What are the six steps in human resource planning?
- ➤ What factors make it difficult to recruit qualified employees?
- ➤ What are the six steps in the selection process?

Lecture Outline

A. **TRAINING AND DEVELOPMENT** involves all attempts to improve performance by increasing an employee's ability to perform through learning.

1. Training is short-term skills oriented; development is long-term career oriented.

2. The process of creating training and development programs includes:

   a. **ASSESSING THE NEEDS** of the organization and the skills of the employees to determine training needs.

   b. **DESIGNING TRAINING ACTIVITIES** to meet the identified needs.

   c. **EVALUATING THE EFFECTIVENESS** of the training.

B. **TRAINING AND DEVELOPMENT ACTIVITIES.**

1. **EMPLOYEE ORIENTATION** programs range from formal programs to informal programs which acquaint the new employee with the organization and its policies and procedures.

2. **ON-THE-JOB TRAINING.**

   a. In an **ON-THE-JOB TRAINING PROGRAM,** employees immediately start their tasks. They learn by doing or watching others.

Lecture Notes

OT ACETATE 11-6
Do Employers Feel Workers Are "Ready" for Work?

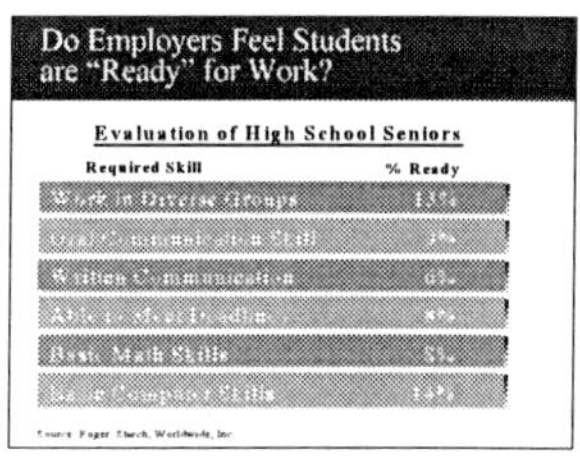

Comments:

1. Students should be very interested in the information on this acetate. As they can see, employers do not have a very high opinion of student's abilities coming out of high school.
2. See if students concur with the evaluation of employers about student's preparation. It's particularly important to emphasize the low marks employers attach to student abilities in written communication and basic math skills. Ask students if the information is accurate, who's fault is it that student work readiness is so poor?
3. This is a good time to pitch for student electives such as composition courses and basic oral communications. Some programs require such courses but some have them as electives. Students should be aware of the importance employers attach to such skills in the communication's age.

Lecture Outline

b. This type of training is **EASY AND EFFECTIVE** for learning low skill, repetitive jobs, **BUT CAN BE DISASTROUS** if used in areas demanding more knowledge and expertise.

3. **APPRENTICE PROGRAMS.**

   a. **APPRENTICESHIP PROGRAMS** involve a period of time when a learner works alongside a skilled worker to learn the skills and procedures of a craft.

   b. Many skilled crafts require a new worker to serve several years as an apprentice.

   c. There may be more but shorter apprenticeship programs in the future as jobs require more intense training.

4. **OFF-THE-JOB TRAINING** consists of internal and external programs to develop skills and to foster personal development that occurs away from the workplace (conferences, workshops, etc.)

5. **VESTIBULE TRAINING** takes place in schools where equipment is used which is similar to that used on the job (i.e. computer school.)

6. **JOB SIMULATION** is the use of equipment that duplicates the job conditions and tasks

Lecture Notes

so that an employee can learn without endangering himself or the company's expensive equipment (pilots, astronauts, etc.)

C. **MANAGEMENT DEVELOPMENT.**

1. **MANAGERS NEED SPECIAL TRAINING**—They must learn communication, planning, management, and human relation skills.

2. **MANAGEMENT DEVELOPMENT** is the process of training and educating employees to become good managers and then developing managerial skills over time.

3. **MANAGEMENT DEVELOPMENT PROGRAMS INCLUDE THE FOLLOWING:**

   a. **ON-THE-JOB COACHING** by a senior manager.

   b. **UNDERSTUDY POSITIONS** as assistants who participate in planning and other managerial functions.

   c. **JOB ROTATION** to expose managers to different functions of the organization.

   d. **OFF-THE-JOB COURSES AND TRAINING** expose managers to the latest concepts and create a sense of camaraderie.

D. **NETWORKING.**

Lecture Notes

LECTURE ENHANCER 11-6
Mimic Your Way Upward

The real power in groups is not the person with the biggest title, but the person being mimicked. (See complete lecture enhancer on page 11.66.)

Lecture Outline

1. **NETWORKING** is the process of establishing and maintaining contacts with key managers in one's own organization and in other organizations and using those contacts to weave strong relationships that serve as informal development systems.

2. **MENTORS** are corporate managers who supervise, coach, and guide selected lower-level employees by introducing them to the right people and just acting as their organizational sponsors.

E. **DIVERSITY IN MANAGEMENT DEVELOPMENT.**

1. Since most older managers are male, women often have more difficulty finding mentors and entering the network.

2. "Men only" clubs were declared illegal, allowing women access to areas where contacts are made.

3. African-American managers also are learning the benefits of networking.

4. Principles to develop female and minority managers:

   a. Grooming women and minorities for management positions is the key to long-term profitability.

Lecture Notes

b. The best women and minorities will become harder to attract and retain.

c. More women and minorities means that businesses can serve female and minority customers better.

VI. APPRAISING EMPLOYEE PERFORMANCE TO GET OPTIMUM RESULTS.

▶ **LEARNING GOAL 6.** Trace the six steps in appraising employee performance.

A. A **PERFORMANCE APPRAISAL** is an evaluation of the performance level of employees against established standards to make decisions about promotions, compensation, additional training, or firing.

B. The six **STEPS OF PERFORMANCE APPRAISALS ARE:**

1. **ESTABLISH PERFORMANCE STANDARDS.**
2. **COMMUNICATE THOSE STANDARDS.**
3. **EVALUATE PERFORMANCE.**
4. **DISCUSS RESULTS WITH EMPLOYEES.**
5. **TAKE CORRECTIVE ACTION.**
6. **USE THE RESULTS TO MAKE DECISIONS.**

C. The latest form of performance appraisal is the **360 REVIEW** because it uses feedback from all

Lecture Notes

OT ACETATE 11-8
Major Uses of Performance Appraisals

Major Uses of Performance Appraisals

- To identify training needs.
- To use as a promotion tool.
- To recognize workers' achievements.
- To evaluate the hiring process.
- To judge the effectiveness of the orientation process.
- To use as a basis for terminating workers.

Comments:

1. Appraising employee performance is one of the least preferred tasks of managers. The class may have a difficult time associating with this assessment since it's doubtful many of them have encountered such responsibility in their previous employment. You might want to refer to your own difficulty in appraising performance of students. They don't realize it's often very difficult for professors to accurately measure what students know. This acetate carefully lists the major uses of performance appraisals from a managerial perspective. Students familiar with performance appraisals often feel they are primarily used for discipline.
2. If you take this discussion a bit deeper, you might want to get into some of the problems associated with managers' performance appraisals, such as:
   a. **Halo Effects** - this happens if the evaluator assigns a basic rating to an employee on the basis of their overall impression of the person being rated. They lose objectivity in terms of what they should exactly be appraising.
   b. **Leniency or Harshness** - evaluators are often either too lenient or too harsh in their evaluation of employees. This can lead to employee confusion and rather strange employee performance histories.
   c. **Central Tendency** - in this situation, evaluators avoid high or low ratings. Instead they rate everyone as being about average. This can lead highly motivated performers to cut back on their efforts.
   d. **Recency** - often evaluators lose focus on the period being evaluated. For example, in a semi-annual evaluation, they may only consider the employee's performance over the past two weeks. This time span would not be a fair or accurate measurement of performance.
3. If you follow the techniques listed, students should have no difficulty understanding how both manager and employee can benefit from the performance appraisal process.

CRITICAL THINKING EXERCISE 11-1
Appraise Your Own Performance

See complete exercise on page 11.77.

TRANSPARENCY MASTER 82
Making Appraisals and Reviews More Effective
(Figure 11.4 on text page 330)

(Transparency Masters begin on page 11.90.)

directions in the organization: up, down, and all around.

VII. COMPENSATING EMPLOYEES: ATTRACTING AND KEEPING THE BEST.

▶ **LEARNING GOAL 7.** Summarize the objectives of employee compensation programs and describe various pay systems and fringe benefits.

A. Compensation is one of the main marketing tools used to attract qualified employees.

1. The long-term success of a firm may depend on how well it can control employee costs.

2. The primary cost of service operations is the cost of labor.

3. Manufacturing firms have asked employees to take reductions in wages to make the firm more competitive.

4. Compensation and benefit packages are begin given special attention.

B. The **OBJECTIVES** of compensation and benefit programs include:

1. **ATTRACTING QUALIFIED WORKERS.**

2. **PROVIDING PRODUCTIVITY INCENTIVES.**

3. **KEEPING VALUED EMPLOYEES.**

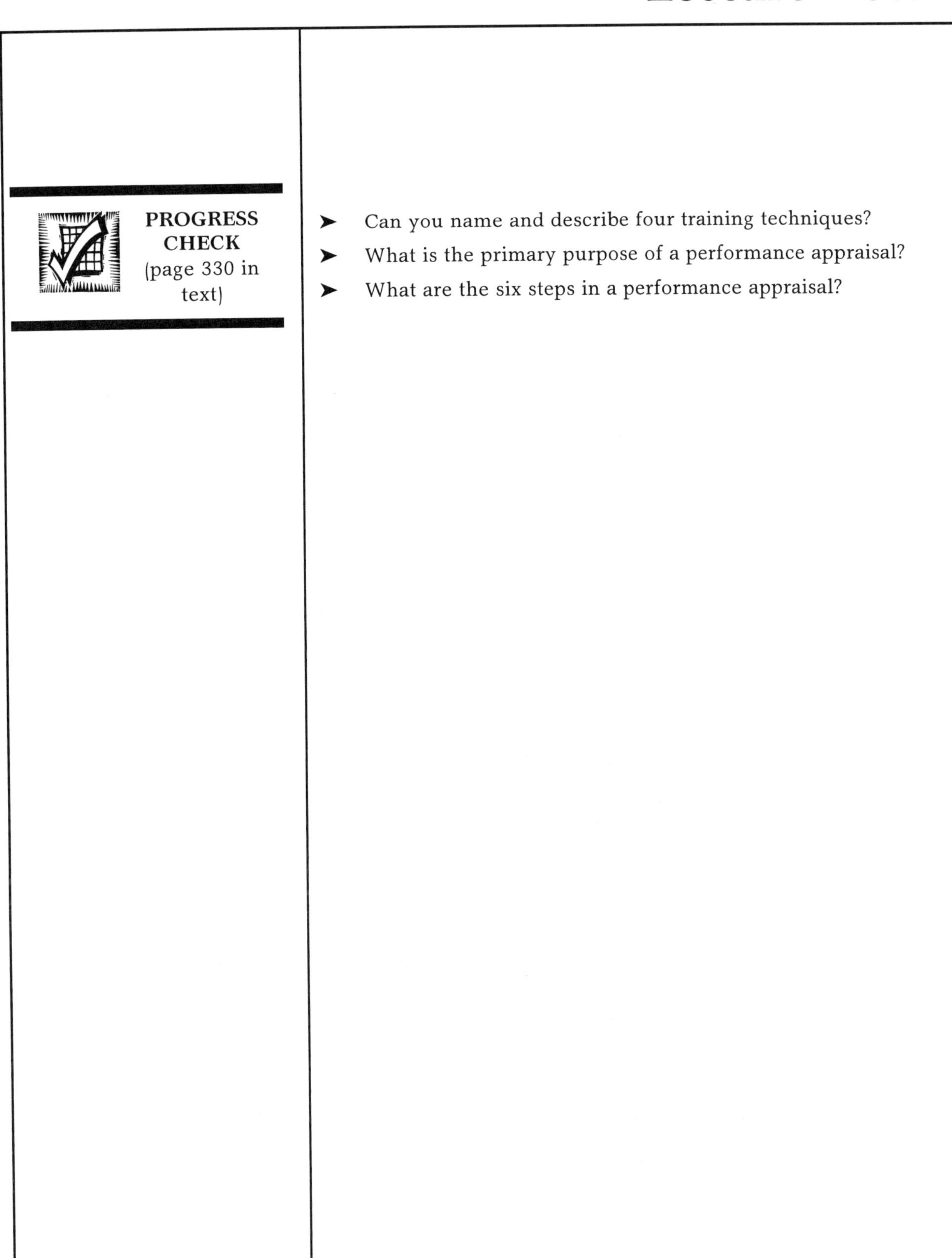

PROGRESS CHECK
(page 330 in text)

- Can you name and describe four training techniques?
- What is the primary purpose of a performance appraisal?
- What are the six steps in a performance appraisal?

Lecture Outline

4. **MAINTAINING A COMPETITIVE EDGE** by increasing productivity.

5. **PROTECTING EMPLOYEES FROM LAYOFFS, ETC.**

C. **PAY SYSTEMS.**

1. Pay systems include:
    a. **SALARY SYSTEMS** are fixed compensation programs (managers.)
    b. **HOURLY WAGE** or **DAYWORK** (blue-collar and clerical workers.)
    c. **PIECEWORK** means that employees are paid according to the number of items they produce (manufacturing.)
    d. **COMMISSION** (salespeople.)
    e. **BONUS PLANS** are earned for accomplishing or surpassing certain objectives (executives, salespeople.)
    f. **PROFIT-SHARING** give employees some share of profits over their normal pay.
2. Many companies use the **HAY SYSTEM,** based on job tiers each of which has a strict pay range.
3. Another system begins with base pay and gives all employees the same percent merit raise.

Lecture Notes

LECTURE ENHANCER 11-7
Teamwork Calls for Team Compensation

In many companies the movement toward cross-functional teams has proceeded much faster than the systems needed to support the change. (See complete lecture enhancer on page 11.67.)

CRITICAL THINKING EXERCISE 11-2
Expanding the Workforce

See complete exercise on page 11.78.

Lecture Outline

D. **COMPENSATING TEAMS.**

1. Compensating teams is a complex issue.
2. Some studies have shown that team-based pay programs may not be effective.
3. **SKILL-BASED PAY** is related to the growth of both the individual and the team.
    a. Base pay is raised when team members learn and apply new skills.
    b. The skill-based pay system is complex, and it is difficult to correlate skill acquisition to bottom-line gains.
4. In **GAIN-SHARING SYSTEMS,** bonuses are based on improvements over a performance baseline.
5. It is important to reward individual team players, also.

E. **FRINGE BENEFITS.**

1. **FRINGE BENEFITS** include vacation pay, pensions plans, and health plans that provide additional compensation to employees.
    a. In recent years benefit programs grew faster than wages.
    b. Many employees want more fringe benefits instead of more salary to avoid higher taxes.

OT ACETATE 11-10
Unusual Benefits Offered to Workers

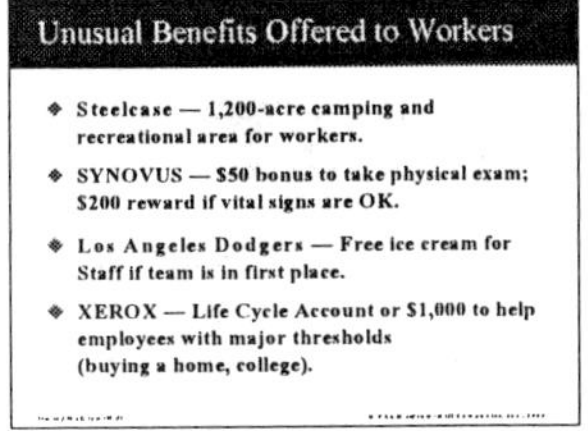

Comments:

1. Students should like this acetate for its uniqueness however, it does enforce an important point nonetheless. Company benefits vary considerably company by company. These are some rather interesting examples.
2. In case you might want to relate a few more unique benefit offerings:
   a. Fannie Mae offers workers ten paid hours a month for volunteer work
   b. J.P. Morgan gives a free lunch every day for all employees at 60 Wall Street.
   c. Moog Industries offers 35 extra vacation days on the tenth year of service and every five years thereafter.
   d. Deloitte & Touche gives bonuses of $1,500 to $10,000 to employees that recommend new hires.
   e. Xerox has a life cycle account of $10,000 to help employees cross major thresholds such as buying a first house or financing college tuition.
3. Benefits are a key part of the compensation package and companies seem to be getting more and more creative. Ask the class if they know of any unique type of benefit plan available through a particular employer.

OT ACETATE 11-9
Employers Offering Family-Friendly Benefits

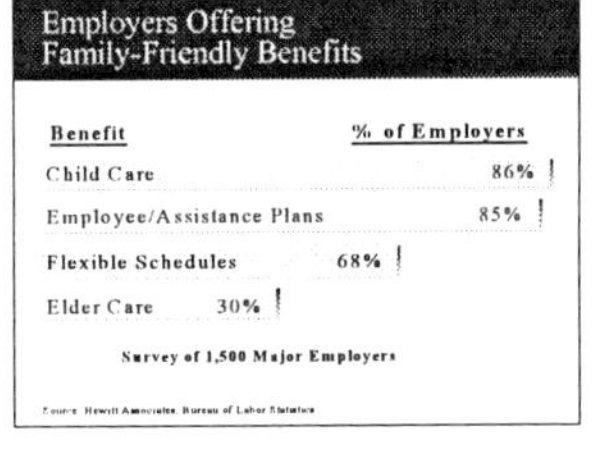

Comments:

1. Employees are concerned more than ever with balancing a successful career with the responsibilities of family life. Companies have made concerted efforts to change the workplace and make it more family-friendly. However, many critics contend that changing the attitudes of managers is a far more difficult task. This acetate identifies family-friendly benefits offered by employers and the percentage of employers offering such assistance.
2. Pressures of balancing work and family has accelerated during the 1990s. Some statistics that reinforce this fact are:
   a. In 1996 62% of married couples were dual earners. The number was 44% in 1967.
   b. In 1996, 65% of mothers with children under 6 were in the labor force. The number was 39% in 1975
   c. In 1997, 86% of new mothers returned to the workforce within 6 months of giving birth.
   d. In 1991 only 66% of employers offered any form of child-care benefit. In 1997 the number was 86%
   e. In 1991 53% of employers offered flexible scheduling; in 1997 the number grew to 68%
3. With these numbers it's obvious the issue of balancing work and family will not go away. Business must respond and as the acetate shows employers are making progress.

Lecture Outline

2. Fringe benefits can include everything from paid vacations to child care programs, use of the company condo, and more.

3. Some companies offer **CAFETERIA-STYLE FRINGE BENEFITS** from which employees can choose the benefits they want based on their personal needs.

4. Because of the cost of administering benefit programs, many companies are contracting with outside companies (**OUTSOURCING**) to run their benefit plans.

VIII. SCHEDULING EMPLOYEES.

▶ **LEARNING GOAL 8.** Explain scheduling plans managers use to adjust to workers' needs.

A. Managers and workers are demanding more flexibility and responsiveness from their jobs.

B. **FLEXTIME PLANS** allow employees some freedom in choosing their own hours.

1. Most flextime plans include a period known as **CORE TIME** in which all employees are expected to be at work.

2. There are disadvantages, as well.

   a. It does not work in assembly-line processes or for shift work.

   b. Managers often have to work longer days in order to supervise employees.

Lecture Notes

LECTURE ENHANCER 11-8
Changing Family Issues: Caring for a Dependent Adult

One company found that nearly one in five of its workers said they had adult relatives who depended on them for care. (See complete lecture enhancer on page 11.69.)

OT ACETATE 11-11
Percentage of Employers That Grant Family Leave

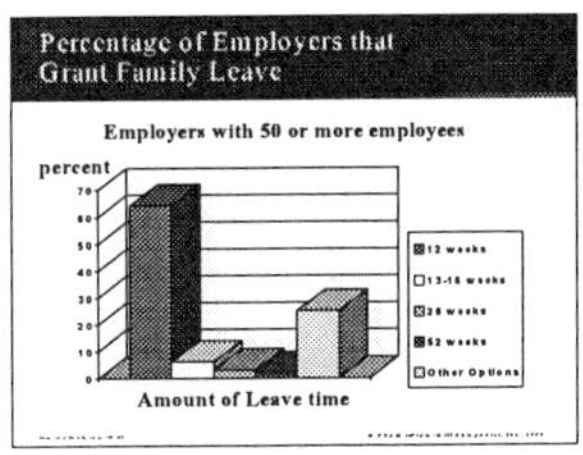

Comments:

1. Federal law requires that workers get 12 weeks unpaid leave for birth, adoption, and serious illness of the worker or their child, spouse, or parent. This acetate gives the percentages of employers that provide different levels of family leave.
2. As the acetate notes, the information covers firms with 50 or more employees. Congress has considered legislation to expand family leave benefits but to date no expansion has been passed. It is interesting to note to students that many European countries have **paid** family leave benefits for employees that can extend up to 2 years.

TRANSPARENCY MASTER 83
A Flextime Chart
(Figure 11.5 on text page 334)

(Transparency Masters begin on page 11.88.)

LECTURE ENHANCER 11-9
Irregular Hours and Worker Health

One in five working Americans works other than daytime hours. These workers are more likely to suffer from digestive disorders, heart disease, and emotional problems. (See complete lecture enhancer on page 11.70.)

Lecture Outline

c. Flextime makes communication more difficult.

d. Some employees could abuse the system.

C. **COMPRESSED WORKWEEKS** allow employees to concentrate their work hours in a fewer number of days rather than working five days a week.

1. There are advantages for employees in working only four days.

2. But some employees get tired working such long hours, and productivity could decline.

D. **HOME-BASED AND OTHER MOBILE WORK**.

1. Nearly nine million U.S. workers work at home.

2. To be successful, a home-based worker must have the discipline to stay focused on the work.

3. Telecommuting can be a cost saver for employers.

E. **JOB SHARING PLANS** are plans that allow two employees to share the same job.

1. Job sharing lets parents work part-time while their children are in school.

2. **BENEFITS INCLUDE:**

Lecture Notes

OT ACETATE 11-12
Job-Oriented Motivational Techniques

Job-Oriented Motivational Techniques

- Job Enrichment & Redesign
- Telecommuting
- Flextime
- Compressed Workweeks
- Work and Job Sharing

Comments:

1. Students should recall the discussion of job enrichment and telecommuting from previous chapters. If you think they need a quick refresher, its helps to offer it. Chapter 11 covers specific scheduling techniques that are often motivators to workers. The most familiar of these is flextime or compressed workweeks. Ask students if any of them work in jobs that offer these options. We have had many firefighters over the years. Many of them said they like the job because of the compressed work schedules that are offered.
2. Ask students which of these techniques would be the most attractive to them. Also question if certain jobs (such as police, or some production lines) by nature cannot use these techniques. Lots of options available here.
3. Company reasons for establishing flexible work plans is discussed in the next acetate.

OT ACETATE 11-13
Company's Reasons for Establishing Flexible Work Plans

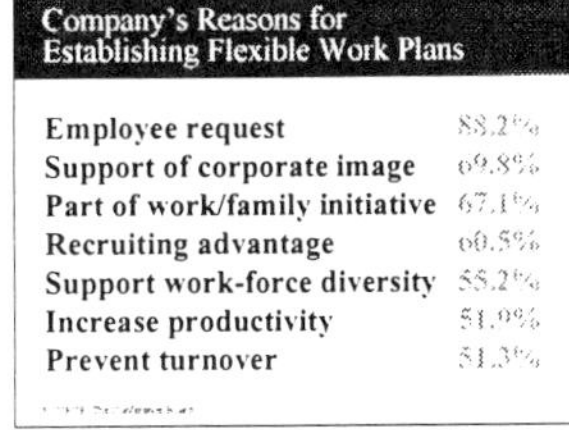

Comments:

1. This acetate lists the primary reasons why companies establish flexible work systems.
2. It's interesting to get student perspectives about such plans as flextime and compressed workweeks. Some students may have experience working in such systems. Once again, It might be helpful for them to relate what they consider to be the pro's and con's of such systems.
3. Flexible work plans have taken on a new direction with the growth of home-based businesses and flex-place options. Flex-place options allow workers to come into the office or stay at home to accomplish specific job requirements. If your campus is involved in distance learning programs, this will fit in nicely with the information in the acetate. Check and see if students think flexible work situations will grow or diminish in the future work environment. Odds are they will grow.

CRITICAL THINKING
(page 335 in text)

What effects have dual-career families had on the human resource function? What problems can arise when family members work together in the same firm? What is your reaction to employees who date one another?

a. Employment opportunities for those who cannot or prefer not to work full-time.

b. A high level of enthusiasm and productivity.

c. Reduced absenteeism and tardiness.

d. Ability to schedule people into peak demand periods.

3. Disadvantages: having to hire, train, motivate, and supervise twice as many people.

4. Most firms have found the benefits outweigh the disadvantages.

IX. MOVING EMPLOYEES UP, OVER, AND OUT.

▶ **LEARNING GOAL 9.** Describe the ways employees can move through a company: promotion, reassignment, termination, and retirement.

A. Employees don't always stay in the position they were initially hired to fill.

B. **PROMOTING AND REASSIGNING EMPLOYEES.**

1. Promotions are **COST-EFFECTIVE** ways to improve **EMPLOYEE MORALE.**

2. Due to the prevalence of flatter corporate structures, it is more common today for workers to transfer over to a new position than to move up to one.

Lecture Notes

PROGRESS CHECK (page 335 in text)

- Can you name and describe five alternative compensation techniques?
- What advantages do compensation plans such as profit sharing offer an organization?

LECTURE ENHANCER 11-10
Caught in the Crossfire: Managing Family Firms

One of the most complex groups to manage is the family firm, with its formal-informal group interrelationships. (See complete lecture enhancer on page 11.71.)

SUPPLEMENTAL CASE 11-2
The Dangers of Firing Employees

See complete case on page 11.85.

LECTURE ENHANCER 11-11
Using the Exit Interview as Control

Feedback on problems is the only way to prevent them from reoccurring. One often-overlooked way of getting this feedback from employees is through the exit interview. (See complete lecture enhancer on page 11.73.)

Lecture Outline

C. **TERMINATING EMPLOYEES.**

1. Downsizing and restructuring, increasing customer demands for greater value, and the relentless pressure of global competition and shifts in technology have human resource managers struggling to manage layoffs and firings.

2. The **COST OF TERMINATING** employees is so high that managers choose to use **TEMPORARY EMPLOYEES** or **OUTSOURCE** certain functions.

3. **"EMPLOYMENT AT WILL."**

   a. **"EMPLOYMENT AT WILL"** meant that managers had as much freedom to fire workers as workers had to leave voluntarily.

   b. Most states now have written employment laws that limit the **"AT WILL" DOCTRINE** to protect employees from wrongful firing.

D. **RETIRING EMPLOYEES.**

1. Another tool used to downsize companies is to offer early retirement benefits to entice older workers to resign.

2. The advantage of offering early retirement benefits rather than laying off employees is

TRANSPARENCY MASTER 84
How to Avoid Wrongful Discharge Lawsuits *(Figure 11.6 on text page 337)*

TM 84

(Transparency Masters begin on page 11.90.)

that early retirement offers **INCREASE THE MORALE OF THE SURVIVING EMPLOYEES.**

3. Retiring senior workers increases **PROMOTION OPPORTUNITIES** for younger employees.

X. LAWS AFFECTING HUMAN RESOURCE MANAGEMENT.

▶ **LEARNING GOAL 10.** Illustrate the effects of legislation on human resource management.

A. Legislation has made hiring, promoting, firing, and managing employee relations complex and subject to legal complications.

B. One of the most important laws ever passed by Congress was the **CIVIL RIGHTS ACT OF 1964.**

1. **TITLE VII** of the act prohibits discrimination in hiring, firing, compensation, apprenticeships, training, terms, conditions, or privileges of employment based on race, religion, creed, sex, or national origin (age was added later.)

2. Specific language in the law often made its enforcement difficult.

C. The **EQUAL EMPLOYMENT OPPORTUNITY ACT (EEOA)** was added as an amendment to Title VII in 1972.

Lecture Notes

OT ACETATE 11-14 and **OT ACETATE 11-15**
What Do You Know About Equal Employment Opportunity Law?

What Do You Know About Equal Employment Opportunity Laws?
Decide if the following statements are true or false
It's okay to ask any applicant whether he or she has an automobile.
It's appropriate to ask applicants to attach photographs to their applications.
During interviews, it's appropriate to ask an applicant his or her age.
It's appropriate to ask if an applicant is a naturalized U.S. citizen.
It's not appropriate to ask an applicant about past work experience.

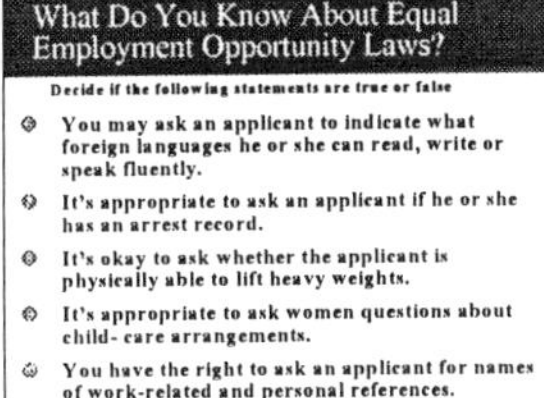

Comments:

1. The importance of understanding Equal Employment Law is emphasized in this acetate.
2. Students often have a variety of opinions related to these questions. It leads to spirited discussion as to the benefits/shortcomings of equal employment law.
3. The short quiz highlights some of the particulars involved in Equal Employment Law most people never consider. The answers to the questions are as follows:
    1. FALSE. This is irrelevant unless the job requires working in one's car.
    2. FALSE. This is considered inappropriate to protect applicants from possible recruiter bias.
    3. TRUE. This would be a violation of the Age Discrimination in Employment Act of 1967.
    4. FALSE. This is considered non-essential in measuring potential job performance and could lead to possible recruiter bias.
    5. FALSE. You can and should ask about an applicant's past work experience.
    6. TRUE. You can ask this question if language fluency is required in the job only.
    7. TRUE. You should not inquire about arrests since they do not imply convictions or guilt.
    8. TRUE. This can be asked only if the job requires such lifting.
    9. TRUE. This question can only be asked if it is asked of all applicants.
    10. TRUE. You can ask for the information but cannot ask any questions from the references that could be construed as discriminatory.

Lecture Outline

1. It established the EEOC which issues guidelines for administering equal employment opportunity.

2. Congress gave the EEOC broad powers, making it a formidable regulatory force.

D. **AFFIRMATIVE ACTION.**

1. **AFFIRMATIVE ACTION** are activities designed to increase opportunities for minorities and women.

2. The EEOC enforces affirmative action, which is designed to "right past wrongs" made against women and minorities.

3. This has led to problems including **REVERSE DISCRIMINATION,** the feeling of unfairness unprotected groups have when protected groups are given preference.

E. The **CIVIL RIGHTS ACT OF 1991** expanded the remedies available to victims of discrimination by amending Title VII of the CRA of 1964.

F. **LAWS PROTECTING THE DISABLED AND OLDER EMPLOYEES.**

1. The **VOCATIONAL REHABILITATION ACT** (1973).

   a. The Act extended the same protection given to minorities and women to people with disabilities.

LECTURE ENHANCER 11-12
Dismantling the Glass Ceiling

Two decades of equal-opportunity initiatives have succeeded in drawing women into the work force and getting them moving up the career ladder. But across a range of industries, the top rungs remain as frustratingly out of reach as ever. (See complete lecture enhancer on page 11.74.)

LEGAL BRIEFCASE

(Box in text, page 338)

"Government Legislation"

b. Businesses cannot discriminate against people with disabilities on the basis of their physical or mental handicap.

2. The **AMERICANS WITH DISABILITIES ACT OF 1990 (ADA)** requires that disabled applicants be given the same consideration for employment as people without disabilities.

   a. It requires that businesses make "reasonable accommodations" to people with disabilities.

   b. Most companies are having more trouble making cultural changes than structural changes to be accommodating.

3. In 1997, the EEOC issues new guidelines for the ADA that tell employers how they are to treat workers and applicants with mental disabilities.

4. The **AGE DISCRIMINATION IN EMPLOYMENT ACT** protects older employees (40-69.)

   a. It outlawed mandatory retirement before age 70.

   b. Many companies are voluntarily phasing out mandatory retirement after age 70.

G. **EFFECTS OF LEGISLATION.**

Lecture Notes

1. Legislation affects all areas of human resource management.

2. **IN SUMMARY:**

   a. Employers must be sensitive to the legal rights of their employees.

   b. Legislation affects all areas of human resource management.

   c. It is sometimes legal to go beyond providing equal rights for minorities and women to provide special employment to correct discrimination in the past.

   d. New court cases and legislation continuously change human resource management; it is important to keep current.

XI. SUMMARY AND REVIEW.

Lecture Notes

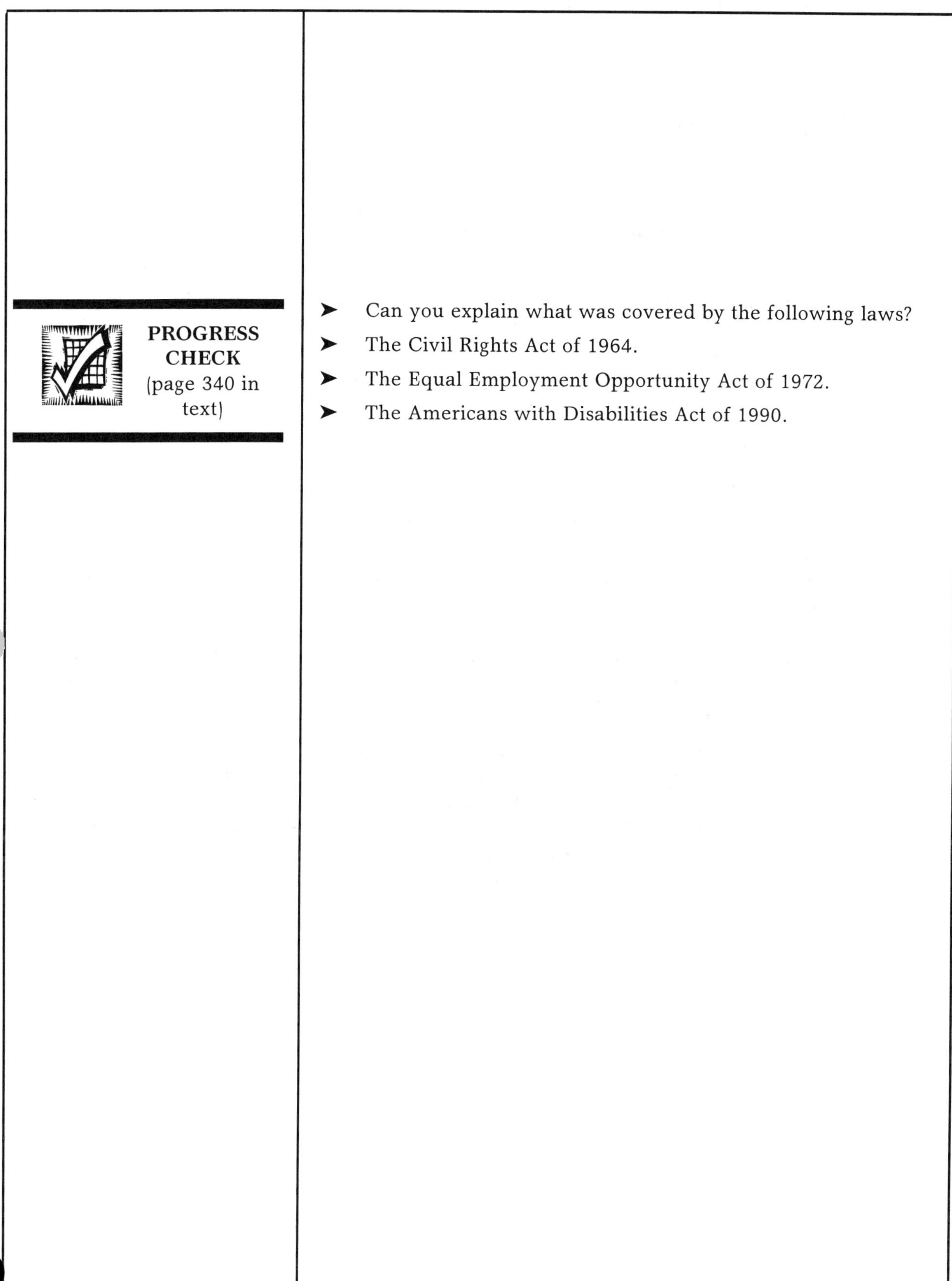

PROGRESS CHECK (page 340 in text)

- Can you explain what was covered by the following laws?
- The Civil Rights Act of 1964.
- The Equal Employment Opportunity Act of 1972.
- The Americans with Disabilities Act of 1990.

Answers to Practicing Management Decisions

CASE ONE

DUAL-CAREER PLANNING

1. *What are some of the issues you can see developing because of dual-career families? How is this affecting children in such families?*

Issues include the problem of relocation, in that one spouse may receive a promotion calling for a move, leaving the other behind or needing to find a new job in a new location. Other issues include the allocation of home chores, child care, increased affluence, and vacation schedules. Children are affected by not having a parent at home after school (latch key children), by not spending as much time with parents, and by the increase affluence. (Students know as much about this as anyone, so their input is invaluable here).

2. *What kind of corporate policies need changing to adapt to these new realities?*

There is a need for more part-time jobs for spouses who desire to work less than a full day, more flextime schedules, more daycare programs, more flexible leave time for illness and other emergencies, more flexible vacation schedules, and less frequent location changes.

3. *What can newlywed couples do to minimize the problems of dual careers? What are the advantages of dual careers? Disadvantages? How can a couple achieve the advantages with a minimum number of problems?*

Couples need to sit down and plan their careers as a team. That may mean postponing having children for a while. It may also mean deciding ahead of time what is to be done if one or the other is asked to move. Household chores need to be divided, and each partner must be clear about who is going to do what, when, and how often. Such things are best put in writing to minimize conflicts later. Most of all, dual careers call for constant open communication, flexibility, and regard for the other.

CASE TWO

VIDEO CASE: WORKPLACE TRENDS

1. *What are the advantages and disadvantages of companies offering creative perks and special programs to workers in the workplace?*

The advantages are employee morale, less turnover, more productivity, and more references from employees for other workers. The disadvantages include the costs involved, the time involved, and the jealously of workers who don't qualify or can't use the programs for some reason.

2. *Do you think the number and variety of perks will continue to grow or do you think this is just a management fad that will fade in the future?*

The number of perks will likely grow as firms compete with each other for employees. This is especially true in high-tech areas where supply is low and demand high for workers.

3. *What other perks might companies consider to lower stress levels and increase employee productivity?*

Other perks might include time sharing, flexible work weeks, time off for rest and relaxation (sabbatical), exercise rooms and classes, stress seminars, massages, and more. Lots more. Let your students brainstorm this answer.

Lecture Enhancers

LECTURE ENHANCER 11-1

WANTED: A GLOBAL BOSS

Any time there's a big international merger, there are inevitable worries about "culture clash." When Marjorie Scardino, a tall, wisecracking Texan, was named to head Britain's blue-blooded Pearson publishing firm in November 1996, the company's stock plunged for a day in London. In 1997 Ford Motor named Henry Wallace, a Scottish executive, to take over its Mazda unit. As the first *gaijin* in memory to head a major Japanese company, he faced a nation of skeptics. "Ford sends people who don't speak Japanese at all," grumbled one business leader in Hiroshima, Mazda's hometown.

But Wallace's bad Japanese—he gets tutoring once a week—hardly matters these days. Nor does Scardino's Texarkana drawl grate much on British ears. With surprising speed, the big multinationals—and many small ones—have come to speak the same language and inhabit a common culture. The global environment has bred a new kind of executive, the global boss, who is breaking down cultural barriers.

How does one qualify as a topnotch global boss? First, learn their language. Global managers speak a combination of straight-shooting American pragmatism, Japanese-inspired management ideas (like *kaizen*, or continuous improvement), and M.B.A. jargon ("strategic resource allocation.") They're tough, smart, and flexible enough to survive in the global economy.

Another must: "benchmarking." This buzzword means measuring your company against the best practices of other companies worldwide. Smart global bosses personally benchmark themselves against world executives like the late Coca-Cola's Roberto Goizueta and GE's Jack Welch—two of the world's most successful multinational managers.

Big companies must go global to be near the billions of new consumers and to find the best deal worldwide on wages, taxes, and local talent. That takes a savvy global boss. Paul Ray Jr., a New York headhunter, describes a search he did for a semiconductor company. "They were looking for someone [who understands why] the chips were designed in India, water-etched in Japan, diced and mounted in Korea, assembled in Thailand, encapsulated in Singapore, and distributed" everywhere, he says. "About one in a million fits that description."

Indeed, there aren't enough global bosses to go around—even if many companies haven't yet figured out that they need them. (Few large U.S. companies, for instance, have foreigners on their boards.) The coming of the global boss is less a revolution than culture creep. Why, for example, don't we hear much about the Japanese way of doing business, as we did in the '80s? Mostly because everyone has adopted it. Today American execs chant "TQM" in their sleep and the Japanese idolize Bill Gates.

For global bosses, even time zones are a competitive edge. George Everhart, the American president of Fujitsu PC in Milpitas, California, tells how his team worked nonstop for months to develop software for Fujitsu's brand-new Lifebook notebook computers, the kind of cutting-edge product that just has to beat the competition to market. "When the work had been done in Japan, they would ship it here in the morning, our time. We did validation testing, wrote it up, and shipped the results back to them in the evening."

That sense of cross-border trust is a big step for a Japanese firm, says Everhart. So was Fujitsu's decision to put him, a former Apple exec, in charge. His Tokyo bosses, he says, "no longer think in terms of local control of worldwide enterprise." Like global bosses everywhere, they can't afford to.

LECTURE ENHANCER 11-2

THE CLERICAL EVOLUTION

We think of the clerical field as being dominated by women, but in its early years the reverse was true. A century ago offices were off-limits to women; stenographers and secretaries were always men. Some famous former secretaries: Mark Twain, Lyndon Johnson, and Carl Sandburg.

Changes began about 1870 when there were more office jobs than men to fill them. By 1900 a quarter of all clerical workers in the United States were women. During the first world war, the percentage rose as thousands of male office workers left to fight the war and women took over their jobs.

Women encountered strong opposition from their male co-workers, who felt that they were losing their jobs to women who would accept much lower salaries and worse working conditions. One 1909 survey found that only about half of the offices surveyed had separate restrooms for men and women.

Men's working conditions weren't much better. As secretary to the novelist Sinclair Lewis, writer John Hersey took dictation, chauffeured his boss around, and bought him chocolates. Novelist John O'Hara worked as a secretary for columnist Heywood Broun in 1930 for $35 a week. He did, however, receive free lunch at Broun's penthouse apartment.

LECTURE ENHANCER 11-3

HIRING METHODS EMPLOYERS USE MOST

A study of 2,300 human resource specialists conducted showed that employers use a number of methods to hire employees. The most frequently used methods are listed.

METHOD	PERCENT WHO USE THE METHOD
"Walk-ins"	99%
Resumes	98%
Recruitment advertising	91%
Employee referrals	56%
Private contingency employment agencies	24%
Public employment agencies	18%
Search firms on retainer	5%
Computer database recruiting services	3%
Job fairs	1%
Direct mail	1%

LECTURE ENHANCER 11-4

MEMORABLE JOB INTERVIEWS

The world's largest temporary personnel service for accounting, bookkeeping, and information systems, Accountemps, recently conducted a nationwide survey of executives about the most unusual job interview they ever conducted. Some of the results:

- "Apologized for being late, said he accidently locked his clothes in his closet."
- "Applicant walked in and inquired why he was here."
- "Shortly after sitting down, she brought out a line of cosmetics and started a strong sales pitch."
- "Man brought in his five children and cat."
- "Said if I hired him, I'd soon learn to regret it."
- "Arrived with a snake around her neck. Said she took her pet everywhere."
- "When asked about loyalty, showed a tattoo of his girlfriend's name."

LECTURE ENHANCER 11-5

TESTING AND DIVERSITY

The vast majority of American companies use some form of employment testing, whether through interviews or more formal methods, as a tool for guiding their hiring decisions. But the growing ethnic diversity of the U.S. work force, and the corresponding need to eliminate the potential for discrimination in hiring, have put the efficacy of some of those tests in doubt.

On many widely used tests of verbal aptitude, intelligence, and psychological fitness, some minority groups consistently score at a level lower than the norm because certain concepts translate badly to their language or culture. The discrepancies have sparked controversy over whether the tests are fair, and employers and test designers have scrambled to find solutions.

Increasingly, the designers of tests are "norming" them, or subjecting them to a statistical overhaul designed to insure that they measure skills fairly across cultural boundaries. Human-resource executives seeking to insure fair testing practices now contact their test suppliers to make sure their tests are normed. In addition, some tests that have posed problems for minorities are now available in alternate versions that reduce score differences resulting from cultural factors.

You can circumvent test troubles in your workplace by modifying or tailoring the testing involved in your hiring. Before seeking candidates for an open job, analyze the position to determine exactly what skills it demands and what kind of tests best apply to it. Generally speaking, the more job-specific the test, the more likely it will fairly rate a potential employee's abilities, regardless of his or her ethnic background.

Common sense can help eliminate some anxieties about diversity. Fairness and productivity need to be balanced. Hiring a woman with only rudimentary English to run your customer service department would tip the scales too far. But giving her a fair shot at the jobs she can perform is the just course to follow.

LECTURE ENHANCER 11-6

MIMIC YOUR WAY UPWARD

A meeting at Microsoft Corporation: Cofounder and CEO Bill Gates is talking with top executives. As he talks, he starts rocking back and forth in his chair. Seated around him, several of his managers are soon rocking and bobbing. Gates pushes his glasses up on his nose from time to time; his associates push their glasses up.

This hypothetical meeting demonstrates what psychologists call "modeling," "mirroring," or "patterning." Subordinates show an unerring tendency to copy their boss's mannerisms, dress, and sometimes even choice of cars. It's an acceptable mode of behavior up to a point. In fact it may be a compliment. The real power in groups is not the person with the biggest title, but the person being mimicked.

When an employee believes he can evoke interest from a boss, he or she will fly on the same airline, order the same salad at lunch, or wear the same kind of cuff links. The danger of such behavior comes when it becomes overdone or steps on the boss's ego. One young assistant wore a plaid suit to please his boss, who always wore plaid. The boss promptly ordered him home to change clothes. The subordinate had diluted the boss's uniqueness.

Mimicking can lead to career advancement by showing that the individual "fits" in the organizational culture. This benefit may not be available to all, however. Minorities and foreigners often find it puzzling to decipher the nonverbal traits of a boss of a different culture or sex. That reluctance to mirror the boss may play at least a small role when minorities and foreigners are overlooked for top jobs. They are viewed as not "marching to the same drummer."

LECTURE ENHANCER 11-7

TEAMWORK CALLS FOR TEAM COMPENSATION

In many companies the movement toward cross-functional teams has proceeded much faster than the systems needed to support the change. Technological and training systems are keeping up, but the performance appraisal and compensation systems in many cases are lagging. A recent study of 4,500 teams in more than 500 organizations found that 80 percent of the firms still based compensation solely on individual performance. The ultimate goal, however, is to reward individuals based on group performance. A separate study of *Fortune* 1000 firms found that the number of such plans was quite small, but since most teams had only been in operation for a short time (three years or less) most believe this circumstance will change. Guidelines currently being used to design team incentive systems include:

1. **Formulate team awards that reinforce the cross-functional team concept.** The belief among team members should be that none of them can win unless they all win. In a major New York bank, for example, measurable goals were established for product sales, customer service, and profitability. All personnel are included on cross-functional teams to reach those goals. No one wins in terms of bonuses unless all three objectives are achieved. Initial results have exceeded management's highest expectations.

2. **Any individual rewards must reinforce the cross-functional team concept.** The compensation system must be designed from scratch to reward team efforts, not reconfigured from a functional base due to the likelihood that team members will tend to be more loyal to their function than the team if the function controls the funds

3. **Bring the rewards down to the team level.** Gainsharing and profit-sharing plans are too far removed from the team to offer true incentives for teamwork. There should always be a clear, direct connection between team success and team rewards.

4. **Reward individual team players also.** Outstanding team players-those that go beyond what is required and make an outstanding individual contribution to the firm-should be separately recognized for their additional contribution. Some firms use knowledge-based pay to reward individuals. At Johnsonville Foods in Sheboygan Falls, Wisconsin, for example, employees are paid the market value of their jobs. When they master a series of skills, they receive a raise. Bonuses are also given those who exceed quality and efficiency standards or teach teammates something new

5. **Use noncash as well as cash rewards.** Team members are often motivated by such things as free vacation trips, briefcases, home computers, or some other noncash reward.

6. **Use informal methods of reward until the team compensation plan is in place.** Teams can be mentioned in company newsletters or bulletin boards. Verbal recognition can be given at staff meetings. Teams can be sent to baseball games or similar events, or given team-building symbols such as shirts, coffee mugs, and other gifts with the team name and goals on them.

Measuring and rewarding individual performance on teams while at the same time rewarding team performance can be tricky. Nonetheless, it can be done. Football players are rewarded as a team when the team goes to the play-offs and Super Bowl, but they are paid individually as well. Companies are now experimenting with and developing similar incentive programs.

LECTURE ENHANCER 11-8

CHANGING FAMILY ISSUES: CARING FOR A DEPENDENT ADULT

As the Baby Boom generation approaches mid-century, their parents' generation are retiring. And more and more U.S. workers are finding themselves responsible for caring for an adult relative.

The typical worker who provides care to an adult relative is about 40, married, and has children at home. The worker spends about nine hours a week making phone calls, paying bills, and shopping for a dependent adult relative. And they worry about it at work. Sometimes they have to leave early or take a day off.

That's what EMC Insurance Companies found in a survey of its 900 employees in the Des Moines, Iowa, area. The results are consistent with many national studies.

Kathy Krogmeier, benefits specialist at EMC, said the company found that nearly one in five of its workers who responded said they had adult relatives who depended on them for care. Seventy-six percent of its employees responded to the survey.

Sixty-one percent of the caregivers were women. Half of the respondents said they have children at home. Two-thirds were in their 30s or 40s. Seventy percent are married and more than half have income—usually a spouse's earnings—in addition to their earnings at EMC. Almost all said they've occasionally rearranged work schedules to care for an adult relative.

Ninety-five percent said they have been late or left early, and 75 percent said they missed a full day. Eighty-two percent said they've used vacation time to provide care.

LECTURE ENHANCER 11-9

IRREGULAR HOURS AND WORKER HEALTH

One in five working Americans—20 million people—works other than daytime hours. The length of the shifts and time of day vary, from consistent nights to rotating schedules. The number of shift workers is expected to grow as advances in computers, telecommunications, and transportation bind the U.S. economy ever closer to markets in different time zones.

Studies show that up to 80 percent have trouble sleeping. Over time, sleep loss combined with other strains from irregular hours can affect health and job performance. In the case of a trucker or nuclear power plant operator, the results can be deadly.

The *Wall Street Journal* has estimated that shift work costs companies $70 billion a year in lost productivity, medical bills, and industrial accidents. Shift workers are more likely to suffer from digestive disorders, heart disease, and emotional problems. Some research suggests women are at a slightly higher risk of miscarriage.

Researchers say that shift work disrupts the body's circadian rhythms—the 24-hour cycles cued to light and darkness that regulate everything from heart rate and hormones to digestion and alertness. Daytime sleepers, who often complain of noise and other distractions, may be waking up prematurely simply because their body temperatures are rising from an early morning low. One psychologist has concluded that sleep deprivation is a bigger problem in the work place than even drugs.

However, 15 percent to 20 percent of shift workers prefer their unconventional hours. Some like the solitude and relative lack of supervision, others the chance to go to school, run errands when everyone else is at work, or spend time with their children. But most people who work irregular hours do so because it's required or they can't get another job. And shift work pays a little better, up to 10 percent more in the U.S.

LECTURE ENHANCER 11-10

CAUGHT IN THE CROSSFIRE: MANAGING FAMILY FIRMS

One of the most complex groups to manage is the family firm, with its formal-informal group interrelationships. These firms are growing in importance. Some 75 percent of U.S. companies are family owned or controlled. One third of the Fortune 500 companies are family firms. They produce 60 percent of the gross national product, and they grew faster than non-family firms did in the last decade.

The conflicts involved in managing a working group composed of relatives is familiar to Dennis Miller. As chief operating officer of a small electrical-supplies distributor, Miller normally would have plenty to say about the departure of key executives. But when two top managers resigned, Miller stayed out of the discussions. His reason: The executives who left were the chairman's children.

Three sons of Chairman Abraham Brand worked at Standard Electric Supply Co. when Miller joined the Wilmington, Mass., firm in 1988. One son quit in 1990, and another left in 1995. Both times, Miller says, he carefully avoided entangling himself in the matter.

Why the reticence? Miller says he knew a nonfamily manager at another family business who took sides and paid dearly for his mistake. A family member had privately solicited the manager's opinion in a dispute he was having with his kin, Miller says. The manager sided with the family member who sought his view, assuming the conversation would remain confidential. But, in the heat of a contentious meeting that the manager attended, the family member passed on the manager's comments to his relatives to prove that other employees backed him. The manager's "relationship with the family was never the same," Miller says.

Getting caught in the crossfire of a family feud is a daily peril for many employees of small family firms. Big corporations controlled by families also have their share of such intrigue, of course—but a small company's size and informality sharply increase workers' vulnerability to the fallout from family rivalries.

Even outsiders who are big fans of family businesses say they can create trying work environments. They often would go home wondering, "Why have I chosen to work with these people?"

Karen Toney was asking herself the same question when she worked for a small family-owned apparel maker in Boston. A father, his sons, and their cousins "were always fighting over the business, doing things behind each other's backs," Toney says. "It was very uncomfortable."

One relative's suspicions about his kin grew into a distrust of all workers, Toney says: The family member began accusing employees of stealing inventory. "He was always lurking around, watching everyone," she adds. After a few years, she says, "it really became impossible for me to stay there."

Toney has since worked for two more family firms, including her current employer, Agar Supply Co. She joined the Boston wholesale food distributor in 1992 as an administrative assistant to the founder's son, Alan Bressler, who is the company's president. Alan Bressler's daughter Karen runs a company division.

In contrast to the clothing manufacturer, Agar reminded Toney of the virtue of working for a business owned by relatives. Even for outsiders such as herself, "it feels like a big family," she says. Indeed, a paternalistic culture fosters high levels of job security and a sense of well-being at many family-owned companies, authorities say.

But the family atmosphere can create problems, too. Becoming an adopted family member may create expectations that outsiders, like kin, put in long hours for only modest pay. On top of that, nonfamily employees often don't receive stock as compensation—giving them less of a stake in improving the company.

Without equity or a shot at the presidency, a post usually reserved for the founder's son or daughter, nonfamily employees often leave after reaching a certain management level. The parting may be bitter for managers who have watched family members of lesser ability ascend to the top. In cases where the boss's child is perceived as getting a free ride, it creates resentment and jealousy. It can demoralize the nonfamily work force.

For nonfamily executives, perhaps the touchiest predicament is having to manage heirs apparent on their way up.

Of course, problems don't always materialize in that area. As vice president of Mazon Associates Inc., a family-owned commercial-finance firm in Irving, Texas, Kathie Schroeder served as a mentor for the two daughters of company founder Helma Mazon. Schroeder says Mazon and her husband, who is the company's president, "really wanted their daughters to be treated just like the other employees"—a potentially daunting commission for an outsider.

But Schroeder's strong social ties with Mazon—which predated their business relationship—made the task much easier. The women had met and become friends 12 years earlier, when both served as officers of a local branch of the American Association of University Women.

LECTURE ENHANCER 11-11

USING THE EXIT INTERVIEW AS CONTROL

Feedback on problems is the only way to prevent them from reoccurring. One often-overlooked way of getting this feedback from employees is through the exit interview. Interviews with employees who voluntarily leave the organization serve a dual purpose. For the employee, exit interviews are a chance to say many things they haven't been able to say before. For employers, the interviews can be an excellent source of information. Many companies, however, do not conduct exit interviews or conduct them ineffectively.

A good exit interview should consist of structured and unstructured questions. If the employee is counting on a reference, he or she may be unwilling to be too truthful. To put the employee at ease and get honest information, some human resource professionals recommend writing the reference in advance and letting the employee know at the beginning of the interview. Then questions such as the following can be used to get honest information about the company as a whole.

"What did you like most about working here?" This helps gain insight into how the employee perceives the corporate culture. At AT&T one of the answers most frequently heard is that they appreciated the benefits package. When exiting employees mention this, it reaffirms to the company that the investment in benefits is paying off.

"What do you feel good about having accomplished?" This helps determine what responsibilities gave the employee a sense of accomplishment.

"If you were in charge here, what would you change?" This question is used to give the employee a chance to figuratively change the work environment. Prepare for a candid answer.

"What best helped you achieve your goals?" This is where managers find out which employee-support systems are working and which are not. If, for example, the vice president's open door policy was useful in getting some project underway, the policy could be encouraged among other senior management.

"What did you dislike about the work environment here?" An exit interview survey at a Boston hospital showed that twenty percent said they had problems with the work schedule and 15 percent said they disliked their direct supervisor. This information encouraged hospital administrators to implement schedule alternatives and management training for supervisors.

Finally, the exit interview information should be used. Managers at AT&T produce a twice-yearly, in-depth analysis of exit-interview findings which are presented to the senior vice president of human resources. The information is used to reexamine policies, make suggestions for change, and generally help retain skilled employees. Some of the best ideas have come from people who are leaving.

LECTURE ENHANCER 11-12

DISMANTLING THE GLASS CEILING

Two decades of equal-opportunity initiatives have succeeded in drawing women into the work force and getting them moving up the career ladder. But across a range of industries, the top rungs remain as frustratingly out of reach as ever.

"Anyone who thinks the glass ceiling has been shattered is probably a white male," said Carolyn Leighton, executive director of the International Network of Women in Technology, based in Sherman Oaks, California. "It's pretty dismal out there when 46 percent of the work force are women, yet only 5 percent of that number are top executives.

Companies can make it easier for women and minorities to climb the corporate ladder by heeding the recommendations of the Glass Ceiling Commission, a panel created by the 1991 Civil Rights Act and chaired by former Labor Secretary Robert B. Reich. The panel's suggestions for toppling job-advancement barriers include the following:

- Demonstrate commitment. A company's CEO should communicate its dedication to workforce diversity and enact policies that promote it.
- Hold line managers accountable for progress by including diversity in all strategic business plans. In addition, performance appraisals, compensation incentives, and other evaluation measures must reflect this priority.
- Use affirmative action as a tool to ensure that all qualified individuals can compete based on ability and merit.
- Expand your universe of candidates. Cull prospects from noncustomary sources who may have nontraditional backgrounds and experiences.
- Prepare minorities and women for senior positions. Establish mentoring programs, for example, and give these employees access to core areas of the business and developmental opportunities.
- Educate all employees about the strengths and challenges of gender, racial, ethnic, and cultural differences.
- Initiate family-friendly programs that help men and women balance their work and family responsibilities.

Critical Thinking Exercises

Name: ____________________

Date: ____________________

CRITICAL THINKING EXERCISE 11-1

APPRAISE YOUR OWN PERFORMANCE

The text describes job analysis as the process used to answer the question, "What do people with a particular job title actually do?" It is simply a matter of listing all the tasks a person in that job must do. One of the job titles you have right now is college student. Let's analyze that job—take a few minutes to jot down five of the most important tasks college students do.

How well do you do your job as student? Use this exercise to appraise your own performance. The text identifies the first step of appraising performance as setting performance standards. Next to each task you listed, write down a standard you might use to measure performance (for example, if one of your tasks was "to read the text," the performance standard might be "completes the text reading assignment before each class meeting."

Now for the moment of truth. By each performance standard rate how well you meet the standard using a scale of 1 (not even close) to 10 (meets it all the time.) After you rate each standard, average your score. How did you do? If you are unhappy with your score, remember one important step in performance appraisal is to take corrective action!

TASKS OF BEING A COLLEGE STUDENT	PERFORMANCE STANDARDS	RATING (1 = low, 10 = high)
____________	____________	____________
	____________	
____________	____________	____________
	____________	
____________	____________	____________
	____________	
____________	____________	____________
	____________	
____________	____________	____________
	____________	

TASKS OF BEING A COLLEGE STUDENT	PERFORMANCE STANDARDS	RATING (1 = low, 10 = high)
______________	______________	______
	______________	
______________	______________	______
	______________	
______________	______________	______
	______________	

Average: ______

ANSWERS TO CRITICAL THINKING EXERCISE 11-1

It is not easy to set up performance criteria for anyone, including yourself. It is also difficult to assign scores to a person, especially when that person is close to you, as employees usually are. It is even more difficult to be objective when you are evaluating yourself. All of this becomes clear when you do this exercise. Did anyone rate themselves below average? (Below a 7?) What does this tell you about rating systems?

Name: ____________________

Date: ____________________

CRITICAL THINKING EXERCISE 11-2

EXPANDING THE WORKFORCE

You are the human resource manager for Twinkle Toes Tap Shoes, Inc. Twinkle Toes is considering expanding its operations in order to double its current $1.5 million in sales in five years. This means production must double. It will require expanding the workforce and payroll. You have been asked to project the staffing levels and payroll costs necessary to expand. You report that in addition to the current work force the following personnel will be required:

- Two additional sales representatives.
- Two additional secretaries (both Level 6.)
- Ten additional assembly-line operators (Level 4) for the production department.
- Three additional materials handlers (Level 4) for the production department.

Now you must estimate the costs of adding these personnel to the payroll. Use the attached chart "Future Payroll Estimates" to compute your projection figures (assume the current pay scales remain unchanged.) Use the chart to answer the following questions:

1. What is the projected annual payroll cost?

2. If Twinkle Toes does double its sales in five years, what percentage of sales will payroll be in five years? What percentage is it today?

3. Would you recommend the expansion? Why?

CRITICAL THINKING EXERCISE 11-2 (continued)

FUTURE PAYROLL ESTIMATES

POSITION	PAY SCALE	PRESENT STAFF	PRESENT PAYROLL	PROJECTED STAFF	PROJECTED PAYROLL
MANAGEMENT					
Level 24	$60,000	1	$60,000	________	________
Level 18	$40,000	1	$40,000	________	________
Level 11					
CLERICAL					
Level 10	$20,000	2	$40,000	________	________
Level 6	$15,000	3	$45,000	________	________
PRODUCTION					
Level 14	$25,000	3	$75,000	________	________
Level 10	$18,000	1	$18,000	________	________
Level 8	$15,000	2	$30,000	________	________
Level 5	$12,000	2	$24,000	________	________
Level 4	$10,000	13	$130,000	________	________
SALES					
Level 10	$25,000	5	$125,000	________	________
TOTALS		36	$677,000	________	________

ANSWERS TO CRITICAL THINKING EXERCISE 11-2

FUTURE PAYROLL ESTIMATES

POSITION	PAY SCALE	PRESENT STAFF	PRESENT PAYROLL	PROJECTED STAFF	PROJECTED PAYROLL
MANAGEMENT					
Level 24	$60,000	1	$60,000	1	$60,000
Level 18	$40,000	1	$40,000	1	$40,000
Level 11					
CLERICAL					
Level 10	$20,000	2	$40,000	2	$40,000
Level 6	$15,000	3	$45,000	5	$75,000
PRODUCTION					
Level 14	$25,000	3	$75,000	3	$75,000
Level 10	$18,000	1	$18,000	1	$18,000
Level 8	$15,000	2	$30,000	1	$30,000
Level 5	$12,000	2	$24,000	2	$24,000
Level 4	$10,000	13	$130,000	26	$260,000
SALES					
Level 10	$25,000	5	$125,000	7	$175,000
TOTALS		36	$677,000	53	$887,000

1. *What is the projected annual payroll cost?*

   Projected annual payroll cost is $887,000.

2. *If Twinkle Toes does double its sales in five years, what percentage of sales will payroll be in five years? What percentage is it today?*

   Projected percentage of sales: $887,000/3,000,000 = 29.5%
   Current percentage: $677,000/1,500,000 = 45%

3. *Would you recommend the expansion? Why?*

   Yes, the cost figures are good and the potential is good. The percentage of sales devoted to payroll expenses will decrease significantly with the expansion.

Supplemental Cases

CASE 11-1

HUMAN RESOURCE PLANNING AND WOMEN WORKERS

The steadily increasing flow of women into the work force has caused human resource planners and chief executive officers to consider women's needs more carefully when doing human resource planning.

Affirmative action laws are partially responsible for increasing the number of women in the workplace. Another cause of the influx of women is demographics: the work force is no longer expanding in the traditional way, since population growth has slowed. As companies expand and the population doesn't, HR managers will have to hire more women and minorities to fill their needs for employees. This is causing some employers to incorporate benefits in their overall benefit package that are especially addressed to women.

Among the more important issues for both males and females is how to balance work and family. Human resource planners are responding to this need by adding new benefits such as parental leave. Some businesses are against mandatory parental leave because it is costly to hire temporary help to replace parents while they are taking leave. Federal legislation has been proposed requiring up to 18 weeks of leave for both parents. In some countries, such as Canada, France, Sweden, and West Germany, parental leave is already part of an employers benefits by law.

Maternity leave is a controversial area of human resources planning that has divided women's groups. Some say women should be guaranteed paid maternity leave and that they will give them the same job or a similar one when they return. These groups claim that when women leave their jobs to have children it has a negative effect on their careers that doesn't affect men. Women thus lose seniority since career ladders are not designed for people who take leave. On the other hand, the National Association for Women (NOW) believes that if mandatory leave laws are passed, the laws will cause employers not to hire women of child-bearing age.

One option that is becoming more popular is to offer women benefits in a "cafeteria plan." basically, that means that women are able to choose from a variety of benefits to suit their individual needs. A parent may choose parental leave, for example, while a single women may choose an extra week of vacation.

Child care is another area where companies are beginning to provide assistance to parents. IBM, for example, has set up a referral service to help employees find day care in the community. Other countries, such as France, Belgium, Italy, Israel, and Canada, have day care systems that are subsidized by the government to help ease the financial burden on parents. In many cases in the U.S., a mother's salary may barely cover the cost of keeping a child in day care.

Other benefits that can help parents manage work while raising a family, and also benefit employers because they reduce the need for parents to spend time at work dealing with family issues are: flextime, part-time work with partial benefits, and job-sharing.

Flextime allows workers to come in during a 2-hour period and leave within a 2-hour period, as long as they are at work between certain hours known as core time. A new arrangement for part-time workers allows them to reduce their worktime and keep some proportion of their benefits. Job sharing means that two workers share a job and a salary, along with benefits.

A company called Chicken Soup in Minneapolis provides day care for ill children so that parents won't have to stay home from work when a child is ill. Many large corporations, such as 3M, Dayton Hudson, and First Bank Systems, have provided funding for the project.

DISCUSSION QUESTIONS FOR CASE 11-1:

1. Have companies done enough to adjust to women in the workplace?

2. Which of the issues mentioned so far do you feel is most important? Why?

3. What else could companies do, if anything, to assist women workers? Would you recommend that they do that?

ANSWERS TO DISCUSSION QUESTIONS FOR CASE 11-1:

1. *Have companies done enough to adjust to women in the workplace?*

   Some companies have, but many have done little or nothing. In the future, all companies will have to do something because women will make up a huge part of the labor force, especially in the service sector. Focus should be on families, not just women.

2. *Which of the issues mentioned so far do you feel is most important? Why?*

   The most important issue is freedom to choose options in benefits. Not all families have children and need day care, flextime, etc. Also too much emphasis on families is unfair to those without families. Flexible systems can be fair to all.

3. *What else could companies do, if anything, to assist women workers? Would you recommend that they do that?*

   It is not wise to focus on women in isolation. It is best to study families and work and home situations. More work may be done at home and sent over computer lines to work. More part-time and flextime schedules could be made. The women and men in the class may have several good suggestions.

CASE 11-2

THE DANGERS OF FIRING EMPLOYEES

At one time, it was relatively easy for managers to fire an employee as long as they didn't violate any laws such as the Civil Rights Act. That is no longer true. Since the 1970s, courts have chipped away at the so-called employment-at-will doctrine, which declared that workers could be fired for almost any reason or in some cases for no reason. Beverly Hills attorney H. Bradley Jones proclaimed that wrongful discharge "is even more dangerous than medical malpractice . . . since few insurance companies sell insurance coverage to protect employers against wrongful discharge lawsuits." NAS Insurance Services Inc. in California offers insurance for companies sued for wrongful discharge. It has been estimated that only 2 out of every 1,000 employees is fired unjustly, but that amounts to some 55,000 workers a year.

The number of cases and size of awards are increasing. For example, a Montana woman who was released from her job after 28 years was awarded $94,170 in economic damages, $100,000 for emotional distress and $1.3 million in punitive damages. The Montana Supreme Court upheld a jury's judgment that declared a long-term employee has an expectation of continued employment provided the employee's work performance has been satisfactory. (Montana is the only state where firing employees without just cause is illegal. All other states are considered "at-will" states.) Awards such as this are causing employers to be much more cautious about whom they fire and how. Since fired employees use everything from employee handbooks to informal comments as evidence in wrongful discharge suits, corporate personnel manuals are becoming more detailed to protect firms against legal action. For example, the Del E. Webb Corporation struck the word permanent from employee descriptions. Some companies even go to the point now of leasing rather than hiring employees.

Many companies have added new provisions to their job applications. The statements say that the applicant acknowledges that the employer is free to terminate workers at will—sometimes without cause and without notice. According to Ron Pilenzo, president of the Society for Human Resource Management, the purpose of such at-will statements is to inform applicants that they are not being offered guaranteed lifetime employment.

The situation doesn't promise to become easier. Courts are asking judges and juries to decide what is good cause and what is fair—concepts that are unclear and elusive at best. In addition, several states are considering legislation that would limit instances in which an employer could fire workers.

DISCUSSION QUESTIONS FOR CASE 11-2:

1. What are the implications for personnel departments of new legal rulings against firing for unjust cause?

2. If you were an employer, would you put more effort into screening and training employees, given these rulings? Who may be hurt by such changes? Who may benefit?

3. What is your reaction to the courts' becoming involved in hiring, training, screening, and firing practices of business firms? Is it a positive step toward better employee treatment or not?

ANSWERS TO DISCUSSION QUESTIONS FOR CASE 11-2:

1. *What are the implications for personnel departments of new legal rulings against firing for unjust cause?*

   Human resource managers have to rethink their whole attitude toward employees. They are not a resource, like materials, that can be used and tossed aside when not needed. Rather, employees must be viewed as semipermanent members of the organization who must be carefully selected, trained, motivated, developed, and retrained when necessary. An insensitive human resource manager could be sued and face all kinds of legal problems if he or she is not aware of these new rulings.

2. *If you were an employer, would you put more effort into screening and training employees, given these rulings? Who may be hurt by such changes? Who may benefit?*

   Naturally, a prudent employer would put more effort into screening and training to be sure an employee fits into the organization. This hurts those marginal workers who could be major contributors if given a chance, but who are more risky. This includes those who do not have the needed education, certain minorities and disabled, and those with no experience. Those who benefit are people who already have jobs, those with needed education and training, and those with experience. By making it harder to fire employees, the government may be hurting those who are in most need of help.

3. *What is your reaction to the courts' becoming involved in hiring, training, screening, and firing practices of business firms? Is it a positive step toward better employee treatment or not?*

   It can be a positive step, but it shows a lack on the part of businesses to solve their own problems. It is best to keep out of the courts and the legislature if possible. They must deal with groups, when most problems involve individuals. Making policy for groups based on individual problems is not a good idea. Flexibility is the key, and laws usually limit rather than foster flexibility.

Transparency Masters

TRANSPARENCY MASTER 78	Chapter Outline
TRANSPARENCY MASTER 79	Human Resource Management *(Figure 11.1 on text page 316)*
TRANSPARENCY MASTER 80	Job Analysis *(Figure 11.2 on text page 320)*
TRANSPARENCY MASTER 81	Employee Sources *(Figure 11.3 on text page 322)*
TRANSPARENCY MASTER 82	Making Appraisals and Reviews More Effective *(Figure 11.4 on text page 330)*
TRANSPARENCY MASTER 83	A Flextime Chart *(Figure 11.5 on text page 334)*
TRANSPARENCY MASTER 84	How to Avoid Wrongful Discharge Lawsuits *(Figure 11-6 on text page 337)*

Chapter Outline

CHAPTER 11
HUMAN RESOURCE MANAGEMENT: FINDING AND KEEPING THE BEST EMPLOYEES

PROFILE: Madye H. Whitehead and Charles Henson of Design Alternatives

I. WORKING WITH PEOPLE IS JUST THE BEGINNING.

A. Developing the Ultimate Resource.

B. The Human Resource Challenge.

II. DETERMINING YOUR HUMAN RESOURCES NEEDS.

III. RECRUITING EMPLOYEES FROM A DIVERSE POPULATION.

IV. SELECTING EMPLOYEES WHO WILL BE PRODUCTIVE.

A. Outsourcing: Common Alternative Staffing Options.

V. TRAINING AND DEVELOPING EMPLOYEES FOR OPTIMUM PERFORMANCE.

A. Management Development.

1. Importance of Networking.

B. Diversity in Management Development.

VI. APPRAISING EMPLOYEE PERFORMANCE TO GET OPTIMUM RESULTS.

VII. COMPENSATING EMPLOYEES: ATTRACTING AND KEEPING THE BEST.

Chapter Outline

A. Pay Systems.

B. Compensating Teams.

C. Fringe Benefits.

VIII. SCHEDULING EMPLOYEES THAT MEET ORGANIZATIONAL AND EMPLOYEE NEEDS.

A. Flextime Plans.

B. Home-Based and Other Mobil Work.

C. Job-Sharing Plans.

IX. MOVING EMPLOYEES UP, OVER, AND OUT.

A. Promoting and Reassigning Employees.

B. Terminating Employees.

C. Retiring Employees.

X. LAWS AFFECTING HUMAN RESOURCE MANAGEMENT.

A. Laws Protecting the Disabled and Older Employees.

B. Effects of Legislation.

X. SUMMARY AND REVIEW.

Human Resource Management

(Figure 11.1 on text page 316)

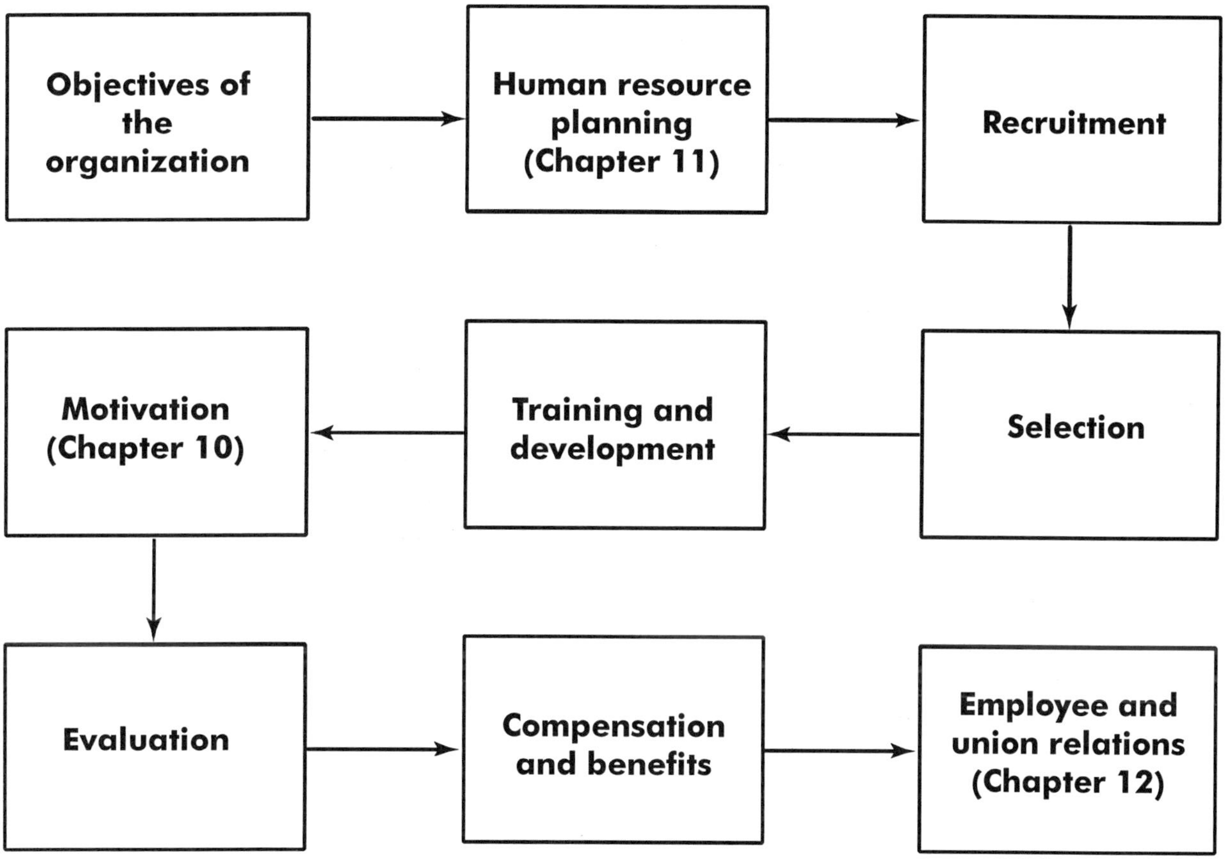

Objectives of the organization → Human resource planning (Chapter 11) → Recruitment → Selection → Training and development → Motivation (Chapter 10) → Evaluation → Compensation and benefits → Employee and union relations (Chapter 12)

Job Analysis
(Figure 11.2 on text page 320)

JOB ANALYSIS

Observe current sales representatives doing the job.
Discuss job with sales managers.
Have current sales reps keep a diary of their activities.

JOB DESCRIPTION

Primary objective is to sell Fiberrific to food stores in Territory Z. Duties include servicing accounts and maintaining positive relationships with clients. Responsibilities include

- Introducing the new cereal to store managers in the area.
- Helping the store managers estimate the volume to order.
- Negotiating prime shelf space.
- Explaining sales promotion activities to store managers.
- Stocking and maintaining shelves in stores that wish such service.

JOB SPECIFICATIONS

Characteristics of the person qualifying for this job include

- Two years' sales experience.
- Positive attitude.
- Well-groomed appearance.
- Good communication skills.
- High school diploma and two years of college credit.

Employee Sources

(Figure 11.3 on text page 322)

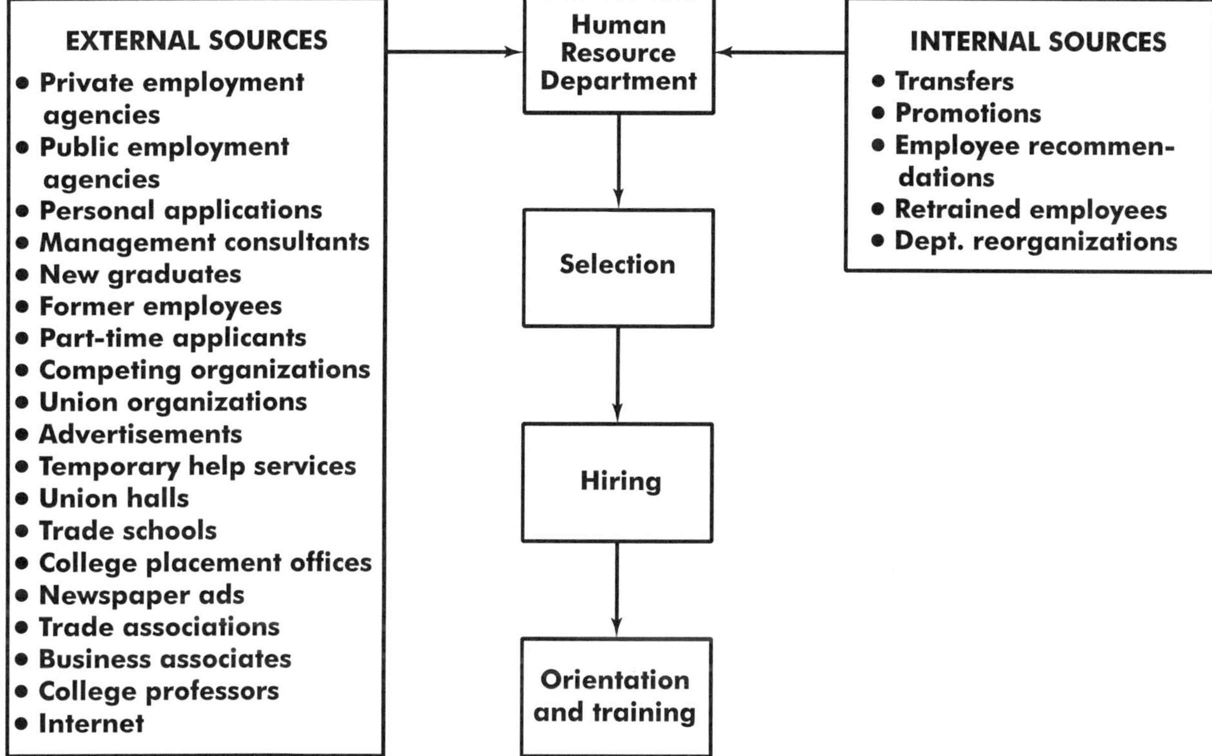

TM-82

Making Appraisals and Reviews More Effective
(Figure 11.4 on text page 330)

MAKING APPRAISALS AND REVIEWS MORE EFFECTIVE

1. **DON'T** attack the employee personally. Critically evaluate his or her work.
2. **DO** allow sufficient time, without distractions, for appraisal. (Take the phone off the hook or close the office door.)
3. **DON'T** make the employee feel uncomfortable or uneasy. Never conduct an appraisal where other employees are present (such as on the shop floor).
4. **DO** include the employee in the process as much as possible. (Let the employee prepare a self-improvement program.)
5. **DON'T** wait until the appraisal to address problems with the employee's work that have been developing for some time.
6. **DO** end the appraisal with positive suggestions for employee improvement.

A Flextime Chart

(Figure 11.5 on text page 334)

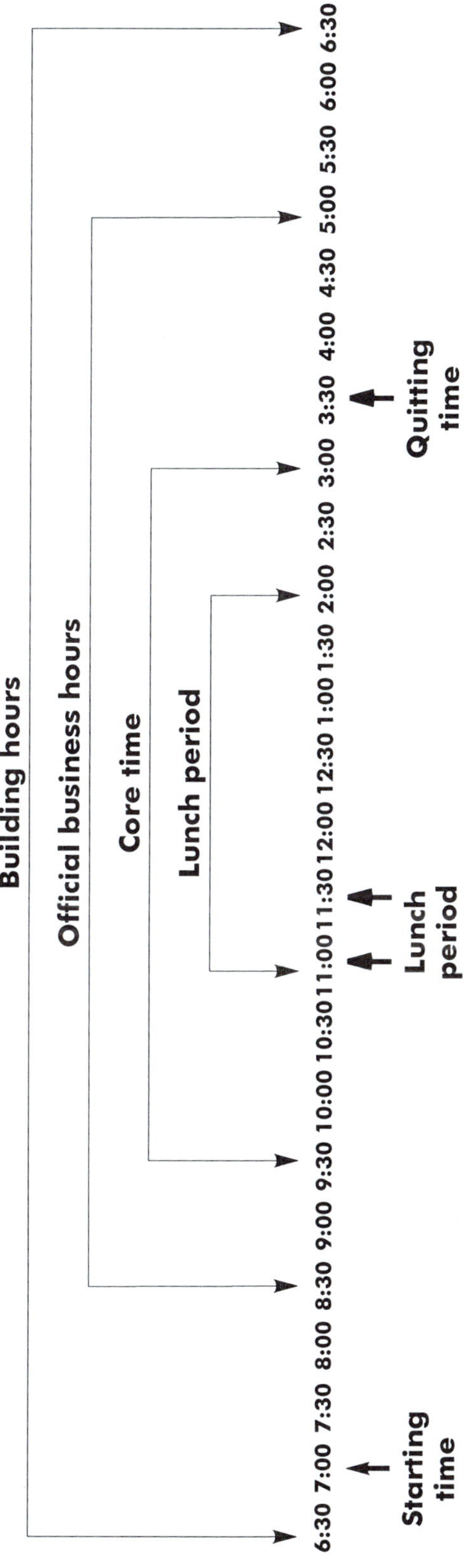

How to Avoid Wrongful Discharge Lawsuits
(Figure 11.6 on text page 337)

CONSULTANTS OFFER THIS ADVICE TO MINIMIZE THE CHANCE OF A LAWSUIT FOR WRONGFUL DISCHARGE:

- Prepare before hiring by requiring recruits to sign a statement that retains management's freedom to terminate at will.
- Don't make unintentional promises by using such terms as permanent employment.
- Document reasons before firing and make sure you have an unquestionable business reason for the firing.
- Fire the worst first and be consistent in discipline.
- Buy out bad risks by offering severance pay in exchange for a signed release from any claims.
- Be sure to give employees the true reasons they are being fired. If you do not, you cannot reveal it to a recruiter asking for a reference without risking a defamation lawsuit.
- Disclose the reasons for an employee's dismissal to that person's potential new employers. For example, if you fired an employee for dangerous behavior and you withhold that information from your references, you can be sued if the employee commits a violent act at his or her next job.

Sources: "When Firing Can Backfire," *The Washington Post*, March 2, 1997, p. H4; and Edward Felsenthal, "Justices Let Former Employees Sue over Bad References," *The Wall Street Journal Interactive Edition*, February 18, 1997.